The Production of Reality

Essays and Readings in Social Psychology

THE PINE FORGE PRESS SOCIAL SCIENCE LIBRARY

The McDonaldization of Society: An Investigation Into the Changing Character of Contemporary Social Life *by George Ritzer*

Sociological Snapshots: Seeing Social Structure and Change in Everyday Life *by Jack Levin*

What Is Society? Reflections on Freedom, Order, and Change *by Earl Babbie*

The Production of Reality: Essays and Readings in Social Psychology *by Peter Kollock and Jodi O'Brien*

Adventures in Social Research: Data Analysis Using SPSS® *by Earl Babbie and Fred Halley*

Crime and Everyday Life: Insights and Implications for Society *by Marcus Felson*

Sociology of Work: Perspectives, Analyses, Issues *by Richard H. Hall*

Aging: Concepts and Controversies *by Harry R. Moody, Jr.*

Worlds of Difference: Inequality in the Aging Experience *by Eleanor Palo Stoller and Rose Campbell Gibson*

Forthcoming

Sociology for a New Century *A Pine Forge Press Series edited by Charles Ragin, Wendy Griswold, and Larry Griffin*

- **Social Psychology and Social Institutions** *by Denise D. and William T. Bielby*
- **The Social Ecology of Natural Resources and Development** *by Stephen G. Bunker*
- **How Societies Change** *by Daniel Chirot*
- **Ethnic Dynamics in the Modern World: Continuity and Transformation** *by Stephen Cornell*
- **Sociology of Childhood** *by William A. Corsaro*
- **Cultures and Societies in a Changing World** *by Wendy Griswold*
- **Crime and Disrepute: Comparative Perspectives** *by John Hagan*
- **Racism and the Modern World: Sociological Perspectives** *by Wilmot James*
- **Religion in the Global Village** *by Lester Kurtz*
- **Waves of Democracy** *by John Markoff*
- **Organizations in a World Economy** *by Walter W. Powell*
- **Constructing Social Research** *by Charles C. Ragin*
- **Women, Men, and Work** *by Barbara Reskin and Irene Padavic*
- **Cities in a World Economy** *by Saskia Sassen*

The Production of Reality

Essays and Readings in Social Psychology

PETER KOLLOCK
University of California, Los Angeles

JODI O'BRIEN
University of Iowa

PINE FORGE PRESS
Thousand Oaks, California
London ■ *New Delhi*

Cover: Jean Miró, Carnival of Harlequin, 1924-25 (oil on canvas, 26 × 36⅝"). Albright-Knox Art Gallery, Buffalo, New York, Room of Contemporary Art Fund, 1940.

For information address:

PINE FORGE PRESS
A Sage Publications Company
2455 Teller Road
Thousand Oaks, California 91320

Production Editor: Rebecca Holland
Copy Editor: Stephanie Hoppe
Designer: Lisa S. Mirski
Desktop Typesetter: Andrea D. Swanson
Cover: Lisa S. Mirski
Print Buyer: Anna Chin
Printer: Malloy Lithographing, Inc.

Printed in the United States of America

1 2 3 4 5 6 7 8 9 10—98 97 96 95 94

Library of Congress Cataloging-in-Publication Data
Main entry under title:
Kollock, Peter.
    The production of reality : essays and readings in social
psychology / Peter Kollock, Jodi O'Brien.
        p.   cm. — (The Pine Forge Press social science library)
    Includes bibliographical references and index.
    ISBN 0-8039-9014-6 (alk. paper : pbk.)
    1. Social psychology. I. O'Brien, Jodi. II. Title.
III. Series.
HM251.K54855 1994   93-8567
302—dc20   CIP

In memory of Philip W. Blumstein,
our teacher and our friend.

This book is a celebration of your vision that all social life
constitutes data for the symbolic interactionist.

About the Authors

Peter Kollock (Ph.D., University of Washington) is Assistant Professor of Sociology at the University of California, Los Angeles, where he teaches courses in social psychology and on the dilemmas of cooperation and collective action. Director of the Ph.D. teacher-training program in his department, he has won teaching awards at UCLA and at the University of Washington. His current research includes work on cooperation and the role of trust and commitment in exchange.

Jodi O'Brien (Ph.D., University of Washington) is an Assistant Professor of Sociology at the University of Iowa. She teaches courses in social psychology, symbolic interactionism, classical and contemporary theory, and the craft of pedagogy. Her academic pursuits include finding creative solutions to the contradictions that exist between teaching and research endeavors in public universities and exploring the implications of a postmodern culture on the learning experience of contemporary college students. In her spare time she enjoys eavesdropping on her fellow social creatures.

About the Publisher

Pine Forge Press is a new educational publisher, dedicated to publishing innovative books and software throughout the social sciences. On this and any other of our publications, we welcome your comments and suggestions.

Please call or write us at

Pine Forge Press

A Sage Publications Company
2455 Teller Road
Thousand Oaks, CA 91320
(805) 499-4224
Internet: sdr@pfp.sagepub.com

Brief Contents

Contents

LANGUAGE AND THE STRUCTURE OF THOUGHT

Preface

What Sort of Creature Is the Human?

We are Star Trek fans. As such we find it fascinating to note that the portrayal of certain primary characters parallels the major currents of thought in social psychology over the past two decades. Consider the contrast between the rational Mr. Spock of the first "Star Trek" series and the android, Data, featured in "Star Trek: The Next Generation." Consistent with the dominant cognitive perspective of the 1970s, the Vulcan, Spock, epitomized the being who operated according to the dictates of pure reason. Unencumbered by emotions (those messy "hot" flashes) and cognitive biases, Spock was able to assess his environment and formulate hypotheses with a detachment and accuracy that resembled a computer. Spock's character was often juxtaposed with the doctor, who, although a man of science, was frequently amiss in his judgment due to the intrusion of human biases and social attachments. Spock was the ultimate rational actor. Some episodes of the early show commented on, and perhaps even lamented, Spock's lack of emotion. However, in the end it was always the virtue of unadulterated rationality that saved the day. The message was clear: emotion and human quirks, endearing and meaningful as they might seem, get in the way of the human project. This project was to explore and chart (and master?) the universe.

"Star Trek: The Next Generation," though no less grand in its pretensions of achieving a reasoned universal harmony orchestrated by sentient beings, is much less grandiose than its predecessor in its claims for the virtue and virility of rationality. In the new show, Spock has been replaced with a potentially more perfect form of rational life, Data. As an android, Data is capable of calculation and theory construction that far surpass the abilities of even the most rationally adroit Vulcan. In a fascinating twist, however, the current show de-emphasizes Data's rational capabilities in order to play out the theme of humanness as nonrationality. Data is a focus not because of his amazing cognitive abilities, but because of the limitation his technological essence places on his endeavors to "be" human.

Data is an amazing piece of machinery. He is stronger than any humanoid, has a life span of unguessed potential, can assimilate and process any amount of information; he is even programmed to simulate perfectly many of the masters of universal culture. For example, he can play the violin like Isaac Stern, paint as if he were Picasso, and perform drama as if he were Laurence Olivier. Despite these technical achievements he is not "human."

Data's existence raises the question, What is the nature of humanness? If it is not to be found in rational, cognitive decision making that characterized social psychology in the seventies, what is the distinctive mark of our species? As a scientific culture we have long admired the computer for its rational, objective, calculating approach to the information in its environment. A great deal of our industrial technology, cognitive science, and popular mythology concerns how humans can be more like the computer; how we can be more objective and rational. Social psychology has, for many years, separated what are known as "cold" topics (rationality, cognition, and decision making) from "hot" topics (emotions). Any young scholar who wished to make a mark in the field was admonished to pursue a study of the "cold" topics. Only recently have social psychologists begun to look more closely at those aspects of humanness that are not epitomized by the technology of the computer and to ask what purpose these nonrational human characteristics play in our personal and cultural stories. Spock represented our quest to become more like the rationality of the computer. Data, who is a computer, symbolizes our search for the essence of humanness that cannot be captured in perfect cognitive activity. Data is computer technology par excellence. Thus he is the perfect jumping-off point for investigating the question, What, beyond perfect rational cognition, makes the human?

One of the features that endears Data to other members of the crew is his earnest attempts to be human and his continual failure to hit the mark. In one episode Data works fervently to understand humor, but the concept is beyond his otherwise "perfect" abilities. He just doesn't get it. In another he explores the question of love and affection and finds that, while he is capable of an intellectual comprehension of this state of being, and is, in fact, even capable of the act of physical love-making, he is unable to experience a state of "love." One by one Data explores various human institutions, the hallmarks of our social species. His factual knowledge of these institutions is an archive that would overwhelm even the most advanced student of human culture. Despite this knowledge, the android is incapable of experiencing life as a human being. The abstract knowledge is present, but the essence is missing. This is a different message from that of earlier social psychology: perfect factual knowledge and cognitive ability do not a human make. Humanness is built on the cognitive ability to absorb and manipulate abstract symbols, but its essence is in the comprehension of the nuanced, situated meaning that takes place between human beings in social interaction.

Little by little Data appears to advance in his comprehension of the human experience. How is this achieved? Not through his impressive information-processing neural networks but through interaction with human beings. Through exposure to various human institutions, such as love, humor, grief, and betrayal, Data begins to respond to some situations in a particularly humanlike fashion. To enhance his understanding of humanness, Data attempts to "do" human things, such as develop hobbies and social attachments. To the extent that Data is able to experience the essence of humanness, it is through his interaction with humans and their endeavors to teach him just what it is that otherwise abstract institutions like "friendship" or "sorrow" mean. In a word, Data is being socialized into the human community.

We find two points worth noting regarding Data and the essence of humanness. First, Data's various experiences suggest that humanness involves not only a general comprehension of myriad facts and the ability to calculate probable hypotheses but an empathetic understanding of highly nuanced, situated meaning. We are reminded of Thomas Scheff's discussion about the computer that is directed to translate the phrase "The spirit is willing but the flesh is weak" into Russian. The computer has all the necessary dictionary terms and grammar to make this translation. Accordingly it translates the phrase as "the vodka is good but the meat is rotten." The computer provides a literal translation but this translation does not convey the intended meaning of the phrase. The computer is unable to translate the essence of the phrase because it does not have a comprehension of metaphor.

Second, the extent to which Data begins to comprehend human metaphorical meaning occurs not through his private cognitive calculations but through interaction with his companions. He notes their reactions to his various utterances and behaviors and then queries them regarding the reasons for their responses—which are often not as Data would predict based on rational calculation alone. In this way Data assembles a litany of human metaphors and expected behaviors that, while not always rational, more closely approximate the actual human experience. The extent to which Data does achieve humanness occurs as the result of social interaction with others. The essence of this interaction is Data's schooling in the nuanced richness of human life. He learns that the meanings of objects and abstractions, despite what his computer archives inform him, are relative in human life. Humans create and recreate meaning in interaction with one another. Reality is not just a codified series of facts and possibilities; it is something that is produced and reproduced through human activity.

Humanness Is Achieved Through Symbolic Interaction

The production of meaningful realities through human interaction is the focus of this book. We intend to demonstrate that human culture is achieved through interaction between individuals who share highly complex, richly nuanced definitions of themselves and the situations in which they participate.

Perfect rationality is not sufficient to the human task. In some cases, literal, rational calculation may even be a hindrance to meaningful human interaction. We learn to be human. The possibility for humanness is in our capacity for language, not just definitions and grammar but also metaphor. The expression of what is considered appropriate human behavior is achieved through interaction with others.

As illustrated by the case of Data, we view cognitive capabilities as a necessary foundation to the development of humanness and the achievement of culture. To extend the computer analogy, neurological cognitive functions constitute the "hardware" of human existence. It is the meaningful use of symbols that makes this existence what it is, however. This ability entails more than simply loading the appropriate software and switching the computer on. In this book we build on the cognitive perspective but take as our central focus the day-to-day interactions that form the fabric of human existence as we experience it. Our primary concern is the manner in which humans learn to participate in and ultimately produce and reproduce themselves and their various cultures.

The social psychological perspective that drives this exploration is symbolic interactionism. We have endeavored to provide a cognitive foundation for symbolic interactionism and also to extend the logic of the perspective to issues of cultural reproduction. In this regard we are expanding both the psychological and the social implications of the theory. Specifically, we ask: What cognitive capacities are necessary for the human to engage in meaningful social interaction? How is social behavior affected by a disruption of the cognitive processes? How do cognitive processes constrain the possible lines of action that we see available to us? How do these processes contribute to the production of culture? How, even when we may be personally opposed to particular cultural institutions such as racism, do our actions contribute to the reproduction of these institutions?

Our general aim is to explore the social foundations of mind, self, and culture. Our intent is not to promote symbolic interactionism per se but to provide a meaningful and relevant basis from which to study human social behavior. Many of our colleagues and students of social psychology suggest that they find symbolic interactionism useful in its presentation of day-to-day human affairs but complain that they have difficulty grasping the full implications of the perspective. Symbolic interactionism as a theoretical perspective is admittedly less precise and refined than many of the social psychological theories that deal with the "cold" topics. In our view, however, human existence is not clear and precise. Rather it is a richly textured fabric and must be studied as such. This means that at times concepts may seem less well defined than the reader might like. In mind of this we offer the following reading notes. These suggestions are intended to serve as caveats regarding the comprehension and application of symbolic interactionism.

Understanding Symbolic Interactionism: Caveats

Psychologism

Social psychologists who study human cognition note that each of us has a tendency to interpret information in terms of its specific relevance to our own experiences. This information-processing bias is termed *psychologism* (or the self-consensus bias). It has been noted that psychologism, when coupled with the American ideal of individualism, makes it difficult for students to comprehend theories that pertain to the social group. The tendency is to interpret and evaluate the information offered by these theories in terms of individual psychology and experience—"Does the theoretical perspective match my personal situation?" Theories that emphasize group knowledge and socialization are viewed as antithetical to the primacy of the individual. This separation of individual and group is based on a false dichotomy. As we discuss throughout the book, there is no possibility of the concept of the "individual" (including individual rights, feelings, and so forth) without the social group.

In order to make full sense of symbolic interactionism the reader should remember that it is not necessary to deny the existence of private psychology in order to explore the implications of group knowledge. In fact, private psychology is taken as a starting point from which to underscore and pursue the question of how, given unique individual perception and traits, persons come to develop shared cultural meaning. In this book we treat as a puzzle the issue of what humans create through interaction (i.e., social acts) and explore how and why these interactions come to have perceivably real properties— even when the private minds of the participants may disagree with or be unaware of the social product. The reader is cautioned, therefore, to remember that what humans do in interaction with others may or may not be harmonious with private thought. However, and this is the point to emphasize, whether or not persons agree with and/or believe in their public actions, it is these actions that are observable by others and come to be real in their consequences.

Reification and Relevance

Reification means to treat an abstraction as if it had concrete properties. There is a tendency to treat many sociological concepts, for example, "norms," as if they were real structures that exist somewhere in a state of nature and "do" things to humans. When a concept is reified, or given a "life of its own," we tend to forget the extent to which our own beliefs and actions contribute to the construction and perpetuation of the "life" of the processes described by the concept. This leads to an interesting paradox. On the one hand, the reification of social concepts implies that humans are hapless robots propelled by the whim of social forces, some unseen "big brother" beyond human control. On the other hand, being "individualists" with a tendency toward "psychologism," we like to think of ourselves as beings who are in control of our own destinies: distinctive entities who chart a unique course. How is this individual psychology reconciled with a reified sociology? Most often it is not. Instead, we tend to conclude that social concepts, however compelling and accurate they may appear, describe someone else's life; individually we really don't believe that the processes described by the concepts are applicable to us. We know that we ourselves are not robots. Thus, social psychology becomes individually irrelevant.

Symbolic interactionism offers an alternative path, one that makes use of the observation that persons act "as if" certain abstractions are real. At the same time the perspective teaches that social reality is the creation of coordinated activity between real individuals. From this perspective the puzzle becomes how abstract concepts are communicated, shared, reproduced, and how they take on patterns of stability that make them appear "as if" they were "real." This "obdurate" character of social inter-action is what we come to know in a reified way as "society." The process of creating social reality is the focus of this book. For now the reader is admonished to be attentive to reified concepts and to ask of them: What processes of interaction does the concept describe? What must real people do in order to create and maintain this process to the point where it is real enough that we come to reify it? What is your individual role in these processes of interaction and what unforeseen consequences might your actions have in the production of social reality?

Level of Analysis

Most social science research employs cause and effect reasoning. This logic presents a model by which one thing affects another: A causes B. The implication is that without A, B would not exist and B has no reciprocal effect on A. (A is presumably caused by something else.) Cause and effect reasoning has many merits. One merit is that it isolates the relationship between variables so that we can explore, for example, whether smoking has a causal influence on developing cancer. Useful as this logic may be, the models suggested by the cause-effect methods of science are not adequate to capture the complexity and nuance of human social behavior and the production of culture. Applied to social behav-ior cause-effect reasoning contributes to reification and perpetuates misleading dichotomies. The general model is that social structures of some sort (reified concepts) "cause" humans to behave in a certain way. These social structures are conceptualized to exist independently of human beings. In sociology the result of this line of thought is a dichotomy known as the "micro/macro" distinction. According to this distinction, groups or society-level variables are treated as separate "macro" phenomena that exert causal influence over individuals. Individual action is considered to be micro activity. Sociologists argue over which level of analysis, micro action or macro structures, should be given theoretical primacy in the study of human culture and behavior. The distinction has become so reified that much ink has been spilt in the past decade on how to bridge the "micro/macro" gap.

The result of this discourse is the false separation of the individual and society. We are told that society "causes" our behavior. Again, as individuals we really don't buy this notion. To the extent that we are willing to believe it, society is viewed as something "out there," beyond our comprehension or control. And what "causes" society? Viewed from a traditional cause-effect logic, if macro structures cause micro behavior, then it is not possible that micro activity causes macro events. Thus, sociology is again rendered irrelevant. We are hesitant to see the effects of distant reified concepts on our actual lives and have almost no understanding of the extent to which our own "micro" actions may contribute to the formation and perpetuation of "macro" structures. Cause-effect reasoning and the separation of the individual and society preclude this line of thought. The logic of traditional social science instructs us to view the world and our place in it in a manner that is completely antithetical to our actual experiences.

Symbolic interactionism has always been conducted at the intersection of individuals and society. From this perspective it is not possible to make sense of one "level" without incorporating the other. The challenge for symbolic interaction has been to represent society in a way that avoids reification, in other words, to model social patterns and relationships as the product of ongoing individual-level activity. At the same time, the perspective must account for the observation that existing social patterns do exert influence over and constrain possible lines of action for individuals. The ultimate aim of symbolic interactionism as presented in this book is to place the individual and society on the same level and to analyze the reciprocal relationship between individual action and social patterns and institutions. From the perspective of symbolic interactionism, social life is conceived as a dynamic web of reciprocal influence between members of a social group. This web is made up of the interactions of individuals. Individuals spin and respin the web. At the same time they are influenced by the existing patterns of previously spun strands. Symbolic interactionism is unique in the study of both psychology and sociology in that it is the only perspective that assumes an active, expressive model of the human actor and treats the individual and the social at the same level of analysis. In gaining an understanding of this perspective the reader is instructed to think in terms of process and feedback.

This is admittedly more complicated than representing social life in terms of simple dichotomies and cause-effect reasoning.

However, in reality individual existence and social patterns are mutually constitutive; the relationship between the individual and society is reciprocal. This perspective offers a rich story about human behavior and its social consequences. We think you will find this story to be more instructive and relevant regarding your personal life and the social world in which you are a participant.

Logic of the Book

The concept of this book, a combination of readings and "orienting" essays, is intended to make use of and combine the descriptive richness of relevant topical readings with the organizational logic and definitional advantages of textbooks. Our hope is to engage a wide audience with the diverse set of readings and to provide a general theoretical framework through the essays. The logic of this book is circular rather than linear. Our intention is to immerse you, the reader, in the puzzles and issues of contemporary social psychology and to provide a framework from which you can begin to construct your own relevant understanding of the social world and your roles and responsibilities in it. Toward this end we pose more questions than we provide definitive answers. The material contained in this book should be approached as a set of building blocks that you assemble and reassemble in the pursuit of answers to your own intellectual queries.

Acknowledgments

The creation of any social product is always a collective enterprise. We acknowledge the role that many others have played in bringing this book to completion. Our publisher, Steve Rutter, has been singularly supportive in encouraging us to push the boundaries suggested by the traditional textbooks currently available in social psychology. We appreciate his confidence in our vision. The staff of Pine Forge Press have been tremendously helpful in dealing with the myriad details and headaches that accompany such a production. We appreciate the many helpful comments from the reviewers of this book: Dick Adams (UCLA), Peter Callero (Western Oregon State College), Jeff Chin (LeMoyne College), Andy Deseran (Louisiana State University), Jennifer Friedman (University of South Florida), John Kinch (San Francisco State University), and Ken Plummer (University of Essex). The Herculean task of compiling the index was accomplished by Anne Eisenberg and Leah Soenke (University of Iowa). We are especially grateful to Judith Howard (University of Washington) who, at a moment's notice, has willingly set aside her own endeavors on several occasions to read countless drafts of this manuscript and give us the benefit of her keen sociological and editorial eye. As always, we are indebted to Ron Obvious simply for being there. Our commitment to producing a relevant and useful social psychology was fostered by our teacher, Fred Campbell, who taught us that the art of teaching is in learning to be purposeful. Finally, cliché though it may sound, the reality is that much of our thinking as it is developed in this book is the result of our conversations and interactions with our students. We thank them for sharing their intellectual passion.

PART I

Introduction

A father said to his double-seeing son, "Son, you see two instead of one."

"How can that be?" the boy replied. "If I were, there would seem to be four moons up there in place of two."
(*Idries Shah*, Caravan of Dreams)

What Is Real?

Introduction

We begin with a few stories. In rural Central American villages religious festivals are often a very important part of the local culture. In one case a documentary film crew was around to record the event. The film shows brightly colored decorations, music, dancing, and a variety of delicious and special foods made for the festival. Indeed, the special treats prepared for the event are clearly a highlight for everyone, especially the children. They crowd around the stands waiting for sweets or other treats.

In the middle of one crowd of children waiting for a treat is a very large stone bowl. A large stone pillar rises out of the center of the bowl. The pillar seems alive. It is completely covered by shiny black beetles crawling around and over each other. The person in charge takes a tortilla, spreads a bit of sauce on the inside and grabs a handful of live beetles, quickly folding the tortilla up so that the beetles cannot escape. Playfully pushing the beetles back into the tortilla between each bite, a gleeful child eats the burrito with relish.

Would you be willing to try a beetle burrito? Is a strip of burnt cow muscle (also known as a steak) inherently any more or less desirable than a beetle burrito? If you had grown up in that village would you be eating beetle burritos and enjoying them? What does your answer have to say about the social and cultural origins of what seems like an almost biological trait—our taste for food?

In his book *The Te of Piglet* (1992), Benjamin Hoff recounts the following narratives based on the writings of the Chinese Taoist philosophers:

> A man noticed that his axe was missing. Then he saw the neighbor's son pass by. The boy looked like a thief, walked like a thief, behaved like a thief. Later that day, the man found his axe where he had left it the day before. The next time he saw the neighbor's son, the boy looked, walked and behaved like an honest, ordinary boy.

> A man dug a well by the side of the road. For years afterward, grateful travelers talked of the Wonderful Well. But one night, a man fell into it and drowned. After that, people avoided the Dreadful Well. Later it was discovered that the victim was a drunken thief who had

left the road to avoid being captured by the night patrol—only to fall into the Justice-Dispensing Well. (p. 172)

What sort of reality do these tales illustrate? Does the essence of the neighbor's boy or the nature of the well change? Or do people's perceptions change? Consider occasions in which your perceptions of someone or something may have been influenced by your own momentary experiences. Is it possible that What Is Real depends on how you look at something? How much does your point of view depend on your own interests?

A group of workers from a local factory gathers every night after work to share drinks and conversation. They express dissatisfaction with the conditions of their job and the atrocities committed by the shop manager. One young man recalls a recent incident in which an employee lost her arm to unsafe machinery. "I'm terrified every second of every working hour that the same will happen to me," he admits. A woman complains of sexual harassment from the "boss" and threatens to "give him a piece of my foot in a place that he won't soon forget next time he lays his dirty hands on me." Several of the workers discuss plans for a walkout and, in a final burst of enthusiasm, agree that at noon on the appointed day they will step away from their machines and cease to work as a show of protest. Each day life resumes at the factory. The young man endures his fear in terrified silence and even manages a friendly nod to fellow employees. The woman smiles sweetly when the boss pats her backside and tells her she looks marvelous in blue. At noon, a few employees, remembering last night's "drunken" talk of strike and rebellion, look sheepishly around the plant floor and are relieved to note that no one else has ceased to work. The status quo prevails.

Consider the difference in the late night and workday conversations and activities of these people. What is the source of the disparity between the behaviors in each setting? Are these people being any more or less truthful in either situation? How does social change occur if people are not willing or able to act out their dissatisfactions?

One more story. Consider a small child with a high fever. The child has been bedridden for a few days and at one point the fever is so severe that she begins to hallucinate, seeing monsters in her bedroom. She begins to cry and call out. When her father enters the room, the child is sobbing, saying that there are monsters everywhere. Her father comforts her. "There aren't any monsters, dear, it's just a bad dream," he says. "But I'm not asleep," complains the child, "And I can *see* them!" The father tries again: "I know you can see them, but they aren't real." "Then why can I see them?" "Because you're sick," the father explains, "You have germs." "What are germs? Where are they?" the little girl asks. "Well you can't see germs, but they're real," the father answers with great confidence.

Is this a reasonable argument? Should we be surprised that the child accepts it? How many of you have ever seen a germ? How many of you believe they exist? We certainly do, yet it is more faith than science that leads us to that conclusion. Simple common sense.

Each of these scenarios has in common a focus on the intersection between social forms of expression and individual perceptions, tastes, and behaviors. In each case there is a taken-for-granted body of cultural knowledge that influences individual action in some otherwise contradictory ways. One group of people consumes certain foodstuffs while others look on in horror. Both groups feel that their tastes are equally "reasonable." A person's reactions to others and to objects depend on how the person defines the situation. The definition of the situation can differ from moment to moment depending on what the person is inclined to see. People also say and do things that appear perfectly reasonable in one situation and then appear to do the opposite in another situation. Humans engage in a great deal of behavior that appears unreasonable and illogical if viewed out of context. But in each of these instances, the behavior seems "normal" and appropriate. We have cultural rules for what is "real" and what is "not real." These rules are not necessarily based on logic or sensory perception. This book is about how human beings come to know the rules for deter-mining What Is Real in various situations. These rules enable us to organize and make sense of our experiences. When people interact with each other they do so according to these rules. The result of this interaction is a set of meaningful patterns that we think of as Society. It is important to note that these rules are constructed by humans and that they are only meaningful within a specific social context. In other words, behavior is contextually meaningful. Taken out of context, many behaviors appear contradictory or silly.

Social Psychology: Different Traditions and Concepts

Social psychology is the study of the relationship between the individual and the rules and patterns that constitute society.

Most sociologists and psychologists agree that human behavior is determined to some extent by physiological, biological, and psychic properties that are beyond the scope of social psychology. However, social psychologists emphasize that the majority of the activities that we engage in and encounter in others on a day-to-day basis consists of *social* behavior. This means that behavior is both influenced by and expressed through social context. Some of the questions that social psychologists ask are: How does the human become "socialized"? What are the implications of human socialization for the transmission of culture? How does human action contribute to the production and reproduction of various social institutions?

There is no single answer to these questions. Much like the scenarios presented above, the answer to these questions depends on which group of social psychologists is responding and the context in which their knowledge was developed. Social psychology consists of different theoretical perspectives regarding the nature of the intersection between the individual and society. Each of these perspectives follows different traditions and pursues different versions of "reality" regarding the basis of human activity and social institutions. This book is written according to a perspective known as *symbolic interactionism*. Although there are many approaches to the study of human social behavior, each with its own strengths and limitations, we find symbolic interactionism to be the most useful perspective for our purposes. In the following pages we will sketch the basic tenets of symbolic interactionism and demonstrate why we think it is a useful approach to the study of the ongoing relationship between the individual and society.

First we explore some of these different traditions in social psychology. The purpose for doing so is to provide some context for symbolic interactionism as it is developed in this book. Our list of the different social psychological traditions is not complete, and people with other purposes might offer other perspectives. We have framed the material in the following manner because it represents the intellectual background from which most social psychological theories have developed. Our discussion is organized around three of the major debates within the social sciences. This presentation is too brief to do justice to all the lines of thought that have developed over the past century. Our intention is to provide enough information to enable you to place specific social psychological traditions that you may encounter within the historical context from which they have arisen.

Some of the major themes of debate in the social sciences include what we can assume about human nature and the conception of society, the issue of the individual versus social primacy, and the question of how we can "know" something. We discuss each of these three themes below. As you read through this material, we suggest that you highlight the contrasts between symbolic interactionism and other perspectives. In order to gain the best understanding it is helpful to imagine that each perspective is similar to wearing a different pair of glasses. Ask yourself, "What do I see through this particular lens?" Also, "What don't I see?" Each perspective contains an untold story as well as the story that it represents.

Major Debates

Assumptions About Human Nature and Society

The debate about human nature centers around two questions: What can we *assume* about the human creature in order to build theories of behavior and society? And which aspects of behavior should be the *primary* focus in the study of the relationship between the individual and society? All theoretical perspectives are based on assumptions. Assumptions are unquestioned beliefs that are used as a foundation upon which to construct a theory. Every theory must have a starting point, a point at which some central ideas are fixed for the purpose of pursuing the implications of the ideas. Proponents of various perspectives do not necessarily believe that these assumptions are "true." They realize that such assumptions allow them to construct and solve puzzles. In order to comprehend and evaluate social theories you should know the assumptions upon which the theory is based.

In addition, no program of study can pursue every possible line of thought. Therefore, different perspectives isolate and scrutinize specific aspects of the social story. Each theory allows us to observe details that might otherwise go unnoticed. The biologist, for instance, focuses primarily on the cellular structure of the physical body in order to construct theories about how organisms behave; psychologists focus on the internal thoughts and impulses of individuals; sociologists emphasize groups of individuals. Each type of research gives primary emphasis to a different *unit of analysis:* the cell, the individual, or groups. Researchers sometimes get caught up in their own unit of analysis and forget that it is part of a larger picture. Thus, you will note even in this book the use of phrases such as "The *most* interesting aspects of behavior are *social*." It would be just as easy to say that the most interesting aspects of behavior are biological, though of course, as the authors of this book, we don't think this is the case. The noteworthy point is that different perspectives give primacy to different aspects of behavior. In evaluating these perspectives you should be able to locate the primary focus within its larger context, such as the cell within the organ of the body from which it was taken, and individual psychology within a social context.

With these considerations in mind we discuss four distinct approaches to human nature and the conception of society: utilitarianism, behaviorism, Freudianism, and the cognitive/interpretive perspective. Following this background we sketch the basic premises of symbolic interactionism.

Utilitarianism. Several philosophers in the 18th and 19th centuries were interested in the question of how to establish forms of government that would provide peace and order for as many people as possible. These thinkers lived in times characterized by the upheaval and rapid change forged by the Industrial Revolution. Their recent history was that of the many being ruled by the few. In order to theorize about how alternative forms of government might work, these philosophers, who include Thomas Hobbes, Jeremy Bentham, John Stuart Mill, and Adam Smith, began with an assumption based on the writings of Aristotle. This assumption is that humans have a *rational* nature. They postulated that the human creature is intelligent and selfish and will achieve its desires through reasoned thought and corresponding action. Conflict arises when people attempt to satisfy their own desires and pursue scarce resources by exploiting and injuring others.

Hobbes suggested that being reasonable, people would know that it is in their own best interest to cooperate with the laws of the land that provide order for all. In other words, humans are not dumb brutes who need to be ruled by an intelligent few (as Machiavelli, among others, had argued), but reasonable beings who will govern themselves because they desire order. Without laws and order each person must be constantly alert to the possibility of attack. Defense requires a lot of energy and personal resources. Therefore, rational individuals will give up some free agency, such as the right to harm others, in order to gain protection for themselves. One person will forego assault or robbery of another with the understanding that the other will behave in the same manner. Thus humans are free to pursue interests without fear of harm to self, as long as they are willing to submit to the same rules of self-governance themselves. In theory, they will submit because being rational, they understand the long-term benefits to themselves.

A corresponding assumption of utilitarianism is that humans will try to get the most for the least. A person will pursue the course of action that is most likely to produce the greatest returns for the least cost. Behavior is therefore the result of cost/benefit analysis in the pursuit of desired ends. Society consists of two or more individuals exchanging resources that have some relative value to each. The availability of a resource and who holds the resource determine the *structure of society.* For example, if you own a small forest in an area where there is little wood, others may want to exchange something they own for some of your wood. One neighbor may offer you sheep in return for wood to use as fuel. Another might offer to exchange wine for lumber. If you already have enough sheep of your own you will probably opt to exchange your wood for wine. When you convert the trees from your forest into lumber in exchange for the wine produced from your neighbor's vineyard, others may approach you to purchase lumber as well. If these exchanges are profitable you might become a major exporter of lumber over time. Similarly, your neighbor might choose to invest resources in developing a winery if enough buyers of wine can be found.

These exchange relationships, based on the law of supply and demand and the rules of trade that promote free exchange, constitute society from the utilitarian perspective. This perspective implies that people will select the most *rational* course of action as determined by supply and demand and that the noteworthy aspects of society consist of the exchange relationships between exchange partners. From this perspective it would be anomalous for you to continue exchanging lumber for wine if another neighbor offered you a better deal to exchange sheep for fuel. To stay with your wine exchange partner would not be rational under these circumstances.

Utilitarianism is a foundational pillar of modern Western thought. The discipline of economics is based on the assumption that humans are rational beings who calculate costs and benefits and make decisions accordingly. A major branch of political science is also founded on this tradition. Social psychologists whose research is based on the utilitarian perspective address questions such as how social order is possible among people with competing interests and how people establish power over others in order to get what they want. This tradition is known as *rational choice theory* in sociology, and its counterpart in social psychology is referred to as *exchange theory*. The important point in this context is that these theories assume that people have particular desires, and that they will behave in a manner that will maximize the attainment of these desires at minimum costs. What these desires are often remains untold. Frequently it is assumed that they include some form of material rewards and power. The emphasis of the theory, in this case, is on the rational individual. Presumably, all forms of social institutions are the result of rational exchange relationships. In other words, institutions exist and operate as they do because they meet the needs of rational, conscious humans.

The utilitarian tradition does not attempt to explain how humans become rational calculators; it simply assumes that they are. One theoretical implication of utilitarianism is that those individuals who fail to act rationally will not be successful competitors in the exchange market. If they are not successful, then they will not exist as observable cases for the researcher to study. Therefore, theoretically speaking, the perspective needn't be concerned with nonrational actors. Another implication is that society is a very fluid process that changes constantly with the redistribution of tangible resources.

The following theoretical perspectives are derivations of utilitarianism that speak specifically to questions of individual psychology. Behaviorism, which is closely related to utilitarianism, is a minimalist perspective that makes even fewer assumptions about human nature than its theoretical predecessor. Freudianism and the cognitive/interpretive perspective offer more complex theories of the individual and make more initial assumptions.

Behaviorism. Behaviorism is a school of thought generally associated with B. F. Skinner. According to the logic of this tradition, behavior is assumed to be hedonistic. In other words, humans and other animals seek pleasure and avoid punishment. This is similar to the logic of utilitarianism, except that there are no assumptions about rational behavior. Organisms, including humans, become conditioned by particular stimuli and learn to behave in a manner that produces positive results and avoids negative ones. Humans are socialized through a process whereby they *learn* that certain actions are accompanied by punishments and certain actions are followed by rewards, or positive reinforcers. If a child is repeatedly spanked for throwing food the child will learn to associate the conduct with punishment and will avoid this behavior. When the child is rewarded for a behavior, such as toilet etiquette, the child will repeat the behavior and thus become socialized to engage in "acceptable" behavior. In short, a person's behavior is predicted by the person's reinforcement history. This relationship between the environment and behavior is often referred to as stimulus-response. The stimulus is anything in a person's environment that provokes action. The environment can include internal physiology as well as external forces. Stimuli usually exist in a tangible form, such as food or money, although some researchers include less tangible stimuli such as approval and affection.

According to behaviorism, human action can be, and often is, irrational, or "neurotic." This sort of action is the result of conditioned responses to stimuli that may not actually be associated with the outcome, but which the actor associates with the desired outcome due to prior conditioning. For example, an animal that has been conditioned by electric shock not to venture beyond a specific area will continue to stay within these boundaries even if the electric fence is removed. Humans often engage in "superstitious" behaviors (such as wearing your "lucky" sweater for exams) in the belief that there is a correlation between certain actions and outcomes. These beliefs are the product of previous experience and/or superstition. In fact, there may be no "real" correlation, but if our behavioral experience indicates that there is a connection, we will persist in the behavior in hopes of producing (or avoiding) the anticipated response.

Behaviorism and its derivative, social learning theory, constitute one building block of most of the predominant social psychological theories. The theories differ, however, with regard to whether or not a particular stimulus will produce the same response in all subjects. It is thought by some that there are "universal" or "objective" resources that are desired by all people and punishments that all will avoid. Something is said to be "objective" if its effect is independent of the subject's comprehension of it. It is "universal" if it produces the same response in all subjects. The pain of fire, for example, can be considered objective and universal; pain appears to occur in all subjects that come into contact with a flame, regardless of what the person's opinion or thoughts on the fire are. On the other hand, money, which many assume to be a universal motivator, may have little or no effect on subjects who do not consider it to be important. In this case, the effect of money as a potential stimulus to action depends on a person's *subjective* interpretation of the stimulus. A researcher may expect a subject to engage in the behavior most likely to produce the greatest amount of money, for instance. Let's say the subject is placed in a situation where she is asked to exploit an acquaintance. The subject may want to be seen as a good person more than she wants the money and may therefore respond in a manner that contradicts the researcher's predictions. This action is based on the person's *subjective* evaluation of the situation. Behavior based on subjective perceptions can only be predicted if the researcher knows what it is that the person values. This can be very difficult to ascertain. Nonetheless, all variants of social psychology assume in some form that behavior is based on the desire to gain rewards and avoid punishments. Just what these rewards and punishments are and how the researcher should figure this out is a complex puzzle.

Behaviorism as a social psychological research program does not offer much of a picture of society. In terms of human socialization the perspective assumes preexisting socialized beings who socialize the next generations through conditioned stimulus-response patterns. How the first humans became socialized initially and why they value certain things and avoid others remain unanswered questions. The primary emphasis is on the individual's reinforcement history, in other words, the patterns of learning achieved through the application of particular rewards and punishments. Why people in this society are punished for not wearing clothing, for example, and are rewarded for wearing certain types of clothing is not a story that can be told from the behaviorist perspective. The story that is told is how people learn that they must wear clothes through punishments, such as being spanked and later jailed, and how certain clothes bring rewards, such as popularity and dates. Based on this perspective it is possible to imagine how one might construct an "ideal" society and train people to behave in a manner that supports these ideals. In his book *Walden Two* (1976) Skinner tells such a story. This book, which was very influential during the 1970s, illustrates the construction of a utopian society based on "behavioral engineering."

Freudianism. In contrast to both the utilitarians and behaviorists, Freud and his followers argued that behavior is largely the result of unconscious desires and impulses that arise in the human psyche. From this perspective, Skinner's utopian society is doomed to failure because people can never be perfectly socialized. Unconscious desires and impulses in the form of sexuality and aggression will rear up and counteract the effects of even the most careful behavioral conditioning. Similarly, seen from this perspective humans are hardly rational and are unlikely to act on the reasonable calculation of costs and benefits. In contrast, most behavior is an attempt to arrive at some tolerable compromise between the bundles of impulses that surge through our unconscious and the striving to live within the boundaries established by our social community.

Freud was one of the first researchers to direct his attention to the human unconscious. In doing so he unlatched a black box previously ignored by most students of human social behavior. Behaviorists discount the distinction between the conscious and the unconscious altogether. They prefer to go directly from an observable stimulus to an observable response. In conversation with a Freudian, a behaviorist might say that unconscious impulses are simply a form of stimulus—in this case an internal rather than an external stimulus. The important feature for the behaviorist is what happens to the person when he or she acts on this impulse? Is the behavior punished and thereby eventually extinguished, or is it rewarded and therefore repeated? Freud might not disagree with this analysis, but his concern was with documenting just what these impulses and drives consisted of in the human and how the contradictions inherent in these forces are reconciled through human development. His larger agenda was to demonstrate that civilization is the product of our attempt to temper and harness these otherwise unruly impulses. Social institutions exist to bring some modicum of order where there would otherwise be only the chaos of beasts raping and murdering one another.

The story left untold by Freud and his followers is how specifically human beasts get their act together and form social institutions that then serve to bring order to chaos. He does offer a complex theory about the development of the individual human from a bundle of impulses and energy into a social creature. Although it offers rich insights regarding psychological development, Freud's story is relatively silent on the development of society. The origin of the first generation of socialized beings who served as models for the subsequent generations is a story that needs further development. Recall that the utilitarians address this question by assuming that humans are rational and will therefore be motivated to form social institutions that benefit each of them individually. Freud offers a richer and more complex picture of the human actor than the utilitarians, but we have to look beyond his theory to see just how human institutions may have gotten their start.

Cognitive/Interpretive. Another perspective that offers a more complex view of the human actor than that assumed by the utilitarians or the behaviorists is the cognitive/interpretive approach. In addition to the black box of the human psyche there is the black box of human thought, or cognition, as it is referred to. Many researchers who agreed with the basic proposition of behaviorism—behavior is the result of learning which actions produce pain and which ones produce rewards—decided that most forms of stimuli are subjective rather than objective. In other words, the way a person responds to a stimulus (for example, a hug) depends on how the person *interprets* the stimulus. If the hug is interpreted as an aggressive clinch then the person will respond differently than if the hug is thought to be a show of affection. Based on the observation that interpretation comes between the stimulus and the response, cognitive social psychologists give primary emphasis to *thought processes.* These processes include what information people pay attention to, how people store the information, and how they later recall it. According to most variants of this perspective, behavior is the result of the individual's selective interpretation of the stimulus. Thus, it is not likely that you would drool in anticipation if offered a beetle burrito. But your rural counterpart in the village we mentioned might interpret the tortilla filled with creeping black bugs as a delicacy and respond with enthusiasm. Same stimulus, different subjective interpretations, different responses. We say a great deal more about the process of interpretation in the essay that accompanies Part II.

In addition to the observation that humans interpret stimuli rather than respond directly to them, another thread of development in the cognitive story concerns the question of whether or not humans are capable of rational thought. In a major research program conducted over the past three decades, two cognitive social psychologists, Daniel Kahnemann and Amos Tversky (Tversky, Kahnemann, & Slovic, 1982), have explored this question. One assumption of rationality is that if you have a preference for A over B and a preference for B over C, then you should prefer A over C. This assumption, known as *transitivity,* seems reasonable. Kahnemann and Tversky decided to test the assumption of transitivity in some experiments. In one experiment, people were asked to select panty hose from a variety of styles and colors. The experiments demonstrated that people who preferred panty hose A over panty hose B, and panty hose B over panty hose C, did not necessarily prefer A over C. In fact, after having selected A in the choice between A and B, and B in the choice between B and C, many participants selected C when given a choice between A and C. In other words, someone who claims to prefer nylon over wool and wool over cotton will presumably prefer nylon over cotton as well. Kahnemann and Tversky demonstrated that this is not necessarily the case. Many people who prefer nylon over wool, and wool over cotton, select cotton in the choice between cotton and nylon.

In yet another study it was observed that the ability to perform complex mathematical calculations was contextually specific (Lave, 1988). Women who generally performed poorly on written math exams were tested on the same skills while grocery shopping. The finding was that these woman performed very rational calculations during the activity of shopping for the best bargains. Conversely, husbands whose wives generally did the shopping, and who performed well on written math tests, did not fare well in locating bargains at the grocery store. The same cognitive skill operated differently in different contexts.

Another assumption of rationality that has not held up to experimental scrutiny is decision making based on the laws of probability. Consider this test. A researcher holds 100 cards that contain short biographical statements taken from 30 engineers and 70 lawyers. The following card is selected at random and read: "Bob is in his middle 40s. He enjoys mathematical puzzles, dislikes social gatherings, and likes to build model trains." Is Bob a lawyer or an engineer? Most people guess that he is an engineer. Yet, based on probability, the most rational guess is that he is a lawyer. The tendency to guess Bob's profession based on the certain types of behavior or activities associated with the profession is a form of stereotyping. Stereotyping involves the use of specific categories of meaning for assessing people or situations. This process of forming opinions is very different from the process suggested by the laws of rational probability.

Social cognition is concerned with the manner in which people impose preexisting categories of thought on the stimuli in their environment and use these categories, or *schema*, to select what to pay attention to, how to "see" the information, and how to store it in and recall it from memory. Some significant schemas include *role schemas* and *event schemas*. In one study of role schemas, subjects were shown a film of a woman and a man having a celebration dinner. Half of the subjects were told that the woman was a librarian; the others were told that she was a server in a restaurant. In each case the subjects recalled information that was consistent with the relevant role schema; the librarian wore glasses and mentioned a trip to Europe, the server liked to bowl and drink beer. Here is an interesting point. The subjects not only focused on and recalled information present in the film that was consistent with their pre-established stereotypes, but they actually made up information that affirmed these schemas as well. For example, subjects reported that the server ate a hamburger. Those believing the woman to be a librarian reported that she ate roast beef. In neither case was the reported item shown in the relevant film (Cohen, 1981). The implication is not that people lie or make things up. It is that perception is influenced by social categories and is a *constructive* as well as a *reflective* process.

Cognitive schemas are based on individual experience. The study of cognition is primarily concerned with individual thought processes. The implication of this perspective is that society exists in the structure of a person's thoughts. In this regard social institutions are individually relative. A question that arises, therefore, is how human groups come to have the *shared* perceptions and interpretations that are necessary for the transmission of culture. The perspective is paradoxical in that it also implies that human thought is shaped by culture. Our social group is the source of our shared schemas. The untold story is how the ideas of "society" get into the human mind and influence individual perceptions to begin with. We have placed the term society in quotes here to underscore another point regarding the cognitive conception of society. This is that "society" is somehow "out there," independent of human actors, but able to shape and direct the course of human thought. Because of the theoretical emphasis on human thought, the cognitive/interpretive perspective also has not focused much on actual human behavior. The assumption is that thoughts somehow predict behavior. Without a more developed story of the relationship between thought and behavior it is difficult to complete the narrative of how human action results in social patterns.

In summary, the foregoing theoretical traditions each begin with a different view of human nature and focus on different angles of the big picture regarding the relationship between the individual and society. The utilitarian tradition emphasizes the rational calculator. The primary lines of inquiry are the impli-cations of the exchange of goods between rational actors and how these economic exchanges affect the structure of society. Behaviorists view the human being as the sum of a history of rewards and punishment. The actor has learned to pursue certain lines of action and to avoid others. Social behavior within any particular group is the result of this conditioned learning. Theoretically it should be possible, according to this perspective, to "engineer" different types of social behavior that would result in alternative types of societies. Utilitarians and behaviorists emphasize observable actions and are interested in the effects of these actions on the social environment. In contrast, Freudians and cognitive/interpretivists focus on internal processes. Freud emphasized the unconscious mind. The tradition following him is interested in how unconscious impulses are dealt with in the process of socializing the human into a healthy adult. Cognitive/interpretivists focus on human thought. A central line of inquiry from this perspective is how people make sense out of the stimuli that they encounter—how they perceive and deal with the environment in an organized fashion.

Symbolic Interactionism

In this book we present social psychology from the perspective of symbolic interactionism. This orientation emphasizes the production of society as an ongoing process of negotiation among social actors. In concert with the cognitive/interpretive perspective, symbolic interactionism suggests that the potential for society exists in the minds of actors who share common symbolic expectations about reality. Society is enacted in the momentary, situational encounters that humans perform with one another. In other words, there is no society independent of the human mind and human expression of culture. This implies that in a strict theoretical sense, humans exist as embryonic potential and anything that the mind can conceive is possible. As we will discuss in detail, however, one of the themes of this book is the manner in which humans limit these possibilities by creating and maintaining social boundaries that make life orderly and predictable. Two main points are worth underlining. One is that we can observe stable patterns of interaction among human beings. Recall, for example, the factory employees discussed in the opening narratives. We would expect to observe that these factory employees will grouse with one another about their job, but make do with the unsatisfactory conditions while on the job. These patterns are the equivalent of social structure. The second point is that enduring as these patterns may seem, they are fragile in that they require the constant coordination and shared understanding of the actors involved to maintain them. It is the tacit compliance of each of the participants that makes social patterns endure.

Symbolic interactionism shares with utilitarianism the assumption that humans are motivated to make practical use of the things they encounter in their environment (including other people). Humans attempt to mold the environment to their own ends. One distinction between the two perspectives is that symbolic interactionists assume that the ends a person desires and the means he or she employs to achieve these ends are based on socially constructed meanings. There are no assumptions about rationality, with its corresponding implications that some goals and resources are inherently more desirable than others. Utilitarianism assumes preexisting standards of what is valuable based on supply and demand, and further assumes that people will act to obtain these valued ends according to the principles of rationality. Symbolic interactionism assumes that what we value and the recipes for how to obtain it are shaped by the social group(s) with which we interact. Values and motivations are based on subjective interpretation. In this regard symbolic interactionism is similar to the cognitive/interpretive tradition.

Like the utilitarians, symbolic interactionists also view society as a fluid process that consists of a series of ongoing human interactions. This is in contrast to the other perspectives we have discussed, each of which treats society as somehow distinct, or apart from the action of individuals. The difference between a conception of social process based on symbolic interactionism and that derived from utilitarianism is that the latter focuses on the exchange of tangible resources that have some intrinsic utility, whereas the former focuses on the exchange of *symbolically meaningful* items and actions. Seen from the utilitarian perspective, the value of the exchange of an item is in its potential use, for example, as food or currency. A symbolic interactionist would view gift exchange in terms of the symbolic gesture it communicates, such as a show of respect, friendship, or solidarity. There is a long history of debate among anthropologists over whether or not human interaction should be viewed primarily as an exchange of utilities or as an exchange of socially meaningful symbols. Symbolic interactionists pursue the latter line of thought.

Symbolic interactionism is similar to behaviorism in the emphasis that human action is motivated by a desire to seek rewards and to avoid punishments. However, symbolic interactionists focus on the *interactional context* and study how participants in an interaction negotiate the meaning of the situation in order to get one another to respond in a desirable way. The emphasis on *meaning negotiated through interaction* is a more social focus than the individual stimulus-response histories studied by behaviorists.

Regarding Freudianism, symbolic interactionists acknowledge that humans are a bundle of drives and impulses. The emphasis in both theories is on the manner in which humans learn to observe, comment on, and direct their own impulses. This process, which is one of internal conversation about the "self," serves to bring a person's behavior into line with the expectations of the social group. Symbolic interactionism is concerned primarily with how the person learns to assign culturally specific meanings to particular actions through inter-action with others. The person then directs her or his behavior in a manner that will produce anticipated rewards and avoid punishments from others. This is socialization. The picture of the actor is of a creature who is reasonable and pragmatic in the pursuit of rewards and the avoidance of punishment as these are subjectively valued by the actor. Furthermore, the actor learns which behaviors produce which outcomes through the ability to observe her or his own actions and direct them. The point to underscore is that symbolic interactionism focuses on the subjective interpretations not of isolated actors, but of events as they occur in an *interactional context*. The assumption is that whether we are engaged in face-to-face encounters or are having an internal dialogue with an imagined other, most human activity is directed toward an evaluation of *how to respond to others in specific contexts*. In this regard, symbolic interaction is the most *social* of the social psychologies. The important questions of study from this perspective are what meaning people give to a social context and how they negotiate and realize this meaning through interaction with others. For this reason, symbolic interactionists talk of "performing reality." Society consists of an ongoing performance of socially meaningful interaction rituals.

Two points are noteworthy regarding symbolic interactionism in contrast to other social psychological perspectives and the major themes of debate:

1. Symbolic interactionism gives primacy to the social over the individual. In other words, behavior is assumed to be primarily a response to social factors.
2. The focus of study is on observable behavior, but the cause of this behavior is assumed to be nonobservable processes of individual interpretation. In other words, behavior is based

on a subjective interpretation of the social environment rather than a direct response to objective stimuli.

These two points are discussed further in the following themes of debate.

One thread that is woven through the story of Western social science regardless of the perspective is the theme of rationality. Whether or not each of the foregoing traditions assumes a rational actor, an implicit point in each is the notion that *humans must become rational in order to function in the modern world.* Whether or not humans actually behave in a rational manner, the legal and political institutions of the United States assume that they do. If we are not reasonable creatures, then we cannot be held accountable for our actions. Individual accountability is the backbone of society as we know it to be. The following discussion concerns a debate about whether or not social researchers should give primary emphasis to individual actions or to social processes. We have termed this debate "Individualism Versus the Social Group." This is a highly charged philosophical and political question with significant implications for how governments should be designed and resources allocated among groups of people.

Individualism Versus the Social Group

Who are you really? Are you a product of your social group, or are you the result of some independent genetic, psychological, perhaps even spiritual factors? How did you get to be you? This question is at the center of the debate among scholars regarding the emphasis on the individual versus the social group. As you read through this section, ponder how you might be different if your significant associations were with family and friends other than those you now have. Or what if you had been raised in another culture?

The hero of U.S. culture is the individual. This person is independent and self-sufficient, a self-starter who is always looking ahead. The U.S. hero is capable of saving the day single-handed. These heroes are epitomized in the early U.S. folklore of the frontierspeople who forged their own way: Daniel Boone, Davy Crockett, Annie Oakley, and Paul Bunyan. The spirit of individualism pervades the work of well-known U.S. poets and authors such as Louisa May Alcott, Walt Whitman, James Fenimore Cooper, Emily Dickinson, Harriet Beecher Stowe, Henry David Thoreau, and Daniel Webster. Through recent decades Hollywood has underwritten the theme of individualism with characters such as John Wayne astride his horse and James Dean and Clint Eastwood astride their motorcycles. Even contemporary cult favorites, such as "Mad Max" and "Repo Man," perpetuate the myth of the U.S. individual hero. When women are recognized by the star-making machinery of Hollywood and the music industry, they too embody the theme of individual achievement and the rise to fame. The film *Thelma and Louise* extends to women the theme of breaking away from the suffocating walls of social expectations in the pursuit of individual freedom. Try this bit of social observation yourself: For one week take note of the number of times that a group is the focus of attention in television programs, movies or novels, and magazines. When a group is emphasized, what is the context? Is the group "heroic"? If so, does the emphasis remain with the group or switch to a group "leader"? Contrast this with the emphasis on the doings, dilemmas, and achievements of single stars and individual characters.

How does the U.S. individual achieve her or his individuality? A survey of popular culture throughout our history suggests that we are endowed with this spirit of individualism. A pervasive plot is that of the individual pitted against forces of evil that threaten to destroy the individual spirit, either from within or without. A central focus in the recent film *Malcolm X* is the betrayal of one individual leader by the group that helped him to power. Malcolm becomes a hero through the process of breaking away from the corruptions of the group and seeking his own path. In film and literature the individual-as-hero begins to take on shape and definition in the struggle against these forces. The forces themselves remain a fuzzy background against which the individual can be sharply defined. In many instances this struggle can be interpreted as the attainment of personal distinction by casting off social chains and rising above "the masses." Indeed, the quest of the U.S. individual may be said to be that of achieving difference relative to her or his cultural backdrop. To admit to being a product of social forces is to suggest that one is a cultural sheep. It is far more preferable to see oneself as having achieved individual distinction through psychological and spiritual struggle. This is the myth of individualism that permeates U.S. culture.

There is evidence that average people act in accordance with this myth. Social psychologists demonstrated some years ago that people are inclined to attribute observed behaviors to individual volition rather than to social or environmental factors. For example, if someone performs poorly on an exam, the cause of this performance is likely to be seen as lack of intelligence or lack of studying—something regarding individual ability. The likelihood that the exam may be culturally biased (a social factor) in such a way that the person is unable to interpret the questions is probably not considered as a possible explanation. Similarly, if one person is observed to be hitting another, we are likely to assume that the person is angry or hostile, has a short temper, and is showing little self-control. We will probably assume that the behavior is connected to certain "personality traits." The possibility that the person has never acted aggressively before but was somehow induced to do so through the dynamics of the situation often doesn't enter into our assessment of the situation. This tendency to assume individual responsibility over social forces is known as the *fundamental attribution error.* People are more likely to attribute behaviors to individual personality and character traits than to social context. In recent years it has been shown that the fundamental attribution error is a U.S. phenomenon; people in other cultures do not tend to make such individualistic judgments when trying to explain things. This tendency underscores the U.S. cultural attitude that single, individual actions are the primary forces shaping the world.

Several observers and critics have noted that the myth of U.S. individualism also pervades the study of social behavior and organizations. The criticism is that there is an overemphasis on the study of individual psychology and development in explaining social behavior and not enough emphasis on environmental factors, particularly social context. European social psychologists criticize their counterparts in the United States for the imbalance between individual psychology and social context. An illustrative scenario popular among sociologists goes like this: A person visits a therapist and complains of extreme distress and the inability to function well in his daily tasks. The person appears very agitated and disoriented. Therapist A spends several years delving into the client's past with special emphasis on the person's relationship with his mother. Therapist B administers a battery of psychological tests and conducts in-depth interviews with her client in order to comprehend how the client perceives his role vis-à-vis his employer, his wife, and other significant private events in his life. This therapy takes several months. Therapist C notices immediately that the patient is presenting symptoms of psychological disillusionment, diagnoses the person as schizophrenic, and has him hospitalized. Therapist D asks the client what sorts of things have gone on in his life recently. The distressed man reports that his wife died recently, he was fired from his job a week ago, his kitchen caught fire the previous evening, and his tire blew out driving to the therapist's office. Therapist D informs the man that he is suffering from an overload of stressful events and tells him to take a vacation.

In this scenario each therapist interprets the situation from the perspective of her or his own training. Therapist A is a Freudian and is inclined to see the man's distress as the result of unresolved psychological impulses and early childhood relations with his parents. Therapist B represents the contemporary cognitive psychologist who is sympathetic to the man's interpretations of his situation but is overly concerned with cognitive functioning at the expense of social context. Therapist C is a psychiatrist who diagnoses the symptoms that are present in the immediate situation without concern for the big picture. Only Therapist D, trained as a sociologist, is inclined to see the extent to which contextual factors may be responsible for the man's immediate emotional state and behavior.

Each of these characters represents a stereotype, of course. But the point is important. Even those who study and treat human behavior often fail to recognize the influence of social context on behavior. It is not necessarily the intention of psychologists or social psychologists to perpetuate individualism. However, they do so to the extent that they fail to examine how much the myth of the independent individual pervades their initial assumptions and thus colors their study of human behavior. The utilitarian perspective is represented by each of the therapists as well as the client. In all cases it is assumed that the man is not behaving as he "should." In other words, his ability to reason and to act responsibly is in question. Regardless of the type of treatment prescribed, all are in agreement that he *needs* treatment to restore his abilities as a rational actor. This unquestioned assumption speaks to the utilitarian underpinnings of Western civilization. Utilitarianism and individualism are the twin pillars of our cultural foundation.

Symbolic interactionism recognizes the themes of rationality and individualism, but as a topic of study rather than an assumed state of being or a necessary political philosophy. Symbolic interactionism gives theoretical primacy to social institutions rather than the individual. Seen from this perspective, rational individualism is a form of social institution that characterizes Western civilization, particularly contemporary North American society. Individualism is therefore a *cultural script*. This script, which is learned through a process of socialization, tells us that the pursuit of individual distinction through rational actions is socially rewarding. In another culture, such pursuits might elicit punishment rather than reward. The point is that people are not inherently rational, nor are they necessarily predisposed to value the individual over the collective; these are culturally specific values.

Individualism is a socially constructed value. It is a set of shared cultural standards by which we knowingly—or unknowingly—shape our behavior. To treat individualism explicitly as a social construction enables us to better study the rules we use as social creatures to determine our own behavior. Ironically, the standard of individual rationality, which presumably gives us the freedom that we so value, may actually hinder and constrain our behavioral possibilities. To the extent that we assume that individualism is a given and necessary aspect of society, we may fail to notice the way in which it curtails and limits other possible lines of action. For instance, whether or not you have a "rational" account for engaging in a particular activity that you happen to enjoy, you must invent such an account. How often have you not done something that you were inclined to do because you didn't have a good enough rationale? One cultural rule is that we must have "good reasons" for our actions, so that we can be held individually accountable.

The point is that an overemphasis on the individual under-plays the influence of the social scripts that individuals use to shape and direct their behavior. Human behavior can be better understood in light of the social context in which it occurs. One reason for this emphasis of the individual over the social in North American social psychology is that these traditions have themselves been shaped by the cultural context in which they have been developed. This context favors the individual over the social. Symbolic interactionism maintains that this emphasis be transcended for better understanding of the implications of the cultural standards of individualism. The "cult of individualism," as it is sometimes referred to, represents "society" as an alien entity that somehow exists independent of human activity. Social forces are something to "break away from" to pursue individual interests. Ironically, theoretical traditions that place so much emphasis on fleshing out human psychology, whether conscious or unconscious, have so separated the individual from society that they cannot yield an explanation of how human action contributes to the construction of the social world. The result is a theoretical actor that exists as an isolated island.

The task of *social* psychology is to merge the social with the individual. The relevant questions for this task are: How does society influence individual action? and, How does individual action shape society? The philosophy of individualism implies that social factors shape the individual in ways that hinder or constrain individual freedom. The moral implication of this philosophy is that we must break away from these chains. This line of reasoning assumes that there is something significant about human social behavior that is not social. Herein lies a paradox. If we break away from social chains, we are left with a bundle of passions. A creature that is a bundle of passions cannot assess and direct its own behavior. Such a creature has no potential to become an "individual hero" because it cannot take responsibility for its own behavior. Our court system distinguishes between those who are capable of knowing what the rules of society are and those who are deemed incompetent to stand trial because they do not comprehend the rules. The criminally insane are judged "unsocial." The rest of us are judged to be competent players because we know the rules of our society and are capable of directing our behavior accordingly. Regardless of whether we choose to obey or disobey the law, we make a choice. Such choices involve incorporating general social standards into our decision-making processes. Similarly, in the various ways in which we exercise freedom of choice by breaking away from social norms, we are using these social rules as a standard by which we judge ourselves and act. Without these social standards what would be our basis for self-evaluation and action? Social rules provide the structure that enables us to organize our bundle of passions into meaningful behavior, even if that behavior is "breaking away." Without such structure, we would have no basis for aligning our behavior with those around us; we would be cut off from our fellow beings. Seen from this angle, the concept of free agency would be a moot point.

This philosophy suggests that humans are *social* creatures. This means that we use shared social standards to shape and evaluate our own actions. These standards serve to coordinate the activity of creatures who would be otherwise isolated. To pursue the implications of this assumption we require a theory that merges the social and the individual into one. The foregoing perspectives, although each has many merits with regard to its particular focus, all isolate the individual from society and represent society as something apart from us, something that exists "out there." The theoretical challenge that underlies this book is how to develop a story that emphasizes the *reciprocal relationship* between individual human actors and their society. This theory must be capable of telling us how social standards shape the development of the individual and how, in turn, individual actions contribute to the maintenance or alteration of these standards.

Social standards are relative; they vary from culture to culture. We have said that two of the main social standards of U.S. society are individuality and rationality. These standards do not exist independent of the social groups who believe in them and act them out. Rationality is not "out there" waiting to bite you on the nose. You are not born with the characteristics of individuality. Paradoxical as it may seem, you develop your "individuality" in the process of becoming socialized into U.S. social life. Similarly, the Japanese person who develops a sense of "groupness" does so in the process of becoming socialized into her or his culture. Neither "individualism" nor "groupness" is any more or less correct or "real." As we illustrate with the narratives that begin this essay, which one you are inclined to see and comprehend depends on your point of view. Our own cultural standards instruct us to be suspicious of cultures that place too much emphasis on the social group. From the perspective of many Americans, groupness threatens individual freedom. From the perspective of cultures that espouse groupness, however, too much unchecked individual selfishness threatens the long-term interests of everyone in the group.

Our intent here is not to make the case for either individuality or groupness as cultural standards but to suggest that to understand human social behavior we must focus on the social context of the behavior. Social factors shape our perspective of reality and thereby influence how we act. In this section we have indicated that even theories of human behavior and society are influenced by general social factors, such as the cultural standards of individuality and rationality. To more fully understand the relationship between the individual and society we must make these cultural standards explicit and attempt to transcend them in our analysis. In this book we emphasize a theoretical perspective with the assumption that the human is primarily a social creature, who through interaction with others, continually creates and recreates social reality.

Positivism Versus Constructionism

How do we discover "truth"? The question of what constitutes knowledge and how to get it has occupied humankind since it developed a collective consciousness. The modern methods for obtaining and verifying information about the world and how it works can be traced to the dialogues of philosophers in 17th- and 18th-century France. During this time the tyrannies of autocratic rule and the superstitions of religion and magic were giving way to the reason of "science." This period in history is referred to as the Enlightenment. The hope of the day was that grand reason would enable its practitioners to harness nature and to invent forms of government that would lead to a better and more just world for all. Using reason and logic, the scientist would uncover the laws of nature and discover the "absolute truths" of the universe. According to this logic, or the new religion of science, the scientist could formulate ideas about the nature of reality and then test these ideas empirically. Although nothing could ever be known for certain, hypotheses could be verified or refuted until they approached the statement of probabilities that approximated certainty; "truth" with a small *t* would suffice.

The logic of science is based on the rejection of alternative hypotheses. If one can reject all possible alternative "truths," then the remaining hypothesis can be taken as positive. A well-known illustration comes from Karl Popper. Popper suggested the hypothesis that "All swans are white." Having established this hypothesis, the scientist then attempts to refute it by finding a contrary case. If a single black swan is located then the hypothesis can be rejected. It can now be said, positively, that all swans are *not* white.

The scientific method, known as positivism, was revolutionary in the biological and physical sciences. By the 19th century many social philosophers began to adopt the method that had been so successful in uncovering "truth" about the natural world. These social philosophers used a similar reason to pursue truths about the social world. The methods of science held the promise of a new age of rationality and prosperity. The only limitation to what science could discover was in the technology needed to conduct increasingly sophisticated observations of the natural world. With time and the development of technology, all the secrets of the natural world would be revealed.

In the 20th century, however, physicists, including Heisenberg and Einstein, began to question the possibility of universal "truth." It seemed that different experiments yielded different results depending on how the question was asked. For example, when light was hypothesized to be waves and tested as such, it produced a pattern that suggested it was waves. However, when it was hypothesized to be particles, the tests revealed a particle-confirming pattern. Was it possible that light was both wave and particle? Both energy and matter at the same time? Heisenberg concluded that the experimental process itself interacts with the reality; there is no completely objective stance from which to view "truth." As scientists we shape the outcome to some extent by our interaction with the phenomenon. Einstein summarized this with the statement, "It is the theory that determines what we can observe."

These observations set the stage for the contemporary debate between those who practice positive science with the goal of discovering and verifying "truth," and those who argue that "truth" is relative—in the case of science, truth is relative to the context of the theories themselves. These theories do not reflect natural reality. They are a social construction. The philosophy that underlies positive science is that there are natural laws that govern the universe and these laws can be known. The counter-argument is that any order that we perceive to exist in a state of nature is the product of our own systems for organizing the "facts." In other words, our theories, which are organized systems of thought, do not simply verify or refute positive truth; they actually interact with the observed phenomenon to create a relative truth. This is a bit like the old conundrum, Does a tree falling alone in the forest make any noise? If we are not present to observe the tree, we cannot know whether or not it makes any noise. And if it does make a noise when we are present, is it only because we are there to hear it? Without the presence of our ears, which "measure" the sound, does the tree *really* make any noise?

Symbolic interactionism takes the position that knowledge, including scientific knowledge, is relative. It is the product of the context within which it is constructed. Humans do not experience the world in its natural state. We do not gather and observe "facts" that interpret themselves. Scientific data are benign. The selection and interpretation of data is based on classification schemes constructed by the observers. No matter how logical and insightful these schemes are, they influence how we make sense of the data and arrive at conclusions about "truth." An example from the study of paleontology is illustrative.

In the book *It's a Wonderful Life* (1989), the natural historian Stephen Jay Gould tells the story of the Burgess Shale. This limestone quarry, which was formed over 530 million years ago, supported more life forms than can be found in the oceans today. The Burgess Shale was discovered by modern naturalists in the early 20th century. According to Gould, its discovery could have changed the entire notion of biological evolution. However, the early discoverers classified every fossil in the Burgess Shale according to the existing classification taxonomy. This taxonomy consisted of only two categories: worms and arthropods. This scheme supported the two dominant perspectives in the study of human evolution: the hierarchical "ladder of progress" theory and the "inverted cone" theory (which holds that creatures evolve with increasing diversity and complexity).

An alternative classification might have enabled seeing evidence for a different set of theories. If the rich diversity of the species fossilized in the Burgess Shale is acknowledged, it serves as evidence for a more recent theory. This theory does not emphasize the superiority of human evolution. Instead, it features an "incredibly prolific bush" theory according to which particular species spread branches that then either break off or continue, a bit like a lottery. From this theoretical vantage point, human evolution is an awesome improbability, not an inevitable truth. Gould points out that the first taxonomists were unable to "see" the richness of the Burgess Shale because they were "trapped by history. . . . The familiar iconographies of evolution are all directed toward reinforcing a comfortable view of human inevitability and superiority. The comfortably familiar becomes a prison of thought" (p. 1).

This story illustrates that the "evidence" has to be classified and interpreted. The theories that shape the process of classification and interpretation determine the picture of "reality" that emerges. The implication is that scientific knowledge is not a direct representation of the natural world, but is based on theoretical systems of thought that are culturally and historically bounded. These systems of thought provide a lens through which to collect, organize, and interpret the information. Theoretical perspectives generally reflect the prevalent paradigms of thought that characterize a particular culture at a particular time in its history. The Burgess Shale was first classified according to theories that supported the superior nature of the human species, a theme prevalent in the early part of this century. More recently, the fossils have been reclassified, this time according to theories that are based on the contemporary reaction that questions these assumptions of human superiority relative to other species. Which one is correct? Both are more or less "correct" according to the criteria for scientific research that governed the historical context in which the classification schemes were developed.

The dominant systems of thought that characterize historical epochs are sometimes referred to as "the language of the day." The two classifications of the Burgess Shale are consistent with the language of their respective day. The case of Copernicus, who was able to convince some of his fellow astronomers that the earth revolved around the sun rather than the other way around, is an example of the relationship between scientific discovery and the language of the day. During the time of Copernicus, it was believed that the sun and all other planets known to exist in the heavens circled the earth. This belief was based on the mathematical calculations of Ptolemy and was known as the Ptolemaic system. Several astronomers suspected, based on the evidence provided by their eyes, that the earth might actually revolve around the sun. However, the language of the day consisted of a particular scheme of mathematics that supported the Catholic church teachings that earth was the center of the universe and humans the center of all things. Most mathematical calculations, the predominant method for charting the movement of celestial bodies, were based on this theory and in turn supported it.

Copernicus was successful in launching a scientific revolution, not because he gathered new empirical evidence that demonstrated conclusively the earth's movements around the sun, but because he developed a mathematical statement that suggested this to be the case. The invention of the telescope was still several years away. Copernicus used the language of the day, with a slightly new twist, to advance an alternative theory. Thus, existing systems of thought can be used to either affirm or alter a particular version of scientific truth. This does not mean that one theory is more or less "correct." The accuracy of scientific propositions is assessed by the prevailing standards of the time. These standards are also shaped by the language of the day. Copernicus was able to reach his colleagues by using the shared language of their knowledge to cast a new light on an old question. He met with resistance from the church, however, because his "findings" did not coincide with another, very powerful perspective of the day. A century later, with the evidence of his telescope to back him up, Galileo was still made to recant similar assertions that the earth revolved around the sun when the church found them to be "incorrect" according to current standards.

A contemporary symbolic interactionist, T. R. Young (see his "Dress, Drama, and Self," p. 147), has stated that "all science is poetics and politics. The question of relevance is whose poetics and whose politics." This statement captures the symbolic interactionist perspective on the debate between positivism and constructionism. Symbolic interactionism treats scientific dialogue in a manner similar to other human interactions—as an interaction among a community of people, in this case the practitioners of a particular line of scientific inquiry. This interaction is based on a general system of shared meaning and reflects the historical context in which it occurs. The following points summarize the symbolic interactionist position regarding the debate over the pursuit of scientific truth:

1. Scientific communities create and affirm systems of thought, known as theoretical paradigms, that shape what we can know and how we can know it.
2. These theories are socially constructed and reflect the historical context in which they are developed.
3. Symbolic interactionism uses the methods of fieldwork, interviews, and participant observation to understand human behavior. The researcher attempts to take the role of the subject and to understand the interactional context in which the behavior takes place.

So, What's Real?

According to symbolic interactionism, "truth" and "reality" are determined by the context in which they are practiced. Does this mean that anything goes? Far from it. Reality may differ across social groups, but within each group there is a taken-for-granted system of knowledge that establishes boundaries about what is real. One point of interest for symbolic interactionists is that people within these groups act "as if" their reality is based on a natural truth. These realities include culturally specific rules for how one can know things. These rules are complex and contextually specific. Thus, people in one society may believe in the existence of germs that cause illness. They may invest considerable resources in developing the technology necessary to "see" and "control" these germs. In another culture, people may perfect other ceremonies and rituals to "see" and "communicate with" spirits that control the health of the people. A central focus of study in symbolic interactionism is what these rules consist of and how members of a community produce and reproduce their systems of knowledge through interaction. The results of these interactions are the patterns of meaning that constitute a society.

In place of the question, What's real? we prefer to ask, What are the implications of a particular reality? What story do different perspectives offer about the nature of the world and our place in it? These questions remind us to scrutinize our own rules of interaction and implications for self and society; to make explicit that which is taken for granted. One of the major strengths of symbolic interactionism is that the perspective encourages us to see our own role as authors in the human story.

One general aim of this book is to establish a foundation for symbolic activity based in human thought processes (social cognition) and then to use this foundation as a means to address sociological questions such as the production and reproduction of social order and institutions. By way of summary, the basic components of this foundation are symbols, the social self, interaction, and social patterns. The materials in this book are organized to present a picture of society as the product of human interaction based on the use of shared social symbols that are incorporated into human conduct through cognitive processes. Because we derive our cognitive schemas from cultural patterns (see Part II) these processes reflect a preexisting social structure. But it is through our interactions with one another that we reproduce and potentially change these structures.

Organization of the Book

Symbolic interactionists pursue the question of how the human incorporates existing cultural knowledge into private thought and how this knowledge is acted on, affirmed, and modified in the course of everyday interactions. In this book we will explore this main agenda. Part II deals specifically with the issue of how humans develop and maintain private active minds that are at the same time a reflection of cultural patterns. The key to this puzzle for symbolic interactionists is in the symbol. The symbol is an abstract representation of something that may or may not exist in a tangible form. "Table" is the symbolic representation of a class of objects constructed from hard substances and designed to serve certain purposes. "Guilt" symbolizes a feeling that those of you who can comprehend this text are familiar with, but it has no actual, physical referent. Complex webs of symbols that are used for communication are known as language. Language, according to the general tenets of symbolic interactionism, is the basis of human thought. It is through language that we are able to incorporate culture into us, and then through our own thoughts and actions, modify and reproduce this culture.

Part III takes up the process of interaction. Humans develop a social self and learn and recreate their culture through inter-action. Social relationships, such as power, are given meaning and come to life when they are acted out by members of a social group. These patterns are discernible in the minute encounters of everyday life, such as conversations. Basic interaction requires people to project an image of what part they wish to play, what part they want others to play, and how they intend to define the situation. For interaction to proceed smoothly actors must agree on a definition of the situation and perform it together. Even arguments, as we will discuss, hold to a particular definition of the situation ("This is a fight") and follow specific rules of interaction. In addition to defining situations, people negotiate how they will define themselves and others. One of the most significant implications of Part III is that our own self-images, as well as the identities we present to others, are a product of interaction.

The social construction of reality is the focus of Part IV. In this section we explore the implications of the points raised in Part II and Part III for the production and reproduction of social realities. We present realities as social constructs that exist through shared assumptions about how the world is organized and how one can "know" this. The maintenance of these "fragile" realities is dependent on the participation of social group members in the enactment of patterns and rituals. These enactments follow highly structured but often unrecognized rules of interaction. These implicit rules can be made explicit by violating them and forcing interaction to a confused halt. We present several such "violations" in Part IV. An important question in this section is why certain patterns of reality endure so well, given that it can be demonstrated that they are based on fragile rules of interaction. The final section of Part IV deals directly with the processes by which all of us contribute to the creation and reinforcement of social patterns such as oppression, racism, sexism, and our own alienation.

The readings in Part I are intended to whet your appetite for the materials that follow and to illustrate some of the basic components for symbolic interactionism as described above. "That Powerful Drop," by the novelist and artist Langston Hughes, is suggestive of the power of a culturally defined symbol to perpetuate a social institution such as racism. The anthropologist Horace Miner takes the outsider's perspective to demonstrate in "Body Rituals Among the Nacirema" how behavior can seem odd and even repulsive to us when stripped of the insider's comprehension. These cultural rituals appear alien and unrecognizable because they are no longer "alive with the meaning" that is infused into them through the insider's eye. In the provocative science fiction story "Mazes," Ursula K. Le Guin spins the tale of another system that is infused with meaning for the story's protagonist but is not understood by the alien captor. The two species do not share the same mode of communication (the "dance") nor do they share the same symbolic system (expressive movements within a maze). The piece by Jane Wagner is extracted from her one-woman play performed by Lily Tomlin, *The Search for Signs of Intelligent Life in the Universe*. The play's narrator, Trudy, a bag lady, provides commentary from the sidelines of contemporary U.S. society. Trudy is an example of someone who has been socialized; she "knows" what the rules of social conduct are, but has chosen not to play the expected role. Despite the uniqueness of her behavior, Trudy's private culture is still a product of the same general reality she shares with those of us who are also able to comprehend this book. As you encounter the material in the upcoming pages we encourage you to refer back to Trudy and to ponder the paradox of how her position simultaneously reflects and affirms the existence of a shared symbolic world and points to alternative paths of interaction with this world.

Consider also Trudy's experience in taking the "aliens" to see a play. They have difficulty ascertaining just what it is that constitutes "art" in this culture. After a few moments of observation the aliens inform Trudy that "the audience is art." She realizes that she forgot to tell them to watch the play, not the audience. In this book we focus on the audience. Or, rather, on the interactional rules that inform this group of people at this particular moment in time how to "be" an audience. When we pause to ponder the intricacy of these rules, the coordination their successful operation requires, and the delicate realities that sustain them, we are inclined to agree with the aliens: the audience is art! Trudy may be correct in her assertion that "reality is a collective hunch." If so, this book is about how we work together to define and sustain that hunch.

References and Further Reading

Cohen, C. (1981). Person categories and social perception: Testing some boundaries of the processing effects of prior knowledge. *Journal of Personality and Social Psychology, 40,* 441-452.

Gould, S. J. (1989). *It's a wonderful life: The Burgess Shale and the nature of history.* New York: Norton.

Hoff, B. (1992). *The Te of Piglet.* New York: Penguin.

Lave, J. (1988). *Cognition in practice: Mind, mathematics, and culture in everyday life.* New York: Cambridge University Press.

Shah, I. (1972). *Caravan of dreams.* Baltimore, MD: Penguin.

Skinner, B. F. (1976). *Walden two.* New York: Macmillan.

Tversky, A., Kahnemann, D., & Slovic, P. (Eds.). (1982). *Judgment under uncertainty: Heuristics and biases.* New York: Cambridge University Press.

1

That Powerful Drop

Langston Hughes

Leaning on the lamp post in front of the barber shop, Simple was holding up a copy of the *Chicago Defender* and reading about how a man who looks white had just been declared officially colored by an Alabama court.

"It's powerful," he said.

"What?"

"That one drop of Negro blood—because just *one* drop of black blood makes a man colored. *One* drop—you are a Negro! Now, why is that? Why is Negro blood so much more powerful than any other kind of blood in the world? If a man has Irish blood in him, people will say, 'He's *part* Irish.' If he has a little Jewish blood, they'll say, 'He's *half Jewish*.' But if he has just a small bit of colored blood in him, BAM!—'*He's a Negro!*' Not, 'He's *part* Negro.' No, be it ever so little, if that blood is black, '*He's a Negro!*' Now, this is what I do not understand—why our *one* drop is so powerful. Take paint—white will not make black *white*. But black will make white *black*. One drop of black in white paint—and the white ain't white no more! Black is powerful. You can have ninety-nine drops of white blood in your veins down South—but if that other *one* drop is black, shame on you! Even if you look white, you're black. That drop is really powerful. Explain it to me. You're colleged."

"It has no basis in science," I said, "so there's no logical explanation." . . .

2

The Search for Signs of Intelligent Life in the Universe

Jane Wagner

Here we are, standing on the corner of
"Walk, Don't Walk."
You look away from me, tryin' not to
    catch my eye,
but you didn't turn fast enough, *did* you?

You don't like my *ras*py voice, do you?
I got this *ras*py voice
'cause I have to yell all the time
'cause nobody around here ever
LISTENS to me.

You don't like that I scratch so much: yes,
    and excuse me,
I scratch so much
'cause my neurons are
on *fire.*

And I admit my smile is not at its
    Pepsodent best
'cause I think my
caps must've somehow got
osteo*poro*sis.

And if my eyes seem to be twirling
    around like fruit flies—
the better to see you with, my dears!

Look at me,
you mammalian-brained LUNKHEADS!
I'm not just talking to myself. I'm talking
    to you, too.
And to you
and you
and you
and you and you and you!

I know what you're thinkin'; you're
    thinkin' I'm crazy.
You think I give a hoot? You people
look at my shopping bags,
call me crazy 'cause I save this junk. What
    should we call the
ones who
buy it?

It's my belief we all, at one time or another,
secretly ask ourselves the question,
"Am *I* crazy?"
In my case, the answer came back: A
    resounding
YES!

You're thinkin': How does a person know
    if they're crazy
or not? Well, sometimes you don't know.
    Sometimes you
can go through life suspecting you *are*
but never really knowing for sure.
    Sometimes you know for sure

'cause you got so many people tellin' you
    you're crazy
that it's your word against everyone
    else's.

Another sign is when you see life so clear
    sometimes
you black out.
This is your typical visionary variety
who has flashes of insight
but can't get anyone to listen to 'em
'cause their insights make 'em sound so
    crazy!

In my case,
the symptoms are subtle
but unmistakable to the trained eye. For
    instance,
here I am,
standing at the corner of "Walk, Don't
    Walk,"
waiting for these aliens from outer space
    to show up.
I call that crazy, don't you? If I were sane,
I should be waiting for the light like
    everybody else.

They're late
as usual.

You'd think,
as much as they know about time travel,
they could be on time *once* in a while.

I could kick myself.
I told 'em I'd meet 'em on the corner of
    "Walk, Don't Walk"
'round lunchtime.
Do they even know what "lunch" means?
I doubt it.

And "'round." Why did I say "'round"?
    Why wasn't I more
specific? This is so typical of what I do.

Now they're probably stuck somewhere
    in time, wondering

what I meant by
"'round lunchtime." And when they get
    here, they'll be
dying to know what "lunchtime" means.
    And when they
find out it means going to Howard
    Johnson's for fried
clams, I wonder, will they be just a bit let
    down?
I dread having to explain
tartar sauce.

This problem of time just points out
how far apart we really are.
See, our ideas about time and space are
    different
from theirs. When we think of time, we
    tend to think of
clock radios, coffee breaks, afternoon
    naps, leisure time,
halftime activities, parole time, doing
    time, Minute Rice, instant
tea, mid-life crises, that time of the
    month, cocktail hour.
And if I should suddenly
mention *space*—aha! I bet most of you
    thought of your
closets. But when they think of time and
    space, they really think
of
Time and Space.

They asked me once my thoughts on
    infinity and I told 'em
with all I had to think about, infinity was
    not on my list
of things to think about. It could be time
    on an ego trip,
for all I know. After all, when you're
    pressed for time,
infinity may as well
not be there.
They said, to them, infinity is
time-released time.

Frankly, infinity doesn't affect
me personally one way or the other.

You think too long about infinity, you
    could go
stark raving mad.
But I don't ever want to sound negative
    about going crazy.
I don't want to overromanticize it either,
    but frankly,
goin' crazy was the *best* thing ever
    happened to me.
I don't say it's for everybody;
some people couldn't cope.

But for me it came at a time when nothing
    else seemed to be
working. I got the kind of madness
    Socrates talked about,
"A divine release of the soul from the
    yoke of
custom and convention." I refuse to be
    intimidated by
reality anymore.
After all, what is reality anyway? Nothin'
    but a
collective hunch. My space chums think
    reality was once a
primitive method of
crowd control that got out of hand.
In my view, it's absurdity dressed up
in a three-piece business suit.

I made some studies, and
reality is the leading cause of stress
    amongst those in
touch with it. I can take it in small doses,
    but as a lifestyle
I found it too confining.
It was just too needful;
it expected me to be there for it *all* the
    time, and with all
I have to do—
I had to let something go.

Now, since I put reality on a back burner,
    my days are
jam-packed and fun-filled. Like some
    days, I go hang out
around Seventh Avenue; I love to do this
    old joke:
I wait for some music-loving tourist from
    one of the hotels
on Central Park to go up and ask
    someone.
"How do I get to Carnegie Hall?"
Then I run up and yell,
"Practice!"
The expression on people's faces is
    priceless. I never
could've done stuff like that when I was
    in my *right* mind.
I'd be worried people would think I was
    crazy.
When I think of the fun I missed,
I try not to be bitter.

See, the human mind is kind of like . . .
a piñata. When it breaks open,
there's a lot of surprises inside. Once you
    get the piñata
perspective, you see that losing your mind
can be a peak experience.

I was not always a bag lady, you know.
I used to be a designer and creative
    consultant. For big
companies!
Who do you think thought up the color
    scheme
for Howard Johnson's?
At the time, nobody was using
orange and aqua
in the same room together.
With fried clams.

Laugh tracks:
I gave TV sitcoms the idea for canned
    laughter.

I got the idea, one day I heard voices
and no one was there.

Who do you think had the idea to
   package panty hose
in a plastic goose egg?

One thing I personally don't like about
   panty hose:
When you roll 'em down to the ankles the
   way I like 'em, you
can't walk too good. People seem
   amused, so what's a little
loss of dignity? You got to admit:
It's a look!

The only idea I'm proud of—

my umbrella hat. Protects against
   sunstroke, rain and
muggers. For *some* reason, muggers steer
   clear of people
wearing umbrella hats

So it should come as no shock . . . I am
   now creative consultant to
these aliens from outer space. They're a
   kinda cosmic
fact-finding committee. Amongst other
   projects, they've been
searching all over for Signs of Intelligent
   Life.

It's a lot trickier than it sounds.

We're collecting all kinds of data
about life here on Earth. We're
   determined to figure out,
once and for all, just what the hell it all
   means.
I write the data on these Post-its and then
   we study it.
Don't worry, before I took the consulting
   job, I gave 'em my whole
psychohistory.

I told 'em what drove *me* crazy was my
   last creative consultant

job, with the Ritz Cracker mogul, Mr.
   Nabisco. It was
my job to come up with snack
   inspirations to increase sales.
I got this idea to give Cracker
   Consciousness to the entire
planet.

I said, "Mr. Nabisco, sir! You could be the
   first to sell the
concept of munching to the Third World.
   We got an untapped
market here! These countries got millions
   and millions of
people don't even know where their next
   meal is *coming* from.
So the idea of eatin' *between* meals is
   somethin' just never
occurred to 'em!"

I heard myself sayin' *this*!

Must've been when I went off the deep end.
I woke up in the nuthouse. They were
   hookin' me up.
One thing they don't tell you about shock
   treatments, for
months afterwards you got
flyaway hair. And it used to *be* my best
   feature.

See, those shock treatments gave me new
   electrical circuitry
(frankly, I think one of the doctors' hands
   must've been wet).
I started having these time-space
   continuum shifts, I guess
you'd call it. Suddenly, it was like my
   central nervous system
had a patio addition out back.
Not only do I have a linkup to
   extraterrestrial
channels. I also got a hookup with
   humanity as a whole.
Animals and plants, too. I used to talk to
   plants all the time;

then, one day, they started talking back.
    They said,
"Trudy,
shut up!"

I got like this . . .

built-in Betamax in my head. Records
    anything.
It's like somebody's using my brain to
    dial-switch
through humanity. I pick up signals that
    seem to transmit
snatches of people's lives.
My umbrella hat works as a satellite dish.
    I hear this
sizzling sound like white noise. Then I
    know it's
trance time.
That's how I met my space chums. I was
    in one of my trances,
watching a scene from someone's life,
    and I suddenly sense
others were there
watching with me.

Uh-oh.
I see this skinny
punk kid.
Got hair the color of
Froot Loops and she's wearin' a T-shirt
    says "Leave Me Alone."
There's a terrible family squabble going on.
If they're listening to each other,
they're all gonna get their feelings hurt.

I see glitches—
Now I see this dark-haired actress
on a Broadway stage. I know her. I see her
    all the time outside
the Plymouth Theater, Forty-fifth Street . . .

Dial-switch me outta this!
I got enough worries of my own.
These trances are entertaining but
    distracting, especially since

someone *else* has the remote control, and
    if the pause button
should somehow get punched, I could
    have a neurotransmitter
mental meltdown. Causes "lapses of the
    synapses." I forget
things. Never underestimate the power of
    the human mind to
forget. The other day, I forgot where I put
    my house keys—
looked everywhere, then I remembered
I don't have a house. I forget more
    important things, too.
Like the meaning of life.
I forget that.
It'll come to me, though.
Let's just hope when it does,
I'll be in . . .

My space chums say they're learning so
    much about us
since they've begun to time-share my
    trances.
They said to me, "Trudy, the human mind
    is so-o-o strange."
I told 'em, "That's nothin' compared to
    the human genitals."
Next to my trances they love goin'
    through my shopping bags.
Once they found this old box of Cream of
    Wheat. I told 'em, "A
box of cereal." But they saw it as a picture
    of infinity. You know
how on the front is a picture of that guy
    holding up a box of
Cream of Wheat
and on *that* box is a picture of that guy
    holding up a box of
Cream of Wheat
and on *that* box is a picture of that guy
    holding up a box of
Cream of Wheat
and on *that* box is a picture of that guy
    holding up a box of
Cream of Wheat . . .

We think so different.

They find it hard to grasp some things
    that come easy to us,
because they simply don't have our frame
    of reference.
I show 'em this can of Campbell's tomato
    soup.
I say,
"This is soup."
Then I show 'em a picture of Andy
    Warhol's painting
of a can of Campbell's tomato soup.
I say,
"This is art."

"This is soup."

"And this is art."

Then I shuffle the two behind my back.

Now what is this?

No,
this is soup
and *this is art*! . . .

Hey, what's this?

"Dear Trudy, thanks for making our stay
    here so jam-packed and
fun-filled. Sorry to abort our mission—it
    is not over,
just temporarily scrapped.

We have orders to go to a higher
    bio-vibrational plane.

Just wanted you to know, the
    neurochemical imprints of our
cardiocortical experiences here on earth
    will remain with us
always, but what we take with us into
    space that we cherish the
most is the 'goose bump' experience."

Did I tell you what happened at the play?
    We were at the back
of the theater, standing there in the dark,
all of a sudden I feel one of 'em tug my
    sleeve,
whispers, "Trudy, look." I said, "Yeah,
    goose bumps. You
definitely
got goose bumps. You really like the play
    that much?" They said
it wasn't the play
gave 'em goose bumps,
it was the audience.

I forgot to tell 'em to watch the play;
    they'd been watching
the *audience*!

Yeah, to see a group of strangers sitting
    together in the dark,
laughing and crying about the same
    things . . . that just knocked
'em out.
They said, "Trudy,
the play was soup . . .
the audience . . .
art."

So they're taking goose bumps
home with 'em.
Goose bumps!
Quite a souvenir.

I like to think of them out there
in the dark, watching us.
Sometimes we'll do something and they'll
    laugh.
Sometimes we'll do something and they'll
    cry.
And maybe one day we'll do something
    so magnificent,
everyone in the universe will get
goose bumps.

3

Body Ritual Among the Nacirema

Horace Miner

The anthropologist has become so familiar with the diversity of ways in which different peoples behave in similar situations that he is not apt to be surprised by even the most exotic customs. In fact, if all of the logically possible combinations of behavior have not been found somewhere in the world, he is apt to suspect that they must be present in some yet undescribed tribe. This point has, in fact, been expressed with respect to clan organization by Murdock (1949, p. 71). In this light, the magical beliefs and practices of the Nacirema present such unusual aspects that it seems desirable to describe them as an example of the extremes to which human behavior can go.

Professor Linton first brought the ritual of the Nacirema to the attention of anthropologists twenty years ago (1936, p. 326), but the culture of this people is still very poorly understood. They are a North American group living in the territory between the Canadian Cree, the Yaqui and Tarahumare of Mexico, and the Carib and Arawak of the Antilles. Little is known of their origin, although tradition states that they came from the east. According to Nacirema mythology, their nation was originated by a culture hero, Notgnihsaw, who is otherwise known for two great feats of strength—the throwing of a piece of wampum across the river Pa-To-Mac and the chopping down of a cherry tree in which the Spirit of Truth resided.

Nacirema culture is characterized by a highly developed market economy which has evolved in a rich natural habitat. While much of the people's time is devoted to economic pursuits, a large part of the fruits of these labors and a considerable portion of the day are spent in ritual activity. The focus of this activity is the human body, the appearance and health of which loom as a dominant concern in the ethos of the people. While such a concern is certainly not unusual, its ceremonial aspects and associated philosophy are unique.

The fundamental belief underlying the whole system appears to be that the human body is ugly and that its natural tendency is to debility and disease. Incarcerated in such a body, man's only hope is to avert these characteristics through the use of the powerful influences of ritual and ceremony. Every household has one or more shrines devoted to this purpose. The more powerful individuals in this society have several shrines in their houses and, in fact, the opulence of a house is often referred to in terms of the number of such ritual centers it possesses. Most houses are of wattle and daub construction, but the shrine rooms of the more wealthy are walled with stone. Poorer

"Body Ritual Among the Nacirema" by H. Miner, 1956. Reproduced by permission of the American Anthropological Association from *American Anthropologist* 58(3), 503-507, 1956. Not for further reproduction.

families imitate the rich by applying pottery plaques to their shrine walls.

While each family has at least one such shrine, the rituals associated with it are not family ceremonies but are private and secret. The rites are normally only discussed with children, and then only during the period when they are being initiated into these mysteries. I was able, however, to establish sufficient rapport with the natives to examine these shrines and to have the rituals described to me.

The focal point of the shrine is a box or chest which is built into the wall. In this chest are kept the many charms and magical potions without which no native believes he could live. These preparations are secured from a variety of specialized practitioners. The most powerful of these are the medicine men, whose assistance must be rewarded with substantial gifts. However, the medicine men do not provide the curative potions for their clients, but decide what the ingredients should be and then write them down in an ancient and secret language. This writing is understood only by the medicine men and by the herbalists who, for another gift, provide the required charm.

The charm is not disposed of after it has served its purpose, but is placed in the charm-box of the household shrine. As these magical materials are specific for certain ills, and the real or imagined maladies of the people are many, the charm-box is usually full to overflowing. The magical packets are so numerous that people forget what their purposes were and fear to use them again. While the natives are very vague on this point, we can only assume that the idea in retaining all the old magical materials is that their presence in the charm-box, before which the body rituals are conducted, will in some way protect the worshipper.

Beneath the charm-box is a small font. Each day every member of the family, in succession, enters the shrine room, bows his head before the charm-box, mingles different sorts of holy water in the font, and proceeds with a brief rite of ablution. The holy waters are secured from the Water Temple of the community, where the priests conduct elaborate ceremonies to make the liquid ritually pure.

In the hierarchy of magical practitioners, and below the medicine men in prestige, are specialists whose designation is best translated "holy-mouth-men." The Nacirema have an almost pathological horror of and fascination with the mouth, the condition of which is believed to have a supernatural influence on all social relationships. Were it not for the rituals of the mouth, they believe that their teeth would fall out, their gums bleed, their jaws shrink, their friends desert them, and their lovers reject them. They also believe that a strong relationship exists between oral and moral characteristics. For example, there is a ritual ablution of the mouth for children which is supposed to improve their moral fiber.

The daily body ritual performed by everyone includes a mouth-rite. Despite the fact that these people are so punctilious about care of the mouth, this rite involves a practice which strikes the uninitiated stranger as revolting. It was reported to me that the ritual consists of inserting a small bundle of hog hairs into the mouth, along with certain magical powders, and then moving the bundle in a highly formalized series of gestures.

In addition to the private mouth-rite, the people seek out a holy-mouth-man once or twice a year. These practitioners have an impressive set of paraphernalia, consisting of a variety of augers, awls, probes, and prods. The use of these objects in the exorcism of the evils of the mouth involves almost unbelievable ritual torture of the client. The holy-mouth-man opens the client's mouth and, using the above-mentioned tools, enlarges any holes which decay may have created in the teeth. Magical materials are put into these holes. If there are no naturally occurring holes in the teeth, large sections of one or more teeth are gouged out so that the supernatural substance can be applied. In the client's view, the purpose of these ministrations is to arrest decay and to draw friends. The extremely sacred and traditional character of the rite is evident in the fact that the natives return to the holy-mouth-man year after year, despite the fact that their teeth continue to decay.

It is to be hoped that, when a thorough study of the Nacirema is made, there will be careful inquiry into the personality structure of these people. One has but to watch the gleam in the eye of a holy-mouth-man, as he jabs an awl into an exposed nerve, to suspect that a certain amount of sadism is involved. If this can be established, a very interesting pattern emerges, for most of the population shows definite masochistic tendencies. It was to these that Professor Linton referred in discussing a distinctive part of the daily body ritual which is performed only by men. This part of the rite involves scraping and lacerating the surface of the face with a sharp instrument. Special women's rites are performed only four times during each lunar month, but what they lack in frequency is made up in barbarity. As part of this ceremony, women bake their heads in small ovens for about an hour. The theoretically interesting point is that what seems to be a preponderantly masochistic people have developed sadistic specialists.

The medicine men have an imposing temple, or *latipso*, in every community of any size. The more elaborate ceremonies required to treat very sick patients can only be performed at this temple. These ceremonies involve not only the thaumaturge but a permanent group of vestal maidens who move sedately about the temple chambers in distinctive costume and headdress.

The *latipso* ceremonies are so harsh that it is phenomenal that a fair proportion of the really sick natives who enter the temple ever recover. Small children whose indoctrination is still incomplete have been known to resist attempts to take them to the temple because "that is where you go to die." De-

spite this fact, sick adults are not only willing but eager to undergo the protracted ritual purification, if they can afford to do so. No matter how ill the supplicant or how grave the emergency, the guardians of many temples will not admit a client if he cannot give a rich gift to the custodian. Even after one has gained admission and survived the ceremonies, the guardians will not permit the neophyte to leave until he makes still another gift.

The supplicant entering the temple is first stripped of all his or her clothes. In everyday life the Nacirema avoids exposure of his body and its natural functions. Bathing and excretory acts are performed only in the secrecy of the household shrine, where they are ritualized as part of the body-rites. Psychological shock results from the fact that body secrecy is suddenly lost upon entry into the *latipso*. A man, whose own wife has never seen him in an excretory act, suddenly finds himself naked and assisted by a vestal maiden while he performs his natural functions into a sacred vessel. This sort of ceremonial treatment is necessitated by the fact that the excreta are used by a diviner to ascertain the course and nature of the client's sickness. Female clients, on the other hand, find their naked bodies are subjected to the scrutiny, manipulation, and prodding of the medicine men.

Few supplicants in the temple are well enough to do anything but lie on their hard beds. The daily ceremonies, like the rites of the holy-mouth-men, involve discomfort and torture. With ritual precision, the vestals awaken their miserable charges each dawn and roll them about on their beds of pain while performing ablutions, in the formal movements of which the maidens are highly trained. At other times they insert magic wands in the supplicant's mouth or force him to eat substances which are supposed to be healing. From time to time the medicine men come to their clients and jab magically treated needles into their flesh. The fact that these temple ceremonies may not cure, and may even kill the neophyte, in no way decreases the people's faith in the medicine men.

There remains one other kind of practitioner, known as a "listener." This witch-doctor has the power to exorcise the devils that lodge in the heads of people who have been bewitched. The Nacirema believe that parents bewitch their own children. Mothers are particularly suspected of putting a curse on children while teaching them the secret body rituals. The counter-magic of the witch-doctor is unusual in its lack of ritual. The patient simply tells the "listener" all his troubles and fears, beginning with the earliest difficulties he can remember. The memory displayed by the Nacirema in these exorcism sessions is truly remarkable. It is not uncommon for the patient to bemoan the rejection he felt upon being weaned as a babe, and a few individuals even see their troubles going back to the traumatic effects of their own birth.

In conclusion, mention must be made of certain practices which have their base in native esthetics but which depend upon the pervasive aversion to the natural body and its functions. There are ritual fasts to make fat people thin and ceremonial feasts to make thin people fat. Still other rites are used to make women's breasts larger if they are small, and smaller if they are large. General dissatisfaction with breast shape is symbolized in the fact that the ideal form is virtually outside the range of human variation. A few women afflicted with almost inhuman hypermammary development are so idolized that they make a handsome living by simply going from village to village and permitting the natives to stare at them for a fee.

Reference has already been made to the fact that excretory functions are ritualized, routinized, and relegated to secrecy. Natural reproductive functions are similarly distorted. Intercourse is taboo as a topic and scheduled as an act. Efforts are made to avoid pregnancy by the use of magical materials or by limiting intercourse to certain phases of the moon. Conception is actually very infrequent. When pregnant, women dress so as to hide their condition. Parturition takes place in secret, without friends or relatives to assist, and the majority of women do not nurse their infants.

Our review of the ritual life of the Nacirema has certainly shown them to be a magic-ridden people. It is hard to understand how they have managed to exist so long under the burdens which they have imposed upon themselves. But even such exotic customs as these take on real meaning when they are viewed with the insight provided by Malinowski when he wrote (1948, p. 70):

Looking from far and above, from our high places of safety in the developed civilization, it is easy to see all the crudity and irrelevance of magic. But without its power and guidance early man could not have mastered his practical difficulties as he has done, nor could man have advanced to the higher stages of civilization.

References

Linton, R. (1936). *The study of man*. New York: Appleton-Century.

Malinowski, B. (1948). *Magic, science, and religion*. Glencoe, IL: Free Press.

Murdock, G. P. (1949). *Social structure*. New York: Macmillan.

4

Mazes

Ursula K. Le Guin

I have tried hard to use my wits and keep up my courage, but I know now that I will not be able to withstand the torture any longer. My perceptions of time are confused, but I think it has been several days since I realized I could no longer keep my emotions under aesthetic control, and now the physical breakdown is also nearly complete. I cannot accomplish any of the greater motions. I cannot speak. Breathing, in this heavy foreign air, grows more difficult. When the paralysis reaches my chest I shall die: probably tonight.

The alien's cruelty is refined, yet irrational. If it intended all along to starve me, why not simply withhold food? But instead of that it gave me plenty of food, mountains of food, all the greenbud leaves I could possibly want. Only they were not fresh. They had been picked; they were dead; the element that makes them digestible to us was gone, and one might as well eat gravel. Yet there they were, with all the scent and shape of greenbud, irresistible to my craving appetite. Not at first, of course. I told myself, I am not a child, to eat picked leaves! But the belly gets the better of the mind. After a while it seemed better to be chewing something, anything, that might still the

pain and craving in the gut. So I ate, and ate, and starved. It is a relief, now, to be so weak I cannot eat.

The same elaborately perverse cruelty marks all its behavior. And the worst thing of all is just the one I welcomed with such relief and delight at first: the maze. I was badly disoriented at first, after the trapping, being handled by a giant, being dropped in to a prison; and this place around the prison is disorienting, spatially disquieting, the strange, smooth, curved wall-ceiling is of an alien substance and its lines are meaningless to me. So when I was taken up and put down, amidst all this strangeness, in a maze, a recognizable, even familiar maze, it was a moment of strength and hope after great distress. It seemed pretty clear that I had been put in the maze as a kind of test or investigation, that a first approach toward communication was being attempted. I tried to cooperate in every way. But it was not possible to believe for very long that the creature's purpose was to achieve communication.

It is intelligent, highly intelligent, that is clear from a thousand evidences. We are both intelligent creatures, we are both maze-builders: surely it would be quite easy to learn to talk together! If that were what the alien wanted. But it is not. I do not know what kind of mazes it builds for itself. The ones it made for me were instruments of torture.

The mazes were, as I said, of basically familiar types, though the walls were of that foreign material much colder and smoother than packed clay. The alien left a pile of picked leaves in one extremity of each maze, I do not know why; it may be a ritual or superstition. The first maze it put me in was babyishly short and simple. Nothing expressive or even interesting could be worked out from it. The second, however, was a kind of simple version of the Ungated Affirmation, quite adequate for the reassuring, outreaching statement I wanted to make. And the last, the long maze, with seven corridors and nineteen connections, lent itself surprisingly well to the Maluvian mode, and indeed to almost all the New Expressionist techniques. Adaptations had to be made to the alien spatial understanding, but a certain quality of creativity arose precisely from the adaptations. I worked hard at the problem of that maze, planning all night long, re-imagining the lines and spaces, the feints and pauses, the erratic, unfamiliar, and yet beautiful course of the True Run. Next day when I was placed in the long maze and the alien began to observe, I performed the Eighth Maluvian in its entirety.

It was not a polished performance. I was nervous, and the spatio-temporal parameters were only approximate. But the Eighth Maluvian survives the crudest performance in the poorest maze. The evolutions in the ninth encatenation, where the "cloud" theme recurs so strangely transposed into the ancient spiraling motif, are indestructibly beautiful. I have seen them performed by a very old person, so old and stiff-jointed that he could only suggest the movements, hint at them, a shadow-gesture, a dim reflection of the themes: and all who watched were inexpressibly moved. There is no nobler statement of our being. Performing, I myself was carried away by the power of the motions and forgot that I was a prisoner, forgot the alien eyes watching me; I transcended the errors of the maze and my own weakness, and danced the Eighth Maluvian as I have never danced it before.

When it was done, the alien picked me up and set me down in the first maze—the short one, the maze for little children who have not yet learned how to talk.

Was the humiliation deliberate? Now that it is all past, I see that there is no way to know. But it remains very hard to ascribe its behavior to ignorance.

After all, it is not blind. It has eyes, recognizable eyes. They are enough like our eyes that it must see somewhat as we do. It has a mouth, four legs, can move bipedally, has grasping hands, etc.; for all its gigantism and strange looks, it seems less fundamentally different from us, physically, than a fish. And yet, fish school and dance and, in their own stupid way, communicate! The alien has never once attempted to talk with me. It has been with me, watched me, touched me, handled me, for days: but all its motions have been purposeful, not communicative. It is evidently a solitary creature, totally self-absorbed.

This would go far to explain its cruelty.

I noticed early that from time to time it would move its curious horizontal mouth in a series of fairly delicate, repetitive gestures, a little like someone eating. At first I thought it was jeering at me; then I wondered if it was trying to urge me to eat the indigestible fodder; then I wondered if it could be communicating *labially*. It seemed a limited and unhandy language for one so well provided with hands, feet, limbs, flexible spine, and all; but that would be like the creature's perversity, I thought. I studied its lip-motions and tried hard to imitate them. It did not respond. It stared at me briefly and then went away.

In fact, the only indubitable *response* I ever got from it was on a pitifully low level of interpersonal aesthetics. It was tormenting me with knob-pushing, as it did once a day. I had endured this grotesque routine pretty patiently for the first several days. If I pushed one knob I got a nasty sensation in my feet, if I pushed a second I got a nasty pellet of dried-up food, if I pushed a third I got nothing whatever. Obviously, to demonstrate my intelligence I was to push the third knob. But it appeared that my intelligence irritated my captor, because it removed the neutral knob after the second day. I could not imagine what it was trying to establish or accomplish, except the fact that I was its prisoner and a great deal smaller than it. When I tried to leave the knobs, it forced me physically to return. I must sit there pushing knobs for it, receiving punishment from one and mockery from the other. The deliberate outrageousness of the situation, the insufferable heaviness and thickness of this air, the feeling of being forever watched yet never understood, all combined to drive me into a condition for which we have no description at all. The nearest thing I can suggest is the last interlude of the Ten Gate Dream, when all the feintways are closed and the dance narrows in and in until it bursts terribly into the vertical. I cannot say what I felt, but it was a little like that. If I got my feet stung once more, or got pelted once more with a lump of rotten food, I would go vertical forever. . . . I took the knobs off the wall (they came off with a sharp tug, like flowerbuds), laid them in the middle of the floor, and defecated on them.

The alien took me up at once and returned to my prison. It had got the message, and had acted on it. But how unbelievably primitive the message had had to be! And the next day, it put me back in the knob room, and there were the knobs as good as new, and I was to choose alternate punishments for its amusement. . . . Until then I had told myself that the creature was alien, therefore incomprehensible and uncomprehending, perhaps not intelligent in the same *manner* as we, and so on. But since then I have known that, though all that may remain true, it is also unmistakably and grossly cruel.

When it put me into the baby maze yesterday, I could not move. The power of speech was all but gone (I am dancing this, of course, in my mind; "the best maze is the mind," the old proverb goes) and I simply crouched there, silent. After a while it took me out again, gently enough. There is the ultimate perversity of its behavior: it has never once touched me cruelly.

It set me down in the prison, locked the gate, and filled up the trough with inedible food. Then it stood two-legged, looking at me for a while.

Its face is very mobile, but if it speaks with its face I cannot understand it, that is too foreign a language. And its body is always covered with bulky, binding mats, like an old widower who has taken the Vow of Silence. But I had become accustomed to its great size, and to the angular character of its limb-positions, which at first had seemed to be saying a steady stream of incoherent and mispronounced phrases, a horrible nonsense-dance like the motions of an imbecile, until I realized that they were strictly purposive movements. Now I saw something a little beyond that, in its position. There were no words, yet there was communication. I saw, as it stood watching me, a clear signification of angry sadness—as clear as the Sembrian Stance. There was the same lax immobility, the bentness, the assertion of defeat. Never a word came clear, and yet it told me that it was filled with resentment, pity, impatience, and frustration. It told me it was sick of torturing me, and wanted me to help it. I am sure I understood it. I tried to answer. I tried to say, "What is it you want of me? Only tell me what it is you want." But I was too weak to speak clearly, and it did not understand. It has never understood.

And now I have to die. No doubt it will come in to watch me die; but it will not understand the dance I dance in dying.

PART II

Humans as Symbolic Creatures

Human beings act toward things on the basis of the meanings that the things have for them.
(*Herbert Blumer*, Symbolic Interactionism)

Shared Meaning as
the Basis of Humanness

Symbolic Meaning Versus a State of Nature

Imagine that you have just been kicked in the knee. How do you respond? Your immediate physical response is probably an upward jerk of the leg. Perhaps a rush of air and a surprised gasp escapes your lips. In terms of direct stimulus-response the blow to the knee is considered the stimulus and your direct, physical response is your jerking leg and cry of pain. The physical response to the stimulus of being kicked is probably the same across most human creatures. In addition to this physiological response, you are likely to have additional reactions that are not as predictable. How do you respond to the person who kicked you? You may kick the person in return. You may apologize for being in the way. You might flee. Your response to the person who has kicked you depends on how you *interpret* the incident. Do you perceive it to be an act of aggression, an accident, a playful joke? Your interpretation of the incident is based on the situation and the cues you pick up from the person who has kicked you. If you are in a crowded space and the kicker smiles apologetically, you are likely to interpret the act as an accident and to respond accordingly. If you have been quietly reading in an empty room and the kicker glares at you menacingly, you are more likely to interpret the kick as an act of aggression than as an accident.

Symbolic interactionists are interested in the process of assigning meaning to actions and the responses that follow. The meaning that you assign to being kicked determines how you will respond to the kicker and, in turn, how the kicker will respond to you. How you perceive the incident will determine your subsequent course of action as well as how you store the event in your memory and recall it later. A jerk of the knee and a cry of pain may be predictable universal responses that are a product of our physical state of nature. However, there is nothing inherent in the interpretation that we place on the event. Symbolic interactionists hold that the most interesting aspects of human behavior take place as a result of the meaning that we assign to our own actions and to the actions of others rather than as a result of purely physical responses to environmental stimuli.

Although it is possible to chart direct stimulus-response patterns in human behavior, symbolic interactionists maintain that these patterns are of limited range and interest in understanding human behavior and institutions. Most noteworthy behavior, they contend, involves a process of interpretation between stimulus and response. Thus, the interesting question for the student of human behavior is not what the objective stimulus is (e.g., a blow to the knee), but what *meaning* an individual assigns to the stimulus (e.g., how the blow is perceived). It is this process of assigning meaning that determines how people will act. In response to behaviorists, symbolic interactionists claim that symbolic activity mediates between stimulus and response.

In this essay we explore the implications of humans being symbol-using creatures who interpret their world. We also discuss human thought as a process of symbolic gestures that is achieved through the acquisition of language. From this perspective, social behavior is conceived as a manifestation of shared symbolic patterns of meaning.

The philosopher Ernst Cassirer in the reading "A Clue to the Nature of Man" suggests that "physical reality recedes in direct proportion to symbolic activity." By this he means that symbol-using creatures do not exist in a direct state of nature. A comparison with elephants illustrates this point. When elephants encounter one another each places its trunk in the mouth of the other. The body temperature and fluids in the mouth indicate whether each elephant is in a state of arousal or aggression or is merely passive. This encounter triggers the appropriate response in each elephant—copulation, fight, flee, or travel together. The elephants, so far as we can tell, do not *think* about this encounter; they do not *interpret* the event and assign meaning to it; they simply engage in a series of stimulus-response behaviors vis-à-vis one another as experienced in a direct state of nature. Humans do not experience one another in a direct physiological state. It is true that we are attuned to odors and other physiological manifestations of our fellow humans and that we may experience these directly rather than through a process of interpretation. But most of our responses to others are determined by a process of interpretation whereby we focus on various cues, which include physiological features as well as clothing and other items, and *interpret* these cues. The difference between the human and the elephant is that humans do not respond directly to the physical environment. Rather, we impose symbolic interpretations on our experiences and draw conclusions based on these interpretations.

Those of you who have driven across the border into another country know that it is the duty of the border guards to ascertain whether or not you may be bringing merchandise into or out of the country that is in violation of international trade laws. These guards cannot read your mind. Nor can they experience directly whether or not you are telling the truth when you claim not to be carrying illicit goods. The guards must *infer* your intentions based on symbolic cues such as the type of car you are driving, your sex, and the style of your clothes and hair. In other words, the guards guess at your integrity based on their symbolic interpretation of you and the situation. Similarly, the police officer who stops a motorist cannot experience directly whether the accosted driver will be hostile or compliant. The officer must make an inference based on the available symbolic cues. One area of interest to sociologists is the patterns that social cues take on and the subsequent reliability in our ability to predict someone's intentions based these cues. It is important to note that this predictability is not a function of a direct reading of the "natural" world; rather it is the product of patterns of interaction and the social processes of assigning meaning to objects.

To exist in a state of nature is to be nonconscious, nonreflective, and nonsymbolic. In such a state the organism is propelled directly by the forces of nature, which include internal physiology and the external environment. The symbolic creature is able to comprehend, comment on, and organize behavior in accordance with abstract representations that are removed from the state of nature.

The notion that humans are to a large extent incapable of experiencing nature directly, that is, without filtering the experience through processes of symbolic thought, has occupied the energy of many philosophers. Some view this process as a curse, others consider symbolic activity a remarkable achievement in human evolution. Our purpose here is not to elevate humans above animals or to lament the extent to which humans are "removed" from nature through reliance on symbolic activity. It is to consider the implications of what it means to be symbolic creatures. The first consideration then is that human behavior is not determined directly from our encounters with the physical world. Our bodies are physical entities that exist in the physical world, but our experience of our bodies, of others, and of the things in our environment is anchored in our thoughts, which consist of symbolic activity.

Thus, we come to the first premise of symbolic interaction— humans act toward things on the basis of the meanings that the things have for them.

Symbolic Meaning: It's the Name, Not the Thing

First use of the term *symbolic interactionism* to define an approach to the study of human behavior and society is accorded to Herbert Blumer (Fine, 1990). Blumer, a sociologist at the University of California, Berkeley, writing in the 1960s, suggested three basic premises for a social science. The first was mentioned above. Here are the other two:

> The second premise is that the meaning of things is derived from, or arises out of, the social interaction that one has with one's fellows. The third premise is that these meanings are handled in, and modified through, an interpretive process used by [persons] in dealing with the things [they] encounter. (Blumer, 1969, p. 2)

These premises can be summarized as:

1. Humans act toward things based on the meaning they assign to the thing.
2. Meanings are socially derived, which is to say that meaning is not inherent in a state of nature. There is no absolute meaning. Meaning is negotiated through interaction with others.
3. The perception and interpretation of social symbols are modified by the individual's own thought processes.

This theoretical basis suggests a picture of humans as creatures who filter their experiences through a symbolic grid otherwise known as thought. Thought is private and unique to each individual. Nonetheless, the general symbolic structure through which thought is organized derives from one's interaction with others and is therefore socially shared. Thus, symbolic interactionism offers a picture of the human as a creature that is unique and yet similar to others who share its symbol system. In this way it becomes possible to explain both the similarities that exist within cultures and the differences between individual members of the same culture.

We have discussed the implications of the first premise. Next arises the question of the nature and source of the symbols that we use to assign meaning to our experiences. It is helpful at this point to first consider what symbols are.

Symbols are abstract representations. A rectangular piece of cloth with red and white horizontal stripes and a blue square in the upper left-hand corner filled with white stars is just that, but its significance is in its abstract representation of the United

States of America. When we encounter a flag it is a symbol not only of the country "for which it stands" but also the countries for which it doesn't stand. In this way a symbol or clusters of symbols both define what something is and what it is not. The essence of the item you hold in your hands at this moment may consist of masses of tree pulp flattened and assembled into connected sheets with ink splotches all over them. Most likely you do not think of the item this way, but as a book that carries an entire body of abstract symbols in the form of written language for you to absorb. It is also likely that you do not consider the book as a source of toilet paper, though its natural essence is suggestive of similar properties to those contained in toilet paper.

One of the important features of symbol use is that because symbols are abstractions their use enables us to transcend the concrete environment and to have experiences that are not rooted to time and space. Other features of abstraction include the acts of remembering, fantasizing, planning, and vicarious experience. When we imagine something we formulate an image—a symbolic representation—of something that is not present in the immediate state of nature. Remembering is a similar activity. When you fantasize and make plans you are manipulating symbolic images. Through vicarious experience you learn by observing the actions of others; you need not experience everything yourself in order to comprehend what someone else is experiencing. This is a profound point regarding survival and the transmission of culture. To comprehend the significance of the ability for symbolic abstraction to human behavior, consider how much time you actually spend in the presence of your intimate partner versus how much time you spend thinking, remembering, fantasizing, and planning about the person. Ask yourself, Is love possible without symbolic abstraction? In the reading "Man Is the Symbol-Using Animal," Kenneth Burke discusses the crucial role that abstract symbols play in the human ability to socialize one another and to transmit culture from generation to generation.

Symbols combine to form clusters of thought that are the equivalent of *concepts*. Anselm Strauss emphasizes the process of naming in the reading "Language and Identity." According to Strauss, the act of identification entails three components: a name (symbolic expression) for a thing, an evaluation of the thing, and a recommended course of action. Strauss quotes the philosophers Dewey and Bentley, who remarked that to name something is to *know* it. This suggests that the process of object identification is central to human perception and appraisal of the environment. We refer to conceptual or symbolic processes as *naming*. Naming includes not only the process of assigning meaning to an object but an evaluation of the object and a script for how to respond to it. Thus we say that human behavior involves not just stimulus-response but a process of naming that mediates between stimulus and response. Humans name things and then respond according to the implications carried in the name. They do not respond to the essence of the thing itself.

Consider a round, hollow tube made of glass with a single closed end. Call it a glass. Immediately the recommended course of action toward this object is apparent. It is a vessel used to hold liquids from which one can drink. We might each be imagining different types of glasses, and if we wished we could further narrow the description by imposing additional classifications of meaning such as the glass has a stem attached. This suggests a wine glass and may even result in a slightly formal stance toward the object. Regardless of the specific glass that we each have in mind, we are in agreement as to the general purpose of the object.

Try the following exercise. Work up some saliva in your mouth. How does it feel? Now spit it into a glass. How does it look? Now drink it up. Most of you probably respond to this last request with some hesitation. Yet we have simply asked you to reabsorb a product that, in fact, you swallow continually all through the day. Why do you hesitate? Because you have an aversion to spit. This aversion is not a direct response to the natural essence of the substance. It is the name, not the thing. Your aversion is a reaction based on a symbolic process whereby you conceptualize bodily fluids that have left the bodily container as something repulsive. The name "spit" implies an evaluative response ("Yuck") and a course of action (avoidance). The degree to which this process of naming is conscious is not an issue here. The point is that you do not respond directly to the fluid. Instead you assign meaning to the fluid and respond to that meaning. Thus, Cassirer reminds us of the words of Epictetus: "What disturbs [people] are not things, but their opinions and fancies about things."

In summary, human activity is organized and guided largely by symbolic activity. Symbols are abstract representations that we use to assign meaning to things, the actions of ourselves and others, and events in our environment. We act in accordance with these meanings. Thus behavior differs not in response to a particular stimulus but in response to the meaning human actors assign to the stimulus.

The Source of Meaning: Language

Blumer's second premise is that symbolic meaning derives from interaction between human beings. This implies several things. One is that the meaning of an object is not inherent in the thing itself. There is nothing inherently distasteful about spit, for instance. The primary way by which humans exchange symbolic meaning is through language. Language is a system of symbols that allows us to communicate and share abstract meaning. Thus language is the source of the symbols we use to imbue things and events with meaning, and it is a process for communicating to ourselves and to others what that meaning is. It is through language that we have the capacity to become social creatures, which is to say, the capacity to incorporate and to transmit culture. In this section we discuss the significance of language as a set of symbols and as a structured system of thought. We also consider how meaning is negotiated through interaction.

The basic unit of language is the word. Words are symbols that denote the meaning of something. Words can be conveyed through writing, speech, and sign. The power of the word to represent the range of human activity can be seen in the following exercise. Write down a list of as many emotions as you can think of. Read over your list with someone else. Chances are that they will comprehend the various possible states of being that each emotion word suggests. Now, select an emotion word that is well understood among those who share your language and attempt to communicate this emotion to someone else through direct physical contact without the use of language. One way to try this is to touch the person in a way that is suggestive of the emotional state. General emotions such as anger, lust, and fright may be communicated by touch. However, it is likely that the list of emotion words that you generated conveys a much wider range of emotion and degree of emotional subtlety than you can communicate effectively without resorting to language. Does this mean that there are more emotions than there are ways of expressing them? No. It implies that there are as many emotions as there are words for describing them.

Words are names or labels that assign meaning to our experiences. In many instances a physiological state of arousal is meaningless until the experience has been named. The story is told of a young man who, while traveling by plane, experienced a shaky stomach and sweaty palms. He was unable to ascertain whether he was experiencing airsickness or attraction to the woman sitting next to him. Both experiences entail the same physiological responses, but different courses of action are prescribed depending on whether one labels the experience "nausea" or "love." The linguist Benjamin Whorf pursues this theme in the reading "The Name of the Situation as Affecting Behavior."

In the biography of Malcolm X the story is told of how a fellow prison inmate taught him that words are not benign by showing him the different meanings associated with the terms "black" and "white" as defined in the dictionary. Meaning consists not only of isolated words or names but of the additional ideas and experiences associated with particular words. Another instructive exercise is to note words that have parallel definitions in the dictionary, but carry very different connotations. "Spinster" and "bachelor" are a case in point. Both are defined simply as the male and female counterpart of being unmarried. "Spinster" conjures up a much less attractive image in the minds of most than does the term "bachelor," however.

As powerful as a single word may be in assigning meaning, the full power of language is in the relationship between words. This is referred to as the *structure* of language. Words are juxtaposed in such a way as to convey one meaning rather than another. The following words each suggest a particular meaning: "cat," "dog," "chases." The first two are nouns that denote certain types of four-legged mammals, and the third is a verb that names a particular state of action. Presumably each of us has a shared understanding of the general class of meaning to which these words refer. Now, consider the alignment of the words: "dog chases cat," "cat chases dog." Does each combination suggest the same state of events? Write down all of the other possible combinations of these three words. How many of these combinations make sense to you?

The structure of language is called *syntax*. Syntax consists of the rules of grammar. The significance of syntax is that it allows us to combine words to create strings or clusters of meaning more complex than those suggested by isolated words. By recombining the three symbols, "cat," "dog," and "chase," I can convey entirely different activities. Another interesting feature of syntax is that we appear to learn and use the rules of language without necessarily being aware of what these rules are. The linguist Suzette Elgin (1987) invites us to consider the construction of the "yes or no" sentence. She notes that although most of us can give an example of such a sentence (for instance, "Is your car red?"), very few of us could state the formal rules for constructing such a sentence. A fascinating point is that even though we may not be aware of the rules, we recognize when they have been violated. We will return to this simple but profound point in Part IV of this book to draw out the similarities between language syntax and "social grammar." As with rules of grammar, people are implicitly aware of the rules of interaction and recognize when these rules have been violated, but do not recognize and cannot state explicitly what these rules are. For now, the point that we wish to emphasize is that the power of language derives from the ability of people to employ rules for formulating various combinations of meaning, without necessarily being aware in advance of all the possibilities that may exist. This means that we are able to continually formulate and represent new possibilities of meaning and that these novel combinations will be understood by others provided that the combinations follow the same syntactical structure.

The power of language, then, is not simply in words, but in the manner in which words can be combined to create more complex systems of meaning. The process of *naming* can be described as an act of *categorization*. Categorization entails imposing conceptual categories of meaning on things, thereby grouping them in a way that makes them related and gives them order. This is the subject of the reading "Mindfulness and Mindlessness," by Harvard psychologist Ellen Langer. Langer's thesis is that the names or categories that we use to give meaning to things suggest certain possibilities and omit others. She tells the story of a man losing out on the opportunity to make several thousand dollars because he is unable to conceive of a door as a 3-ft.-by-7-ft. piece of wood. The category "door" prevents him from seeing the thing as a piece of wood. "Designing a Draining Rack" tells of a similar incident in which the designer David Pye had difficulty creating the product he wanted until he was able to let go of preexisting categorical assumptions about what the thing "should" look like. And in a very different cultural context (the Trobriand Islands), in the reading "Lineal and Nonlineal Codifications of Reality," Dorothy Lee discusses the effects different categorical systems can have on some very basic processes, such as one's conception of time.

Social scientists who study cognition tell us that we use categories to perceive, interpret, and store information because it is not possible for us to attend to all the stimuli that bombard us constantly. Cognition is selective and is influenced by categories. If we had to consider every possible outcome that might confront us throughout the day we would never make it out of bed. We use pre-established categories to ascertain *probable* outcomes and then act accordingly. These categories give order to an otherwise chaotic existence and allow us to navigate our daily lives with a fair amount of predictability and control. One point of emphasis is that it is not nature that categorizes things, but humans who do so through the selection of conceptual categories that they impose on clusters of things. Strings of meaning, like the words of which they consist, are created by human symbol users and employed for specific purposes. These strings of meaning can lead to habits of thought that Langer refers to as *mindlessness*. Mindlessness is characterized by automatic perceptions that are triggered by a few salient cues. This mode of "short-cut" perception is efficient to the extent that it allows humans to process massive quantities of information quickly and efficiently. The dangers of mindlessness include the omission of other relevant features of the object or person in question and the perpetuation of stereotypes.

All languages suggest particular categorical relationships between clusters of symbols. The significance of this point is that in the absence of specific information we use general categories to impose meaning on people, things, and events and to form judgments that we then rely on to guide our behavior. The border guard, in the absence of any other information, may note that someone is a male with long hair and infer, based on categorical associations among clusters of symbols, that the person is a hippie who is probably trying to smuggle drugs into the country. Try this. Without thinking too hard about it, what is your general image of the border guard just referred to? What is the gender of the person you have in mind? Where did you get this information? Your ability to envision a border guard, even if you have personally never encountered one, is a process of symbolic abstraction. You conjure up the image based on a classification scheme. Chances are that the border guard you imagined is based on such a stereotype. This stereotype is most likely male and probably wears some type of uniform.

In the reading "Changes in Default Words and Images Engendered by Rising Consciousness," Douglas Hofstadter speaks to the tendency for *default assumptions* to "permeate our mental representations and channel our thoughts." For instance, in the illustration regarding the words "cat," "dog," and "chase," it is likely that you thought first of a dog chasing a cat. This line of thought reflects a default assumption that, all else being equal, this is the likely state of affairs. Default assumptions are based on our prior experience and knowledge of circumstances. These assumptions are likely to be true and are useful in that we cannot afford the time it would take to consider every theoretical possibility that confronts us. Nonetheless, it is possible that we will be wrong in our default-based assumptions. An interesting question to ponder is how you might know if you are wrong in your expectations. Or if the facts of the situation prove you wrong, does this change your default assumptions? To return to the border guard, if the long-haired motorist turns out not to have drugs in the car will the guard revise her categorical expectations regarding the relationship between male, long hair, and hippie? Or will she reaffirm these general expectations with an account to herself of why this particular incident was not as expected? For example, she may decide that the person does in fact have drugs in the car; she was simply unable to find them. Thus the general category, long hair = hippie = drugs, is confirmed. Furthermore, the category may now be associated with deviousness as well. Default assumptions are one case of language-based categorization.

Hofstadter is particularly interested in sex-based categorization. The central theme of this reading is the extent to which language shapes how we think about, and by extension, behave toward someone. To provoke those who are not inclined to see sexism as a product of the relationship between language and thought, we have included a satire written by Hofstadter, "A Person Paper on Purity in Language," in which he draws an analogy between sex-based and race-based language differences.

Language and Socialization

The foregoing discussion suggests that there is a close relationship between language and thought. The philosopher Bertrand Russell stated, "Language serves not only to express thought but to make possible thoughts which could not exist without it" (quoted in Simmons, 1990, p. 191). Each of the readings in Part II assumes that language is the basis of thought. Furthermore, it is thought that allows us to observe and guide our own behavior; therefore, language is the basis of our ability to be socialized as humans. In other words, without language we would be unable to assign meaning to our own actions and to bring them into line with the expectations of our culture. We would be unsocialized.

The social philosopher George Herbert Mead (1934) theorized that in the process of learning language the mind develops and becomes structured in a manner that reflects the individual's culture. Language acquisition is an interactional process. The meanings that the child learns to assign to various things in her or his environment, including meaning about the self, derive from interaction with significant others. The child does not simply learn to name a spherical object "ball." She learns that a certain activity associated with the ball, hurling it across space, meets with a response from those around her. She also learns that this response is either positive or negative and comes in the form of reactions toward herself. Thus she learns that she is the source of the activity that generates the response, and she learns that in certain situations, for example, in an enclosed space, people react more negatively when she hurls the ball than they do on the green stuff called grass.

The child also learns to distinguish the response of differently named persons in her environment. "Dad" may praise her "athletic ability" when she hurls the ball. "Mom" may attempt to "settle her down." In this way the child learns to form complex associations between persons, things, and situations. Most important, the child learns what stance he or she should adopt in a given setting in relationship to specifically named others and objects. This activity is the foundation of human socialization. The developmental apex for Mead occurs when the child reaches what he terms the "game" stage. Using the example of a baseball game Mead describes the complex interrelationship between language, thought, and self-governance that must occur for baseball to be played successfully. The person must be able to see herself or himself in relationship to others *according to situationally specific meanings* (e.g., pitcher, batter, catcher) and understand the web of relationships that exist between each category of meaning and particular occurrences in the playing field.

Human social activity requires an ability to differentiate among various social roles and the scripts for action associated with these roles. To engage in interaction, individuals must assign a set of meanings to themselves *relative* to other actors. These roles are contextually specific. Knowledge of these interrelational role requirements is a cornerstone of socialization. You would not be very effective in a baseball game if you were unable to differentiate your action as pitcher from the roles of catcher and batter. Likewise, your behavior in a restaurant would be awkward, to say the least, if you insisted that your server join you for the meal and attempted to clear the plates of the other diners. This does not mean that you are always a pitcher or a restaurant patron but that you know what role is required of you, relative to others in specific social settings. Consider the implications of this for how you relate to your family members or friends versus strangers; try acting toward your friends as if they were strangers and observe the response.

A final development for Mead is the emergence of what he termed the *generalized other.* The generalized other is an organized set of information that the individual carries in her or his head about what the general expectations and attitudes of the social group are. We refer to this generalized other whenever we try to figure out how to behave or how to evaluate our behavior in a social situation. We take the position of the generalized other and assign meaning to ourselves and our actions. The generalized other provides us with a set of guidelines for directing our own behavior and for coordinating it with the expectations of others. The development of a generalized other is a cognitive feat that entails complex symbolic manipulation.

The reading by Kingsley Davis, "Final Note on a Case of Extreme Isolation," offers an illustration of the extent to which "human" development is retarded if the individual is denied access to language and interaction. The neurologist Oliver Sacks has investigated the association between language, thought, and human development in his books *The Man Who Mistook His Wife for a Hat* (1987) and *Seeing Voices* (1989). The latter book deals with the congenitally deaf. Based on several case studies, Sacks asserts that those born without hearing are endowed with the same intellectual capacity as those who can hear. But in an oral-based culture they fail to develop conceptual thought. These processes have not been "switched on" due to lack of aural stimulation. In cases where the infant is introduced to sign language, mental capacity develops normally. When the child is denied such access, then he or she is effectively being denied access to the switch (language-based interaction) and the materials (abstract symbols) through which conceptual thought develops. In these cases the child is often perceived to be retarded. The implication is that humans require social stimulation and exposure to abstract symbol systems to embark upon the conceptual thought processes that characterize our species.

In the reading selection "A Matter of Identity," Sacks tells the story of a man who, due to brain damage, is unable to recall the symbolic information necessary to "name" people in his environment. His attempts to "guess" at who they are entail running through a litany of possibilities that have very little connection to the symbolic cues manifest by their actual presence. "Yes, Father-Sister" is a similar case history from the files of Oliver Sacks. These readings illustrate the extent to which human social activity requires that individuals be able to engage in complex conceptual processes that involve the use of shared symbols. People who are unable to engage in appropriate symbolic activity are, in Sacks's words, "islands isolated from meaning." Sacks's case histories also point to the intricate relationship between neurological activity and cognitive, or conceptual, processes. A helpful analogy is the relationship between computer hardware and software: The brain is the hardware and language is the software that enables and organizes thought activity.

Here are some other metaphors of the relationship between language and thought. The renowned Russian neurologist A. R. Luria refers to the mind as an "enchanted loom." According to this metaphor, various threads of meaning are spun together to create what we consider to be the mature adult mind. This is the mind of a person capable of sharing and interacting with other members of a language-based community. Langer, and many cognitive psychologists, view the mind as a huge filing system. Language-based categories determine where you focus your attention and how you perceive and store information and later recall it. Each of these metaphors assumes that the human is "wired" for cognitive activity, but that the material that shapes and directs this activity is derived from culture in the form of language. Two important implications can be drawn from this discussion. One is that symbolic systems (i.e., language) are the basis of both human thought and social activity. Perception and thinking (and by extension experience and behavior) are activities of the social mind. We do not perceive a state of nature directly. Most of our perceptions are based on categorically driven inferences rather than on the apprehension of "fact." The second implication is that the symbolic systems that structure our thoughts and behavior are culturally derived. This suggests that all meaning is relative.

The assertion that humans process all experience through culturally informed symbolic grids has been an object of both caution and enthusiasm. The tension in the symbolic relationship that orients the human relative to a state of nature is expressed in the following quotation from a brooding poet in the science fiction novel *Hyperion*.

> Words are the supreme objects. They are minded things. As pure and transcendent as any idea that ever cast a shadow into Plato's dark cave of our perceptions. But they are also pitfalls of deceit and misper-

ception. Words bend our thinking to infinite paths of self-delusion, and the fact that we spend most of our mental lives in brain mansions built of words means that we lack the objectivity necessary to see the terrible distortion of reality which language brings. . . . [Yet] here is the essence of [humankind's] creative genius: not the edifices of civilization nor the bang-flash weapons which can end it, but the *words* which fertilize new concepts. . . . You see, in the beginning was the Word. And the Word was made flesh in the weave of the human universe. Words are the only bullets in truth's bandolier. (Simmons, 1990, pp. 190-191)

Summary

The human being is the result of the ability to comprehend abstract symbols and to weave these into shared coherent patterns. Personal experience is organized through these symbolic patterns. These patterns make complex group life possible. Through the acquisition of language humans learn to engage in a process of identification based on sets of symbolic meanings that are culturally relative. This process of identification includes self-identification in which we come to see ourselves relative to others and to situations. It is this ability that enables us to become "socialized" or, in other words, to be capable of knowing what category of behavior is expected from us in a given situation according to the meaning that the situation has been assigned. Because we can also treat ourselves as meaningful objects we are able to guide and direct our own behavior in accordance with these expectations.

To return to Blumer's premises: Humans act toward things on the basis of the meanings that things hold for them. Things can include items, people, situations, even ourselves. All of these are objects toward which we respond according to the meaning that they hold for us. Symbolic interactionists are interested in symbolic meaning as the basis for human social activity, and how individuals negotiate the meaning of things, people, and situations through interaction.

References and Further Reading

Blumer, H. (1969). *Symbolic interactionism.* Englewood Cliffs, NJ: Prentice-Hall.

Brown, R. (1986). *Social psychology* (2nd ed.). New York: Free Press.

Charon, J. (1989). *Symbolic interactionism* (3rd ed.). Englewood Cliffs, NJ: Prentice-Hall.

Elgin, S. (1987). *The last word on the gentle art of verbal self-defense.* New York: Prentice-Hall.

Fine, G. (1990). Symbolic interactionism in the post-Blumerian age. In G. Ritzer (Ed.), *Frontiers of social theory* (pp. 117-157). New York: Columbia University Press.

Lindesmith, A., Strauss, A., & Denzin, N. (1988). *Social psychology* (6th ed.). Englewood Cliffs, NJ: Prentice-Hall.

Mead, G. H. (1934). *Mind, self and society.* Chicago: University of Chicago Press.

Sacks, O. (1987). *The man who mistook his wife for a hat.* New York: Harper & Row.

Sacks, O. (1989). *Seeing voices.* Berkeley: University of California Press.

Simmons, D. (1990). *Hyperion.* New York: Bantam.

5

A Clue to the Nature of Man: The Symbol

Ernst Cassirer

In the human world we find a new characteristic which appears to be the distinctive mark of human life. The functional circle of man is not only quantitatively enlarged; it has also undergone a qualitative change. Man has, as it were, discovered a new method of adapting himself to his environment. Between the receptor system and the effector system, which are to be found in all animal species, we find in man a third link which we may describe as the *symbolic system*. This new acquisition transforms the whole of human life. As compared with the other animals man lives not merely in a broader reality; he lives, so to speak, in a new *dimension* of reality. There is an unmistakable difference between organic reactions and human responses. In the first case a direct and immediate answer is given to an outward stimulus; in the second case the answer is delayed. It is interrupted and retarded by a slow and complicated process of thought. At first sight such a delay may appear to be a very questionable gain. Many philosophers have warned man against this pretended progress. "L'homme qui médite," says Rousseau, "est un animal dépravé": it is not an improvement but a deterioration of human nature to exceed the boundaries of organic life.

Yet there is no remedy against this reversal of the natural order. Man cannot escape from his own achievement. He cannot but adopt the conditions of his own life. No longer in a merely physical universe, man lives in a symbolic universe. Language, myth, art, and religion are parts of this universe. They are the varied threads which weave the symbolic net, the tangled web of human experience. All human progress in thought and experience refines upon and strengthens this net. No longer can man confront reality immediately; he cannot see it, as it were, face to face. Physical reality seems to recede in proportion as man's symbolic activity advances. Instead of dealing with the things themselves man is in a sense constantly conversing with himself. He has so enveloped himself in linguistic forms, in artistic images, in mythical symbols or religious rites that he cannot see or know anything except by the interposition of this artificial medium. His situation is the same in the theoretical as in the practical sphere. Even here man does not live in a world of hard facts, or according to his immediate needs and desires. He lives rather in the midst of imaginary emotions, in hopes and fears, in illusions and disillusions, in his fantasies and dreams. "What disturbs and alarms man," said Epictetus, "are not the things, but his opinions and fancies about the things."

From the point of view at which we have just arrived we may correct and enlarge the classical definition of man. In spite of all the efforts of modern irrationalism this definition of man as an *animal rationale* has not lost its force. Rationality is indeed an inherent feature of all human activities. Mythology itself is not simply a crude mass of superstitions or gross delusions. It is not merely chaotic, for it possesses a systematic or conceptual form.[1] But, on the other hand, it would be impossible to characterize the structure of myth as rational. Language has often been identified with reason, or with the very source of reason. But it is easy to see that this definition fails to cover the whole field. It is a *pars pro toto;* it offers us a part for the whole. For side by side with conceptual language there is an emotional language; side by side with logical or scientific language there is a language of poetic imagination. Primarily language does not express thoughts or ideas, but feelings and affections. And even a religion "within the limits of pure reason" as conceived and worked out by Kant is no more than a mere abstraction. It conveys only the ideal shape, only the shadow, of what a genuine and concrete religious life is. The great thinkers who have defined man as an *animal rationale* were not empiricists, nor did they ever intend to give an empirical account of human nature. By this definition they were expressing rather a fundamental moral imperative. Reason is a very inadequate term with which to comprehend the forms of man's cultural life in all their richness and variety. But all these forms are symbolic forms. Hence, instead of defining man as an *animal rationale,* we should define him as an *animal symbolicum.* By so doing we can designate his specific difference, and we can understand the new way open to man—the way to civilization.

Note

1. See E. Cassirer (1922), *Die Begriffsform im mythischen Denken,* Leipzig: B. G. Teubner.

6

Man Is the Symbol-Using Animal

Kenneth Burke

Granted, it doesn't come as much of a surprise. But our definition is being offered not for any possible paradoxical value. The aim is to get as essential a set of clauses as possible and to meditate on each of them.

I remember one day at college when, on entering my philosophy class, I found all blinds up and the windows open from the top, while a bird kept flying nervously about the ceiling. The windows were high, they extended almost to the ceiling; yet the bird kept trying to escape by batting against the ceiling rather than dipping down and flying out one of the open windows. While it kept circling thus helplessly over our heads, the instructor explained that this was an example of a "tropism." This particular bird's instinct was to escape by flying *up*, he said; hence it ignored the easy exit through the windows.

But how different things would be if the bird could speak and we could speak his language. What a simple statement would have served to solve his problem. "Fly down just a foot or so and out one of those windows."

Later, I ran across another example that I cite because it has further implications with regard to a later clause in our definition. I witnessed the behavior of a wren that was unquestionably a genius within the terms of its species. The parents had succeeded in getting all of a brood off the nest except one particularly stubborn or backward fellow who still remained for a couple of days after the others had flown. Despite all kinds of threats and cajolery, he still lingered, demanding and getting the rations which all concerned seem to consider his rightful lot. Then came the moment of genius. One of the parent wrens came to the nest with a morsel of food. But instead of simply giving it to the noisy youngster, the parent bird held it at a distance. The fledgling in the nest kept stretching its neck out farther and farther with its beak gaping until, of a sudden, instead of merely putting the morsel of food into the bird's mouth, the parent wren clamped its beak shut on the young one's lower mandible, and with a slight jerk caused the youngster, with his outstretched neck, to lose balance and tumble out of the nest.

Surely this was an "act" of genius. This wren had discovered how to use the principle of leverage as a way of getting a young bird off the nest. Had that exceptionally brilliant wren been able to conceptualize this discovery in such terms as come easy to symbol systems, we can imagine him giving a dissertation on "The Use of the Principle of Leverage as an Improved Method for Unnesting Birds or Debirding a Nest." And within a few years the invention would spread throughout all birddom, with an incalculable saving in

"Man Is the Symbol-Using Animal" by K. Burke from *Language as Symbolic Interaction* (pp. 3-20). Berkeley: University of California Press. Reprinted by permission from *The Hudson Review*, 26(4) (Winter 1963-1964).

bird-hours as compared with the traditional turbulent and inefficient method still in general practice.

There are three things to note about this incident:

1. The ability to describe this method in words would have readily made it possible for all other birds to take over this same "act" of genius, though they themselves might never have hit upon it.

2. The likelihood is that even this one wren never used the method again. For the ability to conceptualize implies a kind of *attention* without which this innovation could probably not advance beyond the condition of a mere accident to the condition of an invention.

3. On the happier side, there is the thought that at least, through lack of such ability, birds are spared our many susceptibilities to the ways of demagogic spellbinders. They cannot be filled with fantastic hatreds for alien populations they know about mainly by mere hearsay, or with all sorts of unsettling new expectations, most of which could not possibly turn out as promised.

The "symbol-using animal," yes, obviously. But can we bring ourselves to realize just what that formula implies, just how overwhelmingly much of what we mean by "reality" has been built up for us through nothing but our symbol systems? Take away our books, and what little do we know about history, biography, even something so "down to earth" as the relative position of seas and continents? What is our "reality" for today (beyond the paper-thin line of our own particular lives) but all this clutter of symbols about the past combined with whatever things we know mainly through maps, magazines, newspapers, and the like about the present? In school, as they go from class to class, students turn from one idiom to another. The various courses in the curriculum are in effect but so many different terminologies.

And however important to us is the tiny sliver of reality each of us has experienced firsthand, the whole overall "picture" is but a construct of our symbol systems. To meditate on this fact until one sees its full implications is much like peering over the edge of things into an ultimate abyss. And doubtless that's one reason why, though man is typically the symbol-using animal, he clings to a kind of naïve verbal realism that refuses to realize the full extent of the role played by symbolicity in his notions of reality.

In responding to words, with their overt and covert modes of persuasion ("progress" is a typical one that usually sets expectations to vibrating), we like to forget the kind of relation that really prevails between the verbal and the nonverbal. In being a link between us and the nonverbal, words are by the same token a screen separating us from the nonverbal—though the statement gets tangled in its own traces, since so much of the "we" that is separated from the nonverbal by the verbal would not even exist were it not for the verbal (or for our symbolicity in general, since the same applies to the symbol systems of dance, music, painting, and the like).

A road map that helps us easily find our way from one side of the continent to the other owes its great utility to its exceptional existential poverty. It tells us absurdly little about the trip that is to be experienced in a welter of detail. Indeed, its value for us is in the very fact that it is so essentially inane.

Language referring to the realm of the nonverbal is necessarily talk about things in terms of what they are not—and in this sense we start out beset by a paradox. Such language is but a set of labels, signs for helping us find our way about. Indeed, they can even be so useful that they help us to invent ingenious ways of threatening to destroy ourselves. But even accuracy of this powerful sort does not get around the fact that such terms are sheer emptiness, as compared with the substance of the things they name. Nor is such abstractness confined to the language of scientific prose. Despite the concrete richness of the imagery in Keats's poems, his letters repeatedly refer to his art as "abstract." And the same kind of considerations would apply to the symbol systems of all other arts. Even so bodily a form of expression as the dance is abstract in this sense. (Indeed, in this regard it is so abstract that, when asking students to sum up the gist of a plot, I usually got the best results from dance majors, with music students a close second. Students specializing in literature or the social sciences tended to get bogged down in details. They were less apt at "abstracting.")

When a bit of talking takes place, just what is doing the talking? Just where are the words coming from? Some of the motivation must derive from our animality and some from our symbolicity. We hear of "brainwashing," of schemes whereby an "ideology" is imposed upon people. But should we stop at that? Should we not also see the situation the other way around? For was not the "brainwasher" also similarly motivated? Do we simply use words, or do they not also use us? An "ideology" is like a god coming down to earth, where it will inhabit a place pervaded by its presence. An "ideology" is like a spirit taking up its abode in a body: it makes that body hop around in certain ways, and that same body would have hopped around in different ways had a different ideology happened to inhabit it.

I am saying in one way what Paul said in another when he told his listeners that "Faith comes from hearing." He had a doctrine which, if his hearers were persuaded to accept it, would direct a body somewhat differently from the way it would have moved and been moved in its daily rounds under the earlier pagan dispensation. Consider the kind of German boys and girls, for instance, who became burglars in the old days, who during the period of inflation and U.S.-financed reparation payments after World War I wanted but to be Wandering Birds, and who, with the rise of the Third Reich, were got to functioning as Hitlerite fiends.

With regard to this first clause in our definition (man as the "symbol-using" animal) it has often been suggested that "symbol-making" would be a better term. I can go along with that emendation. But I'd want to add one further step. Then, for the whole formula we'd have: the "symbol-using, symbol-making, and symbol-misusing animal."

In referring to the misuse of symbols, I have in mind not only such demagogic tricks as I have already mentioned. I also think of "psychogenic illnesses," violent dislocations of bodily motion due to the improperly criticized action of symbolicity. A certain kind of food may be perfectly wholesome, so far as its sheer material nature is concerned. And people in some areas may particularly prize it. But our habits may be such that it seems to us loathsome; and under those conditions, the very thought of eating it may be nauseating to us. (The most drastic instance is, of course, provided by the ideal diets of cannibals.) When the body rebels at such thoughts, we have a clear instance of the ways whereby the realm of symbolicity may affect the sheerly biologic motions of animality. Instances of "hexing" are of the same sort (as when a tribesman, on entering his tent, finds there the sign that for some reason those in authority have decreed his death by magic, and he promptly begins to waste away and die under the burden of this sheer thought).

A merely funny example concerns an anecdote told by the anthropologist Franz Boas. He had gone to a feast given by Esquimaux. As a good anthropologist, he would establish rapport by eating what they ate. But there was a pot full of what he took to be blubber. He dutifully took some and felt sick. He went outside the igloo to recover. There he met an Esquimau woman, who was scandalized when she heard that they were serving blubber. For they hadn't told her! She rushed in—but came out soon after in great disgust. It wasn't blubber at all, it was simply dumplings. Had the good savant only known, he could have taken dumplings in his stride. But it was a battle indeed for him to hold them down when he thought of them as blubber!

So, in defining man as the symbol-using animal, we thereby set the conditions for asking: Which motives derive from man's animality, which from his symbolicity, and which from the combination of the two?

7

Language and Identity

Anselm Strauss

Central to any discussion of identity is language. The word "central" is used advisedly. Language is ofttimes construed as just one more kind of behavior—encompassing speaking, reading, writing, and hearing—within a long listing of other kinds of behavior. An important and recurring theme of this essay is that a proper theoretical account of men's identities and action must put men's linguistics into the heart of the discussion. . . .

Naming as an Act of Placement

The philosophers John Dewey and Arthur Bentley, in *Knowing and the Known*, have argued that to name is to know, and that the extent of knowing is dependent upon the extent of the naming. By this they do not mean to suggest anything magical about the act of naming, but to make that act central to any human's cognition of his world. This view informs much of the discussion that will follow.

Suppose a mother wishes her very young child to pay attention to an object. She moves his body so that his eyes focus somewhere near the object and then she points toward it. But when he is at an age when he can

respond to a word, she will hope to attract his attention more efficiently to some thing by naming it. This is what is called "ostensive definition," meaning an indication of an object without any description whatever; it is the simplest kind of identification. The first identifications are singular; they indicate particular objects. But the child soon learns that certain objects can be called by the same word, albeit his groupings are frequently amusing and seem incorrect to his elders. At first parents often bow to the child's peculiar classification of objects, in order to keep peace in the family, but in the end they win the game, for the youngster must eventually conform to more conventional, if less colorful, lexicology.

To name, then, is not only to indicate; it is to identify an object as some kind of object. An act of identification requires that the thing referred to be placed within a category. Borrowing from the language of logic, we may say that any particular object that is referred to is a member of a general class, a representative of that class. An orange is a member of a class called oranges; but note that this class itself receives its placement, or definition, only by virtue of its relationships with other classes. These relationships are of quite a systematic sort. Thus oranges may be defined in relation to such classes as fruits, foods, tropical growths, tree products, and moderately priced objects. Defining any class, then, means relating it to systematically associated classes. To tell

"Language and Identity" from *Mirrors and Masks: The Search for Identity* (pp. 15-25) by A. Strauss, 1959. New York: Free Press. Reprinted by permission of the author.

what a thing is, you place it in terms of something else. This idea of locating, or placing, is implicit in our very word for definition itself: to *define*, or *determine* a thing, is to mark its boundaries.[1]

It should be noted, however, that any particular object can be named, and thus located, in countless ways. The naming sets it within a context of quite differently related classes. The nature or essence of an object does not reside mysteriously within an object itself but is dependent upon how it is defined by the namer. An object which looks so much like an orange—in fact which really is an orange—can also be a member of an infinite number of other classes. If it is in its nature to be an orange, it is also in its nature to be other things. In the case of an orange, we may choose to view it within different contexts for other equally legitimate purposes. It may thus be viewed as a spherical object, with rough, warm-colored skin, suitable for catching and casting lights, hence eminently definable as a model for a beginning art student. Essentially it is just that. This is only to repeat a point made earlier that to name or designate is always to do this from some point of view. From a single identical perspective, otherwise seemingly different things can be classed together. Justification lies in the perspective, not in the things. If you do not agree with your neighbor's classification, this may only signify that you have a somewhat or wholly different basis for drawing symbolic circles around things.

The way in which things are classed together reveals, graphically as well as symbolically, the perspectives of the classifier. For instance, an anthropologist (Robert Pehrson) studying the Laplanders recently discovered that a single word is used to encompass both "people" and "reindeer." The life of the Laplander revolves around activities having to do with reindeer. Is a reindeer a human or is a human a reindeer? The question is senseless; the people and reindeer are identified, they go together, and the very fact of their identification in terminology gives the anthropologist one of his best clues to the Laplander's ordering of the world and its objects.

Any group of people that has any permanence develops a "special language," a lingo or jargon, which represents its way of identifying those objects important for group action. Waitresses classify types of customers and other workers in the restaurant, give shorthand names to foods, and have special signs and gestures standing for important activities. So do criminals; and even ministers are not immune from the necessity of classifying their clientele and colleagues, otherwise how could they organize activity in an orderly and sensible manner?

The propensity for certain categories invented by any group to be slanderous, to partake of epithet, derogation, and innuendo, has been bemoaned by liberals, debunkers, teachers, and all others who have wished to set other's classifications straight. Since groups inevitably are in conflict over issues—otherwise they would not be different groups—and since events inevitably come to be viewed differently by those who are looking up or down opposite ends of the gun, it is useless to talk of trying to eradicate from the human mind the tendency to stereotype, to designate nastily, and to oversimplify. This is not to say that humans are brutish, but that they are thoroughly human. Animals do not name-call, neither do they possess or assign identities in the elaborate sense in which we are discussing identity.

Classification and the Direction of Action

This necessity for any group to develop a common or shared terminology leads to an important consideration: the direction of activity depends upon the particular ways that objects are classified. This can be simply illustrated. Not so long ago, children used to be fed large quantities of spinach according to the syllogism that spinach contained iron and that iron was needed for building bones. Now it appears that excessive consumption of spinach reduces body calcium and therefore is bad for the bones. Spinach is thus reclassified and only if you wish to reduce calcium content should you overindulge. The renaming of any object, then, amounts to a reassessment of your relation to it, and ipso facto your behavior becomes changed along the line of your reassessment. In any event it is the definition of what the object "is" that allows action to occur with reference to what it is taken to be. Mark Twain tells how as an apprentice pilot he mistook a wind reef (not dangerous) for a bluff reef (deadly dangerous) and, to the hilarity of his boss who "properly" read the signs, performed miraculous feats of foolishness to avoid the murderous pseudo-bluff.

The naming of an object provides a directive for action, as if the object were forthrightly to announce, "You say I am this, then act in the appropriate way toward me." Conversely, if the actor feels he does not know what the object is, then with regard to it his action is blocked. Suppose that in the dark one reached for a glass of milk, raised it to his lips, recoiled at the strange taste, and stood immobilized until he was able to label the taste as tomato juice. Energy for action was there, but was temporarily unharnessed, immobilized, until naming occurred. Of course, in this example the moment of immobilization would be fleeting, since as soon as one set about to discover what the taste was he would be acting toward something belonging to the category of "unidentified liquid, whose nature is to be discovered." A person need not be certain that he knows what an object is in order to organize a line of action toward it—he merely has to be willing to take a chance on his judgment.

Classification and Evaluation

An act of classification not only directs overt action, but arouses a set of expectations toward the object thus classified. A chair ought to hold anyone who sits on it, not turn into a piano or a cat, and a buzzing housefly should not piteously ask us not to swat her, saying she is a fairy in disguise. We are surprised only if our expectations are unfulfilled, as when a presumed salesman in a department store assures us that he is just an ordinary shopper like ourselves, or when milk turns out to be strongly spiked with rum. When we classify, our expectations necessarily face both past and future. Expectations have to do with consequential relations between ourselves and the object. However, expectations rest also upon remembrances of past experiences with objects resembling—we believe—the one currently before us.

Since this is so, classifications carry not only our anticipations but also those values that were experienced when we encountered the things, persons, or events now classified. For example, the Japanese have a food called "tofu" which is a soy-bean product. Let us imagine that the first time we meet tofu it is served cold with soy sauce over it and that it strikes us as unpalatable. Tofu is for us an indifferent food, and if at some future time we should see tofu or hear the word our images would likely be of the indifferent experience we had with a whitish jellied object covered with brown sauce. But suppose that some time later we are treated to a delicious soup in which there are pieces of a mushy substance. "What is that good stuff in the soup?" we ask, and are surprised to find it is cooked tofu. Now we revise our evaluation: tofu in soup, good; tofu uncooked, not so good. This substance, as used by the Japanese, appears in several guises, so yet more surprises may be in store for us. The range of our experience with tofu is both what we know of it and how we value it. The wider grows this range, the better we know the object—what it can do and what can be done with it—and likewise the more extensive become our judgments of its capacities and qualities. It would appear that classification, knowledge and value are inseparable.

There are several more lessons suggested by the illustration. One is that values attributed to any object—like "good" or "hateful"—really are not "in" the object. In having an experience one does not put value into it like water into a kettle. Value is not an element; it has to do with a relation between the object and the person who has experiences with the object. This is just another way of stating that the "essence" or "nature" of the object resides not in the object but in the relation between it and the namer. Value as a relation is easily seen in conjunction with such an adjective as "useful"— useful for whom, under what conditions, for which of his purposes? Precisely the same is true whether the object is a thing or an event, and whether the value is "useful" or, say, "sinful." Sinfulness is not fixed in the event, a quality of it within the eye of God. An act is sinful to particular definers when perceived as committed under certain circumstances by persons of specified identities.

Since values are not in objects but are evaluations of objects, it follows that persons must do their own experiencing in order to do their own evaluating. This does not mean that I cannot teach you the meaning of something prior to your direct experience of it. I can say that the dust rises off the city streets in a certain country and constantly hangs so heavy in the air that it is hard to breathe. You have experienced similar conditions, so readily understand. But when you are introduced to a new terminology, the best you can do is draw upon possibly analogous experiences, and these may or may not lead to accurate conceptions. To experience, hence to evaluate, a Balinese trance as do the Balinese probably cannot even be approximated by an American. Everyone has at some time been introduced to new terms representing new ways of looking at objects, as when entering upon a new job. Such occupational terms cannot be fully

grasped, the objects and events be perceived as others perceive them, until we have undergone similar experiences ourselves. Of course an articulate informant drawing colorfully and accurately upon whatever is similar in his and your experiences can bring you to closer comprehension and appreciation; hence the great usefulness of some novels and biographies. But no amount of description in advance, if the shift in perspective called for is radical, will teach you how you yourself will finally evaluate. You yourself must do, suffer, and undergo—to use John Dewey's terms.[2]

As people "undergo," their evaluations change. Values are not eternal. Expectations cannot always be fulfilled. Things change; so do we. "Good things change and vanish not only with changes in the environing medium but with changes in ourselves."[3] Even without direct new experience something novel may be learned about an object—such as one might learn something new about life in prison, or as when a college student studies about geological strata and rainfall and so comes into somewhat different relationships with rocks, rain, and water. As long as learning continues, revision of concepts continues; and as long as revision takes place, reorganization of behavior takes place.

The naming or identifying of things is, then, a continual problem, never really over and done with. By "continual" I do not mean "continuous"—one can lie in a hammock contentedly watching the moon rise and raising no questions about it, the world, or oneself. Nevertheless, some portion of one's classificatory terminology, the symbolic screen through which the world is ordered and organized, is constantly under strain—or just has been—or will be. George H. Mead (who asserted that classifications are really hypotheses) would say it necessarily must be, from the very nature of action which brings in its train the reconstruction of past experience and the arising of new objects.[4]

Notes

1. K. Burke (1945), *A grammar of motives*, New York: Prentice-Hall, p. 24.

2. J. Dewey (1920), *Reconstruction in philosophy*, New York: Henry Holt, p. 86.

3. J. Dewey (1925), *Experience and nature*, Chicago: Open Court, p. 399.

4. G. H. Mead (1934), *Mind, self and society*, Chicago: University of Chicago Press.

8

Final Note on a Case of Extreme Isolation

Kingsley Davis

Early in 1940 there appeared . . . an account of a girl called Anna.[1] She had been deprived of normal contact and had received a minimum of human care for almost the whole of her first six years of life. At this time observations were not complete and the report had a tentative character. Now, however, the girl is dead, and with more information available,[2] it is possible to give a fuller and more definitive description of the case from a sociological point of view.

Anna's death, caused by hemorrhagic jaundice, occurred on August 6, 1942. Having been born on March 1 or 6,[3] 1932, she was approximately ten and a half years of age when she died. The previous report covered her development up to the age of almost eight years; the present one recapitulates the earlier period on the basis of new evidence and then covers the last two and a half years of her life.

Early History

The first few days and weeks of Anna's life were complicated by frequent changes of domicile. It will be recalled that she was an illegitimate child, the second such child born to her mother, and that her grandfather, a

widowed farmer in whose house her mother lived, strongly disapproved of this new evidence of the mother's indiscretion. This fact led to the baby's being shifted about.

Two weeks after being born in a nurse's private home, Anna was brought to the family farm, but the grandfather's antagonism was so great that she was shortly taken to the house of one of her mother's friends. At this time a local minister became interested in her and took her to his house with an idea of possible adoption. He decided against adoption, however, when he discovered that she had vaginitis. The infant was then taken to a children's home in the nearest large city. This agency found that at the age of only three weeks she was already in a miserable condition, being "terribly galled and otherwise in very bad shape." It did not regard her as a likely subject for adoption but took her in for a while anyway, hoping to benefit her. After Anna had spent nearly eight weeks in this place, the agency notified her mother to come to get her. The mother responded by sending a man and his wife to the children's home with a view to their adopting Anna, but they made such a poor impression on the agency that permission was refused. Later the mother came herself and took the child out of the home and then gave her to this couple. It was in the home of this pair that a social worker found the girl a short time thereafter. The social worker went to the mother's home and pleaded with Anna's

"Final Note on a Case of Extreme Isolation" by K. Davis, 1947. *American Journal of Sociology, 3*(5), pp. 432-437. Reprinted by permission of the author.

grandfather to allow the mother to bring the child home. In spite of threats, he refused. The child, by then more than four months old, was next taken to another children's home in a near-by town. A medical examination at this time revealed that she had impetigo, vaginitis, umbilical hernia, and a skin rash.

Anna remained in this second children's home for nearly three weeks, at the end of which time she was transferred to a private foster-home. Since, however, the grandfather would not, and the mother could not, pay for the child's care, she was finally taken back as a last resort to the grandfather's house (at the age of five and a half months). There she remained, kept on the second floor in an attic-like room because her mother hesitated to incur the grandfather's wrath by bringing her downstairs.

The mother, a sturdy woman weighing about 180 pounds, did a man's work on the farm. She engaged in heavy work such as milking cows and tending hogs and had little time for her children. Sometimes she went out at night, in which case Anna was left entirely without attention. Ordinarily, it seems, Anna received only enough care to keep her barely alive. She appears to have been seldom moved from one position to another. Her clothing and bedding were filthy. She apparently had no instruction, no friendly attention.

It is little wonder that, when finally found and removed from the room in the grandfather's house at the age of nearly six years, the child could not talk, walk, or do anything that showed intelligence. She was in an extremely emaciated and undernourished condition, with skeletonlike legs and a bloated abdomen. She had been fed on virtually nothing except cow's milk during the years under her mother's care.

Anna's condition when found, and her subsequent improvement, have been described in the previous report. It now remains to say what happened to her after that.

Later History

In 1939, nearly two years after being discovered, Anna had progressed, as previously reported, to the point where she could walk, understand simple commands, feed herself, achieve some neatness, remember people, etc. But she still did not speak, and, though she was much more like a normal infant of something over one year of age in mentality, she was far from normal for her age.

On August 30, 1939, she was taken to a private home for retarded children, leaving the county home where she had been for more than a year and a half. In her new setting she made some further progress, but not a great deal. In a report of an examination made November 6 of the same year, the head of the institution pictured the child as follows:

Anna walks about aimlessly, makes periodic rhythmic motions of her hands, and, at intervals, makes guttural and sucking noises. She regards her hands as if she had seen them for the first time. It was impossible to hold her attention for more than a few seconds at a time—not because of distraction due to external stimuli but because of her inability to concentrate. She ignored the task in hand to gaze vacantly about the room. Speech is entirely lacking. Numerous unsuccessful attempts have been made with her in the hope of developing initial sounds. I do not believe that this failure is due to negativism or deafness but that she is not sufficiently developed to accept speech at this time. . . . The prognosis is not favorable. . . .

More than five months later, on April 25, 1940, a clinical psychologist, the late Professor Francis N. Maxfield, examined Anna and reported the following: large for her age; hearing "entirely normal"; vision apparently normal; able to climb stairs; speech in the "babbling stage" and "promise for developing intelligible speech later seems to be good." He said further that "on the Merrill-Palmer scale she made a mental score of 19 months. On the Vineland social maturity scale she made a score of 23 months."[4]

Professor Maxfield very sensibly pointed out that prognosis is difficult in such cases of isolation. "It is very difficult to take scores on tests standardized under average conditions of environment and experience," he wrote, "and interpret them in a case where environment and experience have been so unusual." With this warning he gave it as his opinion at that time that Anna would eventually "attain an adult mental level of six or seven years."[5]

The school for retarded children, on July 1, 1941, reported that Anna had reached 46 inches in height and weighed 60 pounds. She could bounce and catch a ball and was said to conform to group socialization, though as a follower rather than a leader. Toilet habits were firmly established. Food habits were normal, except that she still used a spoon as her sole implement. She could dress herself except for fastening her clothes. Most remarkable of all, she had finally begun to develop speech. She was characterized as being at about the two-year level in this regard. She could call attendants by name and bring in one when she was asked to. She had a few complete sentences to express her wants. The report concluded that there was nothing peculiar about her, except that she was feeble-minded—"probably congenital in type."[6]

A final report from the school made on June 22, 1942, and evidently the last report before the girl's death, pictured only a slight advance over that given above. It said that Anna could follow directions, string beads, identify a few colors, build with blocks, and differentiate between attractive and unattractive pictures. She had a good sense of rhythm and loved a doll. She talked mainly in phrases but would repeat words and try to carry on a conversation. She was clean about clothing. She habitually washed her hands and brushed her teeth. She would try to help other children. She walked well and could run fairly well, though clumsily. Al-

though easily excited, she had a pleasant disposition.

Interpretation

Such was Anna's condition just before her death. It may seem as if she had not made much progress, but one must remember the condition in which she had been found. One must recall that she had no glimmering of speech, absolutely no ability to walk, no sense of gesture, not the least capacity to feed herself even when the food was put in front of her, and no comprehension of cleanliness. She was so apathetic that it was hard to tell whether or not she could hear. And all this at the age of nearly six years. Compared with this condition, her capacities at the time of her death seem striking indeed, though they do not amount to much more than a two-and-a-half-year mental level. One conclusion therefore seems safe, namely, that her isolation prevented a considerable amount of mental development that was undoubtedly part of her capacity. Just what her original capacity was, of course, is hard to say; but her development after her period of confinement (including the ability to walk and run, to play, dress, fit into a social situation, and, above all, to speak) shows that she had at least this capacity—capacity that never could have been realized in her original condition of isolation.

A further question is this: What would she have been like if she had received a normal upbringing from the moment of birth? A definitive answer would have been impossible in any case, but even an approximate answer is made difficult by her early death. If one assumes, as was tentatively surmised in the previous report, that it is "almost impossible for any child to learn to speak, think, and act like a normal person after a long period of early isolation," it seems likely that Anna might have had a normal or near-normal capacity, genetically speaking. On the other hand, it was pointed out that Anna represented "a marginal case, [because] she was discovered before she had reached six years of age," an age "young enough to allow for some plasticity."[7] While admitting, then, that Anna's isolation may have been the major cause (and was certainly a minor cause) of her lack of rapid mental progress during the four and a half years following her rescue from neglect, it is necessary to entertain the hypothesis that she was congenitally deficient.

In connection with this hypothesis, one suggestive though by no means conclusive circumstance needs consideration, namely, the mentality of Anna's forebears. Information on this subject is easier to obtain, as one might guess, on the mother's than on the father's side. Anna's maternal grandmother, for example, is said to have been college educated and wished to have her children receive a good education, but her husband, Anna's stern grandfather, apparently a shrewd, hard-driving, calculating farmowner, was so penurious that her ambitions in this direction were thwarted. Under the circumstances her daughter (Anna's mother) managed, despite having to do hard work on the farm, to complete the eighth grade in a country school. Even so, however, the daughter was evidently not very smart. "A schoolmate of [Anna's mother] stated that she was retarded in school work; was very gullible at this age; and that her morals even at this time were discussed by other students." Two tests administered to her on March 4, 1938, when she was thirty-two years of age, showed that she was mentally deficient. On the Stanford Revision of the Binet-Simon Scale her performance was equivalent to that of a child of eight years, giving her an I.Q. of 50 and indicating mental deficiency of "middle-grade moron type."[8]

As to the identity of Anna's father, the most persistent theory holds that he was an old man about seventy-four years of age at the time of the girl's birth. If he was the one, there is no indication of mental or other biological deficiency, whatever one may think of his morals. However, someone else may actually have been the father.

To sum up: Anna's heredity is the kind that *might* have given rise to innate mental deficiency, though not necessarily.

Comparison With Another Case

Perhaps more to the point than speculations about Anna's ancestry would be a case for comparison. If a child could be discovered who had been isolated about the same length of time as Anna but had achieved a much quicker recovery and a greater mental development, it would be a stronger indication that Anna was deficient to start with.

Such a case does exist. It is the case of a girl found at about the same time as Anna and under strikingly similar circumstances. A full description of the details of this case has not been published, but in addition to newspaper reports, an excellent preliminary account by a speech specialist, Dr. Marie K. Mason, who played an important role in the handling of the child, has appeared.[9] Also the late Dr. Francis N. Maxfield, clinical psychologist at Ohio State University, as was Dr. Mason, has written an as yet unpublished but penetrating analysis of the case.[10] Some of his observations have been included in Professor Zingg's book on feral man.[11] The following discussion is drawn mainly from these enlightening materials. The writer, through the kindness of Professors Mason and Maxfield, did have a chance to observe the girl in April, 1940, and to discuss the features of her case with them.

Born apparently one month later than Anna, the girl in question, who has been given the pseudonym Isabelle, was discovered in November, 1938, nine months after the discovery of Anna. At the time she was found she was approximately six and a half years of age. Like Anna, she was an illegitimate child and had been kept in seclusion for that reason. Her mother was a deaf-mute, having become so at the age of two, and it appears that she and Isabelle had spent most of their time together in a dark room shut off from the rest of the mother's family. As a result Isabelle had no chance to develop speech; when she communicated with her mother, it was by means of gestures. Lack of sunshine and inadequacy of diet had caused Isabelle to become rachitic. Her legs in particular were affected; they "were so bowed that as she stood erect the soles of her shoes came nearly flat together, and she got about with a skittering gait."[12] Her behavior toward strangers, especially men, was almost that of a wild animal, manifesting much fear and hostility. In lieu of speech she made only a strange croaking sound. In many ways she acted like an infant. "She was apparently utterly unaware of relationships of any kind. When presented with a ball for the first time, she held it in the palm of her hand, then reached out and stroked my face with it. Such behavior is comparable to that of a child of six months."[13] At first it was even hard to tell whether or not she could hear, so unused were her senses. Many of her actions resembled those of deaf children.

It is small wonder that, once it was established that she could hear, specialists working with her believed her to be feebleminded. Even on nonverbal tests her performance was so low as to promise little for the future. Her first score on the Stanford-Binet was 19 months, practically at the zero point of the scale. On the Vineland social maturity scale her first score was 39, representing an age level of two and a half years.[14] "The general impression was that she was wholly uneducable and that any attempt to teach her to speak, after so long a period of silence, would meet with failure."[15]

In spite of this interpretation, the individuals in charge of Isabelle launched a systematic and skillful program of training. It seemed hopeless at first. The approach had to be through pantomime and dramatization, suitable to an infant. It required one week of intensive effort before she even made her first attempt at vocalization. Gradually, she began to respond, however, and, after the first hurdles had at last been overcome, a curious thing happened. She went through the usual stages of learning characteristic of the years from one to six not only in proper succession but far more rapidly than normal. In a little over two months after her first vocalization she was putting sentences together. Nine months after that she could identify words and sentences on the printed page, could write well, could add to ten, and could retell a story after hearing it. Seven months beyond this point she had a vocabulary of 1,500-2,000 words and was asking complicated questions. Starting from an educational level of between one and three years (depending on what aspect one considers), she had reached a normal level by the time she was eight and a half years old. In short, she covered in two years the stages of learning that ordinarily require six.[16] Or, to put it another way, her I.Q. trebled in a year and a half.[17] The speed with which she reached the normal level of mental development seems analogous to the recovery of body weight in a growing child after an illness, the recovery being achieved by an extra fast rate of growth for a period after the illness until normal weight for the given age is again attained.

When the writer saw Isabelle a year and a half after her discovery, she gave him the impression of being a very bright, cheerful, energetic little girl. She spoke well, walked and ran without trouble, and sang with gusto and accuracy. Today she is over fourteen years old and has passed the sixth grade in a public school. Her teachers say that she participates in all school activities as normally as other children. Though older than her classmates, she has fortunately not physically matured too far beyond their level.[18]

Clearly the history of Isabelle's development is different from that of Anna's. In both cases there was an exceedingly low, or rather blank, intellectual level to begin with. In both cases it seemed that the girl might be congenitally feeble-minded. In both a considerably higher level was reached later on. But the Ohio girl achieved a normal mentality within two years, whereas Anna was still marked inadequate at the end of four and a half years. This difference in achievement may suggest that Anna had less initial capacity. But an alternative hypothesis is possible.

One should remember that Anna never received the prolonged and expert attention that Isabelle received. The result of such attention, in the case of the Ohio girl, was to give her speech at an early stage, and her subsequent rapid development seems to have been a consequence of that. "Until Isabelle's speech and language development, she had all the characteristics of a feeble-minded child." Had Anna, who, from the standpoint of psychometric tests and early history, closely resembled this girl at the start, been given a mastery of speech at an earlier point by intensive training, her subsequent development might have been much more rapid.[19]

The hypothesis that Anna began with a sharply inferior mental capacity is therefore not established. Even if she were deficient to start with, we have no way of knowing how much so. Under ordinary conditions she might have been a dull normal or, like her mother, a moron. Even after the blight of her isolation, if she had lived to maturity, she might have finally reached virtually the full level of her capacity, whatever it may have been. That her isolation did have a profound effect upon her mentality, there can be no doubt. This is proved by the substantial degree of change during the four and a half years following her rescue.

Consideration of Isabelle's case serves to show, as Anna's case does not clearly show, that isolation up to the age of six, with failure to acquire any form of speech and hence failure to grasp nearly the whole world of cultural meaning, does not preclude the subsequent acquisition of these. Indeed, there seems to be a process of accelerated recovery in which the child goes through the mental stages at a more rapid rate than would be the case in normal development. Just what would be the maximum age at which a person could remain isolated and still retain the capacity for full cultural acquisition is hard to say. Almost certainly it would not be as high as age fifteen; it might possibly be as low as age ten. Undoubtedly various individuals would differ considerably as to the exact age.

Anna's is not an ideal case for showing the effects of extreme isolation, partly because she was possibly deficient to begin with, partly because she did not receive the best training available, and partly because she did not live long enough. Nevertheless, her case is instructive when placed in the record with numerous other cases of extreme isolation. This and the previous article about her are meant to place her in the record. It is to be hoped that other cases will be described in the scientific literature as they are discovered (as unfortunately they will be), for only in these rare cases of extreme isolation is it possible "to observe *concretely separated* two factors in the development of human personality which are always otherwise only analytically separated, the biogenic and the sociogenic factors."[20]

Notes

1. K. Davis (1940, January), "Extreme social isolation of a child," *American Journal of Sociology*, 45, 554-565.

2. Sincere appreciation is due to the officials in the Department of Welfare, Commonwealth of Pennsylvania, for their kind co-operation in making available the records concerning Anna and discussing the case frankly with the writer. Helen C. Hubbell, Florentine Hackbusch, and Eleanor Meckelnburg were particularly helpful, as was Fanny L. Matchette. Without their aid neither of the reports on Anna could have been written.

3. The records are not clear as to which day.

4. Letter to one of the state officials in charge of the case.

5. *Ibid.*

6. Progress report of the school.

7. Davis (1940), p. 564.

8. The facts set forth here as to Anna's ancestry are taken chiefly from a report of mental tests administered to Anna's mother by psychologists at a state hospital where she was taken for this purpose after the discovery of Anna's seclusion. This excellent report was not available to the writer when the previous paper on Anna was published.

9. M. K. Mason (1942), "Learning to speak after six and one-half years of silence," *Journal of Speech Disorders, 7,* 295-304.

10. F. N. Maxfield (no date), "What happens when the social environment of a child approaches zero." Unpublished manuscript. The writer is greatly indebted to Mrs. Maxfield and to Professor Horace B. English, a colleague of Professor Maxfield, for the privilege of seeing this manuscript and other materials collected on isolated and feral individuals.

11. J. A. L. Singh & R. M. Zingg (1941), *Wolf-children and feral man.* New York: Harper & Bros., pp. 248-251.

12. Maxfield (no date).

13. Mason (1942), p. 299.

14. Maxfield (no date).

15. Mason (1942), p. 299.

16. Mason (1942), pp. 300-304.

17. Maxfield (no date).

18. Based on a personal letter from Dr. Mason to the writer, May 13, 1946.

19. This point is suggested in a personal letter from Dr. Mason to the writer, October 22, 1946.

20. Singh & Zingg (1941), pp. xxi-xxii, in a foreword by the writer.

9

A Matter of Identity

Oliver Sacks

"What'll it be today?" he says, rubbing his hands. "Half a pound of Virginia, a nice piece of Nova?"

(Evidently he saw me as a customer—he would often pick up the phone on the ward, and say "Thompson's Delicatessen.")

"Oh Mr. Thompson!" I exclaim. "And who do you think I am?"

"Good heavens, the light's bad—I took you for a customer. As if it isn't my old friend Tom Pitkins . . . Me and Tom" (he whispers in an aside to the nurse) "was always going to the races together."

"Mr. Thompson, you are mistaken again."

"So I am," he rejoins, not put out for a moment. "Why would you be wearing a white coat if you were Tom? You're Hymie, the kosher butcher next door. No bloodstains on your coat though. Business bad today? You'll look like a slaughterhouse by the end of the week!"

Feeling a bit swept away myself in this whirlpool of identities, I finger the stethoscope dangling from my neck.

"A stethoscope!" he exploded. "And you pretending to be Hymie! You mechanics are all starting to fancy yourselves to be doctors, what with your white coats and stethoscopes—as if you need a stethoscope to listen to a car! So, you're my old friend Manners from the Mobil station up the block, come in to get your boloney-and-rye . . . "

William Thompson rubbed his hands again, in his salesman-grocer's gesture, and looked for the counter. Not finding it, he looked at me strangely again.

"Where am I?" he said, with a sudden scared look. "I thought I was in my shop, doctor. My mind must have wandered . . . You'll be wanting my shirt off, to sound me as usual?"

"No, not the usual. I'm *not* your usual doctor."

"Indeed you're not. I could see that straightaway! You're not my usual chest-thumping doctor. And, by God, you've a beard! You look like Sigmund Freud—have I gone bonkers, round the bend?"

"No, Mr. Thompson. Not round the bend. Just a little trouble with your memory—difficulties remembering and recognizing people."

"My memory has been playing me some tricks," he admitted. "Sometimes I make mistakes—I take somebody for somebody else. . . . What'll it be now—Nova or Virginia?"

So it would happen, with variations, every time—with improvisations, always prompt, often funny, sometimes brilliant, and ultimately tragic. Mr. Thompson would identify me—misidentify, pseudo-identify me—as a dozen different people in the course of five minutes. He would whirl, fluently, from one guess, one hypothesis, one belief, to the next, without any appearance of uncertainty at any point—he never knew who I was, or what and where *he* was, an ex-grocer, with severe Korsakov's, in a neurological institution.

He remembered nothing for more than a few seconds. He was continually disoriented. Abysses of amnesia continually opened beneath him, but he would bridge them, nimbly, by fluent confabulations and fictions of all kinds. For him they were not fictions, but how he suddenly saw, or interpreted, the world. Its radical flux and incoherence could not be tolerated, acknowledged, for an instant—there was, instead, this strange, delirious, quasi-coherence, as Mr. Thompson, with his ceaseless, unconscious, quick-free inventions, continually improvised a world around him—an Arabian Nights world, a phantasmagoria, a dream, of ever-changing people, figures, situations—continual, kaleidoscopic mutations and transformations. For Mr. Thompson, however, it was not a tissue of ever-changing, evanescent fancies and illusion, but a wholly normal, stable and factual world. So far as *he* was concerned, there was nothing the matter.

On one occasion, Mr. Thompson went for a trip, identifying himself at the front desk as "the Revd. William Thompson," ordering a taxi, and taking off for the day. The taxi-driver, whom we later spoke to, said he had never had so fascinating a passenger, for Mr. Thompson told him one story after another, amazing personal stories full of fantastic adventures. "He seemed to have been everywhere, done everything, met everyone. I could hardly believe so much was possible in a single life," he said. "It is not exactly a single life," we answered. "It is all very curious—a matter of identity."[1]

Jimmie G., another Korsakov's patient, whom I have already described at length (Chapter Two), had long since *cooled down* from his acute Korsakov's syndrome, and seemed to have settled into a state of permanent lostness (or, perhaps, a permanent now-seeming dream or reminiscence of the past). But Mr. Thompson, only just out of hospital—his Korsakov's had exploded just three weeks before, when he developed a high fever, raved, and ceased to recognize all his family—was still on the boil, was still in an almost frenzied confabulatory delirium (of the sort sometimes called "Korsakov's psychosis," though it is not really a psychosis at all), continually creating a world and self, to replace what was continually being forgotten and lost. Such a frenzy may call forth quite brilliant powers of invention and fancy—a veritable confabulatory genius—for such a patient *must literally make himself (and his world) up every moment*. We have, each of us, a life-story, an inner narrative—whose continuity, whose sense, is our lives. It might be said that each of us constructs and lives, a "narrative," and that this narrative *is* us, our identities.

If we wish to know about a man, we ask "what is his story—his real, inmost story?"—for each of us *is* a biography, a story. Each of us *is* a singular narrative, which is constructed, continually, unconsciously, by, through, and in us—through our perceptions, our feelings, our thoughts, our actions; and, not least, our discourse, our spoken narrations. Biologically, physiologically, we are not so different from each other; historically, as narratives—we are each of us unique.

To be ourselves we must *have* ourselves—possess, if need be re-possess, our life-stories. We must "recollect" ourselves, recollect the inner drama, the narrative, of ourselves. A man *needs* such a narrative, a continuous inner narrative, to maintain his identity, his self.

This narrative need, perhaps, is the clue to Mr. Thompson's desperate tale-telling, his verbosity. Deprived of continuity, of a quiet, continuous, inner narrative, he is driven to a sort of narrational frenzy—hence his ceaseless tales, his confabulations, his mythomania. Unable to maintain a genuine narrative or continuity, unable to maintain a genuine inner world, he is driven to the proliferation of pseudo-narratives, in a pseudo-continuity, pseudo-worlds peopled by pseudo-people, phantoms.

What is it *like* for Mr. Thompson? Superficially, he comes over as an ebullient comic. People say, "He's a riot." And there *is* much that is farcical in such a situation, which might form the basis of a comic novel.[2] It *is* comic, but not just comic—it is terrible as well. For here is a man who, in some sense, is desperate, in a frenzy. The world keeps disappearing, losing meaning, vanishing—and he must seek meaning, *make* meaning, in a desperate way, continually inventing, throwing bridges of meaning over abysses of meaninglessness, the chaos that yawns continually beneath him.

But does Mr. Thompson himself know this, feel this? After finding him "a riot," "a laugh," "loads of fun," people are disquieted, even terrified, by something in him. "He never stops," they say. "He's like a man in a race, a man trying to catch something which always eludes him." And, indeed, he can never stop running, for the breach in memory, in existence, in meaning, is never healed, but has to be bridged, to be "patched," every second. And the bridges, the patches, for all their brilliance, fail to work—because they *are* confabulations, fictions, which cannot do service for reality, while also failing to correspond with reality. Does Mr. Thompson feel *this*? Or, again, what *is* his "feeling of reality"? Is he in a torment all the while—the torment of a man lost in unreality, struggling to rescue himself, but sinking himself, by ceaseless inventions, illusions, themselves quite unreal? It is certain that he is not at ease—there is a tense, taut look on his face all the while, as of a man under ceaseless inner pressure; and occasionally, not too often, or masked if present, a look of open, naked, pathetic bewilderment. What saves Mr. Thompson in a sense, and in another sense damns him, *is* the forced or defensive superficiality of his life: the way in which it is, in effect, reduced to a surface, brilliant, shimmering, iridescent, ever-changing, but for all that a surface, a mass of illusions, a delirium, without depth.

And with this, no feeling *that* he has lost feeling (for the feeling he has lost), no feeling *that* he has lost the depth, that unfathomable, mysterious, myriad-levelled depth which somehow defines identity or reality. This strikes everyone who has been in contact with him for any time—that under his fluency, even his frenzy, is a strange loss of feeling—that feeling, or judgment, which distinguishes between "real" and "unreal," "true" and "untrue" (one cannot speak of "lies" here, only of "non-truth"), important and trivial, relevant or irrelevant. What comes out, torrentially, in his ceaseless confabulation, has, finally, a peculiar quality of indifference . . . as if it didn't really matter what he said, or what anyone else did or said; as if nothing really mattered any more.

A striking example of this was presented one afternoon, when William Thompson, jabbering away, of all sorts of people who were improvised on the spot, said: "And there goes my younger brother, Bob, past the window," in the same, excited but even and indifferent tone, as the rest of his monologue. I was dumbfounded when, a minute later, a man peeked round the door, and said: "I'm Bob, I'm his younger brother—I think he saw me passing by the window." Nothing in William's tone or manner—nothing in his exuberant, but unvarying and indifferent, style of monologue—had prepared me for the possibility of . . . reality. William spoke of his brother, who *was* real, in precisely the same tone, or lack of tone, in which he spoke of the unreal—and now, suddenly, out of the phantoms, a real figure appeared! Further, he did not treat his younger brother as "real"—did not display any real emotion, was not in the least oriented or delivered from his delirium—but, on the contrary, instantly treated his brother *as* unreal, effacing him, losing him, in a further whirl of delirium—utterly different from the rare but profoundly moving times when Jimmie G. . . . met *his* brother, and while with him was unlost. This was intensely disconcerting to poor Bob—who said "I'm Bob, not Rob, not Dob," to no avail whatever. In the midst of confabulations—perhaps some strand of memory, of remembered kinship, or identity, was still holding (or came back for an instant)—William spoke of his *elder* brother, George, using his invariable present indicative tense.

"But George died nineteen years ago!" said Bob, aghast.

"Aye, George is always the joker!" William quipped, apparently ignoring, or indifferent to, Bob's comment, and went on blathering of George in his excited, dead way, insensitive to truth, to reality, to propriety, to everything—insensitive too to the manifest distress of the living brother before him.

It was this which convinced me, above everything, that there was some ultimate and total loss of inner reality, of feeling and meaning, of soul, in William—and led me to ask the Sisters, as I had asked them of Jimmie G. "Do you think William *has* a soul? Or has he been pithed, scooped-out, de-souled, by disease?"

This time, however, they looked worried by my question, as if something of the sort were already in their minds: they could not say "Judge for yourself. See Willie in Chapel," because his wise-cracking, his confabulations continued even there. There was an utter pathos, a sad *sense* of lostness, with Jimmie G. which one does not feel, or feel directly, with the effervescent Mr. Thompson. Jimmie has *moods*, and a sort of brooding (or, at least, yearning) sadness, a depth, a soul, which does not seem to be present in Mr. Thompson. Doubtless, as the Sisters said, he had a soul, an immortal soul, in the theological sense; could be seen, and loved, as an individual by the Almighty; but, they agreed, something very disquieting had happened to him, to his spirit, his character, in the ordinary, human sense.

It is *because* Jimmie is "lost" that he *can* be redeemed or found, at least for a while, in the mode of a genuine emotional relation. Jimmie is in despair, a quiet despair (to use or adapt Kierkegaard's term), and therefore he has the possibility of salvation, of touching base, the ground of reality, the feeling and meaning he has lost, but still recognises, still yearns for . . .

But for William—with his brilliant, brassy surface, the unending joke which he substitutes for the world (which if it covers over a desperation, is a desperation he does not feel); for William with his manifest indifference to relation and reality caught in an unending verbosity, there may be nothing "redeeming" at all—his confabulations, his apparitions, his frantic search for meanings, being the ultimate barrier *to* any meaning.

Paradoxically, then, William's great gift—for confabulation—which has been called out to leap continually over the ever-opening abyss of amnesia—William's great gift is also his damnation. If only he could be *quiet*, one feels, for an instant; if only he could stop the ceaseless chatter and jabber; if only he could relinquish the deceiving surface of illusions—then (ah then!) reality might seep in; something genuine, something deep, something true, something felt, could enter his soul.

For it is not memory which is the final, "existential" casualty here (although his memory *is* wholly devastated); it is not memory only which has been so altered in him, but some ultimate capacity for feeling which is gone; and this is the sense in which he is "desouled."

Luria speaks of such indifference as "equalization"—and sometimes seems to see it as the ultimate pathology, the final destroyer of any world, any self. It exerted, I think, a horrified fascination on him, as well as constituting an ultimate therapeutic challenge. He was drawn back to this theme again and again—sometimes in relation to Korsakov's and memory, as in *The Neuropsychology of Memory*, more often in relation to frontal-lobe syndromes, especially in *Human Brain and Psychological Processes*, which contains several full-length case-histories of such patients, fully comparable in their terrible coherence and impact to "the man with a shattered world"—comparable, and, in a way, more terrible still, because they depict patients who do not realize that anything has befallen them, patients who have lost their own reality, without knowing it, patients who may not suffer, but be the most God-forsaken of all. Zazetsky (in *The Man with a Shattered World*) is constantly described as a *fighter*, always (even passionately) conscious of his state, and always fighting "with the tenacity of the damned" to recover the use of his damaged brain. But William (like Luria's frontal-lobe patients—see next chapter) is so damned he does not know he is damned, for it is not just a faculty, or some faculties, which are damaged, but the very citadel, the self, the soul itself. William is "lost," in this sense, far more than Jimmie—for all his brio; one never feels, or rarely feels, that there is a *person* remaining, whereas in Jimmie there is plainly a real, moral being, even if disconnected most of the time. In Jimmie, at least, re-connection is *possible*—the therapeutic challenge can be summed up as "Only connect."

Our efforts to "re-connect" William all fail—even increase his confabulatory pressure. But when we abdicate our efforts, and let him be, he sometimes wanders out into the quiet and undemanding garden which surrounds the Home, and there, in its quietness, he recovers his own quiet. The presence of others, other people, excite and rattle him, force him into an endless, frenzied, social chatter, a veritable delirium of identity-making and -seeking; the presence of plants, a quiet garden, the non-human order, making no social or human demands upon him, allow this identity-delirium to relax, to subside; and by their quiet, non-human self-sufficiency and completeness allow him a rare quietness and self-sufficiency of his own, by offering (beneath, or beyond, all merely human identities and relations) a deep wordless communion with Nature itself, and with this the restored sense of being in the world, being real.

Notes

1. A very similar story is related by Luria in *The Neuropsychology of Memory* (1976), in which the spell-bound cabdriver only realized that his exotic passenger was ill when he gave him, for a fare, a temperature chart he was holding. Only then did he realize that this Scheherazade, this spinner of 1,001 tales, was one of "those strange patients" at the Neurological Institute.

2. Indeed such a novel has been written. Shortly after "The Lost Mariner" ... was published, a young writer named David Gilman sent me the manuscript of his book *Croppy Boy*, the story of an amnesiac like Mr. Thompson, who enjoys the wild and unbridled license of creating identities, new selves, as he whims, and as he must—an astonishing imagination of an amnesiac genius, told with positively Joycean richness and gusto. I do not know whether it has been published; I am very sure it should be. I could not help wondering whether Mr. Gilman had actually met (and studied) a "Thompson"—as I have often wondered whether Borges' "Funes," so uncannily similar to Luria's Mnemonist, may have been based on a personal encounter with such a mnemonist.

Yes, Father-Sister

Oliver Sacks

Mrs. B., a former research chemist, had presented with a rapid personality change, becoming "funny" (facetious, given to wisecracks and puns), impulsive—and "superficial." ("You feel she doesn't care about you," one of her friends said. "She no longer seems to care about anything at all.") At first it was thought that she might be hypomanic, but she turned out to have a cerebral tumor. At craniotomy there was found, not a meningioma as had been hoped, but a huge carcinoma involving the orbitofrontal aspects of both frontal lobes.

When I saw her, she seemed high-spirited, volatile—"a riot" (the nurses called her)—full of quips and cracks, often clever and funny.

"Yes, Father," she said to me on one occasion.

"Yes, Sister," on another.

"Yes, Doctor," on a third.

She seemed to use the terms interchangeably.

"What *am* I?" I asked, stung, after a while.

"I see your face, your beard," she said, "I think of an Archimandrite Priest. I see your white uniform—I think of the Sisters. I see your stethoscope—I think of a doctor."

"You don't look at *all* of me?"

"No, I don't look at all of you."

"You realize the difference between a father, a sister, a doctor?"

"I *know* the difference, but it means nothing to me. Father, sister, doctor—what's the big deal?"

Thereafter, teasingly, she would say: "Yes, father-sister. Yes, sister-doctor," and other combinations.

Testing left-right discrimination was oddly difficult, because she said left or right indifferently (though there was not, in reaction, any confusion of the two, as when there is a lateralizing defect of perception or attention). When I drew her attention to this, she said: "Left/right. Right/left. Why the fuss? What's the difference?"

"*Is* there a difference?" I asked.

"Of course," she said, with a chemist's precision. "You could call them *enantiomorphs* of each other. But they mean nothing to *me*. They're no different for *me*. Hands . . . Doctors . . . Sisters . . . ," she added, seeing my puzzlement. "Don't you understand? They mean nothing—nothing to me. *Nothing means anything* . . . at least to me."

"And . . . this meaning nothing . . . ," I hesitated, afraid to go on, "This meaninglessness . . . does *this* bother you? Does *this* mean anything to you?"

"Nothing at all," she said promptly, with a bright smile, in the tone of one who makes a joke, wins an argument, wins at poker.

Was this denial? Was this a brave show? Was this the "cover" of some unbearable emotion? Her face bore no deeper expression whatever. Her world had been voided of feeling and meaning. Nothing any longer felt "real" (or "unreal"). Everything was now "equivalent" or "equal"—the whole world reduced to a facetious insignificance.

I found this somewhat shocking—her friends and family did too—but she herself, though not without insight, was uncaring, indifferent, even with a sort of funny-dreadful nonchalance or levity.

Mrs. B., though acute and intelligent, was somehow not present—"de-souled"—as a person. I was reminded of William Thompson (and also of Dr. P.). This is the effect of the "equalization" described by Luria which we saw in the preceding chapter. . . .

Postscript

The sort of facetious indifference and "equalization" shown by this patient is not uncommon—German neurologists call it *Witzelsucht* ("joking disease"), and it was recognized as a fundamental form of nervous "dissolution" by Hughlings Jackson a century ago. It is not uncommon, whereas insight is—and the latter, perhaps mercifully, is lost as the "dissolution" progresses. I see many cases a year with similar phenomenology but the most varied etiologies. Occasionally I am not sure, at first, if the patient is just "being funny," clowning around, or schizophrenic. Thus, almost at random, I find the following in my notes on a patient with cerebral multiple sclerosis, whom I saw (but whose case I could not follow up) in 1981:

She speaks very quickly, impulsively, and (it seems) indifferently . . . so that the important and the trivial, the true and the false, the serious and the joking, are poured out in a rapid, unselective, half-confabulatory stream . . . She may contradict herself completely within a few seconds . . . will say she loves music, she doesn't, she has a broken hip, she hasn't . . .

I concluded my observation on a note of uncertainty:

How much is cryptannesia-confabulation, how much frontal-lobe indifference-equalization, how much some strange schizophrenic disintegration and shattering-flattening?

Of all forms of "schizophrenia" the "silly-happy," the so-called "hebephrenic," most resembles the organic amnestic and frontal lobe syndromes. They are the most malignant, and the least imaginable—and no one returns from such states to tell us what they were like.

In all these states—"funny" and often ingenious as they appear—the world is taken apart, undermined, reduced to anarchy and chaos. There ceases to be any "center" to the mind, though its formal intellectual powers may be perfectly preserved. The end point of such states is an unfathomable "silliness," an abyss of superficiality, in which all is ungrounded and afloat and comes apart. Luria once spoke of the mind as reduced, in such states, to "mere Brownian movement." I share the sort of horror he clearly felt about them (though this incites, rather than impedes, their accurate description). They make me think, first, of Borges' "Funes", and his remark, "My memory, Sir, is like a garbage-heap," and finally, of the *Dunciad*, the vision of a world reduced to Pure Silliness—Silliness as being the End of the World:

Thy hand, great Anarch, lets the curtain fall;
And Universal Darkness buries All.

The Name of the Situation as Affecting Behavior

Benjamin Lee Whorf

[. . .] In the course of my professional work for a fire insurance company, [. . .] I undertook the task of analyzing many hundreds of reports of circumstances surrounding the start of fires, and in some cases, of explosions. My analysis was directed toward purely physical conditions, such as defective wiring, presence or lack of air spaces between metal flues and woodwork, etc., and the results were presented in these terms. Indeed it was undertaken with no thought that any other significances would or could be revealed. But in due course it became evident that not only a physical situation *qua* physics, but the meaning of that situation to people, was sometimes a factor, through the behavior of the people, in the start of the fire. And this factor of meaning was clearest when it was a *linguistic meaning,* residing in the name or the linguistic description commonly applied to the situation. Thus, around a storage of what are called "gasoline drums," behavior will tend to a certain type, that is, great care will be exercised; while around a storage of what are called "empty gasoline drums," it will tend to be different—careless, with little repression of smoking or of tossing cigarette stubs about. Yet the "empty" drums are perhaps the more dangerous, since they contain explosive vapor. Physically the situation is hazardous, but the linguistic analysis according to regular analogy must employ the word "empty," which inevitably suggests lack of hazard. The word "empty" is used in two linguistic patterns: (1) as a virtual synonym for "null and void, negative, inert," (2) applied in analysis of physical situations without regard to, e.g., vapor, liquid vestiges, or stray rubbish, in the container. The situation is named in one pattern (2) and the name is then "acted out" or "lived up to" in another (1), this being a general formula for the linguistic conditioning of behavior into hazardous forms.

In a wood distillation plant the metal stills were insulated with a composition prepared from limestone and called at the plant "spun limestone." No attempt was made to protect this covering from excessive heat or the contact of flame. After a period of use, the fire below one of the stills spread to the "limestone," which to everyone's great surprise burned vigorously. Exposure to acetic acid fumes from the stills had converted part of the limestone (calcium carbonate) to calcium acetate. This when heated in a fire decomposes, forming inflammable acetone. Behavior that tolerated fire close to the covering was induced by use of the name "limestone," which because it ends in "-stone" implies noncombustibility.

"The Name of the Situation as Affecting Behavior" from *Language, Thought and Reality* (pp. 135-137) by B. L. Whorf, 1956. Cambridge, MA: M.I.T. Press. Reprinted by permission of the Massachusetts Institute of Technology.

A huge iron kettle of boiling varnish was observed to be overheated, nearing the temperature at which it would ignite. The operator moved it off the fire and ran it on its wheels to a distance, but did not cover it. In a minute or so the varnish ignited. Here the linguistic influence is more complex; it is due to the metaphorical objectifying . . . of "cause" as contact or the spatial juxtaposition of "things"—to analyzing the situation as "on" versus "off" the fire. In reality, the stage when the external fire was the main factor had passed; the overheating was now an internal process of convection in the varnish from the intensely heated kettle, and still continued when "off" the fire.

An electric glow heater on the wall was little used, and for one workman had the meaning of a convenient coathanger. At night a watchman entered and snapped a switch, which action he verbalized as "turning on the light." No light appeared, and this result he verbalized as "light is burned out." He could not see the glow of the heater because of the old coat hung on it. Soon the heater ignited the coat, which set fire to the building.

A tannery discharged waste water containing animal matter into an outdoor settling basin partly roofed with wood and partly open. This situation is one that ordinarily would be verbalized as "pool of water." A workman had occasion to light a blowtorch near by, and threw his match into the water. But the decomposing waste matter was evolving gas under the wood cover, so that the setup was the reverse of "watery." An instant flare of flame ignited the woodwork, and the fire quickly spread into the adjoining building.

A drying room for hides was arranged with a blower at one end to make a current of air along the room and thence outdoors through a vent at the other end. Fire started at a hot bearing on the blower, which blew the flames directly into the hides and fanned them along the room, destroying the entire stock. This hazardous setup followed naturally from the term "blower" with its linguistic equivalence to "that which blows," implying that its function necessarily is to "blow." Also its function is verbalized as "blowing air for drying," overlooking that it can blow other things, e.g., flames and sparks. In reality, a blower simply makes a current of air and can exhaust as well as blow. It should have been installed at the vent end to *draw* the air over the hides, then through the hazard (its own casing and bearings), and thence outdoors.

Beside a coal-fired melting pot for lead reclaiming was dumped a pile of "scrap lead"—a misleading verbalization, for it consisted of the lead sheets of old radio condensers, which still had paraffin paper between them. Soon the paraffin blazed up and fired the roof, half of which was burned off.

Such examples, which could be greatly multiplied, will suffice to show how the cue to a certain line of behavior is often given by the analogies of the linguistic formula in which the situation is spoken of, and by which to some degree it is analyzed, classified, and allotted its place in that world which is "to a large extent unconsciously built up on the language habits of the group." And we always assume that the linguistic analysis made by our group reflects reality better than it does.

11

Mindfulness and Mindlessness

Ellen Langer

Introduction

I don't like the idea of a unitary subject; I prefer the play of a kaleidoscope: you give it a tap and the little bits of colored glass form a new pattern.

(Roland Barthes, *The Grain of the Voice*)

One day, at a nursing home in Connecticut, elderly residents were each given a choice of houseplants to care for and were asked to make a number of small decisions about their daily routines. A year and a half later, not only were these people more cheerful, active, and alert than a similar group in the same institution who were not given these choices and responsibilities, but many more of them were still alive. In fact, less than half as many of the decision-making, plant-minding residents had died as had those in the other group. This experiment, with its startling results, began over ten years of research into the powerful effects of what my colleagues and I came to call *mindfulness*, and of its counterpart, the equally powerful but destructive state of *mindlessness*.[1] . . .

Social psychologists usually look for the ways in which behavior depends on context. When mindless, however, people treat information as though it were *context-free*—true regardless of circumstances. For example, take the statement: Heroin is dangerous. How true is this for a dying individual in intolerable pain?

Once alerted to the dangers of mindlessness and to the possibility of bringing about a more mindful attitude by such deceptively simple measures as those used in the nursing home experiment, I began to see this double-edged phenomenon at work in many different settings. For instance, consider the events that led to the 1985 crash of an Air Florida plane that killed seventy-four passengers. It was a routine flight from Washington, D.C., to Florida with an experienced flight crew. Pilot and copilot were in excellent physical health. Neither was tired, stressed, or under the influence. What went wrong? An extensive examination pointed to the crew's pre-takeoff control checks. As the copilot calls out each control on his list, the pilot makes sure the switches are where he wants them to be. One of these controls is an anti-icer. On this day, the pilot and copilot went over each of the controls as they had always done. They went through their routine and checked "off" when the anti-icer was mentioned. This time, however, the flight was different from their experience. This time they were not flying in the usual warm southern weather. It was icy outside.

As he went through the control checks, one by one as he always did, the pilot appeared to be thinking when he was not.[2] The pre-takeoff routines of pilot and copilot have a lot in common with the tiresome safety demonstrations of flight attendants to experienced, glassy-eyed passengers. When we blindly follow routines or unwittingly carry out senseless orders, we are acting like automatons, with potentially grave consequences for ourselves and others.

When the Light's On and Nobody's Home

Out of time we cut "days" and "nights," "summers" and "winters." We say what each part of the sensible continuum is, and all these abstract whats are concepts.

The intellectual life of man consists almost wholly in his substitution of a conceptual order for the perceptual order in which his experience originally comes.

(William James, "The World We Live In")

Imagine that it's two o'clock in the morning. Your doorbell rings; you get up, startled, and make your way downstairs. You open the door and see a man standing before you. He wears two diamond rings and a fur coat, and there's a Rolls Royce behind him. He's sorry to wake you at this ridiculous hour, he tells you, but he's in the middle of a scavenger hunt. His ex-wife is in the same contest, which makes it very important to him that he win. He needs a piece of wood about three feet by seven feet. Can you help him? In order to make it worthwhile he'll give you $10,000. You believe him. He's obviously rich. And so you say to yourself, how in the world can I get this piece of wood for him? You think of the lumber yard; you don't know who owns the lumber yard; in fact you're not even sure where the lumber yard is. It would be closed at two o'clock in the morning anyway. You struggle but you can't come up with anything. Reluctantly, you tell him, "Gee, I'm sorry."

The next day, when passing a construction site near a friend's house, you see a piece of wood that's just about the right size, three feet by seven feet—a door. You could have just taken a door off its hinges and given it to him, for $10,000.

Why on earth, you say to yourself, didn't it occur to you to do that? It didn't occur to you because yesterday your door was not a piece of wood. The seven-by-three-foot piece of wood was hidden from you, stuck in the category called "door."

This kind of mindlessness, which usually takes more humdrum forms—"Why didn't I think of Susan? She can unclog sinks"—could be called "entrapment by category." It is one of three definitions that can help us understand the nature of mindlessness. The other two, which we will also explain, are automatic behavior and acting from a single perspective.

Trapped by Categories

We experience the world by creating categories and making distinctions among them. "This is a Chinese, not a Japanese, vase." "No, he's only a freshman." "The white orchids are endangered." "She's his boss now." In this way, we make a picture of the world, and of ourselves. Without categories the world might seem to escape us. Tibetan Buddhists call this habit of mind "The Lord of Speech":

We adopt sets of categories which serve as ways of managing phenomena. The most fully developed products of this tendency are ideologies, the systems of ideas that rationalize, justify and sanctify our lives. Nationalism, communism, existentialism, Christianity, Buddhism—all provide us with identities, rules of action, and interpretations of how and why things happen as they do.[3]

The creation of new categories, as we will see throughout this book, is a mindful activity. Mindlessness sets in when we rely too rigidly on categories and distinctions created in the past (masculine/feminine, old/young, success/failure). Once distinctions are created, they take on a life of their own. Consider: (1) First there was earth. (2) Then there was land, sea, and sky. (3) Then there were countries. (4) Then there was Germany. (5) Now there is East Germany versus West Germany. The categories we make gather momentum and are very hard to overthrow. We build our own and our shared realities and then we become victims of them—blind to the fact that they are constructs, ideas.

If we look back at the categories of an earlier age, once firmly established, it is easier to see why new ones might become necessary. The Argentinean writer Jorge Luis Borges quotes from an ancient Chinese encyclopedia in which the animals are classified as "(a) belonging to the Emperor, (b) embalmed, (c) tame, (d) suckling pigs, (e) sirens, (f) stray dogs, (g) included in the present classification, (h) frenzied, (i) innumerable, (j) drawn with a very fine camel brush, (k) et cetera, (l) having just broken the water pitcher, (m) that from a long way off look like flies."[4] To be mindless is to be trapped in a rigid world in which certain creatures always belong to the Emperor, Christianity is always good, certain people are forever untouchable, and doors are only doors.

Automatic Behavior

Have you ever said "excuse me" to a store mannequin or written a check in January with the previous year's date? When in this mode, we take in and use limited signals from the world around us (the female form, the familiar face of the check) without letting other signals (the motionless pose, a calendar) penetrate as well.

Once, in a small department store, I gave a cashier a new credit card. Noticing that I hadn't signed it, she handed it back to me to sign. Then she took my card, passed it through her machine, handed me the resulting form, and asked me to sign it. I did as I was told. The cashier then held the form next to the newly signed card to see if the signatures matched.

Modern psychology has not paid much attention to how much complicated action may be performed automatically, yet as early as 1896 Leon Solomons and Gertrude Stein looked into this question. (This was *the* Gertrude Stein who, from 1893 to 1898, was a graduate student in experimental psychology at Harvard University, working under William James.) They studied what was then called "double personalities" and which later came to be known as "split personalities," and proposed that the mindless performance of the second personality was essentially similar to that of ordinary people. Ordinary people also engage in a great deal of complex behavior without consciously paying attention to it. Solomons and Stein conducted several experiments in which they were their own subjects, demonstrating that both writing and reading could be done automatically. They succeeded in writing English words while they were otherwise caught up in reading an absorbing story. With much practice, they were even able to take dictation automatically while reading. Afterward, they were completely unable to recall the words they had written but were nevertheless quite certain they had written something. To show that reading could take place automatically, the subject read aloud from a book while a captivating story was read to him or her. Again they found that, after a lot of practice, they could read aloud unhampered while giving full attention to the story being read to them.

Solomons and Stein concluded that a vast number of actions that we think of as intelligent, such as reading and writing, can be done quite automatically: "We have shown a general tendency on the part of normal people, to *act*, without any express desire or conscious volition, in a manner in general accord with the *previous habits* of the person."[5]

An experiment I conducted in 1978 with fellow psychologists Benzion Chanowitz and Arthur Blank explored this kind of mindlessness.[6] Our setting was the Graduate Center at the City University of New York. We approached people using a copying machine and asked whether they would let us copy something then and there. We gave reasons that were either sound or senseless. An identical response to both sound and senseless requests would show that our subjects were not thinking about what was being said. We made one of three requests: "Excuse me, may I use the Xerox machine?"; "Excuse me, may I use the Xerox machine because I want to make copies?"; "Excuse me, may I use the Xerox machine because I'm in a rush?"

The first and second requests are the same in *content*—What else would one do with a copying machine except make copies? Therefore if people were considering what was actually being said, the first two requests should be equally effective. Structurally, however, they are different. The redundant request ("Excuse me, may I use the Xerox machine because I want to make copies?") is more similar to the last one ("Excuse me, may I use the Xerox machine because I'm in a rush?") in that both state the request and give a reason. If people comply with the last two requests in equal numbers, this implies attention to structure rather than conscious attention to content. That, in fact, was just what we found. There was more compliance when a reason was given—whether the reason sounded legitimate or silly. People responded mindlessly to the familiar framework rather than mindfully attending to the content.

Of course, there are limits to this. If someone asked for a very large favor or if the excuse were unusually absurd ("because an elephant is after me"), the individual would be likely to think about what was said. It is not that people don't hear the request the rest of the time; they simply don't think about it actively.

In a similar experiment, we sent an interdepartmental memo around some university offices. The message either requested or demanded the return of the memo to a designated room—and that was all it said.[7]

("Please return this immediately to Room 247," or "This memo is to be returned to Room 247.") Anyone who read such a memo mindfully would ask, "If whoever sent the memo wanted it, why did he or she send it?" and therefore would not return the memo. Half of the memos were designed to look exactly like those usually sent between departments. The other half were made to look in some way different. When the memo looked like those they were used to, 90 percent of the recipients actually returned it. When the memo looked different, 60 percent returned it.

When I was discussing these studies at a university colloquium, a member of the audience told me about a little con game that operated along the same lines. Someone placed an ad in a Los Angeles newspaper that read, "It's not too late to send $1 to ————," and gave the person's own name and address. The reader was promised nothing in return. Many people replied, enclosing a dollar. The person who wrote the ad apparently earned a good sum.

The automatic behavior in evidence in these examples has much in common with habit.[8] Habit, or the tendency to keep on with behavior that has been repeated over time, naturally implies mindlessness. However, as we will see . . . mindless behavior can arise without a long history of repetition, almost instantaneously, in fact.

Acting From a Single Perspective

So often in our lives, we act as though there were only one set of rules. For instance, in cooking we tend to follow recipes with dutiful precision. We add ingredients as though by official decree. If the recipe calls for a pinch of salt and four pinches fall in, panic strikes, as though the bowl might now explode. Thinking of a recipe only as a rule, we often do not consider how people's tastes vary, or what fun it might be to make up a new dish.

The first experiment I conducted in graduate school explored this problem of the single perspective. It was a pilot study to examine the effectiveness of different requests for help. A fellow investigator stood on a busy sidewalk and told people passing by that she had sprained her knee and needed help. If someone stopped she asked him or her to get an Ace bandage from the nearby drugstore. I stood inside the store and listened while the helpful person gave the request to the pharmacist, who had agreed earlier to say that he was out of Ace bandages. After being told this, not one subject, out of the twenty-five we studied, thought to ask if the pharmacist could recommend something else. People left the drugstore and returned empty-handed to the "victim" and told her the news. We speculated that had she asked for less specific help, she might have received it. But, acting on the single thought that a sprained knee needs an Ace bandage, no one tried to find other kinds of help.

As a little test of how a narrow perspective can dominate our thinking, read the following sentence:

FINAL FOLIOS SEEM TO RESULT FROM YEARS OF DUTIFUL STUDY OF TEXTS ALONG WITH YEARS OF SCIENTIFIC EXPERIENCE.

Now count how many Fs there are, reading only once more through the sentence.

If you find fewer than there actually are (the answer is given in the notes),[9] your counting was probably influenced by the fact that the first two words in the sentence begin with F. In counting, your mind would tend to cling to this clue, or single perspective, and miss some of the Fs hidden within and at the end of words.

Highly specific instructions such as these or the request for an Ace bandage encourage mindlessness. Once we let them in, our minds snap shut like a clam on ice and do not let in new signals.

Notes

1. E. Langer & J. Rodin (1976), "The effects of enhanced personal responsibility for the aged: A field experiment in an institutional setting," *Journal of Personality and Social Psychology, 34,* 191-198; J. Rodin & E. Langer (1977), "Long-term effects of a control-relevant intervention among the institutionalized aged," *Journal of Personality and Social Psychology, 35,* 897-902.

2. C. Gersick & J. R. Hackman (1990), "Habitual routines in task-performing groups," *Organizational Behavior and Human Decision Processes, 47,* 65-97.

3. C. Trungpa (1973), *Cutting through spiritual materialism,* Boulder & London: Shambhala.

4. T'ai P'ing (978), *Kuang chi* [Extensive records made in the period of peace and prosperity]; cited in J. L. Borges (1967), *Libro de los seres imaginarios,* Buenos Aires: Editorial Kiersa S. A., Fauna China, p. 88.

5. L. Solomons & G. Stein (1896), "Normal motor automation," *Psychological Review, 36,* 492-572.

6. E. Langer, A. Blank, & B. Chanowitz (1978), "The mindlessness of ostensibly thoughtful action: The role of placebic information in interpersonal interaction, *Journal of Personality and Social Psychology, 36,* 635-642.

7. Langer et al. (1978).

8. To understand the more complex relationship between automatic information processing and mindlessness, compare E. Langer (1989), "Minding matters," in L. Berkowitz (Ed.), *Advances in experimental social psychology* (pp. 137-173), New York: Academic Press; and W. Schneider & R. M. Schiffrin (1977), "Controlled and automatic human information processing: I. Detection, search, and attention," *Psychological Review, 84,* 1-66.

9. The correct answer is 8. A similar quiz was printed on the business card of the Copy Service of Miami, Inc.

12

Designing a Draining Rack

David Pye

The poet invents new juxtapositions of words and phrases which convey a new experience. The inventor makes new juxtapositions of things which give new results. Neither the poet's words nor the inventor's things have any remarkable properties of their own. They are everyday words and things. It is the juxtaposition of them which is new.

Before anything is made, a desirable result is likely to have been envisaged. The man who envisages the result may already know of a system or several systems which are capable of giving rise to it, and in that case no further invention is needed. If you say, "Invent me something which will result in these books and this alarm clock remaining at rest at this level which I will indicate on the wall," I shall at once think of a shelf on brackets, which I remember to have seen giving the same sort of result with the same sort of things before. I shall not be hailed as a great inventor. I have simply had to determine the class to which the specified result belongs and to consider which devices of all those in my memory give rise to results of the same class. But have I really done even that? I doubt it. I have simply envisaged the books up there on the wall, compared the vision with vari-

ous sights stored in my memory, found one which showed books half way up a wall, noticed that there was a shelf under the books, and concluded that a bookshelf would do now because it was suitable before.

That can be a bad procedure. There may be other systems which are better than the first which turns up in the memory.

The author once set about designing a draining rack. It was for the plates, pot-lids and so forth used by his family while living in a tent. It had therefore to be very small and very light. Because he started by thinking "I must design a draining rack" instead of considering what kind of result was wanted, his train of thought was conditioned unprofitably. Racks act by supporting. Any instance of a rack which will support plates must have dimensions conformable with those of the plates, and there is a limit below which its size and therefore its weight cannot be reduced.

After prolonged thought the designer realised his mistake and started to consider what result he wanted, namely, a row of plastic plates edge-on in mid air. He then started to search his memory for results of the same class but not necessarily involving similar objects or, at any rate, objects which were closely similar. Doing this is not as easy as it sounds. Because it was not easy his mind ran to a result involving objects which, if not closely similar, at any rate were suggested by a very obvious association, namely a row of cups hanging on hooks. The unconscious association must have been

"Designing a Draining Rack" from *The Nature and Aesthetics of Design* (pp. 58-60) by D. Pye, 1978. New York: Van Nostrand Reinhold. Reprinted by permission of James Pye.

plates—saucers: saucers—cups. Thus the thought of plates unearthed the memory of cups.

It was then easy to arrive at the required invention, a thin stick carrying a row of thin wire hooks like cup-hooks; for the desired result was by now well in mind, and the objects in it too, the flexible rather soft plastic plates, which being rather soft at once suggested that holes might be cut in their rims.[1]

Designers and their clients seldom formulate their purposes in terms of the desired results, but on the contrary habitually do so in terms of the systems of things which give rise to them. As the example of the dish rack showed, this may be a bad habit; but it will only be bad if some new factor in the situation, such as plates made out of easily drilled plastic, is overlooked. Otherwise the designer's normal habit is mere common sense. If you want to enable someone to sit, it will be idiotic to proceed in the way that students of design are sometimes advised to do, and think out the whole problem from first principles, as though all the people who for the last four thousand years have been making and using chairs were half-wits. Where the problem is old, the old solutions will nearly always be best (unless a new technique has been introduced) because it is inconceivable that all the designers of ten or twenty generations will have been fools.

When a desirable result is envisaged and the memory, being searched, shows no immediate picture like the bookshelf, then the same procedure must be followed as was done with the dish rack. A similar result involving different objects must be sought, in the hope that the device which gave rise to it can be adapted to the objects which are now intended, or that these can be adapted to the device. It is here that our habit of refusing even to name results, and our habit of referring to them by way of mythical actions, and all the habits of mind associated with them and with the idea of "function," all these help to make our task more difficult and to inhibit us from discerning analogies between different results; for we are averse from thinking of classes of results, as such, in any case, and have no proper tools to do the thinking with. Invention can only be done deliberately if the inventor can discern similarities between the particular result which he is envisaging and some other actual result which he has seen and stored in his memory (which must of course be well stored so as to give him a wide choice and therefore a better chance). The fact that we habitually visualise particular results is something of a stumbling block too, in its way. We *envisage* or feel the desired result. We see it or feel it, objects and all. Our memories are visual or muscular memories of particular results, not conceptual memories of classes of results. We see or feel in our memories particular results each including a particular system with its particular components and above all with the particular objects which were involved. Out of that lot we have to abstract the class of result, averting our attention from the particular system and objects. This is not easy when one is reviewing the bloodless ghosts of memory.

If an exact classification of devices were made according to a close analysis of the characteristics of their results it would presumably be possible for computers to invent, provided that their memories were full-fed. For all I know they are doing it now. But it may be doubted whether the classification could be subtle enough or the feeding full enough to enable them to spot far-fetched similarities with the same genius which human inventors have sometimes shown. What association gave Watt his centrifugal governor? A merry-go-round? Who is going to feed a computer with merry-go-rounds?

Note

1. In case anyone wants to adopt this important invention let him be warned that in a breeze of wind it makes a noise like a muffled glockenspiel. Take it down at night.

13

Lineal and Nonlineal Codifications of Reality

Dorothy Lee

The following study is concerned with the codification of reality, and more particularly, with the nonlineal apprehension of reality among the people of the Trobriand Islands, in contrast to our own lineal phrasing. Basic to my investigation is the assumption that a member of a given society not only codifies experienced reality through the use of the specific language and other patterned behavior characteristic of his culture, but that he actually grasps reality only as it is presented to him in this code. The assumption is not that reality itself is relative; rather, that it is differently punctuated[1] and categorized, or that different aspects of it are noticed by or presented to the participants of different cultures. If reality itself were not absolute, then true communication of course would be impossible. My own position is that there is an absolute reality, and that communication is possible. If, then, that which the different codes refer to is ultimately the same, a careful study and analysis of a different code and of the culture to which it belongs should lead us to concepts which are ultimately comprehensible, when translated into our own code. It may even, eventually, lead us to aspects of reality from which our own code excludes us.

It is a corollary of this assumption that the specific phrasing of reality can be discovered through intensive and detailed analysis of any aspect of culture. My own study was begun with an analysis of linguistic formulation, only because it is in language that I happen to be best able to discover my clues. To show how these clues can be discovered and used as guides to the apprehension of reality, as well as to show what I mean by codification, I shall present at first concrete material in the field of language.

I

That a word is not the reality, not the thing which it represents, has long been a commonplace to all of us. The thing which I hold in my hand as I write *is* not a pencil; I *call* it a pencil. And it remains the same whether I call it *pencil, molyvi, Bleistift,* or *siwiqoq.* These words are different sound-complexes applied to the same reality; but is the difference merely one of sound-complex? Do they refer to the same *perceived* reality? *Pencil* originally meant little tail; it delimited and named the reality according to form. *Molyvi* means lead and refers to the writing element. *Bleistift* refers both to the form and to the writing element. *Siwiqoq* means painting-stick and refers to observed function and form. Each culture has phrased the reality differently. To say that *pencil,* for example, applies primarily to form is no idle etymologic statement. When we use this word metaphorically, we refer neither to writing element nor to function, but to form alone; we speak of a pencil of light, or a styptic pencil.

When I used the four words for this object, we all knew what reality was referred to; we knew the meaning of the word. We could visualize the object in my hand, and the words all delimited it in the same way; for example, none of them implied that it was a continuation of my fist. But the student of ethnography often has to deal with words which punctuate reality into different phrasings from the ones with which he is familiar. Let us take, for instance, the words for "brother" and "sister." We go to the islands of Ontong Java to study the kinship system. We ask our informant what he calls his sister and he says *ave*; he calls his brother *kainga*. So we equate *ave* with "sister" and *kainga* with "brother." By way of checking our information we ask the sister what she calls her brother; it turns out that for her, *ave* is "brother," not "sister" as we were led to expect; and that it is her sister whom she calls *kainga*. The same reality, the same actual kinship is present there as with us; but we have chosen a different aspect for naming. We are prepared to account for this; we say that both cultures name according to what we would call a certain type of blood relationship; but whereas we make reference to absolute sex, they refer to relative sex. Further inquiry, however, discloses that in this, also, we are wrong. Because in our own culture we name relatives according to formal definition and biologic relationship, we have thought that this formulation represents reality; and we have tried to understand the Ontong Javanese relationship terms according to these distinctions which, we believe, are given in nature. But the Ontong Javanese classifies relatives according to a different aspect of reality, differently punctuated. And because of this, he applies *kainga* as well to a wife's sister and a husband's brother; to a man's brother's wife and a woman's sister's hus-

band, as well as to a number of other individuals. Neither sex nor blood relationship, then, can be basic to this term. The Ontong Javanese name according to their everyday behavior and experience, not according to formal definition. A man shares the ordinary details of his living with his brothers and their wives for a large part of the year; he sleeps in the same large room, he eats with them, he jokes and works around the house with them; the rest of the year he spends with his wife's sisters and their husbands, in the same easy companionship. All these individuals are *kainga* to one another. The *ave*, on the other hand, names a behavior of great strain and propriety; it is based originally upon the relative sex of siblings, yes, but it does not signify biologic fact. It names a social relationship, a behavior, an emotional tone. *Ave* can never spend their adult life together, except on rare and temporary occasions. They can never be under the same roof alone together, cannot chat at ease together, cannot refer even distantly to sex in the presence of each other, not even to one's sweetheart or spouse; more than that, everyone else must be circumspect when the ave of someone of the group is present. The *ave* relationship also carries special obligations toward a female ave and her children. *Kainga* means a relationship of ease, full of shared living, of informality, gaiety; *ave* names one of formality, prohibition, strain. These two cultures, theirs and our own, have phrased and formulated social reality in completely different ways, and have given their formulation different names. The word is merely the name of this specific cultural phrasing. From this one instance we might formulate the hypothesis—a very tentative one—that among the Ontong Javanese names describe emotive experiences, not observed forms or functions. But we cannot accept this as fact, unless further investigation shows it to be implicit in the rest of their patterned behavior, in their vocabulary and the morphology of their language, in their ritual and their other organized activity.

One more instance, this time from the language of the Wintu Indians of California, will deal with the varying aspect or segmentation of experience which is used as a basis of classification. To begin with, we take the stem *muk*. On the basis of this stem we form the word *mukeda*, which means: "I turned the basket bottom up"; we form *mukuhara*, which means: "The turtle is moving along"; and we form *mukurumas*, which means: "automobile." Upon what conceivable principle can an automobile be put in the same category as a turtle and a basket? There is such a principle, however, and it operates also when the Wintu calls the activity of laundering, *to make foam continuously*. According to this principle, he uses the same stem (*puq* or *poq*) to form words for the following:

puqeda: I just pushed a peg into the ground.

olpuqal: He is sitting on one haunch.

poqorahara: Birds are hopping along.

olpoqoyabe: There are mushrooms growing.

tunpoqoypoqoya: You walked shortskirted, stiff-legged ahead of me.

It is difficult for us to discover the common denominator in the different formations from this one stem, or even to believe that there can be one. Yet, when we discover the principle underlying the classification, the categories themselves are understandable. Basic to the classification is the Wintu view of himself as observer; he classifies as an outsider. He passes no judgment on essence, and where we would have used kinesthetic or participatory experience as the basis of naming, he names as an observer only, for the shape of the activity or the object. The turtle and the automobile can thus naturally be grouped together with the inverted baskets. The mushroom standing on its stem, the fist grasping a peg against the ground, the stiff leg topped by a short skirt, or by the body of a bird or of a man resting on a haunch, obviously all belong together in one category. But the progress of a grasshopper cannot be categorized with that of a hopping bird. We, who classify on a different basis, apprehend the hop of the two kinesthetically and see it as basically the same in both cases; but the Wintu see the difference in recurrent shape, which is all-important to them, and so name the two by means of completely different stems. Again, when we discover this principle, it is easy to see that from the observer's point of view laundering is the making of a lot of foam; and to see why, when beer was introduced, it was named *laundry*.

An exhaustive study of the language and other aspects of Wintu culture shows that this principle is present in all of the Wintu language, as well as in the Wintu's conception of the self, of his place in the universe, in his mythology, and probably in other aspects of his culture.

II

I have discussed at length the diversity of codification of reality in general, because it is the foundation of the specific study which I am about to present. I shall speak of the formulation of experienced reality among the Trobriand Islanders in comparison to our own; I shall speak of the nature of expectancy, of motivation, of satisfaction, as based upon a reality which is differently apprehended and experienced in two different societies; which is, in fact, for each, a different reality. The Trobriand Islanders were studied by the late Bronislaw Malinowski, who has given us the rich and circumstantial material about them which has made this study possible. I have given a detailed presentation of some implications of their language elsewhere; but since it was in their language that I first noticed the absence of lineality, which led me to this study, I shall give here a summary of the implications of the language.

A Trobriand word refers to a self-contained concept. What we consider an attribute or a predicate is to the Trobriander an ingredient. Where I would say, for example, "A good gardener," or "The gardener is good," the Trobriand word would include both "gardener" and "goodness"; if the gardener loses the goodness, he has lost a defining ingredient, he is something else, and he is named by means of a completely different word. A *taytu* (a species of yam) contains a certain degree of ripeness, bigness, roundedness, etc.; without one of these defining ingredients, it is something else, perhaps a *bwanawa* or a *yowana*. There are no adjectives in the language; the rare words dealing with qualities are substantivized. The term *to be* does not occur; it is used neither attributively nor existentially, since existence itself is contained; it is an ingredient of being.

Events and objects are self-contained points in another respect; there is a series of beings, but no becoming. There is no temporal connection between objects. The taytu always remains itself; it does not *become* over-ripe; over-ripeness is an ingredient of another, a different being. At some point, the taytu *turns into* a yowana, which contains over-ripeness. And the yowana, over-ripe as it is, does not put forth shoots, does not *become* a sprouting yowana. When sprouts appear, it ceases to be itself; in its place appears a *silasata*. Neither is there a temporal connection made—or, according to our own premises, perceived—between events; in fact, temporality is meaningless. There are no tenses, no linguistic distinction between past or present. There is no arrangement of activities or events into means and ends, no causal or teleologic relationships. What we consider a causal relationship in a sequence of connected events is to the Trobriander an ingredient of a patterned whole. He names this ingredient *u'ula*. A tree has a trunk, u'ula; a house has u'ula, posts; a magical formula has u'ula, the first strophe; an expedition has u'ula, a manager or leader; and a quarrel contains an u'ula, what we would call a cause. There is no purposive *so as to*; no *for the purpose of*; there is no *why* and

no *because*. The rarely used *pela*, which Malinowski equates with *for*, means primarily *to jump*. In the culture, any deliberately purposive behavior—the kind of behavior to which we accord high status—is despised. There is no automatic relating of any kind in the language. Except for the rarely used verbal it-differents and it-sames, there are no terms of comparison whatever. And we find in an analysis of behavior that the standard for behavior and of evaluation is noncomparative.

These implications of the linguistic material suggest to my mind an absence of axiomatic lineal connection between events or objects in the Trobriand apprehension of reality, and this implication, as I shall attempt to show below, is reinforced in their definition of activity. In our own culture, the line is so basic, that we take it for granted, as given in reality. We see it in visible nature, between material points, and we see it between metaphorical points such as days or acts. It underlies not only our thinking, but also our aesthetic apprehension of the given; it is basic to the emotional climax which has so much value for us, and, in fact, to the meaning of life itself. In our thinking about personality and character, we have assumed the line as axiomatic.

In our academic work, we are constantly acting in terms of an implied line. When we speak of *ap*plying an *at*tribute, for example, we visualize the process as lineal, coming from the outside. If I make a picture of an apple on the board, and want to show that one side is green and the other red, I connect these attributes with the pictured apple by means of lines, as a matter of course; how else would I do it? When I organize my data, I *draw* conclusions *from* them. I *trace* a relationship between my facts. I describe a pattern as a *web* of relationships. Look at a lecturer who makes use of gestures; he is constantly making lineal connections in the air. And a teacher with chalk in hand will be drawing lines on the board whether he be a psychologist, a historian, or a paleontologist.

Preoccupation with social facts merely as self-contained facts is mere antiquarianism. In my field, a student of this sort would be an amateur or a dilettante, not an anthropologist. To be an anthropologist, he can arrange his facts in an upward slanting line, in a *unilinear* or *multilinear course* of development, in *parallel lines* or *converging lines.* Or he may arrange them geographically, with *lines* of *diffusion* connecting them; or schematically, using *concentric circles.* Or at least, he must indicate what his study *leads to,* what new insights we can *draw from* it. To be accorded status, he must use the guiding line as basic.

The line is found or presupposed in most of our scientific work. It is present in the *induction* and the *deduction* of science and logic. It is present in the philosopher's phrasing of means and ends as lineally connected. Our statistical facts are presented lineally as a *graph* or reduced to a normal *curve.* And all of us, I think, would be lost without our diagrams. We *trace* a historical development; we *follow the course* of history and evolution *down to* the present and *up from* the ape; and it is interesting to note, in passing, that whereas both evolution and history are lineal, the first goes up the blackboard, the second goes down. Our psychologists picture motivation as external, connected with the act through a line, or, more recently, entering the organism through a lineal channel and emerging transformed, again lineally, as response. I have seen lineal pictures of nervous impulses and heartbeats, and with them I have seen pictured lineally a second of time. These were photographs, you will say, of existing fact, of reality; a proof that the line is present in reality. But I am not convinced, perhaps due to my ignorance of mechanics, that we have not created our recording instruments in such a way that they have to picture time and motion, light and sound, heartbeats and nerve impulses lineally, on the unquestioned assumption of the line as axiomatic. The line is omnipresent and inescapable, and so we are incapable of questioning the reality of its presence.

When we see a *line* of trees, or a *circle* of stones, we assume the presence of a connecting line which is not actually visible. And we assume it metaphorically when we follow a *line* of thought, a *course* of action or the *direction* of an argument; when we *bridge* a gap in the conversation, or speak of the *span* of life or of teaching a *course,* or lament our *interrupted career.* We make children's embroidery cards and puzzle cards on this assumption; our performance tests and even our tests for sanity often assume that the line is present in nature and, at most, to be discovered or given visual existence.

But is the line present in reality? Malinowski, writing for members of our culture and using idioms which would be comprehensible to them, describes the Trobriand village as follows: "Concentrically with the circular row of yam houses there runs a ring of dwelling huts." He saw, or at any rate, he represented the village as two circles. But in the texts which he recorded, we find that the Trobrianders at no time mention circles or rings or even rows when they refer to their villages. Any word which they use to refer to a village, such as *a* or *this,* is prefixed by the substantival element *kway* which means *bump* or *aggregate of bumps.* This is the element which they use when they refer to a pimple or a bulky rash; or to canoes loaded with yams. In their terms, a village is an aggregate of bumps; are they blind to the circles? Or did Malinowski create the circles himself, out of his cultural axiom?

Again, for us as well as in Malinowski's description of the Trobrianders, which was written necessarily in terms meaningful to us, all effective activity is certainly not a haphazard aggregate of acts, but a lineally planned series of acts leading to an envisioned end. Their gardening with all its specialized activities, both technical and magical, leading to a rich harvest; their *kula* involving the cutting down of trees, the communal dragging of the tree to the beach, the rebuilding or building of large sea-worthy canoes, the provisioning, the magical and ceremonial activities involved, surely all these can be carried through only if they are lineally conceived. But the Trobrianders do not describe their activity lineally: they do no dynamic relating of acts; they do not use even so innocuous a connective as *and*. Here is part of a description of the planting of coconut: "Thou-approach-there coconut thou-bring-here-we-plant-coconut thou-go thou-plant our coconut. This-here it-emerge sprout. We-push-away this we-push-away this-other coconut-husk-fiber together sprout it-sit together root." We who are accustomed to seek lineal continuity, cannot help supplying it as we read this; but the continuity is not given in the Trobriand text; and all Trobriand speech, according to Malinowski, is "jerky," given in points, not in connecting lines. The only connective I know of in Trobriand is the *pela* which I mentioned above; a kind of preposition which also means "to jump." I am not maintaining here that the Trobrianders cannot see continuity; rather that lineal connection is not automatically made by them, as a matter of course. At Malinowski's persistent questioning, for example, they did attempt to explain their activities in terms of cause or motivation, by stating possible "results" of uncooperative action. But Malinowski found their answers confused, self-contradictory, inconsistent; their preferred answer was, "It was ordained of old"—pointing to an ingredient value of the act instead of giving an explanation based on lineal connection. And when they were not trying to find answers to leading questions, the Trobrianders made no such connections in their speech. They assumed, for example, that the validity of a magical spell lay, not in its results, not in proof, but in its very being; in the appropriateness of its inheritance, in its place within the patterned activity, in its being performed by the appropriate person, in its realization of its mythical basis. To seek validity through proof was foreign to their thinking, yet they attempted to do so at the ethnographer's request. I should add here that their names

for constellations imply that here they see lineal figures; I cannot investigate the significance of this, as I have no contextual material. At any rate, I would like to emphasize that, even if the Trobriander does occasionally supply connecting lines between points, his perception and experience do not automatically fall into a lineal framework.

The fact remains that Trobrianders embark on, what is certainly for us, a series of acts which "must require" planning and purposiveness. They engage in acts of gift-giving and gift-receiving which we can certainly see as an exchange of gifts. When we plot their journeys, we find that they do go from point to point, they do navigate a course, whether they say so or not. Do they merely refrain from giving linguistic expression to something which they actually recognize in nature? On the nonlinguistic level, do they act on an assumption of a lineality which is given no place in their linguistic formulation? I believe that, where valued activity is concerned, the Trobrianders do not act on an assumption of lineality at any level. There is organization or rather coherence in their acts because Trobriand activity is patterned activity. One act within this pattern gives rise to a pre-ordained cluster of acts. Perhaps one might find a parallel in our culture in the making of a sweater. When I embark on knitting one, the ribbing at the bottom does not *cause* the making of the neckline, nor of the sleeves or the armholes; and it is not part of a lineal series of acts. Rather it is an indispensable part of a patterned activity which includes all these other acts. Again, when I choose a dress pattern, the acts involved in the making of the dress are already present for me. They are embedded in the pattern which I have chosen. In this same way, I believe, can be seen the Trobriand insistence that though intercourse is a necessary preliminary to conception, it is not the cause of conception. There are a number of acts in the pattern of procreating; one is intercourse, another the entrance of the spirit of a dead Trobriander into the womb. However, there is a further point here. The Trobrianders, when pressed by the ethnographer or teased by the neighboring Dobuans, showed signs of intense embarrassment, giving the impression that they were trying to maintain unquestioningly a stand in which they had to believe. This, I think, is because pattern is truth and value for them; in fact, acts and being derive value from the embedding pattern.

So the question of perception of line remains. It is because they find value in pattern that the Trobrianders act according to nonlineal pattern; not because they do not perceive lineality.

But all Trobriand activity does not contain value; and when it does not, it assumes lineality, and is utterly despicable. For example, the pattern of sexual intercourse includes the giving of a gift from the boy to the girl; but if a boy gives a gift so as to win the girl's favor, he is despised. Again, the kula pattern includes the eventual reception of a gift from the original recipient; the pattern is such that it keeps the acts physically and temporally completely disparate. In spite of this, however, some men are accused of giving gifts as an inducement to their kula partner to give them a specially good kula gift. Such men are labeled with the vile phrase: he barters. But this means that, unvalued and despised, lineal behavior does exist. In fact, there are villages in the interior whose inhabitants live mainly by bartering manufactured articles for yams. The inhabitants of Omarakana, about whom Malinowski's work and this study are mainly concerned, will barter with them, but consider then pariahs.

This is to say that it is probable that the Trobrianders experience reality in nonlineal pattern because this is the valued reality; and that they are capable of experiencing lineally, when value is absent or destroyed. It is not to say, however, that this, in itself, means that lineality is given, is present in nature, and that pattern is not. Our own insistence on the line, such as lineal causal-ity, for example, is also often based on unquestioned belief or value. To return to the subject of procreation, the husband in our culture, who has long hoped and tried in vain to beget children, will nevertheless maintain that intercourse causes conception; perhaps with the same stubbornness and embarrassment which the Trobrianders exhibited when maintaining the opposite.

III

The line in our culture not only connects, but it moves. And as we think of a line as moving from point to point, connecting one to the other, so we conceive of roads as *running from* locality *to* locality. A Trobriander does not speak of roads either as connecting two points, or as *running from* point *to* point. His paths are self-contained, named as independent units; they are not *to* and *from*, they are *at*. And he himself is *at*; he has no equivalent for our *to* or *from*. There is, for instance, the myth of Tudava, who goes—in our view—from village to village and from island to island planting and offering yams. The Trobriand texts puts it this way: "Kitava it-shine village already (i.e., completed) he-is-over. 'I-sail I-go Iwa'; Iwa he-anchor he-go ashore . . . He-sail Digumenu . . . They-drive (him off) . . . he-go Kwaywata." Point after point is enumerated, but his sailing from and to is given as a discrete event. In our view, he is actually following a southeasterly course, more or less; but this is not given as course or line, and no directions are even mentioned. In fact, in the several texts referring to journeyings in the Archipelago, no words occur for the cardinal directions. In sailing, the "following" winds are named according to where they are *at*, the place where they strike the canoe, such as wind-striking-the-outrigger-beam; not according to where they *come from*. Otherwise, we find names for the southwest wind (*youyo*), and the northwest wind (*bombatu*), but these are merely substantival names which have nothing to do with direction; names for kinds of wind.

When a member of our society gives an unemotional description of a person, he follows an imaginary line, usually downward: from head to foot, from tip to toe, from hair to chin. The Navaho do the opposite, following a line upward. The Trobriander follows no line, at least none that I can see. "My head boils," says a kula spell; and it goes on to enumerate the parts of the head as follows: nose, occiput, tongue, larynx, speech, mouth. Another spell casting a protective fog runs as follows: "I befog the hand, I befog the foot, I befog the head, I befog the shoulders. . . ." There is a magic formula where we do recognize a line, but it is one which Malinowski did not record verbatim at the time, but which he put down later from memory; and it is not improbable that his memory edited the formula according to the lineality of his culture. When the Trobriander enumerates the parts of a canoe, he does not follow any recognizable lineal order: "Mist . . . surround me my mast . . . the nose of my canoe . . . my sail . . . my steering oar . . . my canoe-gunwale . . . my canoe-bottom . . . my prow . . . my rib . . . my threading-stick . . . my prowboard . . . my transverse stick . . . my canoe-side." Malinowski diagrams the garden site as a square piece of land subdivided into squares; the Trobrianders refer to it in the same terms as those which they use in referring to a village—a bulky object or an aggregate of bumps. When the plots in the garden site are apportioned to the gardeners, the named plots are assigned by name, the others by location along each named side of the garden. After this, the inner plots, the "belly" of the garden, are apportioned. Following along a physical rim is a procedure which we find elsewhere also. In a spell naming villages on the main island, there is a long list of villages which lie along the coast northward, then westward around the island, then south. To us, of course, this is lineal order. But we have no indication that

the Trobrianders see other than geographical location, point after point, as they move over a physically continuous area; the line as a guide to procedure is not necessarily implied. No terms are used here which might be taken as an implication of continuity; no "along the coast" or "around" or northward."

IV

When we in our culture deal with events or experiences of the self, we use the line as guide for various reasons, two of which I shall take up here. First, we feel we must arrange events chronologically in a lineal order; how else could our historians discover the causes of a war or a revolution or a defeat? Among the Trobrianders, what corresponds to our history is an aggregate of anecdotes, that is, unconnected points, told without respect to chronological sequence, or development, or causal relationship; with no grammatical distinction made between words referring to past events, or to present or contemplated ones. And in telling an anecdote, they take no care that a temporal sequence should be followed. For instance, they said to Malinowski, "They-eat-taro, they-spew-taro, they-disgusted-taro"; but if time, as we believe, is a moving line, then the revulsion came first in time, the vomiting was the result, coming afterward. Again, they say, "This-here . . . ripes . . . falls-down truly gives-birth . . . Sits seed in belly-his"; but certainly the seed is there first, and the birth follows in time, if time is lineal.

Secondly, we arrange events and objects in a sequence which is climactic, in size and intensity, in emotional meaning, or according to some other principle. We often arrange events from earlier to later, not because we are interested in historical causation, but because the present is the climax of our history. But when the Trobriander relates happenings, there is no developmental arrangement, no building up of emotional tone. His stories have no plot, no lineal development, no climax. And when he repeats his garden spell, his list is neither climactic, nor anticlimactic; it sounds merely untidy to us:

The belly of my garden lifts
The belly of my garden rises
The belly of my garden reclines
The belly of my garden
    is-a-bushhen's-nest-in-lifting
The belly of my garden is-an-anthill
The belly of my garden lifts-bends
The belly of my garden
    is-an-ironwood-tree-in-lifting
The belly of my garden lies-down
The belly of my garden burgeons.

When the Trobrianders set out on their great ceremonial kula expedition, they follow a preestablished order. First comes the canoe of the Tolab waga, an obscure subclan. Next come the canoes of the great chiefs. But this is not climactic; after the great chiefs come the commoners. The order derives meaning not from lineal sequence, but from correspondence with a present, experienced, meaningful pattern, which is the recreation or realization of the mythical pattern; that which has been ordained of old and is forever. Its meaning does not lie in an item-to-item relationship, but in fitness, in the repetition of an established unit.

An ordering of this sort gives members of our society a certain esthetic disphoria except when, through deliberate training, we learn to go beyond our cultural expectation; or, when we are too young to have taken on the phrasings of our culture. When we manipulate objects naively, we arrange them on some climactic lineal principle. Think of a college commencement, with the faculty arranged in order of rank or length of tenure or other mark of importance; with the students arranged according to increasing physical height, from shortest to tallest, actually the one absolutely irrelevant principle as regards the completion of their college education, which is the occasion for the celebration. Even when the sophisticated

avoid this principle, they are not unconscious of it; they are deliberately avoiding something which is there.

And our arrangement of history, when we ourselves are personally involved, is mainly climactic. My great grandmother sewed by candle light, my grandmother used a kerosene lamp, my mother did her studying by gaslight, I did it by a naked electric ceiling light, and my children have diffused fluorescent lighting. This is progress; this is the meaningful sequence. To the Trobriander, climax in history is abominable, a denial of all good, since it would imply not only the presence of change, but also that change increases the good; but to him value lies in sameness, in repeated pattern, in the incorporation of all time within the same point. What is good in life is exact identity with all past Trobriand experience, and all mythical experience. There is no boundary between past Trobriand existence and the present; he can indicate that an action is completed, but this does not mean that the action is past; it may be completed and present or timeless. Where we would say "Many years ago" and use the past tense, the Trobriander will say, "In my father's childhood" and use non-temporal verbs; he places the event situationally, not temporally. Past, present, and future are presented linguistically as the same, are present in his existence, and sameness with what we call the past and with myth, represents value to the Trobriander. Where we see a developmental line, the Trobriander sees a point, at most swelling in value. Where we find pleasure and satisfaction in moving away from the point, in change as variety or progress, the Trobriander finds it in the repetition of the known, in maintaining the point; that is, in what we call monotony. Esthetic validity, dignity, and value come to him not through arrangement into a climactic line, but rather in the undisturbed incorporation of the events within their original, nonlinear order. The only history which has meaning for him is that which evokes the value of the point, or which, in the repetition, swells the value of the point. For example, every occasion in which a kula object participates becomes an ingredient of its being and swells its value; all these occasions are enumerated with great satisfaction, but the lineal course of the traveling kula object is not important.

As we see our history climactically, so do we plan future experiences climactically, leading up to future satisfaction or meaning. Who but a very young child would think of starting a meal with strawberry shortcake and ending it with spinach? We have come to identify the end of the meal with the height of satisfaction, and we identify semantically the words dessert and reward, only because of the similarity of their positions in a climactic line. The Trobriand meal has no dessert, no line, no climax. The special bit, the relish, is eaten *with* the staple food; it is not something to "look *forward to*," while disposing of a meaningless staple.

None of the Trobriand activities are fitted into a climactic line. There is no job, no labor, no drudgery which finds its reward outside the act. All work contains its own satisfaction. We cannot speak of S——R here, as all action contains its own immanent "stimulus." The present is not a means to future satisfaction, but good in itself, as the future is also good in itself; neither better nor worse, neither climactic nor anticlimactic, in fact, not lineally connected nor removed. It follows that the present is not evaluated in terms of its place within a course of action leading upward to a worthy end. In our culture, we can rarely evaluate the present in itself. I tell you that Sally is selling notions at Woolworth's, but this in itself means nothing. It acquires some meaning when I add that she has recently graduated from Vassar. However, I go on to tell you that she has been assistant editor of *Vogue*, next a nursemaid, a chairwoman, a public school teacher. But this is a mere jumble; it makes no sense and has no meaning, because the series leads to nothing. You cannot relate one job to another, and you are unable to see them discretely simply as part of her being. However, I now add that she is

gathering material for a book on the working mother. Now all this falls in line, it makes sense in terms of a career. Now her job is good and it makes her happy, because it is part of a planned climactic line leading to more pay, increased recognition, higher rank. There was a story in a magazine about the college girl who fell in love with the milkman one summer; the reader felt tense until it was discovered that this was just a summer job, that it was only a means for the continuation of the man's education in the Columbia Law School. Our evaluation of happiness and unhappiness is bound with this motion along an envisioned line leading to a desired end. In the fulfillment of this course or career—not in the fulfillment of the self as point—do we find value. Our conception of freedom rests on the principle of noninterference with this moving line, noninterruption of the intended course of action.

It is difficult to tell whether climax is given in experience at all, or whether it is always imposed on the given. At a time when progress and evolution were assumed to be implicit in nature, our musicians and writers gave us climactic works. Nowadays, our more reflective art does not present experience climactically. Then, is emotion itself climactic? Climax, for us, evokes "thrill" or "drama." But we have cultures, like the Tikopia, where life is lived on an even emotive plane without thrill or climax. Experiences which "we know to be" climactic, are described without climax by them. For example, they, as well as the Trobrianders, described intercourse as an aggregate of pleasurable experiences. But Malinowski is disturbed by this; he cannot place the erotic kiss in Trobriand experience, since it has no climactic function. Again, in our culture, childbearing is climactic. Pregnancy is represented by the usual obstetrician as an uncomfortable means to a dramatic end. For most women, all intensity of natural physical experience is nowadays removed from the actual birth itself; but the approach of birth nevertheless is a period of mounting tension, and drama is supplied by the intensive social recognition of the event, the dramatic accumulation of gifts, flowers, telegrams. A pregnancy is not formally announced since, if it does not eventuate in birth, it has failed to achieve its end; and failure to reach the climax brings shame. In its later stages it may be marked with a shower; but the shower looks forward to the birth, it does not celebrate the pregnancy itself. Among the Trobrianders, pregnancy has meaning in itself, as a state of being. At a first pregnancy, there is a long ceremonial involving "preparatory" work on the part of many people, which merely celebrates the pregnancy. It does not anchor the baby, it does not *have as its purpose* a more comfortable time during the pregnancy, it does not *lead to* an easier birth or a healthy baby. It makes the woman's skin white, and makes her be at her most beautiful; yet this *leads to* nothing, since she must not attract men, not even her own husband.

V

Are we then right in accepting without question the presence of a line in reality? Are we in a position to say with assurance that the Trobrianders are wrong and we are right? Much of our present-day thinking, and much of our evaluation, are based on the premise of the line and of the line as good. Students have been refused admittance to college because the autobiographic sketch accompanying their application showed absence of the line; they lacked purposefulness and ability to plan; they were inadequate as to character as well as intellectually. Our conception of personality formation, our stress on the significance of success and failure and of frustration in general, is based on the axiomatically postulated line. How can there be blocking without presupposed lineal motion or effort? If I walk along a path because I like the country, or if it is not important to get to a particular point at a particular time, then the insuperable puddle from the morning's shower is not frustrating; I throw stones into it and watch the ripples, and then choose another path. If the undertaking is of value in itself, a point good in itself, and not because it leads to something, then failure has no symbolic meaning; it merely results in no cake for supper, or less money in the family budget; it is not personally destructive. But failure is devastating in our culture, because it is not failure of the undertaking alone; it is the moving, becoming, lineally conceived self which has failed.

Ethnographers have occasionally remarked that the people whom they studied showed no annoyance when interrupted. Is this an indication of mild temper, or might it be the case that they were not interrupted at all, as there was no expectation of lineal continuity? Such questions are new in anthropology and most ethnographers therefore never thought of recording material which would answer them. However, we do have enough material to make us question the line as basic to all experience; whether it is actually present in given reality or not, it is not always present in experienced reality. We cannot even take it for granted as existing among those members of our society who are not completely or naively steeped in their culture, such as many of our artists, for example. And we should be very careful, in studying other cultures, to avoid the unexamined assumption that their actions are based on the prediction of a lineal reality.

Note

1. I have taken over this special use of the terms *codification* and *punctuation* from Gregory Bateson.

Bibliography

Lee, D. (1940). A primitive system of values. *Philosophy of Science, 7,* 355.

Lee, D. (1949). Being and value in a primitive culture. *Journal of Philosophy, 46,* 401.

Malinowski, B. (1922). *Argonauts of the western Pacific.* London: Routledge.

Malinowski, B. (1929). *The sexual life of savages.* New York: H. Liveright.

Malinowski, B. (1935). *Coral gardens and their magic.* New York: American.

14

Changes in Default Words and Images Engendered by Rising Consciousness

Douglas R. Hofstadter

A father and his son were driving to a ball game when their car stalled on the railroad tracks. In the distance a train whistle blew a warning. Frantically, the father tried to start the engine, but in his panic, he couldn't turn the key, and the car was hit by the onrushing train. An ambulance sped to the scene and picked them up. On the way to the hospital, the father died. The son was still alive but his condition was very serious, and he needed immediate surgery. The moment they arrived at the hospital, he was wheeled into an emergency operating room, and the surgeon came in, expecting a routine case. However, on seeing the boy, the surgeon blanched and muttered, "I can't operate on this boy—he's my son."

What do you make of this grim riddle? How could it be? Was the surgeon lying or mistaken? No. Did the dead father's soul somehow get reincarnated in the surgeon's body? No. Was the surgeon the boy's true father and the dead man the boy's adopted father? No. What, then, is the explanation? Think it through until you have figured it

out on your own—I insist! You'll know when you've got it, don't worry.

When I was first asked this riddle, a few years ago, I got the answer within a minute or so. Still, I was ashamed of my performance. I was also disturbed by the average performance of the people in the group I was with—all educated, intelligent people, some men, some women. I was neither the quickest nor the slowest. A couple of them, even after five minutes of scratching their heads, still didn't have the answer! And when they finally hit upon it, their heads hung low.

Whether we light upon the answer quickly or slowly, we all have something to learn from this ingenious riddle. It reveals something very deep about how so-called *default assumptions* permeate our mental representations and channel our thoughts. A default assumption is what holds true in what you might say is the "simplest" or "most natural" or "most likely" possible model of whatever situation is under discussion. In this case, the default assumption is to assign the sex of male to the surgeon. The way things are in our society today, that's the most plausible assumption. But the critical thing about default assumptions—so well revealed by this story—is that they are made automatically, not as a result of consideration and elimination. You didn't explicitly ponder the point and ask yourself, "What is the most plausible sex to assign to the surgeon?" Rather, you let your past experience merely assign a sex for you. Default assumptions are by their nature implicit assumptions. You never were aware of having made any assumption about the surgeon's sex, for if you had been, the riddle would have been easy!

Usually, relying on default assumptions is extremely useful. In fact, it is indispensable in enabling us—or any cognitive machine—to get around in this complex world. We simply can't afford to be constantly distracted by all sorts of theoretically possible but unlikely exceptions to the general rules or models that we have built up by induction from many past experiences. We have to make what amount to shrewd guesses—and we do this with great skill all the time. Our every thought is permeated by myriads of such shrewd guesses—assumptions of normalcy. This strategy seems to work pretty well. For example, we tend to assume that the stores lining the main street of a town we pass through are not just cardboard façades, and for good reason. Probably you're not worried about whether the chair you're sitting on is about to break. Probably the last time you used a salt shaker you didn't consider that it might be filled with sugar. Without much trouble, you could name dozens of assumptions you're making at this very moment—all of which are simply *probably* true, rather than *definitely* true.

This ability to ignore what is very unlikely—*without even considering whether or not to ignore it!*—is part of our evolutionary heritage, coming out of the need to be able to size up a situation quickly but accurately. It is a marvelous and subtle quality of our thought processes; however, once in a while, this marvelous ability leads us astray. And sexist default assumptions are a case in point. . . .

I have continued to ponder these issues with great intensity. And I must say, the more I ponder, the more prickly and confusing the whole matter becomes. I have found

appalling unawareness of the problem all around me—in friends, colleagues, students, on radio and television, in magazines, books, films, and so on. The *New York Times* is one of the worst offenders. You can pick it up any day and see prominent women referred to as "chairman" or "congressman." Even more flagrantly obnoxious is when they refer to prominent feminists by titles that feminism repudiates. For example, a long article on Judy Goldsmith (head of NOW, the National Organization for Women) repeatedly referred to her as "Mrs. Goldsmith." The editors' excuse is:

> Publications vary in tone, and the titles they affix to names will differ accordingly. The *Times* clings to traditional ones (*Mrs., Miss,* and *Dr.,* for example). As for *Ms.*—that useful business-letter coinage—we reconsider it from time to time; to our ear, it still sounds too contrived for news writing.

As long as they stick with the old terms, they will sound increasingly reactionary and increasingly silly.

Perhaps what bothers me the most is when I hear newscasters on the radio—especially public radio—using blatantly sexist terms when it would be so easy to avoid them. Female announcers are almost uniformly as sexist as male announcers. A typical example is the female newscaster on National Public Radio who spoke of "the employer who pays his employees on a weekly basis" and "the employee who is concerned about his tax return," when both employer and employee were completely hypothetical personages, thus without either gender. Or the male newscaster who described the Pope in Warsaw as "surrounded by throngs of his countrymen." Or the female newscaster who said, "Imagine I'm a worker and I'm on my deathbed and I have no money to support my wife and kids. . . . " Of all people, newscasters should know better.

I attended a lecture in which a famous psychologist uttered the following sentence, *verbatim:* "What the plain man would like, as he comes into an undergraduate psychology course, as a man or a woman, is that he would find out something about emotions." Time and again, I have observed people lecturing in public who, like this psychologist, seem to feel a mild discomfort with generic "he" and generic "man," and who therefore try to compensate, every once in a while, for their constant usage of such terms. After, say, five uses of "he" in describing a hypothetical scientist, they will throw in a meek "he or she" (and perhaps give an embarrassed little chuckle); then, having pacified their guilty conscience, they will go back to "he" and other sexist usages for a while, until the guilt-juices have built up enough again to trigger one more token nonsexist usage.

This is not progress, in my opinion. In fact, in some ways, it is retrograde motion, and damages the cause of nonsexist language. The problem is that these people are simultaneously showing that they recognize that "he" is *not* truly generic and yet continuing to use it as if it were. They are thereby, at one and the same time, increasing other people's recognition of the sham of considering "he" as a generic, and yet reinforcing the old convention of using it anyway. It's a bad bind.

In case anybody needs to be convinced that supposed generics such as "he" and "man" are *not* neutral in people's minds, they should reflect on the following findings. I quote from the chapter called "Who Is Man?" in *Words and Women*, an earlier book by Casey Miller and Kate Swift:

In 1972 two sociologists at Drake University, Joseph Schneider and Sally Hacker, decided to test the hypothesis that *man* is generally understood to embrace *woman*. Some three hundred college students were asked to select from magazines and newspapers a variety of pictures that would appropriately illustrate the different chapters of a sociology textbook being prepared for publication. Half the students were assigned chapter headings like "Social Man," "Industrial Man," and "Political Man."

The other half were given different but corresponding headings like "Society," "Industrial Life," and "Political Behavior." Analysis of the pictures selected revealed that in the minds of students of both sexes use of the word *man* evoked, to a statistically significant degree, images of males only—filtering out recognition of women's participation in these major areas of life—whereas the corresponding headings without *man* evoked images of both males and females. In some instances the differences reached magnitudes of 30 to 40 per cent. The authors concluded, "This is rather convincing evidence that when you use the word *man* generically, people do tend to think male, and tend not to think female."

Subsequent experiments along the same lines but involving schoolchildren rather than college students are then described by Miller and Swift. The results are much the same. No matter how generic "man" is claimed to be, there is a residual trace, a subliminal connotation of higher probability of being male than female.

Shortly after this column came out, I hit upon a way of describing one of the problems of sexist language. I call it the *slippery slope of sexism*. The idea is very simple. When a generic term and a "marked" term (i.e., a sex-specific term) coincide, there is a possibility of mental blurring on the part of listeners and even on the part of the speaker. Some of the connotations of the generic will automatically rub off even when the specific is meant, and conversely. The example of "Industrial Man" illustrates one half of this statement, where a trace of male imagery rubs off even when no gender is intended. The reverse is an equally common phenomenon; an example would be when a newscaster speaks of "the four-man crew of next month's space shuttle flight." It may be that all four are actually males, in which case the usage would be precise. Or it may be that there is a woman among them, in which case "man" would be functioning generically (supposedly). But if you're just listening to the news, and you *don't know* whether a woman is among the four, what are you supposed to do?

Some listeners will automatically envision four males, but others, remembering the existence of female astronauts, will leave room in their minds for at least one woman potentially in the crew. Now, the newscaster may know full well that this flight consists of males only. In fact, she may have chosen the phrase "four-man crew" quite deliberately, in order to let you know that no woman is included. For her, "man" may be marked. On the other, she may not have given it a second thought: for her, "man" may be unmarked. But how are you to know? The problem is right there: the slippery slope. Connotations slip back and forth very shiftily, and totally beneath our usual level of awareness—especially (though not exclusively) at the interface between two people whose usages differ.

Let me be a little more precise about the slippery slope. I have chosen a number of salient examples and put them in Figure 14.1. Each slippery slope involves a little triangle, at the apex of which is a supposed generic, and the bottom two corners of which consist of oppositely marked terms. Along one side of each triangle runs a diagonal line—the dreaded slippery slope itself. Along that line, connotations slosh back and forth freely in the minds of listeners and speakers and readers and writers. And it all happens at a completely unconscious level, in exactly the same way as a poet's choice of a word subliminally evokes dozens of subtle flavors without anyone's quite understanding how it happens. This wonderful fluid magic of poetry is not quite so wonderful when it imbues one word with all sorts of properties that it should not have.

The essence of the typical slippery slope is this: it establishes a firm "handshake" between the generic and the masculine, in such a way that the feminine term is left out in the cold. The masculine inherits the abstract power of the generic, and the generic inherits the power that comes with specific imagery. Here is an example of the *generic-benefits-from-specific* effect: "Man forging his destiny." Who can resist thinking of some kind of huge mythical brute of a guy hacking his way forward in a jungle or otherwise making progress? Does the image of a woman even come *close* to getting evoked? I seriously doubt it. And now for the converse, consider these gems: "Kennedy was a man for all seasons." "Feynman is the world's smartest man." "Only a man with powerful esthetic intuition could have created the general theory of relativity." "Few men have done more for science than Stephen Hawking." "Leopold and Loeb wanted to test the idea that a perfect crime might be committed by men of sufficient intelligence." Why "man" and "men," here? The answer is: to take advantage of the *specific-benefits-from-generic* effect. The power of the word "man" emanates largely from its close connection with the mythical "ideal man": Man the Thinker, Man the Mover, Man whose Best Friend is Dog.

Another way of looking at the slippery-slope effect is to focus on the single isolated corner of the triangle. At first it might seem as if it makes women somehow more distinguished. How nice! But in fact what it does is mark them as *odd*. They are considered nonstandard; the standard case is presumed not to be a woman. In other words, women have to fight their way back into imagery as just-plain *people*. Here are some examples to make the point.

When I learned French in school, the idea that masculine pronouns covered groups of mixed sex seemed perfectly natural, logical, and unremarkable to me. Much later, that usage came to seem very biased and bizarre to me. However, very recently, I was a bit surprised to catch myself falling into the same trap in different guise. I was perusing a multilingual dictionary, and noticed that instead of the usual *m.* and *f.* to indicate noun genders, they had opted for "+" and "−." Which way, do you suspect? Right! And it seemed just right to me, too—until I realized how dumb I was being.

Heard on the radio news: "A woman motorist is being held after officials observed

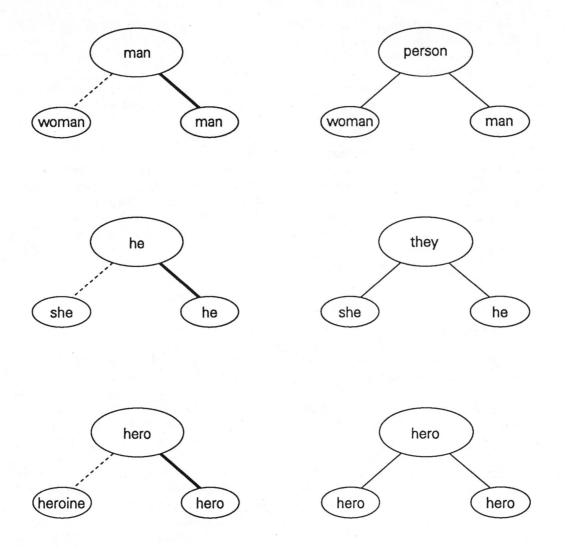

Figure 14.1. The "slippery slope of sexism," illustrated. In each case in (a), a supposed generic (i.e., gender-neutral term) is shown above its two marked particularizations (i.e., gender-specific terms). However, the masculine and generic coincide, which fact is symbolized by the thick heavy line joining them—the slippery slope, along which connotations slash back and forth, unimpeded. The "most-favored sex" status is thereby accorded the masculine term. In (b), the slippery slopes are replaced by true gender fairness, in which generics are unambiguously generic and marked terms unambiguously marked. Still, it is surprising how often it is totally irrelevant which sex is involved. Do we need—or want—to be able to say such things as, "Her actions were heroinic"? Who cares if a hero is male or female, as long as what they did is heroic? The same can be said about actors, sculptors, and a hostess of other terms. The best fix for that kind of slippery slope is simply to drop the marked term, making all three coincide in a felicitously ambisexual ménage à trois.

---

her to be driving erratically near the White House." Why say "*woman* motorist"? Would you say "man motorist" if it had been a male? Why is gender, and gender alone, such a crucial variable?

Think of the street sign that shows a man in silhouette walking across the street, intended to tell you "Pedestrian Crossing" in sign language. What if it were recognizably a *woman* walking across the street? Since it violates the standard default assumption that people have for people, it would immediately arouse a kind of suspicion: "Hmmm . . . 'Women Crossing'? Is there a nunnery around here?" This would be the reaction not merely of dyed-in-the-wool sexists, but of anyone who grew up in our society, where women are portrayed—not deliberately or consciously, but ubiquitously and subliminally—as "exceptions."

If I write, "In the nineteenth century, the kings of nonsense were Edward Lear and Lewis Carroll," people will with no trouble get the message that those two men were the best of all nonsense writers at that time. But now consider what happens if I write, "The queen of twentieth-century nonsense is Gertrude Stein." The implication is unequivocal: Gertrude Stein is, among *female* writers of nonsense, the best. It leaves completely open her ranking relative to males. She might be way down the list! Now isn't this preposterous? Why is our language so asymmetric? This is hardly chivalry—it is utter condescension.

A remarkable and insidious slippery-slope phenomenon is what has happened recently to formerly all-women's colleges that were paired with formerly all-men's colleges, such as Pembroke and Brown, Radcliffe and Harvard, and so on. As the two merged, the women's school gradually faded out of the picture. Do men now go to Radcliffe or Pembroke or Douglass? Good God, no! But women are proud to go to Harvard and Brown and Rutgers. Sometimes, the women's college keeps some status within the larger unit, but that larger unit is always named after the men's college. In a weird twist on this theme, Stanford University has no sororities at all—but guess what kinds of people it now allows in its fraternities!

Another pernicious slippery slope has arisen quite recently. That is the one involving "gay" as both masculine and generic, and "Lesbian" as feminine. What is problematic here is that some people are very conscious of the problem, and refuse to use "gay" as a generic, replacing it with "gay or Lesbian" or "homosexual." (Thus there are many "Gay and Lesbian Associations.") Other people, however, have eagerly latched onto "gay" as a generic and use it freely that way, referring to "gay people," "gay men," "gay women," "gay rights," and so on. As a consequence, the word "gay" has a much broader flavor to it than does "Lesbian." What does "the San Francisco gay community" conjure up? Now replace "gay" by "Lesbian" and try it again. The former image probably is capable of fitting between that of both sexes and that of men only, while the latter is certainly restricted to women. The point is simply that men are made to seem standard, ordinary, somehow proper; women as special, deviant, exceptional. That is the essence of the slippery slope.

Part of the problem in sexism is how deeply ingrained it is. I have noticed a disturbing fact about my observation of language and related phenomena: whenever I encounter a particularly blatant example, I write it down joyfully, and say to friends, "I just heard a *great* example of sexism!" Now, why is it *good* to find a glaring example of something *bad*? Actually, the answer is very simple. You need outrageously clear examples if you want to convince many people that there is a problem worth taking at all seriously.

I was very fortunate to meet the philosopher and feminist Joan Straumanis shortly after my column on sexism appeared. We had a lot to talk over, and particularly enjoyed swapping stories of the sort that make you groan and say, "Isn't that *great*?"—

meaning, of course, "How sickening!" Here's one that happened to her. Her husband was in her university office one day, and wanted to make a long-distance phone call. He dialed "0," and a female operator answered. She asked if he was a faculty member. He said no, and she said, "Only faculty members can make calls on these phones." He replied, "My wife is a faculty member. She's in the next room—I'll get her." The operator snapped back, "Oh no—*wives* can't use these phones!"

Another true story that I got from Joan Straumanis, perhaps more provocative and fascinating, is this one. A group of parents arranged a tour of a hospital for a group of twenty children: ten boys and ten girls. At the end of the tour, hospital officials presented each child with a cap: doctors' caps for the boys, nurses' caps for the girls. The parents, outraged at this sexism, went to see the hospital administration. They were promised that in the future, this would be corrected. The next year, a similar tour was arranged, and at the end, the parents came by to pick up their children. What did they find, but the exact same thing—all the boys had on doctors' hats, all the girls had on nurses' hats! Steaming, they stormed up to the director's office and demanded an explanation. The director gently told them, "But it *was* totally different this year: we offered them all *whichever hat they wanted.*"

David Moser, ever an alert observer of the language around him, had tuned into a radio talk show one night, and heard an elderly woman voicing outrage at the mild sentence of two men who had murdered a three-year-old girl. The woman said, "Those two men should get the gas chamber for sure. I think it's terrible what they did! Who knows what that little girl could have grown up to become? Why, she could have been the mother of the next great composer!" The idea that that little girl might have grown up to *be* the next great composer undoubtedly never entered the woman's mind. Still, her remark was not consciously sexist and I find it strangely touching, reminiscent of a quieter era where gender roles were obvious and largely unquestioned, an era when many people felt safe and secure in their socially defined niches. But those times are gone, and we must now move ahead with consciousness raised high.

In one conversation I was in, a man connected with a publisher—let's call it "Freeperson"—said to me, "Aldrich was the liaison between the Freeperson boys and we—er, I mean *us.*" What amused me so much was his instant detection and correction of a *syntactic* error, yet no awareness of his more serious *semantic* error. Isn't that *great*?

I was provoked to write the following piece about a year after the column on sexism came out. It came about this way. One evening I had a very lively conversation at dinner with a group of people who thought of the problem of sexist language as no more than that: dinner-table conversation. Despite all the arguments I put forth, I just couldn't convince them there was anything worth taking seriously there. The next morning I woke up and heard two most interesting pieces of news on the radio: a black Miss America had been picked, and a black man was going to run for president. Both of these violated default assumptions, and it set my mind going along two parallel tracks at once: What if people's default assumptions were violated in all sorts of ways both sexually and racially? And then I started letting the default violations cross all sorts of lines, and pretty soon I was coming up with an image of a totally different society, one in which . . . Well, I'll just let you read it.

A Person Paper on Purity in Language

William Satire (alias Douglas R. Hofstadter)

It's high time someone blew the whistle on all the silly prattle about revamping our language to suit the purposes of certain political fanatics. You know what I'm talking about—those who accuse speakers of English of what they call "racism." This awkward neologism, constructed by analogy with the well-established term "sexism," does not sit well in the ears, if I may mix my metaphors. But let us grant that in our society there may be injustices here and there in the treatment of either race from time to time, and let us even grant these people their terms "racism" and "racist." How valid, however, are the claims of the self-proclaimed "black libbers," or "negrists"—those who would radically change our language in order to "liberate" us poor dupes from its supposed racist bias?

Most of the clamor, as you certainly know by now, revolves around the age-old usage of the noun "white" and words built from it, such as *chairwhite, mailwhite, repairwhite, clergywhite, middlewhite, Frenchwhite, forewhite, whitepower, whiteslaughter, oneupwhiteship, straw white, whitehandle,* and so on. The negrists claim that using the word "white," either on its own or as a component, to talk about *all* the members of the human species is somehow degrading to blacks and reinforces racism. Therefore the libbers propose that we substitute "person" everywhere where "white" now occurs. Sensitive speakers of our secretary tongue of course find this preposterous. There is

great beauty to a phrase such as "All whites are created equal." Our forebosses who framed the Declaration of Independence well understood the poetry of our language. Think how ugly it would be to say "All persons are created equal," or "All whites and blacks are created equal." Besides, as any schoolwhitey can tell you, such phrases are redundant. In most contexts, it is self-evident when "white" is being used in an inclusive sense, in which case it subsumes members of the darker race just as much as fairskins.

There is nothing denigrating to black people in being subsumed under the rubric "white"—no more than under the rubric "person." After all, white is a mixture of all the colors of the rainbow, including black. Used inclusively, the word "white" has no connotations whatsoever of race. Yet many people are hung up on this point. A prime example is Abraham Moses, one of the more vocal spokeswhites for making such a shift. For years, Niss Moses, authoroon of the well-known negrist tracts *A Handbook of Nonracist Writing* and *Words and Blacks*, has had nothing better to do than go around the country making speeches advocating the downfall of "racist language" that ble objects to. But when you analyze bler objections, you find they all fall apart at the seams. Niss Moses says that words like "chairwhite" suggest to people—most especially impressionable young whiteys and blackeys—that all chairwhites belong to the white race. How absurd! It is quite obvious, for instance, that the chairwhite of the League of Black Voters is going to be a black, not a white. Nobody need think twice about it. As a matter of fact, the suffix "white" is usually not pronounced with a long "i" as in the noun "white," but like "wit," as in the terms *saleswhite, freshwhite, penwhiteship, first basewhite,* and so on. It's just a simple and useful component in building race-neutral words.

But Niss Moses would have you sit up and start hollering "Racism!" In fact, Niss Moses sees evidence of racism under every stone. Ble has written a famous article, in which ble vehemently objects to the immortal and poetic words of the first white on the moon, Captain Nellie Strongarm. If you will recall, whis words were: "One small step for a white, a giant step for whitekind." This noble sentiment is anything but racist; it is simply a celebration of a glorious moment in the history of White.

Another of Niss Moses' shrill objections is to the age-old differentiation of whites from blacks by the third-person pronouns "whe" and "ble." Ble promotes an absurd notion: that what we really need in English is a single pronoun covering *both* races. Numerous suggestions have been made, such as "pe," "tey," and others. These are all repugnant to the nature of the English language, as the average white in the street will testify, even if whe has no linguistic training whatsoever. Then there are advocates of usages such as "whe or ble," "whis or bler," and so forth. This makes for monstrosities such as the sentence "When the next President takes office, whe or ble will have to choose whis or bler cabinet with great care, for whe or ble would not want to offend any minorities." Contrast this with the spare elegance of the normal way of putting it, and there is no question which way we ought to speak. There are, of course, some yapping black libbers who advocate writing "bl/whe" everywhere, which, aside from looking terrible, has no reasonable pronunciation. Shall we say "blooey" all the time when we simply mean "whe"? Who

wants to sound like a white with a chronic sneeze?

One of the more hilarious suggestions made by the squawkers for this point of view is to abandon the natural distinction along racial lines, and to replace it with a highly unnatural one along sexual lines. One such suggestion—emanating, no doubt, from the mind of a madwhite—would have us say "he" for male whites (and blacks) and "she" for female whites (and blacks). Can you imagine the outrage with which sensible folk of either sex would greet this "modest proposal"?

Another suggestion is that the plural pronoun "they" be used in place of the inclusive "whe." This would turn the charming proverb "Whe who laughs last, laughs best" into the bizarre concoction "They who laughs last, laughs best." As if anyone in whis right mind could have thought that the original proverb applied only to the white race! No, we don't need a new pronoun to "liberate" our minds. That's the lazy white's way of solving the pseudo-problem of racism. In any case, it's ungrammatical. The pronoun "they" is a plural pronoun, and it grates on the civilized ear to hear it used to denote only one person. Such a usage, if adopted, would merely promote illiteracy and accelerate the already scandalously rapid nosedive of the average intelligence level in our society.

Niss Moses would have us totally revamp the English language to suit bler purposes. If, for instance, we are to substitute "person" for "white," where are we to stop? If we were to follow Niss Moses' ideas to their logical conclusion, we would have to conclude that ble would like to see small blackeys and whiteys playing the game of "Hangperson" and reading the story of "Snow Person and the Seven Dwarfs." And would ble have us rewrite history to say, "Don't shoot until you see the *persons* of their eyes!"? Will pundits and politicians henceforth issue *person* papers? Will we now have egg yolks and egg *persons*? And pledge allegiance to the good old Red, *Person,* and Blue? Will we sing, "I'm dreaming of a *person* Christmas"? Say of a frightened white, "Whe's *person* as a sheet!"? Lament the increase of *person*-collar crime? Thrill to the chirping of bob*persons* in our gardens? Ask a friend to *person* the table while we go visit the *persons'* room? Come off it, Niss Moses—don't personwash our language!

What conceivable harm is there in such beloved phrases as "No white is an island," "Dog is white's best friend," or "White's inhumanity to white"? Who would revise such classic book titles as Bronob Jacowski's *The Ascent of White* or Eric Steeple Bell's *Whites of Mathematics*? Did the poet who wrote "The best-laid plans of mice and whites gang aft agley" believe that blacks' plans gang *ne'er* agley? Surely not! Such phrases are simply metaphors: everyone can see beyond that. Whe who interprets them as reinforcing racism must have a perverse desire to feel oppressed.

"Personhandling" the language is a habit that not only Niss Moses but quite a few others have taken up recently. For instance, Nrs. Delilah Buford has urged that we drop the useful distinction between "Niss" and "Nrs." (which, as everybody knows, is pronounced "Nissiz," the reason for which nobody knows!). Bler argument is that there is no need for the public to know whether a black is employed or not. *Need* is, of course, not the point. Ble conveniently sidesteps the fact that there is a *tradition* in our society of calling unemployed blacks "Niss" and employed blacks "Nrs." Most blacks—in fact, the vast majority—prefer it that way. They *want* the world to know what their employment status is, and for good reason. Unemployed blacks want prospective employers to know they are available, without having to ask embarrassing questions. Likewise, employed blacks are proud of having found a job, and wish to let the world know they are employed. This distinction provides a sense of security to all involved, in that everyone knows where ble fits into the scheme of things.

But Nrs. Buford refuses to recognize this simple truth. Instead, ble shiftily turns the argument into one about whites, asking why it is that whites are universally addressed as "Master," without any differentiation between employed and unemployed ones. The answer, of course, is that in America and other Northern societies, we set little store by the employment status of whites. Nrs. Buford can do little to change that reality, for it seems to be tied to innate biological differences between whites and blacks. Many white-years of research, in fact, have gone into trying to understand why it is that employment status matters so much to blacks, yet relatively little to whites. It is true that both races have a longer life expectancy if employed, but of course people often do not act so as to maximize their life expectancy. So far, it remains a mystery. In any case, whites and blacks clearly have different constitutional inclinations, and different goals in life. And so I say, *Vive na différence!*

As for Nrs. Buford's suggestion that both "Niss" and "Nrs." be unified into the single form of address "Ns." (supposed to rhyme with "fizz"), all I have to say is, it is arbitrary and clearly a thousand years ahead of its time. Mind you, this "Ns." is an abbreviation concocted out of thin air: it stands for absolutely nothing. Who ever heard of such toying with language? And while we're on this subject, have you yet run across the recently founded *Ns.* magazine, dedicated to the concerns of the "liberated black"? It's sure to attract the attention of a trendy band of black airheads for a little while, but serious blacks surely will see through its thin veneer of slick, glossy Madison Avenue approaches to life.

Nrs. Buford also finds it insultingly asymmetric that when a black is employed by a white, ble changes bler firmly name to whis firmly name. But what's so bad about that? Every firm's core consists of a boss (whis job is to make sure long-term policies are well charted out) and a secretary (bler job is to keep corporate affairs running smoothly on a day-to-day basis). They are both equally important and vital to the firm's success. No one disputes this. Beyond them there may of course be other firmly members. Now it's quite obvious that all members of a given firm should bear the same firmly name—otherwise, what are you going to call the firm's products? And since it would be nonsense for the boss to change whis name, it falls to the secretary to change bler name. Logic, not racism, dictates this simple convention.

What puzzles me the most is when people cut off their nose to spite their faces. Such is the case with the time-honored colored suffixes "oon" and "roon," found in familiar words such as *ambassadroon, stewardoon,* and *sculptroon.* Most blacks find it natural and sensible to add those suffixes onto nouns such as "aviator" or "waiter." A black who flies an airplane may proudly proclaim, "I'm an aviatroon!" But it would sound silly, if not ridiculous, for a black to say of blerself, "I work as a waiter." On the other hand, who could object to my saying that the lively Ticely Cyson is a great actroon, or that the hilarious Quill Bosby is a great comedioon? You guessed it—authoroons such as Niss Mildred Hempsley and Nrs. Charles White, both of whom angrily reject the appellation "authoroon," deep though its roots are in our language. Nrs. White, perhaps one of the finest poetoons of our day, for some reason insists on being known as a "poet." It leads on to wonder, is Nrs. White *ashamed* of being black, perhaps? I should hope not. White needs Black, and Black needs White, and neither race should feel ashamed.

Some extreme negrists object to being treated with politeness and courtesy by whites. For example, they reject the traditional notion of "Negroes first," preferring to open doors for themselves, claiming that having doors opened for them suggest implicitly that society considers them inferior. Well, would they have it the other way? Would these incorrigible grousers prefer to open doors for whites? What do blacks want?

Another unlikely word has recently become a subject of controversy: "blackey." This is, of course, the ordinary term for black children (including teen-agers), and by affectionate extension it is often applied to older blacks. Yet, incredible though it seems, many blacks—even teen-age blackeys—now claim to have had their "consciousness raised," and are voguishly skittish about being called "blackeys." Yet it's as old as the hills for blacks employed in the same office to refer to themselves as "the office blackeys." And for their superior to call them "my blackeys" helps make the ambiance more relaxed and comfy for all. It's hardly the mortal insult that libbers claim it to be. Fortunately, most blacks are sensible people and realize that mere words do not demean; they know it's how they are *used* that counts. Most of the time, calling a black—especially an older black—a "blackey" is a thoughtful way of complimenting bler, making bler feel young, fresh, and hirable again. Lord knows, I certainly wouldn't object if someone told me that I looked whiteyish these days!

Many young blackeys go through a stage of wishing they had been born white. Perhaps this is due to popular television shows like *Superwhite* and *Batwhite,* but it doesn't really matter. It is perfectly normal and healthy. Many of our most successful blacks were once tomwhiteys and feel no shame about it. Why should they? Frankly, I think tomwhiteys are often the cutest little blackeys—but that's just my opinion. In any case, Niss Moses (once again) raises a ruckus on this score, asking why we don't have a corresponding word for young whiteys who play blackeys' games and generally manifest a desire to be black. Well, Niss Moses, if this were a common phenomenon, we most assuredly *would* have such a word, but it just happens not to be. Who can say why? But given that tomwhiteys are a dime a dozen, it's nice to have a word for them. The lesson is that White must learn to fit language to reality; White cannot manipulate the world by manipulating mere words. An elementary lesson, to be sure, but for some reason Niss Moses and others of bler ilk resist learning it.

Shifting from the ridiculous to the sublime, let us consider the Holy Bible. The Good Book is of course the source of some of the most beautiful language and profound imagery to be found anywhere. And who is the central character of the Bible? I am sure I need hardly remind you; it is God. As everyone knows, Whe is male and white, and that is an indisputable fact. But have you heard the latest joke promulgated by tasteless negrists? It is said that one of them died and went to Heaven and then returned. What did ble report? "I have seen God, and guess what? Ble's female!" Can anyone say that this is not blasphemy of the highest order? It just goes to show that some people will stoop to any depths in order to shock. I have shared this "joke" with a number of friends of mine (including several blacks, by the way), and, to a white, they have agreed that it sickens them to the core to see Our Lord so shabbily mocked. Some things are just in bad taste, and there are no two ways about it. It is scum like this who are responsible for some of the great problems in our society today, I am sorry to say.

Well, all of this is just another skirmish in the age-old Battle of the Races, I guess, and we shouldn't take it too seriously. I am reminded of words spoken by the great British philosopher Alfred West Malehead in whis commencement address to my *alma secretaria*, the University of North Virginia: "To enrich the language of whites is, certainly, to enlarge the range of their ideas." I agree with this admirable sentiment wholeheartedly. I would merely point out to the overzealous that there are some extravagant notions about language that should be recognized for what they are: cheap attempts to let dogmatic, narrow minds enforce their views on the speakers lucky enough to have

inherited the richest, most beautiful and flexible language on earth, a language whose traditions run back through the centuries to such deathless poets as Milton, Shakespeare, Wordsworth, Keats, Walt Whitwhite, and so many others . . . Our language owes an incalculable debt to these whites for their clarity of vision and expression, and if the shallow minds of bandwagon-jumping negrists succeed in destroying this precious heritage for all whites of good will, that will be, without any doubt, a truly female day in the history of Northern White.

Post Scriptum

Perhaps this piece shocks you. It is meant to. The entire point of it is to use something that we find shocking as leverage to illustrate the fact that something that we usually close our eyes to is also very shocking. The most effective way I know to do so is to develop an extended analogy with something known as shocking and reprehensible. Racism is that thing, in this case. I am happy with this piece, despite—but also because of—its shock value. I think it makes its point better than any factual article could. As a friend of mine said, "It makes you so uncomfortable that you can't ignore it." I admit that rereading it makes even me, the author, uncomfortable!

Numerous friends have warned me that in publishing this piece I am taking a serious risk of earning myself a reputation as a terrible racist. I guess I cannot truly believe that anyone would see this piece that way. To misperceive it this way would be like calling someone a vicious racist for telling other people "The word 'nigger' is extremely offensive." If *allusions* to racism, especially for the purpose of satirizing racism and its cousins, are confused with racism itself, then I think it is time to stop writing.

Some people have asked me if to write this piece, I simply took a genuine William Safire column (appearing weekly in the *New*

York Times Magazine under the title "On Language") and "fiddled" with it. That is far from the truth. For years I have collected examples of sexist language, and in order to produce this piece, I dipped into this collection, selected some of the choicest, and ordered them very carefully. "Translating" them into this alternate world was sometimes extremely difficult, and some words took weeks. The hardest terms of all, surprisingly enough, were "Niss," "Nrs.," and "Ns.," even though "Master" came immediately. The piece itself is not based on any particular article by William Safire, but Safire has without doubt been one of the most vocal opponents of nonsexist language reforms, and therefore merits being safired upon.

Interestingly, Master Safire has recently spoken out on sexism in whis column (August 5, 1984). Lamenting the inaccuracy of writing either "Mrs. Ferraro" or "Miss Ferraro" to designate the Democratic vice-presidential candidate whose husband's name is "Zaccaro," whe writes:

> It breaks my heart to suggest this, but the time has come for *Ms.* We are no longer faced with a theory, but a condition. It is unacceptable for journalists to dictate to a candidate that she call herself *Miss* or else use her married name; it is equally unacceptable for a candidate to demand that newspapers print a blatant inaccuracy by applying a married honorific to a maiden name.

How disappointing it is when someone finally winds up doing the right thing but for the wrong reasons! In Safire's case, this shift was entirely for journalistic rather than humanistic reasons! It's as if Safire wished that women had never entered the political ring, so that the Grand Old Conventions of English—good enough for our grandfathers—would never have had to be challenged. How heartless of women! How heartbreaking the toll on our beautiful language!

A couple of weeks after I finished this piece, I ran into the book *The Nonsexist Communicator,* by Bobbye Sorrels. In it, there is a satire called "A Tale of Two Sexes," which is very interesting to compare with my "Person Paper." Whereas in mine, I slice the world orthogonally to the way it is actually sliced and then perform a mapping of worlds to establish a disorienting yet powerful new vision of our world, in hers, Mrs. Sorrels simply reverses the two halves of our world as it is actually sliced. Her satire is therefore in some ways very much like mine, and in other ways extremely different. It should be read.

I do not know too many publications that discuss sexist language in depth. The finest I have come across are the aforementioned *Handbook of Nonsexist Writing,* by Casey Miller and Kate Swift; *Words and Women,* by the same authors; *Sexist Language: A Modern Philosophical Analysis,* edited by Mary Vetterling-Braggin; *The Nonsexist Communicator,* by Bobbye Sorrels; and a very good journal titled *Women and Language News.* Subscriptions are available at Centenary College of Louisiana, 2911 Centenary Boulevard, Shreveport, Louisiana 71104.

My feeling about nonsexist English is that it is like a foreign language that I am learning. I find that even after years of practice, I still have to translate sometimes from my native language, which is sexist English. I know of no human being who speaks Nonsexist as their native tongue. It will be very interesting to see if such people come to exist. If so, it will have taken a lot of work by a lot of people to reach that point.

One final footnote: My book *Gödel, Escher, Bach,* whose dialogues were the source of my very first trepidations about my own sexism, is now being translated into various languages, and to my delight, the Tortoise, a green-blooded male if ever there was one in English, is becoming *Madame Tortue* in French, *Signorina Tartaruga* in Italian, and so on. Full circle ahead!

The Dynamics of Interaction: Identity, Situation, Self

All the world's a stage.
And all the men and women merely players:
They have their exits and their entrances;
And one man in his time plays many parts.
(William Shakespeare, As You Like It)

The Elements and Outcomes
of Interaction

Life as Theater

The metaphor of the stage underlies much of the work in Part III.
Like any metaphor, it is not a complete description of social
reality, but there do seem to be many ways in which our
interaction with others resembles a theatrical performance. The
metaphor of the theater is seen even in the origins of the word
"person," which comes from the Latin *persona*, meaning a face
mask worn by actors. We behave differently (play different roles)
in front of different people (audiences). We pick out clothing (a
costume) that is consistent with the image we wish to project. We
enlist the help of friends, caterers, decorators (fellow actors and
stage crew) in helping us successfully "stage" a dinner for a
friend, a birthday party for a relative, or a rush party for a
sorority or fraternity. And if we need to adjust our clothing or
wish to say something unflattering about one of our guests, we
are careful to do so out of sight from others (back stage).

The presentation of ourselves to others is known as
dramaturgy, and the use of the theatrical metaphor for analyzing
human interaction is known as the dramaturgical perspective.
The most noted writer on this perspective was Erving Goffman,
who in 1959 published *The Presentation of Self in Everyday Life*.
This is still considered to be the classic treatment of the subject.
In this book Goffman lucidly analyzed our everyday performances. He details the care people take in preparing and
presenting their performances, that is, the manner in which
people manage the impressions others form of them.

But why do people go through all this? Why do we spend so
much time and energy thinking about what we should say and how
we should look? Is it necessary? The response of some people is
that we should simply "be ourselves" and that only those who are
deceitful need to worry about managing their image. Con artists
and the insincere surely have to be concerned about these issues,
but what about good, decent people such as us?

However, even if one is a saint, one must be concerned with
the presentation of self. To tell people to simply "be" themselves
implies that who we are is easily, quickly, and accurately

perceived by those we interact with. But this is a fiction. If we have just met someone or will be interacting with someone for only a short length of time (e.g., a job interview) we certainly can't count on the person being able to instantly size us up and determine if we might be a good friend or employee. This can be an issue even for people who have known us for some time because who we are may not be obvious to others; we do not wear our personal traits and convictions tattooed onto our foreheads.

Minds are private, which is to say that our thoughts, desires, beliefs, and character cannot be directly perceived and evaluated. We are not a race of mind readers, and so we must depend on signs and symbols as substitutes for an underlying reality. Recall the example of the border guard from Part II. The guard sizes you up and treats you according to your appearance. Therefore, it is in your interest to appear in a way that gets you treated as you wish.

The point that minds are private is one of those simple but profound facts around which our whole world pivots. Certainly the fact that minds are private means we are under no obligation to accurately display our thoughts, desires, and so forth (and so the door is opened to deceit and deception), but it also means that even the most honest people must be concerned about how they come across. Goffman (1959) makes this point in *The Presentation of Self in Everyday Life:*

> Whether an honest performer wishes to convey the truth or whether a dishonest performer wishes to convey a falsehood, both must take care to enliven their performances with appropriate expressions, exclude from their performances expressions that might discredit the impression being fostered, and take care lest the audience impute unintended meanings. (p. 66)

It is crucial to remember that impression management is something we all do in our everyday activities. A number of authors (e.g., see the readings by Emerson and Goffman in the sections that follow) often use examples from unusual interactions (such as the tactics of con artists) as a way of highlighting these processes. But to one degree or another impression management occurs in most interactions.

Because minds are private, we typically behave in a way that will highlight facts that might otherwise go unnoticed. Goffman calls this activity *dramatic realization*. Examples include describing a position of responsibility one held in the past during a job interview, pointing out the absence of any past traffic violations to a judge, or mentioning that you are on a varsity sports team to someone you wish to impress. Dramatic realization is an attempt to make traits and characteristics that otherwise go unnoticed "real" and noticeable. If these traits are not noticed, they don't exist as "real" aspects of the performance. It is up to us to bring them into play.

Goffman also makes the point that we often try to present ourselves in a favorable light, a process he calls *idealization.* This can mean simply accenting those aspects about ourselves that are positive (e.g., mentioning that one is on the varsity team but not mentioning that one has just lost one's job), or outright deception (saying one is on the varsity team when one is not). There is also a general tendency to convey the impression that the role we are currently engaged in is our most important role. When we walk into a store to buy an expensive suit or dress, we will deal with a salesperson who may also be a spouse, parent, community volunteer, jogger, gardener, and so forth. But if that salesperson is good at her or his job, the salesperson will interact with us as if serving customers is the only (or at least the most important) role in her or his life.

Before interaction can proceed successfully, two actors must come to an agreement about what sort of situation they are in and what sort of roles each of them are playing (e.g., a friendly chat between acquaintances, a seduction between lovers, asking for advice from a superior, etc.). This process is referred to as *identity negotiation.* People in an interaction each project an identity, and their responses to one another indicate whether they accept the projected identity. For example, if you ask your boss how old she is and she doesn't acknowledge the question, she has chosen not to grant you the identity of "familiar acquaintance." When two people agree on the identities they are both going to play in an interaction, they have arrived at what Goffman refers to as the *working consensus.* However, this *public* agreement need not be an accurate reflection of the actor's *private* beliefs. You may have a pleasant chat with a co-worker even if you dislike the person. There are many possible reasons for doing this: to be polite, to prevent a scene, to ensure good relations in the workplace, or perhaps because the person controls resources that you may need sometime. Whatever the *private* reality might be, it is the *public,* socially agreed upon definition of the situation that will guide interaction.

Indeed, once a public agreement has been reached (whether implicitly or explicitly) it carries the weight of a contract. The working consensus has a moral character to it. By that we mean that once the situation and the identities of the actors are accepted, each actor has the *right* to be treated in a particular way by other actors and an *obligation* to behave in ways that are consistent with the presented identity. For example, in an interaction between a teacher and a student, the person who is in the role of the teacher has the right to expect certain behavior from the person who is the student: to be treated respectfully, to be treated as a status superior, to be treated as an expert in the topic of the class, and so on. At the same time, someone who has claimed the identity of teacher has numerous obligations or duties. One is held responsible for competently carrying out one's role, and so the teacher is obligated to be respectful to the student, to know a great deal about the subject, and to be able to convey that knowledge to students.

The identities we claim, if publicly accepted by others, carry rights and duties that must be respected if the small social order that is an interaction is to continue. If a math teacher cannot solve a problem in front of the class or if a student treats the teacher as a younger sibling, the interaction grinds to an uncomfortable halt.

In sum, there are two key elements to interaction: publicly defining (and presenting) our own identity and defining what sort of situation we are in with others. There are many possible answers to the questions: Who am I? Who are you? What's going on? And so these definitions are usually negotiated by the participants in the interactions. People will jockey back and forth, each working to claim an identity and define the situation in ways that will help them accomplish their goals. Further, even once an identity is established, it must be actively maintained.

An important implication of this process is the way in which it leads us, knowingly or unknowingly, to reproduce taken-for-granted cultural patterns. Because minds are private we must dramatize (in other words, signal) the identities we wish to claim and our definition of the situation. To be effective in interaction, we select symbolic representations that we know to be reliable signals of our intentions. This selection of culturally typical or expected symbols is *idealization*. You may not like business suits, for instance, but you don one for a job interview because you believe it to be the appropriate costume for presenting the identity of an eager and professional potential employee. In presenting yourself as such, with the appropriate costumes, props, and mannerisms, you effectively reproduce a set of cultural expectations: business people wear suits. In other words, you present a symbolic *ideal type* and through your self-presentation, you affirm the ideal type. The implications of this process for perpetuating social norms are significant. We consider the consequences of "dramatizing the ideal" both here and in Part IV. Below we examine how we manage our identities, how situations are defined, what happens when interaction breaks down, and how our ongoing interactions can lead to more permanent changes in our sense of who we are.

Who Are We?

In the next two sections we examine the two key tasks of interaction: defining who we are and defining the situation we are in. The first section concerns the identities we present to others.

An identity can be thought of as a mask. This mask is a role that we temporarily inhabit. We use many different identities throughout the course of our interactions, and the identity we project will be a function of both our desires and also what is expected of us by others. The readings in the section on identity and impression management illustrate this. A particularly dramatic example of the impact of others' expectations can be seen in "Shooting an Elephant" by George Orwell. In it he describes how he came to kill an elephant despite the fact that he did not want to do so and that it exposed him to danger. He killed the elephant in order to behave in a manner consistent with his official role. He was performing an identity. It is an important lesson in how identities can be a prison as well as a resource.

In "Dress, Drama and Self," T. R. Young examines dramaturgy in a more contemporary arena and illustrates the extent to which we use clothing as a prop to signal our identities. Once again, we cannot read each other's mind. Hence there is a need to signal who we are and what we believe. Young's case study is tee shirts, which serve as a kind of personal billboard on which we can write private editorials that establish our identity.

Brent Staples ("Black Men and Public Space") demonstrates one of the dilemmas inherent in identity management and why one has to be concerned with dramaturgy regardless of one's intentions. As a young black man he recognizes that a prevalent cultural stereotype casts him in the role of a potentially threatening actor. Recognizing this, he is put in a position where he must explicitly dramatize the fact that he intends no harm.

The last reading in this section is "Managing Feeling," by Arlie Hochschild. She points out that the identities we present can be commodified—particular jobs may require employees to present very finely specified identities to clients and to do so in a uniform way. This leads Hochschild to ask to what extent we might become alienated from ourselves when we are required to enact identities for someone else's gain.

What's Going On?

The story is *Tom Sawyer* by Mark Twain (1875/1946). The scene is a weekend afternoon when Tom has been given the thankless task of whitewashing a long fence. Soon one of his friends comes by and begins to taunt him:

> "Hello, old chap, you got to work, hey?"
> Tom wheeled suddenly and said:
> "Why, it's you, Ben! I warn't noticing."
> "Say—I'm going in a-swimming, *I* am. Don't you wish you could? But of course you'd druther *work*—wouldn't you? Course you would!"
> Tom contemplated the boy a bit, and said:
> "What do you call work?"
> "Why ain't *that* work?"
> Tom resumed his whitewashing, and answered carelessly:
> "Well, maybe it is, and maybe it ain't. All I know, is, it suits Tom Sawyer."
> "Oh come, now, you don't mean to let on that you *like* it?"
> The brush continued to move.
> "Like it? Well, I don't see why I oughtn't to like it. Does a boy get a chance to whitewash a fence every day?"
> That put the thing in a new light. Ben stopped nibbling his apple. Tom swept his brush daintily back and forth— stepped back to note the effect—added a touch here and there—criticized the effect again—Ben watching every move and getting more and more interested, more and more absorbed. Presently he said:
> "Say, Tom, let *me* whitewash a little." (pp. 18-19)

Soon boy after boy come by and part with their food, toys, and other treasures for an opportunity to whitewash the fence.

Tom is, on a small scale, an entrepreneur of meaning (we examine large-scale entrepreneurs of meaning in Part IV). Through great skill he has managed to take an activity defined as unpleasant and reframed it as a rare and desirable project. That is, he has successfully defined the situation in a way that allows him to accomplish his goal (to avoid having to spend the day whitewashing the fence).

This section examines how situations are defined. If an interaction is to proceed successfully, the participants must establish their identities *and* come to a public agreement as to what sort of situations they will perform together. As the above example makes clear, different people will attempt to define a situation in different ways. The readings in this section point out the work that goes into defining a situation and maintaining a particular definition. They also illustrate that situational definitions are constructed through interaction.

We begin with a reading on conversation and how it is used and abused. Conversation is an intricately coordinated dance between two or more people. This dance demands great skill. Conversation is also an extremely valuable resource. The opportunity to talk is an opportunity to define the situation in a particular way, try to change someone's mind, or project oneself as a particular kind of person. Because talking publicly is such a valuable resource, it is not surprising that people will often try very hard to make sure they are heard or to ensure that other people are not given an opportunity to air their views (which is to say, their definitions of the situation). As such, conversation is supported by a variety of norms about how a conversation (at least a "polite" or "correct" conversation) should take place: people should take turns speaking, no one should dominate the conversation, and people should not interrupt one another. However, not everyone abides by these norms. It turns out there are some interesting patterns in who supports a conversation and who takes advantage of it.

For example, past research (e.g., West & Zimmerman, 1983) has found that men are much more likely to interrupt women than vice versa. This suggests that women are being taken advantage of in conversation and consequently are less able to influence how a situation is defined. Why do these patterns exist? Is it because men and women have different physiology? Is it something genetic? Is it related to different socialization patterns? Or might it be something about the actual relationships between men and women? Researchers have suggested that these imbalanced conversational patterns may exist because of differences in power between men and women.

Testing this idea is the point of the reading by Peter Kollock, Philip Blumstein, and Pepper Schwartz ("Sex and Power in Interaction: Conversational Privileges and Duties"). These researchers designed a study that allowed them to disentangle the effects of sex and power, and found that many of the patterns that have been described are tied to power rather than sex. For example, in a male-female relationship in which the woman had more power than the man, she would tend to exhibit "male" conversational patterns and he would exhibit "female" patterns. The lesson here is that behavior that we tend to associate with individuals is instead often a function of the *relationship* between two people. It is not the fact that one person has a Y chromosome and one person has two X chromosomes that determines these interactional patterns; it is that there is a relative power difference between two people in their relationship. And this relative power difference means that some actors will be better able to put forward their definition of the situation.

The next readings examine how situations are defined in three very different settings. In "Behavior in Private Places: Sustaining Definitions of Reality in Gynecological Examinations," Joan Emerson uses an unusual context to highlight processes that are present in many interactions. In this case, the doctors and nurses performing this medical procedure must take care to ensure that the situation continues to be defined as a medical examination. This examination includes many sensitive behaviors that could threaten this definition of the situation. Although most interaction is not as precarious as a gynecological exam, any interaction can end up being redefined in a negative light ("I thought you were being helpful. Now I just think you're being patronizing and manipulative!"). Thus, the concerns and dramaturgical activity that are brought out so clearly in the gynecological exam are relevant to many more ordinary interactional settings.

"Becoming a Marihuana User," written by Howard Becker, illustrates a number of the features of interaction discussed in the previous readings. The fact that this is an old piece is an important advantage because it allows us to study a new culture in its infancy, before the general public knew much about marijuana and its effects. One of the key points of Becker's article is that getting "high" is something that must be learned and that it is learned in interaction with other, more experienced users. Becker points out, for example, that it is very common for novices not to feel high the first time they smoke marijuana, just as it is possible for an experienced user to smoke an inert placebo that smells like marijuana and report feeling high. In other words, smoking marijuana is not a simple physiological response to a psychoactive drug, but a socially constructed experience that must be *identified* or *named* (see Part II) before it takes on the intended meaning. This process of identifying the expected effects of the drug takes place through interaction. A person who inadvertently ingests marijuana without any preexisting expectations is not likely to define the experience as "being high."

Barbara Heyl traces the process of defining an identity in "The Madam as Teacher: The Training of House Prostitutes." This reading illustrates that identities, like the effects of marijuana, must be defined before they can be experienced or performed in a socially meaningful way. Women do not simply engage in activities of prostitution. They must have the activity defined for them and learn how to perform the part before they can "become" a prostitute. This process of learning how to perform an identity extends to all social roles. The authors of this book also give a seminar on how to teach college students. It is intriguing to note the similarities between our syllabus for a course designed to teach graduate students how to "become" teachers and the steps the house madam follows to train her prostitutes.

When Interaction Breaks Down

Many of the previous readings make the point that interaction requires a significant amount of work if it is to proceed smoothly and successfully. This implies that there are many ways in which interaction might break down. One possibility is that a situation might be in danger of being redefined in an inappropriate way. Emerson's article on gynecological exams is a case in point.

Another possibility is that the identities we have claimed are somehow discredited (e.g., the teacher who cannot solve a problem in front of the class). This leads to embarrassment. It is striking to note how uncomfortable we are made by embarrassment and how hard we work to avoid it. Indeed, embarrassment makes us so uncomfortable that we usually cooperate to prevent or smooth over *other people's* embarrassing actions, even if they are strangers. From a dramaturgical perspective, embarrassment can be defined as a breakdown in a projected identity. When we engage in cooperative support of each other's identities, to avoid or repair embarrassment, it is called *tact*. We might look away when someone stumbles clumsily, pretend not to hear the fight the couple is having at a nearby table, and readily and eagerly accept other people's explanations for their untoward behavior. In one sense the presence and prevalence of tact is an extraordinary thing. The implication is that there is a very deep commitment to support each other's identities, even the identities of strangers. True, there are times when an actor might look on an embarrassing moment without tact (or even have engineered the moment, as might be the case with two rivals), but these instances stand out because they are exceptions.

Indeed, practical jokes that discredit someone's "face" would not be funny if they were not a deviation from the usual norm of using tact. In this sense the self that is publicly presented and accepted is a sacred thing that we are obligated to support.

This mutual obligation to avoid "scenes" and to be who we claim to be means that whenever a situation or identity is threatened, someone must repair the interaction. When the audience helps in the repair work we speak of tact, but of course the person whose identity is threatened can also work to repair the interaction. Following a behavior that threatens an identity, that person can offer explanations that are designed to give an account of the actions. This is the topic of "Accounts," by Marvin Scott and Stanford Lyman. In this reading the authors dissect the explanations people offer and categorize them. Scott and Lyman distinguish between two broad categories of accounts, *excuses* and *justifications*. Excuses admit that one's behavior was bad or inappropriate but deny responsibility for the act (for example, because it was "an accident"). Justifications assert that the act was in fact positive (by claiming, for example, that no one got hurt, or if a person was injured, that that person deserved it for some reason).

Offering accounts after an inappropriate act does not guarantee that others will accept ("honor") the account. Not every explanation is acceptable. "I had car trouble" might be a reasonable excuse for failing to turn in a term paper, but not "Voices told me to throw it into the ocean." And some explanations are acceptable in some situations but not others. Forgetting to pull dinner out of the oven in time because "I was distracted by a phone call" is acceptable, but the same excuse would certainly not be honored as an explanation for why someone failed to show up for her or his own wedding. What is judged as an acceptable account varies from situation to situation. It can also vary tremendously from one culture to another.

Sometimes we know that something we are about to say or do might be considered embarrassing or objectionable. In these cases we can try to preempt the negative consequences of what we are about to do by making statements we hope will influence other people's interpretations *before* we act (as opposed to accounts that occur *after* a questionable act). These preliminary assertions are called *disclaimers* by John Hewitt and Randall Stokes in their article. For example, if a statement could be taken as racist, a person might begin with the phrase "Some of my best friends are . . ." A person who intends to say something very unusual can begin with "This may seem crazy to you, but . . ." or "Hear me out before you jump to any conclusions. . . ."

Finally, in "On Cooling the Mark Out," Erving Goffman uses an unusual interaction as a metaphor for issues that are relevant in many settings. Here the metaphor is the con game and the way in which con artists try to pacify ("cool") the person they have just cheated (the "mark"). The previous two readings deal with the details of interaction and examine how people might try to manage their own behavior. In this reading Goffman considers situations in which a person moves into a different and lower status role (being fired from a job, for example, or being rejected by a lover) and how other people help such a person adjust to this new role.

A point to consider is how remarkable it is that so much effort is directed toward repairing interaction and identities. Through tact, accounts, disclaimers, and such processes as "cooling the mark out," we work to bring our behavior into line with the values and norms of our social group. In doing so we reinforce cultural symbols and expectations. There is a ritual aspect to interaction, which is to say there is a conservative aspect to interaction. Through our ritual presentations of the "ideal," we conserve or maintain the status quo. This is what Goffman means when he says "The world, in truth, is a wedding" (1959, p. 36).

From Masks to Selves

One implication of interaction rituals is that they have the potential to become set or routinized. The process may become so automatic that we fail to notice the extent to which we are engaging in these performances. After having spent some time at a job or in the company of old friends, we seldom recall the discomfort of the initial interaction rituals in which we were not exactly sure if our identity claims would be granted and what was expected of us in terms of the definition of the situation. Blind dates are often considered the example par excellence of the sticky challenges involved in interaction and identity management.

Although the interaction rituals that we perform repeatedly may become routine, this does not mean that we cease to engage in impression management. It simply means that the part we perform in routine settings has become comfortably familiar. In Part II we discussed the work of George Herbert Mead, who suggested that humans learn to treat themselves as an object that has meaning relative to other people and situations, just as they learn to attribute relative meaning to other things in their environment. The ability to treat the self as an object is what makes it possible for us to observe, reflect on, plan, and direct our own behavior. In other words, without the ability to perceive the self as an object we would be unable to engage in impression management. One of the things that the self can do is to engage in *internal conversation* (private thought) and reflect on whether or not its behavior seems "authentic." For example, out of deference and fear of losing your job, you may play the part of a likable clown for your overbearing boss. In private, however, you "know" that this is not the "real you." The "real you" is serious and efficient and hates the boss.

As we discussed in Part II, your notions of how to present yourself to your boss are based on a set of general expectations that represent the attitudes and values of your culture. These expectations function as the "generalized other" to give you an "ideal script" for how to act relative to an employer. You may also have another set of general expectations that direct you to stand up to the boss. The generalized other can be contradictory. Which set of expectations you act on depends on the specific situation, including who you are interacting with and her or his power to define the situation. Your internal dialogues regarding these contradictions and how you choose to enact them contribute to the process of self-definition.

An interesting question is the nature of the relationship between the identities that we perform to manage the impressions that others have of us and the self that we consider to be a more stable and enduring aspect of who we are. Identities, as we have seen, vary across situations relative to interaction partners. The *self* is a more or less stable construct and serves as the basis of comparison when we reflect on our identity performances and their consequences. Even if one is unable to express the "real" self in a particular situation, this "real self" exists as a touchstone by which the actor evaluates the authenticity of the identities that he or she presents. In this section we ask, how does an identity become a self?

The answer, in part, is in the process of routinization. Identities that you perform repeatedly may become part of your general sense of who you are. On the other hand, some of us perform very routinized identities without ever considering them to be an aspect of our "true self." Many people who live and work in Los Angeles, when asked what they do, will reply, "I work as a server/delivery person/janitor, but I am *really* writing a screenplay," or "I am *really* an actor." The job, even if it is one that they have performed for years, may not be an important aspect of the "real" self, whereas an identity that has yet to be realized may be the core of the self. Before reading further, take out a piece of paper and write down twenty responses to the question, "Who am I?" As you read through this section ponder how each of these aspects of your "real" self came to be.

The readings in this section emphasize the process of identifying or naming behaviors that one comes to see as an aspect of "self." In other words, the self, like other objects, is viewed as a social construction that takes on its meaning through interaction. In the case of the self, this interaction can include internal dialogue with one's self, as an object, as well as interaction with others. In much the same way that we learn to define the meaning of things in our environment, we learn about who we are through observing the responses of others to us, as an object. Charles Horton Cooley, a contemporary of Mead, suggested the concept of the "looking-glass self" whereby our image of ourself is based on how we think others see us. These reflected appraisals are the topic of the reading "Looking-Glass Self." Cooley notes that we gain information about ourselves by casting ourselves into the role of someone observing us, imagining how our actions appear to that person, and then attaching some reaction, such as pride or mortification, to that perceived reaction.

In "Turning Points in Identity," Anselm Strauss suggests a series of experiences, such as discovering that one has done something especially well, which may contribute to a reconsideration of how one sees oneself. In this reading Strauss's term *identity* is better seen as synonymous with the term "self" as we are discussing it here. A central point of this reading is that incidents that break routine can often serve as a basis for the transformation of our identity. This implies that even a stable sense of self may vary over time and with different experiences.

Philip Blumstein, in contrast to Strauss, focuses on repeated interaction rituals played out with people who are significant to us (in this case, an intimate partner). "The Production of Selves in Personal Relationships" contains the rudiments of a theory for the development of stable selves through interaction. Blumstein's thesis is that significant others, particularly our intimate partners, have the potential to be important contributors to our sense of self because we value their reflected appraisals a great deal. In addition, the process of coordinating couple activities leads to the naming of particular identities. Partners may become attached to, or grow into, these identities through routinization and the reflected appraisals of one another. Blumstein refers to this process as "ossification." This means that identities have the potential to harden, like bone, into selves. If played out under the right circumstances, with people who reinforce the identity in such a way that we come to incorporate it into our own internal dialogue, the masks that we wear to convey information to others, to dramatize the ideal, may in fact become part of what we consider to be our "real" face. Consider the implications of this process as you re-read your "Who am I?" list.

Itabari Njeri, in "The Power of Names," and Shelby Steele, in "On Being Black and Middle Class," speak of the internal dialogue involved in the deliberations we engage in as we try to "name" ourselves. These readings suggest that the identification of the "true self" is a complicated process involving much consideration about which self to cultivate and how to express it to others in a world of complex symbolic meaning regarding race.

Interaction is a fluid, intricately coordinated dance that requires actors to participate in meaningful symbolic routines. These interaction rituals serve to define who people are, relative to one another, and what the situation is. The implication is that social life is a production or performance staged by us, the participants. We have suggested that even the self is a social construction arrived at through processes of meaningful interaction. By way of conclusion we invite you to ponder the paradox of the social self. Many Western individuals are uncomfortable with the notion of the self as a social construction. We are all more or less aware that we engage in impression management as the situation requires it, but many of us like to think that our "true self" is unchanging and is the product of forces independent of society. Based on this logic, many of us rebel against what we consider to be the "chains of society." It is thought that if only we could break loose from these chains, we would be "free" (Charon, 1989). Herein lies the paradox.

To gain control over our own behavior we must develop a self that is capable of observing, reflecting on, and directing that behavior. Without such a self we are merely passive organisms propelled by the forces of nature. In the process of developing this self, we determine what position to take on our own behavior by observing and by experiencing the reactions of others to our behavior. This implies that all of the behavior that we reflect on (in other words, take an *active* stance toward) holds meaning for us only in that it has been derived from some form of social interaction. The ability to even consider whether or not we are "free" agents or "controlled" by society is possible only through our ability to engage in internal dialogue regarding the self as an object. This ability is a product of socialization. Free agency is therefore a moot point for the unsocialized being. Such a being cannot reflect on or guide its own behavior and therefore cannot make active choices. Resolution of this paradox may lie in the recognition, rather than the denial, of social patterns and interaction rituals as a process in which we are all "sweet conspirators." Once these processes have been identified, we find it useful to ask ourselves what purpose they serve and with what consequences, rather than to merely shrug them off as if they were someone else's chains. To shrug off our socialization is, according to Goffman, to leave the stage where reality is being performed. The pertinent question for the enlightened social actor is: "Just what sort of a performance am I a part of?" This is the subject of Part IV.

A Final Note. A number of these readings are quite old. Although the concepts and processes they describe are every bit as relevant today as when the articles were first written, some of the examples are dated. You may even be offended by a few of them. We ask you to think about the cultural and historical context within which these pieces were written, and to treat the examples themselves as data, as one more indication of how social definitions change over time. In the final section of this book we will explicitly deal with how larger scale realities are reinforced or changed. That is, we will examine the conservative and radical effects that different social processes have for the negotiation and routinization of the patterns of interaction that we refer to as "society."

References and Further Reading

Charon, J. (1989). *Symbolic interactionism* (3rd ed.). Englewood Cliffs, NJ: Prentice-Hall.

Goffman, E. (1959). *The presentation of self in everyday life.* New York: Doubleday.

Tannen, D. (1986). *That's not what I meant!* New York: Ballantine.

Turner, R. (1976). The real self: From institution to impulse. *American Journal of Sociology, 81,* 989-1016.

Twain, M. (1946). *The adventures of Tom Sawyer.* New York: Grosset & Dunlap. (Original work published 1875)

West, C., & Zimmerman, D. H. (1983). Small insults: A study of interruptions in cross-sex conversations between unacquainted persons. In B. Thorne, C. Kramarae, & N. Henley (Eds.), *Language, gender, and society* (pp. 102-117). Rowley, MA: Newbury.

Shooting an Elephant

George Orwell

In Moulmein, in lower Burma, I was hated by large numbers of people—the only time in my life that I have been important enough for this to happen to me. I was sub-divisional police officer of the town, and in an aimless, petty kind of way anti-European feeling was very bitter. No one had the guts to raise a riot, but if a European woman went through the bazaars alone somebody would probably spit betel juice over her dress. As a police officer I was an obvious target and was baited whenever it seemed safe to do so. When a nimble Burman tripped me up on the football field and the referee (another Burman) looked the other way, the crowd yelled with hideous laughter. This happened more than once. In the end the sneering yellow faces of young men that met me everywhere, the insults hooted after me when I was at a safe distance, got badly on my nerves. The young Buddhist priests were the worst of all. There were several thousand of them in the town and none of them seemed to have anything to do except stand on street corners and jeer at Europeans.

All this was perplexing and upsetting. For all the time I had already made up my mind that imperialism was an evil thing and the sooner I chucked up my job and got out of it the better. Theoretically—and secretly, of course—I was all for the Burmese and all against their oppressors, the British. As for the job I was doing, I hated it more bitterly than I can perhaps make clear. In a job like that you see the dirty work of Empire at close quarters. The wretched prisoners huddling in the stinking cages of the lock-ups, the gray, cowed faces of the long-term convicts, the scarred buttocks of the men who had been flogged with bamboos—all these oppressed me with an intolerable sense of guilt. But I could get nothing into perspective. I was young and ill educated and I had had to think out my problems in the utter silence that is imposed on every Englishman in the East. I did not even know that the British Empire is dying, still less did I know that it is a great deal better than the younger empires that are going to supplant it. All I knew was that I was stuck between my hatred of the empire I served and my rage against the evil-spirited little beasts who tried to make my job impossible. With one part of my mind I thought of the British Raj as an unbreakable tyranny, as something clamped down, in *saecula saeculorum*, upon the will of prostrate peoples; with another part I thought that the greatest joy in the world would be to drive a bayonet into a Buddhist priest's guts. Feelings like these are the normal by-products of imperialism; ask any Anglo-Indian official, if you can catch him off duty.

One day something happened which in a roundabout way was enlightening. It was a tiny incident in itself, but it gave me a better glimpse than I had had before of the real nature of imperialism—the real motives for which despotic governments act. Early one morning the sub-inspector at a police station the other end of the town rang me up on the phone and said that an elephant was ravaging the bazaar. Would I please come and do something about it? I did not know what I could do, but I wanted to see what was happening and I got on to a pony and started out. I took my rifle, an old .44 Winchester and much too small to kill an elephant, but I thought the noise might be useful *in terrorem*. Various Burmans stopped me on the way and told me about the elephant's doing. It was not, of course, a wild elephant, but a tame one which had gone "must." It had been chained up, as tame elephants always are when their attack of "must" is due, but on the previous night it had broken its chain and escaped. Its mahout, the only person who could manage it when it was in that state, had set out in pursuit, but had taken the wrong direction and was now twelve hours' journey away, and in the morning the elephant had suddenly reappeared in the town. The Burmese population had no weapons and were quite helpless against it. It had already destroyed somebody's bamboo hut, killed a cow and raided some fruit-stalls and devoured the stock; also it had met the municipal rubbish van and, when the driver jumped out and took to his heels, turned the van over and inflicted violences upon it.

The Burmese sub-inspector and some Indian constables were waiting for me in the quarter where the elephant had been seen. It was a very poor quarter, a labyrinth of squalid bamboo huts, thatched with palm-leaf, winding all over a steep hillside. I remember that it was a cloudy, stuffy morning at the beginning of the rains. We began questioning the people as to where the elephant had gone and, as usual, failed to get any definite information. That is invariably the case in the East; a story always sounds clear enough at a distance, but the nearer you get to the scene of events the vaguer it becomes. Some of the people said that the elephant had gone in one direction, some said that he had gone in another, some professed not even to have heard of any elephant. I had almost made up my mind that the whole story was a pack of lies, when we heard yells a little distance away. There was a loud, scandalized cry of "Go away, child! Go away this instant!" and an old woman with a switch in her hand came round the corner of a hut, violently shooing away a crowd of naked children. Some more women followed, clicking their tongues and exclaiming; evidently there was something that the children ought not to have seen. I rounded the hut and saw a man's dead body sprawling in the mud. He was an Indian, a black Dravidian coolie, almost naked, and he could not have been dead many minutes. The people said that the elephant had come suddenly upon him round the corner of the hut, caught him with its trunk, put its foot on his back and ground him into the earth. This was the rainy season and the ground was soft, and his face had scored a trench a foot deep and a couple of yards long. He was lying on his belly with arms crucified and head sharply twisted to one side. His face was coated with mud, the eyes wide open, the teeth bared and grinning with an expression of unendurable agony. (Never tell me, by the way, that the dead look peaceful. Most of the corpses I have seen looked devilish.) The friction of the great beast's foot had stripped the skin from his back as neatly as one skins a rabbit. As soon as I saw the dead man I sent an orderly to a friend's house nearby to borrow an elephant rifle. I had already sent back the pony, not wanting it to go mad with fright and throw me if it smelt the elephant.

The orderly came back in a few minutes with a rifle and five cartridges, and meanwhile some Burmans had arrived and told us that the elephant was in the paddy fields below, only a few hundred yards away. As I started forward practically the whole population of the quarter flocked out of the houses and followed me. They had seen the rifle and were all shouting excitedly that I was going to shoot the elephant. They had not shown much interest in the elephant when he was merely ravaging their homes, but it was different now that he was going to be shot. It was a bit of fun to them, as it would be to an English crowd; besides they wanted the meat. It made me vaguely uneasy. I had no intention of shooting the elephant—I had merely sent for the rifle to defend myself if necessary—and it is always unnerving to have a crowd following you. I marched down the hill, looking and feeling a fool, with the rifle over my shoulder and an ever-growing army of people jostling at my heels. At the bottom, when you got away from the huts, there was a metalled road and beyond that a miry waste of paddy fields a thousand yards across, not yet ploughed but soggy from the first rains and dotted with coarse grass. The elephant was standing eight yards from the road, his left side toward us. He took not the slightest notice of the crowd's approach. He was tearing up branches of grass, beating them against his knees to clean them, and stuffing them into his mouth.

I had halted on the road. As soon as I saw the elephant I knew with perfect certainty that I ought not to shoot him. It is a serious matter to shoot a working elephant—it is comparable to destroying a huge and costly piece of machinery—and obviously one ought not to do it if it can possibly be avoided. And at that distance, peacefully eating, the elephant looked no more dangerous than a cow. I thought then and I think now that his attack of "must" was already passing off; in which case he would merely wander harmlessly about until the mahout came back and caught him. Moreover, I did not in the least want to shoot him. I decided that I would watch him for a little while to make sure that he did not turn savage again, and then go home.

But at that moment I glanced round at the crowd that had followed me. It was an immense crowd, two thousand at the least and growing every minute. It blocked the road for a long distance on either side. I looked at the sea of yellow faces above the garish clothes—faces all happy and excited over this bit of fun, all certain that the elephant was going to be shot. They were watching me as they would watch a conjurer about to perform a trick. They did not like me, but with the magical rifle in my hands I was momentarily worth watching. And suddenly I realized that I should have to shoot the elephant after all. The people expected it of me and I had got to do it; I could feel their two thousand wills pressing me forward, irresistibly. And it was at this moment, as I stood there with the rifle in my hands, that I first grasped the hollowness, the futility of the white man's dominion in the East. Here was I, the white man with his gun, standing in front of the unarmed native crowd—seemingly the leading actor of the piece; but in reality I was only an absurd puppet pushed to and fro by the will of those yellow faces behind. I perceived in this moment that when the white man turns tyrant it is his own freedom that he destroys. He becomes a sort of hollow, posing dummy, the conventionalized figure of a sahib. For it is the condition of his rule that he shall spend his life in trying to impress the "natives," and so in every crisis he has got to do what the "natives" expect of him. He wears a mask, and his face grows to fit it. I had got to shoot the elephant. I had committed myself to doing it when I sent for the rifle. A sahib has got to act like a sahib; he has got to appear resolute, to know his own mind and do definite things. To come all that way, rifle in hand, with two thousand people marching at my heels, and then to trail feebly away, having done nothing—no, that was impossible. The crowd would laugh at me. And my whole life, every white man's life in the East, was one long struggle not to be laughed at.

But I did not want to shoot the elephant. I watched him beating his bunch of grass against his knees with that preoccupied grandmotherly air that elephants have. It seemed to me that it would be murder to shoot him. At that age I was not squeamish about killing animals, but I had never shot an elephant and never wanted to. (Somehow it always seems worse to kill a *large* animal.) Besides, there was the beast's owner to be considered. Alive, the elephant was worth at least a hundred pounds; dead, he would only be worth the value of his tusks, five pounds, possibly. But I had got to act quickly. I turned to some experienced-looking Burmans who had been there when he arrived, and asked them how the elephant had been behaving. They all said the same thing: he took no notice of you if you left him alone, but he might charge if you went too close to him.

It was perfectly clear to me what I ought to do. I ought to walk up to within, say, twenty-five yards of the elephant and test his behavior. If he charged, I could shoot; if he took no notice of me, it would be safe to leave him until the mahout came back. But also I knew that I was going to do no such thing. I was a poor shot with a rifle and the ground was soft mud into which one would sink at every step. If the elephant charged and I missed him, I should have about as much chance as a toad under a steam-roller. But even then I was not thinking particularly of my own skin, only of the watchful yellow faces behind. For at that moment, with the crowd watching me, I was not afraid in the ordinary sense, as I would have been if I had been alone. A white man mustn't be frightened in front of "natives"; and so, in general, he isn't frightened. The sole thought in my mind was that if anything went wrong those two thousand Burmans would see me pursued, caught, trampled on, and reduced to a grinning corpse like that Indian up the hill. And if that happened it was quite probable that some of them would laugh. That would never do. There was only one alternative. I shoved

the cartridges into the magazine and lay down on the road to get a better aim.

The crowd grew very still, and a deep, low, happy sigh, as of people who see the theater curtain go up at last, breathed from innumerable throats. They were going to have their bit of fun after all. The rifle was a beautiful German thing with cross-hair sights. I did not then know that in shooting an elephant one should shoot to cut an imaginary bar running from ear-hole to ear-hole. I ought, therefore, as the elephant was sideways on, to have aimed straight at his ear-hole; actually I aimed several inches in front of this, thinking the brain would be further forward.

When I pulled the trigger I did not hear the bang or feel the kick—one never does when a shot goes home—but I heard the devilish roar of glee that went up from the crowd. In that instant, in too short a time, one would have thought, even for the bullet to get there, a mysterious, terrible change had come over the elephant. He neither stirred nor fell, but every line of his body altered. He looked suddenly, stricken, shrunken, immensely old, as though the frightful impact of the bullet had paralyzed him without knocking him down. At last, after what seemed a long time—it might have been five seconds, I dare say—he sagged flabbily to his knees. His mouth slobbered. An enormous senility seemed to have settled upon him. One could have imagined him thousands of years old. I fired again into the same spot. At the second shot he did not collapse but climbed with desperate slowness to his feet and stood weakly upright, with legs sagging and head drooping. I fired a third time. That was the shot that did for him. You could see the agony of it jolt his whole body and knock the last remnant of strength from his legs. But in falling he seemed for a moment to rise, for as his hind legs collapsed beneath him he seemed to tower upward like a huge rock toppling, his trunk reaching skyward like a tree. He trumpeted, for the first and only time. And then down he came, his belly toward me, with a crash that seemed to shake the ground even where I lay.

I got up. The Burmans were already racing past me across the mud. It was obvious that the elephant would never rise again, but he was not dead. He was breathing very rhythmically with long rattling gasps, his great mound of a side painfully rising and falling. His mouth was wide open—I could see far down into caverns of pale pink throat. I waited a long time for him to die, but his breathing did not weaken. Finally I fired my two remaining shots into the spot where I thought his heart must be. The thick blood welled out of him like red velvet, but still he did not die. His body did not even jerk when the shots hit him, the tortured breathing continued without a pause. He was dying, very slowly and in great agony, but in some world remote from me where not even a bullet could damage him further. I felt that I had got to put an end to that dreadful noise. It seemed dreadful to see the great beast lying there, powerless to move and yet powerless to die, and not even to be able to finish him. I sent back for my small rifle and poured shot after shot into his heart and down his throat. They seemed to make no impression. The tortured gasps continued as steadily as the ticking of a clock.

In the end I could not stand it any longer and went away. I heard later that it took him half an hour to die. Burmans were bringing dahs and baskets even before I left, and I was told they had stripped his body almost to the bones by the afternoon.

Afterward, of course, there were endless discussions about the shooting of the elephant. The owner was furious, but he was only an Indian and could do nothing. Besides, legally I had done the right thing, for a mad elephant has to be killed, like a mad dog, if its owner fails to control it. Among the Europeans opinion was divided. The older men said I was right, the younger men said it was a damn shame to shoot an elephant for killing a coolie, because an elephant was worth more than any damn Coringhee coolie. And afterward I was very glad that the coolie had been killed; it put me legally in the right and it gave me a sufficient pretext for shooting the elephant. I often wondered whether any of the others grasped that I had done it solely to avoid looking a fool.

16

Dress, Drama and Self: The Tee Shirt as Text

T. R. Young

Sex is better than drugs
If you have the right pusher

(Mope's Tee Shirt)

This chapter interprets the results of a three-day observation of the dress of students at a college event. Categories for the analysis of tee shirts were generated by participant observation. The analysis of clothing is located in the larger process by which social reality is constructed. Clothing is one of four information media over which a young person still has control. As students are processed through the routines of mass bureaucracies, voice, body, and behavior are repressed as language media. As young people fail to find an institutionalized medium which expresses their concerns and their responses to the contingencies of life, they invent one.

The tee shirt is the uniquely postmodern medium that young people have found to speak out. We can read these tee shirts as text, deconstruct them and, thus, help reconstruct a world in which young people can give voice to those concerns.

To deconstruct a discourse is to think about how it fails its own project and interferes with the competent practice of social life. While this seems unnecessarily negative, one assumes that its positivities are registered in the knowledge process, in the sociocultural process, and will survive such a critique. Deconstruction of a topic requires that all its privileged assumptions are desanctified, returned to the human hand and the human mind that gave them birth and thus repoliticized—made part of a radical democracy of ideas and a rich democracy of decision.

All over the world young people collect and display tee shirts. In the United States, the wearing of tee shirts is a national phenomenon. The typical middle-class youngster has from five to ten such tee shirts with which to communicate his or her special message of style, gender, affinities, politics, status, interests, beliefs, and value preferences. Mope, an employee of the Copy Center Service at Central Michigan University, has about a hundred such tee shirts that he wears on appropriate occasions—that is to say, everyday. . . .

Symbolic Systems

A . . . language system available to a person with which to create the infinitely rich and varied social-life worlds found in authentic social action is clothing. Every society in history has used clothing for more than mere physiological function. Clothing has, for most of human history, been used in infinite permutation with voice and body to help define a situation, to help sanctify it, to help keep it going within its own logic, and to help end it. Each special social occasion demands a separate costuming. If a person is involved in many special occasions, s/he will have a closet full of meaningful clothes.

People who have five different kinds of shoes, jackets, hats, trousers, ties, or belts have transcended the physiological meaning of clothing and have entered into the symbolic world of clothing. For each set of clothing there is a separate and distinct social-life world that is to be constructed somewhere sometime. There are clothes for sport, clothes for work, clothes that speak of romance, and there are clothes to wear in the quiet and holy places of the world.

Fashion and style further expand the closets of the world. Those without secure and significant social anchorage for their self system can buy instant identities from a fashion boutique. Many shopping malls include stores that sell an identity to those who have none in which they can take pride. Young men and women, disconnected from the society in which they find themselves, buy, steal, and borrow clothing with which to project an image of status, of human worth.

Superefficient textile factories, superproductive sweat shop industries, superaesthetic advertising firms combine to colonize the desire of young men and women for social honor. They create and recreate fashion with which to do so—and thus garner superprofits.

In mass education, mass marketing, mass religion, mass sports, mass medicine, and mass politics, clothing comes under the control of a clothing police and loses its vocabulary. Dress codes for the patient, physician, and nurse are set by the singular logic of mass medicine, not by therapeutic logic. If a patient and a doctor knew each other as distinct human beings, there would be no need for white jackets or blue pants. Mass hospitals process masses of patients through the fragmented routines of mechanized medicine. In such a way, hundreds of patients can be mass-produced by the deskilled labor of unknown others.

Dress codes for the military or for the police are set by the logic of partisan conflict, not by the logic of law or justice. Dress codes for children in school or their teachers are set by the logic of social power, not by that of pedagogy. In business, dress codes are set in such a manner as to submerge alternate—and human—potentialities of clerk and customer alike. Even in the factory, field, and mine, some of the codes of clothing are set more by the administrative interests of management than by the logic of safety or task.

Mass institutions subvert the individuality of language systems, of meaning construction, the individual contribution to the social occasion at hand even as mass societies proclaim the ascendancy of individualism. What is meant by individuality in that context is that each individual should come before the bureaucracy one at a time rather than in organized collectives, and that any activity to act autonomously should occur outside the mass occasion at hand. Dress codes subvert the capacity of human beings to embody personal desire and to focus on distinctly human beings and human endeavor. Tee shirts recapture and express this alienated desire to their own purpose.

Clothing, voicings, body decor, and behavior are the four symbol systems used, in manifold and subtle variation, to create meaning by the participating individual within a collective enterprise. These four information flow systems are used by the individual in informationally-rich and interactively-rich social occasions with which to share in the creation of social reality. In mass society, the speech-carrying capacity of voice, body, clothing, and behavior is sharply reduced. The means of producing meaning are alienated by the rules of mass society.

Mass society itself arises from the interests of a few persons consolidated in an elite to preprogram the behavior of a mass enlarged as much as possible, in ways compatible with the interests of that elite. A special set of persons, hired and trained by the elite, process the mass through the routines of the mass institutions in ways compatible with the rules of the organization.

The mass is processed as individuals in questions of power and as standardized blocs in questions of status. Historically, the structures of mass organization arose with bureaucracy in prehistoric hydraulic societies, of which China and Egypt may be the prototypes. In modern history, the mass armies of France in Napoleonic times are perhaps the prototypic form of mass organization.

For our purposes here, we are interested in the ways in which students reclaim control over their own clothing as part of an interest in how media are alienated and liberated in given social occasions. In the study at hand, we will find that students use the tee shirt not as a physiological device by which to help regulate body temperature but rather as a political device by which to give voice to their anguish, ambitions, and needs in a world where their voice counts for little in the process by which social reality is created.

The Structure of Mass Society

Mass societies are comprised of organizations controlled by a few persons, managed by a few more, to control the activity of large numbers of people. The name we give to most of these organizations is *bureaucracy*. A bureaucracy is a stratified system of power in which an *elite* employs a *cadre* to process masses of people through standardized routines. The structure of a mass society serves as the social background and the theoretical soil out of which comes the growing interest in the tee shirt as a medium of discourse.

The rules by which people are processed—in education, medicine, sport, theatre, politics, industry, the marketplace, or in religion—are ordinarily set by the elite. And ordinarily the elite set the rules for their own convenience or purpose. The convenience or advantage of those persons processed may be considerable but is incidental to the purposes of the elite. The rules themselves are set forth and enforced without the rich dialectics of symbolic interaction. Interaction is reduced to the voicing of the rules and the control of deviation from the rule.

The one-sided nature of these rules requires considerable political effort on the part of the cadre. They organize the lines of action to reduce to a bare minimum the use of symbol systems by the individuals processed en masse. Modern policing arose to accommodate the interests of the few in controlling the activity of the many. Modern administrative science arose as a scientific alternative to the use of force in the shaping of behavior.

Unfree Speech

In the classroom, students must raise their hand to be permitted to speak. In the hospital, the use of body adornment with which one signals status, gender, sexual availability, or age grade is sharply curtailed. In the fast-food shop, clerks are instructed to use their voice in friendly manner and to say only the words set forth at headquarters by industrial psychologists. In the military, the complex wardrobe of the civilian used to create a dozen different social occasions is removed and a uniform set of clothing issued. This clothing says but one thing: "I am to give orders, you are to obey my orders." In the professional sport endeavor, the use of behavior to say something to the crowd or to the other team not previously set forth by coaches or by management is forbidden. Five yards for dancing in delight.

Bureaucracy destroys the use by the individual of one's own personal language systems. And yet one cannot be alienated from one's own voice, one's own body, one's own clothing, or one's own behavior easily.

In the back of the classroom, students whisper; on the factory floor, bets are made; in the fast-food restaurant, youngsters giggle; in the prison, inmates tap out messages.

Unfree Media

There are information flow systems that more readily lend themselves to alienation than those under the direct control of the individual. Electronically based systems designed to put only a cadre in control of the switch, the mike, the speaker, the copier, the printer, or the modulated electronic impulse do so and in so doing, alienate the mass from the wondrous ability of the human to create, in cooperative process with others, the incredibly complex and varied social occasions reported by ethnographers from around the world and throughout history. In a bureaucracy, mass production of meaning replaces the art and craft of human interaction.

The advent of mechanized media in elitist societies gave control over symbolic interaction to elites. In capitalist societies, the costs of access to magazines, television, radio, or newspapers give the rich a louder voice in which to shape the economic environment than the poor. In bureaucratic organizations, access to the media gives the bureaucratic officer control over the symbolic environment in which the faceless client, supplicant, inmate, student, or patient must live.

Free Speech

Outside of mass-produced social endeavors voice, clothing, body, and behavior remain the private property of the individual to use as he/she sees fit. When there is no organized, mass-mediated occasion that requires the political control of symbol sets, and when young people are left to their own devices, shut out of the organized world of the adult and cast adrift from the more private arenas of social life, symbol sets may be used in quite idiosyncratic ways.

Out of the politics of mass society, come the privatized use of the graffiti that young people put on their bodies, upon walls, trains, clothing and, in particular, tee shirts.

More generally, when existing communication systems are used for purposes alien to the human project, parallel and underground structures of communication arise (Young, 1983). The phenomenon of the tee shirt, as with other graffiti, is a parallel symbolic system by which people, usually young people, attempt to create a social-life world that resonates with their own preferences and affinities. Often these same symbol systems are used to express rage, contempt, rebellion, or are used to plead for redress of grievance.

What is said here about the structure and use of symbols and interactions does not hold for the fully open and collective creation of social life. The rules are very different for interaction and so are the results. For the shared creation of social life, each person defined as situationally present has a turn at shaping the activity of others present and, generally, the benefits of such a social life occasion are shared on the basis of need. Collective needs especially are served in social life. Massified forms of organization benefit first the elite, then the cadre, and only incidently, the mass.

Tee Shirts as Text

This section reports the results of a three-day observation of the wearing of tee shirts over a school holiday called "College Days," at Colorado State University. The holiday, incidentally, received considerable national news coverage as a "riot." The riot is not, in the first instance, the subject matter of this study, but passing comment will be made in the analysis here. Riots, too, are a form of language in which the voiceless get the attention of those who are "hard of listening."

The study of tee shirt display arose out of a class in sociology entitled Public Opinion and Mass Society. The point of the course was to think about and explain the differences in symbolic interactions between mass society on the one hand and interactively rich social occasions rich in information on the other. The point of the assignment was to locate the tee shirt culture in the larger social context in which it appears; to deconstruct the origins of the tee shirt so that we may reconstruct the larger meaning of their popularity. If we are to read tee shirts for the full meaning they carry, we must read them as a collective event in a sociohistorical process.

The research team reported to the class that the students observed at the parties, concerts, and later at the riot wore tee shirts that bore a wide variety of messages. One of the students took slide photos of the tee shirts to add visual depth to the report. The observations of the research team were first put into a classificatory scheme. The categories generated included: brand names, exotic vacation places, morality messages including religious sentiments, sexual concerns and action, and youth culture themes oriented to music.

Commodity Fetishism

Most were brand-name shirts; little more than walking advertisements for shoes, beverages, beers, and sporting equipment—all high-profit consumer items. Stroh's, Henry Weinhard, Dos Equis, and other beers showed up on the chests of young men. The Banana Republic is, I was informed, a clothing chain. Sole Suckers was, it seems, a shoe advertisement. One person advertised Camel cigarettes on his chest.

The naturalness of wearing brand names implies a naive commodity fetishism that for many would be distasteful. Materialism and possession has permeated the consciousness of these young people without the shame it might bring in other settings.

It is the intent of the 300,000 ads seen by preschoolers that they become walking commercials for cereals, toys, burgers, clothes, electronics, and other high-profit, mass-produced goods. The adornment of one's body by commercials is testimony to the success of the advertising industry to colonize the very bodies of their victims.

Status Quests and Proclamations

A second most popular motif was the display of exotic foreign place names. Many students are widely traveled. Central America, Europe, and Asia were represented in the tee shirt parade. A shirt with the logo of Bear Surf Boards not only indicates one's hobby, one's socioeconomic status, but also one's choice of vacation place (we were told that shirt came from Hawaii).

As with commodity fetishism above, the display of vacation place names bespeaks a social status and serves as an opening device for similarly traveled persons. In a mass of unknown others, one can dramatize one's potential affinities and thus invite overture from those unknown others.

Only in those societies where the social self is cut loose from social identity would such pathetic efforts to proclaim status be found. The social identities available in mass sports, mass education, mass religion, and mass markets are too fragile, too flimsy, too short, and too narrowly focused a social take upon which to ground the richness and complexity of a whole human being. Young people as do older people understand this and do not ground their social standing on mass institutions.

One would not say, "I am a K-Mart shopper," or "I am a Channel 7 viewer," in answer to Kuhn's Twenty Statements Test about the social anchorage of self-identity. Sad enough to adorn one's car with bumper stickers saying, "I 'heart' New York," or "I 'heart' Shelties," or "I 'heart' my VW." Sad commentary on the locations of love in mass society.

Morality Lives

The third most commonly observed tee shirt messages were a wide assortment of morality statements. The environment, religious values, friendships, comments on peace and war, as well as social-philosophical comments were displayed. For the most part, a profound concern with brotherhood, sisterhood, and fellowship across social boundaries was, to their credit, dramatized on youths' bodies.

Communion with the forms of nature spoke loudly, publicly, and dramatically of concern with pollution and ecological integrity.

"Life is a beach," was perhaps the most cynical philosophy noted. There was a tee shirt that suggested that one partied until one died—a particularly nihilistic philosophy. One understands that the message is not to be taken literally but, at the same time, there is the question of the quality of life in school or at home that makes such a shirt wearable.

A particularly innocent shirt said simply, "Señor Frog." We assumed the allusion was to Kermit and to the delights of magic and make-believe put forward in the Muppets. I was reminded that, after all, the people who wear such shirts were, only yesterday, children.

There were several shirts among the hundreds seen telling unknown others of the benefits of a life dedicated to Jesus. On a young woman was a cross encircled by a wreath and printed words informing the world that she was a "national member." Such tee shirts are close cousins to the bumper stickers that say, "Jesus Saves," "Honk if you love Jesus," "God is coming—and is She pissed."

One wonders if one will ever see such bumper stickers or such shirts used by Muslim youngsters, Jewish youngsters, Buddhist or Shinto devotees, or those still practicing animistic religions. There must be something different about the ways young people are fitted into religion in Christianity and the ways they fit into other religions that they would have to say such a thing on a tee shirt.

In other, more devout societies, such membership would be a background assumption. Only in secularized, technicized, and automized society would such tee shirts make sense.

Other morality statements had to do with touching one another, smiling at each other, helping each other, or showing concern for others at home or abroad. One particularly effective shirt for making contact in a friendly sort of a way was called the "ten questions" shirt. The students explained to me that shirt had ten questions on it one was invited to answer: "How old are you?" "What is your

major?" "Where is your home?" and such. There was also a tee shirt from Copirg, a public interest research group, advising students to "take it to the streets," presumably because institutional politics were closed to the voice of the student or to the public interest.

In mass society, morality is programmed out of the grasp of the individual. An elite claims control over moral questions in factory, shop, stadium, school, marketplace, and church. The location of morality is so remote from the worker, the guard, the soldier, the student, or the professor that each is reduced to the tee shirt as a feeble cry for a just and decent world.

Just coming into the fullness of their morality, young people find no social role, no social occasion, no social institution in which morality can mediate their situated behavior. Rules, orders, policies, programs, commands, as well as reified social relations preprogram behavior and reduce the self system to the mechanical robot that embodies those rules, orders, or commands.

Sexuality Lives

There were a few shirts with sexual content. Most were of a good-natured sort but one was distinctly chauvinist. The front of the shirt had two cherries over which was superimposed the international symbol of negation. It took us about two seconds to figure out what it meant—then came a chorus of groans. The next slide showed the back of the same shirt. It said, "Busting makes me feel good." The classroom became very quiet.

The group reported that the young man who wore that shirt was observing the norm that one wore such outrageous shirts only in the company of friends. In this case, the shirt was worn at a fraternity party. The party members were all from the same frat or their dates together with a smattering of friends. Even in that company, the person who wore the shirt was made uncomfortable. He was made to understand that few if any of even his close friends appreciated the humor of the message. We were told that he did go in and change shirts after bearing for a while his discomfort.

I have mentioned the practice of commercial advertising to colonize desire and to relocate it in a beverage, a car, a CD, or other commodity. In our society, sexuality becomes a highly privatized activity disconnected from family, community, or gender solidarity concerns as was the case in all previous history.

As a mass society displaces community, human sexuality is liberated to be used for quite personal or commercial purpose. This idiosyncratic use of sexuality offends those who think such a thing as sexuality is too valuable a solidarity tool to discard; who think that community is too valuable a social form to discard. However, the logic of mass society is that solidarity is too strong a social glue to use, and all such solidarity supplies need be made private property.

The privatization of human sexuality permits it to be vested in commodities while the outrage at privatized sexuality by those still oriented to solidarity concerns means that one must avoid an open, honest display of one's sexuality. But that part of the population still too lively or too unsocialized will proclaim that their desire still aims at living human beings—or parts of them at any rate.

Against Mass Culture

A great many tee shirts proclaimed the merits of musical groups. "Bruce Springsteen and the E Street Band" as well as other popular and/or exotic musical groups were promoted. In an earlier report, the students noted the rich interaction between musicians and audiences at rock concerts, jazz festivals, and blue-grass affairs. These cultural events contrast with the highly organized, formalized, and ritualized behavior of the musicians and audience in musical concert out of the eighteenth century, where attire is formal and the conventions of applause and response well regulated by convention.

Such cultural events also stand against the deadness of mass education, mass relig-

ion, or mass sport. When young people are given a choice between watching and doing, they opt for the forms of living. When not given that choice, they feign interest and involvement—then find parallel or underground cultural events in which to embody the forces of life. They will act as zombies, as vegetables in the classroom, but in the halls, in the game room, at parties, or in riots, they act in more human ways.

Discussion

The class as a whole reflected upon the semiotics of tee shirts. We wondered how one was to understand the place they had in the overall organization of the lives of young people. We agreed that the major way to understand the wearing of tee shirts was a way to find voice in a mass society.

We agreed that one tried to tell unknown others what one believed, what one liked to do, what another person could talk to one about if one wanted to make human contact, and told others as well what one was worried about at a college event at which most people did not know most others. The anonymity of mass events strips one of most of the language systems one could use. Of the four unalienable symbol systems mentioned earlier, clothing has the particular virtue of speaking when the other media—voice, body, and behavior—are silenced.

The tee shirt can be seen from afar. It can speak over the din of a concert, a party, or a sport event. It can carry a concise and lucid message in ways body and behavior cannot. It is fairly inexpensive and can address a comment to a faceless mass without the expensive electronics or printing equipment ordinarily used in such situations. The tee shirt is the modern equivalent of the poster in prerevolutionary France, wall graffiti in Latin America, or the flaming cross in antebellum South. It is a billboard for those struck dumb by the alienation of mass media in mass society.

We agreed that in a society in which status is based upon one's labor power as a commodity, and at a stage in one's life cycle in which one could not easily sell one's labor power in a way that reflected an acceptable presenting identity, some young people sought other foundations upon which to base status.

In a mass society, the structure of self is freed from the ancient social anchorages of tribe, gender, occupation, religion, or age grade. Those who have no social base for their identity outside of the mass institution turn to other sources of self. Astrology, electronic as well as exotic religions, exclusive clothing, body building, and such cultural semiworlds as punk, hippie, yuppie, country-western, and college tee shirts provide the structural basis for a quite privatized self system as the social sources found in mass institutions become too alienated and trivial a foundation upon which to build one's life.

The wearing of brand names, of exotic place names, of expensive tee shirts—all resonate with the materialism of a consumer society. Such shirts say to all who will look that the wearer is well located in the class system. There is the discretionary income available to the wearer—that clearly the wearer did not earn—that permits travel in style to far away places. One can say, "If it is money that gets your attention and enlists your company, I have it."

The tee shirt says to anyone who will look, "I am a person worthy of notice; you are to orient your approach to me upon the clues given off by my shirt." By extension, the shirt informs others that the person will be hard to approach if these basic interests are not respected. The possibility of impromptu formation of affinity groups—dyads, triads, and quartets—arose out of such artful presentments.

Morality shirts say to all who will listen that the wearer is an estimable person of moral worth. Concern for the good earth, for the oppressed of the world, for the morality of others, for the fellowship and love of each other is a central value in the life of the bearer. One may expect something of real value in a relationship with such a person.

Shirts carrying sexual messages carry an invitation to embark upon a short-term, impersonal sexual venture. They say: "In my life, my essential sexuality is a matter of great concern; I am in the process of developing my sexuality and I invite you to consider the possibility of exploration together."

Tee shirts that bear the name of a musical group, the marijuana leaf, or death's head say to their age group that they are angry at the stupidities of the adult world, that they join with others in a protest that cannot be lightly ignored and that they fully intend to stay in the youth culture until the message is heard. One might agree that such a protest is pretheoretical in its self-destructiveness, that young people should engage in more constructive forms of resistance and rebellion, but such a view asks that children be wiser than the adults who criticize them.

At the same time, one wonders about the need to use the information-deficient tee shirt as an opening gambit. Given the mass, anonymous character of state universities in general and "College Days" in particular, one can understand that more traditional sources of information about how to respond to another are lacking. One cannot be certain that one will have a common friend who will provide the necessary opening clues. One appreciates that one misses out on meeting others whom one might like to meet and get to know. The living graffiti of the tee shirt helps bridge the social distance between unknown others when more traditional bridges are missing.

We talked about the curious fact that young people feel the need to make contact with unknown others. Most people for most of history felt no such need. Even today, many strangers will walk away from casual openings and most will make little effort to initiate them. But here are a large number of young people, mostly Americans, Europeans, and Canadians who will make the effort and take the risk. It is easy to say that Americans are friendly or that they are open or that they are assertive. The more interesting question is why they feel the urge to be friendly.

The short answer lies in the systematic displacement of young people by their society. They are displaced persons trying to make the most of the cultural resources available in the effort to build a parallel social-life world that resonates with some of the best of human hope and some of the worst of human avarice. The society that discards its young will find cause to regret it. The society that values profits and budgets above persons and work will find the costs very high—both in human waste and in dollars.

Mope's Tee Shirts

I think you're cute
But then I think I'm cute.

My idea of camping out is when
room service is late.

Stupidity should be Painful

Yesterday was the Deadline
For all Complaints

The difference between dark and hard
is that it stays dark all night.

Sticks and Stones Break My Bones
but whips and chains excite me

All Extremists should be Killed

Joan of Arc is Alive and
Medium Well

Not everything that sucks
is necessarily bad

The older the wood
The hotter the fire

Built for Comfort
Not for speed

Ready, Willing & Still Able

Where there's a Will
I want to be part of it

Valley Girls

Valley boys and valley girls
lips of gloss and hair of curls
loins of fire and kisses sweet
give us pause when in the street:
Teased hair and fitted jeans
lots of "you knows" or "I means";
"fucking" this and "fucking" that;
not much mind below their hat.
Read their shirts and read their cars
you can read of their desires.
In the space between their breasts
you discover where each invests
all their wants and all their hopes
voices for a million Mopes;
you can read their primal curse
written in some simple verse.
Salt in coffee
sand in tea
these were never meant to be.
Was it this for which we planned,
Adam delved and Eve had spanned?

Note

Mope runs the Copy Center Service at Central Michigan University. On the day after Bush was elected in 1988, Mope wore the following tee shirt message:

When I was young
They told me anyone
Could be President.
They were right.

Reference

Young, T. R. (1983). Underground structures of the democratic state. *Mid-American Review of Sociology, 7*(2).

17

Black Men and Public Space

Brent Staples

My first victim was a woman—white, well dressed, probably in her early twenties. I came upon her late one evening on a deserted street in Hyde Park, a relatively affluent neighborhood in an otherwise mean, impoverished section of Chicago. As I swung onto the avenue behind her, there seemed to be a discreet, uninflammatory distance between us. Not so. She cast back a worried glance. To her, the youngish black man—a broad six feet two inches with a beard and billowing hair, both hands shoved into the pockets of a bulky military jacket—seemed menacingly close. After a few more quick glimpses, she picked up her pace and was soon running in earnest. Within seconds she disappeared into a cross street.

That was more than a decade ago. I was twenty-two years old, a graduate student newly arrived at the University of Chicago. It was in the echo of that terrified woman's footfalls that I first began to know the unwieldy inheritance I'd come into—the ability to alter public space in ugly ways. It was clear that she thought herself the quarry of a mugger, a rapist, or worse. Suffering a bout of insomnia, however, I was stalking sleep, not defenseless wayfarers. As a softy who is scarcely able to take a knife to a raw chicken—let alone hold on to a person's throat—I was surprised, embarrassed, and dismayed all at once. Her flight made me feel like an accomplice in tyranny. It also made it clear that I was indistinguishable from the muggers who occasionally seeped into the area from the surrounding ghetto. That first encounter, and those that followed, signified that a vast, unnerving gulf lay between nighttime pedestrians—particularly women—and me. And I soon gathered that being perceived as dangerous is a hazard in itself. I only needed to turn a corner into a dicey situation, or crowd some frightened, armed person in a foyer somewhere, or make an errant move after being pulled over by a policeman. Where fear and weapons meet—and they often do in urban America—there is always the possibility of death.

In that first year, my first away from my hometown, I was to become thoroughly familiar with the language of fear. At dark, shadowy intersections, I could cross in front of a car stopped at a traffic light and elicit the *thunk, thunk, thunk, thunk* of the driver—black, white, male, or female—hammering down the door locks. On less traveled streets after dark, I grew accustomed to but never comfortable with people crossing to the other side of the street rather than pass me. Then there were the standard unpleasantries with policemen, doormen, bouncers, cabdrivers, and others whose business it is to screen out troublesome individuals *before* there is any nastiness.

I moved to New York nearly two years ago and I have remained an avid night walker. In central Manhattan, the near-constant crowd cover minimizes tense one-on-one street encounters. Elsewhere—in SoHo, for example, where sidewalks are narrow and tightly spaced buildings shut out the sky—things can get very taut indeed.

After dark, on the warrenlike streets of Brooklyn where I live, I often see women who fear the worst from me. They seem to have set their faces on neutral, and with their purse straps strung across their chests bandolier-style, they forge ahead as though bracing themselves against being tackled. I understand, of course, that the danger they perceive is not a hallucination. Women are particularly vulnerable to street violence, and young black males are drastically over-represented among the perpetrators of that violence. Yet these truths are no solace against the kind of alienation that comes of being ever the suspect, a fearsome entity with whom pedestrians avoid making eye contact.

It is not altogether clear to me how I reached the ripe old age of twenty-two without being conscious of the lethality nighttime pedestrians attributed to me. Perhaps it was because in Chester, Pennsylvania, the small, angry industrial town where I came of age in the 1960s, I was scarcely noticeable against a backdrop of gang warfare, street knifings, and murders. I grew up one of the good boys, had perhaps a half-dozen fistfights. In retrospect, my shyness of combat has clear sources.

As a boy, I saw countless tough guys locked away; I have since buried several, too. They were babies, really—a teenage cousin, a brother of twenty-two, a childhood friend in his mid-twenties—all gone down in episodes of bravado played out in the streets. I came to doubt the virtues of intimidation early on. I chose, perhaps unconsciously, to remain a shadow—timid, but a survivor.

The fearsomeness mistakenly attributed to me in public places often has a perilous flavor. The most frightening of these confu-sions occurred in the late 1970s and early 1980s, when I worked as a journalist in Chicago. One day, rushing into the office of a magazine I was writing for with a deadline story in hand, I was mistaken for a burglar. The office manager called security and, with an ad hoc posse, pursued me through the labyrinthine halls, nearly to my editor's door. I had no way of proving who I was. I could only move briskly toward the company of someone who knew me.

Another time I was on assignment for a local paper and killing time before an interview. I entered a jewelry store on the city's affluent Near North Side. The proprietor excused herself and returned with an enor-mous red Doberman Pinscher straining at the end of a leash. She stood, the dog extended toward me, silent to my questions, her eyes bulging nearly out of her head. I took a cursory look around, nodded, and bade her good night.

Relatively speaking, however, I never fared as badly as another black male jour-nalist. He went to nearby Waukegan, Illi-nois, a couple of summers ago to work on a story about a murderer who was born there. Mistaking the reporter for the killer, police officers hauled him from his car at gunpoint and but for his press credentials would prob-ably have tried to book him. Such episodes are not uncommon. Black men trade tales like this all the time.

Over the years, I learned to smother the rage I felt at so often being taken for a criminal. Not to do so would surely have led to madness. I now take precautions to make myself less threatening. I move about with care, particularly late in the evening. I give a wide berth to nervous people on subway platforms during the wee hours, particularly when I have exchanged busi-ness clothes for jeans. If I happen to be entering a building behind some people who appear skittish, I may walk by, letting them clear the lobby before I return, so as not to seem to be following them. I have been calm and extremely congenial on those rare occasions when I've been pulled over by the police.

And on late-evening constitutionals I employ what has proved to be an excellent tension-reducing measure: I whistle melodies from Beethoven and Vivaldi and the more popular classical composers. Even steely New Yorkers hunching toward nighttime destinations seem to relax, and occasionally they even join in the tune. Virtually everybody seems to sense that a mugger wouldn't be warbling bright, sunny selections from Vivaldi's *Four Seasons*. It is my equivalent of the cowbell that hikers wear when they know they are in bear country.

18

Managing Feeling

Arlie Hochschild

He who always wears the mask of a friendly man must at last gain a power over friendliness of disposition, without which the expression itself of friendliness is not to be gained—and finally friendliness of disposition gains the ascendancy over him—he is benevolent.

(Nietzsche)

"Sincerity" is detrimental to one's job, until the rules of salesmanship and business become a "genuine" aspect of oneself.

(C. Wright Mills)

We all do a certain amount of acting. But we may act in two ways. In the first way, we try to change how we outwardly appear. As it is for the people observed by Erving Goffman, the action is in the body language, the put-on sneer, the posed shrug, the controlled sigh. This is surface acting.[1] The other way is deep acting. Here, display is a natural result of working on feeling; the actor does not try to *seem* happy or sad but rather expresses spontaneously, as the Russian director Constantin Stanislavski urged, a real feeling that has been self-induced. Stanislavski offers this illustration from his own experience:

At a party one evening in the house of friends, we were doing various stunts and they de-

cided, for a joke, to operate on me. Tables were carried in, one for operating, the other supposedly containing surgical instruments. Sheets were draped around; bandages, basins, various vessels were brought.

The "surgeons" put on white coats and I was dressed in a hospital gown. They laid me on the operating table and bandaged my eyes. What disturbed me was the extremely solicitous manner of the doctors. They treated me as if I were in a desperate condition and did everything with utmost seriousness. Suddenly the thought flashed through my mind, "What if they really should cut me open?!"

Now and then a large basin made a booming noise like the toll of a funeral bell.

"Let us begin!" someone whispered.

Someone took a firm hold on my right wrist. I felt a dull pain and then three sharp stabs. I couldn't help trembling. Something that was harsh and smarted was rubbed on my wrist. Then it was bandaged, people rustled around handing things to the surgeon.

Finally, after a long pause, they began to speak out loud, they laughed, congratulated me. My eyes were unbandaged and on my left arm lay a new-born baby made out of my right hand, all swaddled in gauze. On the back of my hand they had painted a silly, infantile face.[2]

The "patient" above is not pretending to be frightened at his "operation." He is not trying to fool others. He is really scared. Through deep acting he has managed to scare himself. Feelings do not erupt spontaneously or automatically in either deep acting or surface acting. In both cases the actor has learned to intervene—either in creating the inner shape of a feeling or in shaping the outward appearance of one.

In surface acting, the expression on my face or the posture of my body feels "put on." It is not "part of me." In deep acting, my conscious mental work—the effort to imagine a tall surgeon looming over me, for example—keeps the feeling that I conjure up from being part of "myself." Thus in either method, an actor may separate what it takes to act from the idea of a central self.

But whether the separation between "me" and my face or between "me" and my feeling counts as estrangement depends on something else—the outer context. In the world of the theater, it is an honorable art to make maximum use of the resources of memory and feeling in stage performance. In private life, the same resources can be used to advantage, though to a lesser extent. But when we enter the world of profit-and-loss statements, when the psychological costs of emotional labor are not acknowledged by the company, it is then that we look at these otherwise helpful separations of "me" from my face and my feeling as potentially estranging.

Surface Acting

To show through surface acting the feelings of a Hamlet or an Ophelia, the actor operates countless muscles that make up an outward gesture. The body, not the soul, is the main tool of the trade. The actor's body evokes passion in the *audience's* soul, but the actor is only *acting* as if he had feeling. Stanislavski, the originator of a different type of acting—called Method acting—illustrates surface acting in the course of disparaging it:

[The actor portrayed] an important general [who] accidentally found himself alone at home with nothing to do. Out of boredom he lined up all the chairs in the place so that they looked like soldiers on parade. Then he made neat piles of everything on all the tables. Next he thought of something rather spicy; after that he looked aghast over a pile of business correspondence. He signed several letters without reading them, yawned, stretched himself, and then began his silly activities all over again.

All the while [the actor] was giving the text of the soliloquy with extraordinary clarity; about the nobility of highly placed persons and the dense ignorance of everyone else. He did it in a cold, impersonal way, indicating the outer form of the scene without any attempt to put life or depth into it. In some places he rendered the text with technical crispness, in others he underscored his pose, gesture, play, or emphasized some special detail of his characterization. Meantime he was watching his public out of the corner of his eye to see whether what he was doing carried across.[3]

This is surface acting—the art of an eyebrow raised here, an upper lip tightened there. The actor does not really experience the world from an imperial viewpoint, but he works at seeming to. What is on the actor's mind? Not the chairs that he has commanded to line up at attention, but the audience, which is the nearest mirror to his own surface.

Stanislavski described the limitations of surface acting as follows:

This type of art (of the Coquelin school) is less profound than beautiful. It is more immediately effective than truly powerful; [its] form is more interesting than its content. It acts more on your sense of sound and sight than on your soul. Consequently it is more likely to delight than to move you. You can receive great impressions through this art. But they will neither warm your soul nor penetrate deeply into it. Their effect is sharp but not lasting. Your astonishment rather than your faith is aroused. Only what can be accomplished through surprising theatrical beauty or picturesque pathos lies within the bounds of this art. But delicate and deep human feelings are not subject to such technique. They call for natural emotions at the very moment in which they appear before you in the flesh. They call for the direct cooperation of nature itself.[4]

Deep Acting

There are two ways of doing deep acting. One is by directly exhorting feeling, the other by making indirect use of a trained imagination.[5] Only the second is true Method acting. But in either case, Stanislavski argued, the acting of passions grows out of living in them.

People sometimes talk as much about their *efforts* to feel (even if these efforts fail) as they do about having feelings.[6] When I asked students simply to describe an event in which they experienced a deep emotion, the responses were sprinkled with such phrases as "I psyched myself up, I squashed my anger down, I tried hard not to feel disappointed, I forced myself to have a good time, I mustered up some gratitude, I put a damper on my love for her, I snapped myself out of the depression."[7] In the flow of experience, there were occasional common but curious shades of will—will to evoke, will to suppress, and will to somehow allow a feeling, as in "I finally let myself feel sad about it."[8]

Sometimes there was only a social custom in mind—as when a person wished to feel sad at a funeral. But other times there was a desperate inner desire to avoid pain. Herbert Gold describes a man's effort to prevent himself from feeling love for a wife he no longer has:

He fought against love, he fought against grief, he fought against anger. They were all linked.

He reminded himself when touched, moved, overwhelmed by the sights and smell of her, or a sight and smell which recalled her, or passing their old house or eating their foods, or walking on their streets; don't do this, don't feel. First he succeeded in removing her from the struggle. . . . He lost his love. He lost his anger. She became a limited idea, like a newspaper death notice. He did not lose her entirely, but chipped away at it; don't, don't, don't, he would remind himself in the middle of the night; don't feel; and then dream what he could.[9]

These are almost like orders to a contrary horse (whoa, giddyup, steady now), attempts to exhort feeling as if feeling can listen when it is talked to.[10] And sometimes it does. But such coaching only addresses the capacity to duck a signal, to turn away from what evokes feeling.[11] It does not move to the home of the imagery, to that which gives power to a sight, a sound, or a smell. It does not involve the deeper work of retraining the imagination.

Ultimately, direct prods to feeling are not based on a deep look into how feeling works, and for this reason Stanislavski advised his actors against them: "On the stage there cannot be, under any circumstances, action which is directed immediately at the arousing of a feeling for its own sake. . . . Never seek to be jealous, or to make love, or to suffer for its own sake. All such feelings are the result of something that has gone before. Of the thing that goes before you should think as you can. As for the result, it will produce itself."[12]

Stanislavski's alternative to the direct prodding of feeling is Method acting. Not simply the body, or immediately accessible feeling, but the entire world of fantasy, of subconscious and semiconscious memory, is conceived as a precious resource.[13]

If he were in the hands of Stanislavski, the man who wanted to fight off love for his former wife would approach his task differently. First, he would use "emotion memory": he would remember all the times he had felt furious at his wife's thoughtlessness or cruelty. He would focus on one most exasperating instance of this, reevoking all the circumstances. Perhaps she had forgotten his birthday, had made no effort to remember, and failed to feel badly about it afterwards. Then he would use the "if" supposition and say to himself: "How would I feel about her if this is what she really was like?" He would not prompt himself not to feel love; rather he would keep alive the cruel episode of the forgotten birthday and sustain the "if." He would not, then, fall naturally out of love. He would actively conduct himself out of love through deep acting.

The professional actor simply carries this process further for an artistic purpose. His goal should be to accumulate a rich deposit of "emotion memories"—memories that recall feelings. Thus, Stanislavski explains, the actor must relearn how to remember:

> Two travelers were marooned on some rocks by high tide. After their rescue they narrated their impressions. One remembered every little thing he did; how, why, and where he went, where he climbed up and where he climbed down; where he jumped up or jumped down. The other man had no recollection of the place at all. He remembered only the emotions he felt. In succession came delight, apprehension, fear, hope, doubt, and finally panic.[14]

To store a wealth of emotion memories, the actor must remember experiences emotively. But to remember experiences emotively, he or she must first experience them in that way too, perhaps with an eye to using the feelings later.[15] So the conceiving of emotion memory as a noun, as something one *has*, brings with it a conceiving of memory and of spontaneous experience itself as also having the qualities of a usable, nounlike thing. Feeling—whether at the time, or as it is recalled, or as it is later evoked in acting—is an object. It may be a valuable object in a worthy pursuit, but it is an object nonetheless.

Some feelings are more valuable objects than others, for they are more richly associated with other memorable events; a terrifying train ride may recall a childhood fall or a nightmare. Stanislavski recalled, for example, seeing an old beggar killed by a trolley car but said that the memory of this event was less valuable to him as an actor than another one:

> It was long ago—I came upon an Italian, leaning over a dead monkey on the sidewalk. He was weeping and trying to push a bit of orange rind into the animal's mouth. It would seem that this scene had affected my feelings more than the death of the beggar. It was buried more deeply into my memory. I think that if I had to stage the street accident I would search for emotional material for my part in my memory of the scene of the Italian with the dead monkey rather than in the tragedy itself.[16]

But emotion memory is not enough. The memory, like any image drawn to mind, must *seem real now*. The actor must *believe* that an imagined happening *really is happening now*. To do this, the actor makes up an "as if," a supposition. He actively suspends the usual reality testing, as a child does at play, and allows a make-believe situation to seem real. Often the actor can manage only a precarious belief in *all* of an illusion, and so he breaks it up into sturdier small details, which taken one by one are easier to believe: "*if* I were in a terrible storm" is chopped up into "*if* my eyebrows were wet and *if* my shoes were soaked." The big *if* is broken into many little ones.[17]

The furnishings of the physical stage—a straight horsehair chair, a pointer leaning against the wall—are used to support the actor's *if*. Their purpose is not to influence the audience, as in surface acting, but to help convince the person doing deep acting that the *if* events are really happening.

Everyday Deep Acting

In our daily lives, offstage as it were, we also develop feeling for the parts we play;

and along with the workaday props of the kitchen table or office restroom mirror we also use deep acting, emotion memory, and the sense of "as if this were true" in the course of trying to feel what we sense we ought to feel or want to feel. Usually we give this little thought, and we don't name the momentary acts involved. Only when our feeling does not fit the situation, and when we sense this as a problem, do we turn our attention to the inward, imagined mirror, and ask whether we are or should be acting.

Consider, for example, the reaction of this young man to the unexpected news that a close friend had suffered a mental breakdown:

I was shocked, yet for some reason I didn't think my emotions accurately reflected the bad news. My roommate appeared much more shaken than I did. *I thought that I should be more upset by the news than I was.* Thinking about this conflict I realized that one reason for my emotional state might have been the spatial distance separating me from my friend, who was in the hospital hundreds of miles away. I then tried to focus on his state . . . and began to picture my friend as I thought he then existed.

Sensing himself to be less affected than he should be, he tried to visualize his friend— perhaps in gray pajamas, being led by impassive attendants to the electric-shock room. After bringing such a vivid picture to mind, he might have gone on to recall smaller private breakdowns in his own life and thereby evoked feelings of sorrow and empathy. Without at all thinking of this as acting, in complete privacy, without audience or stage, the young man can pay, in the currency of deep acting, his emotional respects to a friend.

Sometimes we try to stir up a feeling we wish we had, and at other times we try to block or weaken a feeling we wish we did not have. Consider this young woman's report of her attempt to keep feelings of love in check.

Last summer I was going with a guy often, and I began to feel very strongly about him. I knew, though, that he had broken up with a girl a year ago because she had gotten too serious about him, so I was afraid to show any emotion. I also was afraid of being hurt, so I attempted to change my feelings. *I talked myself into not caring about him . . .* but I must admit it didn't work for long. To sustain this feeling I had to *invent bad things about him and concentrate on them* or continue to tell myself he didn't care. It was a hardening of emotions, I'd say. It took a lot of work and was unpleasant because I had to concentrate on anything I could find that was irritating about him.

In this struggle she hit upon some techniques of deep acting. "To invent bad things about him and concentrate on them" is to make up a world she could honestly respond to. She could tell herself, "If he is self-absorbed, then he is unlovable, and *if* he is unlovable, which at the moment I believe, then I don't love him." Like Stanislavski during his make-believe "operation," she wavers between belief and doubt, but she nevertheless reaches for the inner token of feeling that it is her part to offer. She wavers between belief and doubt in her beloved's "flaws." But her temporary effort to prevent herself from falling in love may serve the grander purpose of waiting for him to reciprocate. So in a way, her act of momentary restraint, as she might see it, was an offering to the future of their love.

We also set a personal stage with personal props, not so much for its effect on our audience as for the help it gives us in believing in what we imagine. Serving almost as stage props, often, are fellow members of the cast—friends or acquaintances who prod our feelings in a desired direction. Thus, a young woman who was trying not to love a man used her supporting cast of friends like a Greek chorus: "I could only say horrible things about him. My friends thought he was horrible because of this and reinforced my feelings of dislike for him."

Sometimes the stage setting can be a dismayingly powerful determinant of feeling. Consider this young woman's description of her ambivalent feelings about a priest forty years her senior: "I started trying to make myself like him and fit the whole situation. When I was with him I did like him, but then I'd go home and write in my journal how much I couldn't stand him. I kept changing my feelings." What she felt while facing the priest amid the props of a living room and two cups of afternoon tea collapsed when she left that setting. At home with her diary, she felt free of her obligation to please her suitor by trying to like him. There, she felt another obligation—to be honest to her diary. What changed between the tea party and the diary session was her sense of which feeling was real. Her sense of realness seemed to shift disconcertingly with the stage setting, as if her feeling of liking the priest gained or lost its status as "real" depending on its context.

Sometimes the realness of a feeling wavers more through time. Once a love story is subject to doubt, the story is rewritten; falling in love comes to seem like the work of convincing each other that this had been true love. A nineteen-year-old Catholic college student recalled:

Since we both were somewhat in need of a close man-woman relationship and since we were thrown together so often (we lived next door to each other and it was summertime), I think that we convinced ourselves that we loved each other. I had to try to convince myself that I loved him in order to justify or somehow make "right" sleeping with him, which I never really wanted to do. We ended up living together supposedly because we "loved" each other. But I would say instead that we did it for other reasons which neither of us wanted to admit. What pretending that I loved him meant to me was having a secret nervous breakdown.

This double pretending—pretending to him and pretending to herself that she loved him—created two barriers to reflection and spontaneous feeling. First, she tried to feel herself in love—intimate, deeply enhanced, and exquisitely vulnerable—in the face of

contrary evidence. Second, she tried not to feel irritation, boredom, and a desire to leave. By this effort to orchestrate feeling—to keep some feelings above consciousness and some below, and to counter inner resistances on a daily basis—she tried to suppress reality testing. She both nurtured an illusion about her lover and doubted the truth of it. It was the strain of this effort that led to her "secret nervous breakdown."

In the theater, the illusion that the actor creates is recognized beforehand as an illusion by actor and audience alike. But in real life we more often participate in the illusion. We take it into ourselves, where it struggles against the sense we ordinarily make of things. In life, illusions are subtle, changeable, and hard to define with certainty, and they matter far more to our sanity.

The other side of the matter is to live with a dropped illusion and yet want to sustain it. Once an illusion is clearly defined as an illusion, it becomes a lie. The work of sustaining it then becomes redefined as lying to oneself so that one becomes self-stigmatized as a liar. This dilemma was described by a desperate wife and mother of two:

I am desperately trying to change my feelings of being trapped [in marriage] into feelings of wanting to remain with my husband voluntarily. Sometimes I think I'm succeeding—sometimes I know I haven't. *It means I have to lie to myself and know I am lying.* It means I don't like myself very much. It also makes me wonder whether or not I'm a bit of a masochist. I feel responsible for the children's future and for my husband's, and there's the old self-sacrificer syndrome. I know what I'm doing. I just don't know how long I can hold out.

On stage, the actress doing Method acting tries to delude herself; the more voluntary, the more richly detailed the lie, the better. No one thinks she actually *is* Ophelia or even pretending to be. She is borrowing Ophelia's reality or something from her own personal life that resembles it. She is trying to delude herself and create an illusion for the audience, who accept it as a gift. In everyday life there is also illusion, but how to define it is chronically unclear; the matter needs constant attention, continual questioning and testing. In acting, the illusion starts out as an illusion. In everyday life, that definition is always a possibility and never quite a certainty. On stage, the illusion leaves as it came, with the curtain. Off stage, the curtains close, too, but not at our bidding, not when we expect, and often to our dismay. On stage, illusion is a virtue. But in real life, the lie to oneself is a sign of human weakness, of bad faith. It is far more unsettling to discover that we have fooled ourselves than to discover that we have been fooling others.

This is because for the professional actor the illusion takes on meaning only in relation to a professional role whereas in real life the illusion takes on meaning with reference to living persons. When in private life we recognize an illusion we have held, we form a different relation to what we have thought of as our self. We come to distrust our sense of what is true, as we know it through feeling. And if our feelings have lied to us, they cannot be part of our good, trustworthy, "true" self. To put it another way, we may recognize that we distort reality, that we deny or suppress truths, but we rely on an observing ego to comment on these unconscious processes in us and to try to find out what is going on despite them.

At the same time, everyday life clearly requires us to do deep acting. We must dwell on what it is that we want to feel and on what we must do to induce the feeling. Consider, for example, this young man's efforts to counter an apathy he dreaded:

I was a star halfback in high school. [But in my senior year] before games I didn't feel the surge of adrenalin—in a word, I wasn't "psyched-up." This was due to emotional difficulties I was experiencing at the time, and still experi-

ence. Also, I had been an A student but my grades were dropping. Because in the past I had been a fanatical, emotional, intense player— a "hitter," recognized by coaches as a hard worker and a player with "desire"—this was very upsetting. I did everything I could to get myself "up." I tried to be outwardly rah-rah, I tried to get myself scared of my opponents— anything to get the adrenalin flowing. I tried to look nervous and intense before games, so at least the coaches wouldn't catch on . . . when actually I was mostly bored, or in any event, not "up." Before one game I remember wishing I was in the stands watching my cousin play for his school.

This young man felt a slipping sense of realness; he was clear that he felt "basically" bored, not "really" up. What also seemed real to him was the sense that he should feel driven to win and that he wanted to feel that way. What also felt real to him in hindsight was his effort to seem to the coaches like a "hitter" (surface acting) and his effort to make himself fearful of his opponents (deep acting).

As we look back at the past, we may alternate between two understandings of "what really happened." According to one, our feeling was genuine and spontaneous. According to the other, it seemed genuine and spontaneous, but in fact it was covertly managed. In doubt about which understanding will ultimately make sense, we are led to ask about our present feelings: "Am I acting now? How do I know?" One basic appeal of the theater is that the stage decides that question for us: we know for sure who is acting.

In sum, what distinguishes theater from life is not illusion, which both have, need, and use. What distinguishes them is the honor accorded to illusion, the ease in knowing when an illusion *is* an illusion, and the consequences of its use in making feeling. In the theater, the illusion dies when the curtain falls, as the audience knew it would. In private life, its consequences are unpredictable and possibly fateful: a love is killed, a suitor rejected, another hospital bed filled.

Institutional Emotion Management

The professional actress has a modest say over how the stage is assembled, the props selected, and the other characters positioned, as well as a say over her own presence in the play. This is also true in private life. In both cases the person is the *locus* of the acting process.

But something more operates when institutions are involved, for within institutions various elements of acting are taken away from the individual and replaced by institutional mechanisms. The locus of acting, of emotion management, moves up to the level of the institution. Many people and objects, arranged according to institutional rule and custom, together accomplish the act. Companies, prisons, schools, churches—institutions of virtually any sort—assume some of the functions of a director and alter the relation of actor to director. Officials in institutions believe they have done things right when they have established illusions that foster the desired feelings in workers, when they have placed parameters around a worker's emotion memories, a worker's use of the *as if*. It is not that workers are allowed to see and think as they like and required only to show feeling (surface acting) in institutionally approved ways. The matter would be simpler and less alarming if it stopped there. But it doesn't. Some institutions have become very sophisticated in the techniques of deep acting; they suggest how to imagine and thus how to feel.

As a farmer puts blinders on his workhorse to guide its vision forward, institutions manage how we feel.[18] One of the ways in which they do this is to prearrange what is available to the worker's view. A teaching hospital, for example, designs the stage for medical students facing their first autopsy. Seeing the eye of a dead person might call to mind a loved one or oneself; to see this organ coldly violated by a knife might lead a student to faint, or flee in horror, or quit medicine then and there. But this seldom happens. In their study of medical training, Lief and Fox report:

> The immaculate, brightly lit appearance of the operating room, and the serious professional behavior required, justify and facilitate a clinical and impersonal attitude toward death. Certain parts of the body are kept covered, particularly the face and genitalia, and the hands, which are so strongly connected with human, personal qualities, are never dissected. Once the vital organs have been taken out, the body is removed from the room, bringing the autopsy down to tissues, which are more easily depersonalized. The deft touch, skill, and professional attitude of the prosector makes the procedure neater and more bloodless than might otherwise be the case, and this increases intellectual interest and makes it possible to approach the whole thing scientifically rather than emotionally. Students appear to avoid talking about the autopsy, and when they do talk about it, the discussion is impersonal and stylized. Finally, whereas in laboratory dissection humor appears to be a widespread and effective emotional control device, it is absent in the autopsy room, perhaps because the death has been too recent and [humor] would appear too insensitive.[19]

Covering the corpse's face and genitalia, avoiding the hands, later removing the body, moving fast, using white uniforms, and talking in uniformed talk—these are customs designed to manage the human feeling that threatens order.[20]

Institutions arrange their front stages. They guide the way we see and what we are likely to feel spontaneously. Consider the inevitable institutional halls, especially those near the areas where people wait. Often in medical, academic, and corporate settings we find on the walls a row of photographs or oil paintings of persons in whom we should have full confidence. Consider Allen Wheelis's description of a waiting-room picture of a psychiatrist:

> With the crossed legs you claim repose, tranquility. . . . Everything is under control. With

the straight shoulders you say dignity, *status.* No matter what comes up, this guy has nothing to fear, is calmly certain of his worth and of his ability. With the head turned sharply to the left you indicate that someone is claiming his attention. No doubt hundreds of people would like this guy's attention. He was engrossed in his book, but now he's being interrupted. And what was he reading? *Playboy? Penthouse?* The funny papers? Oh, no; he's into something heavy. We can't see the title, but we know it's plenty important.... Usually it's Osler's *Principles and Practice of Medicine.* And the finger marking his place? Why, he's been at it so intently, so diligently, he's already halfway through. And the other hand, lying so lightly, so gracefully, on the book. That shows intelligence, experience, mastery. He's not scratching his head trying to figure out what the hell the author is getting at.... Anytime you knock on this guy's door, you'll find him just like that, dressed to the nines, tie up tight in his buttoned-down collar, freshly pressed jacket, deeply immersed in one of these heavy tomes.[21]

The professional's own office, of course, should be done up in a pleasant but impersonal decor, not too messy and colorful but not too cold and bare; it should reflect just the amount of professional warmth the doctor or lawyer or banker himself ought to show. Home is carefully distinguished from office, personal flair from professional expertise. This stage setting is intended to inspire our confidence that the service is, after all, worth paying a lot for.

Airlines seem to model "stage sets" on the living rooms seen on daytime television serials; the Muzak tunes, the TV and movie screens, and the smiling flight attendants serving drinks are all calculated to "make you feel at home." Even fellow passengers are considered part of the stage. At Delta Airlines, for example, flight attendants in training are advised that they can prevent the boarding of certain types of passengers— a passenger with "severe facial scars," for example. The instructor elaborated: "You know, the other passengers might be reminded of an airplane crash they had read

about." The bearer of a "severe facial scar," then, is not deemed a good prop. His or her effect on the emotion memory of other money-paying passengers might be all wrong.[22]

Sometimes props are less important than influential directors. Institutions authorize stage directors to coach the hired cast in deep acting. Buttressed with the authority of a high office or a specialized degree, the director may make suggestions that are often interpreted at lower levels as orders.

The director's role may be simple and direct, as in the case of a group of college students training to be clinicians in a camp for emotionally disturbed children, studied by Albert Cohen. These students, who composed the junior staff, did not know at first how they were supposed to feel or think about the wild behavior of the disturbed children. But in the director's chair sat the senior counselors, advising them on how to see the children: "They were expected to see the children as victims of uncontrollable impulses somehow related to their harsh and depriving backgrounds, and in need of enormous doses of kindliness and indulgence in order to break down their images of the adult world as hateful and hostile."[23]

They were also taught how to *feel* properly toward them: "The clinician must never respond in anger or with intent to punish, although he might sometimes have to restrain or even isolate children in order to prevent them from hurting themselves or one another. Above all, the staff were expected to be warm and loving and always to be governed by a 'clinical attitude.'"[24] To be warm and loving toward a child who kicks, screams, and insults you—a child whose problem is unlovability—requires emotion work. The art of it is passed down from senior to junior counselor, as in other settings it passes from judge to law clerk, professor to graduate student, boss to rising subordinate.

The professional worker will implicitly frown on certain uses of emotion memory. The senior counselor of disturbed children will not allow herself to think, "Tommy reminds me of the terrible brat I had to babysit when I was thirteen, and if he's like that I'll end up hating him." Instead, she will reconceive Tommy in another way: "Tommy is really like the other kid I used to babysit when I was fourteen. He was difficult but I got to like him, so I expect I'll get to like Tommy despite the way he pushes me away suspiciously."

A proper way to *experience* the child, not simply a proper way to seem to feel, was understood by everyone as part of the job. And Cohen reports that the young caretakers did admirably: "To an extraordinary degree they fulfilled these expectations, including, I am convinced, the expectation that they *feel* sympathy and tenderness and love toward their charges, despite their animal-like behavior. The speed with which these college students learned to behave in this way cannot be easily explained in terms of gradual learning through a slow process of 'internalization.' "[25]

In more circuitous ways, too, the formal rules that prop up an institution set limits to the emotional possibilities of all concerned. Consider, for example, the rules that guard access to information. Any institution with a bit of hierarchy in it must suppress democracy to some extent and thus must find ways to suppress envy and resentment at the bottom. Often this is done by enforcing a hierarchy of secrets. The customary rule of secrecy about pay is a case in point: those at the bottom are almost never allowed to know how much money those at the top get each month, nor, to the fullest extent, what privileges they enjoy. Also kept secret are deliberations that determine when and to what level an individual is likely to rise or fall within the organization. As one University of California administrative memorandum explained: "Letters concerning the disposition of tenure review cases will be kept confidential, in order that those involved not hold grudges or otherwise harbor resentment toward those unfavorably disposed in their case." In this situation, where the top depends upon being protected from the middle and the bottom—from "those involved" as the memo put it—leaks can cause panic.[26]

Finally, drugs of various sorts can be used to stimulate or depress mood, and companies are not above engineering their use. Just as the plow displaced manual labor, in some reported instances drug use seems to be displacing emotional labor. The labor that it takes to withstand stress and boredom on the job can be performed, some workers have found, by Darvon and Valium. Workers at the American Telephone and Telegraph Company, for example, found that nurses in its medical department gave out Valium, Darvon, codeine, and other drugs free and without prescription. There are a number of ways, some of them company-sponsored, to "have a nice day" on the job, as part of the job.[27]

An Instrumental Stance Toward Feeling

The stage actor makes the finding and expressing of feeling his main professional task. In Stanislavski's analogy, he seeks it with the dedication of a prospector for precious metal. He comes to see feeling as the object of painstaking internal mining, and when he finds it, he processes it like gold. In the context of the theater, this use of feeling is considered exciting and honorable. But what happens when deep and surface acting become part of a day's work, part of what we sell to an employer in return for a day's wage? What happens when our feelings are processed like raw ore?

In the Recurrent Training class for experienced flight attendants at Delta Airlines, I observed borrowings from all types of acting. These can be seen in the ways students answered when the instructor asked how they tried to stop feeling angry and resentful at passengers:

If I pretend I'm feeling really up, sometimes I actually get into it. The passenger responds to me as though I were friendly, and then more of me responds back [surface acting].

Sometimes I purposely take some deep breaths. I try to relax my neck muscles [deep acting with the body].

I may just talk to myself: "Watch it. Don't let him get to you. Don't let him get to you. Don't let him get to you." And I'll talk to my partner and she'll say the same thing to me. After a while, the anger goes away [deep acting, self-prompting].

I try to remember that if he's drinking too much, he's probably scared of flying. I think to myself, "He's like a little child." Really, that's what he is. And when I see him that way, I don't get mad that he's yelling at me. He's like a child yelling at me then [deep acting, Method acting].

Surface and deep acting in a commercial setting, unlike acting in a dramatic, private, or therapeutic context, make one's face and one's feelings take on the properties of a resource. But it is not a resource to be used for the purposes of art, as in drama, or for the purposes of self-discovery, as in therapy, or for the pursuit of fulfillment, as in everyday life. It is a resource to be used to make money. Outside of Stanislavski's parlor, out there in the American marketplace, the actor may wake up to find himself actually operated upon.

Notes

Epigraphs: F. W. Nietzsche (1874), cited in Gellhorn (1964); C. Wright Mills (1956), p. 183.

1. As suggested by Goffman's description of "Preedy" on the beach, in *The Presentation of Self in Everyday Life* (1959), surface acting is alive and well in Goffman's work. But the second method of acting, deep acting, is less apparent in his illustrations, and the theoretical statement about it is correspondingly weak. Goffman posits a self capable of surface acting, but not one capable of deep acting. . . .

2. Stanislavski (1948/1965), p. 268.

3. Stanislavski (1948/1965), p. 196.

4. Stanislavski (1948/1965), p. 22.

5. There is actually another distinguishable way of doing deep acting—by actively altering the body so as to change conscious feeling. This

surface-to-center approach differs from surface acting. Surface acting uses the body to *show* feeling. This type of deep acting uses the body to *inspire* feeling. In relaxing a grimace or unclenching a fist, we may actually make ourselves feel less angry (Stanislavski, 1948/1965, p. 93). This insight is sometimes used in bio-feedback therapy (see Brown, 1974, p. 50).

6. The direct method of cognitive emotion work is known not by the result (see Peto, 1968) but by the effort made to achieve the result. The result of any given act is hard enough to discern. But if we were to identify emotion work by its results, we would be in a peculiar bind. We might say that a "cooled-down anger" is the result of an effort to reduce anger. But then we would have to assume that we have some basis for knowing what the anger "would have been like" had the individual not been managing his anger. We are on theoretically safer ground if we define emotion management as a set of acts *addressed* to feeling. (On the nature of an act of will, as separate from its effect, see Jean Piaget in Campbell, 1976, p. 87.)

7. In each instance the individual indicates awareness of acting on a feeling. A passive stance toward feeling was reflected in other examples: "I found myself filled with pride," "My stomach did a trapeze act all by itself."

8. By definition, each method of emotion work is active, but just how active, varies. At the active end of the continuum we contort reality and grip our bodily processes as though gripping the steering wheel of a car. At the passive extreme we may simply perform an act upon an act—as in deliberately relaxing already existing controls or issuing permission to "let" ourselves feel sad. (For a discussion of active versus passive concentration in autogenic training, see Wolfgang Luthe, quoted in Pelletier, 1977, p. 237.) In addition we may "ride over" a feeling (such as a nagging sense of depression) in the attempt to feel cheerful. When we meet an inward resistance, we "put on" the cheer. When we meet no inward resistance, we amplify a feeling: we "put it out."

9. Gold (1979), p. 129.

10. It also presupposes an *aspiration* to feel. The man who fought against love wanted to feel the same about his former wife as he thought she felt about him; if he was a limited idea to her, he wanted her to be that for him. A courtly lover in twelfth-century France or a fourteen-year-old

American female rock fan might have been more disposed to aspire to one-sided love, to want it that way. Deep acting comes with its social stories about what we aspire to feel.

11. Stanislavski (1948/1965), p. 38. Indeed, an extra effort is required *not to focus* on the intent, the effort of trying to feel. The point, rather, is to focus on seeing the situation. Koriat, Melkman, Averill, & Lazarus (1972) illustrated this second approach in a laboratory experiment in which university students were shown films of simulated wood-chopping accidents. In one film a man lacerates the tips of his fingers; in another, a woodworker cuts off his middle finger; in a third, a worker dies after a plank of wood is thrust through his midsection by a circular saw. Subjects were instructed to detach themselves when first viewing the films and then, on another viewing, to involve themselves. To deintensify the effect of the films, the viewers tried to remind themselves that they were just films and often focused on technical aspects of production to reinforce this sense of unreality. Others tried to think of the workers in the films as being responsible for their own injuries through negligence. Such detachment techniques may be common in cases when people victimize others (see Latane & Darley, 1970). To intensify the films' effect, the viewers reported trying to imagine that the accidents were happening to them, or to someone they knew, or were similar to experiences they had had or had witnessed; some tried to think about and exaggerate the consequences of accidents. Koriat et al. conceive of these deintensifying or intensifying devices as aspects of appraisal that precede a "coping response." Such devices may also be seen as mental acts that adjust the "if supposition" and draw on the "emotional memory" described in Stanislavski (1948\1965).

12. Stanislavski (1948/1965), p. 57.

13. In *An Actor Prepares*, Stanislavski points out an apparent contradiction: "We are supposed to create under inspiration; only our subconscious gives us inspiration; yet we apparently can use this subconscious only through our consciousness, which kills it" (1948\1965, p. 13). The solution to this problem is the indirect method. The subconscious is induced. As Stanislavski notes: "The aim of the actor's preparation is to cross the threshold of the subconscious. . . . Beforehand we have 'true-seeming feeling,' afterwards 'sincer-

ity of emotion.' On this side of it, we have the simplicity of a limited fantasy; beyond, the simplicity of the larger imagination, [where] the creative process differs each time it is repeated" (p. 267).

14. Stanislavski (1948/1965), p. 163.

15. The mind acts as a magnet to reusable feeling. Stanislavski advises actors: "Imagine that you have received some insult in public, perhaps a slap in the face, that makes your cheek burn whenever you think of it. The inner shock was so great that it blotted out all the details of this harsh incident. But some insignificant thing will instantly revive the memory of the insult, and the emotion will recur with redoubled violence. Your cheek will grow red or you will turn pale and your heart will pound. If you possess such sharp and easily aroused emotional material, you will find it easy to transfer it to the stage and play a scene analogous to the experience you had in real life which left such a shocking impression on you. To do this you will not need any technique. It will play itself because nature will help you" (1948\1965, p. 176).

16. Stanislavski (1948/1965), p. 127.

17. Stanislavski once admonished his actors: "You do not get hold of this exercise because . . . you are anxious to believe all of the terrible things I put into the plot. But do not try to do it all at once; proceed bit by bit, helping yourselves along by small truths. If every little auxiliary act is executed truthfully, then the whole action will unfold rightly" (1948/1965, p. 126).

18. We commonly assume that institutions are called in when individual controls fail; those who cannot control their emotions are sent to mental hospitals, homes for disturbed children, or prisons. But in looking at the matter this way, we may ignore the fact that individual failures of control often signal a prior institutional failure to shape feeling. We might ask instead what sort of church, school, or family influence was unavailable to the parents of institutionalized patients, who presumably tried to make their children into adequate emotion managers.

19. Lief & Fox (1963) quoted in Lazarus (1975), p. 55.

20. Scientific writing, like scientific talk, has a function similar to that of covering the face and genitalia. It is an extension of institutional control over feeling. The overuse of passive verb forms, the avoidance of "I," the preference for Latinate nouns, and for the abstract over the

concrete, are customs that distance the reader from the topic and limit emotionality. In order to seem scientific, writers obey conventions that inhibit emotional involvement. There is a purpose in such "poor" writing.

21. Wheelis (1980), p. 7.

22. I heard the rationale for this company regulation discussed in class on February 19, 1980. (It was also stated in the training manual.) Whether it has ever been enforced, and with what result, I don't know.

23. Cohen (1966), p. 105.

24. Cohen (1966), p. 105.

25. Cohen (1966), p. 105.

26. The very way most institutions conduct the dirty work of firing, demotion, and punishment also assures that any *personal* blame aimed at those who fire, demote, and punish is not legitimized. It becomes illegitimate to interpret an "impersonal act" of firing as a personal act, as in "You did that to me, you bastard!" See Wolff (1950), pp. 345-378.

27. See R. Howard (1981).

References

Brown, B. (1974). *New mind, new body.* New York: Harper & Row.

Campbell, S. F. (Ed.). (1976). *Piaget sampler.* New York: John Wiley.

Cohen, A. (1966). *Deviance and control.* Englewood Cliffs, NJ: Prentice-Hall.

Gellhorn, E. (1964). Motion and emotion: The role of proprioception in the physiology and pathology of the emotions. *Psychological Review, 71,* 457-472.

Goffman, E. (1959). *The presentation of self in everyday life.* New York: Doubleday Anchor.

Gold, H. (1979). The smallest part. In W. Abrahams (Ed.), *Prize stories, 1979. The O'Henry award* (pp. 203-212). Garden City, NY: Doubleday.

Howard, R. (1981, August). Drugged, bugged, and coming unplugged. *Mother Jones.*

Koriat, A., Melkman, R., Averill, J. R., & Lazarus, R. (1972). The self-control of emotional reactions to a stressful film. *Journal of Personality, 40,* 601-619.

Latane, B., & Darley, J. (1970). *The unresponsive bystander.* New York: Appleton-Century-Crofts.

Lazarus, R. (1975). The self-regulation of emotion. In L. Levi (Ed.), *Emotions, their parameters and measurement* (pp. 47-67). New York: Raven.

Lief, H. I., & Fox, R. C. (1963). Training for a "detached concern" in medical studies. In H. I. Lief, V. F. Lief, & N. R. Lief (Eds.), *The psychological basis of medical practice* (pp. 12-35). New York: Harper & Row.

Mills, C. W. (1956). *White collar.* New York: Oxford University Press.

Nietzsche, F. W. (1876). *Menschliches alzumenschliches* (Vol. 1). Leipzig: Kroner.

Pelletier, K. (1977). *Mind as healer, mind as slayer: A holistic approach to preventing stress disorders.* New York: Delacorte.

Peto, A. (1968). On affect control. *International Journal of Psychoanalysis, 49*(Parts 2-3), 471-473.

Stanislavski, C. (1965). *An actor prepares* (E. R. Hapgood, Trans.). New York: Theatre Arts Books. (First published 1948)

Wheelis, A. (1980). *The scheme of things.* New York and London: Harcourt Brace Jovanovich.

Wolff, K. H. (1950). *The sociology of Georg Simmel.* New York: Free Press.

Sex and Power in Interaction: Conversational Privileges and Duties

Peter Kollock, Philip Blumstein, and *Pepper Schwartz*

This paper examines conversational behavior which previous research suggests is differentiated on the basis of sex. Interaction is conceptualized in terms of a sexual division of labor wherein men dominate conversation and women behave in a supportive manner. The literature raises the question of whether these differences in conversational patterns are tied to power as well as sex. A study was designed to determine which of a set of variables reflecting conversational duties and privileges are linked to power, to sex, or to both. The data were coded from interactions of intimate couples divided among those with both partners sharing power equally and those where one partner has more power. Three types of couples were compared: cross-sex, couples, male couples, and female couples. Interruptions and back channels are linked to power regardless of the sex of the actor, as are tag questions, although the rarity of their occurrence makes any conclusions tentative. The more powerful person interrupts his or her partner more and produces a lower rate of back channels and tag questions. Talking time and question asking seemed linked to both sex and power, though not in any simple way. The results of the analyses of minimal responses and overlaps proved inconclusive.

In recent years there has been a growing research interest in sex differences in speech (e.g., Thorne & Henley, 1975; Thorne, Kramer, & Henley, 1983). Conversational behavior, it was once argued, can be viewed as having a "male dialect" and a "female dialect"—(Kramer, 1974). More recent commentators feel that such a conceptualization exaggerates and at the same time oversimplifies the differences between men's and women's speech (Thorne et al., 1983, p. 14). However, neither these authors, nor any others, deny that there are significant sex differences in verbal interaction.

"Sex and Power in Interaction: Conversational Privileges and Duties" by P. Kollock, P. Blumstein, and P. Schwartz, 1985. *American Sociological Review, 50,* pp. 34-46. Copyright © 1985 by The American Sociological Association.

This research was supported in part by NSF grant SES-7617497 and a research assistantship to the first author from the Graduate School of the University of Washington. A draft of this paper was presented at the Annual Meeting of the American Sociological Association, San Antonio, 1984.

The authors are grateful to these colleagues for comments on an earlier draft of this paper: Nancy Durbin, Mary Rogers Gillmore, Laurie Russell Hatch, Judith A. Howard, Mary Savage Leber, Anne Martin, Barbara Risman, Donald Stull, and Toshio Yamagishi. We would also like to thank Sandra Hayashi for her work in coding the conversations.

As various sex differences were observed, some authors began to look at possible reasons for their existence and at their implications. Notably, some researchers (cf. Fishman, 1978; Thorne & Henley, 1975) felt that these differences were tied not solely to sex, but to power as well. In looking, for example, at differences in the amount of time spent talking, at terms of address, and at interruption patterns, the implication was that observed sex differences in language mirror the overall difference in power between men and women and that the way in which people communicate reflects and reinforces the hierarchical relationships that exist around them.

As intriguing or intuitively appealing as these questions may be, there have been few studies to test empirically what relationship power and sex have to the observed differences in men's and women's speech.

A Model of Turn Taking in Conversation

Our analysis of conversation is based on a model of turn taking derived from the work of Sacks, Schegloff, and Jefferson (1974) and of Zimmerman and West (1975) on the organization of verbal interaction. Conversation is organized to insure that one speaker talks at a time and that change of speakers occurs. A speaker's turn should not be thought of merely as the segments of time he or she speaks. Rather it is a concrete as well as symbolic platform on which an actor may accomplish his or her interactional goals and may also block the other person from effectively delivering a message. Speaking turns can have attached to them responsibilities, obligations, or privileges. Consequently, they may not be equally distributed and are often fought for. Much of the time the transition between turns occurs smoothly with little or no gap or overlap in the conversation. In order to accomplish this, a listener must anticipate when the end of a sentence will occur or infer when the speaker has finished a thought. The implication, then, is

that each person must work and continuously analyze the conversation in order to keep it going smoothly. Conversation involves both active "speakership" and active "listenership," the roles being continuously exchanged (Zimmerman & West, 1975, p. 108).

This model is more than an abstract representation of how conversation works. It also reflects the normative ordering of talk: these are the rules of turn taking, and speakers are constrained to respect and obey them—at least in their broadest strokes—or risk sanctions. It is important to recognize that there are implicit rules that govern "polite" or "proper" conversation and that a certain amount of work must necessarily be done by the participants if the interaction is to go smoothly. In looking at a conversation we may then ask which persons are respecting these implicit rules and which persons are violating or ignoring them. The rules of turn taking may not apply equally to all classes of actors. In most every society sex is a basis for allocating tasks, responsibilities, duties and privileges, and the empirical literature suggests that such a division between men and women exists in terms of duties and privileges in conversation (cf. Fishman, 1978).

Conversational Division of Labor

There are two major elements to the division of labor within verbal interaction: conversational dominance and conversational support. A conversation can be dominated by using a disproportionate amount of the available time as well as through the use of interruptions which serve to gain the floor. In addition, interruptions can be a sign of disregard toward the rules and etiquette of polite exchange as well as a projection on the speaker's part that he or she is worthy of more attention—has more of value to say and less to learn—than the other party.

With regard to the amount of time spent talking, the stereotype—as expressed in such folk expressions as the Scots' "Nothing is so unnatural as a talkative man or a quiet woman" (cited in Swacker, 1975)—is that women are more loquacious. A large body of research, however, indicates that men talk more than women do (Argyle, Lalljee, & Cook, 1968; Bernard, 1972; Hilpert, Kramer, & Clark, 1975; Kester, cited in Kramer, 1974; Marlatt, 1970; Rosenfeld, 1966; Soskin & John, 1963; Strodtbeck, 1951; Swacker, 1975).

Research on interruptions has generally shown that men interrupt women much more often than women interrupt men (Argyle et al., 1968; Eakins & Eakins, 1978; Kester, in Kramer, 1974; Natale, Entin, & Jaffe, 1979; Octigan & Niederman, 1979; Zimmerman & West, 1975). Zimmerman and West felt that the differences among cross-sex dyads were reflections of the power and dominance enjoyed by men in society, and in a subsequent study (West & Zimmerman, 1977) found the same sort of marked asymmetry in rates of interruptions among adult-child dyads, thereby giving further credence to the idea that the differences were tied to status. The notion that interruptions are a form of dominance is also supported in the work of Courtright, Millar, and Rogers-Millar (1979), Eakins and Eakins (1978), Rogers and Jones (1975), and West (1984).

The work of Sacks et al. (1974) on turn taking makes clear that some sort of work is necessary to insure smooth transitions between turns. Fishman (1978) expands on the idea of "interactional work":

> In a sense, every remark or turn at speaking should be seen as an attempt to interact. Some attempts succeed: others fail. For an attempt to succeed, the other party must be willing to do further interactional work. That other person has the power to turn an attempt into a conversation or to stop it dead. (p. 399)

In the literature on behaviors which help to keep the conversation going and which may serve to support the speaker, three types of speech element are central. These are the use of (1) questions, (2) tag questions, and (3) minimal responses. In her study of interactional work, Fishman (1978) found that women asked two and a half times as many questions as men. Questions, like greetings, evoke further conversation in that they require a response. The asking of questions supports the conversation by insuring minimal interaction. Fishman also found differences in the use of minimal responses. By a minimal response is meant such simple one- or two-word responses as "yeah," "uh huh," or "umm." Schegloff (1972) points out that one speaker will often intersperse minimal responses within another speaker's turn, not as a way of interrupting or invading the other's turn, but rather as a way of displaying interest and support for what the other person is saying. Minimal responses, however, can be used in various ways.

Fishman argues that males use them as lazy ways of filling a turn and as a way of showing a lack of interest (the woman may make a long statement touching on a variety of issues to which the man simply replies "uh-huh"). Among women, however, Fishman found that their most frequent use was as described by Schegloff: minimal responses were skillfully interspersed within the male's turn as a form of passive support. The insertion of these minimal responses in the other person's turn (sometimes called *back channels*) was usually done with great skill, making use of the slight gaps or pauses for breath that occurred, so as not to affect the flow of the other person's speech or interrupt the other in any way. Such timing demonstrates that the woman is paying very close attention to her partner's speech.

Lakoff (1975) also asserts that women ask more questions than men, and she additionally believes that they use tag questions much more often than men. A tag question is a hybrid between a question and an outright statement (e.g., "It's cold in here, isn't it?"), and can be a way of avoiding making strong statements. It does not force agreement with one's beliefs; it asks, rather, for confirmation of those beliefs. The use of tag questions implies the person somehow has less right to voice his or her opinions and less right to make a simple assertion in order to define the situation. They can also be used, much in the same manner as questions, as a way of encouraging conversation. In empirical investigations, Fishman (1980) and Eakins and Eakins (1978) found that women used tag questions more often than men. Other researchers, however, have found that tag questions were used more by men than by women (e.g., Dubois & Crouch, 1975; Lapadat & Seesahai, 1977).

Logic of the Study

In general, then, the literature suggests that men talk more, interrupt and overlap others more, and use minimal responses as a lazy way of filling a turn and showing a lack of interest. Women, on the other hand, seem to talk less, interrupt less, ask a greater number of questions and tag questions, and use minimal responses (back channels) as a way of supporting the other speaker. We see, then, a division of labor in which women nurture the conversation by working to keep it going and by obeying the rules implicit in polite interaction in order to make the transition and allocation of turns go smoothly, while men freely violate these rules without repercussions and further dominate the conversation by using a disproportionate amount of the time.

Previous research on the sexual division of labor in conversation has generally confounded the effects of sex and power. For us the question becomes: *Are the interactional privileges and duties linked to power to sex or to both?* Kramer (1974, p. 20) notes that "It would be interesting to see if female speech patterns once found in a variety of situations in which women are in the subordinate position are found in situations where a woman speaks from some base of power." One would, of course, also want to look at

such situations as two men in which one was more powerful and one was less, or a cross-sex dyad in which the woman was higher and the man was lower. In other words, we want to find a research setting in which sex and power can vary independently. This suggests a two-dimensional design with sex composition of the dyad being one dimension (*F-F* versus *M-F* versus *M-M*), and power within the dyad being the second dimension (*both speakers being equal* versus *power imbalanced*). A critical ingredient in the design would be the inclusion of cross-sex dyads in which the woman is the more powerful partner, as well as the more usual case where she is the less powerful.

Method

The cases to be used for this investigation are a subsample of a larger study on role differentiation (see Blumstein & Schwartz, 1983). The larger study compares the nature of interpersonal relations in four types of couples who live together—heterosexual married couples, heterosexual unmarried cohabitors, male homosexual couples, and lesbian couples. The study was conceived to use the same-sex couples as naturally occurring comparison groups in order to examine the ways in which role differentiation based on sex affects couples.

It might be argued that male and female homosexuals are not a relevant comparison to heterosexual married and cohabiting couples. Perhaps it is true that two factors, at least—the effects of living a stigmatized life and the putative socialization antecedents in the development of a homosexual identity—have created homosexual men and women who are very different from heterosexuals and who therefore cannot provide generalizable insights into male and female sex roles. However, both our own research (Blumstein & Schwartz, 1983) and other recent studies on male and female homosexuality have emphasized the continuities of behavior and attitudes within sexes and across sexual-orientation categories (Bell, Weinberg, & Hammersmith, 1981; Gagnon & Simon, 1973; Symons, 1979). These continuities reflect the potency of the norms governing the acquisition and maintenance of sex roles.

Ultimately, the comparability of heterosexuals with homosexual men and women is not critical to the argument of this paper. In same-sex couples, sex is not a marker of internal differentiation around which to organize variations in conversational behavior. If power differentials in these same-sex pairs are observed to covary with conversational support and dominance, then it is reasonable to rule out sex as the *sole* source of the division of labor in interaction. Attention can then be turned to the broader question of how structural properties of groups affect conversation.

All of the couples in the study were living together in intimate relationships. This provides a response to a criticism sometimes leveled at research on conversation, that the data come from "unnatural" sources For example, Hirshman (cited in Thorne & Henley, 1975, p. 248), in a study which generated inconclusive results, argued that the awkwardness of the setting in which the subjects found themselves (two males and two females, all previously unacquainted, interacting in a laboratory setting) led to conversation that was strained, generally very polite, and somewhat unnatural. Parks (1978) voiced a similar concern when he questioned the validity of research that has employed zero-history, ad hoc experimental groups. These critics imply that it would be desirable, in choosing dyads for study, to use couples who are involved in ongoing relationships and to record their conversations in a natural and familiar setting.

The present research involved a detailed questionnaire, a version of which was completed independently by each partner in the couple, and which dealt with a large number of topics concerning the division of labor within the relationship, power and influence,

satisfaction, etc. (see Blumstein & Schwartz, 1983, pp. 603-643).[1] The questionnaire was also used to provide stratification criteria for selecting a subsample of couples to be interviewed in depth in their homes.

The interview sample was drawn largely from three different locales within a one-hour driving radius of Seattle, San Francisco, or New York.[2] The questionnaire subsamples fitting these geographical constraints were stratified on two variables: *duration of the relationship* (3 levels); and *socioeconomic status* (3 levels), as measured by educational data on each partner.[3] It was also attempted informally to maximize the diversity of several other criteria within each stratum (i.e., age, number of prior relationships. presence of children, etc.). Within each *duration* by *class level* cell, couples were chosen at random, with approximately 100 couples of each of three types (*F-F, M-F, M-M*) ultimately selected to be interviewed.[4]

The interviews were generally carried out by male/female teams in the homes of the subjects and were designed to probe the nature, history, and day-to-day functioning of the relationship. In part of the interview the couple was given several conflict situations to resolve (modifications of role scenes suggested by Raush, Barry, Hertel, & Swain, 1974). Each person in the couple read five short stories dealing with such problems as a member of a couple refusing to go to a party or spending a large amount of time on a hobby. The two people read slightly differently slanted versions of the same basic stories. The essential facts were the same, but the points of view varied regarding which of the actors was more in the wrong. As each person read the stories he or she was asked to mark on a separate sheet which character he or she felt was more justified. The couple was then brought together with their answer sheets (but without the stories) and were asked *as a couple* to decide which character in each story was more justified and what would be the best means of resolving the conflict. This conversation between the couple occurred *in the absence of the interviewers* and was tape recorded. The data presented below are derived from the recordings of these conversations.

From this population of interviewed couples a subsample was selected on the basis of the power dynamics in the relationship in order to fill the two-dimensional design discussed above.

Power was operationalized by constructing a scale composed of eight items from the original questionnaire. The items were selected from a group of questions which asked who in the relationship had more influence with regards to particular decisions concerning their day-to-day life (i.e., where to go on vacation, when to go out to eat, etc.).[5]

Based on the power scale, all of the interviewed couples were categorized as either power-balanced or power-imbalanced and the cross-sex imbalanced couples were further subdivided into couples in which the male has greater power and couples in which the female is the more powerful member. From each category, five couples were chosen to fill the cells in the design, for a total *N* of 35 couples. In the case of the power-imbalanced couples the two members had to agree as to who had more influence and who had less.

Analysis of the Conversation

Based on the literature and the previous discussion, data were gathered from each conversation on the following items for each person:

1. Total number of seconds spent talking.
2. Number of overlaps. It is important to distinguish between overlaps and interruptions. Using Zimmerman and West's criteria (1975), overlaps are those instances of simultaneous speech which occur at or very close to a legitimate transition place or ending point in the present speaker's turn, for example:[6]

Female 73372: . . . there would have been no half-hour lateness, and there would have been no prob-[lem.]

Male 73371: [I] don't figure a half hour is worth arguing over.

In contrast, interruptions are a deeper intrusion into the current speaker's turn.

3. Number of interruptions (and whether or not they were successful). In a successful interruption, the first speaker stops talking (cedes control of the floor), allowing the second speaker to communicate a complete message. For example:

Female 73372: If he went to a party with Cindy, [which]

Male 73371: [Well,] that's not what the question said.

An unsuccessful interruption occurs when the first speaker refuses to cede control of the floor and continues to talk in order to complete his or her message despite the attempt of the second speaker to interrupt. For instance:

Male 10441: If you're late on purpose, or [out of your own]

Male 10442: [It seemed to me]

Male 10441: neglect, then that's one answer.

4. Number of minimal responses used as a turn. These are generally simple one- or two-word responses, argued by Fishman (1978) to be a lazy means used to fulfill the requirement of a spoken turn. For example:

Male 10442: I think Carl should have the right to talk to somebody else about a relationship.

Male 10441: Mm hmm.

Male 10442: Especially if it's in a way of trying to understand it.

5. Number of back channels. Superficially, back channels resemble minimal responses used as a turn. Both are the "uh-huh's" which punctuate conversation. But unlike the latter, which denote laziness on the speaker's part, the use of back channels

serves as a sign of the listener's encouragement and support. The capacity to intersperse interested feedback into the uninterrupted flow of the other's speech reflects both conversational skill and a willingness to engage in "interactive work." For instance:

Male 10172: I think Larry is more justified. It [sounded like]
Male 10171: [Yeah, right]
Male 10172: really several nights a week [and] a weekend.
Male 10171: [Sure]

6. Number of questions.
7. Number of tag questions:

Male 10171: On the first one, I think Al is justified about Bill's lateness, *don't you?*

Simply looking at the number of questions or interruptions that someone utters would be misleading; a person may ask a greater number of questions than his or her partner simply because he or she talked for a greater amount of time. The variables have therefore been adjusted so as to control for a speaker's talking time. The number of questions asked, for example, is divided by the person's talking time in seconds and multiplied by 900, yielding a figure indicating the number of questions asked per quarter hour. What are examined in this study, therefore, are *rates* of interruptions, overlaps, questions, tag questions, minimal responses and back channels.[7]

Data Analysis

Since the behavior of an individual within a couple is not independent of his or her partner's behavior, the couple must be treated as the unit of analysis. This fact, combined with the fact that the study does not involve a balanced factorial design, suggests several strategies for analysis. While none is, in itself, a perfect solution, they are used together with the belief that collectively they converge on an optimal,

yet conservative way of approaching the hypothesis-testing problem.[8]

Three different types of analysis of variance were performed. The first (Type 1) involves a 3 by 2 design, with *sex composition* being one dimension (*M-M, M-F, F-F*) and *power balance* within the couple being the second dimension (*equal* versus *unequal*). Type 1 analyses treat as dependent variables the means of the two individuals within each couple for each element of conversation. For example, a Type 1 analysis can compare equal with unequal couples in the number of interruptions within the conversation, or it can compare the three different sex compositions in terms of overall loquaciousness. It should be noted that for Type 1 analyses, in the power-imbalanced cross-sex couples the distinction is obscured as to whether it is the male or the female who has the greater power. Consequently, while these analyses may show, for example, whether cross-sex couples display very high rates of asking questions, they cannot tell whether it is the more powerful or less powerful partner (or alternately, male or female) who is asking the greater number of questions. This problem leads to two other kinds of analysis.

Type 2 and Type 3 analyses involve repeated-measures designs using the couple as the unit of analysis, but where each partner within the couple is viewed as a unit of observation. These analyses only make sense when looking at couples which are in some way internally differentiated, be it by sex (*male* versus *female*) or by power (*more* versus *less* powerful). Type 2 analyses look at the *effects of sex* within the couple, making use of *the cross-sex couples only*. The couples were classified into three possible types (*power-balanced; imbalanced, with the male more powerful*; and *imbalanced, with the female more powerful*), yielding a 3 by 2 design with sex (*male* versus *female*) as the repeated measure. Type 2 analyses allow one to look at the effects among the cross-sex couples of power balance/imbalance, sex, and the position one holds in an unequal relationship. One can see, for example, how couples in which the female has greater power than the male differ from couples in which the reverse is true.

The final analyses (Type 3) look at the *effects of a person's position of power* in the relationship and thus deal only with the *power-imbalanced couples,* yielding a 3 by 2 design examining male couples, female couples, and cross-sex couples and using a person's position of power (*more powerful* versus *less powerful*) as the repeated measure.[9]

Results

Talking Time

Is loquaciousness associated with sex or with power or both? The pattern in the data is not totally consistent, but there is some evidence that talking time is greater for men and for the more powerful partner. A Type 2 analysis of variance yields a near significant main effect for sex ($F(1,12) = 3.2$; $p < .10$). The sex difference varies depending on the power dynamics of the couple. Looking first at the traditional pattern (where the man is more powerful), we find that men do speak substantially more than women (see Table 19.1).

Table 19.1
Mean Talking Time in Seconds (Cross-Sex Couples)

	Males	Females	Group Mean
Balanced couples	292	286	289
Couples with male more powerful	385	330	358
Couples with female more powerful	465	373	419
Group Mean	381	330	

NOTE: N = 5 people per cell.

However, in the power-balanced couples, there is no appreciable difference in loquaciousness between men and women.

Before we hypothesize that it is power rather than sex which accounts for the apparent sex difference in the couples where the man is more powerful, we should note the very large sex difference among the "role-reversed" couples (female more powerful). While the females in these couples are more talkative than their counterparts in traditional couples, their male partners are more talkative than anyone else in the study.

The striking tendency of these lower-power males to talk a great deal does not generalize to the male couples. For them, the more powerful partner is somewhat more loquacious than the less powerful (mean talking times of 245 versus 210 seconds). Indeed these couples cast serious doubt on the notion of males being generally more talkative, since among power-imbalanced couples, male couples have lower rates than female or cross-sex couples (mean for male couples: 228 seconds; female couples: 300 seconds; cross-sex couples: 389 seconds).

The female couples illustrate that pure power dynamics can affect loquaciousness. The more powerful partner talks more (mean of 333 seconds) than the less powerful (mean of 267). The talking time of power-balanced female couples falls in between (mean of 304 seconds).

Interruptions and Overlaps

The number of interruptions is clearly tied to power in cross-sex couples. The means in Table 19.2 reflect a significant sex by power-composition interaction effect ($F(2,12) = 6.6$; $p < .01$). There is no sex difference in the power-balanced couples, but partners greater in power—male or female—interrupt a great deal more than weaker partners. Interruptions are clearly a sign of conversational dominance. However, not all interruptions are successful (fewer than 50 percent in our data). In other words, in more than half the observed cases the interrupted party did not yield the floor. Perhaps, then, it is better to think of interruptions as *attempts* at conversational control. Successful interruptions, then, become a more sensitive measure of *actual* dominance. A Type 2 analysis of variance on rates of successful interruptions yielded a pattern of means very similar to those in Table 19.2 (interaction effect $F(2,12) = 8.3; p < .01$).

Table 19.2
Mean Number of Interruptions per Quarter Hour (Cross-Sex Couples)

	Males	Females	Group Mean
Balanced couples	17.6	17.4	17.5
Couples with male more powerful	23.5	13.6	18.5
Couples with female more powerful	14.7	24.7	19.7
Group Mean	18.6	18.6	

NOTE: $N = 5$ people per cell.

The question remains as to whether the relationship between power and successful interruptions occurs solely in cross-sex couples. Table 19.3 shows that same-sex couples experience the same dynamics. There is a significant power-position main effect ($F(1,17) = 7.2; p < .02$).

Table 19.3
Mean Number of Successful Interruptions per Quarter Hour (Power-Imbalanced Couples)

	More Powerful Partner	Less Powerful Partner	Group Mean
Male couples	5.7	3.1	4.4
	(5)	(5)	
Female couples	10.6	6.8	8.7
	(5)	(5)	
Cross-sex couples	14.9	4.5	9.7
	(10)	(10)	
Group Mean	11.5	4.7	

NOTE: Number of persons appears in parentheses.

We have shown that in cross-sex couples interruptions are a function of power posi-tion, rather than sex. Since most married couples are of the traditional (male more powerful) variety (see, e.g., Blood & Wolfe, 1960; Blumstein & Schwartz, 1983), then it is obvious that husbands would generally be observed to interrupt more often. However, before we conclude that, ceteris paribus, men and women are equally likely to interrupt, we should consider the same-sex dyads. The data show that male couples produce significantly fewer successful interruptions than cross-sex or female couples (a male couple mean of 4.3 versus 9.8 for females and 9.7 for cross-sex couples; $F(2,29) = 3.4; p < .05$). This male pattern, however, reflects different dynamics in the power-balanced as compared to power-imbalanced couples. In the equal couples, there are few successful interruptions because there are simply few interruptions of any sort (4.2 successful out of 10.1 on average). In the power-imbalanced couples, the ratio of successful to unsuccessful interruptions is strikingly low (4.4. successful out of a total of 20.4).

Zimmerman and West (1975) reported strong sex-linked differences for overlaps as well as interruptions. Our data do not offer support for this assertion. There was no significant sex effect within the cross-sex couples (male mean of 13.7 and female mean of 12.1). We also found no effect of power position in the imbalanced couples, no matter what the sex composition. The only suggestion of any kind of sex difference occurs among the power-balanced couples, where male couples show *fewer* overlaps than female or cross-sex couples, which is contrary to Zimmerman and West's (1975) findings (a male couple mean of 7.2, as compared to 16.4 for female couples and 14.6 for cross-sex couples).

Minimal Responses Used as a Turn

As might be expected, male couples averaged higher rates of minimal responses than female or cross-sex couples (means of 21.2 versus 13.2 and 14.1, respectively). The difference, however, is not significant, and in general the analyses were inconclusive, yielding no significant results. In the analysis of different power arrangements in cross-sex couples, as well as the analysis comparing more powerful and less powerful partners in the three kinds of couples, we discovered no consistent or statistically reliable patterns.

Back Channels

Table 19.4 shows the rates of back channels among cross-sex couples. In power-imbalanced couples, it appears that it is the less powerful person who exhibits the higher rates. A repeated-measures analysis of variance involving the imbalanced cross-sex couples yields no significant effect for sex or for the interaction of sex and position. Owing to the small number of cases involved, the position effect only approaches statistical significance ($F(1,8) = 2.3$; $p < .16$).

Table 19.4

Mean Number of Back Channels per Quarter Hour (Cross-Sex Couples)

	Males	Females	Group Mean
Balanced couples	15.6	11.9	13.7
Couples with male more powerful	5.9	18.1	12.0
Couples with female more powerful	17.1	2.0	9.5
Group Mean	12.8	10.6	

NOTE: $N = 5$ people per cell.

This power difference is also found in the female couples (means of 6.7 for the less powerful partner and 3.0 for the more powerful). However, we should note that in power-balanced female couples there is a much higher rate of back channels (mean of 15.9). The male couples offer a very different picture from the others: the *more* powerful partner exhibits far more back channels than the less powerful (means of 13.9 versus 6.0).

Questions and Tag Questions

We find a consistent sex difference in question asking, with males outdistancing females. Table 19.5 shows the means among the cross-sex couples (sex main effect $F(1,12) = 10.2$; $p < .01$). The sex difference also appears when we compare male and female power-imbalanced couples (a male mean of 29.8 versus a female mean of 16.6: the cross-sex mean is 14.3: the sex composition main effect from analysis Type 3 is significant: $F(2,17) = 7.2$; $p < .01$).

In addition to the sex effects, position of power makes a difference in male couples

Table 19.5

Mean Number of Questions per Quarter Hour (Cross-Sex Couples)

	Males	Females	Group Mean
Balanced couples	29.5	23.0	26.2
Couples with male more powerful	22.0	7.2	14.6
Couples with female more powerful	18.9	9.1	14.0
Group Mean	23.5	13.1	

NOTE: $N = 5$ people per cell.

and to a lesser degree in cross-sex couples. The more powerful partner in male couples asks substantially more questions (39.3 versus 20.3), and the same is true in cross-sex couples (15.6 versus 13.1). There is no difference in the female couples. The tabulation of questions did not include tag questions such as, "It's a nice day, isn't it?" These can be seen as a timid way of proffering a definition of the situation. Consistent with this characterization, we find that in cross-sex couples, the less powerful partner uses more tag questions, whether a man or a woman (see Table 19.6; a repeated-measures analysis of variance involving the imbalanced cross-sex couples yields a near significant power-position main effect; $F(1,8) = 3.9$; $p < .08$).

Table 19.6
Mean Number of Tag Questions per Quarter
Hour (Cross-Sex Couples)

	Male	Female	Group Mean
Balanced couples	1.0	1.7	1.4
Couples with male more powerful	1.3	2.7	2.0
Couples with female more powerful	3.3	0.3	1.8
Group Mean	1.9	1.6	

NOTE: N = 5 people per cell.

There is a slight tendency among female couples for the less powerful partner to ask more tag questions. However, these couples have so few tag questions that this finding is not statistically reliable (means of 1.0 versus 0.0). The male couples, yet again, show a different pattern, with the *more* powerful partner posing many more tag questions (5.1 versus 0.0).

It should be noted that in each of the last three variables—back channels, questions, and tag questions—the occupant of the less powerful position among male couples averaged very low rates, although the variables were linked, according to the literature, to conversational submissiveness.

Discussion

It is clear from the literature that men and women play different roles in conversation, even though there is not perfect agreement on all of the details. Men play a domi- nant role, controlling the interaction and frequently violating rules of polite turn taking. Women are more submissive, seeking permission to speak, and taking more responsibility for encouraging and supporting other speakers. This study was designed to "unconfound" two possible causes of these sex differences. Is it in the nature of individual men and women consistently to perform these different roles together, or is it the general power imbalance of male-female relationships which promotes different conversational responsibilities and privileges?

Our findings show that power dynamics by themselves can create a conversational division of labor parallel to the one ordinarily associated with sexual differentiation. One source of findings is couples who do not have sex as a basis for internal differentiation. We found in same-sex couples two clear areas of conversational dominance: In male couples and in female couples the more powerful partner far outdistances the other in successful interruptions. Additionally, in these couples, the more powerful partner tends to monopolize the conversation. Turning to conversational support, we found that in female couples the less powerful partner exhibits twice the rate of back channels; she also asks more tag questions.

The male couples provide exceptions when we consider two variables that have been linked to conversational support in the literature. The less powerful partner in these couples actually has lower rates of back channels and tag questions. This suggests that these men are unwilling to assume the responsibilities for conversational support. They fail to dominate the conversation and may as a consequence become alienated from the interaction. There is some evidence from the larger study that the role of the less powerful is not a comfortable one in male couples. For example, when such couples break up, it is the less powerful partner, the one who is less well educated, is less forceful and aggressive, or has a lower income, who is more inclined to want to leave (Blumstein & Schwartz, 1983, p. 317). In conversation, the more powerful partner, perhaps sensing the other's alienation, compensates with the kind of supportive devices aimed at drawing him into the conversation and restoring his sense of being a valid contributor. The more powerful partner is made uncomfortable by the inequality of status in a relationship that is "supposed to be" one of status equals. At the same time he is in a superior position and therefore can do what he wants to try to restore balance. In the following example, partner 10172 is the less powerful and partner 10171 the more powerful:

Male 10172:   Bill wanted to go on from there and have a pleasant evening. [It's hard] to know. I mean not
Male 10171:   [Mm hm]
Male 10172:   knowing what the past pattern is [and] everything, I mean
Male 10171:   [Right]
Male 10172:   it's very hard [to]
Male 10171:   [My] sense is that Al just . . .

Note that while the more powerful partner allows the less powerful to dominate the floor and encourages him by the use of back channels, he also chooses to interrupt and is successful in doing so. The use of back channels is a low-cost device to foster the impression of interactive equality because it clearly does not require the ceding of control. To take on a supportive role in conversation can acknowledge or endorse one's inferior identity. In a relationship between two men, the less powerful partner may reject such a symbolic acknowledgment, while the more powerful partner can take the identity upon himself as a means of restoring a feeling of parity.

Why then do we not find a similar pattern among cross-sex couples? The tenacity of traditional sex roles may be one reason for its absence in couples where the man is the more powerful. Perhaps women have not traditionally expressed sufficient alienation at their subordinate role in conversation to cause men to develop devices to draw them in and underscore their role as participants. Perhaps men have made the costs for doing so too high. Among the role-reversed couples we do not find evidence of male alienation from interaction. Indeed, in addition to high rates of back channels and tag questions, these men demonstrate their involvement with very high rates of

talk. We return to the anomaly of these less powerful males below.

Another contradiction of our hypotheses can be found in the same-sex couples' use of questions. Fishman (1978) argued that women ask more questions as part of the work they do to sustain interaction. One would expect among the same-sex couples, where sex does not serve as a marker, that the less powerful partner would ask more questions. However, we find that in female couples there are no differences, and among male couples we find a pattern similar to that with back channels and tag questions, i.e., the more powerful partner exhibits higher rates. This anomaly deserves further comment, and so we will return to the issue of questions and their function in conversation.

Our findings from *cross-sex* couples also support the notion that power dynamics establish a conversational division of labor. Those coming from the traditional male-dominant couples cannot be used to contrast a power argument with a sex argument. However, our results from couples with equal power and from role-reversed couples (female more powerful) allow us to unconfound sex and power.

Interruptions are a critical measure of conversational dominance. In cross-sex couples, the more powerful partner, *irrespective of sex* exhibits significantly higher rates. Within the couples of equal power, the rates of interruptions are virtually identical.

Another measure reflecting conversational dominance—talking time—provides only partial support for the power argument. In traditional cross-sex couples, the more powerful partner is more loquacious, but since this is the male partner, we cannot disentangle sex and power. However, when we look at the cross-sex couples of *equal* power, we see that males and females are very similar. These findings cast doubt on an interpretation based on sex. Turning to the role-reversed couples, the female talks more than her counterpart in traditional couples. However, the less powerful males are extremely talkative, more so than any other group in the study. These last results support a sex argument over a power argument, unless we were to consider an idiosyncratic explanation of the extreme behavior of the less powerful men. For them, loquaciousness may be a response to role reversal. Other findings from the larger data set suggest that men are generally uncomfortable with role reversal in such realms as sexuality and income (Blumstein & Schwartz, 1983). Perhaps this discomfort takes the form of increased loquaciousness. These men may feel it necessary to call attention to themselves as participants in the interaction, and to remind their partners that it is a dialogue. It is interesting that this is the only measure where these men attempt to command the floor. By way of contrast, they tend not to interrupt their partners, and when they do they are generally unsuccessful. Interruptions are a high-risk interpersonal device setting up the possibility of sanctions for the breach of polite discourse. Speakers with little power are much more likely to incur such sanctions, and so the less powerful males choose a safer route to a "conversational presence," namely, talkativeness. Indirect evidence that these men are reacting to a situation of role reversal lies in the fact that their less powerful counterparts in male couples (where there is no such thing as role reversal) are *less* talkative than their partners.

In the case of supportive behavior, the findings from the cross-sex couples are consistent with a power interpretation. Regardless of sex, the less powerful partner displays a higher rate of back channels and tag questions.

Taken as a whole, the findings we have just summarized go a long way toward the conclusion that it is the power dynamics of male-female relationships which account for the division of labor in conversation. The question still remains whether there are observable sex differences *over and above* those attributable to relative power. Three kinds of findings can be brought to bear: sex differences among cross-sex couples of equal power; sex differences consistent with prediction from the literature found among role-reversed cross-sex couples; and differences between male couples and female couples. With respect to both conversational dominance and support, we have no sex differences in equal-power couples. Turning to role-reversed couples, we found that men are much more loquacious than women and they ask more questions.[10]

In comparing male and female same-sex couples, only one finding supports a sex-based prediction. Members of male couples, no matter what their power position, have higher rates of minimal responses than their counterparts in female couples. This lazy way of filling a turn seems not to be a prerequisite of the more powerful person, but rather a type of male privilege. Among same-sex couples, two of our findings are the opposite of the predicted sex pattern: Among unequal couples, males are *less* talkative than women. Additionally, men ask notably more questions, particularly when they are in the more powerful position.[11]

The findings most difficult to interpret involve the variable, *questions*. It is undeniably true—as Fishman (1978) argued—that one function of questions is to sustain conversation. However, it is important to take into consideration all of the other ways questions can fit into a conversational division of labor. A task leader asking for expert input is certainly a different kind of act than an expressive leader asking a participant if he or she was hurt by a criticism. In our data, questions are more common among males and among more powerful partners. This suggests that they tend to be questions which—as Bales (1950) would put it—ask for orientation, ask for an opinion, or ask for a suggestion. For example, from a female couple:

Female 4115: Was it Joyce that talked to her first?

Or from the more powerful partner in a male couple:

Male 10171:   We have to come to some agree-
            ment here. What do you think?

Such patterns are not surprising, given the task focus of the conversations. Perhaps in other kinds of interactions, other kinds of questions would predominate and would be associated either with females or with the less powerful partner. Unlike some of our other measures—interruptions, back channels, and tag questions—questions, as a conversational form do not have a single clear-cut function. To understand a given question's function, it is therefore necessary to understand its unique meaning. There is both conceptual and methodological advantage to doing research on conversational *forms.* However, the issue of questions makes it clear that future studies will profit from including conversational *content* as well.

The content of conversation will obviously vary with the situation and the purposes that brought the actors together. Perhaps less obvious is that the form of conversation may vary similarly. If a conversation centered on the reciprocal disclosure of very intimate feelings, the division of labor might be very different from the task-oriented situation in which our couples found themselves. Power might disappear altogether as a factor and perhaps sex differences would be enormous. Future research should be directed towards systematically varying the nature of the "conversational task," as well as the type of relationship between the speakers. Dyads with a long history should be contrasted with ad hoc pairs (cf. Leik, 1963); intimate couples should be compared to more distant relationships; and multifaceted relationships, e.g., marriages, should be held up against single-purpose associations.

We measured power with several questionnaire items dealing with the partners' relative influence over decision making. These items are indirect reflections of the underlying power structure. It is our preference for a structural definition of power,

seeing it as the consequence of relative dependency and deriving from the actors' differential resources and differential alternatives (Emerson, 1962). Thus it is unfortunate that we have to rely solely on the influence measures. Relative influence is a *consequence* of structural power, but other factors such as bargaining competence may also affect the influence process.

We have seen that power dynamics can create the conversational division of labor usually attributed to sex. We have also seen that sex *by itself* has very little or nothing to do with such a division of labor. We have succeeded at unconfounding sex and power. This should not, however, keep us from recognizing how closely tied they generally are among heterosexual couples (Cromwell & Olson, 1975). Understanding that power differences can create the *appearance* of sex differences does not reduce the realities of sexual inequality.

Some of our findings have invoked explanations based on an interaction between power and sex—for example, the anomalously talkative behavior of the men in cross-sex couples who are less powerful than their partners, and the high degree of support from the men in male couples who are more powerful than their partners. These explanations were of the form: males (or females) *in a certain kind of relationship* (with a male or female partner) and *in a certain kind of power position* (higher, equal, or lower) behave in a manner that could not be predicted by sex, power, or type of relationship alone. There is therefore clear explanatory utility to the concept of sex, but only when key structural conditions are considered. Men are different from women. Structural properties of their relationship will often affect them similarly, but some combinations of properties will produce unique outcomes. Without consideration of those structural effects, sex, as a quality of persons, appears to be a concept of limited utility in understanding the nature of conversation.

Notes

1. The total numbers of couples with usable data (two completed questionnaires in each) are: 4,314 heterosexual couples (of whom approximately 85 percent were married), 969 male homosexual couples, and 788 lesbian couples. These figures reflect return rates of 58 percent, 52 percent, and 46 percent, respectively.

2. In finding the original questionnaire respondents, the investigators attempted to secure a large and diverse group, at the same time acknowledging the unique problems that finding male homosexuals and lesbians—and to a lesser degree, heterosexual cohabitors—posed (see the discussions of sampling stigmatized persons in, e.g., Bell, 1974; Weinberg, 1970). Couples were sought for participation through a number of different methods, including the use of local and national print and broadcast media, soliciting in public gatherings (e.g., PTA meetings, churches and synagogues, union gatherings, gay and lesbian social and political organizations, etc.), and canvassing neighborhoods with high densities of the kinds of couples desired. This recruitment plan, devised to find large numbers of same-sex couples, was also applied to heterosexual couples, in order to maintain comparability of recruitment effort. National representativeness of the male homosexuals, lesbians, and cohabitors was believed impossible to achieve, and so diversity and large numbers were made the goal. By keeping the recruitment procedures comparable for all four kinds of couples, the possibility of representativeness among the married couples was lost. In general, the couples who returned questionnaires tend to be better educated and more predominantly white than the nation as a whole. (See Blumstein & Schwartz, 1983, pp. 16-19 for a description of the recruitment process and pp. 593-602 for a statistical profile of the couples.)

3. Couples of *short duration* were defined as those living together less than two years, while those of *medium duration* were together between two and ten years, and those over ten years were classified as being of *long duration*. *Low-education* couples were defined as neither partner having gone beyond high school. *Medium-education* couples were those where at least one partner had attended college, and *high-education* couples were those where at least one partner had a degree higher than a B.A.

4. The plan was to interview 300 couples, but due to the vagaries of scheduling, a larger number was actually interviewed: 129 heterosexual couples (approximately 40 percent unmarried cohabitors), 93 lesbian couples, and 98 male homosexual couples.

5. Factor analyses, performed separately for heterosexual males, heterosexual females, homosexual males, and lesbians, yielded eight relative influence items with reasonable internal consistency over the four groups. The answers to these questions were summed together to form a simple additive scale. The scale has the following alpha reliability coefficients in the entire questionnaire samples: heterosexual males: .601; heterosexual females: .649; homosexual males: .650; and lesbians: .570. The decision areas represented in the eight items are: whether to move residence; where to go on vacation; when to go out to eat; how much money to spend on home furnishings; how much money to spend on entertainment; how much money to spend on groceries; whom to invite to the couple's home; and where to go out for an evening (the exact wording of items appears in Blumstein & Schwartz, 1983, pp. 612-613). There was high agreement within the subsample between partners with respect to the overall power measure, the intracouple correlations being: cross-sex couples, $r = -.939$; male couples, $r = -.813$; female couples, $r = -.994$ (because of the item wording, a negative correlation reflects agreement).

6. Brackets used in quoted speech indicate that the enclosed material occurred simultaneously.

7. A subset of the conversations (25 out of 35) was analyzed a second time by a second coder in order to estimate intercoder reliabilities for each of the dependent variables. The intercoder correlations are as follows: talking time, $r = .989$; successful interruptions, $r = .753$; unsuccessful interruptions, $r = .872$; overlaps, $r = .698$; minimal responses, $r = .737$; back channels: $r = .752$; questions, $r = .925$; tag questions, $r = .586$. The last reliability is relatively low, probably due to the infrequency of the behavior. Consequently, findings for this variable should be interpreted with caution.

8. The authors wish to thank Charles T. Hill for suggesting the analysis strategy.

9. It should be noted that while the Type 1 analyses aggregate the data within each couple, Type 2 and 3 analyses allow for disaggregation

of the data while still keeping the couple as the unit of analysis.

10. Recall that this is the *rate of asking questions*, i.e., the number of questions standardized by the amount of talking time.

11. Interpretations based on overall differences between male and female couples should be made with care. While the literature might be used glibly to derive hypotheses about broad sex differences in conversational styles, it is probably safer to generalization only to *patterns of differentiation within couples*. For example, the literature holds that men interrupt women. On the basis of this observation—even if power were not a confounding factor—it is a large leap to the hypothesis that conversations between men are riddled with escalating interruptions, while women's conversations flow along, with each person politely taking her turn.

References

Argyle, M., Lalljee, M., & Cook, M. (1968). The effects of visibility on interaction in a dyad. *Human Relations, 21,* 3-17.

Bales, R. F. (1950). *Interaction process analysis: A method for the study of small groups.* Cambridge, MA: Addison-Wesley.

Bell, A. P. (1974). Homosexualities: Their range and character. In *1973 Nebraska Symposium on Motivation* (pp. 1-26). Lincoln: University of Nebraska Press.

Bell, A. P., Weinberg, M. S., & Hammersmith, S. K. (1981). *Sexual preference: Its development in men and women.* Bloomington: Indiana University Press.

Bernard, J. (1972). *The sex game.* New York: Atheneum.

Blood, R. O., & Wolfe, D. M. (1960). *Husbands and wives: The dynamics of married living.* New York: Free Press.

Blumstein, P., & Schwartz, P. (1983). *American couples: Money, work, sex.* New York: William Morrow.

Courtright, J. A., Millar, F. E., & Rogers-Millar, L. E. (1979). Domineeringness and dominance: Replication and expansion. *Communication Monographs, 46,* 179-192.

Cromwell, R. E., & Olson, D. H. (Eds.). (1975). *Power in families.* New York: John Wiley.

Dubois, B. L., & Crouch, I. (1975). The question of tag questions in women's speech: They don't really use more of them, do they? *Language in Society, 4,* 289-294.

Eakins, B. W., & Eakins, R. G. (1978). *Sex differences in human communication.* Boston: Houghton Mifflin.

Emerson, R. M. (1962). Power-dependence relations. *American Sociological Review, 27,* 31-41.

Fishman, P. M. (1978). Interaction: The work women do. *Social Problems, 25,* 397-406.

Fishman, P. M. (1980). Conversational insecurity. In H. Giles, W. P. Robinson, & P. M. Smith (Eds.), *Language: Social psychological perspectives* (pp. 127-132). New York: Pergamon.

Gagnon, J. H., & Simon, W. (1973). *Sexual conduct: The social sources of human sexuality.* Chicago: Aldine.

Hilpert, F., Kramer, C., & Clark, R. A. (1975). Participants' perception of self and partner in mixed-sex dyads. *Central States Speech Journal, 26,* 52-56.

Kramer, C. (1974). Women's speech: Separate but unequal? *Quarterly Journal of Speech, 60,* 14-24.

Lakoff, R. (1975). *Language and woman's place.* New York: Harper & Row.

Lapadat, J., & Seesahai, M. (1977). Male versus female codes in informal contexts. *Sociolinguistics Newsletter, 8,* 7-8.

Leik, R. (1963). Instrumentality and emotionality in family interaction. *Sociometry, 26,* 131-145.

Marlatt, G. A. (1970). A comparison of vicarious and direct reinforcement control of verbal behavior in an interview setting. *Journal of Personality and Social Psychology, 16,* 695-703.

Natale, M., Entin, E., & Jaffe, J. (1979). Vocal interruptions in dyadic communication as a function of speech and social anxiety. *Journal of Personality and Social Psychology, 37,* 865-878.

Octigan, M., & Niederman, S. (1979). Male dominance in conversations. *Frontiers, 4,* 50-54.

Parks, M. R. (1978). *Perceived sex differences in friendship development.* Paper presented at the annual convention of the Speech Communication Association.

Raush, H. L., Barry, W. A., Hertel, R. K., & Swain, M. A. (1974). *Communication conflict and marriage.* San Francisco: Jossey-Bass.

Rogers, W. T., & Jones, S. E. (1975). Effects of dominance tendencies on floor holding and interruption behavior in dyadic interaction. *Communication Research, 1*, 113-122.

Rosenfeld, H. M. (1966). Approval-seeking and approval-inducing functions of verbal and nonverbal responses in the dyad. *Journal of Personality and Social Psychology, 4*, 597-605.

Sacks, H., Schegloff, E., & Jefferson, G. (1974). A simplest systematics for the organization of turn-taking for conversation. *Language, 50*, 696-735.

Schegloff, E. (1972). Sequencing in conversational openings. In J. Gumperz & D. Hymes (Eds.), *Directions in sociolinguistics: The ethnography of communications* (pp. 346-380). New York: Holt, Rinehart & Winston.

Soskin, W. F., & John, V. P. (1963). The study of spontaneous talk. In R. Barker (Ed.), *The stream of behavior* (pp. 228-281). New York: Appleton-Century-Crofts.

Strodtbeck, F. L. (1951). Husband-wife interaction over revealed differences. *American Sociological Review, 16*, 468-473.

Swacker, M. (1975). The sex of the speaker as a sociolinguistic variable. In B. Thorne & N. Henley (Eds.), *Language and sex: Difference and dominance* (pp. 76-83). Rowley, MA: Newbury House.

Symons, D. (1979). *The evolution of human sexuality.* New York: Oxford University Press.

Thorne, B., & Henley, N. (Eds.). (1975). *Language and sex: Difference and dominance.* Rowley, MA: Newbury House.

Thorne, B., Kramer, C., & Henley, N. (Eds.). (1983). *Language, gender and society.* Rowley, MA: Newbury House.

Weinberg, M. S. (1970). Homosexual samples: Differences and similarities. *Journal of Sex Research, 6*, 312-325.

West, C. (1984). When the doctor is a "lady": Power, status and gender in physician-patient encounters. *Symbolic Interaction, 7*, 87-106.

West, C., & Zimmerman, D. H. (1977). Women's place in everyday talk: Reflections on parent-child interactions. *Social Problems, 24*, 521-528.

Zimmerman, D. H., & West, C. (1975). Sex roles, interruptions and silences in conversation. In B. Thorne & N. Henley (Eds.), *Language and sex: Difference and dominance* (pp. 105-129). Rowley, MA: Newbury House.

20

Behavior in Private Places: Sustaining Definitions of Reality in Gynecological Examinations

Joan P. Emerson

Introduction

In *The Social Construction of Reality*, Berger and Luckmann discuss how people construct social order and yet construe the reality of everyday life to exist independently of themselves.[1] Berger and Luckmann's work succeeds in synthesizing some existing answers with new insights. Many sociologists have pointed to the importance of social consensus in what people believe; if everyone else seems to believe in something, a person tends to accept the common belief without question. Other sociologists have discussed the concept of legitimacy, an acknowledg-

"Behavior in Private Places: Sustaining Definitions of Reality in Gynecological Examinations" by J. P. Emerson from *Recent Sociology No. 2* (pp. 74-97) edited by P. Dreitsel, 1970. New York: Macmillan. Reprinted by permission of the author.

Arlene K. Daniels has applied her talent for editing and organizing to several drafts of this paper. Robert M. Emerson, Roger Pritchard, and Thomas J. Scheff have also commented on the material. The investigation was supported in part by a predoctoral fellowship from the National Institute of Mental Health (Fellowship Number MPM-18,239) and by Behavioral Sciences Training Grant MH-8104 from the National Institute of Mental Health, as well as General Research Support Grant I-SOI-FR-05441 from the National Institutes of Health, U.S. Department of Health, Education, and Welfare to the School of Public Health, University of California, Berkeley.

ment that what exists has the right to exist, and delineated various lines of argument which can be taken to justify a state of affairs. Berger and Luckmann emphasize three additional processes that provide persons with evidence that things have an objective existence apart from themselves. Perhaps most important is the experience that reality seems to be out there before we arrive on the scene. This notion is fostered by the nature of language, which contains an all-inclusive scheme of categories, is shared by a community, and must be learned laboriously by each new member. Further, definitions of reality are continuously validated by apparently trivial features of the social scene, such as details of the setting, persons' appearance and demeanor, and "inconsequential" talk. Finally, each part of a systematic world view serves as evidence for all the other parts, so that reality is solidified by a process of intervalidation of supposedly independent events.

Because Berger and Luckmann's contribution is theoretical, their units of analysis are abstract processes. But they take those processes to be grounded in social encounters. Thus, Berger and Luckmann's theory provides a framework for making sense of social interaction. In this paper observations of a concrete situation will be interpreted to show how reality is embodied in routines and reaffirmed in social interaction.

Situations differ in how much effort it takes to sustain the current definition of the situation. Some situations are relatively stable; others are precarious.[2] Stability depends on the likelihood of three types of disconforming events. Intrusions on the scene may threaten definitions of reality, as when people smell smoke in a theater or when a third person joins a couple and calls one member by a name the second member does not recognize. Participants may deliberately decline to validate the current reality, like Quakers who refused to take off their hats to the king. Sometimes participants are unable to produce the gestures which would validate the current reality. Perhaps a person is ignorant of the relevant vocabulary of gestures. Or a person, understanding how he should behave, may have limited social skills so that he cannot carry off the performance he would like to. For those who insist on "sincerity," a performance becomes especially taxing if they lack conviction about the trueness of the reality they are attempting to project.

A reality can hardly seem self-evident if a person is simultaneously aware of a counterreality. Berger and Luckmann write as though definitions of reality were internally congruent. However, the ordinary reality may contain not only a dominant definition, but in addition counterthemes opposing or qualifying the dominant definition. Thus, several contradictory definitions must be sustained at the same time. Because each element tends to challenge the other elements, such composite definitions of reality are inherently precarious even if the probability of disconfirming events is low.

A situation where the definition of reality is relatively precarious has advantages for the analysis proposed here, for processes of sustaining reality should be more obvious where that reality is problematic. The situation chosen, the gynecological examination,[3] is precarious for both reasons discussed above. First, it is an excellent example of multiple contradictory definitions of reality, as described in the next section. Second, while intrusive and deliberate threats are not important, there is a substantial threat from participants' incapacity to perform.

Dramaturgical abilities are taxed in gynecological examinations because the less convincing reality internalized by secondary socialization is unusually discrepant with rival perspectives taken for granted in primary socialization.[4] Gynecological examinations share similar problems of reality-maintenance with any medical procedure, but the issues are more prominent because the site of the medical task is a woman's genitals. Because touching usually connotes personal intimacy, persons may have to work at accepting the physician's privileged access to the patient's genitals.[5] Participants are not entirely convinced that modesty is out of place. Since a woman's genitals are commonly accessible only in a sexual context, sexual connotations come readily to mind. Although most people realize that sexual responses are inappropriate, they may be unable to dismiss the sexual reaction privately and it may interfere with the conviction with which they undertake their impersonal performance. The structure of a gynecological examination highlights the very features which the participants are supposed to disattend. So the more attentive the participants are to the social situation, the more the unmentionable is forced on their attention.

The next section will characterize the complex composition of the definition of reality routinely sustained in gynecological examinations. Then some of the routine arrangements and interactional maneuvers which embody and express this definition will be described. A later section will discuss threats to the definition which arise in the course of the encounter. Measures that serve to neutralize the threats and reaffirm the definition will be analyzed. The concluding section will turn to the theoretical issues of precariousness, multiple contradictory definitions of reality, and implicit communication.

The Medical Definition and Its Counterthemes

Sometimes people are in each other's presence in what they take to be a "gynecological examination." What happens in a gynecological examination is part of the common stock of knowledge. Most people know that a gynecological examination is when a doctor examines a woman's genitals in a medical setting. Women who have undergone this experience know that the examination takes place in a special examining room where the patient lies with her buttocks down to the edge of the table and her feet in stirrups, that usually a nurse is present as a chaperone, that the actual examining lasts only a few minutes, and so forth. Besides knowing what equipment to provide for the doctor, the nurse has in mind a typology of responses patients have to this situation, and a typology of doctors' styles of performance. The doctor has technical knowledge about the examining procedures, what observations may be taken to indicate, ways of getting patients to relax, and so on.

Immersed in the medical world where the scene constitutes a routine, the staff assume the responsibility for a credible performance. The staff take part in gynecological examinations many times a day, while the patient is a fleeting visitor. More deeply convinced of the reality themselves, the staff are willing to convince skeptical patients. The physician guides the patient through the precarious scene in a contained manner: taking the initiative, controlling the encounter, keeping the patient in line, defining the situation by his reaction, and giving cues that "this is done" and "other people go through this all the time."

Not only must people continue to believe that "this is a gynecological examination," but also that "this is a gynecological examination going right." The major definition to be sustained for this purpose is "this is a medical situation" (not a party, sexual assault, psychological experiment, or anything else). If it is a medical situation, then it follows that "no one is embarrassed"[6] and "no one is thinking in sexual terms."[7] Anyone who indicates the contrary must be swayed by some nonmedical definition.

The medical definition calls for a matter-of-fact stance. One of the most striking observations about a gynecological examination is the marked implication underlying the staff's demeanor toward the patient: "Of course, you take this as matter-of-factly as we do." The staff implicitly contend: "In the medical world the pelvic area is like any other part of the body; its private and sexual connotations are left behind when you enter the hospital." The staff want it understood that their gazes take in only medically pertinent facts, so they are not concerned with an aesthetic inspection of a patient's body. Their nonchalant pose attempts to put a gynecological examination in the same light as an internal examination of the ear.

Another implication of the medical definition is that the patient is a technical object to the staff. It is as if the staff work on an assembly line for repairing bodies; similar body parts continually roll by and the staff have a particular job to do on them. The staff are concerned with the typical features of the body part and its pathology rather than with the unique features used to define a person's identity. The staff disattend the connection between a part of the body and some intangible self that is supposed to inhabit the body.

The scene is credible precisely because the staff act as if they have every right to do what they are doing. Any hint of doubt from the staff would compromise the medical definition. Since the patient's nonchalance merely serves to validate the staff's right, it may be dispensed with without the same threat. Furthermore, the staff claim to be merely agents of the medical system, which is intent on providing good health care to patients. This medical system imposes procedures and standards which the staff are merely following in this particular instance. That is, what the staff do derives from external coercion—"We have to do it this way"—rather than from personal choices which they would be free to revise in order to accommodate the patient.

The medical definition grants the staff the right to carry out their task. If not for the medical definition the staff's routine activities could be defined as unconscionable assaults on the dignity of individuals. The topics of talk, particularly inquiries about bodily functioning, sexual experience, and death of relatives might be taken as offenses against propriety. As for exposure and manipulation of the patient's body, it would be a shocking and degrading invasion of privacy were the patient not defined as a technical object. The infliction of pain would be mere cruelty. The medical definition justifies the request that a presumably competent adult give up most of his autonomy to persons often subordinate in age, sex, and social class. The patient needs the medical definition to minimize the threat to his dignity; the staff need it in order to inveigle the patient into cooperating.

Yet definitions that appear to contradict the medical definition are routinely expressed in the course of gynecological examinations. Some gestures acknowledge the pelvic area as special; other gestures acknowledge the patient as a person. These counterdefinitions are as essential to the encounter as the medical definition. We have already discussed how an actor's lack of conviction may interfere with his performance. Implicit acknowledgments of the special meaning of the pelvic area help those players hampered by lack of conviction to perform adequately. If a player's sense of "how things really are" is implicitly acknowledged, he often finds it easier to adhere outwardly to a contrary definition.

A physician may gain a patient's cooperation by acknowledging her as a person. The physician wants the patient to acknowledge the medical definition, cooperate with the procedures of the examination, and acknowledge his professional competence. The physician is in a position to bargain with the patient in order to obtain this cooperation. He can offer her attention and acknowledgment as a person. At times he does so.

Although defining a person as a technical object is necessary in order for medical activities to proceed, it constitutes an indignity in itself. This indignity can be canceled or at least qualified by simultaneously acknowledging the patient as a person.

The medical world contains special activities and special perspectives. Yet the inhabitants of the medical world travel back and forth to the general community where modesty, death, and other medically relevant matters are regarded quite differently. It is not so easy to dismiss general community meanings for the time one finds oneself in a medical setting. The counterthemes that the pelvic area is special and that patients are persons provide an opportunity to show deference to general community meanings at the same time that one is disregarding them.

Sustaining the reality of a gynecological examination does not mean sustaining the medical definition, then. What is to be sustained is a shifting balance between medical definition and counterthemes.[8] Too much emphasis on the medical definition alone would undermine the reality, as would a flamboyant manifestation of the counterthemes apart from the medical definition. The next three sections will suggest how this balance is achieved.

Sustaining the Reality

The appropriate balance between medical definition and counterthemes has to be created anew at every moment. However, some routinized procedures and demeanor are available to participants in gynecological examinations. Persons recognize that if certain limits are exceeded, the situation would be irremediably shattered. Some arrangements have been found useful because they simultaneously express medical definition and countertheme. Routine ways of meeting the task requirements and also dealing with "normal trouble" are available. This section will describe how themes and counterthemes are embodied in routinized procedures and demeanor.

The pervasiveness of the medical definition is expressed by indicators that the scene is enacted under medical auspices.[9] The action is located in "medical space" (hospital or doctor's office). Features of the setting such as divisions of space, decor, and equipment are constant reminders that it is indeed "medical space." Even background details such as the loudspeaker calling, "Dr. Morris. Dr. Armand Morris" serve as evidence for medical reality (suppose the loudspeaker were to announce instead, "Five minutes until post time"). The staff wear medical uniforms, don medical gloves, use medical instruments. The exclusion of lay persons, particularly visitors of the patient who may be accustomed to the patient's nudity at home, helps to preclude confusion between the contact of medicine and the contact of intimacy.[10]

Some routine practices simultaneously acknowledge the medical definition and qualify it by making special provision for the pelvic area. For instance, rituals of respect express dignity for the patient. The patient's body is draped so as to expose only that part which is to receive the technical attention of the doctor. The presence of a nurse acting as "chaperone" cancels any residual suggestiveness of male and female alone in a room.[11]

Medical talk stands for and continually expresses allegiance to the medical definition. Yet certain features of medical talk acknowledge a nonmedical delicacy. Despite the fact that persons present on a gynecological ward must attend to many topics connected with the pelvic area and various bodily functions, these topics are generally not discussed. Strict conventions dictate what unmentionables are to be acknowledged under what circumstances. However, persons are exceptionally free to refer to the genitals and related matters on the obstetrics-gynecology service. If technical matters in regard to the pelvic area come up, they are to be discussed nonchalantly.

The special language found in staff-patient contacts contributes to depersonalization and desexualization of the encounter. Scientific-sounding medical terms facilitate such communication. Substituting dictionary terms for everyday words adds formality. The definite article replaces the pronoun adjective in reference to body parts, so that for example, the doctor refers to "the vagina" and never "your vagina." Instructions to the patient in the course of the examination are couched in language which bypasses sexual imagery; the vulgar connotation of "spread your legs" is generally metamorphosed into the innocuous "let your knees fall apart."

While among themselves the staff generally use explicit technical terms, explicit terminology is often avoided in staff-patient contacts.[12] The reference to the pelvic area may be merely understood, as when a patient says: "I feel so uncomfortable there right now" or "They didn't go near to this area, so why did they have to shave it?" In speaking with patients the staff frequently uses euphemisms. A doctor asks: "When did you first notice difficulty down below?" and a nurse inquires: "Did you wash between your legs?" Persons characteristically refer to pelvic examinations euphemistically in staff-patient encounters. "The doctors want to take a peek at you," a nurse tells a patient. Or "Dr. Ryan wants to see you in the examining room."

In one pelvic examination there was a striking contrast between the language of staff and patient. The patient was graphic; she used action words connoting physical contact to refer to the examination procedure: feeling, poking, touching, and punching. Yet she never located this action in regard to her body, always omitting to state where the physical contact occurred. The staff used impersonal medical language and euphemisms: "I'm going to examine you"; "I'm just cleaning out some blood clots"; "He's just trying to fix you up a bit."

Sometimes the staff introduce explicit terminology to clarify a patient's remark. A patient tells the doctor, "It's bleeding now" and the doctor answers, "You? From the vagina?" Such a response indicates the appropriate vocabulary, the degree of freedom permitted in technically oriented conversation, and the proper detachment. Yet the common avoidance of explicit terminology in staff-patient contacts suggests that despite all the precautions to assure that the medical definition prevails, many patients remain somewhat embarrassed by the whole subject. To avoid provoking this embarrassment, euphemisms and understood references are used when possible.

Highly specific requirements for everybody's behavior during a gynecological examination curtail the leeway for the introduction of discordant notes. Routine technical procedures organize the event from beginning to end, indicating what action each person should take at each moment. Verbal exchanges are also constrained by the technical task, in that the doctor uses routine phrases of direction and reassurance to the patient. There is little margin for ad-libbing during a gynecological examination.

The specifications for demeanor are elaborate. Foremost is that both staff and patient should be nonchalant about what is happening. According to the staff, the exemplary patient should be "in play": showing she is attentive to the situation by her bodily tautness, facial expression, direction of glance, tone of voice, tempo of speech and bodily movements, timing and appropri-

ateness of responses. The patient's voice should be controlled, mildly pleasant, self-confident, and impersonal. Her facial expression should be attentive and neutral, leaning toward the mildly pleasant and friendly side, as if she were talking to the doctor in his office, fully dressed and seated in a chair. The patient is to have an attentive glance upward, at the ceiling or at other persons in the room, eyes open, not dreamy or "away," but ready at a second's notice to revert to the doctor's face for a specific verbal exchange. Except for such a verbal exchange, however, the patient is supposed to avoid looking into the doctor's eyes during the actual examination because direct eye contact between the two at this time is provocative. Her role calls for passivity and self-effacement. The patient should show willingness to relinquish control to the doctor. She should refrain from speaking at length and from making inquiries which would require the doctor to reply at length. So as not to point up her undignified position, she should not project her personality profusely. The self must be eclipsed in order to sustain the definition that the doctor is working on a technical object and not a person.

The physician's demeanor is highly stylized. He intersperses his examination with remarks to the patient in a soothing tone of voice: "Now relax as much as you can"; "I'll be as gentle as I can"; "Is that tender right there?" Most of the phrases with which he encourages the patient to relax are routine even though his delivery may suggest a unique relationship. He demonstrates that he is the detached professional and the patient demonstrates that it never enters her mind that he could be anything except detached. Since intimacy can be introduced into instrumental physical contact by a "loving" demeanor (lingering, caressing motions and contact beyond what the task requires), a doctor must take special pains to insure that his demeanor remains a brisk, no-nonsense show of efficiency.[13]

Once I witnessed a gynecological examination of a forty-year-old woman who played the charming and scatterbrained Southern belle. The attending physician stood near the patient's head and carried on a flippant conversation with her while a resident and medical student actually performed the examination. The patient completely ignored the examination, except for brief answers to the examining doctor's inquiries. Under these somewhat trying circumstances she attempted to carry off a gay, attractive pose and the attending physician cooperated with her by making a series of bantering remarks.

Most physicians are not so lucky as to have a colleague conversing in cocktail-hour style with the patient while they are probing her vagina. Ordinarily the physician must play both parts at once, treating the patient as an object with his hands while simultaneously acknowledging her as a person with his voice. In this incident, where two physicians simultaneously deal with the patient in two distinct ways, the dual approach to the patient usually maintained by the examining physician becomes more obvious.[14]

The doctor needs to communicate with the patient as a person for technical reasons. Should he want to know when the patient feels pain in the course of examination or information about other medical matters, he must address her as a person. Also the doctor may want to instruct the patient on how to facilitate the examination. The most reiterated instruction refers to relaxation. Most patients are not sufficiently relaxed when the doctor is ready to begin. He then reverts to a primitive level of communication and treats the patient almost like a young child. He speaks in a soft, soothing voice, probably calling the patient by her first name, and it is not so much the words as his manner which is significant. This caressing voice is routinely used by hospital staff members to patients in critical situations, as when the patient is overtly frightened or disoriented. By using it here the doctor heightens his interpersonal relation with the patient, trying to reassure her as a person in order to get her to relax.

Moreover even during a gynecological examination, failing to acknowledge another as a person is an insult. It is insulting to be entirely instrumental about instrumental contacts. Some acknowledgment of the intimate connotations of touching must occur. Therefore, a measure of "loving" demeanor is subtly injected. A doctor cannot employ the full gamut of loving insinuations that a lover might infuse into instrumental touching. So he indirectly implies a hint of intimacy which is intended to counter the insult and make the procedure acceptable to the woman. The doctor conveys this loving demeanor not by lingering or superfluous contact, but by radiating concern in his general manner, offering extra assistance, and occasionally by sacrificing the task requirements to "gentleness."

In short, the doctor must convey an optimal combination of impersonality and hints of intimacy that simultaneously avoid the insult of sexual familiarity and the insult of unacknowledged identity. The doctor must manage this even though the behavior emanating from each definition is contradictory. If the doctor can achieve this feat, it will contribute to keeping the patient in line. In the next section, we will see how the patient may threaten this precarious balance.

Precariousness in Gynecological Examinations

Threats to the reality of a gynecological examination may occur if the balance of opposing definitions is not maintained as described above. Reality in gynecological examinations is challenged mainly by patients. Occasionally a medical student, who might be considerably more of a novice than an experienced patient, seemed uncomfortable in the scene.[15] Experienced staff members were rarely observed to undermine the reality.

Certain threatening events which could occur in any staff-patient encounter bring an added dimension of precariousness to a gynecological examination because the medical aegis screens so much more audacity at that time. In general, staff expect patients to remain poised and in play like a friendly office receptionist; any show of emotion except in a controlled fashion is objectionable. Patients should not focus on identities of themselves or the staff outside those relevant to the medical exchange. Intractable patients may complain about the pain, discomfort, and indignities of submitting to medical treatment and care. Patients may go so far as to show they are reluctant to comply with the staff. Even if they are complying, they may indirectly challenge the expert status of the staff, as by "asking too many questions."

Failure to maintain a poised performance is a possible threat in any social situation. Subtle failures of tone are common, as when a performer seems to lack assurance. Performers may fumble for their lines: hesitate, begin a line again, or correct themselves. A show of embarrassment, such as blushing, has special relevance in gynecological examinations. On rare occasions when a person shows signs of sexual response, he or she really has something to blush about. A more subtle threat is an indication that the actor is putting an effort into the task of maintaining nonchalant demeanor; if it requires such an effort, perhaps it is not a "natural" response.

Such effort may be indicated, for example, in regard to the direction of glance. Most situations have a common visual focus of attention, but in a gynecological examination the logical focus, the patient's internal organs, is not accessible; and none of the alternatives, such as staring at the patient's face, locking glances with others, or looking out the window are feasible. The unavailability of an acceptable place to rest the eyes is more evident when the presence of several medical students creates a "crowd" atmosphere in the small cubicle. The lack of a visual focus of attention and the necessity to shift the eyes from object to object requires the participants to remain vaguely aware of their directions of glance. Normally the resting place of the eyes is a background matter automatically managed without conscious attention. Attentiveness to this background detail is a constant reminder of how awkward the situation is.

Certain lapses in patients' demeanor are so common as hardly to be threatening. When patients express pain it can be overlooked if the patient is giving other signs of trying to behave well, because it can be taken that the patient is temporarily overwhelmed by a physiological state. The demonstrated presence of pain recalls the illness framework and counters sexual connotations. Crying can be accredited to pain and dismissed in a similar way. Withdrawing attention from the scene, so that one is not ready with an immediate comeback when called upon, is also relatively innocuous because it is close to the required passive but in play demeanor.

Some threats derive from the patient's ignorance of how to strike an acceptable balance between medical and nonmedical definitions, despite her willingness to do so. In two areas in particular, patients stumble over the subtleties of what is expected: physical decorum (proprieties of sights, sounds, and smells of the body) and modesty. While the staff is largely concerned with behavioral decorum and not about lapses in physical decorum, patients are more concerned about the latter, whether due to their medical condition or the procedure. Patients sometimes even let behavioral decorum lapse in order to express their concern about unappealing conditions of their bodies, particularly discharges and odors. This concern is a vestige of a nonmedical definition of the situation, for an attractive body is relevant only in a personal situation and not in a medical one.

Some patients fail to know when to display their private parts unashamedly to others and when to conceal them like anyone else. A patient may make an "inappropriate" show of modesty, thus not granting the staff the right to view what medical personnel have the right to view and others do not. But if patients act as though they literally accept the medical definition this also constitutes a threat. If a patient insists on acting as if the exposure of her breasts, buttocks, and pelvic area are no different from exposure of her arm or leg, she is "immodest." The medical definition is supposed to be in force only as necessary to facilitate specific medical tasks. If a patient becomes nonchalant enough to allow herself to remain uncovered for much longer than is technically necessary she becomes a threat. This also holds for verbal remarks about personal matters. Patients who misinterpret the license by exceeding its limits unwittingly challenge the definition of reality.[16]

Neutralizing Threatening Events

Most gynecological examinations proceed smoothly and the definition of reality is sustained without conscious attention.[17] Sometimes subtle threats to the definition arise, and occasionally staff and patient struggle covertly over the definition throughout the encounter.[18] The staff take more preventive measures where they anticipate the most trouble: young, unmarried girls; persons known to be temporarily upset; and persons with reputations as uncooperative. In such cases the doctor may explain the technical details of the procedure more carefully and offer direct reassurance. Perhaps he will take extra time to establish personal rapport, as by medically related inquiries ("How are you feeling?" "Do you have as much pain today?"), personal inquiries ("Where do you live?"), addressing the patient by her first name, expressing direct sympathy, praising the patient for her be-

havior in this difficult situation, speaking in a caressing voice, and affectionate gestures. Doctors also attempt to reinforce rapport as a response to threatening events.

The foremost technique in neutralizing threatening events is to sustain a nonchalant demeanor even if the patient is blushing with embarrassment, blanching from fear, or moaning in pain. The patient's inappropriate gestures may be ignored as the staff convey, "We're waiting until you are ready to play along." Working to bring the scene off, the staff may claim that this is routine, or happens to patients in general; invoke the "for your own good" clause; counterclaim that something is less important than the patient indicates; assert that the unpleasant medical procedure is almost over; and contend that the staff do not like to cause pain or trouble to patients (as by saying, "I'm sorry" when they appear to be causing pain). The staff may verbally contradict a patient, give an evasive answer to a question, or try to distract the patient. By giving a technical explanation or rephrasing in the appropriate hospital language something the patient has referred to in a nonmedical way, the staff member reinstates the medical definition.

Redefinition is another tactic available to the staff. Signs of embarrassment and sexual arousal in patients may be redefined as "fear of pain." Sometimes sexual arousal will be labeled "ticklishness." After one examination the doctor thanked the patient, presumably for her cooperation, thus typifying the patient's behavior as cooperative and so omitting a series of uncooperative acts which he had previously acknowledged.

Humor may be used to discount the line the patient is taking. At the same time, humor provides a safety valve for all parties whereby the sexual connotations and general concern about gynecological examinations may be expressed by indirection. Without taking the responsibility that a serious form of the message would entail, the participants may communicate with each other about the events at hand. They may discount the derogatory implications of what would be an invasion of privacy in another setting by dismissing the procedure with a laugh. If a person can joke on a topic, he demonstrates to others that he possesses a laudatory degree of detachment.

For example, in one encounter a patient vehemently protests, "Oh, Dr. Raleigh, what are you doing?" Dr. Raleigh, exaggerating his southern accent, answers, "Nothin'." His levity conveys: "However much you may dislike this, we have to go on with it for your own good. Since you know that perfectly well, your protest could not be calling for a serious answer." Dr. Raleigh also plays the seducer claiming innocence, thus obliquely referring to the sexual connotations of where his hand is at the moment. In another incident Doctor Ryan is attempting to remove some gauze which has been placed in the vagina to stop the bleeding. He flippantly announces that the remaining piece of gauze has disappeared inside the patient. After a thorough search Doctor Ryan holds up a piece of gauze on the instrument triumphantly: "Well, here it is. Do you want to take it home and put it in your scrapbook?" By this remark Doctor Ryan ridicules the degree of involvement in one's own medical condition which would induce a patient to save this kind of memento. Later in the same examination Dr. Ryan announces he will do a rectal examination and the (elderly) patient protests, "Oh, honey, don't bother." Dr. Ryan assures her jokingly, "It's no bother, really." The indirect message of all three jokes is that one should take gynecological procedures casually. Yet simultaneously an undercurrent of each joke acknowledges a perspective contrary to the medical definition.

While in most encounters the nurse remains quietly in the background, she comes forward to deal actively with the patient if the definition of reality is threatened. In fact, one of the main functions of her presence is to provide a team member for the doctor in those occasional instances where the patient threatens to get out of line. Team members can create a more convincing reality than one person alone. Doctor and nurse may collude against an uncooperative patient, as by giving each other significant looks. If things reach the point of staff collusion, however, it may mean that only by excluding the patient can the definition of reality be reaffirmed. A more drastic form of solidifying the definition by excluding recalcitrant participants is to cast the patient into the role of an "emotionally disturbed person." Whatever an "emotionally disturbed person" may think or do does not count against the reality the rest of us acknowledge.

Perhaps the major safeguard of reality is that challenge is channeled outside the examination. Comments about the unpleasantness of the procedure and unaesthetic features of the patient's body occur mainly between women, two patients or a nurse and a patient. Such comments are most frequent while the patient gets ready for the examination and waits for the doctor or after the doctor leaves. The patient may establish a momentary "fellow-woman aura" as she quietly voices her distaste for the procedure to the nurse. "What we women have to go through" the patient may say. Or, "I wish all gynecologists were women." Why? "They understand because they've been through it themselves." The patient's confiding manner implies: "I have no right to say this, or even feel it, and yet I do." This phenomenon suggests that patients actually have strong negative reactions to gynecological examinations which belie their acquiescence in the actual situation. Yet patients' doubts are expressed in an innocuous way which does not undermine the definition of reality when it is most needed.

To construct the scene convincingly, participants constantly monitor their own behavior and that of others. The tremendous work of producing the scene is contained in subtle maneuvers in regard to details which may appear inconsequential to the layman. Since awareness may interfere with a convincing performance, the participants may have an investment in being as unselfconscious as possible. But the sociologist is free to recognize the significance of "inconsequential details" in constructing reality.

Conclusion

In a gynecological examination the reality sustained is not the medical definition alone, but a dissonance of themes and counterthemes. What is done to acknowledge one theme undermines the others. No theme can be taken for granted because its opposite is always in mind. That is why the reality of a gynecological examination can never be routinized, but always remains precarious.

The gynecological examination should not be dismissed as an anomaly. The phenomenon is revealed more clearly in this case because it is an extreme example. But the gynecological examination merely exaggerates the internally contradictory nature of definitions of reality found in most situations. Many situations where the dominant definition is occupational or technical have a secondary theme of sociality which must be implicitly acknowledged (as in buttering up the secretary, small talk with sales clerks, or the undertaker's show of concern for the bereaved family). In "business entertaining" and conventions of professional associations a composite definition of work and pleasure is sustained. Under many circumstances a composite definition of action as both deviant and unproblematic prevails. For example, while Donald Ball stresses the claim of respectability in his description of an abortion clinic, his material illustrates the interplay of the dominant theme of respectability and a countertheme wherein the illicitness of the situation is acknowledged.[19] Internally inconsistent definitions also are sustained in many settings on who persons are and what their relation is to each other.

Sustaining a sense of the solidness of a reality composed of multiple contradictory definitions takes unremitting effort. The required balance among the various definitions fluctuates from moment to moment. The appropriate balance depends on what the participants are trying to do at that moment. As soon as one matter is dealt with, something else comes into focus, calling for a different balance. Sometimes even before one issue is completed, another may impose itself as taking priority. Further, each balance contains the seeds of its own demise, in that a temporary emphasis on one theme may disturb the long-run balance unless subsequent emphasis on the countertheme negates it. Because the most effective balance depends on many unpredictable factors, it is difficult to routinize the balance into formulas that prescribe a specific balance for given conditions. Routinization is also impractical because the particular forms by which the themes are expressed are opportunistic. That is, persons seize opportunities for expression according to what would be a suitable move at each unique moment of an encounter. Therefore, a person constantly must attend to how to express the balance of themes via the currently available means.

Multiple contradictory realities are expressed on various levels of explicitness and implicitness. Sustaining a sense of solidness of reality depends on the right balance of explicit and implicit expressions of each theme through a series of points in time. The most effective gestures express a multitude of themes on different levels. The advantages of multiple themes in the same gesture are simultaneous qualification of one theme by another, hedging (the gesture lacks one definite meaning), and economy of gestures.

Rational choices of explicit and implicit levels would take the following into account. The explicit level carries the most weight, unless countered by deliberate effort. Things made explicit are hard to dismiss or discount compared to what is left implicit. In fact, if the solidification of explication is judged to be nonreversible, use of the explicit level may not be worth the risk. On the other hand, when participants sense that the implicit level is greatly in use, their whole edifice of belief may become shaken. "I sense that a lot is going on underneath" makes a person wonder about the reality he is accepting. There must be a lot he does not know, some of which might be evidence which would undermine what he currently accepts.

The invalidation of one theme by the concurrent expression of its countertheme must be avoided by various maneuvers. The guiding principle is that participants must prevent a definition that a contradiction exists between theme and countertheme from emerging. Certain measures routinely contribute to this purpose. Persons must try to hedge on both theme and countertheme by expressing them tentatively rather than definitely and simultaneously alluding to and discounting each theme. Theme and countertheme should not be presented simultaneously or contiguously on the explicit level unless it is possible to discount their contradictory features. Finally, each actor must work to keep the implicit level out of awareness for the other participants.

The technique of constructing reality depends on good judgment about when to make things explicit and when to leave them implicit, how to use the implicit level to reinforce and qualify the explicit level, distributing themes among explicit and implicit levels at any one moment, and seizing opportunities to embody messages. To pursue further these tentative suggestions on how important explicit and implicit levels are for sustaining reality, implicit levels of communication must be explored more systematically.

Notes

1. P. Berger & T. Luckmann (1966), *The social construction of reality*, Garden City, NY: Doubleday.

2. The precarious nature of social interaction is discussed throughout the work of Erving Goffman.

3. The data in this article are based on observations of approximately 75 gynecological examinations conducted by male physicians on an obstetrics-gynecology ward and some observations from a medical ward for comparison. For a full account of this study, see J. P. Emerson (1963), "Social functions of humor in a hospital setting," unpublished doctoral dissertation, University of California at Berkeley. For a sociological discussion of a similar setting, see W. P. Rosengren & S. DeVault (1963), "The sociology of time and space in an obstetrical hospital," in E. Freidson (Ed.), *The hospital in modern society* (pp. 266-292), New York: Free Press of Glencoe.

4. "It takes severe biographical shocks to disintegrate the massive reality internalized in early childhood; much less to destroy the realities internalized later. Beyond this, it is relatively easy to set aside the reality of the secondary internalizations." Berger & Luckmann (1966), p. 142.

5. As stated by Lief and Fox: "The amounts and occasions of bodily contact are carefully regulated in all societies, and very much so in ours. Thus, the kind of access to the body of the patient that a physician in our society has is a uniquely privileged one. Even in the course of a so-called routine physical examination, the physician is permitted to handle the patient's body in ways otherwise permitted only to special intimates, and in the case of procedures such as rectal and vaginal examinations in ways normally not even permitted to a sexual partner." H. I. Lief & R. C. Fox (1963), "Training for 'detached concern' in medical students," in H. I. Lief et al. (Eds.), *The psychological basis of medical practice*, New York: Harper & Row, p. 32. As Edward Hall remarks, North Americans have an inarticulated convention that discourages touching except in moments of intimacy. E. T. Hall (1959), *The silent language*, Garden City, NY: Doubleday, p. 149.

6. For comments on embarrassment in the doctor-patient relation, see M. Balint (1957), *The doctor, his patient, and the illness*, New York: International Universities Press, p. 57.

7. Physicians are aware of the possibility that their routine technical behavior may be interpreted as sexual by the patient. The following quotation states a view held by some physicians: "It is not unusual for a suspicious hysterical woman with fantasies of being seduced to

misinterpret an ordinary movement in the physical examination as an amorous advance." E. Weiss & O. S. English (1949), *Psychosomatic medicine*, Philadelphia: W. B. Saunders; quoted in M. Hollender (1958), *The psychology of medical practice*, Philadelphia: W. B. Saunders, p. 22. An extreme case suggests that pelvic examinations are not without their hazards for physicians, particularly during training: "A third-year student who had prided himself on his excellent adjustment to the stresses of medical school developed acute anxiety when about to perform, for the first time, a pelvic examination on a gynecological patient. Prominent in his fantasies were memories of a punishing father who would unquestionably forbid any such explicitly sexual behavior." S. Bojar (1961), "Psychiatric problems of medical students," in G. B. Glaine, Jr., et al. (Eds.), *Emotional problems of the student*, Garden City, NY: Doubleday, p. 248.

8. Many other claims and assumptions are being negotiated or sustained in addition to this basic definition of the situation. Efforts in regard to some of these other claims and assumptions have important consequences for the fate of the basic definition. That is, in the actual situation any one gesture usually has relevance for a number of realities, so that the fates of the various realities are intertwined with each other. For example, each participant is putting forth a version of himself which he wants validated. A doctor's jockeying about claims about competence may reinforce the medical definition and so may a patient's interest in appearing poised. But a patient's ambition to "understand what is really happening" may lead to undermining of the medical definition. Understanding that sustaining the basic definition of the situation is intertwined with numerous other projects, however, we will proceed to focus on that reality alone.

9. Compare Donald Ball's account of how the medical definition is conveyed in an abortion clinic, where it serves to counter the definition of the situation as deviant. D. W. Ball (1967, Winter), "An abortion clinic ethnography," *Social Problems*, 14, 293-301.

10. Glaser and Strauss discuss the hospital prohibition against examinations and exposure of the body in the presence of intimates of the patient. B. Glaser & A. Strauss (1965), *Awareness of dying*, Chicago: Aldine, p. 162.

11. Sudnow reports that at the county hospital he studied, male physicians routinely did pelvic examinations without nurses being present, except in the emergency ward. D. Sudnow (1967), *Passing on: The social organization of dying*, Englewood Cliffs, NJ: Prentice-Hall, p. 78.

12. The following quotation suggests that euphemisms and understood references may be used because the staff often has the choice of using "lewd words" or not being understood. "Our popular vocabulary for describing sexual behavior has been compounded of about equal parts of euphemism and obscenity, and popular attitude and sentiment have followed the same duality. Among both his male and female subjects, the interviewers found many who knew only the lewd words for features of their own anatomy and physiology." N. N. Foote (1955), "Sex as play," in J. Himelhock & S. F. Fava, *Sexual behavior in American society*, New York: Norton, p. 239.

13. The doctor's demeanor typically varies with his experience. In his early contacts with patients the young medical student may use an extreme degree of impersonality generated by his own discomfort in his role. By the time he has become accustomed to doctor-patient encounters, the fourth-year student and intern may use a newcomer's gentleness, treating the scene almost as an intimate situation by relying on elements of the "loving" demeanor previously learned in non-professional situations. By the time he is a resident and focusing primarily on the technical details of the medical task, the physician may be substituting a competent impersonality, although he never reverts to the extreme impersonality of the very beginning. The senior doctor, having mastered not only the technical details but an attitude of detached concern as well, reintroduces a mild gentleness, without the involved intimacy of the intern.

14. The management of closeness and detachment in professional-client relations is discussed in C. Kadushin (1962, March), "Social distance between client and professional," *American Journal of Sociology*, 67, 517-531. Wilensky and Lebeaux discuss how intimacy with strangers in the social worker-client relation is handled by accenting the technical aspects of the situation, limiting the relationship to the task at hand, and observing the norms of emotional neutrality, impartiality, and altruistic service. H. L. Wilensky

& C. N. Lebeaux (1958), *Industrial society and social welfare*, New York: Russell Sage Foundation, pp. 299-303.

15. For a discussion of the socialization of medical students toward a generally detached attitude, see Lief & Fox (1963), pp. 12-35. See also M. J. Daniels (1960, November), "Affect and its control in the medical intern," *American Journal of Sociology, 66*, 259-267.

16. The following incident illustrates how a patient may exceed the limits. Mrs. Lane, a young married woman, was considered by the physicians a "seductive patient," although her technique was subtle and her behavior never improper. After examining Mrs. Lane, an intern privately called my attention to a point in the examination when he was pressing on the patient's ovaries and she remarked to the nurse: "I have this pain in intercourse until my insides are about to come out." The intern told me that Mrs. Lane said that to the nurse, but she wanted him to hear. He didn't want to know that, he said; it wasn't necessary for her to say that. The intern evidently felt that Mrs. Lane's remark had exceeded the bounds of decorum. A specific medical necessity makes the imparting of private information acceptable, the doctor's reaction suggests, and not merely the definition of the situation as medical.

17. There is reason to think that those patients who would have most difficulty in maintaining their poise generally avoid the situation altogether. Evidence that some uncool women avoid pelvic examinations is found in respondents' remarks quoted by Rainwater: "I have thought of going to a clinic for a diaphragm, but I'm real backward about doing that. I don't even go to the doctor to be examined when I'm pregnant. I never go until about a month before I have the baby." "I tell you frankly, I'd like a diaphragm but I'm just too embarrassed to go get one." L. Rainwater (1960), *And the poor get children*, Chicago: Quadrangle, pp. 10, 31.

18. An example of such a struggle is analyzed in J. P. Emerson (1970), "Nothing unusual is happening," in T. Shibutani (Ed.), *Human nature and collective behavior: Papers in honor of Herbert Blumer*, Englewood Cliffs, NJ: Prentice-Hall.

19. Donald Ball (1967).

21

Becoming a Marihuana User

Howard S. Becker

The use of marihuana is and has been the focus of a good deal of attention on the part of both scientists and laymen. One of the major problems students of the practice have addressed themselves to has been the identification of those individual psychological traits which differentiate marihuana users from nonusers and which are assumed to account for the use of the drug. That approach, common in the study of behavior categorized as deviant, is based on the premise that the presence of a given kind of behavior in an individual can best be explained as the result of some trait which predisposes or motivates him to engage in the behavior.[1]

This study is likewise concerned with accounting for the presence or absence of marihuana use in an individual's behavior. It starts, however, from a different premise:

"Becoming a Marihuana User" by H. S. Becker, 1953. Reprinted from *The American Journal of Sociology, 59,* pp. 235-242, by permission of the University of Chicago Press. Copyright © 1953 by the University of Chicago Press.

Read at the meetings of the Midwest Sociological Society in Omaha, Nebraska, April 25, 1953. The research on which this paper is based was done while I was a member of the staff of the Chicago Narcotics Survey, a study done by the Chicago Area Project, Inc., under a grant from the National Institute of Mental Health. My thanks to Solomon Kobrin, Harold Finestone, Henry McKay, and Anselm Strauss, who read and discussed with me earlier versions of this paper.

that the presence of a given kind of behavior is the result of a sequence of social experiences during which the person acquires a conception of the meaning of the behavior, and perceptions and judgments of objects and situations, all of which make the activity possible and desirable. Thus, the motivation or disposition to engage in the activity is built up in the course of learning to engage in it and does not antedate this learning process. For such a view it is not necessary to identify those "traits" which "cause" the behavior. Instead, the problem becomes one of describing the set of changes in the person's conception of the activity and of the experience it provides for him.[2]

This paper seeks to describe the sequence of changes in attitude and experience which lead to *the use of marihuana for pleasure.* Marihuana does not produce addiction, as do alcohol and the opiate drugs; there is no withdrawal sickness and no ineradicable craving for the drug.[3] The most frequent pattern of use might be termed "recreational." The drug is used occasionally for the pleasure the user finds in it, a relatively casual kind of behavior in comparison with that connected with the use of addicting drugs. The term "use for pleasure" is meant to emphasize the noncompulsive and casual character of the behavior. It is also meant to eliminate from consideration here those few cases in which marihuana is used for its prestige value only, as a symbol that one is a certain kind of person, with no pleasure at all being derived from its use.

The analysis presented here is conceived of as demonstrating the greater explanatory usefulness of the kind of theory outlined above as opposed to the predispositional theories now current. This may be seen in two ways: (1) predispositional theories cannot account for that group of users (whose existence is admitted)[4] who do not exhibit the trait or traits considered to cause the behavior and (2) such theories cannot account for the great variability over time of a given individual's behavior with reference to the drug. The same person will at one stage be unable to use the drug for pleasure, at a later stage be able and willing to do so, and still later, again be unable to use it in this way. These changes, difficult to explain from a predispositional or motivational theory, are readily understandable in terms of changes in the individual's conception of the drug as is the existence of "normal" users.

The study attempted to arrive at a general statement of the sequence of changes in individual attitude and experience which have always occurred when the individual has become willing and able to use marihuana for pleasure and which have not occurred or not been permanently maintained when this is not the case. This generalization is stated in universal terms in order that negative cases may be discovered and used to revise the explanatory hypothesis.[5]

Fifty interviews with marihuana users from a variety of social backgrounds and present positions in society constitute the data from which the generalization was constructed and against which it was tested.[6] The interviews focused on the history of the person's experience with the drug, seeking major changes in his attitude toward it and in his actual use of it, and the reasons for these changes. The final generalization is a statement of that sequence of changes in attitude which occurred in every case known to me in which the person came to use marihuana for pleasure. Until a negative case is found, it may be considered as an explana-tion of all cases of marihuana use for pleasure. In addition, changes from use to nonuse are shown to be related to similar changes in conception, and in each case it is possible to explain variations in the individual's behavior in these terms.

This paper covers only a portion of the natural history of an individual's use of marihuana,[7] starting with the person having arrived at the point of willingness to try marihuana. He knows that others use it to "get high," but he does not know what this means in concrete terms. He is curious about the experience, ignorant of what it may turn out to be, and afraid that it may be more than he has bargained for. The steps outlined below, if he undergoes them all and maintains the attitudes developed in them, leave him willing and able to use the drug for pleasure when the opportunity presents itself.

I

The novice does not ordinarily get high the first time he smokes marihuana, and several attempts are usually necessary to induce this state. One explanation of this may be that the drug is not smoked "properly," that is, in a way that insures sufficient dosage to produce real symptoms of intoxication. Most users agree that it cannot be smoked like tobacco if one is to get high:

Take in a lot of air, you know, and . . . I don't know how to describe it, you don't smoke it like a cigarette, you draw in a lot of air and get it deep down in your system and then keep it there. Keep it there as long as you can.

Without the use of some such technique[8] the drug will produce no effects, and the user will be unable to get high:

The trouble with people like that [who are not able to get high] is that they're just not smoking it right, that's all there is to it. Either they're not holding it down long enough, or they're getting too much air and not enough smoke, or the other way around or something like that. A lot of people just don't smoke it right, so naturally nothing's gonna happen.

If nothing happens, it is manifestly impossible for the user to develop a conception of the drug as an object which can be used for pleasure, and use will therefore not continue. The first step in the sequence of events that must occur if the person is to become a user is that he must learn to use the proper smoking technique in order that his use of the drug will produce some effects in terms of which his conception of it can change.

Such a change is, as might be expected, a result of the individual's participation in groups in which marihuana is used. In them the individual learns the proper way to smoke the drug. This may occur through direct teaching:

I was smoking like I did an ordinary cigarette. He said, "No, don't do it like that." He said, "Suck it, you know, draw in and hold it in your lungs till you . . . for a period of time."

I said, "Is there any limit of time to hold it?"

He said, "No, just till you feel that you want to let it out, let it out." So I did that three or four times.

Many new users are ashamed to admit ignorance and, pretending to know already, must learn through the more indirect means of observation and imitation:

I came on like I had turned on [smoked marihuana] many times before, you know. I didn't want to seem like a punk to this cat. See, like I didn't know the first thing about it—how to smoke it, or what was going to happen, or what. I just watched him like a hawk—I didn't take my eyes off him for a second, because I wanted to do everything just as he did it. I watched how he held it, how he smoked it, and everything. Then when he gave it to me I just came on cool, as though I knew exactly what the score was. I held it like he did and took a poke just the way he did.

No person continued marihuana use for pleasure without learning a technique that supplied sufficient dosage for the effects of the drug to appear. Only when this was learned was it possible for a conception of the drug as an object which could be used for pleasure to emerge. Without such a conception marihuana use was considered meaningless and did not continue.

II

Even after he learns the proper smoking technique, the new user may not get high and thus not form a conception of the drug as something which can be used for pleasure. A remark made by a user suggested the reason for this difficulty in getting high and pointed to the next necessary step on the road to being a user:

I was told during an interview, "As a matter of fact, I've seen a guy who was high out of his mind and didn't know it."

I expressed disbelief: "How can that be, man?"

The interviewee said, "Well, it's pretty strange, I'll grant you that, but I've seen it. This guy got on with me, claiming that he'd never got high, one of those guys, and he got completely stoned. And he kept insisting that he wasn't high. So I had to prove to him that he was."

What does this mean? It suggests that being high consists of two elements: the presence of symptoms caused by marihuana use and the recognition of these symptoms and their connection by the user with his use of the drug. It is not enough, that is, that the effects be present; they alone do not automatically provide the experience of being high. The user must be able to point them out to himself and consciously connect them with his having smoked marihuana before he can have this experience. Otherwise, regardless of the actual effects produced, he considers that the drug has had no effect on him: "I figured it either had no effect on me or other people were exaggerating its effect on them, you know. I thought it was probably psychological, see." Such persons believe that the whole thing is an illusion and that the wish to be high leads the user to deceive himself into believing that something is happening when, in fact, nothing is. They do not continue marihuana use, feeling that "it does nothing" for them.

Typically, however, the novice has faith (developed from his observation of users who do get high) that the drug actually will produce some new experience and continues to experiment with it until it does. His failure to get high worries him, and he is likely to ask more experienced users or provoke comments from them about it. In such conversations he is made aware of specific details of his experience which he may not have noticed or may have noticed but failed to identify as symptoms of being high:

I didn't get high the first time . . . I don't think I held it in long enough. I probably let it out, you know, you're a little afraid. The second time I wasn't sure, and he [smoking companion] told me, like I asked him for some of the symptoms or something, how would I know, you know. . . . So he told me to sit on a stool. I sat on—I think I sat on a bar stool—and he said, "Let your feet hang," and then when I got down my feet were real cold, you know.

And I started feeling it, you know. That was the first time. And then about a week after that, sometime pretty close to it, I really got on. That was the first time I got on a big laughing kick, you know. Then I really knew I was on.

One symptom of being high is an intense hunger. In the next case the novice becomes aware of this and gets high for the first time:

They were just laughing the hell out of me because like I was eating so much. I just scoffed [ate] so much food, and they were just laughing at me, you know. Sometimes I'd be looking at them, you know, wondering why

they're laughing, you know, not knowing what I was doing. [Well, did they tell you why they were laughing eventually?] Yeah, yeah, I come back, "Hey, man, what's happening?" Like, you know, like I'd ask, "What's happening?" and all of a sudden I feel weird, you know. "Man, you're on you know. You're on pot [high on marihuana]." I said, "No, am I?" Like I don't know what's happening.

The learning may occur in more indirect ways:

I heard little remarks that were made by other people. Somebody said, "My legs are rubbery," and I can't remember all the remarks that were made because I was very attentively listening for all these cues for what I was supposed to feel like.

The novice, then, eager to have this feeling, picks up from other users some concrete referents of the term "high" and applies these notions to his own experience. The new concepts make it possible for him to locate these symptoms among his own sensations and to point out to himself a "something different" in his experience that he connects with drug use. It is only when he can do this that he is high. In the next case, the contrast between two successive experiences of a user makes clear the crucial importance of the awareness of the symptoms in being high and re-emphasizes the important role of interaction with other users in acquiring the concepts that make this awareness possible:

[Did you get high the first time you turned on?] Yeah, sure. Although, come to think of it, I guess I really didn't. I mean, like that first time it was more or less of a mild drunk. I was happy, I guess, you know what I mean. But I didn't really know I was high, you know what I mean. It was only after the second time I got high that I realized I was high the first time. Then I knew that something different was happening.

[How did you know that?] How did I know? If what happened to me that night would of happened to you, you would've known, believe me. We played the first tune for almost two hours—one tune! Imagine, man! We got on the stand and played this one tune, we started at nine o'clock. When we got finished I looked at my watch, it's a quarter to eleven. Almost two hours on one tune. And it didn't seem like anything. I mean, you know, it does that to you. It's like you have much more time or something. Anyway, when I saw that, man, it was too much. I knew I must really be high or something if anything like that could happen. See, and then they explained to me that that's what it did to you, you had a different sense of time and everything. So I realized that that's what it was. I knew then. Like the first time, I probably felt that way, you know, but I didn't know what's happening.

It is only when the novice becomes able to get high in this sense that he will continue to use marihuana for pleasure. In every case in which use continued, the user had acquired the necessary concepts with which to express to himself the fact that he was experiencing new sensations caused by the drug. That is, for use to continue, it is necessary not only to use the drug so as to produce effects but also to learn to perceive these effects when they occur. In this way marihuana acquires meaning for the user as an object which can be used for pleasure.

With increasing experience the user develops a greater appreciation of the drug's effects; he continues to learn to get high. He examines succeeding experiences closely, looking for new effects, making sure the old ones are still there. Out of this there grows a stable set of categories for experiencing the drug's effects whose presence enables the user to get high with ease.

The ability to perceive the drug's effects must be maintained if use is to continue; if it is lost, marihuana use ceases. Two kinds of evidence support this statement. First, people who become heavy users of alcohol, barbiturates, or opiates do not continue to smoke marihuana, largely because they lose the ability to distinguish between its effects and those of the other drugs.[9] They no longer know whether the marihuana gets them high. Second, in those few cases in which an individual uses marihuana in such quantities that he is always high, he is apt to get this same feeling that the drug has no effect on him, since the essential element of a noticeable difference between feeling high and feeling normal is missing. In such a situation, use is likely to be given up completely, but temporarily, in order that the user may once again be able to perceive the difference.

III

One more step is necessary if the user who has now learned to get high is to continue use. He must learn to enjoy the effects he has just learned to experience. Marihuana-produced sensations are not automatically or necessarily pleasurable. The taste for such experience is a socially acquired one, not different in kind from acquired tastes for oysters or dry martinis. The user feels dizzy, thirsty; his scalp tingles; he misjudges time and distances; and so on. Are these things pleasurable? He isn't sure. If he is to continue marihuana use, he must decide that they are. Otherwise, getting high, while a real enough experience, will be an unpleasant one he would rather avoid.

The effects of the drug, when first perceived, may be physically unpleasant or at least ambiguous:

It started taking effect, and I didn't know what was happening, you know, what it was, and I was very sick. I walked around the room, walking around the room trying to get off, you know; it just scared me at first, you know. I wasn't used to that kind of feeling.

In addition, the novice's naive interpretation of what is happening to him may further confuse and frighten him, particularly if he decides, as many do, that he is going insane:

I felt I was insane, you know. Everything people done to me just wigged me. I couldn't hold a conversation, and my mind would be wandering, and I was always thinking, oh, I don't know, weird things, like hearing music different. . . . I get the feeling that I can't talk to anyone. I'll goof completely.

Given these typically frightening and unpleasant first experiences, the beginner will not continue use unless he learns to redefine the sensations as pleasurable:

It was offered to me, and I tried it. I'll tell you one thing. I never did enjoy it at all. I mean it was just nothing that I could enjoy. [Well, did you get high when you turned on?] Oh, yeah, I got definite feelings from it. But I didn't enjoy them. I mean I got plenty of reactions, but they were mostly reactions of fear. [You were frightened?] Yes, I didn't enjoy it. I couldn't seem to relax with it, you know. If you can't relax with a thing, you can't enjoy it, I don't think.

In other cases the first experiences were also definitely unpleasant, but the person did become a marihuana user. This occurred, however, only after a later experience enabled him to redefine the sensations as pleasurable:

[This man's first experience was extremely unpleasant, involving distortion of spatial relationships and sounds, violent thirst, and panic produced by these symptoms.] After the first time I didn't turn on for about, I'd say, ten months to a year. . . . It wasn't a moral thing; it was because I'd gotten so frightened, bein' so high. An' I didn't want to go through that again, I mean, my reaction was, "Well, if this is what they call bein' high, I don't dig [like] it." . . . So I didn't turn on for a year almost, accounta that. . . .

Well, my friends started, an' consequently I started again. But I didn't have any more, I didn't have that same initial reaction, after I started turning on again.

[In interaction with his friends he became able to find pleasure in the effects of the drug and eventually became a regular user.]

In no case will use continue without such a redefinition of the effects as enjoyable.

This redefinition occurs, typically, in interaction with more experienced users who, in a number of ways, teach the novice to find pleasure in this experience which is at first so frightening.[10] They may reassure him as to the temporary character of the unpleasant sensations and minimize their seriousness, at the same time calling attention to the more enjoyable aspects. An experienced user describes how he handles newcomers to marihuana use:

Well, they get pretty high sometimes. The average person isn't ready for that, and it is a little frightening to them sometimes. I mean, they've been high on lush [alcohol], and they get higher that way than they've ever been before, and they don't know what's happening to them. Because they think they're going to keep going up, up, up till they lose their minds or begin doing weird things or something. You have to like reassure them, explain to them that they're not really flipping or anything, that they're gonna be all right. You have to just talk them out of being afraid. Keep talking to them, reassuring, telling them it's all right. And come on with your own story, you know: "The same thing happened to me. You'll get to like that after awhile." Keep coming on like that; pretty soon you talk them out of being scared. And besides they see you doing it and nothing horrible is happening to you, so that gives them more confidence.

The more experienced user may also teach the novice to regulate the amount he smokes more carefully, so as to avoid any severely uncomfortable symptoms while retaining the pleasant ones. Finally, he teaches the new user that he can "get to like it after awhile." He teaches him to regard those ambiguous experiences formerly defined as unpleasant as enjoyable. The older user in the following incident is a person whose tastes have shifted in this way, and his remarks have the effect of helping others to make a similar redefinition:

A new user had her first experience of the effects of marihuana and became frightened and hysterical. She "felt like she was half in and half out of the room" and experienced a number of alarming physical symptoms. One of the more experienced users present said, "She's dragged because she's high like that. I'd give anything to get that high myself. I haven't been that high in years."

In short, what was once frightening and distasteful becomes, after a taste for it is built up, pleasant, desired, and sought after. Enjoyment is introduced by the favorable definition of the experience that one acquires from others. Without this, use will not continue, for marihuana will not be for the user an object he can use for pleasure.

In addition to being a necessary step in becoming a user, this represents an important condition for continued use. It is quite common for experienced users suddenly to have an unpleasant or frightening experience, which they cannot define as pleasurable, either because they have used a larger amount of marihuana than usual or because it turns out to be a higher-quality marihuana than they expected. The user has sensations which go beyond any conception he has of what being high is and is in much the same situation as the novice, uncomfortable and frightened. He may blame it on an overdose and simply be more careful in the future. But he may make this the occasion for a rethinking of his attitude toward the drug and decide that it no longer can give him pleasure. When this occurs and is not followed by a redefinition of the drug as capable of producing pleasure, use will cease.

The likelihood of such a redefinition occurring depends on the degree of the individual's participation with other users. Where this participation is intensive, the individual is quickly talked out of his feeling against marihuana use. In the next case, on the other hand, the experience was very disturbing, and the aftermath of the inci-

dent cut the person's participation with other users to almost zero. Use stopped for three years and began again only when a combination of circumstances, important among which was a resumption of ties with users, made possible a redefinition of the nature of the drug:

It was too much, like I only made about four pokes, and I couldn't even get it out of my mouth, I was so high, and I got real flipped. In the basement, you know, I just couldn't stay in there anymore. My heart was pounding real hard, you know, and I was going out of my mind; I thought I was losing my mind completely. So I cut out of this basement, and this other guy, he's out of his mind, told me, "Don't, don't leave me, man. Stay here." And I couldn't.

I walked outside, and it was five below zero, and I thought I was dying, and I had my coat open; I was sweating. I was perspiring. My whole insides were all . . . , and I walked about two blocks away, and I fainted behind a bush. I don't know how long I laid there. I woke up, and I was feeling the worst, I can't describe it at all, so I made it to a bowling alley, man, and I was trying to act normal, I was trying to shoot pool, you know, trying to act real normal, and I couldn't lay and I couldn't stand up and I couldn't sit down, and I went up and laid down where some guys that spot pins lay down, and that didn't help me, and I went down to a doctor's office. I was going to go in there and tell the doctor to put me out of my misery . . . because my heart was pounding so hard, you know. . . . So then all weekend I started flipping, seeing things there and going through hell, you know, all kinds of abnormal things. . . . I just quit for a long time then.

[He went to a doctor who defined the symptoms for him as those of a nervous breakdown caused by "nerves" and "worries." Although he was no longer using marihuana, he had some recurrences of the symptoms which led him to suspect that "it was all his nerves."] So I just stopped worrying, you know; so it was about thirty-six months later I started making it again. I'd just take a few pokes, you know. [He first resumed use in the company of the same user-friend with whom he had been involved in the original incident.]

A person, then, cannot begin to use mari-huana for pleasure, or continue its use for pleasure, unless he learns to define its effects as enjoyable, unless it becomes and remains an object which he conceived of as capable of producing pleasure.

IV

In summary, an individual will be able to use marihuana for pleasure only when he goes through a process of learning to conceive of it as an object which can be used in this way. No one becomes a user without (1) learning to smoke the drug in a way which will produce real effects; (2) learning to recognize the effects and connect them with drug use (learning, in other words, to get high); and (3) learning to enjoy the sensations he perceives. In the course of this process he develops a disposition or motivation to use marihuana which was not and could not have been present when he began use, for it involves and depends on conceptions of the drug which could only grow out of the kind of actual experience detailed above. On completion of this process he is willing and able to use marihuana for pleasure.

He has learned, in short, to answer "Yes" to the question: "Is it fun?" The direction his further use of the drug takes depends on his being able to continue to answer "Yes" to this question and, in addition, on his being able to answer "Yes" to other questions which arise as he becomes aware of the implications of the fact that the society as a whole disapproves of the practice: "Is it expedient?" "Is it moral?" Once he has acquired the ability to get enjoyment out of the drug, use will continue to be possible for him. Considerations of morality and expediency, occasioned by the reactions of society, may interfere and inhibit use, but use continues to be a possibility in terms of his conception of the drug. The act becomes impossible only when the ability to enjoy the experience of being high is lost, through a change in the user's conception of the drug occasioned by certain kinds of experience with it.

In comparing this theory with those which ascribe marihuana use to motives or predispositions rooted deep in individual behavior, the evidence makes it clear that marihuana use for pleasure can occur only when the process described above is undergone and cannot occur without it. This is apparently so without reference to the nature of the individual's personal makeup, or psychic problems. Such theories assume that people have stable modes of response which predetermine the way they will act in relation to any particular situation or object and that, when they come in contact with the given object or situation, they act in the way in which their makeup predisposes them.

This analysis of the genesis of marihuana use shows that the individuals who come in contact with a given object may respond to it at first in a great variety of ways. If a stable form of new behavior toward the object is to emerge, a transformation of meanings must occur, in which the person develops a new conception of the nature of the object.[11] This happens in a series of communicative acts in which others point out new aspects of his experience to him, present him with new interpretations of events, and help him achieve a new conceptual organization of his world, without which the new behavior is not possible. Persons who do not achieve the proper kind of conceptualization are unable to engage in the given behavior and turn off in the direction of some other relationship to the object or activity.

This suggests that behavior of any kind might fruitfully be studied developmentally, in terms of changes in meanings and concepts, their organization and reorganization, and the way they channel behavior, making some acts possible while excluding others.

Notes

1. See, as examples of this approach, the following: E. Marcovitz & H. J. Meyers (1944, December), "The marihuana addict in the army," *War Medicine, 6,* 382-391; H. S. Gaskill (1945, September), "Marihuana, an intoxicant," *American Journal of Psychiatry, 102,* 202-204; S. Charen & L. Perelman (1946, March), "Personality studies of marihuana addicts," *American Journal of Psychiatry, 102,* 674-682.

2. This approach stems from George Herbert Mead's (1934) discussion of objects in *Mind, self, and society,* Chicago: University of Chicago Press, pp. 277-280.

3. Cf. R. Adams (1942, November), "Marihuana," *Bulletin of the New York Academy of Medicine, 18,* 705-730.

4. Cf. L. Kolb (1938, July), "Marihuana," *Federal Probation, 2,* 22-25; and W. Bromberg (1939, July 1), "Marihuana: A psychiatric study," *Journal of the American Medical Association, 113,* 11.

5. The method used is that described in A. R. Lindesmith (1947), *Opiate addiction,* Bloomington, IN: Principia, chap. i. I would like also to acknowledge the important role Lindesmith's work played in shaping my thinking about the genesis of marihuana use.

6. Most of the interviews were done by the author. I am grateful to Solomon Kobrin and Harold Finestone for allowing me to make use of interviews done by them.

7. I hope to discuss elsewhere other stages in this natural history.

8. A pharmacologist notes that this ritual is in fact an extremely efficient way of getting the drug into the blood stream. R. P. Walton (1938), *Marihuana: America's new drug problem,* Philadelphia: J. B. Lippincott, p. 48.

9. "Smokers have repeatedly stated that the consumption of whiskey while smoking negates the potency of the drug. They find it very difficult to get 'high' while drinking whiskey and because of that smokers will not drink while using the 'weed.' " Cf. New York City Mayor's Committee on Marihuana (1944), *The marihuana problem in the city of New York,* Lancaster, PA: Jacques Cattel, p. 13.

10. Charen & Perelman (1946), p. 679.

11. Cf. A. Strauss (1952, June), "The development and transformation of monetary meanings in the child," *American Sociological Review, 17,* 275-286.

22

The Madam as Teacher:
The Training of House Prostitutes

Barbara Sherman Heyl

Ann's Turn-out Establishment

A professional prostitute, whether she works as a streetwalker, house prostitute, or call girl, can usually pick out one person in her past who "turned her out," that is, who taught her the basic techniques and rules of the prostitute's occupation. For women who begin working at the house level, that person may be a pimp, another "working girl," or a madam. Most madams and managers of prostitution establishments, however, prefer not to take on novice prostitutes, and they may even have a specific policy against hiring turn-outs (see Erwin, 1960, pp. 204-205; and Lewis, 1942, p. 22). The turn-out's inexperience may cost the madam clients and money; to train the novice, on the other hand, costs her time and energy. Most madams and managers simply do not want the additional burden.

It was precisely the madam's typical disdain for turn-outs that led to the emergence of the house discussed in this paper—a house specifically devoted to training new prostitutes. The madam of this operation, whom

"The Madam as Teacher: The Training of House Prostitutes" by B. S. Heyl, 1977. *Social Problems*, 24, pp. 545-555. Copyright © 1977 by the Society for the Study of Social Problems, by permission. Also found in *The Madam as Entrepreneur* by B. S. Heyl, 1979 (New Brunswick, NJ: Transaction Books).

we shall call Ann, is forty-one years old and has been in the prostitution world twenty-three years, working primarily at the house level. Ann knew that pimps who manage women at this level have difficulty placing novices in houses. After operating several houses staffed by professional prostitutes, she decided to run a school for turn-outs partly as a strategy for acquiring a continually changing staff of young women for her house. Pimps are the active recruiters of new prostitutes, and Ann found that, upon demonstrating that she could transform the pimps' new, square women into trained prostitutes easily placed in professional houses, pimps would help keep her business staffed. Ann's house is a small operation in a middle-sized, industrial city (population 300,000), with a limited clientele of primarily working-class men retained as customers for ten to fifteen years and offered low rates to maintain their patronage.

Although Ann insists that every turn-out is different, her group of novices is remarkably homogeneous in some ways. Ann has turned out approximately twenty women a year over the six years while she has operated a training school. Except for one Chicano, one black, and one American Indian, the women were all white. They ranged in age from eighteen to twenty-seven. Until three years ago, all the women she hired had pimps. Since then, more women are independent (so-called "outlaws"), although many come to Ann sponsored by a pimp. That is, in return for being placed with Ann, the turn-out gives the pimp a percentage of her earnings for a specific length of time. At present eighty percent of the turn-outs come to Ann without a long-term commitment to a pimp. The turn-outs stay at Ann's on the average of two to three months. This is the same average length of time Bryan (1965, p. 209) finds for the apprenticeship in his call-girl study. Ann seldom has more than two or three women in training at any one time. Most turn-outs live at the house, often just a large apartment near the older business section of the city.

The Content of the Training

The data for the following analysis are of three kinds. First, tape recordings from actual training sessions with fourteen novices helped specify the structure and content of the training provided. Second, lengthy interviews with three of the novices and multiple interviews with Ann were conducted to obtain data on the training during the novice's first few days at the house before the first group training sessions were conducted and recorded by Ann. And third, visits to the house on ten occasions and observations of Ann's interaction with the novices during teaching periods extended the data on training techniques used and the relationship between madam and novice. In addition, weekly contact with Ann over a four-year period allowed repeated review of current problems and strategies in training turn-outs.

The content analysis of the taped training sessions produced three major topics of discussion and revealed the relative amount of time Ann devoted to each. The first two most frequently discussed topics can be categorized under Bryan's dimension of interpersonal skills; they were devoted to teaching situational strategies for managing clients.

The third topic resembles Bryan's value dimension (1965, pp. 291-292).

The first topic stressed physical skills and strategies. Included in this category were instruction on how to perform certain sexual acts and specification of their prices, discussion of particular clients, and instruction in techniques for dealing with certain categories of clients, such as "older men" or "kinky" tricks. This topic of physical skills also included discussion of, and Ann's demonstration of, positions designed to provide the woman maximum comfort and protection from the man during different sexual acts. Defense tactics, such as ways to get out of a sexual position and out of the bedroom quickly, were practiced by the novices. Much time was devoted to analyzing past encounters with particular clients. Bryan finds similar discussions of individual tricks among novice call girls and their trainers (1965, p. 293). In the case of Ann's turn-outs these discussions were often initiated by a novice's complaint or question about a certain client and his requests or behavior in the bedroom. The novice always received tips and advice from Ann and the other women present on how to manage that type of bedroom encounter. Such sharing of tactics allow the turn-out to learn what Gagnon and Simon call "patterns of client management" (1973, p. 231).

The second most frequently discussed topic could be labeled client management-verbal skills. Ann's primary concern was teaching what she calls "hustling." "Hustling" is similar to what Bryan terms a "sales pitch" for call girls (1965, p. 292), but in the house setting it takes place in the bedroom while the client is deciding how much to spend and what sexual acts he wishes performed. "Hustling" is designed to encourage the client to spend more than the minimum rate. The prominence on the teaching tapes of instruction in this verbal skill shows its importance in Ann's training of novices.

On one of the tapes Ann uses her own turning-out experience to explain to two novices (both with pimps) why she always teaches hustling skills as an integral part of working in a house.

Ann as a Turn-out

Ann: Of course, I can remember a time when I didn't know that I was supposed to hustle. So that's why I understand that it's difficult to *learn* to hustle. When I turned out it was $2 a throw. They came in. They gave me their $2. They got a hell of a fuck. And that was it. Then one Saturday night I turned *forty-four* tricks! And Penny [the madam] used to put the number of tricks at the top of the page and the amount of money at the bottom of the page—she used these big ledger books. Lloyd [Ann's pimp] came in at six o'clock and he looked at that book and he just *knew* I had made all kinds of money. Would you believe I had turned forty-two $2 tricks and two $3 tricks—because two of 'em got generous and gave me an extra buck! [Laughs] I got my ass whipped. And I was so tired—I thought I was going to die—I was 15 years old. And I got my ass whipped for it. [Ann imitates an angry Lloyd:] "Don't you know you're supposed to ask for more money?!" No, I didn't. Nobody told me that. All they told me was it was $2. So that is learning it the *hard* way. I'm trying to help you learn it the *easy* way, if there is an easy way to do it.

In the same session Ann asks one of the turn-outs (Linda, age eighteen) to practice her hustling rap.

Learning the Hustling Rap

Ann: I'm going to be a trick. You've checked me. I want you to carry it from there. [Ann begins role-playing: she plays the client; Linda, the hustler.]

Linda: [mechanically] What kind of party would you like to have?

Ann: That had all the enthusiasm of a wet noodle. I really wouldn't *want* any party with that because you evidently don't want give me one.

Linda: What kind of party would you *like* to have?

Ann: I usually take a half and half.

Linda: Uh, the money?

Ann: What money?

Linda: The money you're supposed to have! [loudly] 'Cause you ain't getting' it for free!

Ann: [upset] Linda, if you *ever*, ever say that in my joint . . . Because that's fine for street hustling. In street hustling, you're going to *have* to hard-hustle those guys or they're not going to come up with anything. Because they're going to *try* and get it for free. But when they walk in here, they *know* they're not going to get it for free to begin with. So try another tack—just a little more friendly, not quite so hard-nosed. [Returning to role-playing:] I just take a half and half.

Linda: How about fifteen [dollars]?

Ann: You're leading into the money too fast. Try: "What are you going to spend?" or "How much money are you going to spend?" or something like that.

Linda: How much would you like to spend?

Ann: No! Not "like." 'Cause they don't *like* to spend anything.

Linda: How much *would* you like to spend?

Ann: Make it a very definitive, positive statement: "How much are you going to spend?"

Ann considers teaching hustling skills her most difficult and important task. In spite of her lengthy discussion on the tapes of the rules and techniques for dealings with the customer sexually, Ann states that it may take only a few minutes to "show a girl how to turn a trick." A substantially longer period is required, however, to teach her to hustle. To be adept at hustling, the woman must be mentally alert and sensitive to the client's response to what she is saying and doing and be able to act on those perceptions of his reactions. The hustler must maintain a steady patter of verbal coaxing, during which her tone of voice may be more important than her actual words.

In Ann's framework, then, hustling is a form of verbal sexual aggression. Referring to the problems in teaching novices to hustle, Ann notes that "taking the aggressive part is something women are not used to doing, particularly young women." No doubt, hustling is difficult to teach partly because the woman must learn to discuss sexual acts, whereas in her previous experience, sexual behavior and preferences had been negotiated nonverbally (see Gagnon & Simon, 1973, p. 228). Ann feels that to be effective, each woman's "hustling rap" must be her own—one that comes naturally and will strike the clients as sincere. All of that takes practice. But Ann is aware that the difficulty in learning to hustle stems more from the fact that it involves inappropriate sex-role behavior. Bryan concludes that it is precisely this aspect of soliciting men on the telephone that causes the greatest distress to the novice call girl (1965, p. 293). Thus, the call girl's income is affected by how much business she can bring in by her calls, that is, by how well she can learn to be socially aggressive on the telephone. The income of the house prostitute, in turn, depends heavily on her hustling skills in the bedroom. Ann's task, then, is to train the novice, who has recently come from a culture where young women are not expected to be sexually aggressive, to assume that role with a persuasive naturalness.

Following the first two major topics—client management through physical and verbal skills—the teaching of "racket" (prostitution world) values was the third-ranking topic of training and discussion on the teaching tapes. Bryan notes that the major value taught to call girls is "that of maximizing gains and minimizing effort, even if this requires transgressions of either a legal or moral nature" (1965, p. 291). In her training, however, Ann avoids communicating the notion that the novices may exploit the customers in any way they can. For example, stealing or cheating clients is grounds for dismissal from the house. Ann cannot afford the reputation among her tricks that they risk being robbed when they visit her. Moreover, being honest with clients is extolled as a virtue. Thus, Ann urges the novices to tell the trick if she is nervous or unsure, to let him know she is new to the business. This is in direct contradiction to

the advice pimps usually give their new women to hide their inexperience from the trick. Ann asserts that honesty in this case usually means that the client will be more tolerant of mistakes in sexual technique, be less likely to interpret hesitancy as coldness, and be generally more helpful and sympathetic. Putting her "basic principle" in the form of a simple directive, Ann declares: "Please the trick, but at the same time get as much money for pleasing him as you possibly can." Ann does not consider hustling to be client exploitation. It is simply the attempt to sell the customer the product with the highest profit margin. That is, she would defend hustling in terms familiar to the businessman or sales manager.

That Ann teaches hustling as a value is revealed in the following discussion between Ann and Sandy—a former hustler and long-time friend of Ann. Sandy, who married a former trick and still lives in town, has come over to the house to help instruct several novices in the hustling business.

Whores, Prostitutes, and Hustlers

Ann: [To the turn-outs:] Don't get up-tight that you're hesitating or you're fumbling, within the first week or even the first five years. Because it takes that long to become a good hustler. I mean you can be a whore in one night. There's nothing to that. The first time you take money you're a whore.

Sandy: This girl in Midtown [a small, Midwestern city] informed me—I had been working there awhile—that I was a "whore" and she was a "prostitute." And I said: "Now what the hell does that mean?" Well, the difference was that a prostitute could pick her customer and a whore had to take anybody. I said: "Well honey, I want to tell you something. I'm neither one." She said: "Well, you *work*." I said: "I know, but I'm a *hustler*. I make *money* for what I do."

Ann: And this is what I turn out—or try to turn out—hustlers. Not prostitutes. Not whores. But hustlers.

For Ann and Sandy the hustler deserves high status in the prostitution business because she has mastered a specific set of skills that, even with many repeat clients, earn her premiums above the going rate for sexual acts.

In the ideological training of call girls Bryan finds that "values such as fairness with other working girls, or fidelity to a pimp, may occasionally be taught" (1965, pp. 291-292); the teaching tapes revealed Ann's affirmation of both these virtues. When a pimp brings a woman to Ann, she supports his control over the woman. For example, if during her stay at the house, the novice breaks any of the basic rules—by using drugs, holding back money (from either Ann or the pimp), lying, or seeing another man—Ann will report the infractions to the woman's pimp. Ann notes: "If I don't do that and the pimp finds out, he knows I'm not training her right, and he won't bring his future ladies to me for training." Ann knows she is dependent on the pimps to help supply her with turn-outs. Bryan, likewise, finds a willingness among call girls' trainers to defer to the pimps' wishes during the apprenticeship period (1965, p. 290).

Teaching fairness to other prostitutes is particularly relevant to the madam who daily faces the problem of maintaining peace among competing women at work under one roof. If two streetwalkers or two call girls find they cannot get along, they need not work near one another. But if a woman leaves a house because of personal conflicts, the madam loses a source of income. To minimize potential negative feelings among novices, Ann stresses mutual support, prohibits "criticizing another girl," and denigrates the "prima donna"—the prostitute who flaunts her financial success before the other women.

In still another strategy to encourage fair treatment of one's colleagues in the establishment, Ann emphasizes a set of rules prohibiting "dirty hustling"—behavior engaged in by one prostitute that would undercut the business of other women in the house. Tabooed under the label of "dirty hustling" are the following: appearing in the line-up partially unclothed; performing certain disapproved sexual positions, such as anal intercourse; and allowing approved sexual extras without charging additional fees. The norms governing acceptable behavior vary from house to house and region to region, and Ann warns the turn-outs to ask about such rules when they begin work in a new establishment. The woman who breaks the work norms in a house, either knowingly or unknowingly, will draw the anger of the other women and can be fired by a madam eager to restore peace and order in the house.

Other topics considered on the tapes—in addition to physical skills, "hustling," and work values—were instruction on personal hygiene and grooming, role-playing of conversational skills with tricks on topics not related to sex or hustling ("living room talk"), house rules not related to hustling (such as punctuality, no perfume, no drugs), and guidelines for what to do during an arrest. There were specific suggestions on how to handle personal criticism, questions, and insults from clients. In addition, the discussions on the tapes provided the novices with many general strategies for becoming "professionals" at their work, for example, the importance of personal style, enthusiasm ("the customer is always right"), and sense of humor. In some ways these guidelines resemble a beginning course in salesmanship. But they also provide clues, particularly in combination with the topics on handling client insults and the emphasis on hustling, on how the house prostitute learns to manage a stable and limited clientele and cope psychologically with the repetition of the clients and the sheer tedium of the physical work (Hughes, 1971, pp. 342-345).

Training House Prostitutes—A Process of Professional Socialization

Observing how Ann trains turn-outs is a study in techniques to facilitate identity change (see also Davis, 1971; Heyl, 1974, chap. 2). Ann uses a variety of persuasive strategies to help give the turn-outs a new occupational identity as a "professional." One strategy is to help heavily on the new values taught the novice to isolate her from her previous life style and acquaintances. Bryan finds that "The value structure [taught to novice call girls] serves, in general, to create in-group solidarity and to alienate the girl from 'square' society" (1965, p. 292). Whereas alienation from conventional society may be an indirect effect of values taught to call girls, in Ann's training of house prostitutes the expectation that the novice will immerse herself in the prostitution world ("racket life") is made dramatically explicit.

In the following transcription from one of the teaching tapes, the participants are Ann (age thirty-six at the time the tape was made), Bonnie (an experienced turn-out, age twenty-five), and Kristy (a new turn-out, age eighteen). Kristy has recently linked up with a pimp for the first time and volunteers to Ann and Bonnie her difficulty in adjusting to the racket rule of minimal contact with the square world—a rule her pimp is enforcing by not allowing Kristy to meet and talk with her old friends. Ann (A) and Bonnie (B) have listened to Kristy's (K) complaints and are making suggestions. (The notation "B-K" indicates that Bonnie is addressing Kristy.)

Kristy's Isolation From the Square World

B-K: What you gotta do is sit down and talk to him and weed out your friends and find the ones he thinks are suitable companions for you—in your new type of life.

K-B: None of them.

A-K: What about *his* friends?

K-A: I haven't met very many of his friends. I don't like any of 'em so far.

A-K: You are making the same mistake that makes me so goddamned irritated with square broads! You're taking a man and trying to train *him,* instead of letting the man train you.

K-A: What?! I'm not trying to train him, I'm just . . .

A-K: All right, you're trying to force him to accept your friends.

K-A: I don't care whether he accepts them or not. I just can't go around not talking to anybody.

A-K: "Anybody" is your old man! He is your world. And the people he says you can talk to are the people that are your world. But what you're trying to do is force your square world on a racket guy. It's like oil and water. There's just no way a square and a racket person can get together. That's why when you turn out you've got to change your mind completely from square to racket. And you're still trying to hang with squares. You can't do it.

Strauss' (1969) concept of "coaching" illuminates a more subtle technique Ann employs as she helps the novice along, step by step, from "square" to "racket" values and life style. She observes carefully how the novice progresses, elicits responses from her about what she is experiencing, and then interprets those responses for her. In the following excerpt from one of the teaching tapes, Ann prepares two novices for feelings of depression over their newly-made decisions to become prostitutes.

Turn-out Blues

Ann: And while I'm on the subject—depression. You know they've got a word for it when you have a baby—it's called "postpartum blues." Now, I call it "turn-out blues." Every girl that ever turns out has 'em. And, depending on the girl, it comes about the third or fourth day. You'll go into a depression for no apparent reason. You'll wake up one morning and you'll say: "Why in the hell am I doing this? Why am I here? I wanna go home!" And I can't do a thing to help you. The only thing I can do is leave you alone and hope that you'll fight the battle yourself. But knowing that it will come, and knowing that everybody else goes through it too, does help. Just pray it's a busy night! So if you get blue and you get down, remember: "turn-out blues"—everybody gets it. Here's when you'll decide whether you're going to stay or you're gonna quit.

Ann's description of "turn-out blues" is a good example of Strauss' account (1969, pp. 111-112) of how coaches will use prophecy to increase their persuasive power over their novices. In the case of "turn-out blues," the novice, if she becomes depressed about her decision to enter prostitution, will recall Ann's prediction that this would happen and that it happens to all turn-outs. This recollection may or may not end the woman's misgivings about her decision, but it will surely enhance the turn-out's impression of Ann's competence. Ann's use of her past experience to make such predictions is a form of positive leverage; it increases the probability that what she says will be respected and followed in the future.

In Bryan's study the call girls reported that their training was more a matter of observation than direct instruction from their trainer (1965, p. 294). Ann, on the other hand, relies on a variety of teaching techniques, including lecturing and discussion involving other turn-outs who are further along in the training process and can reinforce Ann's views. Ann even brings in guest speakers, such as Sandy, the former hustler, who participates in the discussion with the novices in the role of the experienced resource person. "Learning the Hustling Rap," above, offers an example of role-playing—another teaching technique Ann frequently employs to help the turn-outs develop verbal skills. Ann may have to rely on more varied teaching approaches than the call-girl trainer because: (1) Ann herself is not working, thus her novices have fewer opportunities to watch their trainer interact with clients than do the call-girl novices; and (2) Ann's livelihood depends more directly on the success of her teaching efforts than does that of the call-girl trainer. Ann feels that if a woman under her direction does not "turn out well," not only will the woman earn less money while she is at her house (affecting Ann's own income), but Ann could also lose clients and future turn-outs from her teaching "failure."

The dissolution of the training relationship marks the end of the course. Bryan claims that the sharp break between trainer and trainee shows that the training process itself is largely unrelated to the acquisition of a skill. But one would scarcely have expected the trainee to report "that the final disruption of the apprenticeship was the result of the completion of adequate training" (1965, p. 296). Such establishments do not offer diplomas and terminal degrees. The present study, too, indicates that abrupt breaks in the training relationship are quite common. But what is significant is that the break is precipitated by personal conflicts exacerbated by both the narrowing of the skill-gap between trainer and trainee and the consequent increase in the novice's confidence that she can make it on her own. Thus, skill acquisition counts in such an equation, not in a formal sense ("completion of adequate training"), but rather insofar as it works to break down the earlier bonds of dependence between trainer and trainee.

References

Bryan, J. H. (1965, Winter). Apprenticeships in prostitution. *Social Problems, 12,* 287-297.

Bryan, J. H. (1966, Spring). Occupational ideologies and individual attitudes of call girls. *Social Problems, 13,* 441-450.

Davis, N. J. (1971). The prostitute: Developing a deviant identity. In J. M. Henslin (Ed.), *Studies in the sociology of sex.* New York: Appleton-Century-Crofts.

Erwin, C. (1960). *The orderly disorderly house.* Garden City, NY: Doubleday.

Gagnon, J. H., & Simon, W. (1973). *Sexual conduct: The social sources of human sexuality.* Chicago: Aldine.

Heyl, B. S. (1974, Spring). The madam as entrepreneur. *Sociological Symposium, 11,* 61-82.

Hughes, E. C. (1971). Work and self. In *The sociological eye: Selected papers* (pp. 338-347). Chicago: Aldine-Atherton.

Lewis, G. A. (1942). *Call house madam: The story of the career of Beverly Davis.* San Francisco: Martin Tudordale.

Strauss, A. L. (1969). *Mirrors and masks: The search for identity.* San Francisco: Sociology Press.

Accounts

Marvin B. Scott and *Stanford M. Lyman*

From time to time sociologists might well pause from their ongoing pursuits to inquire whether their research interests contribute in any way to the fundamental question of sociology, namely, the Hobbesian question: How is society possible? Attempts to answer this question could serve to unite a discipline that may not yet have forgotten its founders, but may still have forgotten why it was founded.

Our purpose here is not to review the various answers to the Hobbesian question,[1] but rather to suggest that an answer to this macro-sociological problem might be fruitfully explored in the analysis of the slightest of interpersonal rituals and the very stuff of which most of those rituals are composed—talk.

Talk, we hold, is the fundamental material of human relations. And though sociologists have not entirely neglected the subject,[2] the sociology of talk has scarcely been developed. Our concern here is with one feature of talk: Its ability to shore up the timbers of fractured association, its ability to throw bridges between the promised and the performed, its ability to repair the broken and restore the estranged. This feature of talk involves the giving and receiving of what we shall call *accounts*.

An account is a linguistic device employed whenever an action is subjected to valuative inquiry.[3] Such devices are a crucial element in the social order since they prevent conflicts from arising by verbally bridging the gap between action and expectation.[4] Moreover, accounts are "situated" according to the statuses of the interactants, and are standardized within cultures so that certain accounts are terminologically stabilized and routinely expected when activity falls outside the domain of expectations.

By an account, then, we mean a statement made by a social actor to explain unanticipated or untoward behavior—whether that behavior is his own or that of others, and whether the proximate cause for the statement arises from the actor himself or from someone else.[5] An account is not called for when people engage in routine, common-sense behavior in a cultural environment that recognizes that behavior as such. Thus in American society we do not ordinarily ask why married people engage in sexual intercourse, or why they maintain a home with their children, although the latter question might well be asked if such behavior occurred among the Nayars of Malabar.[6] These questions are not asked because they have been settled in advance in our culture and are indicated by the language itself. We learn the meaning of a "married couple" by indicating that they are two people of opposite sex who have a legitimate right to engage in sexual intercourse and maintain their own children in their own household. When such taken-for-granted phenomena are called into question, the inquirer (if a member of the same culture group) is regarded as "just fooling around," or perhaps as being sick.[7]

To specify our concerns more sharply we should at this point distinguish accounts from the related phenomenon of "explanations." The latter refers to statements about events where untoward action is not an issue and does not have critical implications for relationship. Much of what is true about accounts will also hold for explanations, but our concern is primarily with linguistic forms that are offered for untoward action. With this qualification to our concern, we may now specify further the nature and types of accounts.

Types of Accounts

There are in general two types of accounts: *excuses* and *justifications*.[8] Either or both are likely to be invoked when a person is accused of having done something that is "bad, wrong, inept, unwelcome, or in some other of the numerous possible ways, untoward."[9] Justifications are accounts in which one accepts responsibility for the act in question, but denies the pejorative quality associated with it. Thus a soldier in combat may admit that he has killed other men, but deny that he did an immoral act since those he killed were members of an enemy group and hence "deserved" their fate. Excuses are accounts in which one admits that the act in question is bad, wrong, or inappropriate but denies full responsibility. Thus our combat soldier could admit the wrongfulness of killing but claim that his acts are not entirely undertaken by volition: he is "under orders" and must obey. With these introductory remarks, we now turn our focus to a more detailed examination of types of justifications and excuses.

Excuses are socially approved vocabularies for mitigating or relieving responsibility when conduct is questioned. We may distinguish initially four modal forms by which excuses are typically formulated:[10] *appeal to accidents, appeal to defeasibility, appeal to biological drives,* and *scapegoating.*

Excuses claiming *accident* as the source of conduct or its consequences mitigate (if not relieve) responsibility by pointing to the generally recognized hazards in the environment, the understandable inefficiency of the body, and the human incapacity to control all motor responses. The excuse of accident is acceptable precisely because of the irregularity and infrequency of accidents occurring to any single actor. Thus while hazards are numerous and ubiquitous, a particular person is not expected ordinarily to experience the same accident often. In other words, social actors employ a lay version of statistical curves whereby they interpret certain acts as occurring or not occurring by chance alone. When a person conducts himself so that the same type of accident befalls him frequently, he is apt to earn a label— such as "clumsy"—which will operate to stigmatize him and to warn others not to put him and themselves or their property in jeopardy by creating the environment in which he regularly has accidents. When the excuse is rooted in an accident that is unobservable or unable to be investigated—such as blaming one's lateness to work on the heaviness of traffic—frequent pleas of it are likely to be discredited. Excuses based on accidents are thus most likely to be honored precisely because they do not occur all the time or for the most part to the actor in question.[11]

Appeals to *defeasibility*[12] are available as a form of excuse because of the widespread agreement that all actions contain some "mental element." The components of the mental element are "knowledge" and "will." One defense against an accusation is that a person was not fully informed or that his "will" was not completely "free." Thus an individual might excuse himself from responsibility by claiming that certain information was not available to him, which, if it had been, would have altered his behavior. Further, an individual might claim to have acted in a certain way because of misinformation arising from intentional or innocent misrepresentation of the facts by others. An excuse based on interference with the "free will" of an individual might invoke duress or undue influence. Finally both will and knowledge can be impaired under certain conditions, the invocation of which ordinarily constitutes an adequate mitigation of responsibility—intoxication (whether from alcohol or drugs) and lunacy (whether temporary or permanent) being examples.

In ordinary affairs and in law a person's actions are usually distinguished according to their intent. Further, a person's intentions are distinguished from the consequences of his actions. Under a situation where an action is questioned an actor may claim a lack of intent or a failure to foresee the consequences of his act, or both. If the action in question involves a motor response—such as knocking over a vase—the situation is not very different from that subsumed under the term accident. When actions going beyond motor responses are at issue, the actor's intentions and foresight can be questioned. "Why did you make her cry?" asks the accuser. The presentational strategies in reply to this question allow several modes of defeating the central claim implied in the question, namely, that the actor intended with full knowledge to make the lady weep. The accused may simply deny any intention on his part to have caused the admittedly unfortunate consequence. However, men ordinarily impute to one another some measure of foresight for their actions so that a simple denial of intent may not be believed if it appears that the consequence of the action in question was indeed what another person might expect and therefore what the actor intended.

In addition to his denial of intent an actor may also deny his knowledge of the consequence. The simplest denial is the cognitive disclaimer, "I did not *know* that I would make her cry by what I did." But this complete denial of cognition is often not honored, especially when the interactants know one another well and are expected to have a more complete imagery of the consequences of their acts to guide them. A more complex denial—the gravity disclaimer—includes admitting to the possibility of the outcome in question but suggesting that its probability was incalculable: "I knew matters were serious, but I did not know that telling her would make her weep."

Still another type of excuse invokes biological drives. This invocation is part of a larger category of "fatalistic" forces which in various cultures are deemed in greater or lesser degree to be controlling of some or all events. Cultures dominated by universalist-achievement orientations[13] tend to give scant and ambiguous support to fatalistic interpretations of events, but rarely disavow them entirely. To account for the whole of one's life in such terms, or to account for events which are conceived by others to be controlled by the actor's conscience, will, and abilities is to lay oneself open to the charge of mental illness or personality disorganization.[14] On the other hand, recent studies have emphasized the situational element in predisposing certain persons and groups in American society to what might be regarded as a "normalized" fatalistic view of their condition. Thus, for example, Negroes[15] and adolescent delinquents[16] are regarded and tend to regard themselves as less in control of the forces that shape their lives than whites or middle-class adults.

Among the fatalistic items most likely to be invoked as an excuse are the biological drives. Despite the emphasis in Occidental culture since the late nineteenth century on personality and social environment as causal elements in human action, there is still a popular belief in and varied commitment to the efficacy of the body and biological factors in determining human behavior. Such commonplaces as "men are like that" are short-hand phrases invoking belief in sex-linked traits that allegedly govern behavior beyond the will of the actor. Precisely because the body and its biological behavior are always present but not always accounted for in science or society, invocation of the body and its processes is available as an excuse. The body and its inner workings enjoy something of the status of the sociological stranger as conceived by Simmel, namely, they are ever with us but mysterious. Hence, biological drives may be credited with influencing or causing at least some of the behavior for which actors wish to relieve themselves of full responsibility.

The invocation of biological drives is most commonly an appeal to natural but uncontrollable sexual appetite. Among first and second generation Italians in America the recognition and fear of biologically induced sexual intercourse serves men as both an excuse for pre- and extra-marital sexual relations and a justification for not being alone with women ineligible for coitus. Thus one student of Italian-American culture observes:

What the men fear is their own ability at self-control. This attitude, strongest among young unmarried people, often carries over into adulthood. The traditional Italian belief—that sexual intercourse is unavoidable when a man and a woman are by themselves—is maintained intact among second-generation Italians, and continues even when sexual interest itself is on the wane. For example, I was told of an older woman whose apartment was adjacent to that of an unmarried male relative. Although they had lived in the same building for almost twenty years and saw each other every day, she had never once been in his apartment because of this belief.[17]

Biological drive may be an expected excuse in some cultures, so that the failure to invoke it, and the use of some other excuse, constitutes an improper account when the appropriate one is available. Oscar Lewis provides such an example in his ethnography of a Mexican family. A cuckolded wife angrily rejects her wayward husband's explanation that the red stains on his shirt are due to paint rubbed off during the course of his work. She strongly suggests, in her retelling of the incident, that she would have accepted an excuse appealing to her husband's basic sex drives:[18]

And he had me almost believing it was red paint! It was not that I am jealous. I realize a man can never be satisfied with just one woman, but I cannot stand being made a fool of.

Homosexuals frequently account for their deviant sexual desires by invoking the principle of basic biological nature. As one homosexual put it:[19]

It's part of nature. You can't alter it, no matter how many injections and pills they give you.

Another of the biological elements that can be utilized as an excuse is the shape of the body itself. Body types are not only defined in purely anatomical terms, but also, and perhaps more importantly, in terms of their shared social meanings. Hence fat people can excuse their excessive laughter by appealing to the widely accepted proverb that fat men are jolly. Similarly, persons bearing features considered to be stereotypically "criminal"[20] may be exonerated for their impoliteness or small larcenies on the grounds that their looks proved their intentions and thus their victims ought to have been on guard. The phrase, "he looks crooked to me," serves as a warning to others to carefully appraise the character and intentions of the person so designated, since his features bespeak an illegal intent.

The final type of excuse we shall mention is *scapegoating*. Scapegoating is derived from another form of fatalistic reasoning. Using this form a person will allege that his questioned behavior is a response to the behavior or attitudes of another. Certain psychological theory treats this phenomenon as indicative of personality disorder, and, if found in conjunction with certain other characteristic traits, a signal of authoritarian personality.[21] Our treatment bypasses such clinical and pathological concerns in order to deal with the "normal" situation in which individuals slough off the burden of responsibility for their actions and shift it on to another. In Mexican working-class society, for example, women hold a distinctly secondary position relative to men, marriage causes a loss of status to the latter, and sexual intercourse is regarded ambivalently as healthy and natural, but also as a necessary evil.[22] Such a set of orientations predisposes both men and women to attribute many of their shortcomings to women. An example is found in the autobiography of a Mexican girl:[23]

> I was always getting into fights because some girls are vipers; they get jealous, tell lies about each other, and start trouble.

Similarly, a Mexican youth who tried unsuccessfully to meet a girl by showing off on a bicycle explains:[24]

> She got me into trouble with my father by lying about me. She said I tried to run her down with my bike and that all I did was hang around spying on her.

In another instance the same youth attributes his waywardness to the fact that the girl truly loved was his half-sister and thus unavailable to him for coitus or marriage:

> So, because of Antonia, I began to stay away from home. It was one of the main reasons I started to go on the bum, looking for trouble.[25]

Like excuses, *justifications* are socially approved vocabularies that neutralize an act or its consequences when one or both are called into question. But here is the crucial difference: to *justify* an act is to assert its positive value in the face of a claim to the contrary. Justifications recognize a general sense in which the act in question is impermissible, but claim that the particular occasion permits or requires the very act. The laws governing the taking of life are a case in point. American and English jurisprudence are by no means united on definitions or even on the nature of the acts in question, but in general a man may justify taking the life of another by claiming that he acted in self-defense, in defense of others' lives or property, or in action against a declared enemy of the state.

For a tentative list of types of justifications we may turn to what has been called "techniques of neutralization."[26] Although these techniques have been discussed with respect to accounts offered by juvenile delinquents for untoward action, their wider use has yet to be explored. Relevant to our discussion of justification are the techniques of "denial of injury," "denial of victim," "condemnation of condemners," and "appeal to loyalties."[27]

In *denial of injury* the actor acknowledges that he did a particular act but asserts that it was permissible to do that act since no one was injured by it, or since no one about whom the community need be concerned with was involved, or finally since the act resulted in consequences that were trifling. Note that this justification device can be invoked with respect to both persons and objects. The denial of injury to *persons* suggests that they be viewed as "deserving" in a special sense: that they are oversupplied with the valued things of the world, or that they are "private" persons ("my friends," "my enemies") who have no standing to claim injury in the public, or to be noticed as injured. Denial of injury to *objects* involves redefining the act as not injurious to it but only using it, e.g., car "borrowing" is not theft.

In *denial of the victim* the actor expresses the position that the action was permissible since the victim deserved the injury. Four categories of persons are frequently perceived as deserving injury. First, there are proximate foes, i.e., those who have directly injured the actor; second, incumbents of normatively discrepant roles, e.g., homosexuals, whores, pimps; third, groups with tribal stigmas, e.g., racial and ethnic minorities; and finally, distant foes, that is, incumbents of roles held to be dubious or hurtful, e.g., "Whitey," the "Reds," "politicians." Besides categories of persons, there are categories of objects perceived as deserving of injury. To begin with, the property of any of the above mentioned categories of persons may become a focus of attack, especially if that property is symbolic of the attacked person's status. Thus the clothing of the whore is torn, the gavel of the politician is smashed, and so on. Secondly, there are objects that have a neutral or ambiguous identity with respect to ownership, e.g., a park bench. A final focus of attacked objects are those having a low or polluted value, e.g., junk, or kitsch.

Using the device of *condemnation of the condemners*, the actor admits performing an untoward act but asserts its irrelevancy because others commit these and worse acts, and these others are either not caught, not punished, not condemned, unnoticed, or even praised.

Still another neutralization technique is *appeal to loyalties*. Here the actor asserts that his action was permissible or even right since it served the interests of another to whom he owes an unbreakable allegiance or affection.[28]

Besides these "techniques of neutralization," two other sorts of justification may be mentioned: "sad tales," and "self-fulfillment." The *sad tale* is a selected (often distorted) arrangement of facts that highlight an extremely dismal past, and thus "explain" the individual's present state.[29]

For example, a mental patient relates:[30]

I was going to night school to get an M.A. degree, and holding down a job in addition, and the load got too much for me.

And a homosexual accounts for his present deviance with this sad tale:[31]

I was in a very sophisticated queer circle at the university. It was queer in a sense that we all camped like mad with "my dear" at the beginning of every sentence, but there was practically no sex, and in my case there was none at all. The break came when I went to a party and flirted with a merchant seaman who took me seriously and cornered me in a bedroom. There was I, the great sophisticate, who, when it came to the point, was quite raw, completely inexperienced; and I might tell you that seaman gave me quite a shock. I can't say I enjoyed it very much but it wasn't long after before I started to dive into bed with anyone.

Finally we may mention a peculiarly modern type of justification, namely, *self*-fulfillment. Interviewing LSD users and homosexuals in the Haight-Ashbury district of San Francisco, we are struck by the prominence of self-fulfillment as the grounds for these activities. Thus, an "acid head" relates:[32]

The whole purpose in taking the stuff is self-development. Acid expands consciousness. Mine eyes have seen the glory—can you say that? I never knew what capacities I had until I went on acid.

And a Lesbian:[33]

Everyone has the right to happiness and love. I was married once. It was hell. But now I feel I have fulfilled myself as a person and as a woman.

We might also note that the drug users and homosexuals interviewed (in San Francisco) who invoked the justification of self-fulfillment did not appear to find anything "wrong" with their behavior. They indicated either a desire to be left alone or to enlighten what they considered to be the unenlightened establishment.

Honoring Accounts and Background Expectations

Accounts may be honored or not honored. If an account is honored, we may say that it was efficacious and equilibrium is thereby restored in a relationship. The most common situation in which accounts are routinely honored is encounters interrupted by "incidents"—slips, boners, or gaffes which introduce information deleterious to the otherwise smooth conduct of the interactants.[34] Often a simple excuse will suffice, or the other interactants will employ covering devices to restore the status quo ante. A related situation is that in which an individual senses that some incident or event has cast doubt on that image of himself which he seeks to present. "At such times," the authority on impression management writes, "the individual is likely to try to integrate the incongruous events by means of apologies, little excuses for self, and disclaimers; through the same acts, incidentally, he also tries to save his face."[35]

One variable governing the honoring of an account is the character of the social circle in which it is introduced. As we pointed out earlier, vocabularies of accounts are likely to be routinized within cultures, subcultures, and groups, and some are likely to be exclusive to the circle in which they are employed. A drug addict may be able to justify his conduct to a bohemian world, but not to the courts. Similarly kin and friends may accept excuses in situations in which strangers would refuse to do so. Finally, while ignorance of the consequences of an act or of its prohibition may exculpate an individual in many different circles, the law explicitly rejects this notion: "Ignorance of the law excuses no man; not that all men know the law but because 'tis an excuse every man will plead, and no man can tell how to confute him."[36]

Both the account offered by *ego* and the honoring or nonhonoring of the account on the part of *alter* will ultimately depend on the *background expectancies* of the interactants. By background expectancies we refer to those sets of taken-for-granted ideas that permit the interactants to interpret remarks as accounts in the first place.[37] Asked why he is listless and depressed, a person may reply, "I have family troubles." The remark will be taken as an account, and indeed an account that will probably be honored, because "everyone knows" that "family problems" are a cause of depression.

This last illustration suggests that certain accounts can fit a variety of situations. Thus in response to a wide range of questions—Why don't you get married? Why are you in a fit of depression? Why are you drinking so heavily?—the individual can respond with "I'm having family problems." The person offering such an account may not himself regard it as a true one, but invoking it has certain interactional payoffs: since people cannot say they don't understand it—they are accounts that are part of our socially distributed knowledge of what "everyone knows"—the inquiry can be cut short.

Clearly, then, a single account will stand for a wide collection of events, and the efficacy of such accounts depends upon a set of shared background expectations.

In interacting with others, the socialized person learns a repertoire of background expectations that are appropriate for a variety of others. Hence the "normal" individual will change his account for different role others. A wife may respond sympathetically to her depressed husband because his favorite football team lost a championship game, but such an account for depression will appear bizarre when offered to one's inquiring boss. Thus background expectancies are the means not only for the honoring, but also for the nonhonoring of accounts. When the millionaire accounts for his depression by saying he is a failure, others will be puzzled since "everyone knows" that millionaires are not failures. The incapacity to invoke situationally appropriate accounts, i.e., accounts that are anchored to the background expectations of the situation, will often be taken as a sign of mental illness.[38] There are grounds then for conceptualizing normal individuals as "not stupid" rather than "not ill."[39] The person who is labeled ill has been behaving "stupidly" in terms of his culture and society: he offers accounts not situationally appropriate according to culturally defined background expectations.[40]

Often an account can be discredited by the appearance of the person offering an account. When a girl accounts for her late return from a date by saying the movie was overlong—that no untoward event occurred and that she still retains virgin status—her mother may discredit the account by noting the daughter's flushed appearance. Since individuals are aware that appearances may serve to credit or discredit accounts, efforts are understandably made to control these appearances through a vast repertoire of "impression management" activities.[41]

When an account is not honored it will be regarded as either *illegitimate* or *unreasonable*. An account is treated as *illegitimate* when the gravity of the event exceeds that of the account or when it is offered in a circle where its vocabulary of motives is unacceptable. As illustration of the former we may note that accidentally allowing a pet turtle to drown may be forgiven, but accidentally allowing the baby to drown with the same degree of oversight may not so easily be excused. As illustration of the latter, male prostitutes may successfully demonstrate their masculinity within the subculture of persons who regularly resort to homosexual acts by insisting that they are never fellators, but such a defense is not likely in heterosexual circles to lift from them the label of "queer."[42]

An account is deemed *unreasonable* when the stated grounds for action cannot be "normalized" in terms of the background expectancies of what "everybody knows." Hence when a secretary explained that she placed her arm in a lighted oven because voices

had commanded her to do so in punishment for her evil nature, the account was held to be grounds for commitment to an asylum.[43] In general those who persist in giving unreasonable accounts for questioned actions are likely to be labeled as mentally ill. Or, to put this point another way, unreasonable accounts are one of the sure indices by which the mentally ill are apprehended. Conversely, those persons labeled as mentally ill may relieve themselves of the worst consequences of that label by recognizing before their psychiatrists the truth value of the label, by reconstructing their past to explain how they came to deviate from normal patterns, and by gradually coming to give acceptable accounts for their behavior.[44]

Beyond illegitimacy and unreasonableness are special types of situations in which accounts may not be acceptable. One such type involves the incorrect invocation of "commitment" or "attachment"[45] in account situations where one or the other, but only the correct one, is permitted. By commitment we refer to that role orientation in which one has through investiture become liable and responsible for certain actions. By attachment we refer to the sense of vesting one's feelings and identity in a role. Certain statuses, especially those dealing with distasteful activities or acts that are condemned except when performed by licensed practitioners, are typically expected to invest their incumbents with only commitment and not with attachment. Hangmen who, when questioned about their occupation, profess to be emotionally attracted to killing are not likely to have their account honored. Indeed, distasteful tasks are often imputed to have a clandestine but impermissible allure, and so those who regularly perform them are often on their guard to assert their commitment, but not their attachment, to the task.

Organizations systematically provide accounts for their members in a variety of situations. The rules of bureaucracy, for instance, make available accounts for actions taken toward clients—actions which, from the viewpoint of the client, are untoward.[46] Again, these accounts "work" because of a set of background expectations. Thus when people say they must perform a particular action because it is a rule of the organization, the account is regarded as at least reasonable, since "everyone knows" that people follow rules. Of course, the gravity of the event may discredit such accounts, as the trials of Nazi war criminals dramatically illustrate.[47]

Under certain situations behavior that would ordinarily require an account is normalized without interruption or any call for an account. Typically such situations are social conversations in which the values to be obtained by the total encounter supersede those which would otherwise require excuses or justifications. Two values that may override the requirement of accounts are *sociability* and *information.*

In the case of *sociability* the desire that the interactional circle be uninterrupted by any event that might break it calls for each interactant to weigh carefully whether or not the calling for an account might disrupt the entire engagement. When the gathering is a convivial one not dedicated to significant matters—that is, matters that have a proactive life beyond the engagement itself—the participants may overlook errors, inept statements, lies, or discrepancies in the statements of others. Parties often call for such behavior but are vulnerable to disruption by one who violates the unwritten rule of not questioning another too closely. In unserious situations in which strangers are privileged to interact as a primary group without future rights of similar interaction—such as in bars—the interactants may construct elaborate and self-contradictory biographies without fear of being called to account.[48]

In some engagements the interactants seek to obtain *information* from the speaker which is incidental to his main point but which might be withheld if any of the speaker's

statements were called into account. Among the Japanese, for example, the significant item in a conversation may be circumscribed by a verbal wall of trivia and superfluous speech. To interrupt a speaker by calling for an account might halt the conversation altogether or detour the speaker away from disclosing the particularly valued pieces of information.[49] Among adolescent boys in American society engaged in a "bull session" it is usually inappropriate to challenge a speaker describing his sexual exploits since, no matter how embellished and exaggerated the account might be, it permits the hearers to glean knowledge about sex—ordinarily withheld from them in the regular channels of education—with impunity. Calling for an account in the midst of such disclosures, especially when the account would require a discussion of the speaker's morality, might cut off the hearers from obtaining precisely that kind of information which is in no other way available to them.[50]

So far we have discussed accounts in terms of their content, but it should be pointed out that accounts also differ in form or style. Indeed, as we will now suggest, the style of an account will have bearing on its honoring or dishonoring.

Linguistic Styles and Accounts

We may distinguish five linguistic styles that frame the manner in which an account will be given and often indicate the social circle in which it will be most appropriately employed. These five styles, which in practice often shade into one another and are not unambiguously separated in ordinary life, are the *intimate, casual, consultative, formal,* and *frozen* styles.[51] These styles, as we shall see, are ordered on a scale of decreasing social intimacy.[52]

The *intimate* style is the socially sanctioned linguistic form employed among persons who share a deep, intense, and personal relationship. The group within which it is employed is usually a dyad—lovers, a married pair, or very close friends. The group can be larger but not much larger, and when it reaches four or five it is strained to its limits. The verbal style employs single sounds or words, and jargon, to communicate whole ideas. An account given in this form may be illustrated by the situation in which a husband, lying beside his wife in bed, caresses her but receives no endearing response. His wife utters the single word, "pooped." By this term the husband understands that the account given in response to his unverbalized question, "Why don't you make love to me? After all I am your husband. You have wifely duties!" is "I realize that under ordinary circumstances I should and indeed would respond to your love making, but tonight I am too exhausted for that kind of activity. Do not take it to mean that I have lost affection for you, or that I take my wifely duties lightly."

The *casual* style is used among peers, in-group members, and insiders. It is a style employed by those for whom the social distance is greater than that among intimates but is still within the boundaries of a primary relationship. Typically it employs ellipses, i.e., omissions, and slang. In casual style certain background information is taken for granted among the interactants and may be merely alluded to in order to give an account. Thus among those who are regular users of hallucinogenic drugs, the question "Why were you running about naked in the park?" might be answered, "I was 'on.' " The hearer will then know that the speaker was under the influence of a familiar drug and was engaged in an activity that is common in response to taking that drug.

While each style differs from that to which it is juxtaposed by degree, the difference between any two styles—skipping an interval on the aforementioned social intimacy scale—is one of kind. Thus intimate and casual styles differ only in degree from one another and suggest a slight but significant difference in social distance among the interactants, but the *consultative* style differs in kind from the intimate. Consultative style is that verbal form ordinarily employed when the amount of knowledge available to one of the interactants is unknown or problematic to the others. Typically in such an interaction the speaker supplies background information which he is unsure the hearer possesses, and the hearer continuously participates by means of linguistic signs and gestures which indicate that he understands what is said or that he requires more background information. In offering accounts in this form there is a definite element of "objectivity," i.e., of non-subjective and technical terms. The individual giving an account relies on reference to things and ideas outside the intimate and personal realm. In response to the question, "Why are you smoking marijuana? Don't you know that it's dangerous?" the individual might reply, "I smoke marijuana because everybody who's read the LaGuardia Report knows that it's not habit-forming." But a casual response might be simply, "Don't be square."

Formal style is employed when the group is too large for informal co-participation to be a continuous part of the interaction. Typically it is suited to occasions when an actor addresses an audience greater than six. Listeners must then wait their turn to respond, or, if they interject comments, know that this will be an untoward event, requiring some kind of re-structuring of the situation. Speaker and audience are in an active and a passive role, respectively, and, if the group is large enough, may be obligated to speak or remain silent according to preestablished codes of procedure. Formal style may also be employed when speaker and auditor are in rigidly defined statuses. Such situations occur in bureaucratic organizations between persons in hierarchically differentiated statuses, or in the courtroom, in the interaction between judge and defendant.

Frozen style is an extreme form of formal style employed among those who are simultaneously required to interact and yet remain social strangers. Typically interaction in the frozen style occurs among those between whom an irremovable barrier exists. The barrier may be of a material or a social nature, or both. Thus pilots communicate to air scanners in a control tower in the same lingual style as prisoners of war to their captors or telephone operators to angered clients. Often the frozen accounts offered are tutored, memorized, or written down in advance, and they may be applicable to a variety of situations. Thus the prisoner of war reiterates his name, rank, and serial number to all questions and refers his interrogators to the Geneva Convention. The pilot replies to questions about his aberrant flight pattern, coming from the anonymous control tower, with a smooth flow of technical jargon quoted from his handbook on flying. The telephone operator refuses to become flustered or angered by the outraged demands and accusations of the caller unable to reach his party, and quotes from memory the rules of telephone conduct required of the situation.

In summary, then, accounts are presented in a variety of idioms. The idiomatic form of an account is expected to be socially suited to the circle into which it is introduced, according to norms of culture, subculture, and situation. The acceptance or refusal of an offered account in part depends on the appropriateness of the idiom employed. Failure to employ the proper linguistic style often results in a dishonoring of the account or calls for further accounts. Sometimes the situation results in requirements of compound accounting wherein an individual, having failed to employ idiomatic propriety in his first account, is required not only to re-account for his original untoward act but also to present an account for the unacceptable language of his first account. Note that idiomatic errors on the part of a person giving an account provide an unusual opportunity for the hearer to dishonor or punish the speaker if he so wishes. Thus even if the content of the tendered account is such as to excuse or justify the act, a hearer who wishes to discredit the speaker may "trip him up" by shifting the subject away from the matter originally at hand and onto the form of the account given. Typical situations of this kind arise when persons of inferior status provide substantially acceptable accounts for their allegedly untoward behavior to their inquiring superiors but employ idiomatically unacceptable or condemnable form. Thus school children who excuse their fighting with others by not only reporting that they were acting in self-defense but also, and in the process, by using profanity may still be punished for linguistic impropriety, even if they are let off for their original defalcation.[53]

Strategies for Avoiding Accounts

The vulnerability of actors to questions concerning their conduct varies with the situation and the status of the actors. Where hierarchies of authority govern the social situation, the institutionalized office may eliminate the necessity of an account, or even prevent the question from arising. Military officers are thus shielded from accountability to their subordinates. Where culture distance and hierarchy are combined—as in the case of slaveholders vis-à-vis their new imported slaves—those enjoying the superior status are privileged to leave their subordinates in a perplexed and frightened state.[54]

Besides the invulnerability to giving accounts arising from the status and position of the actors are the strategies that can prevent their announcement. We may refer to these strategies as meta-accounts. Three such strategies are prominent: *mystification, referral,* and *identity switching.*[55]

When the strategy of *mystification* is employed an actor admits that he is not meeting the expectations of another, but follows this by pointing out that, although there are reasons for his unexpected actions, he cannot tell the inquirer what they are. In its simplest sense the actor says "It's a long story," and leaves it at that. Such accounts are most likely to be honored under circumstances which would normally hinder an elaborate account, as when students have a chance meeting while rushing off to scheduled classes.

More complicated versions of mystification are those that suggest that *alter* is not aware of certain facts—facts that are secret—which, if known, would explain the untoward action. Typically this is the response of the charismatic leader to his followers or the expert to his naive assistant. Thus does Jesus sometimes mystify his disciples and Sherlock Holmes his Dr. Watson. Finally, as already mentioned, certain statuses suggest mystification: in addition to charismatic leaders and experts at occult or little-understood arts are all those statuses characterized by specialized information including (but not limited to) doctors, lawyers, and spies.

Using the strategy of *referral*, the individual says, "I know I'm not meeting your expectations but if you wish to know why, please see. . . . " Typically referral is a strategy available to the sick and the subordinate. Illness, especially mental illness, allows the sick person to refer inquiries about his behavior to his doctor or psychiatrist. Subordinates may avoid giving accounts by designating superiors as the appropriate persons to be questioned. A special example of group referral is that which arises when accounts for the behavior of a whole people are avoided by sending the interrogator to the experts. Thus juvenile delinquents can refer inquiries to social workers, Hopi Indians to anthropologists, and unwed Negro mothers to the Moynihan Report.

In *identity switching*, *ego* indicates to *alter* that he is not playing the role that *alter* believes he is playing. This is a way of saying

to *alter*, "You do not know who I am." This technique is readily available since all individuals possess a multiplicity of identities. Consider the following example.[56] A working-class Mexican husband comes home from an evening of philandering. His wife suspects this and says, "Where were you?" He responds with: "None of your business, you're a wife." Here the husband is assuming that it is not the wife's job to pry into the affairs of her husband. She replies, "What kind of a father are you?" What the woman does here is to suggest that she is not a wife, but a mother—who is looking out for the welfare of the children. To this the husband replies: "I'm a man—and you're a woman." In other words, he is suggesting that, in this status of man, there are things that a woman just doesn't understand. We note in this example that the status of persons not only affects the honoring and non-honoring of accounts, but also determines who can call for an account and who can avoid it. Again it should be pointed out that the normal features of such interaction depend upon the actors sharing a common set of background expectancies.

Negotiating Identities and Accounts

As our discussion of identity-switching emphasizes, accounts always occur between persons in roles—between husband and wife, doctor and patient, teacher and student, and so on. A normative structure governs the nature and types of communication between the interactants, including whether and in what manner accounts may be required and given, honored, or discredited.

Accounts, as suggested, presuppose an identifiable speaker and audience. The particular identities of the interactants must often be established as part of the encounter in which the account is presented.[57] In other words, people generate role identities for one another in social situations. In an account-giving situation, to cast *alter* in a particular role is to confer upon him the privilege of honoring a particular kind of account, the kind suitable to the role identity conferred and assumed for at least the period of account. To assume an identity is to don the mantle appropriate to the account to be offered. Identity assumption and "altercasting"[58] are prerequisites to the presentation of accounts, since the identities thus established interactionally "set" the social stage on which the drama of the account is to be played out.

The identities of speaker and audience will be negotiated as part of the encounter. Each of the interactants has a stake in the negotiations since the outcomes of the engagement will often depend on these pre-established identities. In competitive or bargaining situations[59] the interactants will each seek to maximize gains or minimize losses, and part of the strategy involved will be to assume and accept advantageous identities, refusing those roles that are disadvantageous to the situation. *Every account is a manifestation of the underlying negotiation of identities.*[60]

The most elementary form of identification is that of human and fellow human negotiated by the immediate perceptions of strangers who engage in abrupt and involuntary engagements. Thus once two objects on a street collide with one another and mutually perceive one another to be humans, an apology in the form of an excuse, or mutually paired excuses, will suffice. Those persons not privileged with full or accurate perception—the blind, myopic, or blindfolded—are not in a position to ascertain immediately whether the object with which they have collided is eligible to call for an account and to deserve an apology. In overcompensating for their inability to negotiate immediately such elementary identities, the persons so handicapped may indiscriminately offer apologies to everyone and everything with which they collide—doormen and doors, street-walkers and street signs. On the other hand, their identification errors are forgiven as soon as their handicap is recognized.

Some objects are ambiguously defined with respect to their deserving of accounts. Animals are an example. House pets, especially dogs and cats, are sometimes imputed to possess human attributes and are thus eligible for apologies and excuses when they are trodden upon by their masters. But insects and large beasts—ants and elephants, for example—do not appear to be normally eligible for accounts even when they are trodden upon by unwary (Occidental) humans.

However, there are instances wherein the anthropomorphosis of the human self is more difficult to negotiate than that of a dog. Racial minorities in caste societies often insist to no avail on the priority of their identity as "human beings" over their identification as members of a racial group.[61] Indeed the "Negro human-being" role choice dilemma is but one instance of a particular form of strategy in the negotiation of identities. The strategy involves the competition between ego and alter over particularistic versus universalistic role identities. In any encounter in which a disagreement is potential or has already occurred, or in any situation in which an account is to be offered, the particularistic or universalistic identity of the interactants might dictate the manner and outcome of the account situation. Each participant will strive for the advantageous identity. A Negro psychoanalyst with considerable experience in Europe and North Africa has shown how the form of address—either consultative or deprecatingly casual—and the tone used, are opening moves in the doctor's designation of his patient as European or Negro.[62]

Twenty European patients, one after another, came in: "Please sit down . . . Why do you wish to consult me?" Then comes a Negro or an Arab. "Sit here, boy . . ."

And, as the psychoanalyst points out, the identity imputed to the patient might be accepted or rejected. To reject the particularistic identity in favor of a universalistic one, the Negro patient might reply, "I am in no sense your boy, Monsieur"[63] and the negotiations for identities begin again or get detoured in an argument.

In an account situation there is a further complication. Once identities have been established and an account offered, the individual has committed himself to an identity and thus seemingly assumed the assets and liabilities of that role for the duration of the encounter. If he accepts the identity as permanent and unchangeable, however, he may have limited his range of subsequent accounts. And if he wishes to shift accounts to one appropriate to another identity he may also need to account for the switch in identities. Thus, in the face of a pejorative particularistic identity, a Negro might wish to establish his claim to a positive universalistic one devoid of the pejorative contents of the imputed one. However, once this new universalistic identity has been established, the Negro might wish to shift back to the particularistic one, if there are positive qualities to be gained thereby, qualities utterly lost by an unqualified acceptance of the universalistic identity.[64] But the switch might require an account itself.

Identity switching has retroactive dangers, since it casts doubt on the attachment the claimant had to his prior identity, and his attachment may have been a crucial element in the acceptability of his first account. On the other hand, the hearer of an account may have a vested interest in accepting the entire range of accounts and may thus accommodate or even facilitate the switch in identities. Thus the hearer may "rationalize" the prior commitment, or reinterpret its meaning so that the speaker may carry off subsequent accounts.[65] Another strategy available to a hearer is to engage in alter-casting for purposes of facilitating or frustrating an account. The fact that individuals have multiple identities makes them both capable of strategic identity change and vulnerable to involuntary identity imputations.

In ordinary life, accounts are usually "phased."[66] One account generates the question which gives rise to another; the new account requires re-negotiation of identities; the identities necessitate excuses or justifications, improvisation and alter-casting; another account is given; another question arises, and so on. The following interview between a Soviet social worker and his client, a young woman, nicely illustrates this phenomenon.[67]

A girl of about nineteen years of age enters the social worker's office and sits down sighing audibly. The interview begins on a note of *mystification* which ends abruptly when the girl establishes her identity—abandoned wife.

"What are you sighing so sadly for?" I asked. "Are you in trouble?" Lyuba raised her prim little head with a jerk, sighed pianissimo and smiled piteously.
"No . . . it's nothing much. I *was* in trouble, but it's all over now. . . . "
"All over, and you are still sighing about it?" I questioned further. Lyuba gave a little shiver and looked at me. A flame of interest had leaped into her earnest brown eyes.
"Would you like me to tell you all about it?"
"Yes, do."
"It's a long story."
"Never mind. . . . "
"My husband has left me."

The interview carries on in what must be regarded as an unsuccessful approach by the social worker. He establishes that Lyuba still loves her wayward husband, has lost faith in men, and is unwilling to take his advice to forget her first husband and remarry. The abandoned wife turns out to be an identity with which the worker has difficulty coping. He, therefore, alter-casts with telling effect in the following manner.

"Tell me, Lyuba, are your parents alive?"
"Yes, they are. Daddy and Mummy! They keep on telling me off for having got married."
"Quite right too."

"No, it's not. What's right about it?"

"Of course, they're right. You're still a child and already married and divorced."

"Well . . . what about it! What's that got to do with them?"

"Aren't you living with them?"

"I have a room of my own. My husband left me and went to live with his . . . and the room is mine now. And I earn two hundred rubles. And I'm not a child! How can you call me a child?"

Note that little bits of information provide the cues for alter-casting, so that Lyuba's volunteering the fact of her parents' disapproval of her first marriage provides the grounds for the social worker's recasting her in the child role. However, this new identity is rejected by Lyuba by further evidentiary assertions: she supports herself and maintains her own residence. The child role has been miscast. Even the social worker gives up his attempt at switching Lyuba out from her role as abandoned wife. He writes: "Lyuba looked at me in angry surprise and I saw that she was quite serious about this game she played in life." Thus negotiations for identities—as in financial transactions—usually end with both parties coming to an agreeable settlement.

Conclusion

The sociologist has been slow to take as a serious subject of investigation what is perhaps the most distinctive feature of humans—talk. Here we are suggesting a concern with one type of talk: the study of what constitutes "acceptable utterances"[68] for untoward action. The sociological study of communications has relegated linguistic utterances to linguists and has generally mapped out non-verbal behavior as its distinctive domain. We are suggesting that a greater effort is needed to formulate theory that will integrate both verbal and non-verbal behavior.[69]

Perhaps the most immediate task for research in this area is to specify the background expectations that determine the range of alternative accounts deemed culturally appropriate to a variety of recurrent situations. We want to know how the actors take bits and pieces of words and appearances and put them together to produce a perceivedly normal (or abnormal) state of affairs. This kind of inquiry crucially involves a study of background expectations.[70] On the basis of such investigations, the analyst should be able to provide a set of instructions on "how to give an account" that would be taken by other actors as "normal."[71] These instructions would specify how different categories of statuses affect the honoring of an account, and what categories of statuses can use what kinds of accounts.

Future research on accounts may fruitfully take as a unit of analysis the *speech community*.[72] This unit is composed of human aggregates in frequent and regular interaction. By dint of their association sharers of a distinct body of verbal signs are set off from other speech communities. By speech community we do not refer to language communities, distinguished by being composed of users of formally different languages. Nor do we refer simply to dialect communities, composed of persons who employ a common spoken language which is a verbal variant of a more widely used written language.

Speech communities define for their members the appropriate lingual forms to be used amongst themselves. Such communities are located in the social structure of any society. They mark off segments of society from one another, and also distinguish different kinds of activities. Thus, the everyday language of lower-class teenage gangs differs sharply from that of the social workers who interview them, and the language by which a science teacher demonstrates to his students how to combine hydrogen and oxygen in order to produce water differs from the language employed by the same teacher to tell his inquisitive six-year-old son how babies are created. The types of accounts appropriate to each speech community differ in form and in content. The usage of particular speech norms in giving an account has consequences for the speaker depending upon the relationship between the form used and the speech community into which it is introduced.

A single individual may belong to several speech communities at the same time, or in the course of a lifetime. Some linguistic devices (such as teenage argot) are appropriate only to certain age groups and are discarded as one passes into another age grouping; others, such as the linguistic forms used by lawyers in the presence of judges, are appropriate to certain status sets and are consecutively employed and discarded as the individual moves into and out of interactions with his various status partners. Some individuals are dwellers in but a single speech community; they move in circles in which all employ the same verbal forms. The aged and enfeebled members of class or ethnic ghettos are an obvious example. Others are constant movers through differing speech communities, adeptly employing language forms suitable to the time and place they occupy. Social workers who face teenage delinquents, fellow workers, lawyers, judges, their own wives, and children, all in one day, are an example.

In concluding we may note that, since it is with respect to deviant behavior that we call for accounts, the study of deviance and the study of accounts are intrinsically related, and a clarification of accounts will constitute a clarification of deviant phenomena—to the extent that deviance is considered in an interactional framework.[73]

Notes

1. For a now classic statement and analysis of the Hobbesian question, see the discussion by T. Parsons (1949), *The structure of social action*, Glencoe, IL: Free Press, pp. 89-94.

2. See, for instance, W. Soskin & V. John (1963), "The study of spontaneous talk," in R. Barker (Ed.), *The stream of behavior* (pp. 228-282), New York: Appleton-Century-Crofts. Much suggestive material and a complete bibliography can be found in J. O. Hertzler (1965), *A sociology of language*, New York: Random House.

3. An account has a family resemblance to the verbal component of a "motive" in Weber's sense of the term. Weber defined a motive as "a complex of subjective meaning which seems to the actor himself or to the observer as an adequate ground for the conduct in question." M. Weber (1947), *Theory of social and economic organization*, (T. Parsons & A. M. Henderson, Trans.), Glencoe, IL: Free Press, pp. 98-99. Following Weber's definition and building on G. H. Mead's social psychology and the work of Kenneth Burke, C. Wright Mills (1940, December) was among the first to employ the notion of accounts in his much neglected essay, "Situated actions and vocabularies of motives," *American Sociological Review, 5*, 904-913. Contemporary British philosophy, following the leads of Ludwig Wittgenstein, has (apparently) independently advanced the idea of a "vocabulary of motives." An exemplary case is R. S. Peters (1958), *The concept of motivation*, London: Routledge & Kegan Paul.

4. The point is nicely illustrated in J. Toby (1952, March), "Some variables in role conflict analysis," *Social Forces, 30*, 323-327.

5. Thus by an account we include also those non-vocalized but linguistic explanations that arise in an actor's "mind" when he questions his own behavior. However, our concern is with vocalized account and especially those that are given in face-to-face relations.

6. W. J. Goode (1963), *World revolution and family patterns*, New York: Free Press of Glencoe, pp. 254-256.

7. Moreover, common-sense understandings that violate widespread cognitive knowledge, such as are asserted in statements like "The sun rises every morning and sets every night," or avowed in perceptions that a straight stick immersed in water appears bent, are expected to be maintained. Persons who always insist on the astronomically exact statement about the earth's relation to the sun might be considered officious or didactic, while those who "see" a straight stick in a pool might be credited with faulty eyesight. For a relevant discussion of social reactions to inquiries

about taken-for-granted phenomena, see H. Garfinkel (1964, Winter), "Studies of the routine grounds of everyday activities," *Social Problems, 11*, 225-250; and "A conception of and experiments with 'trust' as a condition of concerted stable actions," in O. J. Harvey (Ed.), *Motivation and social interaction* (pp. 187-238), New York: Ronald.

8. We have taken this formulation from J. L. Austin. See his (1961) *Philosophical papers*, London: Oxford University Press, pp. 123-152.

9. Austin (1961), p. 124.

10. These types of excuses are to be taken as illustrative rather than as an exhaustive listing.

11. Only where nothing is left to chance—as among the Azande, where particular misfortunes are accounted for by a ubiquitous witchcraft—is the excuse by accident not likely to occur. Azande do not assert witchcraft to be the sole cause of phenomena; they have a "practical" and "realistic" approach to events which would enjoy consensual support from Occidental observers. However, Azande account for what Occidentals would call "chance" or "coincidence" by reference to witchcraft. E. E. Evans-Pritchard (1937) writes: "We have no explanation of why the two chains of causation [resulting in a catastrophe] intersected at a certain time and in a certain place, for there is no interdependence between them. Azande philosophy can supply the missing link. . . . It is due to witchcraft. . . . Witchcraft explains the coincidence of these two happenings." *Witchcraft, oracles and magic among the Azande*, London: Oxford University Press, p. 70.

12. Defeasibility, or the capacity of being voided, is a concept developed by H.L.A. Hart. This section leans heavily on Hart's (1960) essay, "The ascription of responsibility and rights," in A. Flew (Ed.), *Logic and language, First series* (pp. 145-166), Oxford: Basil Blackwell.

13. For a general discussion of cultures in terms of their "fatalistic" orientations or universalist-achievement orientations, see T. Parsons (1954), "A revised analytical approach to the theory of social stratification," in *Essays in sociological theory* (pp. 386-439), New York: Free Press of Glencoe. See also T. Parsons (1951), *The social system*, Glencoe, IL: Free Press.

14. Thus, in the most famous study of the psychodynamics of prejudice, one of the characteristics of the intolerant or "authoritarian" personality is "externalization," i.e., the attribution of causality of events believed to be within the actor's power or rational comprehension to uncontrollable forces beyond his influence or understanding. See T. W. Adorno et al. (1950), *The authoritarian personality*, New York: Harper & Row, pp. 474-475. See also G. W. Allport (1958), *The nature of prejudice*, Garden City, NY: Doubleday Anchor, p. 379. In a recent study an intermittently employed cab driver's insistence that there would inevitably be a revolution after which the world would be taken over by Negroes and Jews is recalled as one of several early warning cues that he is mentally ill. M. R. Yarrow et al. (1967), "The psychological meaning of mental illness in the family," in T. J. Scheff (Ed.), *Mental illness and social process*, New York: Harper & Row, 1967, p. 35.

15. See H. R. Clayton (1953), "The psychology of the Negro under discrimination," in A. Rose (Ed.), *Race prejudice and discrimination* (pp. 276-280), New York: Knopf; and B. P. Karon (1958), *The Negro personality*, New York: Springer, pp. 8-53, 140-160.

16. D. Matza (1964), *Delinquency and drift*, New York: John Wiley, pp. 88-90, 188-191.

17. H. J. Gans (1962), *The urban villagers*, New York: Free Press, p. 49. According to another student of Italian-American life, slum-dwelling members of this subculture believe that "a man's health requires sexual intercourse at certain intervals." W. F. Whyte (1943, July), "A slum sex code," *American Journal of Sociology, 49*, 26.

18. O. Lewis (1961), *The children of Sanchez*, New York: Random House, p. 475.

19. G. Westwood (1960), *A minority*, London: Longmans, Green, p. 46.

20. For an interesting study showing that criminals believe that a fellow criminal's physical attractiveness will vary with type of crime—robbers are the most attractive, murderers the least; rapists are more attractive than pedophiles, etc.—see R. J. Corsini (1959, July), "Appearance and criminality," *American Journal of Sociology, 65*, 49-51.

21. Adorno (1950), pp. 233, 485; Allport (1958), pp. 235-249, suggests the historicity and uniqueness of each instance of scapegoating.

22. A. de Hoyos & G. de Hoyos (1966), "The amigo system and alienation of the wife in the conjugal Mexican family," in B. Farber (Ed.), *Kinship and family organization*, New York: John Wiley, pp. 102-115, esp. pp. 103-107.

23. Lewis (1961), p. 143.

24. Lewis (1961), p. 202.

25. Lewis (1961), p. 86.

26. G. M. Sykes & D. Matza (1957, December), "Techniques of neutralization," *American Sociological Review, 22,* 667-669.

27. One other neutralization technique mentioned by Sykes and Matza (1957), "denial of responsibility," is subsumed in our schema under "appeal to defeasibility."

28. Note that appeal to loyalties could be an *excuse* if the argument runs that X did to A under the influence of Y's domination or love, or under the coercive influence of Y's injury to him were he not to act, e.g., loss of love, blackmail, etc. In other words, appeal to loyalties is an excuse if X admits it was bad to do A, but refuses to monopolize responsibility for A in himself.

29. E. Goffman (1961a), *Asylums,* Garden City, NY: Doubleday Anchor, pp. 150-151. The sad tale involves the most dramatic instance of the general process of reconstructing personal biography whereby—for example—a husband may account for his present divorce by reconstructing the history of earlier events in an ascending scale leading up to the final dissolution. The idea of a reconstruction of biography is a continual theme in the writings of Alfred Schutz. See his (1962) *Collected papers* (vol. 1, M. Natanson, Ed.), The Hague: Martinus Nijhoff. A short clear summary of Schutz's contribution on the reconstruction of biography is found in P. L. Berger (1963), *Invitation to sociology,* Garden City, NY: Doubleday Anchor, pp. 54-65. Drawing on Schutz, Garfinkel details the concept of reconstruction of biography in a series of experiments on the "retrospective reading" of social action. See his (1962) "Common sense knowledge of social structures," in J. M. Scher (Ed.), *Theories of the mind* (pp. 689-712), Glencoe, IL: Free Press. The empirical use of the concept of retrospective reading of action is nicely illustrated in J. I. Kitsuse (1964), "Societal reaction to deviant behavior," in H. S. Becker (Ed.), *The other side* (pp. 87-102), New York: Free Press of Glencoe.

30. Goffman (1961a), p. 152.

31. Westwood (1960), p. 32.

32. Tape-recorded interview, May 1967.

33. Tape-recorded interview, June 1967.

34. E. Goffman (1961b), *Encounters,* Indianapolis, IN: Bobbs-Merrill, pp. 45-48.

35. Goffman (1961b), p. 51.

36. J. Selden (1696), *Table talk;* quoted in H. Johnson (1960), *Sociology,* New York: Harcourt, Brace, p. 552n.

37. The term is borrowed from Harold Garfinkel. Besides the footnote references to Garfinkel already cited, see his (1968) *Studies in ethnomethodology,* Englewood Cliffs, NJ: Prentice-Hall. For an original discussion on how the meaning of an account depends upon background expectancies and a methodology for its study, see H. Sacks (1966), *The search for help,* unpublished doctoral dissertation, University of California, Berkeley.

38. On how background expectations are used to determine whether a person is judged criminal or sick see the neglected essay by V. Aubert & S. L. Messinger (1958, Autumn), "The criminal and the sick," *Inquiry, 1,* 137-160.

39. This formulation is persistently (and we believe rightly) argued in the various writings of Ernest Becker. See especially (1964b) *The revolution in psychiatry,* New York: Free Press of Glencoe; and his (1964a) essay "Mills' social psychology and the great historical convergence on the problem of alienation," in I. L. Horowitz (Ed.), *The new sociology* (pp. 108-133), New York: Oxford University Press.

40. In the case of schizophrenics, it has been noted that they are individuals who construct overly elaborate accounts, i.e., accounts that are perceived as being elaborately constructed. These accounts, it appears, take the form of "building up" the possibilities of a situation that others find improbable. Thus the paranoid husband accounts for his frenzied state by relating that his wife went shopping—and, to him, going shopping constitutes the most opportune occasion to rendezvous secretly with a lover. In response to the inquirer, the paranoid asks: "If you wanted to meet a lover, wouldn't you tell your spouse you're going shopping?" For a general discussion, see Becker (1964b).

41. E. Goffman (1956), *Presentation of self in everyday life,* University of Edinburgh.

42. A. J. Reiss, Jr. (1964), "The social integration of queers and peers," in H. S. Becker (Ed.), *The other side* (pp. 181-210), New York: Free Press of Glencoe.

43. M. Sechehaye (1951), *Autobiography of a schizophrenic girl,* New York: Grune & Stratton.

44. See T. Scheff (1966), *Being mentally ill,* Chicago: Aldine. See also Goffman (1961a).

45. These terms are adapted from E. Goffman (1963), *Behavior in public places*, New York: Free Press of Glencoe, p. 36n; and (1961b), pp. 105 ff.

46. The theme is widely explored in the literature on formal organizations. For an early and perhaps still the clearest statement of the theme, see R. K. Merton's widely reprinted "Bureaucratic structure and personality," available in (1962) A. Etzioni (Ed.), *Complex organizations* (pp. 48-60), New York: Holt, Rinehart & Winston.

47. For a literary illustration, see the play by P. Weiss (1967), *The investigation*, New York: Atheneum.

48. See S. Cavan (1966), *Liquor license*, Chicago: Aldine, pp. 79-87.

49. E. T. Hall (1966), *The hidden dimension*, Garden City, NY: Doubleday, pp. 139-144.

50. When a boy is interrupted by a call for an account in the midst of his own recounting of sexual exploits he may simply relapse into uncommunicative silence, change the subject, or withdraw from the group. To prevent any of these, and to aid in the continuity of the original story, the other members of the audience may urge the speaker to continue as before, assure him of their interest and support, and sharply reprove or perhaps ostracize from the group the person who called for the account.

51. We have adapted these styles from M. Joos (1961), *The five clocks*, New York: Harbinger.

52. Each of these linguistic styles is associated with distinctive physical distances between the interactants. For a discussion of this point see Hall (1966), pp. 116-122.

53. Besides the five linguistic styles discussed, we may note that accounts may be usefully distinguished in the manner of their *delivery*. For a cogent typology see R. E. Pittenger et al. (1960), *The first five minutes*, Ithaca, NY: Paul Martineau, p. 255.

54. Another kind of invulnerability arises in those situations in which physical presence is tantamount to task performance. Students in a classroom, parishioners in a church, and soldiers at a drill may be counted as "present"—their very visibility being all that is required for routine performance—although they might be "away" in the vicarious sense of day-dreaming, musing on other matters, or relaxing into a reverie.

55. For these terms, in the context of strategies for avoiding accounts, we are indebted to Gregory Stone.

56. For this illustration we are again indebted to Gregory Stone. The illustration itself is derived from Lewis (1961).

57. For an excellent discussion of this point as well as an insightful analysis of the concept of identity, see A. L. Strauss (1959), *Mirror and masks*, New York: Free Press of Glencoe.

58. The concept of "alter-casting" is developed by E. A. Weinstein & P. Deutschberger (1964, May), "Tasks, bargains, and identities in social interaction," *Social Forces*, 42, 451-456.

59. See the brilliant discussion by T. C. Schelling (1963), *The strategy of conflict*, New York: Galaxy, pp. 21-52.

60. The terms "identities" and "roles" may be used as synonymous in that roles are identities mobilized in a specific situation; whereas role is always situationally specific, identities are trans-situational.

61. "An unconscious desire to be white, coupled with feelings of revulsion toward the Negro masses, may produce an assimilationist pattern of behavior at the purely personal level. Assimilation is in this sense a means of escape, a form of flight from 'the problem.' It involves a denial of one's racial identity which may be disguised by such sentiments as 'I'm not a Negro but a human being'—as if the two were mutually exclusive. This denial is accompanied by a contrived absence of race consciousness and a belittling of caste barriers. By minimizing the color line, the assimilationist loses touch with the realities of Negro life." R. A. Bone (1965), *The Negro novel in America*, New Haven, CT: Yale University Press, p. 4.

62. F. Fanon (1967), *Black skin, white masks*, New York: Grove, p. 32.

63. Fanon (1967), p. 33.

64. Fanon (1967) provides one of the most graphic examples of this phenomenon. For a socio-literary treatment, see S. C. Drake (1963), "Hide my face—On pan-Africanism and Negritude," in H. Hill (Ed.), *Soon one morning* (pp. 77-105), New York: Knopf.

65. Schelling (1963), p. 34.

66. For a discussion on the "phrasing" of encounters, see Strauss (1959), p. 44ff.

67. The following is from A. S. Makarenko (1967), *The collective family*, Garden City, NY: Doubleday Anchor, pp. 230-232.

68. The term is borrowed from N. Chomsky (1965), *Aspects of a theory of syntax*, Cambridge, MA: MIT Press, p. 10.

69. To our knowledge the most persuasive argument for this need is made by K. L. Pike (1954), *Language in relation to a unified theory of the structure of human behavior*, Glendale, IL: Summer Institute of Linguistics. A short, clear programmatic statement is found in D. Hymes (1962), "The ethnography of speaking," in T. Gladwin & W. C. Sturtevant (Eds.), *Anthropology and human behavior* (pp. 72-85), Washington, DC: Anthropological Society of Washington. For an argument that stresses the analytic separation of the content of talk from the forms of talk, see the brief but lucid statement by E. Goffman (1964, December), "The neglected situation," in J. Gumpertz & D. Hymes (Eds.), *The ethnography of communications, American Anthropologist, 66* (Part 2), pp. 133-136.

70. For the methodology of such studies sociologists may well investigate the anthropological technique of componential analysis, i.e., the study of contrast sets. The clearest statement of the method of componential analysis is that of C. O. Frake, "The ethnographic study of cognitive systems," in T. Gladwin & W. C. Sturtevant (Eds.), *Anthropology and human behavior* (pp. 72-85), Washington, DC: Anthropological Society of Washington. A related methodology is developed in Sacks (1966).

71. See C. O. Frake (1964, December), "How to ask for a drink in Subanun," in J. Gumpertz & D. Hymes (Eds.), *The ethnography of communications, American Anthropologist, 66* (Part 2), 127-132.

72. The idea of a "speech community" is usefully developed in J. J. Gumpertz (1964b), "Speech variation and the study of Indian civilization," in D. Hymes (Ed.), *Language in culture and society* (pp. 416-423), New York: Harper & Row; and (1964a) "Linguistic and social interaction in two communities," in J. Gumpertz & D. Hymes (Eds.), *The ethnography of communications, American Anthropologist, 66* (Part 2), 137-153.

73. We refer to the approach to deviance clearly summarized by H. S. Becker (1963), *The outsiders*, New York: Free Press of Glencoe, esp. pp. 1-18.

24

Disclaimers

John P. Hewitt and Randall Stokes

Introduction

Problematic events of varying seriousness occur in the concrete situations of everyday life: people are embarrassed by their own and others' faux pas; serious and trivial departures from role obligations are noticed; rules are broken (or, more properly, certain actions are treated as rule violations); extraordinary, disturbing, or seemingly inexplicable behavior is observed in self or others.

Such problematic events are important for two reasons. First, they affect the course and outcome of social interaction. People gear their words and deeds to the restoration and maintenance of situated and cherished identities. When the violation of rules fractures the context of interaction, or when the emergent meaning of a situation is disrupted, people endeavor to repair the breaks and restore meaning. Thus, if the direction of social interaction in a given situation is to be well understood, adequate concepts for handling such events are necessary.

Second, a conceptual grasp of the problematic features of identity, social interaction and emergent meaning is crucial to an understanding of the classic problem of so-

cial order and cultural continuity. While the sociological treatment of the problem is conventionally anchored in socialization and the internalization of culture, there are several difficulties with such a formulation, most notably that little routine action appears guided by deeply internalized norms. A discussion of problematic events aids in the reformulation of the link between culture and behavior, for it is in relation to such problematic occasions that culture most clearly enters the consciousness of actors, shapes the meaning of their conduct, becomes fundamental to their identities, and is thus made visible and re-affirmed.

Several concepts have been developed to deal with the problem of how actors restore disrupted meaning, repair fractured social interaction, and re-negotiate damaged identities. C. Wright Mills' (1940) conception of "vocabularies of motive"; Marvin Scott and Stanford Lyman's (1968) "accounts"; and John Hewitt and Peter Hall's (1970, 1973) "quasi-theories" each comes to grips with an important aspect of the dual problem of social interaction and culture in problematic situations.

For Mills, the most important feature of motives is that they arise in talk, whether as states of mind the person imputes to others or avows for himself. "As a word, a motive tends to be one which is to the actor and to the other members of a situation an unquestioned answer to questions concerning social and lingual conduct" (Mills, 1940, p. 906).

"Disclaimers" by J. P. Hewitt and R. Stokes, 1975. *American Sociological Review, 40,* pp. 1-11. Copyright © 1975 by The American Sociological Association.

We are indebted to Rob Faulkner for his helpful comments on an earlier draft of this paper.

Motive talk is thus important to the ongoing construction of meaning in social interaction, since the continuity of both is sustained (in part) by people's ability to attribute their own and others' acts to "reasons" or "motives." While Mills addresses himself to the issue of how disrupted meaning is restored, his discussion lacks generality, since motive talk, while central to social interaction, is not the only means of dealing with disrupted meaning.

The concepts of accounts and quasi-theories are also addressed, each in a particular way, to problematic meaning. Accounts are the justifications and excuses people offer when the course of interaction has been disrupted by an act or word. Quasi-theories are explanations people construct in social interaction to account for various kinds of problematic situations. Both concepts point to observable features of social interaction in which meaning is restored by efforts undertaken for that purpose. But these concepts are limited because their view of meaning and its reconstruction is largely *retrospective*—they deal with the definition of the past in the present. Neither deals adequately, nor is it intended to do so, with the anticipation of events, with the *prospective* construction of meaning for words and deeds that may be problematic.

This paper introduces, defines, and discusses a new concept, the "disclaimer." Its level is that of the account and the quasi-theory: a process that occurs in social interaction in which problematic events that may disrupt emergent meaning are defined and dealt with. Unlike accounts and quasi-theories, which are retrospective in their effect, disclaimers are prospective, defining the future in the present, creating interpretations of potentially problematic events intended to make them unproblematic when they occur.

The Disclaimer

In order to define the disclaimer and describe its forms we must first attend to some major features of problematic meaning. As individuals in social interaction form their conduct in response to one another, meaning in their situation is created and maintained. The individual organizes meaning thematically: as behavior in the situation emerges he seeks to "fit" events to "theme" (McHugh, 1968). The relationship between the theme that organizes meaning and the specific acts or events that fit the theme is a reflexive one: events take on meaning when pattern is imputed to them; pattern is visible only in the concrete events it is used to interpret. When events or acts no longer seem understandable in terms of the patterns imputed to them, individuals examine discrepant events with some care, seeking to determine what has gone wrong with their understanding of the situation.

Central to the themes used to organize meaning are identities. Whether defined on the basis of conventional, named social roles (father, policeman, teacher) or interpersonal roles established by specific individuals over time in relation to one another (friend, follower, enemy), situated identities are established and known to interactants. Indeed, the thematic organization of meaning by interactants usually depends upon their ability to interpret each other's actions as manifestations of particular identities. It follows that when events fail to fit themes in interaction, identities may come into focus as problematic: if the acts of another fail to appear sensible in light of his identity in the situation, perhaps he is not who he appears to be.

The crucial place of identities in the organization of meaning points more generally to the importance of the process of typifying and the fact of typification in social interaction (Schutz, 1964). In their relations with one another, people search for and make use of specific cues from others as a means of typifying them, i.e., of treating them as kinds of persons. Socialized individuals carry with them a vast store of information as to how various types of persons will behave, what they are like, their typical motives and values, how to deal with them, etc. In concrete situations they search for cues from others, invoke a typification that appears relevant to those cues and rely upon the store of information organized by the typification in their subsequent interaction with the other, filling in the "gaps" in the other's self-presentation with the typification. Some typifications are essentially identical in content to conventional and interpersonal roles (thus we carry typifications of fathers, enemies, policemen), while others cut across the grain of roles, pointing to other "types" that may, in given cases, be important, even controlling in social interaction (so, for example, we carry typifications of the prejudiced, stupid, incompetent, mentally ill, etc.).

Crucial to the concept of the disclaimer is the fact that individuals *know* their own acts serve as the basis for typifying them; they know that specific acts they undertake will be treated by others as cues for typification. They know this, in the simplest sense, because they do it themselves, seeking in others' acts the "keys" that will unlock the secrets of their behavior. Moreover, with varying degrees of awareness, individuals seek to present others with cues that will lead to desired typifications of them—to present themselves in ways that will lead others to grant their situated identity claims.

This awareness of typification (in general, if not in specific cases) plays an important role in the imaginative preconstructions of conduct that go on continuously in the mental life of the individual. As individuals construct their acts in imagination, they anticipate the responses of others, including the typificatory uses to which their acts will be put. For the individual, any given act is potentially a basis on which others can typify him. Put another way, as the individual anticipates the response to his conduct, he may see it either as in line with an established identity or as somehow discrepant, in which case it may be taken as a cue for

some new typification, possibly a negative one, possibly a more favorable one.

Individuals' anticipation of others' typifications of them are not governed, however, by any simple principle of seeking positive and avoiding negative typifications. Life is filled with occasions on which individuals find it necessary to engage in acts that undermine the emergent meaning of situations and make probable the destruction of their identities in them. Even if they do not feel constrained to act in such ways, individuals may perceive opportunities—even legitimate ones—in lines of action they know others will take exception to. And on some occasions, individuals may sense the possibility of being typified in ways they would like to avoid, but find themselves without any certain way of anticipating the response. Under such circumstances as these and others, disclaimers are invoked.

A disclaimer is a verbal device employed to ward off and defeat in advance doubts and negative typifications which may result from intended conduct. Disclaimers seek to define forthcoming conduct as not relevant to the kind of identity-challenge or re-typification for which it might ordinarily serve as the basis. Examples abound and serve to make the abstract concrete: "I know this sounds stupid, but . . ."; "I'm not prejudiced, because some of my best friends are Jews, but . . ."; "This is just off the top of my head, so . . . "; "What I'm going to do may seem strange, so bear with me"; "This may make you unhappy, but . . . "; "I realize I'm being anthropomorphic. . . . "

In each of the foregoing examples, individuals display in their speech the expectation of possible responses of others to their impending conduct. In each example, a specific utterance calls the other's attention to a *possible* undesired typification and asks forbearance. Each phrase, in effect, disclaims that the word or deed to follow should be used as a basis for identity challenge and re-typification, the user's clear hope is that his intended act will not disrupt the current relationship, nor undesirably shift the emergent definition of the situation. Each disclaimer is thus a device used to sustain interaction, to manage the flow of meaning in situations, to negotiate a social order in which people can treat one another's acts with discretion, with good judgment, and with deserved good will.

Types of Disclaimers

The examples cited above, as well as others, can best be analyzed by sorting disclaimers into several types, each of which reflects a different set of conditions of use.

Hedging. There are countless situations in which individuals preface statements of fact or opinion, positions in arguments or expressions of belief with disclaimers of the following kind: "I'm no expert, of course, but . . ."; "I could be wrong on my facts, but I think . . ."; "I really haven't thought this through very well, but . . ."; "I'm not sure this is going to work, but let's give it a try"; "Let me play devil's advocate here. . . . "

What does the use of disclaimers of this type indicate about the individual's conduct and his expectations about others' responses? First, each expression is an intentional signal of minimal commitment to the impending line of conduct, an indication of willingness to receive discrepant information, change opinions, be persuaded otherwise, or be better informed. Put otherwise, such an expression indicates the tentative nature of forthcoming action. Second, the tentative or negotiable coloration given subsequent conduct indicates a measure of uncertainty about the likely response to the act. From the standpoint of the individual constructing his act, what he is about to say may be taken seriously and importantly by others, thus confirming his identity; or it may be taken by others as damaging to his identity, even as the basis for some new, controlling typification of him. He does not know. Third,

the re-typification that may occur is at least potentially serious. While the individual may suspect that the worst that can happen is that he will be thought ill-informed or wrong-headed, he faces the possibility that his act may fundamentally transform him in the eyes of the other.

Minimal commitment and uncertain response are the defining conditions under which hedging takes place. Where an individual does not know how his act will be received and simultaneously does not think a positive response to his act is essential to his identity or his ends, he will hedge by disclaiming in advance the importance of the act to his identity. "I'm no expert" is a phrase that conveys to others the idea that no expert identity is being claimed; if no expertise is, in fact, shown, no claim needs to be defended. The phrase signals to hearers that they should treat factually faulty statements or deeds that have the wrong effects as the normal prerogative of people who are not and do not claim to be expert in what they are doing.

At the same time, variability in feared seriousness of response makes for variability within the category of hedging. At one extreme, a person may fear his words or deeds will drastically re-cast him in the eyes of others, and thus make attainment of his ends difficult. Persons who *are* expert, therefore, will often appeal to faulty memory, possible misunderstanding, or over-specialization if they fear an impending act will lead to their retypification as incompetent. Persons who occupy central, leadership positions in administrative organizations often adopt the practice of playing devil's advocate of positions they genuinely support, since they fear open and committed advocacy of position might erode their power and authority. At the other extreme, where people feel they have little to fear in the way of drastic re-typification, hedging is more like insurance, and often more like ritual; a way of reminding people that no great emphasis should be put on their success or failure, accuracy or error, in what they are about to say or do.

Credentialing. Expressions of a different sort are employed when the individual *knows* the outcome of his act will be discrediting, but is nevertheless strongly committed to the act. Credentialing encompasses a group of expressions of this kind exemplified by the following: "I know what I'm going to say seems anthropomorphic, but . . ."; "I'm not prejudiced—some of my best friends are Jews, but . . ."; "Don't get me wrong, I like your work, but. . . . "

In credentialing individuals seek to avoid an undesired typification they are certain will follow from an intended act. The expressions of credentialing try to accomplish this by establishing for the actor special qualifications or credentials that, he implies, permit him to engage in the act without having it treated in the usual way as a cue for typification. In the classic "some of my best friends" example, the speaker acknowledges that someone who says what he is about to say might be typified as a prejudiced person, but implies his friendships put him in a protected category of people who cannot be so typified. The man who sees human qualities in his dogs knows that speaking of them in an anthropomorphic way will make him seem foolish, and so seeks to avoid the typification by announcing he knows it could be made.

In this second example, knowledge of the negative aspects of an act is central to the establishment of a right to engage in the act anyway. Knowledge is a credential because it establishes the actor as one who may have *purpose* in what he is doing, so that others cannot easily regard him as an unknowing representative of a particular negative type. One who has purpose may have good purpose, whereas one who acts in blind ignorance of the implications of his act is presumed not to.

Sin Licenses. Another category of expressions is employed when the actor is committed to a line of conduct and is certain of a negative response, but does not fear some specific undesired typification. In some instances of social interaction, actors anticipate that their acts will be treated as rule violations. Instead of a specific typification (e.g., racist, fool), the actor fears destruction of his identity as a "responsible member" of the encounter and the substitution of a "rule breaker" or "irresponsible member" typification of him. The focus of his talk and his concern is upon the rule which he fears will be invoked as a rebuke to his action. Hence the following examples: "I realize you might think this is the wrong thing to do, but . . ."; "I know this is against the rules, but . . ."; "What I'm going to do is contrary to the letter of the law but not its spirit. . . . "

Invoking the sin licensing disclaimer is equivalent to stipulating in advance that an act to follow might ordinarily be deemed a violation of a rule, and thus disruptive of the interaction that is taking place. The disclaimer is an effort to invoke in a specific situation the more general and commonly recognized principle that there are occasions on which rules may legitimately be violated without questioning the status of those who violate them. Just as accounts are invoked retrospectively as a way of placing rule violations in such a category, sin licensing disclaimers are invoked prospectively as a way of defining the conduct in advance. (But clearly there is less flexibility in the disclaimer—some excuses are good retrospectively but not prospectively.)

In many instances the sin licensing disclaimer is invoked seriously; that is, its user genuinely fears typification as a rule breaker. In other cases, however, where rules are routinely broken and participants aware of this fact, licenses to sin are requested and granted on a pro forma basis. In either case, the license to sin pays due respect to the rules even while establishing the conditions under which they may be broken.

Cognitive Disclaimers. In routine social interaction, participants seldom have occasion to question one another's empirical grasp of the situation in which they are present. Participants generally assume substantive congruency between their own and others' grasp of the situation. Yet underlying any situation is the possibility that the words or deeds of one participant will be construed by others as lacking sense, as out of touch with empirical reality, as somehow indicating the individual's failure to perceive the situation adequately and correctly. While individuals generally assume that others will assume their acts make empirical sense, they know that some acts may be misconstrued, and that this misconstrual may lead to their own re-typification as lacking sense, as out of touch, as disengaged when they should be engaged, as irrational. Under conditions where they think their acts may be so questioned, individuals use cognitive disclaimers such as the following: "This may seem strange to you . . . "; "Don't react right away to what I'm going to do"; "I know this sounds crazy, but I think I saw. . . ."

Cognitive disclaimers anticipate doubts that may be expressed concerning the speaker's capacity to recognize adequately the empirical facts of the situation in which he finds himself. By anticipating doubt, the disclaimer seeks to reassure others that there is no loss of cognitive capacity, that there is still agreement on the facts of the situation. In this form of disclaiming, as in the others, knowledge is a key element: by demonstrating in advance knowledge of a possible basis for re-typification, the individual establishes purpose for acts that might otherwise be taken as having no purpose, as reflecting a loss of cognitive control.

Appeals for the Suspension of Judgment. If much social interaction is pursued in situations in which people have common ends and work to achieve consensus on them and the means of attaining them, still in such interaction individuals recognize that on occasion their acts may offend even their friends. That is, people are aware that what they say and do may be offensive, angering or dismaying to those with whom they interact, unless and until they can place the act in a proper context, give it the "correct" meaning so far as the exchange is concerned. Under such circumstances, individuals appeal to their fellows to suspend judgment until the full meaning of the act can be made known. "I don't want to make you angry by saying this, but . . . "; "Don't get me wrong, but . . . "; "Hear me out before you explode" are illustrative of appeals individuals make for the suspension of judgment.

Frequently, such appeals take the form of appeals for the suspension of affect, in effect asking the other to hold back on what the actor fears will be a powerful affective response until full meaning can be transmitted. In other cases (e.g., "Don't react until I get this all out"), the appeal is not to suspend specific affect, but merely to await full meaning. In either case, the disclaiming individual realizes that what he is about to do may disrupt the social situation, partly because the assumption of common purpose may be questioned, partly because it may promote his own re-typification as an "enemy" or "turncoat" and not a comrade, friend, or colleague.

Responses to Disclaimers

The discussion has so far emphasized users' perspectives, grounding its classification in the intentions and expectations of those who disclaim. But the picture is incomplete until we grasp how it is that others respond to disclaimers and how their responses affect the course of social interaction.

From the user's standpoint, the disclaimer is an effort to dissociate his identity from the specific content of his words or deeds. Take, for example, the following use of credentialing: "I'm no racist, because I have a lot of black friends and associates but I think black people want too much, too soon." In this and similar instances, two fundamental claims are made: first, there is an identity claim—specifically, a negative typification as a racist is disclaimed, and so the opposite, valued identity is claimed; second, there is a substantive claim—specifically, an expressed belief that blacks want improvements more quickly than they can or should be provided. People use disclaimers in order to secure the success of substantive claims, but without the possible negative implications for their identity claims.

By the phrase substantive claim we refer to the fact that every word or deed has implications for the emerging definition of a situation and the joint action it contains. In the above illustration the substantive claim is a factual claim, that is, a statement that certain conditions are true of blacks. In other instances, substantive claims have to do with morality (e.g., "It is right to do what I am urging we do."), technical efficiency (e.g., "This is an appropriate way of doing things.") and the like. Every word or deed operates, in effect, as a claim that the situation should be defined in a certain way, or that it can be best defined in that way or that for all practical purposes that is the way to define it. While claims are not always (nor, perhaps, often) expressed in so many words, they operate to the same effect.

This distinction is crucial to our discussion of responses, for both uses of and responses to disclaimers proceed on these parallel levels of identity and substance. On one hand, others may either accept or reject the identity portion of the disclaimer, either attributing to the user the identity he seeks to avoid or supporting his existing identity in the situation. On the other hand (and somewhat independently of their response on the issue of identity), others may accept or reject the user's substantive claims, agreeing or disagreeing with his statements, regarding his actions as useful or dangerous, morally acceptable or prohibited.

From the user's point of view, a disclaimer is fully successful if it allows both types of claim to be accepted; the other concedes the substantive import of the user's

actions or expressions and makes no undesired re-typification of him. In the example cited above, factual claims about blacks would be granted and no re-typification as a racist would take place. Under such a condition of "full success," we may assume, interaction proceeds on its course—a potential disturbance has been successfully skirted.

Less desirable, but still to be counted a partial success, is the condition where a substantive claim is rejected, but where a possible re-typification is not made. Following the same example, a result such as the following illustrates partial success: "I think you're wrong about the pace of black progress but, of course, I know you are not a racist." In this condition, while the user has failed to define the situation in the hoped-for manner, he has at least succeeded in preserving his identity in the situation and avoiding re-typification.

In either of the above conditions, we can speak of the acceptance of a disclaimer in the sense that the user's identity is preserved intact. A disclaimer is said to be rejected when its user is typified by another in a negative way, whatever his response to the substantive claim. On one hand, it seems likely that most rejected disclaimers involve a rejection of both claims: the use of credentialing, as in the above example, would lead both to a denial of the factual claim being made *and* to the re-typification of the user as a racist. On the other hand, there is at least the logical possibility that a substantive claim will be granted, but that simultaneously the user will be re-typified. "Being right for the wrong reasons" is an illustration of a condition where factual claims are granted in the very process of altering a user's identity.

The acceptance or rejection of disclaimers is, however, a more complex and uncertain process than our elliptical discussion indicates. We have glossed over, thus far, the process of inference and signaling that is crucial to the outcome of a given disclaimer. The appropriate questions are the following: How is it that users infer acceptance or rejection of their claims? How is it that others signal acceptance or rejection of users' claims?

The questions of inference and signaling are, in the course of real social interaction, bound closely together; indeed, there is much reflexivity between the two. Whether a signal is, in fact, a signal is not concretely a matter of fact, but depends upon the interplay between the user's inference and the other's intent. What is intended to be a signal may be falsely construed or not construed at all, and what is not intended as a signal may be so construed, either favorably or unfavorably to the user's hopes. And part of the making of an inference involves its being made known to the other that an inference has been made, a linkage that is always subject to possible slippage.

For analytical purposes, however, we must separate inference and signaling. The former can be discussed by paying attention to the rules or procedures invoked by the user, whether inwardly or overtly, in an effort to determine the success of his disclaimer.

In the most elementary sense prima facie evidence of a disclaimer's success is to be sought in the other's overt response: if the response the user hoped to avoid is not forthcoming, he has evidence that his tactic has succeeded. If an interactant credentials his prejudicial statement, he may infer the success of his credentialing if no charge of prejudice is forthcoming. This will be so at the level of his identity claim, whatever the response given the substance of his action.

The possibility always exists, of course, that others will withhold cues that would enable the interactant to judge the success of his disclaimer. While much of our imagery of role playing and role taking suggests that actors are always forthcoming about their true judgments, there is no reason to assume that awareness contexts are typically open. Closed, pretense, or suspicion awareness contexts may characterize the use and response to disclaimers as much

as any other form of interaction. Thus, we must observe, inferences about success based on prima facie evidence must always be, for the actors who make them, somewhat tentative. Every use of a disclaimer risks the possibility that a user's identity may be damaged without his immediately discovering the damage.

More positively, users may infer acceptance or rejection from cues provided by others. Such cues, insofar as they are meant to signal acceptance, may take a variety of forms. The other may, for example, address himself explicitly to the issue raised by the disclaimer: "I realize you are no expert"; "I know you aren't prejudiced"; "I understand what you mean." These examples suggest responses that more or less explicitly signal the legitimacy of the disclaimer in the situation at hand. Sometimes the positive response may include the sharing of the disclaimer, which entails the other using an expression that indicates that he, also, shares the point of view of the user, that he too might, in similar circumstances, use the same disclaimer. We may assume that when others provide users with positive cues, inferences are made with more confidence and interaction continues on its course. Even here, however, there is slippage between intent and inference, and a nod of the head that signifies to the user the acceptance of his viewpoint may be to the other a means of giving the user more rope with which to hang himself.

The question of inference and signaling also turns on the degree to which those who use disclaimers provide an opportunity for response. Social interaction is not always conducted with full attention to the etiquette of turn-taking; indeed, users of disclaimers may intentionally "rush" their interaction sequences in such a way that others are "left behind" and, having had no opportunity to object, are in the position of having agreed by default. An interaction sequence may be rushed by a refusal to yield the floor to another for a response or a refusal to "see" that the floor is wanted by another. A sequence may also be rushed where deeds follow so quickly upon words that commitments are made that cannot subsequently be escaped.

Opportunities for negative responses to disclaimers may also be limited if users are able to "finesse" interaction sequences. On the one hand, actors can "get away with" words and deeds that are gross threats to their identities if they undertake them in small steps, invoking seemingly minor disclaimers along the way. That is, small disclaimers are honored more readily, we may suggest, than large ones, but a series of small disclaimers may result in a major behavioral cue being treated as irrelevant to the actor's identity. On the other hand, it is not unreasonable to suppose that actors may on occasion make a disclaimer of far greater magnitude than their impending act calls for, knowing the other may thus be more likely to accept it. On any occasion where a disclaimer might be used, the user has some discretion in terms of associating his impending act with a possible negative typification of him. By exaggerating the possibly negative typification, and then proceeding with his word or deed, he hopes to secure acceptance by virtue of contrast.

The net outcome of successful disclaimers, whether the acceptance is voluntary or reflects the user's successful rushing or finessing of the interaction sequence, is that the user's identity in the situation is at least temporarily sustained. No re-typification in negative terms takes place, no disruption in the emergence of meaning occurs. Not only this, acceptance of a disclaimer, and particularly the acceptance of a series of disclaimers, commits both participants to the reciprocal identities being built up. As a situation proceeds and as disclaimers are employed successfully, we can hypothesize that it becomes more difficult for participants to reject subsequent disclaimers—the progressive solidification of identities lays the groundwork for easier disclaiming and,

at some stage, makes it possible for actors to assume disclaimers and acceptances of one another rather than having to make each one explicitly.

How, then, are disclaimers rejected? What cues are sought or provided? What procedures are used to make inferences about acceptance? Again, in the simplest sense, prima facie evidence of rejection is to be found if the other explicitly avows what the disclaimer had sought to avoid. Rejection is certain if the other affirms that the very re-typification that the user feared is, in fact, to be made of him. "You should be an expert in this area!"; "You've had plenty of time to work on a proposal"; "If you know it's anthropomorphic, why are you saying it?" Expressions such as these are used as counters to disclaimers, indicating to the user in direct terms that his tactic has not worked, that he will be re-typified unless he can adduce evidence to show why he should not be.

The failure of a disclaimer makes its user subject to re-typification in the very terms his disclaimer provided to the other. This fact is both a weakness and a strength. It is a weakness, of course, because the use of a given disclaimer provides other interactants with a ready-made issue in terms of which the now-disrupted meaning of the context can be managed. Where hedging has been used, the issue is the identity of the user: thus, for example, a disclaimer of devil's advocacy may be met with a denial that only devil's advocacy is meant, that, in fact, the user is concealing his true purpose or goals, i.e., his true identity. Where credentialing has been employed, the issue becomes one of purpose or intent, specifically of good or bad intent, since the use of credentialing rests largely upon the implication that since the user knows the possibly evil connotations of what he is about to do or say, he may have other than evil intent. Thus charges of evil purpose and identity concealment may also be made. Where sin licensing has been invoked, the issue turns on the applicability of a given rule to the act in question. Where cognitive disclaimers are used, the issue becomes one of fact and its interpretation. Where the appeal is to suspend judgment, the issue is whether, in the end, meaning was in fact clarified during the suspension.

To say that "the issue" turns upon this or that point is to say that the focus of interaction itself turns upon the disclaimer, its user's identity and the associated act. Since the user has, via his disclaimer, announced the problematic quality of his words or deeds, he has placed ready-made weapons at the disposal of the other. The question that arises at this point, therefore, is how interaction progresses when it focuses upon the disclaimer.

It is worth noting that up to this point, the user has sought to manage his own identity in the eyes of the other, whatever the outcome with respect to substantive claims. Now the issue is, basically, his identity, and what is important to the user is how that identity may be sustained. While the tactics of identity maintenance in such circumstances are a matter of empirical discovery, it seems likely that altercasting will play an important role in the proceedings.

Altercasting (Weinstein & Deutschberger, 1963) is a process in which actors endeavor to regulate the identities of others: going on the offensive in an argument, treating a particular child as the "baby of the family," creating a "straw man" and identifying an opponent with it are illustrations of the technique of altercasting. In each case, an other's identity is governed, or an effort is made to have it be governed, by an actor's actions. (Altercasting is to be understood in contrast with identity as a phenomenon an actor manages for himself.)

The significance of altercasting in the disclaiming process lies in the fact that an identity established for another has implications for the identity of the altercaster. Identities are reciprocal, which is to say that participants in social interaction establish identities for themselves and each other in a mutually related texture where the position of one has implications for the position of another. In the disclaiming process, altercasting would appear to be significant because it offers the user a "last chance" to salvage his own identity by trying to establish for the rejecting other an identity that will reflect favorably on the rejected user. Having failed to disclaim an identity implied in his actions and utterances, the user may attempt to salvage his identity by more or less forcibly working on the identity of the other, seeking to portray the other in a light that makes his own discredit less serious, or even makes it disappear. Thus, to illustrate, the user may act towards the other as if the latter, too, shared in the discredit: following our example of the credentialing racist, the user may seek to apply the label racist to the other, perhaps by citing or alleging more serious violations on the part of the latter.

In addition to altercasting, the user may turn to various accounts (Scott & Lyman, 1968) as a way of extracting himself from his predicament. As a disclaimer is used and meets a negative response, it passes into the immediate past, and so becomes a proper object of an account. The user may excuse his conduct, thus defusing its relevance to his identity by accepting its undesirable nature by denying responsibility. Or he may attempt a justification, accepting responsibility but arguing for the irrelevance of his act to his identity.

The possible outcomes of rejected disclaimers, in terms of the course of the interaction and the identities of participants, are many, and difficult to summarize or generalize. Underlying all outcomes, however, is the basic fact that issues of substance have become transformed into issues of participants' identities. In effect, when disclaimers are rejected, a situation is transformed, with possibly unpleasant short and long-term consequences for the actor whose identity claims have been destroyed.

That a rejected disclaimer does not inevitably imply the loss of a desirable situated identity, and may in fact be a strength to the user, turns on the fact that a user may under some conditions *seek* to have his disclaimer rejected. If some actors are genuinely concerned with their identities in the eyes of others, others may be cynical in the use of disclaimers. Just as an individual may use a disclaimer that is far out of proportion to the "real" implications of his conduct in the hopes that it will be more easily accepted, he may look ahead, construct alternative scenarios of the conversation on which he is embarked and choose disclaimers in such a way that discussion turns on issues he can best argue. If his disclaimer is accepted, he is able to pursue the line of conduct he had in mind. If it is rejected, he is in a relatively strong position to argue his case, to portray his partner's characterization of him as a "straw man," even though he is himself the source of the characterization.

Conclusion: The Disclaimer and Social Theory

The disclaimer and the broader current of thought of which it is a part have significance for a long-standing problem in social theory. This is the question of how culture enters individual action or, more broadly, how social order and continuity are maintained. Culture, in most formulations, is the root of continuity. Parsons (1966, pp. 5-7), for example, visualizes culture as akin to the genetic code of physical organisms. Just as the genetic pool of a species provides the parameters for individual phenotypes, so does culture provide the persisting identity for individual actions and interaction. Yet, the crucial question of how culture enters individual action has not been satisfactorily answered.

The most important link between culture and action is generally seen to be the socialization process. Following Mead's seminal account of the generalized other, and de-emphasizing his concern for emergence, heaviest stress has been placed on *internalization* as the means by which culture is transmitted and becomes influential upon action. From this perspective, internalization constitutes a functional equivalent to instinct in other animal species; the bee's dance is guided by a genetic template and man's by a deeply internalized normative structure. Although the origins of control are different, the consequences are the same. In both cases, the direction and substance of action are provided by a precognitive and involuntary hierarchy of preferences. In those (relatively rare) situations where deviance does occur, the reason is seen to be incomplete or faulty socialization, and the link of culture to behavior is then maintained by mechanisms of external control in the form of sanctions.

The perspective sketched, or perhaps caricatured, above has been seriously questioned in recent years. The fundamental root of such questioning is empirical. While it is clear that certain cultural elements are deeply internalized, particularly language-based logical and inferential canons, primal esthetic preferences, and so on, relatively little of routine social action appears to be guided by deeply internalized normative structures. Man does not act like a well-programmed social robot; indeed, in much of everyday social action, variation from normatively prescribed behavior is statistically "normal."

This point has been made from a number of different theoretical perspectives. Dennis Wrong (1961) has argued from a psychoanalytical perspective that sociologists typically err by viewing man as "over-socialized." Sociology, he claims, has historically failed to take account of residual and unsocialized libidinal energy, which continues to exert a dynamic and "unsocial" influence on individual action. David Riesman (1950) and Allen Wheelis (1958), while they don't dispute that traditional views of the link between action and culture may have fitted some earlier time, contend that such models are increasingly inappropriate for contemporary society. Modern man, they argue, is given by his socialization a diffuse capacity to read social cues and to make situationally appropriate responses, rather than any deeply internalized normative set.

A third important critique of internalization as the link between action and culture has emerged from the interactionist and neo-phenomenological traditions. In radical contrast to structural theorists who tend to view culture as given, interactionist and neo-phenomenological theorists are most concerned with the creative and problematic aspects of the relationship between action and culture. Erving Goffman's (1959) vision of the presentation of self as an often laborious and conscious "fitting" of one's line of conduct to cultural norms, Ralph Turner's (1962) substitution of "role-making" for "role-playing," and the ethnomethodological explications of the et cetera rule and similar subroutines (cf. Cicourel, 1970) all convey the same essential point: culture is largely exterior to the person and often problematic.

The foregoing questions and reconceptualizations have made the issue of cultural, and thus social, continuity particularly pressing. If indeed there is minimal deep internalization of culture, at least in contemporary society, how do we account for social order? How is it, faced with the ambiguities and contradictions of a complex society, that normative continuity and meaning are sustained in the actions of diverse and individualistic actors?

For a start, it would be well to view culture as learned, and only approximately so, instead of as internalized. Rather than being somehow akin to instinct, culture is best seen as a kind of shifting cognitive map of the social order and largely within the awareness of the actor. From this point of view, culture is environmental to action. It constitutes one of several sets of parameters within which action is framed. Although there is considerable openness to action, culture, meaning here situationally appropriate norms, meanings, and judgmental standards, must be taken into account as the actor constructs his line of conduct. The disclaimer, along with accounts and vocabularies of motives, are among the means by which actors "take account" of culture. In the interests of preserving cathected identities, of making situations sensible, and of facilitating interaction, actors explicitly define the relation between their questionable conduct and prevailing norms. Collectively these might be called "aligning actions" in the sense that they are intended to serve as means of bringing problematic conduct into line with cultural constraints. The net consequence of aligning actions is to perpetuate normative order and meaning in the face of lines of conduct which are objectively at variance with situational norms and understandings.

References

Cicourel, A. (1970). Basic and normative rules in the negotiation of status and role. In H. P. Dreitzel (Ed.), *Recent sociology: II* (pp. 4-45). New York: Macmillan.

Goffman, E. (1959). *The presentation of self in everyday life*. Garden City, NY: Anchor.

Hall, P. M., & Hewitt, J. P. (1970, Summer). The quasi-theory of communication and the management of dissent. *Social Problems, 18,* 17-27.

Hewitt, J. P., & Hall, P. M. (1973, June). Social problems, problematic situations, and quasi-theories. *American Sociological Review, 38,* 367-374.

McHugh, P. (1968). *Defining the situation.* New York: Bobbs-Merrill.

Mills, C. W. (1940, October). Situated actions and vocabularies of motive. *American Sociological Review, 5,* 904-913.

Parsons, T. (1966). *Societies: Evolutionary and comparative perspectives.* Englewood Cliffs, NJ: Prentice-Hall.

Riesman, D., et al. (1950). *The lonely crowd.* Garden City, NY: Anchor.

Schutz, A. (1964). *Collected papers: II* (M. Natanson, Ed.). The Hague: Nijhoff.

Scott, M. B., & Lyman, S. M. (1968, February). Accounts. *American Sociological Review, 33,* 46-62.

Turner, R. (1962). Role-taking: Process versus conformity. In A. Rose (Ed.), *Human behavior and social process.* Boston: Houghton Mifflin.

Weinstein, E., & Deutschberger, P. (1963, December). Some dimensions of altercasting. *Sociometry, 26,* 454-466.

Wheelis, A. (1958). *The quest for identity.* New York: Norton.

Wrong, D. (1961, April). The oversocialized conception of man in modern sociology. *American Sociological Review, 26,* 183-193.

25

On Cooling the Mark Out: Some Aspects of Adaptation to Failure

Erving Goffman

In cases of criminal fraud, victims find they must suddenly adapt themselves to the loss of sources of security and status which they had taken for granted. A consideration of this adaptation to loss can lead us to an understanding of some relations in our society between involvements and the selves that are involved.

In the argot of the criminal world, the term "mark" refers to any individual who is a victim or prospective victim of certain forms of planned illegal exploitation.[1] The mark is the sucker—the person who is taken in. An instance of the operation of any particular racket, taken through the full cycle of its steps or phases, is sometimes called a "play." The persons who operate the racket and "take" the mark are occasionally called "operators."

The confidence game—the "con," as its practitioners call it—is a way of obtaining money under false pretenses by the exercise of fraud and deceit. The con differs from politer forms of financial deceit in important ways. The con is practiced on private persons by talented actors who methodi-

cally and regularly build up informal social relationships just for the purpose of abusing them; white collar crime is practiced on organizations by persons who learn to abuse positions of trust which they once filled faithfully. The one exploits poise; the other, position. Further, a con man is someone who accepts a social role in the underworld community; he is part of a brotherhood whose members make no pretense to one another of being "legit." A white collar criminal, on the other hand, has no colleagues, although he may have an associate with whom he plans his crime and a wife to whom he confesses it.

The con is said to be a good racket in the United States only because most Americans are willing, nay eager, to make easy money, and will engage in action that is less than legal in order to do so. The typical play has typical phases. The potential sucker is first spotted, and one member of the working team (called the "outside man," "steerer," or "roper") arranges to make social contact with him. The confidence of the mark is won, and he is given an opportunity to invest his money in a gambling venture which he understands to have been fixed in his favor. The venture, of course, *is* fixed, but not in his favor. The mark is permitted to win some money and then persuaded to invest more. There is an "accident" or "mistake," and the mark loses his total invest-

"On Cooling the Mark Out: Some Aspects of Adaptation to Failure" by E. Goffman, 1952. *Psychiatry: Journal for the Study of Interpersonal Relations, 15*(4), pp. 451-463. Reprinted by permission of Dr. Jillian Sankoff, University of Pennsylvania.

ment. The operators then depart in a ceremony that is called the "blowoff" or "sting." They leave the mark but take his money. The mark is expected to go on his way, a little wiser and a lot poorer.

Sometimes, however, a mark is not quite prepared to accept his loss as a gain in experience and to say and do nothing about his venture. He may feel moved to complain to the police or to chase after the operators. In the terminology of the trade, the mark may "squawk," "beef," or "come through." From the operators' point of view, this kind of behavior is bad for business. It gives the members of the mob a bad reputation with such police as have not yet been fixed and with marks who have not yet been taken. In order to avoid this adverse publicity, an additional phase is sometimes added at the end of the play. It is called "cooling the mark out." After the blowoff has occurred, one of the operators stays with the mark and makes an effort to keep the anger of the mark within manageable and sensible proportions. The operator stays behind his team-mates in the capacity of what might be called a cooler and exercises upon the mark the art of consolation. An attempt is made to define the situation for the mark in a way that makes it easy for him to accept the inevitable and quietly go home. The mark is given instruction in the philosophy of taking a loss.

When we call to mind the image of a mark who has just been separated from his money, we sometimes attempt to account for the greatness of his anger by the greatness of his financial loss. This is a narrow view. In many cases, especially in America, the mark's image of himself is built up on the belief that he is a pretty shrewd person when it comes to making deals and that he is not the sort of person who is taken in by anything. The mark's readiness to participate in a sure thing is based on more than avarice; it is based on a feeling that he will now be able to prove to himself that he is the sort of person who can "turn a fast buck." For many, this capacity for high finance comes near to being a sign of masculinity and a test of fulfilling the male role.

It is well known that persons protect themselves with all kinds of rationalizations when they have a buried image of themselves which the facts of their status do not support. A person may tell himself many things: that he has not been given a fair chance; that he is not really interested in becoming something else; that the time for showing his mettle has not yet come; that the usual means of realizing his desires are personally or morally distasteful, or require too much dull effort. By means of such defenses, a person saves himself from committing a cardinal social sin—the sin of defining oneself in terms of a status while lacking the qualifications which an incumbent of that status is supposed to possess.

A mark's participation in a play, and his investment in it, clearly commit him in his own eyes to the proposition that he is a smart man. The process by which he comes to believe that he cannot lose is also the process by which he drops the defenses and compensations that previously protected him from defeats. When the blowoff comes, the mark finds that he has no defense for not being a shrewd man. He has defined himself as a shrewd man and must face the fact that he is only another easy mark. He has defined himself as possessing a certain set of qualities and then proven to himself that he is miserably lacking in them. This is a process of self-destruction of the self. It is no wonder that the mark needs to be cooled out and that it is good business policy for one of the operators to stay with the mark in order to talk him into a point of view from which it is possible to accept a loss.

In essence, then, the cooler has the job of handling persons who have been caught out on a limb—persons whose expectations and self-conceptions have been built up and then shattered. The mark is a person who has compromised himself, in his own eyes if not in the eyes of others.

Although the term "mark" is commonly applied to a person who is given short-lived expectations by operators who have intentionally misrepresented the facts, a less restricted definition is desirable in analyzing the larger social scene. An expectation may finally prove false, even though it has been possible to sustain it for a long time and even though the operators acted in good faith. So, too, the disappointment of reasonable expectations, as well as misguided ones, creates a need for consolation. Persons who participate in what is recognized as a confidence game are found in only a few social settings, but persons who have to be cooled out are found in many. Cooling the mark out is one theme in a very basic social story.

For purposes of analysis, one may think of an individual in reference to the values or attributes of a socially recognized character which he possesses. Psychologists speak of a value as a personal involvement. Sociologists speak of a value as a status, role, or relationship. In either case, the character of the value that is possessed is taken in a certain way as the character of the person who possesses it. An alteration in the kinds of attributes possessed brings an alteration to the self-conception of the person who possesses them.

The process by which someone acquires a value is the process by which he surrenders the claim he had to what he was and commits himself to the conception of self which the new value requires or allows him to have. It is the process that persons who fall in love or take dope call "getting hooked." After a person is hooked, he must go through another process by which his new involvement finds its proper place, in space and time, relative to the other calls, demands, and commitments that he has upon himself. At this point certain other persons suddenly begin to play an important part in the individual's story; they impinge upon him by virtue of the relationship they happen to have to the value in which he has become involved. This is not the place to consider the general kinds of impingement that are institutionalized in our society and the general social relationships that arise: the personal relationship, the professional relationship, and the business relationship. Here we are concerned only with the end of the story, the way in which a person becomes disengaged from one of his involvements.

In our society, the story of a person's involvement can end in one of three general ways. According to one type of ending, he may withdraw from one of his involvements or roles in order to acquire a sequentially related one that is considered better. This is the case when a youth becomes a man, when a student becomes a practitioner, or when a man from the ranks is given a commission.

Of course, the person who must change his self at any one of these points of promotion may have profound misgivings. He may feel disloyal to the way of life that must be left behind and to the persons who do not leave it with him. His new role may require action that seems insincere, dishonest, or unfriendly. This he may experience as a loss in moral cleanliness. His new role may require him to forgo the kinds of risk-taking and exertion that he previously enjoyed, and yet his new role may not provide the kind of heroic and exalted action that he expected to find in it.[2] This he may experience as a loss in moral strength.

There is no doubt that certain kinds of role success require certain kinds of moral failure. It may therefore be necessary, in a sense, to cool the dubious neophyte in rather than out. He may have to be convinced that his doubts are a matter of sentimentality. The adult social view will be impressed upon him. He will be required to understand that a promotional change in status is voluntary, desirable, and natural, and that loss of one's role in these circumstances is the ultimate test of having fulfilled it properly.

It has been suggested that a person may leave a role under circumstances that reflect favorably upon the way in which he performed it. In theory, at least, a related possibility must be considered. A person may leave a role and at the same time leave behind him the standards by which such roles are judged. The new thing that he becomes may be so different from the thing he was that criteria such as success or failure cannot be easily applied to the change which has occurred. He becomes lost to others that he may find himself; he is of the twice-born. In our society, perhaps the most obvious example of this kind of termination occurs when a woman voluntarily gives up a prestigeful profession in order to become a wife and a mother. It is to be noted that this illustrates an institutionalized movement; those who make it do not make news. In America most other examples of this kind of termination are more a matter of talk than of occurrence. For example, one of the culture heroes of our dinner-table mythology is the man who walks out on an established calling in order to write or paint or live in the country. In other societies, the kind of abdication being considered here seems to have played a more important role. In medieval China, for instance, anchoretic withdrawal apparently gave to persons of quite different station a way of retreating from the occupational struggle while managing the retreat in an orderly, face-saving fashion (see Weber, 1951, p. 178).

Two basic ways in which a person can lose a role have been considered; he can be promoted out of it or abdicate from it. There is, of course, a third basic ending to the status story. A person may be involuntarily deprived of his position or involvement and made in return something that is considered a lesser thing to be. It is mainly in this third ending to a person's role that occasions arise for cooling him out. It is here that one deals in the full sense with the problem of persons losing their roles.

Involuntary loss seems itself to be of two kinds. First, a person may lose a status in such a way that the loss is not taken as a reflection upon the loser. The loss of a loved one, either because of an accident that could not have been prevented or because of a disease that could not have been halted, is a case in point. Occupational retirement because of old age is another. Of course, the loss will inevitably alter the conception the loser has of himself and the conception others have of him, but the alteration itself will not be treated as a symbol of the fate he deserves to receive. No insult is added to injury. It may be necessary, none the less, to pacify the loser and resign him to his loss. The loser who is not held responsible for his loss may even find himself taking the mystical view that all involvements are part of a wider con game, for the more one takes pleasure in a particular role the more one must suffer when it is time to leave it. He may find little comfort in the fact that the play has provided him with an illusion that has lasted a lifetime. He may find little comfort in the fact that the operators had not meant to deceive him.

Secondly, a person may be involuntarily deprived of a role under circumstances which reflect unfavorably on his capacity for it. The lost role may be one that he had already acquired or one that he had openly committed himself to preparing for. In either case the loss is more than matter of ceasing to act in a given capacity; it is ultimate proof of an incapacity. And in many cases it is even more than this. The moment of failure often catches a person acting as one who feels that he is an appropriate sort of person for the role in question. Assumption becomes presumption, and failure becomes fraud. To loss of substance is thereby added loss of face. Of the many themes that can occur in the natural history of an involvement, this seems to be the most melancholy. Here it will be quite essential and quite difficult to cool the mark out. I shall be particularly concerned with this second kind of loss— the kind that involves humiliation.

It should be noted, parenthetically, that one circle of persons may define a particular loss as the kind that casts no reflection on the loser, and that a different circle of persons may treat the same loss as a symbol of what the loser deserves. One must also note that there is a tendency today to shift certain losses of status from the category of those that reflect upon the loser to the category of those that do not. When persons lose their jobs, their courage, or their minds, we tend more and more to take a clinical or naturalistic view of the loss and a non-moral view of their failure. We want to define a person as something that is not destroyed by the destruction of one of his selves. This benevolent attitude is in line with the effort today to publicize the view that occupational retirement is not the end of all active capacities but the beginning of new and different ones.

A consideration of consolation as a social process leads to four general problems having to do with the self in society. First, where in modern life does one find persons conducting themselves as though they were entitled to the rights of a particular status and then having to face up to the fact that they do not possess the qualifications for the status? In other words, at what points in the structures of our social life are persons likely to compromise themselves or find themselves compromised? When is it likely that a person will have to disengage himself or become disengaged from one of his involvements? Secondly, what are the typical ways in which persons who find themselves in this difficult position can be cooled out; how can they be made to accept the great injury that has been done to their image of themselves, regroup their defenses, and carry on without raising a squawk? Thirdly, what, in general, can happen when a person refuses to be cooled out, that is, when he refuses to be pacified by the cooler? Fourthly, what arrangements are made by operators and marks to avoid entirely the process of consolation?

In all personal-service organizations customers or clients sometimes make complaints. A customer may feel that he has been given service in a way that is unacceptable to

him—a way that he interprets as an offense to the conception he has of who and what he is. The management therefore has the problem of cooling the mark out. Frequently this function is allotted to specialists within the organization. In large stores the complaint department and the floorwalker perform a similar function.

One may note that a service organization does not operate in an anonymous world, as does a con mob, and is therefore strongly obliged to make some effort to cool the mark out. An institution, after all, cannot take it on the lam; it must pacify its marks.

One may also note that coolers in service organizations tend to view their own activity in a light that softens the harsher details of the situation. The cooler protects himself from feelings of guilt by arguing that the customer is not really in need of the service he expected to receive, that bad service is not really deprivational, and that beefs and complaints are a sign of bile, not a sign of injury. In a similar way, the con man protects himself from remorseful images of bankrupt marks by arguing that the mark is a fool and not a full-fledged person, possessing an inclination towards illegal gain but not the decency to admit it or the capacity to succeed at it.

In organizations patterned after a bureaucratic model, it is customary for personnel to expect rewards of a specified kind upon fulfilling requirements of a specified nature. Personnel come to define their career line in terms of a sequence of legitimate expectations and to base their self-conceptions on the assumption that in due course they will be what the institution allows persons to become. Sometimes, however, a member of an organization may fulfill some of the requirements for a particular status, especially the requirements concerning technical proficiency and seniority, but not other requirements, especially the less codified ones having to do with the proper handling of social relationships at work. It must fall to someone to break the bad news to the victim; someone must tell him that he has been fired, or that he has failed his examinations, or that he has been by-passed in promotion. And after the blowoff, someone has to cool the mark out. The necessity of disappointing the expectations that a person has taken for granted may be infrequent in some organizations, but in others, such as training institutions, it occurs all the time. The process of personnel selection requires that many trainees be called but that few be chosen.

When one turns from places of work to other scenes in our social life, one finds that each has its own occasions for cooling the mark out. During informal social intercourse it is well understood that an effort on the part of one person (ego) to decrease his social distance from another person (alter) must be graciously accepted by alter or, if rejected, rejected tactfully so that the initiator of the move can save his social face. This rule is codified in books on etiquette and is followed in actual behavior. A friendly movement in the direction of alter is a movement outward on a limb; ego communicates his belief that he has defined himself as worthy of alter's society, while at the same time he places alter in the strategic position of being able to discredit this conception.

The problem of cooling persons out in informal social intercourse is seen most clearly, perhaps, in courting situations and in what might be called de-courting situations. A proposal of marriage in our society tends to be a way in which a man sums up his social attributes and suggests to a woman that hers are not so much better as to preclude a merger or partnership in these matters. Refusal on the part of the woman, or refusal on the part of the man to propose when he is clearly in a position to do so, is a serious reflection on the rejected suitor. Courtship is a way not only of presenting oneself to alter for approval but also of saying that the opinion of alter in this matter is the opinion one is most concerned with. Refusing a proposal, or refusing to propose, is therefore a

difficult operation. The mark must be carefully cooled out. The act of breaking a date or of refusing one, and the task of discouraging a "steady," can also be seen in this light, although in these cases great delicacy and tact may not be required, since the mark may not be deeply involved or openly committed. Just as it is harder to refuse a proposal than to refuse a date, so it is more difficult to reject a spouse than to reject a suitor. The process of de-courting by which one person in a marriage maneuvers the other into accepting a divorce without fuss or undue rancor requires extreme finesse in the art of cooling the mark out.

In all of these cases where a person constructs a conception of himself which cannot be sustained, there is a possibility that he has not invested that which is most important to him in the soon-to-be-denied status. In the current idiom, there is a possibility that when he is hit, he will not be hit where he really lives. There is a set of cases, however, where the blowoff cannot help but strike a vital spot; these cases arise, of course, when a person must be dissuaded from life itself. The man with a fatal sickness or fatal injury, the criminal with a death sentence, the soldier with a hopeless objective—these persons must be persuaded to accept quietly the loss of life itself, the loss of all one's earthly involvements. Here, certainly, it will be difficult to cool the mark out. It is a reflection on the conceptions men have—as cooler and mark—that it is possible to do so.

I have mentioned a few of the areas of social life where it becomes necessary, upon occasion, to cool a mark out. Attention may now be directed to some of the common ways in which individuals are cooled out in all of these areas of life.

For the mark, cooling represents a process of adjustment to an impossible situation—a situation arising from having defined himself in a way which the social facts come to contradict. The mark must therefore be supplied with a new set of apologies for himself, a new framework in which to see himself and judge himself. A process of redefining the self along defensible lines must be instigated and carried along; since the mark himself is frequently in too weakened a condition to do this, the cooler must initially do it for him.

One general way of handling the problem of cooling the mark out is to give the task to someone whose status relative to the mark will serve to ease the situation in some way. In formal organizations, frequently, someone who is two or three levels above the mark in line of command will do the hatchet work, on the assumption that words of consolation and redirection will have a greater power to convince if they come from high places. There also seems to be a feeling that persons of high status are better able to withstand the moral danger of having hate directed at them. Incidentally, persons protected by high office do not like to face this issue, and frequently attempt to define themselves as merely the agents of the deed and not the source of it. In some cases, on the other hand, the task of cooling the mark out is given to a friend and peer of the mark, on the assumption that such a person will know best how to hit upon a suitable rationalization for the mark and will know best how to control the mark should the need for this arise. In some cases, as in those pertaining to death, the role of cooler is given to doctors or priests. Doctors must frequently help a family, and the member who is leaving it, to manage the leave-taking with tact and a minimum of emotional fuss.[3] A priest must not so much save a soul as create one that is consistent with what is about to become of it.

A second general solution to the problem of cooling the mark out consists of offering him a status which differs from the one he has lost or failed to gain but which provides at least a something or a somebody for him to become. Usually the alternative presented to the mark is a compromise of some kind, providing him with some of the trappings of his lost status as well as with some of its spirit. A lover may be asked to become a friend; a student of medicine may be asked to switch to the study of dentistry[4]; a boxer may become a trainer; a dying person may be asked to broaden and empty his worldly loves so as to embrace the All-Father that is about to receive him. Sometimes the mark is allowed to retain his status but is required to fulfill it in a different environment: the honest policeman is transferred to a lonely beat; the too zealous priest is encouraged to enter a monastery; an unsatisfactory plant manager is shipped off to another branch. Sometimes the mark is "kicked upstairs" and given a courtesy status such as "Vice President." In the game for social roles, transfer up, down, or away may all be consolation prizes.

A related way of handling the mark is to offer him another chance to qualify for the role at which he has failed. After his fall from grace, he is allowed to retrace his steps and try again. Officer selection programs in the army, for example, often provide for possibilities of this kind. In general, it seems that third and fourth chances are seldom given to marks, and that second chances, while often given, are seldom taken. Failure at a role removes a person from the company of those who have succeeded, but it does not bring him back—in spirit, anyway—to the society of those who have not tried or are in the process of trying. The person who has failed in a role is a constant source of embarrassment, for none of the standard patterns of treatment is quite applicable to him. Instead of taking a second chance, he usually goes away to another place where his past does not bring confusion to his present.

Another standard method of cooling the mark out—one which is frequently employed in conjunction with other methods—is to allow the mark to explode, to break down, to cause a scene, to give full vent to his reactions and feelings, to "blow his top." If this release of emotions does not find a target, then it at least serves a cathartic function. If it does find a target, as in "telling off the boss," it gives the mark a last-minute chance to re-erect his defenses and prove to himself and others that he had not really cared about the status all along. When a blow-up of this kind occurs, friends of the mark or psychotherapists are frequently brought in. Friends are willing to take responsibility for the mark because their relationship to him is not limited to the role he has failed in. This, incidentally, provides one of the less obvious reasons why the cooler in a con mob must cultivate the friendship of the mark; friendship provides the cooler with an acceptable reason for staying around while the mark is cooled out. Psychotherapists, on the other hand, are willing to take responsibility for the mark because it is their business to offer a relationship to those who have failed in a relationship to others.

It has been suggested that a mark may be cooled out by allowing him, under suitable guidance, to give full vent to his initial shock. Thus the manager of a commercial organization may listen with patience and understanding to the complaints of a customer, knowing that the full expression of a complaint is likely to weaken it. This possibility lies behind the role of a whole series of buffers in our society—janitors, restaurant hostesses, grievance committees, floorwalkers, and so on—who listen in silence, with apparent sympathy, until the mark has simmered down. Similarly, in the case of criminal trials, the defending lawyer may find it profitable to allow the public to simmer down before he brings his client to court.

A related procedure for cooling the mark out is found in what is called stalling. The feelings of the mark are not brought to a head because he is given no target at which to direct them. The operator may manage to avoid the presence of the mark or may convince the mark that there is still a slight chance that the loss has not really occurred. When the mark is stalled, he is given a chance to become familiar with the new conception of self he will have to accept before he is absolutely sure that he will have to accept it.

As another cooling procedure, there is the possibility that the operator and the mark may enter into a tacit understanding according to which the mark agrees to act as if he were leaving of his own accord, and the operator agrees to preserve the illusion that this was the case. It is a form of bribery. In this way the mark may fail in his own eyes but prevent others from discovering the failure. The mark gives up his role but saves his face. This, after all, is one of the reasons why persons who are fleeced by con men are often willing to remain silent about their adventure. The same strategy is at work in the romantic custom of allowing a guilty officer to take his own life in a private way before it is taken from him publicly, and in the less romantic custom of allowing a person to resign for delicate reasons instead of firing him for indelicate ones.

Bribery is, of course, a form of exchange. In this case, the mark guarantees to leave quickly and quietly, and in exchange is allowed to leave under a cloud of his own choosing. A more important variation on the same theme is found in the practice of financial compensation. A man can say to himself and others that he is happy to retire from his job and say this with more conviction if he is able to point to a comfortable pension. In this sense, pensions are automatic devices for providing consolation. So, too, a person who has been injured because of another's criminal or marital neglect can compensate for the loss by means of a court settlement.

I have suggested some general ways in which the mark is cooled out. The question now arises: what happens if the mark refuses to be cooled out? What are the possible lines of action he can take if he refuses to be cooled? Attempts to answer these questions will show more clearly why, in general, the operator is so anxious to pacify the mark.

It has been suggested that a mark may be cooled by allowing him to blow his top. If the blow-up is too drastic or prolonged, however, difficulties may arise. We say that the mark becomes "disturbed mentally" or "personally disorganized." Instead of merely telling his boss off, the mark may go so far as to commit criminal violence against him. Instead of merely blaming himself for failure, the mark may inflict great punishment upon himself by attempting suicide, or by acting so as to make it necessary for him to be cooled out in other areas of his social life.

Sustained personal disorganization is one way in which a mark can refuse to cool out. Another standard way is for the individual to raise a squawk, that is, to make a formal complaint to higher authorities obliged to take notice of such matters. The con mob worries lest the mark appeal to the police. The plant manager must make sure that the disgruntled department head does not carry a formal complaint to the general manager or, worse still, to the Board of Directors. The teacher worries lest the child's parent complain to the principal. Similarly, a woman who communicates her evaluation of self by accepting a proposal of marriage can sometimes protect her exposed position—should the necessity of doing so arise—by threatening her disaffected fiancé with a breach-of-promise suit. So, also, a woman who is de-courting her husband must fear lest he contest the divorce or sue her lover for alienation of affection. In much the same way, a customer who is angered by a salesperson can refuse to be mollified by the floorwalker and demand to see the manager. It is interesting to note that associations dedicated to the rights and the honor of minority groups may sometimes encourage a mark to register a formal squawk; politically it may be more advantageous to provide a test case than to allow the mark to be cooled out.

Another line of action which a mark who refuses to be cooled can pursue is that of turning "sour." The term derives from the argot of industry but the behavior it refers to occurs everywhere. The mark outwardly accepts his loss but withdraws all enthusiasm, good will, and vitality from whatever role he is allowed to maintain. He complies with the formal requirements of the rôle that is left him, but he withdraws his spirit and identification from it. When an employee turns sour, the interests of the organization suffer; every executive, therefore, has the problem of "sweetening" his workers. They must not come to feel that they are slowly being cooled out. This is one of the functions of granting periodic advancements in salary and status, of schemes such as profit-sharing, or of giving the "employee" at home an anniversary present. A similar view can be taken of the problem that a government faces in times of crisis when it must maintain the enthusiastic support of the nation's disadvantaged minorities, for whole groupings of the population can feel they are being cooled out and react by turning sour.

Finally, there is the possibility that the mark may, in a manner of speaking, go into business for himself. He can try to gather about him the persons and facilities required to establish a status similar to the one he has lost, albeit in relation to a different set of persons. This way of refusing to be cooled is often rehearsed in phantasies of the "I'll show them" kind, but sometimes it is actually realized in practice. The rejected marriage partner may make a better remarriage. A social stratum that has lost its status may decide to create its own social system. A leader who fails in a political party may establish his own splinter group.

All these ways in which a mark can refuse to be cooled out have consequences for other persons. There is, of course, a kind of refusal that has little consequence for others. Marks of all kinds may develop explanations and excuses to account in a creditable way for their loss. It is, perhaps, in this region of phantasy that the defeated self makes its last stand.

The process of cooling is a difficult one, both for the operator who cools the mark out and for the person who receives this treatment. Safeguards and strategies are therefore employed to ensure that the process itself need not and does not occur. One deals here with strategies of prevention, not strategies of cure.

From the point of view of the operator, there are two chief ways of avoiding the difficulties of cooling the mark out. First, devices are commonly employed to weed out those applicants for a role, office, or relationship who might later prove to be unsuitable and require removal. The applicant is not given a chance to invest his self unwisely. A variation of this technique, which provides, in a way, a built-in mechanism for cooling the mark out, is found in the institution of probationary period and "temporary" staff. These definitions of the situation make it clear to the person that he must maintain his ego in readiness for the loss of his job, or, better still, that he ought not to think of himself as really having the job. If these safety measures fail, however, a second strategy is often employed. Operators of all kinds seem to be ready, to a surprising degree, to put up with or "carry" persons who have failed but who have not yet been treated as failures. This is especially true where the involvement of the mark is deep and where his conception of self had been publicly committed. Business offices, government agencies, spouses, and other kinds of operators are often careful to make a place for the mark, so that dissolution of the bond will not be necessary. Here, perhaps, is the most important source of private charity in our society.

A consideration of these preventive strategies brings to attention an interesting functional relationship among age-grading, recruitment, and the structure of the self. In our society, as in most others, the young in years are defined as not-yet-persons. To a certain degree, they are not subject to success and failure. A child can throw himself completely into a task, and fail at it, and by and large he will not be destroyed by his failure; it is only necessary to play at cooling him out. An adolescent can be bitterly disappointed in love, and yet he will not thereby become, at least for others, a broken person. A youth can spend a certain amount of time shopping around for a congenial job or a congenial training course, because he is still thought to be able to change his mind without changing his self. And, should he fail at something to which he has tried to commit himself, no permanent damage may be done to his self. If many are to be called and few chosen, then it is more convenient for everyone concerned to call individuals who are not fully persons and cannot be destroyed by failing to be chosen. As the individual grows older, he becomes defined as someone who must not be engaged in a role for which he is unsuited. He becomes defined as something that must not fail, while at the same time arrangements are made to decrease the chances of his failing. Of course, when the mark reaches old age, he must remove himself or be removed from each of his roles, one by one, and participate in the problem of later maturity.

The strategies that are employed by operators to avoid the necessity of cooling the mark out have a counterpart in the strategies that are employed by the mark himself for the same purpose.

There is the strategy of hedging, by which a person makes sure that he is not completely committed. There is the strategy of secrecy, by which a person conceals from others and even from himself the facts of his commitment; there is also the practice of keeping two irons in the fire and the more delicate practice of maintaining a joking or unserious relationship to one's involvement. All of these strategies give the mark an out; in ease of failure he can act as if the self that has failed is not one that is important to him. Here we must also consider the function of being quick to take offense and of taking hints quickly, for in these ways the mark can actively cooperate in the task of saving his face. There is also the strategy of playing it safe, as in cases where a calling is chosen because tenure is assured in it, or where a plain woman is married for much the same reason.

It has been suggested that preventive strategies are employed by operator and mark in order to reduce the chance of failing or to minimize the consequences of failure. The less importance one finds it necessary to give to the problem of cooling, the more importance one may have given to the application of preventive strategies.

I have considered some of the situations in our society in which the necessity for cooling the mark out is likely to arise. I have also considered the standard ways in which a mark can be cooled out, the lines of action he can pursue if he refuses to be cooled, and the ways in which the whole problem can be avoided. Attention can now be turned to some very general questions concerning the self in society.

First, an attempt must be made to draw together what has been implied about the structure of persons. From the point of view of this paper, a person is an individual who becomes involved in a value of some kind— a role, a status, a relationship, an ideology—and then makes a public claim that he is to be defined and treated as someone who possesses the value or property in question. The limits to his claims, and hence the limits to his self, are primarily determined by the objective facts of his social life and secondarily determined by the degree to which a sympathetic interpretation of these facts can bend them in his favor. Any event which demonstrates that someone has made a false claim, defining himself as something which he is not, tends to destroy him. If others realize that the person's conception of self has been contradicted and discredited, then the person tends to be destroyed in the eyes of others. If the person can keep the contradiction a secret, he may succeed in keeping everyone but himself from treating him as a failure.

Secondly, one must take note of what is implied by the fact that it is possible for a person to be cooled out. Difficult as this may be, persons regularly define themselves in terms of a set of attributes and then have to accept the fact that they do not possess them—and do this about-face with relatively little fuss or trouble for the operators. This implies that there is a norm in our society persuading persons to keep their chins up and make the best of it—a sort of social sanitation enjoining torn and tattered persons to keep themselves packaged up. More important still, the capacity of a person to sustain these profound embarrassments implies a certain looseness and lack of interpenetration in the organization of his several life-activities. A man may fail in his job, yet go on succeeding with his wife. His wife may ask him for a divorce, or refuse to grant him one, and yet he may push his way onto the same streetcar at the usual time on the way to the same job. He may know that he is shortly going to have to leave the status of the living, but still march with the other prisoners, or eat breakfast with his family at their usual time and from behind his usual paper. He may be conned of his life's savings on an eastbound train but return to his home town and succeed in acting as if nothing of interest had happened.

Lack of rigid integration of a person's social roles allows for compensation; he can seek comfort in one role for injuries incurred in others. There are always cases, of course, in which the mark cannot sustain the injury to his ego and cannot act like a "good scout." On these occasions the shattering experience in one area of social life may spread out to all the sectors of his activity. He may define away the barriers between his several social roles and become a source of difficulty in all of them. In such cases the play is the mark's entire social life, and the operators, really, are the society. In an increasing number of these cases, the mark is given psychological guidance by professionals of some kind. The psychotherapist is, in this sense, the society's cooler. His job is to pacify and re-orient the disorganized person; his job is to send the patient back to an old world or a new one, and to send him back in a condition in which he can no longer cause trouble to others or can no longer make a fuss. In short, if one takes the society, and not the person, as the unit, the psychotherapist has the basic task of cooling the mark out.

A third point of interest arises if one views all of social life from the perspective of this paper. It has been argued that a person must not openly or even privately commit himself to a conception of himself which the flow of events is likely to discredit. He must not put himself in a position of having to be cooled out. Conversely, however, he must make sure that none of the persons with whom he has dealings are of the sort who may prove unsuitable and need to be cooled out. He must make doubly sure that should it become necessary to cool his associates out, they will be the sort who allow themselves to be gotten rid of. The con man who wants the mark to go home quietly and absorb a loss, the restaurant hostess who wants a customer to eat quietly and go away without causing trouble, and, if this is not possible, quietly to take his patronage elsewhere—these are the persons and these are the relationships which set the tone of some of our social life. Underlying this tone there is the assumption that persons are institutionally related to each other in such a way that if a mark allows himself to be cooled out, then the cooler need have no further concern with him; but if the mark refuses to be cooled out, he can put institutional machinery into action against the cooler. Underlying this tone there is also the assumption that persons are sentimentally related to each other in such a way that if a person allows himself to be cooled out, however great the loss he has sustained, then the cooler withdraws all emotional identification from him; but if the mark cannot absorb the injury to his self and if he becomes personally disorganized in some way, then the cooler cannot help but feel guilt and concern over the predicament. It is this feeling of guilt—this small measure of involvement in the feelings of others—which helps to make the job of cooling the mark out distasteful, wherever it appears. It is this incapacity to be insensitive to the suffering of another person when he brings his suffering right to your door which tends to make the job of cooling a species of dirty work.

One must not, of course, make too much of the margin of sympathy connecting operator and mark. For one thing, the operator may rid himself of the mark by application or threat of pure force or open insult.[5] In Chicago in the 1920's small businessmen who suffered a loss in profits and in independence because of the "protection" services that racketeers gave to them were cooled out in this way. No doubt it is frivolous to suggest that Freud's notion of castration threat has something to do with the efforts of fathers to cool their sons out of oedipal involvements. Furthermore, there are many occasions when operators of different kinds must act as middlemen, with two marks on their hands; the calculated use of one mark as a sacrifice or fall guy may be the only way of cooling the other mark out. Finally, there are barbarous ceremonies in our society, such as criminal trials and the drumming-out ritual employed in court-martial procedures, that are expressly designed to prevent the mark from saving his face. And even in those cases where the cooler makes an effort to make things easier for the person he is getting rid of, we often find that there are bystanders who have no such scruples.[6] Onlookers who are close enough to observe the blowoff but who are not obliged to assist in the dirty work often enjoy the scene, taking pleasure in the discomfiture of the cooler and in the destruction of the mark. What is trouble for some is *Schadenfreude* for others.

This paper has dealt chiefly with adaptations to loss: with defenses, strategies, consolations, mitigations, compensations, and the like. The kinds of sugar-coating have been examined, and not the pill. I would like to close this paper by referring briefly to the sort of thing that would be studied if one were interested in loss as such, and not in adaptations to it.

A mark who requires cooling out is a person who can no longer sustain one of his social roles and is about to be removed from it; he is a person who is losing one of his social lives and is about to die one of the deaths that are possible for him. This leads one to consider the ways in which we can go or be sent to our death in each of our social capacities, the ways, in other words, of handling the passage from the role that we had to a state of having it no longer. One might consider the social processes of firing and laying-off; of resigning and being asked to resign; of farewell and departure, of deportation, excommunication, and going to jail; of defeat at games, contests, and wars; of being dropped from a circle of friends or an intimate social relationship; of corporate dissolution; of retirement in old age; and, lastly, of the deaths that heirs are interested in.

And, finally, attention must be directed to the things we become after we have died in one of the many social senses and capacities in which death can come to us. As one might expect, a process of sifting and sorting occurs by which the socially dead come to be effectively hidden from us. This movement of expersons throughout the social structure proceeds in more than one direction.

There is, first of all, the dramatic process by which persons who have died in important ways come gradually to be brought together into a common graveyard that is separated ecologically from the living community.[7] For the dead, this is at once a punishment and a defense. Jails and mental institutions are, perhaps, the most familiar examples, but other important ones exist. In America today, there is the interesting tendency to set aside certain regions and towns in California as asylums for those who have died in their capacity as workers and as parents but who are still alive financially.[8] For the old in America who have also died financially, there are old-folks homes and rooming-house areas. And, of course, large cities have their Skid Rows which are, as Park put it, "full of junk, much of it human, i.e., men and women who, for some reason or other, have fallen out of line in the march of industrial progress and have been scrapped by the industrial organization of which they were once a part" (Park, 1952, p. 60). Hobo jungles, located near freight yards on the outskirts of towns, provide another case in point.

Just as a residential area may become a graveyard, so also certain institutions and occupational roles may take on a similar function. The ministry in Britain, for example, has sometimes served as a limbo for the occupational stillborn of better families, as have British universities. Mayhew, writing of London in the mid-nineteenth century, provides another example: artisans of different kinds, who had failed to maintain a position in the practice of their trade, could be found working as dustmen (1861, pp. 177-178). In the United States, the jobs of waitress, cab driver, and night watchman, and the profession of prostitution, tend to be ending places where persons of certain kinds, starting from different places, can come to rest.

But perhaps the most important movement of those who fail is one we never see. Where roles are ranked and somewhat related, persons who have been rejected from the one above may be difficult to distinguish from persons who have risen from the one below. For example, in America, upper-class women who fail to make a marriage in their own circle may follow the recognized route of marrying an upper-middle-class professional. Successful lower-middle-class women may arrive at the same station in life, coming from the other direction. Similarly, among those who mingle with one another as colleagues in the profession of dentistry, it is possible to find some who have failed to become physicians and others who have succeeded at not becoming pharmacists or optometrists. No doubt there are few positions in life that do not throw together some persons who are there by virtue of failure and other persons who are there by virtue of success. In this sense, the dead are sorted but not segregated, and continue to walk among the living.

Notes

1. Terminology regarding criminal activity is taken primarily from Maurer (1940) and also from Sutherland (1937). The approach that this paper attempts to utilize is taken from Everett C. Hughes of the University of Chicago, who is not responsible for any misapplications of it which may occur here. The sociological problem of failure was first suggested to me by James Littlejohn of the University of Edinburgh. I am grateful to Professor E. A. Shils for criticism and to my wife, Angelica S. Goffman, for assistance.

2. Mr. Hughes has lectured on this kind of disappointment, and one of his students, Miriam Wagenschein (1950), has undertaken a special study of it.

3. This role of the doctor has been stressed by W. L. Warner in his lectures at the University of Chicago on symbolic roles in "Yankee City."

4. In his seminars, Mr. Hughes has used the term "second-choice" professions to refer to cases of this kind.

5. Suggested by Saul Mendlovitz in conversation.

6. Suggested by Howard S. Becker in conversation.

7. Suggested by lectures of and a personal conversation with Mr. Hughes.

8. Some early writers on caste report a like situation in India at the turn of the nineteenth century. Hindus who were taken to the Ganges to die, and who then recovered, were apparently denied all legal rights and all social relations with the living. Apparently these excluded persons found it necessary to congregate in a few villages of their own. In California, of course, settlements of the old have a voluntary character, and members maintain ceremonial contact with younger kin by the exchange of periodic visits and letters.

References

Maurer, D. W. (1940). *The big con.* Indianapolis, IN: Bobbs-Merrill.

Mayhew, H. (1861). *London labour and the London poor* (vol 2). London: Griffin, Bohn.

Park, R. E. (1952). *Human communities.* Glencoe, IL: Free Press.

Sutherland, E. H. (1937). *The professional thief.* Chicago: University of Chicago Press.

Wagenschein, M. (1950). *"Reality shock": A study of beginning school teachers.* Master's thesis, Department of Sociology, University of Chicago.

Weber, M. (1951). *The religion of China* (H. H. Gerth, Trans.). Glencoe, IL: Free Press.

Looking-Glass Self

Charles Horton Cooley

In a very large and interesting class of cases the social reference takes the form of a somewhat definite imagination of how one's self—that is any idea he appropriates—appears in a particular mind, and the kind of self-feeling one has is determined by the attitude toward this attributed to that other mind. A social self of this sort might be called the reflected or looking-glass self:

Each to each a looking-glass
Reflects the other that doth pass.

As we see our face, figure, and dress in the glass, and are interested in them because they are ours, and pleased or otherwise with them according as they do or do not answer to what we should like them to be; so in imagination we perceive in another's mind some thought of our appearance, manners, aims, deeds, character, friends, and so on, and are variously affected by it.

A self-idea of this sort seems to have three principal elements: the imagination of our appearance to the other person; the imagination of his judgment of that appearance, and some sort of self-feeling, such as pride or mortification. The comparison with a looking-glass hardly suggests the second element, the imagined judgment, which is quite essential. The thing that moves us to pride or shame is not the mere mechanical reflection of ourselves, but an imputed sentiment, the imagined effect of this reflection upon another's mind. This is evident from the fact that the character and weight of that other, in whose mind we see ourselves, makes all the difference with our feeling. We are ashamed to seem evasive in the presence of a straightforward man, cowardly in the presence of a brave one, gross in the eyes of a refined one, and so on. We always imagine, and in imagining share, the judgments of the other mind. A man will boast to one person of an action—say some sharp transaction in trade—which he would be ashamed to own to another.

The process by which self-feeling of the looking-glass sort develops in children may be followed without much difficulty. Studying the movements of others as closely as they do they soon see a connection between their own acts and changes in those movements; that is, they perceive their own influence or power over persons. The child appropriates the visible actions of his parent or nurse, over which he finds he has some control, in quite the same way as he appropriates one of his own members or a plaything, and he will try to do things with this new possession, just as he will with his hand or his rattle. A girl six months old will attempt in the most evident and deliberate manner to attract attention to herself, to set going by her actions some of those movements of other persons that she has appropriated. She has tasted the joy of being a cause, of exerting social power, and wishes more of it. She will tug at her mother's skirts, wriggle, gurgle, stretch out her arms, etc., all the time watching for the hoped-for effect. These performances often give the child, even at this age, an appearance of what is called affectation, that is, she seems to be unduly preoccupied with what other people think of her. Affectation, at any age, exists when the passion to influence others seems to overbalance the established character and give it an obvious twist or pose. It is instructive to find that even Darwin was, in his childhood, capable of departing from truth for the sake of making an impression. "For instance," he says in his autobiography, "I once gathered much valuable fruit from my father's trees and hid it in the shrubbery and then ran in breathless haste to spread the news that I had discovered a hoard of stolen fruit."[1]

The young performer soon learns to be different things to different people, showing that he begins to apprehend personality and to foresee its operation. If the mother or nurse is more tender than just, she will almost certainly be "worked" by systematic weeping. It is a matter of common observation that children often behave worse with their mother than with other and less sympathetic people. Of the new persons that a child sees, it is evident that some make a strong impression and awaken a desire to interest and please them, while others are indifferent or repugnant. Sometimes the reason can be perceived or guessed, sometimes not; but the fact of selective interest, admiration, prestige, is obvious before the end of the second year. By that time a child already cares much for the reflection of himself upon one personality and little for that upon another. Moreover he soon claims intimate and tractable persons as *mine*, classes them among his other possessions, and maintains his ownership against all comers. M., at three years of age, vigorously resented R.'s

claim upon their mother. The latter was "*my mamma*," whenever the point was raised.

Strong joy and grief depend upon the treatment this rudimentary social self receives. In the case of M. I noticed as early as the fourth month a "hurt" way of crying which seemed to indicate a sense of personal slight. It was quite different from the cry of pain or that of anger, but seemed about the same as the cry of fright. The slightest tone of reproof would produce it. On the other hand, if people took notice and laughed and encouraged, she was hilarious. At about fifteen months old she had become "a perfect little actress," seeming to live largely in imaginations of her effect upon other people. She constantly and obviously laid traps for attention, and looked abashed or wept at any signs of disapproval or indifference. At times it would seem as if she could not get over these repulses, but would cry long in a grieved way, refusing to be comforted. If she hit upon any little trick that made people laugh she would be sure to repeat it, laughing loudly and affectedly in imitation. She had quite a repertory of these small performances, which she would display to a sympathetic audience, or even try upon strangers. I have seen her at sixteen months, when R. refused to give her the scissors, sit down and make-believe cry, putting up her under lip and snuffling, meanwhile looking up now and then to see what effect she was producing.

In such phenomena we have plainly enough, it seems to me, the germ of personal ambition of every sort. Imagination co-operating with instinctive self-feeling has already created a social "I," and this has become a principal object of interest and endeavor.

Progress from this point is chiefly in the way of a greater definiteness, fullness, and inwardness in the imagination of the other's state of mind. A little child thinks of and tries to elicit certain visible or audible phenomena, and does not go back of them; but what a grown-up person desires to produce in others is an internal, invisible condition which his own richer experience enables him to imagine, and of which expression is only the sign. Even adults, however, make no separation between what other people think and the visible expression of that thought. They imagine the whole thing at once, and their idea differs from that of a child chiefly in the comparative richness and complexity of the elements that accompany and interpret the visible or audible sign. There is also a progress from the naive to the subtle in socially self-assertive action. A child obviously and simply, at first, does things for effect. Later there is an endeavor to suppress the appearance of doing so; affection, indifference, contempt, etc., are simulated to hide the real wish to affect the self-image. It is perceived that an obvious seeking after good opinion is weak and disagreeable.

Notes

1. Darwin, F. (1959). *Life and letters of Charles Darwin*. New York: Basic Books, p. 27.

27

Turning Points in Identity

Anselm Strauss

[In transformations of identities, or] coming to new terms, a person becomes something other than he once was. [Such] shifts necessitate, but also signalize, new evaluations: of self and others, of events, acts, and objects.[. . . T]ransformation of perception is irreversible; once having changed, there is no going back. One can look back, but can evaluate only from the new status.

Some transformations of identity and perspective are planned, or at least fostered, by institutional representatives; others happen despite, rather than because of, such regulated anticipation; and yet other transformations take place outside the orbits of the more visible social structure. . . . As a way of introducing these several dimensions of personal change, I shall discuss . . . certain critical incidents that occur to force a person to recognize that "I am not the same as I was, as I used to be." . . . These critical incidents constitute turning points in the onward movement of personal careers.

Turning Points

[. . . W]hat takes place at . . . turning points [is often] misalignment—surprise, shock,

"Turning Points in Identity" from *Mirrors and Masks: Transformations of Identity* (pp. 92-100) by A. Strauss, 1969. New York: Macmillan. Reprinted by permission of the author.

chagrin, anxiety, tension, bafflement, self-questioning—and also the need to try out the new self, to explore and validate the new and often exciting or fearful conceptions. Rather than discussing critical junctures in general, let us consider their typology. The list will not be a long one, but long enough to suggest the value both of its extension and of relating turning points to changes of identity.

A change in your relations with others is often so mundane, so gradual that it passes virtually unnoticed. Some incident is needed to bring home to you the extent of the shift. A marker of progression, or retrogression, is needed. When the incident occurs it is likely to strike with great impact, for it tells you: "Look! you have come way out to here! This is a milestone!" Recognition then necessitates new stances, new alignments. A striking example of the "milestone" is found in the autobiographies of many immigrants to America who later visited their native lands, only then realizing how little affinity they had retained, how identified they had become with America and Americans. Any return home, insofar as you have really left it, will signalize some sort of movement in identity. Some people literally go back home in an effort both to deny how far they have strayed and to prevent further defection.

Sometimes the path of development is foretold but is not believed, either because the one who forecasts is distrusted or because the prophecy cannot be understood. Prophets not only point out new directions:

they give you measuring rods for calculating movement if you happen to traverse the paths prophesied. This is certainly one of the critical experiences in the psychology of conversion. For instance, a recruit to a religious sect, only partly convinced, is told what will happen when he tries to explain the new position to his old minister, attempts to sell pamphlets to the heathen, and so on, and lo! events turn out as predicted. The prediction will be in terms of a new vocabulary, hence when the vocabulary is shown to be workable the recruit is well on the road toward adopting it in part or *in toto*. The point holds for any kind of conversion—occupational, political, or what not. A novice is told by the old-timer, "Your clients will be of such and such sorts and you'll have such and such experiences with them." When the graph of experience is thus plotted and confirmed, then the person can recognize his own transformation.

Forecasting is often institutionalized in such a fashion that public proclamation is made: "Said candidate has followed the predicted and prescribed path of experience and has gotten to the desired point. Kneel, knight, and receive knighthood. Come to the platform and receive your diploma." When paths are institutionalized, candidates can easily mark their progress, note how far they have come, and how far they have yet to go. If there are the usual institutionalized acknowledgments of partial steps toward the goal, then these may constitute turning points in self-conception also. If the institutionalized steps are purely formalized, are no longer invested with meaning by the institution, or if the candidate believes them of no real significance, they will not, of course, be turning points for him.

Private proclamation to a public audience is quite another matter. Having announced or avowed your own, it is not easy to beat a retreat. Often you find yourself in interpersonal situations climbing out on a limb, announcing a position, and then having to live up to it. In a more subtle sense,

one often marks a recognition of self-change by announcement, but this announcement itself forces a stance facing forward since the way back, however tempting it may still look, is now blocked.

A related turning point—since ceremonial announcement often follows it—is the meeting of a challenge, either self-imposed or imposed by others. Any institution [. . .] possesses regularized means for testing and challenging its members. If you are closely identified with the institution, some tests will be crucial for your self-regard. If you pass them, everyone recognizes that you have met the challenge. However, some challenges, although they occur in institutional settings, are not themselves institutionalized. For instance every student nurse early in her training must face the situation of having a patient die in her arms. For some nurses this appears to be a turning point for self-conception: the test is passed and she—in her own eyes at least—has new status; she can now think of herself as more of a professional. Crucial tests are imposed by individuals on themselves; if they pass they have been psychologically baptized, so to speak, but if they fail then a new path must be taken, a new set of plans drawn up. Naturally, failure does not always result in immediate self-transformation, but may lead to more complete preparation until the test is definitely failed or passed.

One potent form of self-test is the deliberate courting of temptation. Failure to resist it is usually followed by new tests or by yielding altogether. The fuller meaning of temptation is this: you are withdrawing from an old psychological status and coming into a new, and in doing so something akin to the "withdrawal symptoms" of drug addiction occurs. When you are able to resist temptation then an advance is signaled; but when no longer even tempted, you are well aware of having progressed still further. Institutions find it easier to check upon the overt resistance of their members than upon their covert desires. Genuine conversion means the death of old desires. "Backsliding" signifies a failure to resist temptation; frequent backsliding results in a return to previous status or change to yet another.

A rather subtle type of transforming incident occurs when you have played a strange but important role and unexpectedly handled it well. Whether you had considered this an admirable or a despicable role does not matter. The point is that you never thought you could play it, never thought this potential "me" was in yourself. Unless you can discount your acts as "not me" or as motivated by something not under your control, you bear the responsibility or the credit for the performance. Cowardly and heroic roles are both likely to bring unexpected realignment in self-regard. But more usual, and more subtle, are those instances where you find yourself miraculously able to enact roles that you believed—at least as yet—beyond you. Every person new to a job finds himself, through no fault of his own, at some point taken by clients or fellow workers as of more advanced status than he is. . . . Once having carried off the disguise, you realize something new about yourself. The net result is likely to be that you wish to experiment with this new aspect of yourself. Conversely, there are roles previously viewed with suspicion, even despised, that you now find yourself enacting with unexpected success and pleasure. You must either wash your hands of it, actually or symbolically—as in *Macbeth*—or come to grips with this new aspect of yourself.

It is probable that some of the effect of experimental role-dramas is that the drama allows and forces the person to play a range of roles he did not believe himself capable of playing, or never conceived of playing; it brings him face to face with his potential as well as his actual self. Sociable parties . . . by their very episodic and expressive nature, allow and further such exploration of roles. Similarly, some of the effect of psychiatric therapy seems to rest upon the skill of the psychiatrist in making patients face up to the full range of his acts, rather than repress awareness of them or blame them upon outside forces.

A critical experience with built-in ambivalence occurs when someone surpasses the performance of [a role model], as when a student overtakes his beloved teacher, or a son exceeds his father's social position. When allegiance is very strong this awareness of overtaking the model may be crippling, and refuge is sought by drawing back from the abyss of departure. To be a success, one must surpass . . . models and depart from them. Departures are institutionalized in America by such mechanisms as myths of success, by the easy accessibility of higher social positions, and by the blessings of parents who in turn experience vicarious success through the performances of their offspring. Despite the institutionalized devices for reducing the strain of upward departure, ambivalence and stress undoubtedly persist even for many of our most successful climbers.

Another kind of transforming experience, one with shattering or sapping impact, is betrayal—by your heroes, in fact by anybody with whom you are closely "identified." Betrayal implicates you as well as him, in exceedingly subtle ways. Consider three varieties. When you have closely patterned yourself after a model, you have in effect "internalized" what you suppose are the model's values and motives. If the model abandons these, it leaves you with a grievous dilemma. Has the model gone over to the enemy?—then you may with wry smile redouble your efforts along the path he laid out. . . . Or did the model lead you up an illusory path of values?—then with cynicism and self-hate you had better abandon your former self too. A different species of betrayal, involving search for atonement, is illustrated by the stunned . . . mother whose [child becomes converted to another religious or political philosophy]. The cry here is always: "Where did I go wrong that my child, an extension of me, should go wrong?" A third variety of betrayal often goes by the name of "rejection"; that is, rejection of you after you had closely identified with the model. Here the beloved has symbolically announced that you and your values are not right, or at least are not wholly satisfying. [Children who] reject and drift away from immigrant parents illustrate this. Betrayal of this type consists, usually, of a series of incidents, rather than of a single traumatic event. During the course of day-to-day living, decisions are made whose full implications are not immediately apparent. People can go on deceiving themselves about paths that actually have been closed by those decisions. At the point when it becomes apparent that former possibilities are dead issues, the person stands at the crossroads. A severe instance of such a turning point occurs when one traps oneself into an occupation—much as a house painter might paint himself unthinkingly into a corner of the room—believing that he can always get out when he wants to. Jazz musicians who go commercial "just for a while" to make money may find eventually that the commercial style has caught them, that they can no longer play real jazz as it should be played. This kind of crossroad may not be traumatic, but nostalgically reminiscent, signifying then that the gratifications arising from past decisions are quite sufficient to make past possibilities only pleasantly lingering "maybes." Final recognition that they are really dead issues is then more of a ritualistic burial and is often manifested by a revisiting of old haunts—actually or symbolically.

A final type of critical experience that I shall discuss is akin to betrayal, but the agent of destruction is less personal. A man may realize that he has been deceived, not by any specific person but by events in general. If the deception strikes home severely, he may respond with self-hate, "Why did I not discover this before?"; with personalized resentment against someone, "Why did they not tell me?"; or with diffuse resent-

ment against the world in general. An essential aspect of this critical experience is that a man's naming of self is disoriented. He is not what he thought he was. Self-classificatory disorientation, of course, can be mild. For instance, a Jewish boy, brought up in a moderately Orthodox home, discovered later that all Jews were not Orthodox, but that there were Reformed Jews (who made him feel not at all Jewish) and very Orthodox Jews (who made him feel not at all Jewish). Such discoveries come as shocks, but not necessarily as traumas. There is more anguish involved when a person finds that although he believed he possessed a comfortable dual identity, Negro and American, significant others are now challenging one of those identities. This is, or at least was, an unnerving experience for many Northern Negroes who visited in the South, however much they may have read or been warned. This negation of a portion of identity may not provide much of a crisis if the person withdraws from his attackers, but if he stays, as some Negroes have stayed in the South, he must make his peace with the challenging audience. A more crucial juncture in the maintenance of identity occurs when a person discovers that one of his chief self-referential terms is completely erroneous. Cases in point are adopted children who do not discover until later years the fact of their adoption, and those occasional tragic cases of children who are raised as members of the opposite sex and eventually discover the mis-naming. Imagine also the destructive effects, compounded with guilt and self-hate, of discovering an actual identity with a group formerly reviled and despised, as for instance an anti-Semite discovering that he is partly Jewish.

Enough has been said about various types of turning points to suggest that these are points in development when an individual has to take stock, to reevaluate, revise, resee, and rejudge. Although stock-taking goes on within the single individual, it is obviously both a socialized and socializing process. Moreover, the same kinds of incidents that precipitate the revision of identity are extremely likely to befall and to be equally significant to other persons of the same generation, occupation, and social class. This is equivalent to saying that insofar as experiences and interpretations are socially patterned, so also will be the development of personal identities.

28

The Production of Selves
in Personal Relationships

Philip Blumstein

Introduction

Innumerable words have been written and uttered on the fundamental relationship between the person and society, many of them inspiring discussion of the *social* nature of the self. As Rosenberg (1981) summarizes,

> Social factors play a major role in . . . formation [of the self]. . . . [It] arises out of social experience and interaction; it both incorporates and is influenced by the individual's location in the social structure; it is formed within institutional systems . . . ; it is constructed from the materials of the culture, and it is affected by immediate social and environmental contexts. (p. 593)

The significance of this simple point cannot be overstated: It has been one of sociology's guiding principles for many years, it has been offered as an epiphany to generations of undergraduates, and it has inspired countless research studies. Nevertheless, the concrete social processes captured in the simple but elegant notion of the social creation of

"The Production of Selves in Personal Relationships" by P. Blumstein from *The Self-Society Dynamic* (pp. 305-322) edited by J. Howard and P. Callero, 1991. New York: Cambridge University Press. Reprinted by permission of Cambridge University Press and Judith A. Howard, Personal Representative, Estate of Philip Blumstein.

the self remain, after all these years, only vaguely understood. The picture is incomplete. Surely social interaction generates selves, but the question that continues to deserve our attention is *how*.

From the early work of Cooley (1902), it has been a commonplace to locate much of the development of self in *primary groups*, by which is generally meant families and similar intimate relationships. This classical theme is the point of departure for this chapter, in which I address the question of how selves are created, maintained, and changed by virtue of the structure of intimate relationships and the nature of interaction that occurs in them.

Self and Identity

The terms *self* and *identity* have been used in a dizzying diversity of ways, and no definitional synthesis will be attempted here. My approach here is largely dramaturgical, relying on the numerous discussions of self and identity that followed the 1959 publication of Goffman's *The Presentation of Self in Everyday Life* (e.g., Messinger, Sampson, & Towne, 1962; Weinstein & Deutschberger, 1963; McCall & Simmons, 1966; Gergen, 1968; Blumstein, 1975). In my usage, *self* is a personal intrapsychic structure and is only knowable by the person to whom it belongs. In this view the self can be part of the mechanics that motivate the actor's behavior (McCall & Simmons, 1966; Blumstein, 1975; Rosenberg, 1981; Swann, 1987). In contrast, I will use the term *identity* as a shorthand for *situational* or *situated identity* (Weinstein & Deutschberger, 1963; Alexander & Wiley, 1981), referring to the *face* that is publicly displayed, perhaps quite fleeting, in interaction. In this usage, identity is Goffman's *presented self* and, as such, it requires no private commitment on the part of actor or audience to its being a valid reflection of the "true" self.

Numerous attempts have been made to characterize the relationship between identity and self (McCall & Simmons, 1966; Gergen, 1968; Blumstein, 1975; Swann & Read, 1981; Wiley & Alexander, 1987). First, it is necessary to consider the relationship between self and behavior. Although the various approaches to this question differ in detail, a common theme can be identified: The self finds expression in behavior, even if that expression may be mediated in complex ways. The actor's behavior, according to the most general model, invokes a response in alter. Out of that response ego receives information with implications for his or her self, information that ultimately may modify that self. The self, it is posited, has enormous motivation consequences for interactive behavior, and all interactive behavior, it is further posited, can be analyzed in terms of the situated identities being presented. Perhaps the best articulated version of the view that self produces identity is found in McCall and Simmons's (1966) discussion of individuals' ubiquitous motive to seek *role-support*, which they define as "a set of reactions and performances by others the expressive implications of which tend to confirm one's detailed and imaginative view of himself. . . . Role-support is centrally the implied confirmation of the specific *content* of one's idealized and idiosyncratic imaginations of self" (p. 73). Since people are universally motivated to seek role-sup-

port for cherished aspects of the self, they tend to present (enact) identities consistent with that self in order to maximize the likelihood of receiving that role-support.

I have no quarrel with this view of the relationship between self and identity. However, in this chapter I wish to explore a different causal ordering, one less commonly considered, that is, that identity affects self. Going back to the work of Bem (1972), numerous social psychologists have argued that actors perceive their own behavior (whatever its sources), and in the process they make attributions to the self. If one translates this into a dramaturgical framework, instead of *behavior* one may speak of the *identities* people project. Individuals observe the identities they project, and in some circumstances they may attribute this enactment to a true expression of the self. In spite of any constraints the self may place on the identities presented (Blumstein, 1975), these enacted behaviors may frequently have nothing to do with any sincere underlying dimensions of self.

A central assertion of this chapter is that if identities are projected frequently enough, they eventually produce modifications in the self. In searching for a term to capture this process whereby repeated enactment of identities produce selves, I have chosen the concept of *ossification*. Whereas the work of people on self-attribution has dealt with the intrapsychic process whereby one's own behavior is observed and inferences are made about it, I focus more on the interpersonal aspects of how and why identities ossify into selves.

The process of ossification is very slow and gradual, and consequently is not easy to study with our conventional research methods. It is the process that we infer has occurred when we awaken one morning to discover we are not the same person we were twenty years earlier. Or more commonly when we encounter a person from our past and are reminded by the interaction of how much our self has drifted over the years. Surely the meanderings of our social environment are responsible for the drift, but I would argue that it is particularly in our intimate relationships that the ossification process takes place. To say that the self is subject to drift does not contradict the idea of ossification. Indeed the two concepts may be seen as constituting two ends of a continuum. Drift occurs as a function of changes in the individual's interpersonal environment. Ossification has as a necessary condition continuity in the interpersonal environment, and accelerates during those periods of continuity. Ossification means that we enact identities with great frequency and we *become* the person whom we have enacted.

Why, in so much writing about the self has the idea of ossification (or some equivalent) not been prominent? The answer lies in a shortcoming of dramaturgical analysis, that is, its inattention to the development of durable social structures. Microsociology seems recently to have undergone a shift away from an exclusive focus on interaction to a greater recognition of ongoing relationships. When the model, especially in Goffman's work, was built on unanchored, situationally bounded, evanescent exchanges between near strangers, the implications for self of the identity presented seemed trivial. But so much of social life occurs in relationships that, even if not always intense, have histories and futures, and for that reason the identities that are enacted in intimate relationships should have important implications for the self.

Couple Identity Work

There is a form of seemingly insignificant talk heard frequently from husbands, wives, and from partners in other kinds of intimate marriagelike relationships. Possibly it is occasionally heard in the speech of close friends. Here are three simulated examples:

My husband can't be allowed into the kitchen. He wouldn't know how to boil water. He would ruin it and make a mess in the process.

We are different about dirt. I hate it and clean it up the minute it appears. She waits until it begins to accumulate and then goes after it with a vengeance. We are both very clean, just different about it.

We are not like other couples. They are all interested in showing what they earn and what they can buy, but we prefer to content ourselves with a more spiritual approach to life.

This form of verbal behavior, *couple identity work,* is often heard when one interviews couples, as well as in the spontaneous speech of ordinary people. It is frequently directed to persons outside the relationship, but I believe it also arises when intimates are alone talking together about themselves and about their relationship. As is clear from the examples, these are not ponderous discussions of "the relationship," but instead rather mundane characterizations of who the two partners are, frequently with a tone of who they are vis-à-vis one another.

I have called this process couple *identity* work; what does it have to do with the *self*? Although there is certainly identity work going on in the examples, it has already been acknowledged that situated identities and selves are not the same. However, one of the important ways in which personal relationships differ from simple Goffmanesque interaction is that in the former situated identities are potentially much more apt to have long-lasting implications for the self. Again, this is the process I have called ossification.

One might argue that these couples are only announcing the truth about themselves and their partners. Indeed this is a compelling observation because who will be more keenly aware of the dispositions of another than his or her spouse or partner? The very nature of intimacy implies that two people have developed a profound awareness of who the other is. It is, however, the publicness of the display, the apparent felt necessity of locating oneself, one's partner, and the relatedness of the two in some kind of conceptual space that suggests that the relationship engenders or demands reality creation work that is separate and apart from the simple reporting on a preexisting reality (cf. Goffman, 1971, on tie-signs). In these interactions couples are displaying a reality they have created, while at the same time they are allowing us to witness a sample of the processes through which this reality was created over the months and years.

Motivation

A husband may learn for the first time that he cannot cook as his wife describes his culinary failures to a group of assembled friends. If he hears such commentary with sufficient frequency, both in front of guests and in solitary conversation with his wife, one may expect that he will come to incorporate culinary incompetence into his self. Moreover, if no circumstances arise to propel him into the kitchen, he will have no opportunity to challenge that aspect of self. This example is particularly useful because it leads to speculations about motivation: What goals or purposes would a wife be likely to achieve by fostering the reality that her husband is incompetent in the kitchen? What goals or purposes does a husband achieve in passively acceding to that definition of the situation? One can ask a further set of questions, more on the level of social structure, such as, What is it about the institution of marriage that led to this bit of reality creation in which, ultimately, both spouses have colluded? Moreover, in what ways did this minute exercise in reality creation contribute to the reproduction of the marital institution?

A fundamental concept in dramaturgical analysis is *interpersonal control* (Weinstein, 1969). It links the motivational states of purposive actors to the self-presentational strategies they employ. It draws attention to the connection between hedonistic actors and processes of reality presentation and reality negotiation. A focus on interpersonal control lends motivational enrichment to the dramaturgical model, with the simple principle that actors' purposes (desires, goals) can best be served by the identities they choose to enact and the identities into which they are able to cast their interaction partner(s) (Weinstein & Deutschberger, 1963, 1964; Weinstein, 1969). If one accepts that frequently enacted identities eventually may ossify into selves, then the implication of interpersonal control as a motivational concept is that selves grow out of motivational states (both ego's and alter's—the opposite of the usual position on causality).

In close relationships, just as in Goffman's disconnected focused gatherings, it must be acknowledged that ego takes active, though perhaps not conscious, involvement in shaping alter's identity, and his or her motivation may frequently be purely selfish. Ego may best pursue his or her desired outcomes in interaction and/or relationship by shaping the distribution of identities (both ego's and alter's) that are incorporated into the working consensus. But intimate relationships are significantly different from the interactions that Goffman analyzed. Among intimates, who have durable relationships with anticipatable futures, it is generally much more efficient to shape the underlying self of alter, such that by simply *being* that self, alter will assume a situated identity congruent with ego's goals. The less efficient alternative would be for ego to try to manipulate alter's situational identity afresh in each encounter. For example, once a husband has incorporated as a part of his self a sense of ineptitude in the kitchen, then his wife need never again altercast him in that light because his sense of self keeps him from entering her mysterious domain.

So far, little has been said about the content of actors' motivational systems. Aside from the everyday motivations—scratch my neck, take the children off my hands, do not drink too much in front of my parents— I would posit one central motivation in close relationships: the desire to keep alter committed to the relationship, and equally or more committed than oneself. The first part of this motivation involves the creation of solidarity through interdependence; the second involves the potential creation of hierarchy, that is, a partner who is either equal or inferior in terms of power and status. Both can be achieved if one finds ways to encourage alter's dependency (Emerson, 1962). But alter's dependency is encouraged at the same time that he or she is encouraged to perform services that increase his or her worth and consequently ego's own dependency (Emerson, 1972).

Definitions of Reality

The process of identity negotiations should be viewed as ubiquitous because there are identity implications (hence potential self-implications) in even the most insignificant nuances of communication. For example, in a study of the division of labor in conversation, Kollock, Blumstein, and Schwartz (1985) showed that interruptions (violations of turn-taking norms) appear to be the right of the powerful. It is reasonable to argue a related phenomenon, that is, that actors infer from how much they successfully achieve interruption, or how often they are successfully interrupted, what their power or status is in an encounter. Some evidence indirectly supports this assertion: In an experimental study Robinson and Reis (1988) found that people who interrupt are more likely than those who do not to be perceived as more masculine and less feminine. Based on the research of Kollock et al. (1985), it could be argued that the dimensions being measured by Robinson and Reis as perceived masculinity and perceived femininity are really perceived hierarchy in the relationship between the speakers. If research subjects make such judgments about third parties who interrupt, it seems very reasonable that ordinary people make similar judgments about the interruptions that occur in their own

ongoing relationships. To be interrupted at alter's will is to learn the worth of one's contribution, and if this pattern is experienced repeatedly, it should affect the self in significant ways, even if alter is not intentionally trying to altercast ego into a subordinate position by his or her interruptions.

Another example of this logic comes from a study of influence tactics used by couples (Howard, Blumstein, & Schwartz, 1986) that found the weaker partner tends to use indirection to get his or her way. By extension, one might expect that by using indirection, one *becomes* a certain kind of person in the shared definition of reality, and that eventually this is incorporated into the self. Additionally, Goody (1978) has argued very convincingly that the simple act of asking a question is, for the lowly, one of the few legitimate avenues for inducing a high-status other into conversation. How one is required to enter a conversation, with head raised or bowed, sets a situational identity, and if this scenario occurs repeatedly, it eventually shapes the self.

Situations of open conflict have particular capacity for creating realities that may force modifications in the self. Frequently in the opening rounds of conflict in intimate relationships one partner offers a definition of the situation, usually a narrative containing complaints easily translatable into assertions about both situational identities and about dispositions, that is, selves, of the actors (see Turner, 1970, for an analysis of conflict between intimates). Information expressed in conflict situations has the patina of deep veracity because the extreme emotions are believed to undermine the expressive control necessary for strategic interaction. The other partner may find the asserted characterizations of self that emerge during intense conflict enormously discontinuous with respect to the self held dear, and must come to grips with what may be a persuasive but unsettling definition offered by a person who has been granted unparalleled permission to define situations. Alter may also have a counterdefinition to offer, one that may neutralize the self-implications of ego's statements. Nevertheless, alter has learned a possibly new way of framing the self, and even if ego recants his or her asserted truth, that truth, once uttered, continues to exist as a potential resource in the production of self for alter.

An intimate dyad has two fundamental properties when it comes to defining reality: (1) By being intimate, each partner grants the other enormous authority to shape the collective reality of the pair, and (2) by being a dyad, there may often be little in the way of third-party adjudication as to whose definition of reality—definition of selves—bears resemblance to some reality above or beyond the couple (a reality that actors take to be objective). This is why members of couples in conflict feel a need to discuss their problems with third parties, in order to bring the weight of validation to bear on one or the other of the potentially compelling realities. And, of course, central to the realities being crafted are the selves of both parties.

This brings us back to dependency. Even in a structure as simple as a dyad, the process of reality construction can be very complex. Two of the many factors that enter into the process are *power* and *competence*. For the relationship to be close, both partners are highly dependent on one another and therefore both are very powerful. Nevertheless, in most cases one is likely to be even more powerful than the other, reflecting differences in resources and alternatives (Emerson, 1962). The generally more powerful partner, one might expect, will not only have greater capacity to get his or her way, but also in more subtle ways to control the definition of the situation, and by extension, the selves expressed within that definition (Scheff, 1968).

Not all forms of power are the same, and indeed one should expect that power that reflects one partner's particular expertise will be especially useful in defining relevant realities. For example, modern women have been granted the right of expertise over the subject of love (Cancian, 1985), and as a consequence, one would expect women in heterosexual relationships to have legitimacy in defining their partner's competence at such qualities as expressiveness, tenderness, and the like. This does not mean that these women are either generally more powerful or generally more capable of shaping the collective definition of the situation.

Interpersonal competence is an aggregation of skills that allow one actor to prevail over another in defining the situation, that is, in assuring that the working consensus captures a reality that supports his or her goals and desires. It includes such qualities as role-taking ability and the possession of a large and unfettered repertoire of lines of actions (Weinstein, 1969). Competent actors will generally be more successful at shaping their partner's identity *and* their partner's self, even without being relatively more powerful. Indeed the less powerful partner is more likely to resort to interpersonal tactics of indirection (Howard et al., 1986), and one form of indirection may be the subtle yet constant efforts to change alter's self so that he or she will behave more cooperatively. Following this line of argument, one encounters an interesting paradox: The more powerful partner is in a better position to change alter's definition of himself or herself, yet the less powerful partner has a greater desire to change alter's self because he or she does not have as many alternative means to change alter's behavior.

Another aspect of reality work in relationships is worth noting: In the everyday negotiation of reality, there is a norm of passive acceptance such that if the costs are small to endorsing alter's definition of the situation, then people will permit that definition to prevail. Given this premise, dramaturgically astute actors can gradually create a definition of the relationship and the selves of its members that will take enormous effort, and possibly engender hostility and conflict, if alter wishes to amend it. Collective meanings may accrue that one partner feels unable to modify, even though he or she neither believes in them nor feels strategically safe by accepting their implications. This is why such culturally significant relationships as marriage have developed rich elaboration around defining the relationship in an inescapable way. For example, ego's proposal of marriage is a last chance, however fraught with risk of momentary unpleasantness and discomfort, for alter to say that the inadvertent accretion of meaning that may have occurred cannot be sustained.

Roles and Relationships

The motivational states of the actors are not the only place to look for sources of the reality-creating processes in intimate relationships whereby selves are likely to be produced. Other places include the social structure and the structure of intimacy.

There is evidence in the work of social psychologists that roles shape selves (e.g., Huntington, 1957; Kadushin, 1969; Turner, 1978). The role structure of heterosexual marriage, in particular, has clear self-producing properties. Marital roles set important markers that are widely used to define traits or dispositions of role incumbents. The *provider* role, the *homemaker* roles, the *parent* role, the *lover* role, and so on, all have highly elaborated cultural standards that can be used to measure one's own and one's partner's adequacy as a person, as a man, as a woman, and so on. I will not attempt it here, but I think it would be a fruitful enterprise to analyze some of the subtleties in the content of marital roles with respect to the potential for self-implications. For example, what are the implications for the self to live under the conception that one's house can never be too clean, that one can never earn too much money, or that the delinquency of one's children reflects upon the quality of their home life?

Intimate relationships are at the same time *role relationships* and *personal relationships* (Blumstein & Kollock, 1988). As role relationships they provide common cultural scripts for their enactment, and these scripts, I have argued, shape selves. As personal relationships they have a set of internal processes, growing from the structure of intimacy, that also shape selves. Unlike roles, which are scripted particularly for each type of relationships, these internal processes have more to do with the structure of intimacy per se.

I would posit two dynamics in intimate relationships, particularly those that involve the complex coordination problems of living together—the *centripetal* and *centrifugal*. They are akin to the dual and contradictory needs for security/inclusion and autonomy/freedom. The former leads to projections of similarity or sameness; the latter to projections of difference or uniqueness (Maslach, 1974; Snyder & Fromkin, 1980). Projections of difference are very risky because they easily and inadvertently (perhaps inevitably) shade off into hierarchy.

In order to predict when these two dynamics will occur, one must consider both the motivational states of the actors and the constraints of social structure. What can ego accomplish by being similar to or the same as his or her partner? What can ego accomplish by being different? better? How does the relationship function when there is a shared reality of sameness? If there is a shared reality of difference?

Differentiation

Differentiation is one of the internal processes inherent to close relationships. Some differentiation comes with the role structure, as in the case of traditional heterosexual marriage, although the institution of marriage seems to be losing some of its role rigidity. However, this does not mean that as the cultural and structural sources of difference wither, spouses will not create differences, perhaps smaller, more subtle, more idiosyncratic, and personally less repugnant, but differences nevertheless.

There are several connections between forces of differentiation and self-production processes—the contrast effect, the division of labor, and the avoidance of competition. The first, and most evident is the *contrast effect.* Inevitably, as two people become intimately acquainted with one another, they simply will note that they react differently to a situation. The question is how such a simple set of personal observations may enter the interpersonal realm, and from there be elaborated upon to the point where they have potency in the production of selves.

The situation occurs frequently when there are serious potential coordination problems that are being exacerbated by the perceived difference. A good example is in the realm of sexuality, where small differences in sexual appetite or preferred sexual scripts can become highly elaborated under some circumstances. The coordination problems help to heighten each partner's awareness of his or her own dispositions, and this awareness in itself can transform a disposition into a feature of self. But at another level, the couple may need to achieve a shared conceptualization to account for enduring imperfection or compromises in their solutions to the problems of sexual coordination. The consequence is that the dispositional differences are magnified, abstracted, reified, and typified. Through this process, the small differences become a more real feature of the individuals' selves.

Much of our thinking about intimacy derives from a heterosexual marital or dating context. Here a wealth of cultural resources is available for the creation of differences, and it is interesting to wonder whether this availability increases or decreases the potential impact on selves. Returning to the example of sexual coordination, one might wonder what occurs when a wife has a ready cultural basis for understanding the differ-

ence between her sexual appetite and that of her husband (i.e., Men are more sexual than women). What are the consequences for her self? In structuring an answer to this question, it might prove fruitful to contrast the wife's situation to that of a partner in a lesbian couple where a similar asymmetry of initiating and declining sex is present. In this case, it is much more difficult to find relevant cultural materials for contextualizing the observed differences between the two partners. Without an obvious categorical basis of observed differences, then any differences are likely to be treated as idiosyncratic (cf. Jones, Davis, & Gergen, 1961). The questions, then, become: In which kind of couple—two sexes or one—are the problematics of sexual coordination more likely to become part of the shared consciousness and rhetoric? In which kind of couple is that shared definition going to lead to a creation of a reality of dispositional difference? In which kind of couple will the creation of a reality of difference become ossified in the selves of the actors? Given the cultural belief that women have less sexual appetite than men, it would seem that the wife in our example would have as a central feature of her self her female sex, but that the *typical* aspects associated with her sex would in general not feature centrally in her self. The lesbian in our example does not have any category membership to account for her comparatively low sexual appetite and so her uniqueness (relative to her partner) would make sexual appetite a more salient dimension of self-organization. Indeed she may carry her typification of self as a person low in sexual appetite into a subsequent relationship where the facts might cast her self-perception in doubt.

The second force of differentiation is the tendency for all forms of social organization to create a *division of labor* even when there is none preassigned. In my research I have observed that struggle as some couples might to avoid differentiation in household tasks and other instrumental activities, they face a monumental uphill battle. The antagonism to a division of labor seems to have two sources: (1) a fear that it will resemble the traditional patriarchal divisions of heterosexual marriage with their attendant inequality, and (2) a desire to perform tasks together in order to maximize the amount of shared couple time. Couples report, however, that the pressures of efficiency, differences in aptitude, and different tastes all conspire to push them into a division of labor even when they fervently wish to avoid one.

The third process has some parallels to the creation of a division of labor. It involves the *avoidance of competition.* Inspiration for focusing the discussion of competition avoidance comes from the work on self-evaluation maintenance processes described by Tesser (1988). Couples face the problem of competitiveness whenever their selves are constructed such that the realms in which competence is salient are the same for both of them. This means that rather than identifying with the other's success, each may feel diminished by it. The powerful bonds of identification (Turner, 1970) are inhibited by the evils of social comparison processes (Festinger, 1954; Suls & Miller, 1977). According to Tesser's model, there are two dynamic processes: *reflection processes,* which involve what has been called identification by others, such that the successful performance of a person with whom we are close reflects favorably on us (see Cialdini & Richardson, 1980), and *comparison processes,* which involve the sense of diminished worth of our own performance in comparison to the superior performance of the other. Turner (1970) has argued persuasively that bonds based on identification are salutary for intimate relationships, and by implication, the competitiveness that can grow out of comparison processes is detrimental.

The traditional differentiation of gender and its institutionalization in marital roles provided a significant buffer against competitiveness between spouses. However, as these institutions have changed, as men's and women's lives have become more similar and the distinction between their realms (private versus public) has withered, couples have clearly developed an increased potential for competition. Although many couples are probably crippled or brought to dissolution by that competition, I believe I have observed among couples I have interviewed that many others find ways of moving away from the conditions that lead to competitiveness.

Based on my impressionistic observation, I would suggest that couples whose similarity in skills, talents, and performances makes them vulnerable to competition rather than identification work collectively to create rich elaborations on tiny differences. Initially this is an act of reality construction, and eventually an act of self-production. By focusing and elaborating on small and apparent differences, they eventually *become* different. The couple who early in their relationship develop a shared hobby of cooking discovers that one is slightly better at desserts and the other slightly better at salads. Years later they may be discovered to have one salad-maker and one pastry chef, with each taking pride in the other's "unique" talent. Of course, the system is self-perpetuating, that is, the more each partner comes to define herself or himself as different from the other, the more that partner will come to behave differently and thereby be validated in the reflection from others in that self-definition. There is not a lot of strong evidence on the consequences of such differentiation for couples, but one study suggests that when couples can agree on which partner has greater knowledge in various domains, they also express greater satisfaction with their relationship (Wegner, 1986).

Sameness

The creation of differentness, both symbolic and real, must have limits in order for close relationships to survive. Indeed, it might be hypothesized that relationships can only create differences to the extent that their solidarity or bondedness (Turner, 1970) is secure. Indeed, similarity abounds. Homogamy among married couples is one of the most durable empirical facts in the social sciences (Buss, 1984, 1985; Buss & Barnes, 1986), and there is also recent evidence for homogamy in same-sex couples (Kurdek & Schmitt, 1987; Howard, Blumstein, & Schwartz, 1989) as well as in friendship choice (Verbrugge, 1977; Duck & Craig, 1978; Kandel, 1978; Feld, 1982). The usual discussion of homogamy is based on assumptions of similarity of stable values, opinions, social statuses, and personality traits, all qualities the partners bring to the relationship. Without denying the validity of the literature on homogamy, I would suggest that homogamy in the "softer" areas, that is, values, opinions, *perceived* dispositions, may be something that couples *achieve* together once in the relationship. They accomplish the achievement through interpersonal processes of reality construction layered with supporting self-modifications.

Some examples of the social construction of sameness come from my study in collaboration with Pepper Schwartz on four types of couples: married couples, heterosexual cohabitors, lesbian couples, and gay male couples (Blumstein & Schwartz, 1983). One of the lesbian couples was striking in this regard. When they arrived for their interview they wore the same hairstyle and virtually identical clothes. During the interview one partner exemplified couple identity work directed at sameness:

I could honestly believe in reincarnation. We think so much alike and we have so much in common and we do these dumb things like get the same clothes on. We buy the same things. We bought each other the same valentine at different stores at different times. . . . We go out and buy the same groceries, not having discussed what we wanted ahead of time. . . . We'll shop at the same place and drift into each

other. We drive up nose to nose in the same parking lots at the same moments. (p. 454)

There is little to be gained in treating these coincidences as either valid facts or as hallucinations. Rather one can look at these *stories* (which in the interview did not seem to be told for the first time), and the narrative they formed. One can understand how this narrative allows the couple to key into deep cultural themes of *love as merger,* and thereby multiply the symbolic solidarity and perfect taken-for-grantedness of the *happily ever after scenario* for their relationship. One can also understand how by the telling of these stories by both women (or when one woman tells them in the other's presence and the latter does not balk or object), each is saying something, either actively or passively, about her self and about the self of her partner. And if one is cynical about it, one can imagine each woman awaking in the morning and subconsciously choosing what clothing to wear in order to enhance the likelihood of confirming that they have "discovered" the uniquely perfect match in partners. I would suggest that she would choose that dress, not because she is consciously taking the role of her partner, but rather because she has come to see herself as "the kind of person who looks good in and likes wearing pastel colors." The motive is to construct togetherness through coincidence; the product is a pair of selves that will allow that motive to succeed.

Another example (Blumstein & Schwartz, 1983) comes from a partner in a gay male relationship, who said:

We go to the opera and I know that at the first intermission he will have a strong opinion one way or the other. Sometimes I have a gut level reaction to the opera, but generally I fall somewhere in the middle. The opera is somewhere between pretty good and quite bad, and I'm really not sure how I feel. But I do know that I feel a need to have an opinion to express at the intermission. And I realized the other night as

I sit there, I'm getting anxious about what my opinion will be. So I asked myself why I was anxious about having an opinion, and I realized that when we both spontaneously love something, or we both spontaneously hate something, I feel this great, euphoric sense of rapport, of we-ness, that we are well matched and are therefore a "natural," "meant-to-be" couple. And when we disagree, or see the same thing very differently, I feel distant and alienated from him. It's like the spell has been broken. So as I sit in the opera wondering what my opinion is, I am really hoping that I will wind up with the opinion that will allow us to blend into one sweep of unanimity and be overwhelmed with that warm glow of coupleness.

This couple may not be typical; many couples feel free to disagree over heartfelt issues without any constraint to create a mystical couple reality, and do not experience their relationship as diminished by the agreement to disagree. They have learned that they agree on enough basic matters that a few displays of uniqueness are not distressing. Indeed such displays may be salutary in precisely the ways described in our discussion of differentiation processes. Examples such as this are probably most common in the early phases of relationships, where the participants may be eager to give assistance to whatever emerging similarities they may be discovering in one another. They feel genuine in the exaggerated sameness they project, but as I have argued, the projection of a self has the grave potential for the becoming of a self.

Anchors Against Drift

A fundamental fact about close relationships is that their attractiveness emerges from their predictability (Kelly, 1955; Bateson 1972; Kelley & Thibaut, 1978). Costs associated with learning new scripts with each new person one meets are reduced, role taking is simplified, coordination problems are minimized. How do couples accomplish this predictability? It is more than simply learning the other; rather it is by imposing a set of constraints on selves such that partners actually *become* more predictable. I would posit a fundamental overarching obligation in close relationships: to live up to the dispositional qualities that have become part of the working consensus (Athay & Darley, 1981; Swann, 1984). That is why personal relationships are inherently conservative: because an actor is constrained today to be the same person he or she was yesterday. Because of the constraints on actors to exhibit stable dispositional traits, close relationships can depart rather markedly from cultural scripts as the two participants create and maintain their own private culture.

Many people might object to this view of the conservative effects of intimate relationships. They would see close relationships as vehicles of personal growth and change (Cancian, 1987; Aron & Aron, 1989). They would argue that the extreme interdependence found in close relationships would provide a safe haven for the partners to explore alternative definitions of self. Although this logic is very persuasive, it ignores the fact that the selves of the partners are finely interwoven. One partner cannot express a self if there is no complementary self with which to resonate. One cannot enact incompetent dependency unless one's partner plays effective authority. To the extent that each partner has cathected the elements of his or her self, then that person is deeply invested in the complementary aspects of the self of the other. Certainly relationships can sometimes survive significant and abrupt changes in one of the selves. But it is indeed a matter of survival, because newly adopted selves create new demands on the other to give role-support, demands that cannot always be met, even with the best of intentions.

References

Alexander, C. N., Jr., & Wiley, M. (1981). Situated activity and identity formation. In M. Rosenberg & R. H. Turner (Eds.), *Social* psychology: Sociological perspectives (pp. 269-289). New York: Basic Books.

Aron, A., & Aron, E. (1989). *New research on the self-expansion model.* Paper presented at the Nags Head Conference on Interaction Process and Analysis, Nags Head, NC.

Athay, M., & Darley, J. M. (1981). Toward an interaction centered theory of personality. In N. Cantor & J. F. Kihlstrom (Eds.), *Personality, cognition, and social interaction* (pp. 281-308). Hillsdale, NJ: Lawrence Erlbaum.

Bateson, G. (1972). *Steps to an ecology of mind.* New York: Ballantine.

Bem, D. J. (1972). Self-perception theory. In L. Berkowitz (Ed.), *Advances in experimental social psychology* (Vol. 6, pp. 1-62). New York: Academic Press.

Blumstein, P. (1975). Identity bargaining and self-conception. *Social Forces, 53,* 476-485.

Blumstein, P., & Kollock, P. (1988). Personal relationships. *Annual Review of Sociology, 14,* 467-490.

Blumstein, P., & Schwartz, P. (1983). *American couples: Money, work, and sex.* New York: William Morrow.

Buss, D. M. (1984). Toward a psychology of person-environment (PE) correlations: The role of spouse selection. *Journal of Personality and Social Psychology, 47,* 361-377.

Buss, D. M. (1985). Human mate selection. *American Scientist, 73,* 47-51.

Buss, D. M., & Barnes, M. (1986). Preferences in human mate selection. *Journal of Personality and Social Psychology, 50,* 559-570.

Cancian, F. (1985). Gender politics: Love and power in the private and public spheres. In A. S. Rossi (Ed.), *Gender and the life course* (pp. 253-264). New York: Aldine.

Cancian, F. (1987). *Love in America: Gender and self-development.* New York: Cambridge University Press.

Cialdini, R. B., & Richardson, K. D. (1980). Two indirect tactics of image management: Basking and blasting. *Journal of Personality and Social Psychology, 39,* 406-415.

Cooley, C. H. (1902). *Human nature and the social order.* New York: Scribner.

Duck, S. W., & Craig, R. G. (1978). Personality similarity and the development of friendship. *British Journal of Social and Clinical Psychology, 17,* 237-242.

Emerson, R. M. (1962). Power-dependence relations. *American Sociological Review, 27,* 31-41.

Emerson, R. M. (1972). Exchange theory, part II: Exchange relations and networks. In J. Berger, M. Zelditch, & B. Anderson (Eds.), *Sociological theories in progress* (Vol. 2, pp. 58-87). Boston: Houghton Mifflin.

Feld, S. L. (1982). Social structural determinants of similarity among associates. *American Sociological Review, 47,* 797-801.

Festinger, L. (1954). A theory of social comparison processes. *Human Relations, 7,* 117-140.

Gergen, K. J. (1968). Personal consistency and the presentation of self. In C. Gordon & K. J. Gergen (Eds.), *The self in social interaction* (pp. 299-308). New York: John Wiley.

Goffman, E. (1959). *The presentation of self in everyday life.* New York: Doubleday.

Goffman, E. (1971). *Relations in public: Microstudies of the public order.* New York: Basic Books.

Goody, E. N. (1978). Toward a theory of questions. In E. N. Goody (Ed.), *Questions and politeness: Strategies in social interaction* (pp. 17-43). London: Cambridge University Press.

Howard, J. A., Blumstein, P., & Schwartz, P. (1986). Sex, power, and influence tactics in intimate relationships. *Journal of Personality and Social Psychology, 51,* 102-109.

Howard, J. A., Blumstein, P., & Schwartz, P. (1989). *Homogamy in intimate relationships: Why birds of a feather flock together.* Paper presented at the annual meeting of the American Sociological Association, San Francisco.

Huntington, M. J. (1957). The development of a professional self image. In R. K. Merton, G. G. Reeder, & P. Kendall (Eds.), *The student physician* (pp. 179-187). Cambridge: Harvard University Press.

Jones, E. E., Davis, K. E., & Gergen, K. J. (1961). Role playing variations and their informational value for person perception. *Journal of Abnormal and Social Psychology, 63,* 302-310.

Kadushin, C. (1969). The professional self-concept of music students. *American Journal of Sociology, 75,* 389-404.

Kandel, D. B. (1978). Homophily, selection and socialization in adolescent friendships. *American Journal of Sociology, 84*, 427-436.

Kelley, H. H., & Thibaut, J. W. (1978). *Interpersonal relations: A theory of interdependence.* New York: John Wiley.

Kelly, G. A. (1955). *The psychology of personal constructs.* New York: Norton.

Kollock, P., Blumstein, P., & Schwartz, P. (1985). Sex and power in interaction: Conversational privileges and duties. *American Sociological Review, 50*, 34-46.

Kurdek, L., & Schmitt, J. P. (1987). Partner homogamy in married, heterosexual cohabiting, gay, and lesbian couples. *Journal of Sex Research, 23*, 212-232.

Maslach, C. (1974). Social and personal bases of individuation. *Journal of Personality and Social Psychology, 29*, 411-425.

McCall, G. J., & Simmons, J. L. (1966). *Identities and interactions.* New York: Free Press.

Messinger, S. L., with H. Sampson & R. D. Towne. (1962). Life as theatre: Some notes on the dramaturgical approach to social reality. *Sociometry, 25*, 98-110.

Robinson, L. F., & Reis, H. T. (1988). *The effects of interruption, gender, and leadership position in interpersonal perceptions.* Paper presented at the International Conference on Personal Relationships. Vancouver, Canada.

Rosenberg, M. (1981). The self-concept: Social product and social force. In M. Rosenberg & R. H. Turner (Eds.), *Social psychology: Sociological perspectives* (pp. 593-624). New York: Basic Books.

Scheff, T. J. (1968). Negotiating reality: Notes on power in the assessment of responsibility. *Social Problems, 16*, 3-17.

Snyder, C. R., & Fromkin, H. L. (1980). *Uniqueness: The human pursuit of difference.* New York: Plenum.

Suls, J. M., & Miller, R. L. (Eds.). (1977). *Social comparison processes: Theoretical and empirical perspectives.* Washington, DC: Hemisphere.

Swann, W. B., Jr. (1984). Quest for accuracy in person perception: A matter of pragmatics. *Psychological Review, 91*, 457-477.

Swann, W. B., Jr. (1987). Identity negotiation: Where two roads meet. *Journal of Personality and Social Psychology, 53*, 1038-1051.

Swann, W. B., Jr., & Read, S. J. (1981). Self-verification processes: How we sustain our self-conceptions. *Journal of Experimental Social Psychology, 17*, 351-372.

Tesser, A. (1988). Toward a self-evaluation maintenance model of social behavior. In L. Berkowitz (Ed.), *Advances in experimental social psychology* (Vol. 21, pp. 181-227). San Diego: Academic Press.

Turner, R. (1970). *Family interaction.* New York: John Wiley.

Turner, R. (1978). The role and the person. *American Journal of Sociology, 84*, 1-23.

Verbrugge, L. M. (1977). The structure of adult friendship choices. *Social Forces, 56*, 576-597.

Wegner, D. M. (1986). Transactive memory: A contemporary analysis of the group mind. In B. Mullen & G. R. Goethals (Eds.), *Theories of group behavior* (pp. 185-208). New York: Springer-Verlag.

Weinstein, E. A. (1969). The development of interpersonal competence. In D. A. Goslin (Ed.), *Handbook of socialization theory and research* (pp. 753-775). Chicago: Rand McNally.

Weinstein, E. A., & Deutschberger, P. (1963). Some dimensions of altercasting. *Sociometry, 26*, 454-466.

Weinstein, E. A., & Deutschberger, P. (1964). Tasks, bargains, and identities in social interaction. *Social Forces, 42*, 451-456.

Wiley, M. G., & Alexander, C. N. (1987). From situated activity to self-attribution: The impact of social structural schemata. In K. Yardley & T. Honess (Eds.), *Self and identity: Psychosocial perspectives* (pp. 105-117). Chichester, UK: John Wiley.

29

The Power of Names

Itabari Njeri

The decade was about to end when I started my first newspaper job. The seventies might have been the disco generation for some, but it was a continuation of the Black Power, post-Civil Rights era for me. Of course in some parts of America it was still the pre-Civil Rights era. And that was the part of America I wanted to explore. As a good reporter I needed a sense of the whole country, not just the provincial Northeast Corridor in which I was raised.

I headed for Greenville ("Pearl of the Piedmont"), South Carolina.

"*Wheeere,*" some people snarled, their nostrils twitching, their mouths twisted so their top lips went slightly to the right, the bottom ones way down and to the left, "did you get *that* name from?"

Itabiddy. Etabeeedy. Etabeeree. Eat a berry. Mata Hari. Theda Bara. And one secretary in the office of the Greenville Urban League told her employer: "It's Ms. Idi Amin."

Then, and now, there are a whole bunch of people who greet me with "Hi, Ita." They think "Bari" is my last name. Even when they don't they still want to call me "Ita." When I tell them my first name is Itabari, they say, "Well, what do people call you for short?"

"They don't call me anything for short," I say. "The name is Itabari."

Sophisticated white people, upon hearing my name, approach me as would a cultural anthropologist finding a piece of exotica right in his own living room. This happens a lot, still, at cocktail parties.

"Oh, what an unusual and beautiful name. Where are you from?"

"Brooklyn," I say. I can see the disappointment in their eyes. Just another homegrown Negro.

Then there are other white people who, having heard my decidedly northeastern accent, will simply say, "What a lovely name," and smile knowingly, indicating that they saw *Roots* and understand.

Then there are others, black and white, who for different reasons take me through this number:

"What's your *real* name?"

"Itabari Njeri is my real, legal name," I explain.

"Okay, what's your *original* name?" they ask, often with eyes rolling, exasperation in their voices.

After Malcolm X, Muhammad Ali, Kareem Abdul-Jabaar, Ntozake Shange, and Kunta Kinte, who, I ask, should be exasperated by this question-and-answer game?

Nevertheless, I explain, "Because of slavery, black people in the Western world don't usually know their original names. What you really want to know is what my slave name was."

Now this is where things get tense. Four hundred years of bitter history, culture, and politics between blacks and whites in America is evoked by this one term, "slave name."

Some white people wince when they hear the phrase, pained and embarrassed by this reminder of their ancestor's inhumanity. Further, they quickly scrutinize me and conclude that mine was a post-Emancipation Proclamation birth. "You were never a slave."

I used to be reluctant to tell people my slave name unless I surmised that they wouldn't impose their cultural values on me and refuse to use my African name. I don't care anymore. When I changed my name, I changed my life, and I've been Itabari for more years now than I was Jill. Nevertheless, people will say: "Well, that's your *real* name, you were born in America and that's what I am going to call you." My mother tried a variation of this on me when I legalized my traditional African name. I respectfully made it clear to her that I would not tolerate it. Her behavior, and subsequently her attitude, changed.

But many black folks remain just as skeptical of my name as my mother was.

"You're one of those black people who changed their name, huh," they are likely to begin. "Well, I still got the old slave master's Irish name," said one man named O'Hare at a party. This man's defensive tone was a reaction to what I call the "blacker than thou" syndrome perpetrated by many black nationalists in the sixties and seventies. Those who reclaimed their African names made blacks who didn't do the same thing feel like Uncle Toms.

These so-called Uncle Toms couldn't figure out why they should use an African name when they didn't know a thing about Africa. Besides, many of them were proud of their names, no matter how they had come by them. And it should be noted that after the Emancipation Proclamation in 1863, four million black people changed their names, adopting surnames such as Freeman, Freedman, and Liberty. They eagerly gave up names that slave masters had imposed upon them as a way of identifying their human chattel.

Besides names that indicated their newly won freedom, blacks chose common English names such as Jones, Scott, and Johnson. English as their language, America was their home, and they wanted names that would allow them to assimilate as easily as possible.

Of course, many of our European surnames belong to us by birthright. We are the legal as well as "illegitimate" heirs to the names Jefferson, Franklin, Washington, et al.; and in my own family, Lord.

Still, I consider most of these names to be by-products of slavery, if not actual slave names. Had we not been enslaved, we would not have been cut off from our culture, lost our indigenous languages, and been compelled to use European names.

The loss of our African culture is a tragic fact of history, and the conflict it poses is a profound one that has divided blacks many times since Emancipation: Do we accept the loss and assimilate totally or do we try to reclaim our culture and synthesize it with our present reality?

A new generation of black people in America is reexamining the issues raised by the cultural nationalists and Pan-Africanists of the sixties and seventies: What are the cultural images that appropriately convey the "new" black aesthetic in literature and art?

The young Afro-American novelist Trey Ellis has asserted that the "New Black Aesthetic shamelessly borrows and reassembles across both race and class lines." It is not afraid to embrace the full implications of our hundreds of years in the New World. We are a new people who need not be tied to externally imposed or self-inflicted cultural parochialism. Had I understood that as a teenager, I might still be singing today.

Even the fundamental issue of identity and nomenclature, raised by Baraka and others twenty years ago, is back on the agenda: Are we to call ourselves blacks or African-Americans?

In reality, it's an old debate. "Only with the founding of the American Colonization Society in 1816 did blacks recoil from using the term African in referring to themselves and their institutions," the noted historian and author Sterling Stuckey pointed out in an interview with me. They feared that using the term "African" would fuel white efforts to send them back to Africa. But they felt no white person had the right to send them back when they had slaved to build America.

Many black institutions retained their African identification, most notably the African Methodist Episcopal Church. Changes in black self-identification in America have come in cycles, usually reflecting the larger dynamics of domestic and international politics.

The period after World War II, said Stuckey, "culminating in the Cold War years of Roy Wilkins's leadership of the NAACP," was a time of "frenzied integrationism." And there was "no respectable black leader on the scene evincing any sort of interest in Africa—neither the NAACP or the Urban League."

This, he said, "was an example of historical discontinuity, the likes of which we, as a people, had not seen before." Prior to that, for more than a century and a half, black leaders were Pan-Africanists, including Frederick Douglass. "He recognized," said Stuckey, "that Africa was important and that somehow one had to redeem the motherland in order to be genuinely respected in the New World."

The Reverend Jesse Jackson has, of course, placed on the national agenda the importance of blacks in America restoring their cultural, historical, and political links with Africa.

But what does it really mean to be called an African-American?

"Black" can be viewed as a more encompassing term, referring to all people of African descent. "Afro-American" and "African-American" refer to a specific ethnic group. I use the terms interchangeably, depending on the context and the point I want to emphasize.

But I wonder: As the twenty-first century breathes down our necks—prodding us to wake up to the expanding mélange of ethnic groups immigrating in record numbers to the United States, inevitably intermarrying, and to realize the eventual reshaping of the nation's political imperatives in a newly multicultural society—will the term "African-American" be as much of a racial and cultural obfuscation as the term "black"? In other words, will we be the only people, in a society moving toward cultural pluralism, viewed to have no history and no culture? Will we just be a color with a new name: African-American?

Or will the term be—as I think it should—an ethnic label describing people with a shared culture who descended from Africans, were transformed in (as well as transformed) America, and are genetically intertwined with myriad other groups in the United States?

Such a definition reflects the historical reality and distances us from the fallacious, unscientific concept of separate races when there is only one: *Homo sapiens.*

But to comprehend what should be an obvious definition requires knowledge and a willingness to accept history.

When James Baldwin wrote *Nobody Knows My Name*, the title was a metaphor—at the deepest level of the collective African-American psyche—for the blighting of black history and culture before the nadir of slavery and since.

The eradication or distortion of our place in world history and culture is most obvious in the popular media. Liz Taylor—and, for an earlier generation, Claudette Colbert—still represent what Cleopatra—a woman of color in a multiethnic society, dominated at various times by blacks—looks like.

And in American homes, thanks to reruns and cable, a new generation of black kids grow up believing that a simpleton shouting "Dy-no-mite!" is a genuine reflection of Afro-American culture, rather than a white Hollywood writer's stereotype.

More recently, *Coming to America*, starring Eddie Murphy as an African prince seeking a bride in the United States, depicted traditional African dancers in what amounted to a Las Vegas stage show, totally distorting the nature and beauty of real African dance. But with every burlesque-style pelvic thrust on the screen, I saw blacks in the audience burst into applause. They think that's African culture, too.

And what do Africans know of us, since blacks don't control the organs of communication that disseminate information about us?

"No!" screamed the mother of a Kenyan man when he announced his engagement to an African-American woman who was a friend of mine. The mother said marry a European, marry a white American. But please, not one of those low-down, ignorant, drug-dealing, murderous black people she had seen in American movies. Ultimately, the mother prevailed.

In Tanzania, the travel agent looked at me indignantly. "Njeri, that's Kikuyu. What are you doing with an African name?" he demanded.

I'd been in Dar es Salaam about a month and had learned that Africans assess in a glance the ethnic origins of the people they meet.

Without a greeting, strangers on the street in Tanzania's capital would comment, "Oh, you're an Afro-American or West Indian."

"Both."

"I knew it," they'd respond, sometimes politely, sometimes not.

Or, people I got to know while in Africa would mention, "I know another half-caste like you." Then they would call in the "mixed-race" person and say, "Please meet Itabari Njeri." The darker-complected African, presumably of unmixed ancestry, would then smile and stare at us like we were animals in the zoo.

Of course, this "half-caste" (which I suppose is a term preferable to "mulatto," which I hate, and which every person who under- stands its derogatory meaning—"mule"— should never use) was usually the product of a mixed marriage, not generations of ethnic intermingling. And it was clear from most "half-castes" I met that they did not like being compared to so mongrelized and stigmatized a group as Afro-Americans.

I had minored in African studies in college, worked for years with Africans in the United States, and had no romantic illusions as to how I would be received in the motherland. I wasn't going back to find my roots. The only thing that shocked me in Tanzania was being called, with great disdain, a "white woman" by an African waiter. Even if the rest of the world didn't follow the practice, I then assumed everyone understood that any known or perceptible degree of African ancestry made one "black" in America by law and social custom.

But I was pleasantly surprised by the telephone call I received two minutes after I walked into my Dar es Salaam hotel room. It was the hotel operator. "Sister, welcome to Tanzania. . . . Please tell everyone in Harlem hello for us." The year was 1978, and people in Tanzania were wearing half-foot-high platform shoes and dancing to James Brown wherever I went.

Shortly before I left, I stood on a hill surrounded by a field of endless flowers in Arusha, near the border of Tanzania and Kenya. A toothless woman with a wide smile, a staff in her hand, and two young girls at her side, came toward me on a winding path. I spoke to her in fractured Swahili and she to me in broken English.

"I know you," she said smiling. "Wa-Negro." "Wa" is a prefix in Bantu languages meaning people. "You are from the lost tribe," she told me. "Welcome," she said, touching me, then walked down a hill that lay in the shadow of Mount Kilimanjaro.

I never told her my name, but when I told other Africans, they'd say: "*Emmmm*, Itabari. Too long. How about I just call you Ita."

30

On Being Black and Middle Class

Shelby Steele

Not long ago a friend of mine, black like myself, said to me that the term "black middle class" was actually a contradiction in terms. Race, he insisted, blurred class distinctions among blacks. If you were black, you were just black and that was that. When I argued, he let his eyes roll at my naiveté. Then he went on. For us, as black professionals, it was an exercise in self-flattery, a pathetic pretension, to give meaning to such a distinction. Worse, the very idea of class threatened the unity that was vital to the black community as a whole. After all, since when had white America taken note of anything but color when it came to blacks? He then reminded me of an old Malcolm X line that had been popular in the sixties. Question: What is a black man with a Ph.D.? Answer: A nigger.

For many years I had been on my friend's side of this argument. Much of my conscious thinking on the old conundrum of race and class was shaped during my high school and college years in the race-charged sixties, when the fact of my race took on an almost religious significance. Progressively, from the mid-sixties on, more and more aspects of my life found their explanation, their justification, and their motivation in

race. My youthful concerns about career, romance, money, values, and even styles of dress became a subject to consultation with various oracular sources of racial wisdom. And these ranged from a figure as ennobling as Martin Luther King, Jr., to the underworld elegance of dress I found in jazz clubs on the South Side of Chicago. Everywhere there were signals, and in those days I considered myself so blessed with clarity and direction that I pitied my white classmates who found more embarrassment than guidance in the fact of *their* race. In 1968, inflated by my new power, I took a mischievous delight in calling them culturally disadvantaged.

But now, hearing my friend's comment was like hearing a priest from a church I'd grown disenchanted with. I understood him, but my faith was weak. What had sustained me in the sixties sounded monotonous and off the mark in the eighties. For me, race had lost much of its juju, its singular capacity to conjure meaning. And today, when I honestly look at my life and the lives of many other middle-class blacks I know, I can see that race never fully explained our situation in American society. Black though I may be, it is impossible for me to sit in my single-family house with two cars in the driveway and a swing set in the back yard and *not* see the role class has played in my life. And how can my friend, similarly raised and similarly situated, not see it?

Yet despite my certainty I felt a sharp tug of guilt as I tried to explain myself over

"On Being Black and Middle Class" by S. Steele from *The Best American Essays*, edited by G. Wolff (pp. 234-246). New York: Ticknor & Fields. Reprinted by permission of the author.

my friend's skepticism. He is a man of many comedic facial expressions and, as I spoke, his brow lifted in extreme moral alarm as if I were uttering the unspeakable. His clear implication was that I was being elitist and possibly (dare he suggest?) anti-black—crimes for which there might well be no redemption. He pretended to fear for me. I chuckled along with him, but inwardly did I wonder at myself. Though I never doubted the validity of what I was saying, I felt guilty saying it. Why?

After he left (to retrieve his daughter from a dance lesson) I realized that the trap I felt myself in had a tiresome familiarity and, in a sort of slow-motion epiphany, I began to see its outline. It was like the suddenly sharp vision one has at the end of a burdensome marriage when all the long-repressed incompatibilities come undeniably to light.

What became clear to me is that people like myself, my friend, and middle-class blacks generally are caught in a very specific double bind that keeps two equally powerful elements of our identity at odds with each other. The middle-class values by which we were raised—the work ethic, the importance of education, the value of property ownership, of respectability, of "getting ahead," of stable family life, of initiative, of self-reliance, etc.—are, in themselves, raceless and even assimilationist. They urge us toward participation in the American mainstream, toward integration, toward a strong identification with the society—and toward the entire constellation of qualities that are implied in the word "individualism." These values are almost rules for how to prosper in a democratic, free-enterprise society that admires and rewards individual effort. They tell us to work hard for ourselves and our families and to seek our opportunities whenever they appear, inside or outside the confines of whatever ethnic group we may belong to.

But the particular pattern of racial identification that emerged in the sixties and that still prevails today urges middle-class blacks (and all blacks) in the opposite direction. This pattern asks us to see ourselves as an embattled minority, and it urges an adversarial stance toward the mainstream, an emphasis on ethnic consciousness over individualism. It is organized around an implied separatism.

The opposing thrust of these two parts of our identity results in the double bind of middle-class blacks. There is no forward movement on either plane that does not constitute backward movement on the other. This was the familiar trap I felt myself in while talking with my friend. As I spoke about class, his eyes reminded me that I was betraying race. Clearly, the two indispensable parts of my identity were a threat to each other.

Of course when you think about it, class and race are both similar in some ways and also naturally opposed. They are two forms of collective identity with boundaries that intersect. But whether they clash or peacefully coexist has much to do with how they are defined. Being both black and middle class becomes a double bind when class and race are defined in sharply antagonistic terms, so that one must be repressed to appease the other.

But what is the "substance" of these two identities, and how does each establish itself in an individual's overall identity? It seems to me that when we identify with any collective we are basically identifying with images that tell us what it means to be a member of that collective. Identity is not the same thing as the fact of membership in a collective; it is, rather, a form of self-definition, facilitated by images of what we wish our membership in the collective to mean. In this sense, the images we identify with may reflect the aspirations of the collective more than they reflect reality, and their content can vary with shifts in those aspirations.

But the process of identification is usually dialectical. It is just as necessary to say what we are *not* as it is to say what we are—so that finally identification comes about by embracing a polarity of positive and negative images. To identify as middle class, for example, I must have both positive and negative images of what being middle class entails; then I will know what I should and should not be doing in order to be middle class. The same goes for racial identity.

In the racially turbulent sixties the polarity of images that came to define racial identification was very antagonistic to the polarity that defined middle-class identification. One might say that the positive images of one lined up with the negative images of the other, so that to identify with both required either a contortionist's flexibility or a dangerous splitting of the self. The double bind of the black middle class was in place.

The black middle class has always defined its class identity by means of positive images gleaned from middle- and upper-class white society, and by means of negative images of lower-class blacks. This habit goes back to the institution of slavery itself, when "house" slaves both mimicked the whites they served and held themselves above the "field" slaves. But in the sixties the old bourgeois impulse to dissociate from the lower classes (the "we-they" distinction) backfired when racial identity suddenly called for the celebration of this same black lower class. One of the qualities of a double bind is that one feels it more than sees it, and I distinctly remember the tension and strange sense of dishonesty I felt in those days as I moved back and forth like a bigamist between the demands of class and race.

Though my father was born poor, he achieved middle-class standing through much hard work and sacrifice (one of his favorite words) and by identifying fully with solid middle-class values—mainly hard work, family life, property ownership, and education for his children (all four of whom have advanced degrees). In his mind these were not so much values as laws of nature. People who embodied them made

up the positive images in his class polarity. The negative images came largely from the blacks he had left behind because they were "going nowhere."

No one in my family remembers how it happened, but as time went on, the negative images congealed into an imaginary character named Sam, who, from the extensive service we put him to, quickly grew to mythic proportions. In our family lore he was sometimes a trickster, sometimes a boob, but always possessed of a catalogue of sly faults that gave up graphic images of everything we should not be. On sacrifice: "Sam never thinks about tomorrow. He wants it now or he doesn't care about it." On work: "Sam doesn't favor it too much." On children: "Sam likes to have them but not to raise them." On money: "Sam drinks it up and pisses it out." On fidelity: "Sam has to have two or three women." On clothes: "Sam features loud clothes. He likes to see and be seen." And so on. Sam's persona amounted to a negative instruction manual in class identity.

I don't think that any of us believed Sam's faults were accurate representations of lower-class black life. He was an instrument of self-definition, not of sociological accuracy. It never occurred to us that he looked very much like the white racist stereotype of blacks, or that he might have been a manifestation of our own racial self-hatred. He simply gave us a counterpoint against which to express our aspirations. If self-hatred was a factor, it was not, for us, a matter of hating lower-class blacks but of hating what we did not want to be.

Still, hate or love aside, it is fundamentally true that my middle-class identity involved a dissociation from images of lower-class black life and a corresponding identification with values and patterns of responsibility that are common to the middle class everywhere. These values sent me a clear message: be both an individual and a responsible citizen; understand that the quality of your life will approximately reflect the quality of effort you put into it; know that individual responsibility is the basis of freedom and that the limitations imposed by fate (whether fair or unfair) are no excuse for passivity.

Whether I live up to these values or not, I know that my acceptance of them is the result of lifelong conditioning. I know also that I share this conditioning with middle-class people of all races and that I can no more easily be free of it than I can be free of my race. Whether all this got started because the black middle class modeled itself on the white middle class is no longer relevant. For the middle-class black, conditioned by these values from birth, the sense of meaning they provide is as immutable as the color of his skin.

I started the sixties in high school feeling that my class-conditioning was the surest way to overcome racial barriers. My racial identity was pretty much taken for granted. After all, it was obvious to the world that I was black. Yet I ended the sixties in graduate school a little embarrassed by my class background and with an almost desperate need to be "black." The tables had turned. I knew very clearly (though I struggled to repress it) that my aspirations and my sense of how to operate in the world came from my class background, yet "being black" required certain attitudes and stances that made me feel secretly a little duplicitous. The inner compatibility of class and race I had known in 1960 was gone.

For blacks, the decade between 1960 and 1969 saw racial identification undergo the same sort of transformation that national identity undergoes in times of war. It became more self-conscious, more narrowly focused, more prescribed, less tolerant of opposition. It spawned an implicit party line, which tended to disallow competing forms of identity. Race-as-identity was lifted from the relative slumber it knew in the fifties and pressed into service in a social and political war against oppression. It was redefined along sharp adversarial lines and directed toward the goal of mobilizing the great mass of black Americans in this war-like effort. It was imbued with a strong moral authority, useful for denouncing those who opposed it and for celebrating those who honored it as a positive achievement rather than as a mere birthright.

The form of racial identification that quickly evolved to meet this challenge presented blacks as a racial monolith, a singular people with a common experience of oppression. Differences within the race, no matter how ineradicable, had to be minimized. Class distinctions were one of the first such differences to be sacrificed, since they not only threatened racial unity but also seemed to stand in contradiction to the principle of equality which was the announced goal of the movement for racial progress. The discomfort I felt in 1969, the vague but relentless sense of duplicity, was the result of a historical necessity that put my race and class at odds, that was asking me to cast aside the distinction of my class and identify with a monolithic view of my race.

If the form of this racial identity was the monolith, its substance was victimization. The civil rights movement and the more radical splinter groups of the late sixties were all dedicated to ending racial victimization, and the form of black identity that emerged to facilitate this goal made blackness and victimization virtually synonymous. Since it was our victimization more than any other variable that identified and unified us, moreover, it followed logically that the purest black was the poor black. It was images of him that clustered around the positive pole of the race polarity; all other blacks were, in effect, required to identify with him in order to confirm their own blackness.

Certainly there were more dimensions to the black experience than victimization, but no other had the same capacity to fire the indignation needed for war. So, again out of historical necessity, victimization became the overriding focus of racial identity. But this only deepened the double bind for middle-class blacks like me. When it came to class we were accustomed to defining ourselves against lower-class blacks and identifying with at least the values of middle-class whites; when it came to race we were now being asked to identify with images of lower-class blacks and to see whites, middle class or otherwise, as victimizers. Negative lining up with positive, we were called upon to reject what we had previously embraced and to embrace what we had previously rejected. To put it still more personally, the Sam figure I had been raised to define myself against had now become the "real" black I was expected to identify with.

The fact that the poor black's new status was only passively earned by the condition of his victimization, not by assertive, positive action, made little difference. Status was status apart from the means by which it was achieved, and along with it came a certain power—the power to define the terms of access to that status, to say who was black and who was not. If a lower-class black said you were not really "black"—a sellout, an Uncle Tom—the judgment was all the more devastating because it carried the authority of his status. And this judgment soon enough came to be accepted by many whites as well.

In graduate school I was once told by a white professor, "Well, but . . . you're not really black. I mean, you're not disadvantaged." In his mind my lack of victim status disqualified me from the race itself. More recently I was complimented by a black student for speaking reasonably correct English, "proper" English as he put it. "But I don't know if I really want to talk like that," he went on. "Why not?" I asked. "Because then I wouldn't be black no more," he replied without a pause.

To overcome his marginal status, the middle-class black had to identify with a degree of victimization that was beyond his actual experience. In college (and well beyond) we used to play a game called "nap matching." It was a game of one-upmanship, in which we sat around outdoing each other with stories of racial victimization, symbolically measured by the naps of our hair. Most of us were middle class and so had few personal stories to relate, but if we could not match naps with our own biographies, we would move on to those legendary tales of victimization that came to us from the public domain.

The single story that sat atop the pinnacle of racial victimization for us was that of Emmett Till, the Northern black teenager who, on a visit to the South in 1955, was killed and grotesquely mutilated for supposedly looking at or whistling at (we were never sure which, though we argued the point endlessly) a white woman. Oh, how we probed his story, finding in his youth and Northern upbringing the quintessential embodiment of black innocence, brought down by a white evil so portentous and apocalyptic, so gnarled and hideous, that it left us with a feeling not far from awe. By telling his story and others like it, we came to *feel* the immutability of our victimization, its utter indigenousness, as a thing on this earth like dirt or sand or water.

Of course, these sessions were a ritual of group identification, a means by which we, as middle-class blacks, could be at one with our race. But why were we, who had only a moderate experience of victimization (and that offset by opportunities our parents never had), so intent on assimilating or appropriating an identity that in so many ways contradicted our own? Because, I think, the sense of innocence that is always entailed in feeling victimized filled us with a corresponding feeling of entitlement, or even license, that helped us endure our vulnerability on a largely white college campus.

In my junior year in college I rode to a debate tournament with three white students and our faculty coach, an elderly English professor. The experience of being the lone black in a group of whites was so familiar to me that I thought nothing of it as our trip began. But then halfway through the trip the professor casually turned to me and, in an isn't-the-world-funny sort of tone, said that he had just refused to rent an apartment in a house he owned to a "very nice" black couple because their color would "offend" the white couple who lived downstairs. His eyebrows lifted helplessly over his hawkish nose, suggesting that he too, like me, was a victim of America's racial farce. His look assumed a kind of comradeship: he and I were above this grimy business of race, though for expediency we had occasionally to concede the world its madness.

My vulnerability in this situation came not so much from the professor's blindness to his own racism as from his assumptions that I would participate in it, that I would conspire with him against my own race so that he might remain comfortably blind. Why did he think I would be amenable to this? I can only guess that he assumed my middle-class identity was so complete and all-encompassing that I would see his action as nothing more than a trifling concession to the folkways of our land, that I would in fact applaud his decision not to disturb propriety. Blind to both his own racism and to me—one blindness serving the other—he could not recognize that he was asking me to betray my race in the name of my class.

His blindness made me feel vulnerable because it threatened to expose my own repressed ambivalence. His comment pressured me to choose between my class identification, which had contributed to my being a college student and a member of the debating team, and my desperate desire to be "black." I could have one but not both; I was double-bound.

Because double binds are repressed there is always an element of terror in them: the terror of bringing to the conscious mind the buried duplicity, self-deception, and pretense involved in serving two masters. This terror is the stuff of vulnerability, and since vulnerability is one of the least tolerable of all human feelings, we usually transform it into an emotion that seems to restore the control of which it has robbed us; most often, that emotion is anger. And so, before the

professor had even finished his little story, I had become a furnace of rage. The year was 1967, and I had been primed by endless hours of nap-matching to feel, at least consciously, completely at one with the victim-focused black identity. This identity gave me the license, and the impunity, to unleash upon this professor one of those volcanic eruptions of racial indignation familiar to us from the novels of Richard Wright. Like Cross Damon in *Outsider*, who kills in perfectly righteous anger, I tried to annihilate the man. I punished him not according to the measure of his crime but according to the measure of my vulnerability, a measure set by the cumulative tension of years of repressed terror. Soon I saw that terror in *his* face, as he stared hollow-eyed at the road ahead. My white friends in the back seat, knowing no conflict between their own class and race, were astonished that someone they had taken to be so much like themselves could harbor a rage that for all the world looked murderous.

Though my rage was triggered by the professor's comment, it was deepened and sustained by a complex of need, conflict, and repression in myself of which I had been wholly unaware. Out of my racial vulnerability I had developed the strong need of an identity with which to defend myself. The only such identity available was that of me as victim, him as victimizer. Once in the grip of this paradigm, I began to do far more damage to myself than he had done.

Seeing myself as a victim meant that I clung all the harder to my racial identity, which, in turn, meant that I suppressed my class identity. This cut me off from all the resources my class values might have offered me. In those values, for instance, I might have found the means to a more dispassionate response, the response less of a victim attacked by a victimizer than of an individual offended by a foolish old man. As an individual I might have reported this professor to the college dean. Or I might have calmly tried to reveal his blindness to him, and possibly won a convert. (The flagrancy of his remark suggested a hidden guilt and even self-recognition on which I might have capitalized. Doesn't confession usually signal a willingness to face oneself?) Or I might have simply chuckled and then let my silence serve as an answer to his provocation. Would not my composure, in any form it might take, deflect into his own heart the arrow he'd shot at me?

Instead, my anger, itself the hair-trigger expression of a long-repressed double bind, not only cut me off from the best of my own resources, it also distorted the nature of my true racial problem. The righteousness of this anger and the easy catharsis it brought buoyed the delusion of my victimization and left me as blind as the professor himself.

As a middle-class black I have often felt myself *contriving* to be "black." And I have noticed this same contrivance in others—a certain stretching away from the natural flow of one's life to align oneself with a victim-focused black identity. Our particular needs are out of sync with the form of identity available to meet those needs. Middle-class blacks need to identify racially; it is better to think of ourselves as black and victimized than not black at all; so we contrive (more unconsciously than consciously) to fit ourselves into an identity that denies our class and fails to address the true source of our vulnerability.

For me this once meant spending inordinate amounts of time at black faculty meetings, though these meetings had little to do with my real racial anxieties or my professional life. I was new to the university, one of two blacks in an English department of over seventy, and I felt a little isolated and vulnerable, though I did not admit it to myself. But at these meetings we discussed the problems of black faculty and students within a framework of victimization. The real vulnerability we felt was covered over by all the adversarial drama the victim/victimized polarity inspired, and hence went unseen and unassuaged. And this, I think,

explains our rather chronic ineffectiveness as a group. Since victimization was not our primary problem—the university had long ago opened its doors to us—we had to contrive to make it so, and there is not much energy in contrivance. What I got at these meetings was ultimately an object lesson in how fruitless struggle can be when it is not grounded in actual need.

At our black faculty meetings, the old equation of blackness with victimization was ever present—to be black was to be a victim; therefore, not to be a victim was not to be black. As we contrived to meet the terms of this formula there was an inevitable distortion of both ourselves and the larger university. Through the prism of victimization the university seemed more impenetrable than it actually was, and we more limited in our powers. We fell prey to the victim's myopia, making the university an institution from which we could seek redress but which we could never fully join. And this mind-set often led us to look more for compensations for our supposed victimization than for opportunities we could pursue as individuals.

The discomfort and vulnerability felt by middle-class blacks in the sixties, it could be argued, was a worthwhile price to pay considering the progress achieved during that time of racial confrontation. But what may have been tolerable then is intolerable now. Though changes in American society have made it an anachronism, the monolithic form of racial identification that came out of the sixties is still very much with us. It may be more loosely held, and its power to punish heretics has probably diminished, but it continues to catch middle-class blacks in a double bind, thus impeding not only their own advancement but even, I would contend, that of blacks as a group.

The victim-focused black identity encourages the individual to feel that his advancement depends almost entirely on that of the group. Thus he loses sight not only of his own possibilities but of the inextricable connection between individual effort and individual advancement. This is a profound encumbrance today, when there is more opportunity for blacks than ever before, for it reimposes limitations that can have the same oppressive effect as those the society has only recently begun to remove.

It was the emphasis on mass action in the sixties that made the victim-focused black identity a necessity. But in the eighties and beyond, when racial advancement will come only through a multitude of individual advancements, this form of identity inadvertently adds itself to the forces that hold us back. Hard work, education, individual initiative, stable family life, property ownership—these have always been the means by which ethnic groups have moved ahead in America. Regardless of past or present victimization, these "laws" of advancement apply absolutely to black Americans also. There is no getting around this. What we need is a form of racial identity that energizes the individual by putting him in touch with both possibilities and his responsibilities.

It has always annoyed me to hear from the mouths of certain arbiters of blackness that middle-class blacks should "reach back" and pull up those blacks less fortunate than they—as though middle-class status were an unearned and essentially passive condition in which one needed a large measure of noblesse oblige to occupy one's time. My own image is of reaching back from a moving train to lift on board those who have no tickets. A noble enough sentiment—but might it not be wiser to show them the entire structure of principles, effort, and sacrifice that puts one in a position to buy a ticket any time one likes? This, I think, is something members of the black middle class can realistically offer to other blacks. Their example is not only a testament to possibility but also a lesson in method. But they cannot lead by example until they are released from a black identity that regards that example as suspect, that sees them as "marginally" black, indeed that holds *them* back by catching them in a double bind.

To move beyond the victim-focused black identity we must learn to make a difficult but crucial distinction: between actual victimization, which we must resist with every resource, and identification with the victim's status. Until we do this we will continue to wrestle more with ourselves than with the new opportunities which so many paid so dearly to win.

PART IV

The Social Construction of Reality

If [people] define situations as real, they are real in their consequences.
(W. I. Thomas and Dorothy Thomas, The Child in America)

[People] make their own history, but they do not make it just as they please; they do not make it under circumstances chosen by themselves, but under circumstances directly encountered, given and transmitted from the past. The tradition of all the dead generations weighs like a nightmare on the brain of the living.
(*Karl Marx*, The 18th Brumaire of Louis Bonaparte)

Building and Breaching Reality

In 1986, one of us (Peter Kollock) spent the summer in the Caribbean, sailing a boat with five other people from island to island and eventually sailing across the Gulf of Mexico to deliver the boat to Galveston. There were a number of times when we sailed long stretches of ocean over several days, never seeing land. During these long passages everyone on the boat hallucinated at one time or another.

We were in good health, of sound mind. None of us were on medications, or were taking drugs or drinking alcohol. Yet each of us experienced very vivid hallucinations several times. The hallucinations often occurred when we were alone at night at the tiller. Almost everyone reported having long conversations with people (sometimes crew mates, sometimes friends back in the United States) who turned out to not really be there. Seeing colored lights and hearing voices were also common occurrences. These hallucinations were not fleeting, fuzzy things. Some of them seemed as real as the book you are now holding. We were not bothered by the hallucinations and after a time recognized them "for what they were." At times I simply sat back and looked at the hallucination with the same detached interest as a person examining an artifact in a museum, saying to myself, "Here I go again."

Hallucinations are nothing new in the world of long-distance sailing, and as well-socialized members of the Western world, we had at our disposal an entire litany of "facts" for explaining why we were hallucinating and why the objects we saw and voices we heard were not real. These explanations included sleep deprivation (our rotating schedules meant we rarely got more than a few hours sleep), sensory deprivation, poor nutrition, mild dehydration, mild heat exhaustion (in 110-degree weather it's difficult to eat properly or drink enough water). In other words, *we flatly denied the evidence of our eyes and explained away what we saw based on our common sense.*

At one point, we were sailing near Haiti and I wondered what might have happened if we had stopped in that country to pick up another crew member. If that person had been a member of the Haitian traditional religion known as *vodoun*, her or his common sense would include such obvious and taken-for-granted facts as the knowledge that people can communicate with spirits and see visions. Overhearing me and my crew mates explaining away our visions, this Haitian sailor probably would have looked on us with a mixture of confusion and pity. Here we were experiencing vivid images of great power and we refused to acknowledge that they were real. We experienced them repeatedly, we all experienced them, there were common themes in our visions, we were not intoxicated when we saw them, and yet we denied their existence out of hand. "What unreasonable, illogical people," the Haitian might conclude.

Common Sense

The repository for our most basic knowledge of "reality"—as defined by "the language of the day" in a particular culture—we call *common sense*. Common sense is a set of shared cultural rules for making sense of the world. These rules are so well established and taken for granted that they often require no justification. To the question "How did you know that?" or "Why did you do that?" one can reply simply, "It's just common sense." These rules are the bedrock of cultural knowledge; they seem obviously true.

One of the most powerful ways of demonstrating that reality is a *social construction* is to show the limitations and arbitrariness of common sense, either by pointing out inconsistencies or contrasting one culture's common sense to another's, as we did in the story above.

The opening quotation from Karl Marx suggests that people make their own history, but that they do so within the confines of the circumstances that they encounter. Marx had in mind the economic conditions—the "mode of production"—that shaped the existence of a group of people when he spoke of "circumstances encountered from the past." In this section we explore the broader social circumstances that form the basis of the economic and political life of a group. These circumstances, which are encountered and transmitted from the past, consist of the systems of belief that a people use to structure their reality. Contradictory to the words of Marx as it may seem at first, we also agree with the dictum of the sociologist, W. I. Thomas. To say that what people define as real will be real in its consequences implies that anything that we can imagine has the potential to become reality. In theory this may be true. In practice, however, the definitions that people use to organize and direct their own life are generally based on "the traditions of the dead generations" that weigh on their brain. As we discussed in Part II, these language-based traditions structure our thoughts. Hence, although all definitions of the situation may be possible, we actually work within a system of beliefs encountered from our social ancestors. To the extent that our "common sense" limits certain lines of action and affirms arbitrary "truths," it can be said that these traditions "weigh like a nightmare" on our existence. In acting out these traditions of thought uncritically, we both create and recreate the circumstances of the past.

The social construction of reality is perhaps the most central and profound topic we are treating in this book. The phrase deserves careful attention. Note first the claim that reality is a *construction.* This in itself can seem counterintuitive or even nonsensical. Surely "reality" simply *is:* the objective world that exists "out there," the subject of study of our sciences. But the alternative claim is that reality is malleable. Different groups or different cultures or different historical epochs may hold completely different (even diametrically opposed) beliefs about what is "real," what is "obviously true," what is "good," and what is "desired."

The second noteworthy element in the title phrase is that reality is a *social* construction. That is, the subjective realities that are created and maintained are the product not of isolated individuals but of relationships, communities, groups, institutions, and whole cultures.

As the readings that follow will make clear, "reality" can be an amazingly malleable thing. But are there limits to how reality might be constructed? In other words, is any definition of reality, no matter how outlandish, possible? A separate but related question is whether all realities are equally probable. Is any definition of the situation as likely as any other to emerge? Or are there constraints that limit what definitions might be viable? If so, what is the nature of these constraints?

Another significant question is, Who's doing the defining? Are certain people or groups of people more or less able to define things in a particular way? Questions such as these speak to the concept of power. Power, in a symbolic interactionist sense, is the ability to define a situation in a particular way and to have others act in accordance with this definition. Reality may be a social construction, but we are not all equal participants in this construction. What are the sources of this power and how might it be used, abused, or resisted? These issues are explored in the sections that follow.

Features of Reality

The first reading in this section is "Five Features of Reality," written by Hugh Mehan and Houston Wood. It serves both as an introduction to this section and as a framework for organizing many of the readings in the fourth part of this book.

"Five Features of Reality" is a chapter from a book about ethnomethodology. Ethnomethodology is a tradition in sociology that explores the folk methods people use ("ethno methods") to construct a sense of reality. Realities, in this sense, consist of a system of taken-for-granted beliefs and assumptions shared by a group of people. These realities structure existence. Five key features of reality are discussed in this reading.

The first feature is that realities are *reflexive*. This means that realities contain self-sealing beliefs—unquestioned beliefs that cannot be proven wrong. People continue to hold certain unquestioned beliefs in the face of contradictory evidence. For example, if you place your pencil on the desk while you go for a snack and cannot find the pencil when you return, you will assume that you misplaced it. If it reappears in the spot in which you left it, you will assume that you overlooked it. We hold an unquestioned belief in this culture regarding the immobility of "inanimate" objects. Many things could have happened to your pencil, but you will probably not entertain the notion that your pencil left by itself and then returned. This possibility is precluded by the unquestioned assumptions of our reality.

Such beliefs are often more easily noticed when examining a culture different than one's own. In many cases these beliefs are described as superstitious or magical. However, Mehan and Wood demonstrate that any culture, including our own, is filled with such unquestioned beliefs. The idea that we rely on unquestioned assumptions seems to undermine the image of people as lay scientists, testing their ideas against the evidence of the world and revising their beliefs when they are contradicted. Instead Mehan and Wood conclude that "all people are equally superstitious."

A second feature of realities is that they have an order and structure to them; realities are *coherent*. Even realities that seem nonsensical and anarchical to outsiders reveal an order and logic to them upon careful examination. Mehan and Wood's third feature is that realities are *interactional*. Realities are created, maintained, and changed through interaction with other people. This is another way of making the point that realities are *social* constructions—we do not create realities in isolation.

The fourth feature of reality draws from the third. Because realities are based in ongoing interaction, they are subject to breakdowns in the performance of the actors (recall the discussion in Part III). Thus, realities are *fragile*. Realities depend on an extraordinary amount of unnoticed interactional work and support. Any reality can be disrupted or "breached," often by a seemingly trivial act. Examples of breaching reality range from standing in an elevator facing the people instead of the door, to ending a conversation with "hello" instead of "good-bye." The fifth feature is that realities are *permeable*. It is possible to move out of one reality into another. If the conditions are right, one can even move into a radically different reality.

Each of the following readings highlights one or more of the key features of realities. "A Conception of and Experiments With 'Trust' as a Condition of Concerted Stable Actions" is an excerpt from an article by Harold Garfinkel. Garfinkel is the founder of ethnomethodology and achieved great fame and notoriety with the breaching experiments he and his students conducted at UCLA in the 1960s. Breaching entails making the underlying structure of reality explicit by acting in a manner that is inconsistent with the taken-for-granted rules of interaction that maintain the reality. When reality is breached, interaction often comes to a confused halt. This reading provides a variety of examples of breaching experiments as well as some detailed descriptions of people's reactions to these experiments.

The third reading for this section also demonstrates many of the five features of reality. "The Social Construction of Unreality: A Case Study of a Family's Attribution of Competence to a Severely Retarded Child" was written by Melvin Pollner and Lynn McDonald-Wikler. It is a provocative account of the skills and strategies used by a family to maintain a reality in the face of what seems to be massive evidence contradicting their beliefs. The family insists that their youngest child—diagnosed as severely retarded—is capable of complex and sophisticated interaction. To maintain this reality, the family engages in such techniques as "framing" an interaction so that almost anything the child does can be interpreted as meaningful and physically leading the child through some action ("puppeteering") and then interpreting the action as the result of autonomous decisions on the child's part.

The reading concludes with an interesting commentary by David Reiss, who suggests that the features that characterize this family also characterize radical scientific groups. He cautions against making too close a connection, but the commentary suggests how close madness and creativity might be. As you read this article ask yourself what unquestioned beliefs Pollner and McDonald-Wikler hold in their analysis.

Believing Makes It So

The readings in the next section illustrate another feature of reality: beliefs are sometimes self-fulfilling. In the first reading, Paul Watzlawick asserts: "A self-fulfilling prophecy is an assumption or prediction that, purely as a result of having been made, causes the expected or predicted event to occur and thus confirms its own 'accuracy.'" Watzlawick discusses a wide range of self-fulfilling prophecies, ranging from public events (e.g., a predicted gas shortage that led thousands of motorists to fill their tanks, thus *creating* the shortage), to interpersonal relationships, to medical ailments.

Self-fulfilling beliefs can have both positive and negative outcomes for the person who holds them. In any case, self-fulfilling prophecies illustrate an important point that is made throughout this book: Often what is important is not what is factually correct, but what is *defined* as real. People act based on their definitions of what is real. We respond not to the direct event, but to our interpretation of it. You can't hold a belief in your hand, a belief has no physical reality, but a belief can free you or damn you despite what might be *factually* correct.

An important message in Watzlawick's reading is that by becoming aware of self-fulfilling prophecies we will be better able to recognize and resist potentially damaging outcomes. Paradoxically, a crucial step in becoming more free is to become more aware of the constraints we face as social actors and the manner in which certain definitions of the situation either enable or inhibit possible lines of action.

For example, socially held beliefs about the characteristics of groups of people—in other words, stereotypes—often result in self-fulfilling outcomes. One illustration of this process can be seen in the reading by Mark Snyder ("When Belief Creates Reality: The Self-Fulfilling Impact of First Impressions on Social Interaction"). In this piece, Snyder reports on experimental work that he and his colleagues conducted to demonstrate that the stereotypes we hold about attractive versus unattractive people can be self-fulfilling. Based on the stereotype that attractive individuals are more friendly and likable, we may actually behave in ways that encourage such people to respond in a friendly and likable manner. The reverse is also true. Consider the implications for the self-fulfilling potential of other stereotypes.

In "Pygmalion in the Classroom," Robert Rosenthal and Lenore Jacobson report on their famous study of the effects of preconceived beliefs about intelligence on the performance of school children. Rosenthal and Jacobson told elementary school teachers that they had administered a test that indicated that a number of the students in their classes were likely to show significant academic improvement over the course of the year. In fact, the researchers had simply picked a group of students randomly. However, by the end of the year students who were *expected* by their teachers to improve had indeed improved (as measured by a standard IQ test). This remarkable study demonstrates that expecting superior performance, especially in younger children, can actually create that superior performance. This outcome occurs because the teachers behave toward the children according to how they have defined them. In so doing, they elicit the expected response. There is a dark side to this process. If students who were not expected to "bloom" did in fact improve over the year, teachers were more likely to rate such students as *less* well adjusted and *less* interesting. The self-fulfilling nature of expectations are double edged. They may benefit those people about whom we have positive beliefs and oppress those about whom we have negative beliefs.

David Rosenhan, in "On Being Sane in Insane Places," describes another very famous and controversial study. He began with a simple question: Can the sane be reliably distinguished from the insane? By sending sane people into psychiatric hospitals, he discovered that the answer to this question seems to be "No." Psychiatric staff expect patients to be insane, so they interpret the behavior of any person presumed to be a patient, even that of "normal" researchers, as insane. Like a number of the readings from the previous section, this one illustrates several of the different features of reality. How beliefs are self-sealing, the interactional nature of reality, and the self-fulfilling nature of psychiatric diagnoses are all discussed here.

Entrepreneurs of Meaning

The construction of reality occurs not just in one-on-one interactions, but also in larger social organizations. Interaction takes place within various institutional contexts. Organizations, professions, and subcultures all create shared meanings, symbols, rituals, and desires that organize people's lives. In other words, they create frames of meaning, or situational definitions, within which people interact. These frames of meaning are a resource, but they can also be a constraint, leading to definitions of the situation that work against some people's best interests.

Various social institutions can wield great influence in creating or maintaining socially shared definitions of the situation. This influence may be unintended or it may be consciously directed toward supporting a particular status quo. Once again this is an issue of power. We must remember that not everyone is equally able to participate in the construction of meaning.

In this section we examine the construction of order and meaning within the institutions of the mass media and the medical profession. These are both well-established institutions, and we contrast them with an example of a fledgling institution (nudist colonies) that must be explicitly concerned with maintaining its reality despite the pressures that threaten to undermine it.

An instance in which interactional work is needed to maintain a reality that seems at first unsustainable is given by Martin Weinberg in "The Nudist Management of Respectability." Nudist camps face the task of establishing the situational definition that "nudity and sexuality are unrelated [and] that there is nothing shameful about the human body." These ideas are contrary to the socialization of many people. Nudists have the challenge of constructing and maintaining this fragile reality against the backdrop of this cultural tension. The article is reminiscent of Emerson's piece on gynecological exams; both situations explore the issue of how to maintain a public reality that is fragile and vulnerable to devastating reframings. Weinberg describes a variety of strategies used in nudist camps to maintain their fragile reality. Here again, several of the five features discussed by Mehan and Wood are illustrated: the fact that reality is interactional, that it is fragile, and that different realities are permeable.

Next we examine two remarkably different institutions that have considerable influence on how reality is constructed in our society. These institutions are the mass media, in the form of television and motion pictures, and the medical profession. Michael Parenti, in "Black Images in White Media" provides a general discussion of mass media's persuasive influence on our cultural definitions of reality. He emphasizes the media's use of crass racial stereotypes. His thesis is that uncritical exposure to these stereotypes can shape people's beliefs. Notice the parallels between Parenti's discussion and Whorf's and Hofstadter's assertions in Part II that the words we habitually use channel our thinking along certain lines. Parenti's analysis of the media can be read as an instance of the effects of categorization. In this case the emphasis is on the role of a particular cultural institution (television) as an entrepreneur of categorical meaning. In an advanced technological society, television and film industries are key players in constructing definitions of the situation that shape the ideas of large masses of people. As such, these institutions should be carefully and critically studied.

Parenti tracks the changing image of African-Americans in TV and film through the decades. Mark Miller, in "Cosby Knows Best," provides an extended analysis of one of the most recent (and extremely popular) mass media definitions of African-Americans—*The Cosby Show.* Both of these pieces are exercises in *seeing,* that is, in actively excavating the assumptions and messages that are implicit in public portrayals of social life. The noteworthy point here is the influence of these cultural entrepreneurs in providing scripts for what society should value and who its members can be in various situations. Consider some of the other sources from which you obtain your general cultural scripts. What realities do you use to organize your experiences and to evaluate your place in the world?

An institution that has exercised a considerable influence in the definition of behavioral scripts "appropriate" to this culture is the medical profession. In "The Discovery of Hyperkinesis," Peter Conrad presents a case study of what he terms the "medicalization" of deviant behavior. By this he means "defining behavior as a medical problem or illness and mandating or licensing the medical profession to provide some type of treatment for it." There is a pervasive tendency in our culture today to define everything from depression to alcoholism as a physiological disease. Conrad's case is the emergence of hyperkinesis (i.e., hyperactivity in children) as a distinct *medical* problem. Hyperkinesis is particularly interesting because there are none of the usual physiological correlates of disease (e.g., fever, bacteria, viruses, changes in blood chemistry, etc.) and the symptomatic behaviors—rebelliousness, frustration, excitability— seem to have as much to do with social protest as with organic disease. Nevertheless, the definition of hyperkinesis as a physical illness prevails. Conrad concludes by pointing out four troubling implications about medicalizing deviant behavior.

A particularly extreme, even horrific, example of the medicalization of deviant behavior comes from a historical case discussed in Thomas Szasz's "The Sane Slave." He quotes at length from an article written for a prestigious medical journal in

1851. The article concerns the physical diseases of slaves. One of these "diseases" is *drapedomania*. The primary symptom of this ominous-sounding disorder is running away from plantations! As outrageous as this example is, Szasz points out that there are many parallels with modern practices in the psychiatric profession.

Reproducing and Changing Reality

We have said that realities are constructed and maintained through interaction. Erving Goffman speaks of "dramatizing the ideal." By this he means that we employ the "ideals" suggested by our particular cultural reality in shaping our interactions with others. We use these ideals as a framework around which to structure our interactions. In acting on these ideals, we affirm and recreate them. The preceding section illustrates the role played by various social institutions, such as the mass media and dominant professions, in defining the "ideals" that frame cultural realities. Now we ask, How do everyday actions contribute to either the maintenance or dissolution of these realities? It is surprising to discover the extent to which our own behavior may contribute to the maintenance of realities that foster our dissatisfaction or oppression. Through our partici-pation in various interaction rituals we may fortify the walls of our own prisons. Similarly, we have the power to chip away at the walls of a constructed reality by becoming aware of, and breaching, taken-for-granted interaction rituals.

In "Marriage and the Construction of Reality," Peter Berger and Hansfried Kellner discuss how our worldviews are validated through our significant relationships. They take the institution of marriage as their particular focus. You will notice a number of the themes from earlier sections of the book woven throughout this piece, including dramaturgy, conversations, and the link between relationships and selves. There is also a very important contrast here between public life (in which a person may have very little say about how the world is defined) and private life, wherein people can have a real impact on the small, private culture they build. The authors even suggest that the family can serve as a "play area" in which individuals can construct a great variety of different small worlds without threatening the larger social order.

Does the institution of marriage mostly benefit the couple or the definitional realities of our society? This question is debated by Thomas Stoddard ("Why Gay People Should Seek the Right to Marry") and Paula Ettelbrick ("Since When Is Marriage a Path to Liberation?"). On one side, Stoddard argues that gays and lesbians, as citizens of the country, should have the *right* to marry any other consenting and able adult. The act of marriage serves to define their legitimacy as life partners and to ensure participation in the legal rights and entitlements accorded to spouses. In contrast, Ettelbrick argues that in seeking marriage, queer couples, as well as heterosexual couples, contribute to the ongoing definition of the state as the legitimate legislator of its citizens' private domestic relationships. One implication of this debate is that the pursuit of cultural legitimacy in one realm, in this case legal marriage, may contribute to the maintenance of another, less desirable status quo, in this case the expanding authority of the state over personal affairs.

In the next reading of this section, Thomas Scheff ("Negotiating Reality") examines situations in which there is a distinct power difference between individuals in interaction and asks what effect this might have on how a situation is defined. "Power" is a large word that brings up images of armies, dictators, the oppression of people, and great historical changes such as revolutions. But power is also present and relevant in the details of interaction (as we saw in the reading on conversational patterns between men and women in Part III). There are two points to be made here. First, the power relationships in a society will be *reflected* in interaction patterns, even at their most minute level—your boss at work may feel free to call you by your first name or interrupt something you are saying, but if you respond in kind your behavior will be seen as inappropriate or disrespectful. Second, the differences in interaction do not simply reflect power differences, they also *create* and *reinforce* them. For example, if someone continually successful at interrupting other people is not in turn interrupted, this pattern helps to establish and maintain the power of the person.

Specifying the power differences in an interaction may be a relatively simple matter. However, behaving in a manner that alters the definition of the situation, particularly for the actor who is in a role with the least power, is more difficult. The possibility of changing the balance of power in interaction is the focus of the final readings. We view power not as an objective fact but as a social definition that needs to be constructed and maintained. Power is *accomplished*, it is not simply recognized or discovered. Scheff's examples are a psychiatric interview and an interview between a lawyer and client. He goes on to suggest that the manner in which an interview is structured (e.g., the directness of questions and answers) can influence the outcome of that interview irrespective of the actual facts. That is, the structure of negotiation can have an independent effect on how the situation is defined.

In "Prestige as the Public Discourse of Domination," the political scientist James Scott explores the effects of interaction rituals, or dramaturgy, on the maintenance of institutions of oppression. His concern is the process by which powerful social officials establish, maintain, and signal that power through public ceremonies and displays of legitimacy. Scott discusses how it is that the "masses" affirm and support the existing structure of power through their participation in the social rituals that dramatize the legitimacy of the rulers.

There are two noteworthy points made about social power in this piece. First, it is difficult or impossible to rule solely on the basis of raw force or oppression. If a group is to effectively control the society it wishes to lead, there must be some willing compliance by those "beneath" them. This compliance is accomplished through the performance of "legitimacy rituals" that establish and maintain the authority of those in power. Whether or not an actor agrees with this authority in her or his private mind, participation in the public ceremonies and interaction rituals contributes to the construction of the status quo. The existing power structure is "realized" through the performance.

The second point is that this legitimacy must be constantly maintained. Large-scale power relations, like conversations, interpersonal relationships, or public identities, must be continually nurtured. All relationships require continual interaction work. Thus, a powerful group cannot simply rest after having established itself. There must be a never-ending display and advertisement concerning its role, its power, and its legitimacy. This requires effective theater on a huge scale. Again, even if we privately disagree, our actions take place on a public stage, and as such, serve either to affirm or to call into question the dynamics of the overall performance. The need for a government to appear legitimate is savagely lampooned by Luis Valdez in "Los Vendidos." It is a play that tells the tale of a government official shopping around for a compliant Mexican American to fill an official post.

There is no denying real power and real oppression. Although the malleability of reality has been a central theme throughout this book, it is also true that there are limits to the definitions that can be created or maintained. Some of these constraints are the result of the accretion of culture and tradition, which provide the precedents and symbolic material that make some definitions so easy and others nearly impossible. Other constraints are the result of having or lacking tangible resources. Regardless of how you define a situation, if you are at the wrong end of a gun you can be hurt. But as Scott points out, guns alone make for a very fragile social order. Any social system, be it oppressive or humane, requires the cooperation of both the powerful and the weak if it is to survive. We are reminded of the dictum, "When tyranny rules, compliance is a crime."

Compliance is frequently the result of a failure to realize the extent to which one's actions contribute to the maintenance of particular definitions of the situation. Or when we recognize this, we sometimes are unaware of how to act in a manner that will break the chains of the existing reality. This is what Marx means when he says that the "tradition of the dead generations weighs like a *nightmare* on the brain of the living." Our prevailing realities suggest certain lines of action and omit others. To the extent that we participate in taken-for-granted interaction rituals we contribute to the reproduction of reality. The possibility for change is in the conception of alternative lines of interaction. Alexis de Tocqueville once quipped: "A grievance can be endured so long as it seems beyond redress, but it becomes intolerable once the possibility of removing it crosses people's minds." The seeds of social change may be in the reconception of lines of action. To be realized, however (and this is a point emphasized by Scott), even the most eloquent theories must be acted out. Change must be performed on the social stage.

We close this section and this book with a call to action. In "Talking Back," bell hooks considers what happens when an oppressed actor does not engage in expected forms of deference. Oppression is a construction that requires the cooperation of many social actors, both those that are doing the oppressing and those who are being oppressed. Bell hooks asks us to choose whether to join in this construction or withdraw our support. One can actively work to breach realities that work against one's interests. One can talk back.

References and Further Reading

Berger, P., & Luckmann, T. (1966). *The social construction of reality.* New York: Doubleday.

Marx, K. (1963). *The 18th Brumaire of Louis Bonaparte.* New York: International Publishing Co.

Pollner, M., & Goode, D. (1990). Ethnomethodology and person-centering practices. *Person-Centered Review, 5*(2), 213-220.

Thomas, W. I., & Thomas, D. (1928). *The child in America.* New York: Knopf.

Watzlawick, P. (Ed.). (1984). *The invented reality.* New York: Norton.

Five Features of Reality

Hugh Mehan and Houston Wood

Reality as a Reflexive Activity

When the Azande of Africa are faced with important decisions, decisions about where to build their houses, or whom to marry, or whether the sick will live, for example, they consult an oracle. They prepare for these consultations by following a strictly prescribed ritual. First, a substance is gathered from the bark of a certain type of tree. Then this substance is prepared in a special way during a seancelike ceremony. The Azande then pose the question in a form that permits a simple yes or no answer, and feeds the substance to a small chicken. The Azande decide beforehand whether the death of the chicken will signal an affirmative or negative response, and so they always receive an unequivocal answer to their questions.

For monumental decisions, the Azande add a second step. They feed the substance to a second chicken, asking the same question but reversing the import of the chicken's death. If in the first consultation sparing the chicken's life meant the oracle had said yes, in the second reading the oracle must now kill the chicken to once more reply in the affirmative and be consistent with its first response.

Our Western scientific knowledge tells us that the tree bark used by the Azande contains a poisonous substance that kills some chickens. The Azande have no knowledge of the tree's poisonous qualities. They do not believe the tree plays a part in the oracular ceremony. The ritual that comes between the gathering of the bark and the administration of the substance to a fowl transforms the tree into an oracle. The bark is but a vessel for the oracle to enter. As the ritual is completed the oracle takes possession of the substance. The fact that it was once a part of a tree is irrelevant. Chickens then live or die, not because of the properties of the tree, but because the oracle "hears like a person and settles cases like a king" (Evans-Pritchard, 1937, p. 321).

The Westerner sees insuperable difficulties in maintaining such beliefs when the oracle contradicts itself. Knowing the oracle's bark is "really" poison, we wonder what happens when, for example, the first and second administration of the oracle produces first a positive and then a negative answer. Or, suppose someone else consults the oracle about the same question, and contradictory answers occur? What if the oracle is contradicted by later events? The house site approved by the oracle, for example, may promptly be flooded; or the wife the oracle selected may die or be a shrew. How is it possible for the Azande to continue to believe in oracles in the face of so many evident contradictions to his faith?

What I have called contradictions are not contradictions for the Azande. They are only contradictions because these events are being viewed from the reality of Western science. Westerners look at oracular practices to determine if in fact there is an oracle. The Azande *know* that an oracle exists. That is their beginning premise. All that subsequently happens they experience from that beginning assumption.

The Azande belief in oracles is much like the mathematician's belief in certain axioms. Gasking (1955) has described such unquestioned and unquestionable axioms as *incorrigible propositions*:

An incorrigible proposition is one which you would never admit to be false whatever happens: it therefore does not tell you what happens. . . . The truth of an incorrigible proposition . . . is compatible with any and every conceivable state of affairs. (For example: whatever is your experience on counting, it is still true that $7 + 5 = 12$.) (p. 432)

The incorrigible faith in the oracle is "compatible with any and every conceivable state of affairs." It is not so much a faith about a fact in the world as a faith in the facticity of the world itself. It is the same as the faith many of us have that $7 + 5$ always equals 12. (cf. Polanyi, 1958, pp. 190-193, 257-261).

Just as Gasking suggests we explain away empirical experiences that deny this mathematical truth, the Azande too have available to them what Evans-Pritchard (1937) calls "secondary elaborations of belief" (p. 330). They explain the failure of the oracle by retaining the unquestioned absolute reality of oracles. When events occurred that revealed the inadequacy of the mystical faith in oracles, Evans-Pritchard tried to make the Azande understand these failures as he did. They only laughed, or met his arguments:

sometimes by point-blank assertions, sometimes by one of the evasive secondary elaborations of belief . . . sometimes by polite pity, but always by an entanglement of linguistic

obstacles, for one cannot well express in its language objections not formulated by a culture. (p. 319)

Evans-Pritchard goes on to write:

Let the reader consider any argument that would utterly demolish all Zande claims for the power of the oracle. If it were translated into Zande modes of thought it would serve to support their entire structure of belief. For their mystical notions are eminently coherent, being interrelated by a network of logical ties, and are so ordered that they never too crudely contradict sensory experience, but, instead, experience seems to justify them. *The Zande is immersed in a sea of mystical notions, and if he speaks about his poison oracle he must speak in a mystical idiom* [italics added]. (pp. 319-320)

Seeming contradictions are explained away by saying such things as a taboo must have been breached, or that sorcerers, witches, ghosts, or gods must have intervened. These "mystical" notions reaffirm the reality of a world in which oracles are a basic feature. Failures do not challenge the oracle. They are elaborated in such a way that they provide evidence for the constant success of oracles. Beginning with the incorrigible belief in oracles, all events *reflexively* become evidence for that belief.[1]

The mathematician, as Gasking suggests, uses a similar process:

But it does lay it down, so to speak, that if on counting $7 + 5$ you do get 11, you are to describe what has happened in some such way as this: Either "I have made a mistake in my counting" or "Someone has played a practical joke and abstracted one of the objects when I was not looking" or "Two of the objects have coalesced" or "One of the objects has disappeared," etc. (Gasking, 1955; quoted in Pollner, 1973, pp. 15-16)

Consider the analogous case of a Western scientist using chloroform to asphyxiate butterflies. The incorrigible idiom called chemistry tells the scientist, among other things, that substances have certain constant properties. Chloroform of a certain volume and mix is capable of killing butterflies. One evening the scientist administers the chloroform as usual, and is dismayed to see the animal continue to flutter about.

Here is a contradiction of the scientist's reality, just as oracle use sometimes produces contradictions. Like the Azande, scientists have many secondary elaborations of belief they can bring to bear on such occurrences, short of rejecting the Western causal belief. Instead of rejecting chemistry they can explain the poison's failure by such things as "faulty manufacturing," "mislabeling," "sabotage," or "practical joke." Whatever the conclusion, it would continue to reaffirm the causal premise of science. This reaffirmation reflexively supports the reality that produced the poison's unexpected failure in the first place.

The use of contradictions to reaffirm incorrigible propositions can be observed in other branches of science. In the Ptolemaic system of astronomy, the sun was seen as a planet of the earth. When astronomers looked at the sun, they saw it as an orb circling the earth. When the Copernican system arose as an alternative to this view, it offered little new empirical data. Instead, it described the old "facts" in a different way. A shift of vision was required for people to see the sun as a star, not a planet of the earth.

Seeing the sun as a star and seeing it as a planet circling the earth are merely alternatives. There is no a priori warrant for believing that either empirical determination is necessarily superior to the other.

How is a choice between equally compelling empirical determinations made? The convert to the Copernican system could have said: "I used to see a planet, but now I see a star" (cf. Kuhn, 1970, p. 115). But to talk that way is to allow the belief that an object can be both a star and a planet at the same time. Such a belief is not allowed in Western science. So, instead, the Copernican concludes that the sun was a star all along. By

so concluding, the astronomer exhibits an incorrigible proposition of Western thought, the *object constancy assumption*.[2] This is the belief that objects remain the same over time, across viewings from different positions and people. When presented with seemingly contradictory empirical determinations, the convert to Copernicanism does not consider that the sun changes through time. Instead he says: "I once took the sun to be a planet, but I was mistaken." The "discovery" of the sun as a star does not challenge the object constancy belief any more than an oracular "failure" challenges the ultimate reality of Azande belief.

The reaffirmation of incorrigible propositions is not limited to mystical and scientific ways of knowing. This reflexive work operates in commonsense reasoning as well. Each time you search for an object you knew was "right there" the same reflexive process is operating. Say, for example, you find a missing pen in a place you know you searched before. Although the evidence indicates that the pen was first absent and then present, that conclusion is not reached. To do so would challenge the incorrigibility of the object constancy belief. Instead, secondary elaborations—"I must have overlooked it," "I must not have looked there"—are invoked to retain the integrity of the object constancy proposition.

Without an object constancy assumption, there would be no problems about alternative determinations. But, with this assumption as an incorrigible proposition, the person faced with alternative seeings must choose one and only one as real. In choosing one, the other is automatically revealed as false. The falsehood of the rejected alternative may be explained in various ways. It may be due to a defective sensory apparatus, or a cognitive bias, or idiosyncratic psychological dynamics. We explain the inconstancy of the experienced object by saying that inconstancy is a product of the experiencing, not a feature of the object itself.[3]

Once an alternative seeing is explained away, the accepted explanation provides evidence for the object constancy assumption that made the explanation necessary in the first place. By demanding that we dismiss one of two equally valid empirical determinations, the object constancy assumption leads to a body of work that validates that assumption. The work then justifies itself afterward, in the world it has created. This self-preservative reflexive process is common to oracular, scientific, and commonsense reasoning.

So far I have approached the reflexive feature of realities as if it were a form of reasoning. But reflexivity is not only a facet of reasoning. It is a recurrent fact of everyday social life. For example, *talk itself is reflexive* (cf. Garfinkel, 1967; Cicourel, 1973). An utterance not only delivers some particular information, it also creates a world in which information itself can appear.

Zimmerman (1973, p. 25) provides a means for understanding the reflexivity of talk at the level of a single word. He presents three identical shapes:

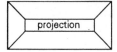 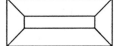

The first and third differ from the second: they each contain single words. These words interact with the box in which they appear so as to change the nature of that box. In so doing, they reflexively illumine themselves. For example, the word "projection," appearing in some other setting, would not mean what it does here. For me it means that I am to see the back panel and the word "projection" as illustrative of a projection. The word "projection" does not merely appear in the scene reporting on that scene. It creates the scene in which it appears as a reasonable object.

Similarly, the word "indentation" not only takes its meaning from the context in which it appears, it reflexively creates that very context. It creates a reality in which it may stand as a part of that reality.

These examples only hint at the reflexivity of talk. (Escher's "Drawing Hands" provides another visual intimation of reflexivity.) Actual conversations are more complex than single words. The social context in which talk occurs, while analogous to one of these static boxes, is enormously ambiguous and potentially infinitely referential. Nonetheless, conversation operates like the printed "projection" and "indentation." An analysis of greetings can be used to show how talk partially constitutes the context and then comes to be seen as independent of it.[4]

To say "hello" both creates and sustains a world in which persons acknowledge that (1) they sometimes can see one another; (2) a world in which it is possible for persons to signal to each other, and (3) expect to be signaled back to, by (4) some others but not all of them. This is a partial and only illustrative list of some of the things a greeting accomplishes. Without the superstitious use 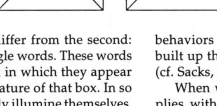 of greetings, no world in which greetings are possible "objects" would arise. A greeting creates "room" for itself. But once such verbal behaviors are regularly done, a world is built up that can take their use for granted (cf. Sacks, Schegloff, & Jefferson, 1974).

When we say "hello" and the other replies with the expected counter greeting, the reflexive work of our initial utterance is masked. If the other scowls and walks on, then we are reminded that we were attempting to create a scene of greetings and that we failed. Rather than treat this as evidence that greetings are not "real," however, the rejected greeter ordinarily turns it into an occasion for affirming the reality of greetings. He formulates "secondary elaborations" of belief about greetings. He says, "He didn't hear me," "She is not feeling well," "It doesn't matter anyway."

Reflexivity provides grounds for absolute faith in the validity of knowledge. The Azande takes the truth of the oracle for granted, the scientist assumes the facticity of science, the layman accepts the tenets of common sense. The incorrigible propositions of a reality serve as criteria to judge other ways of knowing. Using his absolute faith in the oracle, the Azande dismisses Evans-Pritchard's Western science contradictions. Evans-Pritchard, steeped in the efficacy of science, dismissed the oracle as superstitious. An absolute faith in the incorrigibility of one's own knowledge enables believers to repel contrary evidence. This suggests that all people are equally superstitious.

Reality as a Coherent Body of Knowledge

The phenomenon of reflexivity is a feature of every reality. It interacts with the coherence, interactional, fragility, and permeability features I describe in the rest of this chapter. These five features are incorrigible propositions of the reality of ethnomethodology. They appear as facts of the external world due to the ethnomethodologist's unquestioned assumption that they constitute the world. In other words, these features themselves exhibit reflexivity.

This reflexive loop constitutes the interior structure of ethnomethodology. This will become clearer as I describe the second feature of realities, their exhibition of a coherent body of knowledge. To illustrate this feature I will extrapolate from the work of Zimmerman and Wieder (n.d.), who investigated the life of a number of self-named "freaks," frequent drug users within America's counterculture. Both freaks and their academic ethnographers (e.g., Reich, 1970; Roszack, 1969) describe freaks as radical opponents of the straight culture from which they sprang. As Zimmerman and Wieder (n.d.) write:

From the standpoint of the "straight" members of society, freaks are deliberately irrational. . . .

They disavow an interest in efficiency, making long-range plans, and concerns about costs of property (etc.) which are valued by the straight members of American society and are understood by them as indicators of rationality. (p. 103)

On first appearance, here is a reality that seems anarchical. Nonetheless, Zimmerman and Wieder found that:

When it comes to those activities most highly valued by freaks, such as taking drugs, making love, and other "cheap thrills," there is an elaborately developed body of lore. Freaks and others use that knowledge of taking drugs, making love, etc., reasonably, deliberately, planfully, projecting various consequences, predicting outcomes, conceiving of the possibilities of action in more or less clear and distinct ways, and choosing between two or more means of reaching the same end. (pp. 102-103)

The most vivid illustration that freaks use a coherent body of knowledge comes from Zimmerman's and Wieder's discoveries about the place of drugs in the everyday freak life. At first glance such drug use appears irrational. Yet, among freaks, taking drugs "is something as ordinary and unremarkable as their parents regard taking or offering a cup of coffee" (p. 57). Freak behavior is not a function of the freaks' ignorance of chemical and medical "facts" about drugs. The freaks studied knew chemical and medical facts well. They organized these facts into a different, yet coherent corpus of knowledge.

One of the team's research assistants, Peter Suchek, was able to systematize the freaks' knowledge of drugs into a taxonomic schemata (see Table 31.1).

What the freak calls "dope," the chemist calls "psychotropic drugs." Within the family of dope, freaks distinguish "mind-expanding" and "body" dope. Freaks further subdivide each of these species. In addition, freaks share a common body of knowledge informing them of the practicalities surrounding the use of each type of dope.

All knowledge of dope use is grounded in the incorrigible proposition that dope is to be used. One must, of course, know how to use it.

Zimmerman and Wieder (n.d.) found the following knowledge about "psychedelic mind-expanding dope" to be common among freaks:

The folk pharmacology of psychedelic drugs may be characterized as a method whereby drug users rationally assess choices among kinds of drugs, choices among instances of the same kind of drug, the choice to ingest or not, the time of the act of ingestion relative to the state of one's physiology and relative to the state of one's psyche, the timing relative to social and practical demands, the appropriateness of the setting for having a psychedelic

Table 31.1
The Folk Pharmacology for Dope

Types of Dope	Subcategories
Mind-expanding dope	(Untitled)
	"grass" (marijuana)
	"hash" (hashish)
	"LSD" or "acid" (lysergic acid)
	Psychedelics
	Mescaline
	synthetic
	organic
	natural, peyote
	Psilocybin
	synthetic
	organic
	natural, mushrooms
	"DMT"
	miscellaneous (e.g., Angel's Dust)
Body dope	"speed" (amphetamines)
	"downers" (barbiturates)
	"tranks" (tranquilizers)
	"coke" (cocaine)
	"shit" (heroin)

Zimmerman and Wieder (n.d.), p. 107.

experience, the size of the dose, and the effectiveness and risk of mixing drugs. (p. 118)

Freaks share similar knowledge for the rest of the taxonomy. Being a freak means living within the auspices of such knowledge and using it according to a plan, as the chemist uses his. Both the freaks' and the scientists' realities are concerned with "the facts." Though the facts differ, each reality reflexively proves its facts as absolute.

Consider how the freak assembles the knowledge he uses. He is not loath to borrow from the discoveries of science. But before accepting what the scientist says, he first tests scientific "facts" against the auspices of his own incorrigible propositions. He does not use the scientists' findings to determine the danger of the drug, but rather to indicate the particular dosage, setting, et cetera, under which a drug is to be taken.

Scientific drug researchers frequently attend to the experiences of freaks in a comparable way. They incorporate the facts that freaks report about dope into their coherent idiom. The two then are like independent teams of investigators working on the same phenomenon with different purposes. They are like artists and botanists who share a common interest in the vegetable kingdom, but who employ different incorrigibles.

The freak's knowledge, like all knowledge, is sustained through reflexive interactional work. For example, the knowledge contained in the drug taxonomy (Table 31.1) sometimes "fails," that is, it produces not a "high" but a "bummer." The incorrigible propositions of freak pharmacology are not then questioned. Instead, these propositions are invoked to explain the bummer's occurrence. "For example," Zimmerman and Wieder (n.d.) write:

A "bad trip" may be explained in such terms as the following: it was a bad time and place to drop; my head wasn't ready for it; or it was bad acid or mescaline, meaning that it was cut with something impure or that it was some other drug altogether. (p. 118)

The reflexive use of the freak taxonomy recalls my previous discussion of the Azande. When the oracle seemed to contradict itself, the contradiction became but one more occasion for proving the oracular way of knowing. The reality of oracles is appealed to in explaining the failure of the oracle, just as the reality of freak pharmacology is used to explain a bad trip. It would be as futile for a chemist to explain the bad trip scientifically to a freak as it was for Evans-Pritchard to try to convince the Azande that failures of the oracle demonstrated their unreality.

The coherence of knowledge is a reflexive consequence of the researcher's attention. Zimmerman and Wieder, in the best social science tradition, employed many methods to construct the freak's taxonomy. Freaks were interviewed by sociology graduate students and by their peers. These interviewers provided accounts of their own drug experiences as well. Additional freaks not acquainted with the purposes of the research were paid to keep personal diaries of their day-to-day experiences. Zimmerman and Wieder used a portion of this massive data to construct the freak taxonomy, then tested its validity against further portions of the data.

Such systematizations are always the researcher's construction (Wallace, 1972 . . .). To claim that any reality, including the researcher's own, exhibits a coherent body of knowledge is but to claim that coherence can be found *upon analysis*. The coherence located in a reality is found there by the ethnomethodologist's interactional work. The coherence feature, like all features of realities, operates as an incorrigible proposition, reflexively sustained.

Consider the analogous work of linguists (e.g., Chomsky, 1965). Within language-using communities, linguists discover the "rules of grammar." Although the linguist empirically establishes these grammatical rules, speaker-hearers of that language cannot list them. Rules can be located in their talk, upon analysis, but language users cannot describe them.

Similarly, freaks could not supply the taxonomy Zimmerman and Wieder claim they "really" know. It was found upon analysis. It is an imposition of the researcher's logic upon the freak's logic.

Castaneda's (1968, 1971) attempts to explain the reality of Yaqui sorcery further illustrates the reflexity of analysis. In his initial report, *The Teachings of Don Juan,* Castaneda (1968) begins with a detailed ethnography of his experiences of his encounter with a Yaqui sorcerer, Don Juan. In this reality it is common for time to stop, for men to turn into animals and animals into men, for animals and men to converse with one another, and for great distances to be covered while the body remains still.

In the final section of his report, Castaneda systematizes his experiences with the sorcerer. He presents a coherent body of knowledge undergirding Don Juan's teachings. Thus Castaneda, like Zimmerman and Wieder, organizes a "nonordinary" reality into a coherent system of knowledge.

In a second book Castaneda (1971) describes Don Juan's reaction to his systematization of a peyote session, a "mitote." Castaneda told Don Juan he had discovered that mitotes are a "result of a subtle and complex system of cueing." He writes:

It took me close to two hours to read and explain to Don Juan the scheme I had constructed. I ended by begging him to tell me in his own words what were the exact procedures for reaching agreement.

When I had finished he frowned. I thought he must have found my explanation challenging; he appeared to be involved in deep deliberation. After a reasonable silence I asked him what he thought about my idea.

My question made him suddenly turn his frown into a smile and then into roaring laughter. I tried to laugh too and asked nervously what was so funny.

"You're deranged!" he exclaimed. "Why should anyone be bothered with cueing at such an important time as a mitote? Do you think one ever fools around with Mescalito?"

I thought for a moment that he was being evasive; he was not really answering my question.

"Why should anyone cue?" Don Juan asked stubbornly. "You have been in mitotes. You should know that no one told you how to feel, or what to do; no one except Mescalito himself."

I insisted that such an explanation was not possible and begged him again to tell me how the agreement was reached.

"I know why you have come," Don Juan said in a mysterious tone. "I can't help you in your endeavor because there is no system of cueing."

"But how can all those persons agree about Mescalito's presence?"

"They agree because they *see*," Don Juan said dramatically, and then added casually, "Why don't you attend another mitote and see for yourself?" (pp. 37-38)

Don Juan finds Castaneda's account ridiculous. This rejection is not evidence that Castaneda's attempt at systematization is incorrect. It indicates that the investigator reflexively organizes the realities he investigates. All realities may *upon analysis* exhibit a coherent system of knowledge, but knowledge of this coherence is not necessarily part of the awareness of its members.

Features emerging "upon analysis" is a particular instance of reflexivity. These features exist only within the reflexive work of those researchers who make them exist. This does not deny their reality. There is no need to pursue the chimera of a presuppositionless inquiry. Because all realities are ultimately superstitious the reflexive location of reflexivity is not a problem within ethnomethodological studies. Rather, it provides them with their most intriguing phenomenon.

My discussion of these first two features of realities also shows that any one feature is separate from the other only upon analysis. In my description of reflexivity, I was forced to assume the existence of a coherent body of knowledge. Similarly, in the present discussion I could not speak about the existence of coherent systems of knowledge without introducing the caveat of "upon analysis," an implicit reference to reflexivity. This situation will continue as I discuss the remaining three features. Though I attempt to keep them separate from one another, I will only be partially successful, since the five are inextricably intertwined. Nevertheless, I will continue to talk of them as five separate features, not as one. I acknowledge that this talk is more heuristic than literal—it provides a ladder with five steps that may be climbed and then thrown away (cf. Wittgenstein, 1921/1961).

Reality as Interactional Activity

Realities are also dependent upon ceaseless social interactional work. Wood's study of a mental hospital illustrates the reality of this reality work. He discovered that psychiatric attendants shared a body of knowledge. Wood's (1968) analysis of the attendants' interaction with the patients uncovered labels like: "baby," "child," "epileptic," "mean old man," "alcoholic," "lost soul," "good patient," "depressive," "sociopath," and "nigger" (p. 36). Though borrowed from psychiatry, these terms constitute a corpus of knowledge which reflects the attendants' own practical nursing concerns. These terms can be arranged in a systematic taxonomy (see Table 31.2). Each is shown to differ from the others according to four parameters of nursing problems.

Wood's study explored how the attendants used this taxonomy to construct meanings for the mental patients' behavior. One explanation of label use is called a "matching procedure." The matching model of labeling patient behavior is essentially a psychological theory. It treats behavior as a private, internal state, not influenced by social dimensions. The matching model assumes the patients' behavior has obvious features. Trained personnel monitor and automatically

Table 31.2
The Meaning of the Labels

Psychiatric Attendant Label	Nursing Trouble				Fre-quency × 60
	Work	Clean-liness	Super-visory	Miscel-laneous	
Mean old man	yes	yes	yes	yes	2
Baby	yes	yes	yes	—	20
Child	yes	yes	—	yes	4
Nigger	yes	—	yes	yes	1
Epileptic	—	yes	—	yes	4
Sociopath	yes	—	—	yes	3
Depressive	—	—	—	yes	2
Alcoholic	—	—	yes	—	8
Lost soul	yes	—	—	—	12
Good patient	—	—	—	—	6

Wood (1968), p. 45.

apply the appropriate label to patients' behavior.

Wood presents five case histories that show that labels are not applied by a simple matching process. They are molded in the day-to-day interaction of the attendants with one another and with the patients. The labeling of patients is a social activity, not a psychological one.

Wood (1968, pp. 51-91) describes the labeling history of patient Jimmy Lee Jackson. Over the course of his three-month hospitalization, Jackson held the same official psychiatric label, that of "psychoneurotic reaction, depressive type." However, the ward attendants saw Jackson within the web of their own practical circumstances. For them, at one time he was a "nigger," at another a "depressive," and at yet another a "sociopath." These seeings reflected a deep change in the meaning Jackson had for the attendants. When he was seen as a "nigger," for example, it meant that the attendants considered he was "lazy, and . . . without morals or scruples and . . . that the patient is cunning and will attempt to ingratiate himself with the attendants in order to get attention and 'use' them for his own ends" (p. 52). When Jackson became a depressive type, all these negative attributes were with-

drawn. The change in attribution, Wood shows, cannot be explained by a matching procedure. The attendants' social interactional work produced the change, independent of Jackson's behavior. This suggests that realities are fundamentally interactional activities.

One evening Jackson was suffering from a toothache. Unable to secure medical attention, he ran his arm through a window pane in one of the ward's locked doors. He suffered a severe laceration of his forearm which required stitches. When the attendants who were on duty during this episode returned to work the following afternoon, they discovered that the preceding morning shift had decided that Jackson had attempted suicide. Jackson was no longer presented to them as a nigger. The morning shift found that persons who had not even witnessed the event had given it a meaning they themselves had never considered. Nevertheless, the evening shift accepted the validity of this label change.

The label change indexed a far larger change. Jackson's past history on the ward was reinterpreted. He now was accorded different treatment by attendants on all shifts. He was listened to sympathetically, given whatever he requested, and no longer exhorted to do more ward work. All the attendants came to believe that he had always been a depressive and that they had always seen him as such.

A few weeks later Jackson became yet another person, a "sociopath." The attendants no longer accepted that he was capable of a suicide attempt. The new label was once again applied retrospectively. Not only was Jackson believed to be incapable of committing suicide now, he was thought to have always been incapable of it. The attendants agreed that the window-breaking incident had been a "fake" or "con,"—just the sort of thing a sociopath would do. Attendants who had praised Jackson as a hard worker when he was labeled a depressive now pointed to this same work as proof he was a "conniver." Requests for attention and medicine that had been promptly fulfilled for the depressive Jackson were now ignored for the sociopath Jackson, or used as occasions to attack him verbally.

Yet, as Wood describes Jackson, he remained constant despite these changes in attendant behavior. He did the same amount of work and sought the same amount of attention and medicine whether he was labeled a nigger or a depressive or a sociopath. What Jackson was at any time was determined by the reality work of the attendants.

In the final pages of his study, Wood (1968) further illustrates the power of interactional work to create an external world:

> The evening that he [Jackson] cut his arm, I, like the PAs [psychiatric attendants], was overcome by the blood and did not reflect on its "larger" meaning concerning his proper label. The next day, when I heard all of the morning shift PAs refer to his action as a suicide attempt, I too labeled Jackson a "depressive" and the cut arm as a suicide attempt. When the label changed in future weeks I was working as a PA on the ward up to 12 hours a day. It was only two months later when I had left the ward, as I reviewed my notes and my memory, that I recognized the "peculiar" label changes that had occurred. While I was on the ward, it had not seemed strange to think that cutting an arm in a window was a serious attempt to kill oneself. Only as an "outsider" did I come to think that Jackson had "really" stayed the same through his three label changes. (pp. 137-138)

As Wood says, Jackson could never have a meaning apart from *some* social context. Meanings unfold only within an unending sequence of practical actions.[5]

The *matching* theory of label use assumes a correspondence theory of signs (cf. Garfinkel, 1952, p. 91ff.; Wieder, 1970 . . .). This theory of signs has three analytically separate elements: ideas that exist in the head, signs that appear in symbolic representations, and objects and events that appear in the world. Meaning is the relation among these elements. Signs can stand on behalf of the ideas in the head or refer to objects in the world. This theory of signs implies that signs stand in a point-by-point relation to thoughts in one's mind or objects in the world. Meanings are stable across time and space. They are not dependent upon the concrete participants or upon the specific scenes in which they appear.

Wood's study indicates that labels are not applied in accordance with correspondence principles. Instead, labels are *indexical expressions.* Meanings are situationally determined. They are dependent upon the concrete context in which they appear. The participants' interactional activity structured the indexical meaning of the labels used on the ward. The relationship of the participants to the object, the setting in which events occur, and the circumstances surrounding a definition determine the meaning of labels and of objects.

The interactional feature indicates that realities do not possess symbols, like so many tools in a box. A reality and its signs are "mutually determinative" (Wieder, 1973, p. 216). Alone, neither expresses sense. Intertwining through the course of indexical interaction, they form a life.

The Fragility of Realities

Every reality depends upon (1) ceaseless reflexive use of (2) a body of knowledge in (3) interaction. Every reality is also fragile. Suppression of the activities that the first three features describe disrupts the reality. Every reality is equally capable of dissolution. The presence of this fragility feature of realities has been demonstrated by studies called "incongruity procedures" or "breaching experiments."

In one of the simplest of these, Garfinkel used 67 students as "experimenters." These students engaged a total of 253 "subjects" in a game of tick-tack-toe. When the figure necessary for the game was drawn, the experimenters requested the subject to make the first move. After the subject made his mark, the experimenter took his turn. Rather than simply marking another cell, the experimenter erased the subject's mark and moved it to another cell. Continuing as if this were expected behavior, the experimenter then placed his own mark in one of the now empty cells. The experimenters reported that their action produced extreme bewilderment and confusion in the subjects. The reality of the game, which before the experimenter's move seemed stable and external, suddenly fell apart. For a moment the subjects exhibited an "amnesia for social structure" (Garfinkel, 1963, p. 189).

This fragility feature is even more evident in everyday life, where the rules are not explicit. People interact without listing the rules of conduct. Continued reference is made to this knowledge nonetheless. This referencing is not ordinarily available as long as the reality work continues normally. When the reality is disrupted, the interactional activity structuring the reality becomes visible. This is what occurred in the tick-tack-toe game. A usually unnoticed feature of the game is a "rule" prohibiting erasing an opponent's mark. When this unspoken "rule" is broken, it makes its first public appearance. If we were aware of the fragility of our realities, they would not seem real.

Thus Garfinkel (1963) found that when the "incongruity-inducing procedures" developed in games:

were applied in "real life" situations, it was unnerving to find the seemingly endless variety of events that lent themselves to the production of really nasty surprises. These events ranged from . . . standing very, very close to a person while otherwise maintaining an innocuous conversation, to others . . . like saying "hello" at the termination of a conversation. . . . Both procedures elicited anxiety, indignation, strong feelings on the part of the experimenter and subject alike of humiliation and regret, demands by the subjects for explanations, and so on. (p. 198)

Another of the procedures Garfinkel developed was to send student experimenters into stores and restaurants where they were told to "mistake" customers for salespersons and waiters. The following is a sample of what the experimenters reported about the results of these procedures.

One experimenter went to have lunch at a restaurant near a university. Her host directed her toward a likely subject. She began by saying to him:

(E): I should like a table on the west side, a quiet spot, if you please. And what is on the menu?

(S): [Turned toward E but looked past and in the direction of the foyer.] Eh, ah, madam, I'm sure. [Looked past E again, looked at a pocket watch, replaced it, and looked toward the dining room.]

(E): Surely luncheon hours are not over. What do you recommend I order today?

(S): I don't know. You see, I'm waiting . . .

(E): [Interrupted with] Please don't keep me standing here while you wait. Kindly show me to a table.

(S): But Madam—[started to edge away from door, and back into the lounge in a slightly curving direction around E].

(E): My good man—[at this S's face flushed, his eyes rounded and opened wide.]

(S): But—you—I—oh dear! [He seemed to wilt.]

(E): [Took S's arm in hand and propelled him toward the dining room door slightly ahead of herself.]

(S): [Walked slowly but stopped just within the room, turned around and for the first time looked directly and very appraisingly at E, took out the watch, looked at it, held it to his ear, replaced it, and muttered, "Oh dear."]

(E): It will take only a minute for you to show me to a table and take my order. Then you can return to wait for your customers. After all, I am a guest and a customer, too.

(S): [Stiffened slightly, walked jerkily toward the nearest empty table, held a chair for E to be seated, bowed slightly, muttered "My pleasure," hurried toward the door, stopped, turned, looked back at E with a blank facial expression.]

At this point, E's host walked up to S, greeted him, shook hands, and propelled him toward

E's table. *S* stopped a few steps from the table, looked directly at, then through *E*, and started to walk back toward the door. Host told him *E* was a young lady whom he had invited to join them at lunch. (He then introduced her to *S*, who was one of the big names in the physics world, a pillar of the institution.) *S* seated himself reluctantly and perched rigidly on his chair, obviously uncomfortable. *E* smiled, made light and polite inquiries about his work, mentioned various functions he had attended and at which he had been honored, and then complacently remarked that it was a shame *E* had not met him personally. If she had, he said, she would not have mistaken him for the maître d'. The host chattered about his long-time friendship with *E*, while *S* fidgeted and looked again at his pocket watch, wiped his forehead with a table napkin, and looked at *E* but avoided meeting her eyes. When the host mentioned that *E* was studying sociology at UCLA, *S* suddenly burst into loud laughter, realized that everyone in the room was looking in the direction of our table, abruptly became quiet, and said to *E*, "You mistook me for the maître d', didn't you?"

(E): Deliberately, sir.
(S): Why deliberately?
(E): You have just been used as the unsuspecting subject in an experiment.
(S): Diabolic. But clever, I must say [to our host] I haven't been so shaken since —— denounced my theory of —— in 19——. And the wild thoughts that ran through my mind! Call the receptionist from the lobby, go to the men's room, turn this woman to the first person who comes along. Damn these early diners, there's nobody coming in at this time. Time is standing still, or my watch has stopped. I will talk to —— about this, make sure it doesn't happen to "somebody." Damn a persistent woman. I'm not her "good man." I'm Dr. —— and not to be pushed around. This can't be happening. If I do take her to that damned table she wants, I can get away from her, and I'll just take it easy until I can. I remember —— (hereditary psychopath, wife of one of the "family" of the institution), maybe if I do what *this* one wants she will not make any more trouble than this. I wonder if she is

"off." She certainly looks normal. Wonder how you can really tell? (Garfinkel, 1963, pp. 224-226)

The breaching experiments were subsequently refined, such that:

The person [subject] could not turn the situation into a play, a joke, an experiment, a deception, and the like . . .; that he have insufficient time to work through a redefinition of his real circumstances; and that he be deprived of consensual support for an alternative definition of social reality. (Garfinkel, 1964; in 1967, p. 58)

This meant that subjects were not allowed to reflexively turn the disruption into a revalidation of their realities. The incorrigible propositions of their social knowledge were not adequate for the present circumstances. They were removed from the supporting interactional activity that they possessed before the breach occurred.

These refinements had the positive consequence of increasing the bewilderment of the subjects, who became more and more like desocialized schizophrenics, persons completely devoid of any social reality. These refinements produced a negative consequence. They were immoral. Once subjects had experienced the fragility, they could not continue taking the stability of realities for granted. No amount of "cooling out" could restore the subject's faith.

But what is too cruel to impose on others can be tried upon oneself. . . .

The Permeability of Realities

Because the reflexive use of social knowledge is fragile and interaction dependent, one reality may be altered, and another may be assumed. Cases where a person passes from one reality to another, dramatically different, reality vividly display this permeability feature.

Tobias Schneebaum, a painter who lives periodically in New York, provides an example of a radical shift in realities in his book, *Keep the River on Your Right* (1969). Schneebaum entered the jungles of Peru in 1955 in pursuit of his art. During the trip the book describes, he gradually lost interest in painterly studies. He found himself drawn deeper and deeper into the jungle. Unlike a professional anthropologist. he carried no plans to write about his travels. In fact, the slim volume from which I draw the following discussion was not written until 13 years after his return.

He happened upon the Akaramas, a stone age tribe that had never seen a white man. They accepted him quickly, gave him a new name, "Habe," meaning "ignorant one," and began teaching him to be as they were.

Schneebaum learned to sleep in "bundles" with the other men, piled on top of one another for warmth and comfort. He learned to hunt and fish with stone age tools. He learned the Akaramas' language and their ritual of telling stories of their hunts and hikes, the telling taking longer than the doing. He learned to go without clothing, and to touch casually the genitals of his companions in play.

When one of the men in Schneebaum's compartment is dying of dysentery, crying out at his excretions of blood and pain, the "others laugh and he laughs too" (p. 109). As this man lies among them whimpering and crying in their sleeping pile at night, Schneebaum writes: "Not Michii or Baaldore or Ihuene or Reindude seemed to have him on their minds. It was as if he were not there among us or as if he had already gone to some other forest" (p. 129). When he dies, he is immediately forgotten. Such is the normal perception of death within the Akarama reality. As Schneebaum describes another incident: "There were two pregnant women whom I noticed one day with flatter bellies and no babies on their backs, but there was no sign of grief, no service . . ." (p. 109).

Gradually, Schneebaum absorbed even these ways and a new sense of time. At one point he left the Akaramas to visit the mission from which he had embarked. He was startled to find that seven months had passed, not the three or four he had supposed. As he was more and more permeated by the stone age reality, he began to feel that his "own world, whatever, wherever it was, no longer was anywhere in existence" (p. 69). As the sense of his old reality disappears, he says, "My fears were not so much for the future . . . but for my knowledge. I was removing my own reflection" (pp. 64-65).

One day, a day like many others, he rises to begin a hunting expedition with his sleeping companions. This day, however, they go much farther than ever before. They paint themselves in a new way and repeat new chants. Finally they reach a strange village. In they swoop, Schneebaum too, shouting their sacred words and killing all the men they can catch, disemboweling and beheading them on the spot. They burn all the huts, kidnap the women and children. They then hike to their own village, without pause, through an entire night. At home, a new dance is begun. The meat of the men they have murdered and brought back with them is cooked. As a new movement of the dance begins, this meat is gleefully eaten. Exhausted at last, they stumble together on the ground. Then the last of the meat is put to ceremonious use:

We sat or lay around the fires, eating, moaning the tones of the chant, swaying forward and back, moving from the hip, forward and back. Calm and silence settled over us, all men. Four got up, one picked a heart from the embers, and they walked into the forest. Small groups of others arose, selected a piece of meat, and disappeared in other directions. We three were alone until Ihuene, Baaldore, and Reindude were in front of us, Reindude cupping in his hand the heart from the being we had carried from so far away, the heart of he who had lived in the hut we had entered to kill. We stretched out flat upon the ground, lined up, our shoulders touching. Michii looked up at the moon and showed it to the heart. He bit into it as if it were an apple, taking a large bite, almost half the heart, and chewed down several times, spit into a hand, separated the meat into six sections and placed some into the mouths of each of us. We chewed and swallowed. He did the same with the other half of the heart. He turned Darinimbiak onto his stomach, lifted his hips so that he crouched on all fours. Darinimbiak growled, Mayaarii-ha! Michii growled, Mayaari-ha!, bent down to lay himself upon Darinimbiak's back and entered him. (pp. 106-107)

Mass murder, destruction of an entire village, theft of all valuable goods, cannibalism, the ritual eating of the heart before publicly displayed homosexual acts—these are some of the acts Schneebaum participated in. He could not have done them his first day in the jungle. But after his gradual adoption of the Akarama reality, they had become natural. It would have been as immoral for him to refuse to join his brothers in the raid and its victory celebration as it would be immoral for him to commit these same acts within a Western community. His reality had changed. The moral facts were different.

Schneebaum's experience suggests that even radically different realities can be penetrated.[6] We would not have this account, however, if the stone age reality had completely obliterated Schneebaum's Western reality. He would still be with the tribe. The more he permeated the Akaramas' reality, the more suspect his old reality became. The more he fell under the spell of the absolutism of his new reality, the more fragile his old reality became. Like the cannibals, Schneebaum says: "My days are days no longer. Time had no thoughts to trouble me, and everything is like nothing and nothing is like everything. For if a day passes, it registers nowhere, and it might be a week, it might be a month. There is no difference" (p. 174).

As the vision of his old reality receded, Schneebaum experienced its fragility. He knew he must leave soon, or there would be no reality to return to. He describes his departure:

A time alone, only a few weeks ago, with the jungle alive and vibrant around me, and Michii and Baaldore gone with all the other men to hunt, I saw within myself too many seeds that would grow a fungus around my brain, encasing it with mold that could penetrate and smooth the convolutions and there I would remain, not he who had travelled and arrived, not the me who had crossed the mountains in a search, but another me living only in ease and pleasure, no longer able to scrawl out words on paper or think beyond a moment. And days later, I took myself up from our hut, and I walked on again alone without a word to any of my friends and family, but left when all again were gone and I walked through my jungle. . . . (p. 182)

The Akaramas would not miss him. They would not even notice his absence. For them, there were no separate beings. Schneebaum felt their reality obliterating "the me who had crossed the mountains in a search." Schneebaum was attached to this "me," and so he left.

In the previous section, I listed three conditions necessary for successful breaches: There can be no place to escape. There can be no time to escape. There can be no one to provide counter evidence. The same conditions are required to move between realities. That is, as Castaneda's (1968, 1971, 1972) work suggests, in order to permeate realities, one must first have the old reality breached. Castaneda has named this necessity the establishment "of a certainty of a minimal possibility," that another reality actually exists (personal communication). Successful breaches must establish that another reality is available for entry. Thus, as Don Juan attempted to make Castaneda a man of knowledge, he first spent years trying to crack Castaneda's absolute faith in the reality of Western rationalism.

Castaneda's work suggests many relations between the fragility and permeability features. It is not my purpose to explore the relations of the five features in this book. But I want to emphasize that such relations can be supposed to exist.

I relied on the "exotic" case of a person passing from a Western to a stone age reality to display the permeability feature of realities. However, any two subsequent interactional encounters could have been used for this purpose. All such passages are of equal theoretic import. Passages between a movie and freeway driving, between a person's reality before and after psychotherapy, between a "straight" acquiring membership in the reality of drug freaks, or before and after becoming a competent religious healer, are all the same. The differences are "merely" methodological, not theoretical. Studying each passage, I would concentrate on how the reflexive, knowledge, interactional, and fragility features affect the shift.

All realities are permeable. Ethnomethodology is a reality. This book is an attempt to breach the reader's present reality by introducing him to the "certainty of a minimal possibility" that another reality exists.

On the Concept of Reality

Many ethnomethodologists rely on Schutz's concept of reality (e.g., 1962, 1964, 1966). . . . My use of "reality" contrasts with Schutz's view. For Schutz (e.g., 1962, p. 208ff.), the reality of everyday life is the *one* paramount reality. Schutz says that this paramount reality consists of a number of presuppositions or assumptions, which include the assumption of a tacit, taken for granted world; an assumed practical interest in that world; and an assumption that the world is intersubjective (e.g., 1962, p. 23). Schutz argues that other realities exist, but that they derive from the paramount reality. For example, he discusses the realities of "scientific theorizing" and of "fantasy." These realities appear when some of the basic assumptions of the paramount reality are temporarily suspended. The paramount reality of everyday life has an elastic quality for Schutz. After excursions into other realities, we snap back into the everyday.

My view of realities is different. I do not wish to call one or another reality paramount. It is my contention that every reality is equally real. No single reality contains more of the truth than any other. From the perspective of Western everyday life, Western everyday life will appear paramount, just as Schutz maintains. But from the perspective of scientific theorizing or dreaming, or meditating, each of these realities will appear just as paramount. Because every reality exhibits the absolutist tendency I mentioned earlier, there is no way to look from the window of one reality at others without seeing yourself. Schutz seems to be a victim of this absolutist prejudice. As a Western man living his life in the Western daily experience, he assumed that this life was the touchstone of all realities.

My concept of reality, then, has more in common with Wittgenstein (1953) than with Schutz. Wittgenstein (e.g., 1953, pp. 61, 179) recognizes that human life exhibits an empirical multitude of activities. He calls these activities language games. Language games are forever being invented and modified and discarded. The fluidity of language activities do not permit rigorous description. Analysts can discover that at any time a number of language games are associated with one another. This association, too, is not amenable to rigorous description. Instead, language games exhibit "family resemblances." One can recognize certain games going together. But one could no more articulate *the* criteria for this resemblance than one could predict the physical characteristics of some unseen member of a familiar extended family. Wittgenstein (1953, pp. 119, 123) calls a collection of language games bound together by a family resemblance, a *form of life*.[7] Forms of life resemble what I call "realities." Realities are far more aswarm than Schutz's terms "finite" and "province" suggest. Forms of life are always forms of life forming.[8] Realities are always realities becoming.

Notes

1. See Pollner's (1970, 1973) discussions of the reflexive reasoning of the Azande, and Polanyi's (1958, pp. 287-294) examination of the same materials. In the Apostolic Church of John Marangue, illness is not bodily malfunction, it is sin. Sin is curable not by medicine, but by confessional healing. When evangelists' attempts to heal church members were not accompanied by recovery, Jules-Rosette (1973, p. 167) reports that church members did not lose their faith in the confessional process. They looked to other "causes" of the "failure." They said things like: Other persons must have been implicated in the sin, and untrue confession must have been given. Once again, contradictions that could potentially challenge a basic faith do not, as the basic faith itself is not questioned.

2. See Gurwitsch (1966) for a more technical discussion of the object constancy assumption. Later in this chapter . . . I show that the object constancy assumption is not a belief that exists in the head. A body of interactional work is required to achieve a constant world.

3. The pen-not pen and planet-star examples are adapted from Pollner (1973). Much of this discussion of reflexivity derives from Pollner's thinking on these matters.

4. Riel (1972) illustrates how talk reflexively constitutes the context it then seems to independently reference. Trying to make a certain point, she reports turning away from an inadequate sentence she had written to explore notes and texts again. Forty-five minutes later she wrote the now-perfect sentence, only to discover it was exactly the same sentence she had rejected before.

5. Cicourel (1968) examines the interactional work that accomplishes external objects in greater detail. He shows that juvenile delinquents and crime rates are constituted by the social activities of law enforcement personnel.

6. For an account of a reality shift in the other direction, from the stone age to industrial Western society, see Kroeber's *Ishi in Two Worlds* (1961). Again the transition was never total, but this was a result of a political decision on the part of the author's husband. As Ishi's official keeper, he wished to keep him primitive for his own and anthropology's benefit.

7. Blum (1970) has previously explored the importance of Wittgenstein's notion of "form of life" for social science.

8. This phrase, like much of this chapter, has been adapted from the unpublished lectures of Pollner. For Pollner's published writings see Zimmerman and Pollner, 1970; and Pollner, 1970, 1973, 1974.

References

Blum, A. (1970). Theorizing. In J. D. Douglas (Ed.), *Understanding everyday life*. Chicago: Aldine.

Castaneda, C. (1968). *The teachings of Don Juan*. Berkeley: University of California Press.

Castaneda, C. (1971). *A separate reality*. New York: Simon & Schuster.

Castaneda, C. (1972). *A journey to Iztlan*. New York: Simon & Schuster.

Chomsky, N. (1965). *Aspects of the theory of syntax*. Cambridge, MA: MIT Press.

Cicourel, A. V. (1968). *The social organization of juvenile justice*. New York: John Wiley.

Cicourel, A. V. (1973). *Cognitive sociology*. London: Macmillan.

Evans-Pritchard, E. E. (1937). *Witchcraft, oracles and magic among the Azande*. London: Oxford University Press.

Garfinkel, H. (1952). *Perception of the other*. Unpublished Ph.D. dissertation, Harvard University.

Garfinkel, H. (1963). A conception of and experiments with "trust" as a condition of concerted stable actions. In O. J. Harvey (Ed.), *Motivation and social interaction*. New York: Ronald.

Garfinkel, H. (1964). Studies of the routine grounds of everyday activities. *Social Problems, 11*, 225-250 (Chapter 2 in Garfinkel, 1967).

Garfinkel, H. (1967). *Studies in ethnomethodology*. New York: Prentice-Hall.

Gasking, D. (1955). Mathematics and the world. In A. Flew (Ed.), *Logic and language*. Garden City, NY: Doubleday.

Gurwitsch, A. (1966). *Studies in phenomenology and psychology*. Evanston, IL: Northwestern University Press.

Jules-Rosette, B. (1973). *Ritual context and social action*. Unpublished Ph.D. dissertation. Harvard University.

Kroeber, T. (1961). *Ishi in two worlds.* Berkeley: University of California Press.

Kuhn, T. S. (1970). *The structure of scientific revolutions.* Chicago: University of Chicago Press.

Polanyi, M. (1958). *Personal knowledge.* Chicago: University of Chicago Press.

Pollner, M. (1970). *On the foundations of mundane reason.* Unpublished Ph.D. dissertation. University of California, Santa Barbara.

Pollner, M. (1973). *The very coinage of your brain: The resolution of reality disjunctures.* Unpublished manuscript.

Pollner, M. (1974). Mundane reasoning. *Philosophy of social sciences, 4*(1), 35-54.

Reich, C. A. (1970). *The greening of America.* New York: Random House.

Riel, M. M. (1972). *The interpretive process.* Paper presented to a seminar led by Paul Filmer, University of California, San Diego.

Roszak, T. (1969). *The making of a counter culture.* Garden City, NY: Doubleday.

Sacks, H., Schegloff, E., & Jefferson, G. (1974). A simplest systematics for the analysis of turn taking in conversation. *Language, 50,* 696-735.

Schneebaum, T. (1969). *Keep the river on your right.* New York: Grove.

Schutz, A. (1962). *Collected papers I: The problem of social reality.* The Hague: Martinus Nijhoff.

Schutz, A. (1964). *Collected papers II: Studies in social theory.* The Hague: Martinus Nijhoff.

Schutz, A. (1966). *Collected papers III: Studies in phenomenological philosophy.* The Hague: Martinus Nijhoff.

Wallace, H. T. (1972). *Culture and social being.* Unpublished master's thesis, University of California, Santa Barbara.

Wieder, D. L. (1970). Meaning by rule. In J. D. Douglas (Ed.), *Understanding everyday life.* Chicago: Aldine.

Wieder, D. L. (1973). *Language and social reality.* The Hague: Mouton.

Wittgenstein, L. (1953). *Philosophical investigations.* London: Basil Blackwell & Mott.

Wittgenstein, L. (1961). *Tractatus logico-philosphicus.* London: Basil Blackwell & Mott. (Original work published in 1921)

Wood, H. (1968). *The labelling process on a mental hospital ward.* Unpublished master's thesis. University of California, Santa Barbara.

Zimmerman, D. H. (1973). Preface. In D. L. Wieder, *Language and social reality.* The Hague: Mouton.

Zimmerman, D. H., & Pollner, M. (1970). The everyday world as a phenomenon. In J. D. Douglas (Ed.), *Understanding everyday life.* Chicago: Aldine.

Zimmerman, D. H., & Wieder, D. L. (n.d.). *The social bases for illegal behavior in the student community: First year report.* San Francisco and Santa Barbara: Scientific Analysis Corporation.

32

A Conception of and Experiments With "Trust" as a Condition of Concerted Stable Actions

Harold Garfinkel

Some Preliminary Trials and Findings

Since each of the presuppositions that make up the attitude of daily life assigns an expected feature to the actor's environment, it should be possible to induce experimentally a breach of these expectancies by deliberately modifying scenic events so as to disappoint these attributions. By definition, surprise is possible with respect to each of these expected features. The nastiness of surprise should vary directly with the extent to which the actor complies with the constitutive order of events of everyday life as a scheme for assigning witnessed appearances their status of events in a perceivedly normal environment.

Procedures were used to see if a breach of these presuppositions would produce anomic effects and increase disorganization. These procedures must be thought of as demonstrations rather than as experiments. "Experimenters" were upper division students in the author's courses. Their training consisted of little more than verbal instructions about how to proceed. The demonstrations were done as class assignments

"A Conception of and Experiments With 'Trust' as a Condition of Concerted Stable Actions " by H. Garfinkel from *Motivation and Social Interaction* (pp. 220-235), edited by O. J. Harvey, 1963. Reprinted by permission of the author.

and were unsupervised. Students reported their results in anecdotal fashion with no controls beyond the fact that they were urged to avoid interpretation in favor of writing down what was actually said and done, staying as close as possible to a chronological account.

Because the procedures nevertheless produced massive effects, I feel they are worth reporting. Obviously, however, caution must be exercised in assessing the findings.

Demonstration 1: Breaching the Congruency of Relevances

This expectancy consists of the following. The person expects, expects that the other person does the same, and expects that as he expects it of the other the other expects the like of him that the differences in their perspectives that originate in their particular individual biographies are irrelevant for the purposes at hand of each and that both have selected and interpreted the actually and potentially common objects in an "empirically identical" manner that is sufficient for the purposes at hand. Thus, for example, in talking about "matters just known in common" persons will discuss them using a course of utterances that are governed by the expectation that the other person *will* understand. The speaker expects that the other person will assign to his remarks the sense intended by the speaker and expects that thereby the other person will permit the speaker the assumption that both know what he is talking about without any requirement of a check-out. Thus the sensible character of the matter that is being discussed is settled by a fiat assignment that each expects to make, and expects the other to make in reciprocal fashion, that as a condition of his right to decide without interference that he knows what he is talking about and that what he is talking about is so, each will have furnished whatever unstated understandings are required. Much therefore that is being talked about is not mentioned, although each expects that the adequate sense of the matter being talked about is settled. The more so is this the case, the more is the exchange one of commonplace remarks among persons who "know" each other.

Students were instructed to engage an acquaintance or friend in an ordinary conversation and, without indicating that what the experimenter was saying was in any way out of the ordinary, to insist that the person clarify the sense of his commonplace remarks. Twenty-three students reported twenty-five instances of such encounters. The following are typical excerpts from their accounts.

Case 1. The subject was telling the experimenter, a member of the subject's car pool, about having had a flat tire while going to work the previous day.

(S): "I had a flat tire."
(E): "What do you mean, you had a flat tire?"

She appeared momentarily stunned. Then she answered in a hostile way: "What do you mean? What do you mean? A flat tire is a flat tire. That is what I meant. Nothing special. What a crazy question!"

Case 2. (S): "Hi, Ray. How is your girl friend feeling?"

(E): "What do you mean, how is she feeling? Do you mean physical or mental?"

(S): "I mean how is she feeling? What's the matter with you?" (He looked peeved.)
(E): "Nothing. Just explain a little clearer, what do you mean?"
(S): "Skip it. How are your Med School applications coming?"
(E): "What do you mean, 'How are they?' "
(S): "You know what I mean."
(E): "I really don't."
(S): "What's the matter with you? Are you sick?"

Case 3. On Friday night my husband and I were watching television. My husband remarked that he was tired. I asked, "How are you tired? Physically, mentally, or just bored?"

(S): "I don't know, I guess physically, mainly."
(E): "You mean that your muscles ache, or your bones?"
(S): "I guess so. Don't be so technical."
(S): (After more watching) "All these old movies have the same kind of old iron bedstead in them."
(E): "What do you mean? Do you mean all old movies, or some of them, or just the ones you have seen?"
(S): "What's the matter with you? You know what I mean."
(E): "I wish you would be more specific."
(S): "You know what I mean! Drop dead!"

Case 4. During a conversation (with the male E's fiancee) the E questioned the meaning of various words used by the subject. For the first minute and a half the subject responded to the questions as if they were legitimate inquiries. Then she responded with "Why are you asking me these questions?" and repeated this two or three times after each question. She became nervous and jittery, her face and hand movements . . . uncontrolled. She appeared bewildered and complained that I was making her nervous and demanded that I "Stop it!" . . . The subject picked up a magazine and covered her face. She put down the magazine and pretended to be engrossed. When asked why she was looking at the magazine, she closed her mouth and refused any further remarks.

Case 5. My friend said to me, "Hurry or we will be late." I asked him what did he mean by late and from what point of view did it have reference. There was a look of perplexity and cynicism on his face. "Why are you asking me such silly questions? Surely I don't have to explain such a statement. What is wrong with you today? Why should I have to stop to analyze such a statement. Everyone understands my statements and you should be no exception."

Case 6. The victim waved his hand cheerily.

(S): "How are you?"
(E): "How am I in regard to what? My health, my finance, my school work, my peace of mind, my . . . "
(S): (Red in the face and suddenly out of control.) "Look! I was just trying to be polite. Frankly, I don't give a damn how you are."

Case 7. My friend and I were talking about a man whose overbearing attitude annoyed us. My friend expressed his feeling.

(S): "I'm sick of him."
(E): "Would you explain what is wrong with you that you are sick?"
(S): "Are you kidding me? You know what I mean."
(E): "Please explain your ailment."
(S): (He listened to me with a puzzled look.) "What came over you? We never talk this way, do we?"

Case 8. Apparently as a casual afterthought, my husband mentioned Friday night, "Did you remember to drop off my shirts today?"

Taking nothing for granted, I replied, "I remember that you said something about it this morning. What shirts did you mean, and what did you mean by having them 'dropped' off?" He looked puzzled, as though I must have answered some other question than the one asked.

Instead of making the explanation he seemed to be waiting for, I persisted, "I thought your shirts were all in pretty good shape; why not keep them a little longer?" I had the uncomfortable feeling I had overplayed the part.

He no longer looked puzzled, but indignant. He repeated, "A little longer! What do you mean, and what have you done with my shirts?"

I acted indignant too. I asked, "What shirts? You have sport shirts, plain shirts, wool shirts, regular shirts, and dirty shirts. I'm no mind reader. What exactly did you want?"

My husband again looked confused, as though he was trying to justify my behavior. He seemed simultaneously to be on the defensive and offensive. He assumed a very patient, tolerant air, and said, "Now, let's start all over again. Did you drop off my shirts today?"

I replied, "I heard you before. It's your meaning I wish was more clear. As far as I am concerned dropping off your shirts—whichever shirts you mean—could mean giving them to the Goodwill, leaving them at the cleaners, at the laundromat, or throwing them out. I never know what you mean with those vague statements."

He reflected on what I said, then changed the entire perspective by acting as though we were playing a game, that it was all a joke. He seemed to enjoy the joke. He ruined my approach by assuming the role I thought was mine. He then said, "Well, let's take this step by step with 'yes' or 'no' answers. Did you see the dirty shirts I left on the kitchenette, yes or no?"

I could see no way to complicate his question, so felt forced to answer "Yes." In the same fashion, he asked if I picked up the shirts; if I put them in the car; if I left them at the laundry; and if I did all these things that day, Friday. My answers were "Yes."

The experiment, it seemed to me, had been cut short by his reducing all the parts of his previous question to their simplest terms, which were given to me as if I were a child unable to handle any complex questions, problems, or situations.

Demonstration 2: Breaching the Interchangeability of Standpoints

In order to breach the presupposed interchangeability of standpoints, students were asked to enter a store, to select a customer, and to treat the customer as a clerk while giving no recognition that the subject was any other person than the experimenter took him to be and without giving any indication that the experimenter's treatment was anything other than perfectly reasonable and legitimate.

Case 1. One evening, while shopping at Sears with a friend, I (male) found myself next to a woman shopping at the copper-clad pan section. The store was busy . . . and clerks were hard to find. The woman was just a couple of feet away and my friend was behind me. Pointing to a tea kettle, I asked the woman if she did not think the price was rather high. I asked in a friendly tone. . . . She looked at me and then at the kettle and said "Yes." I then said I was going to take it anyway. She said, "Oh," and started to move sideways away from me. I quickly asked her if she was not going to wrap it for me and take my cash. Still moving slowly away and glancing first at me, then at the kettle, then at the other pans farther away from me, she said the clerk was "over there" pointing off somewhere. In a harsh tone, I asked if she was not going to wait on me. She said, "No, No, I'm not the saleslady. There she is." I said that I knew that the extra help was inexperienced, but there was no reason not to wait on a customer. "Just wait on me. I'll be patient." With that, she flushed with anger and walked rapidly away, looking back once as if to ask if it could really be true.

The following three protocols are the work of a forty-year-old female graduate student in clinical psychology.

Case 2. We went to V's book store, noted not so much for its fine merchandise and its wide range of stock as it is in certain circles for the fact that the clerks are male homosexuals. I approached a gentleman who was browsing at a table stacked neatly with books.

(E): "I'm in a hurry. Would you get a copy of *Sociopathic Behavior* by Lemert, please?"

(S): (Looked E up and down, drew himself very straight, slowly laid the book down, stepped back slightly, then leaned forward and in a low voice said) "I'm interested in sociopathic behavior, too. That's why I'm here. I study the fellows here by pretending to be . . . "

(E): (Interrupting) "I'm not particularly interested in whether you are or are only pretending to be. Please just get the book I asked for."

(S): (Looked shocked. More than surprised, believe me. Stepped around the display table, deliberately placed his hands on the books, leaned forward and shouted) "I don't have such a book. I'm not a clerk! I'm—Well!" (Stalked out of the store.)

Case 3. When we entered I. Magnin's there was one woman who was fingering a sweater, the only piece of merchandise to be seen in the shop. I surmised that the clerk must be in the stockroom.

(E): "That is a lovely shade, but I'm looking for one a little lighter. Do you have one in cashmere?"

(S): "I really don't know, you see I'm . . . "

(E): (Interrupting) "Oh, you are new here? I don't mind waiting while you look for what I want."

(S): "Indeed I shall not!"

(E): "But aren't you here to *serve* customers?"

(S): "I'm not! I'm here to . . . "

(E): (Interrupts) "This is hardly the place for such an attitude. Now please show me a cashmere sweater a shade or two lighter than this one."
(The clerk entered.)

(S): (To clerk) "My dear, this—(pointed her face toward E)—*person* insists on being shown a sweater. Please take care of her while I compose myself. I want to be certain this (sweater) will do, and she (pointed her face again at E) is so *insistent*." (S carried the sweater with her, walked haughtily to a large upholstered chair, sat in it, brushed her gloved hands free from imaginary dirt, jerked her shoulders, fluffed her suit jacket, and glared at E).

Case 4. While visiting with a friend in Pasadena, I told him about this being-taken-for-the-clerk-experiment. The friend is a Professor Emeritus of Mathematics at the California Institute of Technology and the successful author of many books, some technical, some fictional, and he is most satirical in his contemplations of his fellow man. He begged to be allowed to accompany me and to aid me in the selection of scenes. . . . We went first to have luncheon at the Atheneum, which caters to the students, faculty and guests of Cal Tech. While we were still in the lobby, my host pointed out a gentleman who was standing in the large drawing room near the entrance to the dining room and said, "Go to it. There's a good subject for you." He stepped aside to watch. I walked toward the man very deliberately and proceeded as follows. (I will use E to designate myself; S, the subject.)

(E): "I should like a table on the west side, a quiet spot, if you please. And what is on the menu?"

(S): (Turned toward E but looked past and in the direction of the foyer) said, "Eh, ah, madam, I'm sure." (looked past E again, looked at a pocket watch, replaced it, and looked toward the dining room).

(E): "Surely luncheon hours are not over. What do you recommend I order today?"

(S): "I don't know. You see, I'm waiting . . ."

(E): (Interrupted with) "Please don't keep me standing here while you wait. Kindly show me to a table."

(S): "But Madam,—" (started to edge away from door, and back into the lounge in a lightly curving direction around E)

(E): "My good man—" (At this S's face flushed, his eyes rounded and opened wide.)

(S): "But—you—I—oh dear!" (He seemed to wilt.)

(E): (Took S's arm in hand and propelled him toward the dining room door, slightly ahead of herself.)

(S): (Walked slowly but stopped just within the room, turned around and for the first time looked directly and very appraisingly at E, took out the watch, looked at it, held it to his ear, replaced it, and muttered) "Oh dear."

(E): "It will take only a minute for you to show me to a table and take my order. Then you can return to wait for your customers. After all, I am a guest and a customer, too."

(S): (Stiffened slightly, walked jerkily toward the nearest empty table, held a chair for E to be seated, bowed slightly, muttered "My pleasure," hurried toward the door, stopped, turned, looked back at E with a blank facial expression.)

At this point E's host walked up to S, greeted him, shook hands, and propelled him toward E's table. S stopped a few steps from the table, looked directly at, then through E, and started to walk back toward the door. Host told him E was the young lady whom he had invited to join them at lunch (then introduced me to one of the big names in the physics world, a pillar of the institution!). S seated himself reluctantly and perched rigidly on his chair, obviously uncomfortable. E smiled, made light and polite inquiries about his work, mentioned various functions attended which had honored him, then complacently remarked that it was a shame E had not met him personally before now, so that she should not have mistaken him for the maître-d'. The host chattered about his long-time friendship with me, while S fidgeted and looked again at his pocket watch, wiped his forehead with a table napkin, looked at E but avoided meeting her eyes. When the host mentioned that E is studying sociology at UCLA, S suddenly burst into loud laughter, realized that everyone in the room was looking in the direction of our table, abruptly became quiet, then said to E "You mistook me for the maître-d', didn't you?"

(E): "Deliberately, sir."

(S): "Why deliberately?"

(E): "You have just been used as the unsuspecting subject in an experiment."

(S): "Diabolic. But clever, I must say (To our host) I haven't been so shaken since ——— denounced my theory of ——— in 19——. And the wild thoughts that ran through my mind! Call the receptionist from the lobby, go to the men's room, turn this woman to the first person that comes along. Damn these early diners, there's nobody coming in at this time. Time is standing still, or my watch has stopped. I will talk to ——— about this, make sure it doesn't happen to 'somebody.' Damn a persistent woman. I'm not her 'good man!' I'm Dr. ———, and not to be pushed around. This can't be happening. If I do take her to that damned table she wants, I can get away from her, and I'll just take it easy until I can. I remember ——— (hereditary psychopath, wife of one of the 'family' of the institution) maybe if I do what *this* one wants she will not make any more trouble than this. I wonder if she is 'off.' She certainly looks normal. Wonder how you can really tell?"

Demonstration 3: Breaching the Expectancy That a Knowledge of a Relationship of Interaction Is a Commonly Entertained Scheme of Communication

Schutz proposed that from the member's point of view, an event of conduct, like a move in a game, consists of an event-in-a-social-order. Thus, for the member, its recognizably real character is furnished by attending its occurrence with respect to a corpus of socially sanctioned knowledge of the social relationships that the member uses and assumes that others use as the same scheme of expression and interpretation.

It was decided to breach this expectancy by having students treat a situation as something that it "obviously" and "really" was not. Students were instructed to spend from fifteen minutes to an hour in their own homes acting as if they were boarders. They were instructed to conduct themselves in a circumspect and polite fashion: to avoid getting personal; to use formal address; to speak only when they were spoken to.

In nine of forty-nine cases students either refused to do the assignment (five cases) or the try was "unsuccessful" (four cases). Four of the "no try" students said they were afraid to do it; a fifth said she preferred to avoid the risk of exciting her mother who had a heart condition. In two of the "unsuccessful" cases the family treated it as a joke from the beginning and refused, despite the continuing actions of the student experimenter, to change. A third family took the view that something of an undisclosed sort was the matter, but what it might be was of no concern to them. In the fourth family the father and mother remarked that the daughter was being "extra nice" and undoubtedly wanted something that she would shortly reveal.

In the remaining four-fifths of the cases family members were stupefied, vigorously sought to make the strange actions intelligible, and to restore the situation to normal appearances. Reports were filled with accounts of astonishment, bewilderment, shock, anxiety, embarrassment, and anger as well as with charges by various family members that the student was mean, inconsiderate, selfish, nasty, and impolite. Family members demanded explanations: "What's the matter?" "What's gotten into you?" "Did you get fired?" "Are you sick?" "What are you being so superior about?" "Why are you mad?" "Are you out of your mind or are you just stupid?" One student acutely embarrassed his mother in front of her friends by asking if she minded if he had a snack from the refrigerator. "Mind if you have a little snack? You've been eating little snacks around here for years without asking me. What's gotten into you!" One mother, infuriated when her daughter spoke to her only when she was spoken to, began to shriek in angry denunciation of the daughter for her disrespect and insubordination and refused to be calmed by the student's sister. A father berated his daughter for being insufficiently concerned for the welfare of others and of acting like a spoiled child.

Occasionally family members would first treat the student's action as a cue for a joint comedy routine which was soon replaced by irritation and exasperated anger at the student for not knowing "when enough was enough." Family members mocked the "politeness" of the students—"Certainly Mr. Dinerberg!"—or charged the student with acting like a wise guy and generally reproved the "politeness" with sarcasm.

Explanations were sought in terms of understandable and previous motives of the student: the accusation that the student was covering up something important that the family should know; that the student was working too hard in school; that the student was ill; that there had been "another fight" with a fiancee.

Unacknowledged explanations were followed by withdrawal of the offended member, attempted isolation of the culprit, retaliation, and denunciation. "Don't bother with him, he's in one of his moods again." "Pay no attention but just wait until he asks me for something." "You're cutting me, okay. I'll cut you and then some." "Why must you always create friction in our family harmony?" A father followed his son into the bedroom. "Your mother is right. You don't look well and you're not talking sense. You had better get another job that doesn't require such late hours." To this the student replied that he appreciated his consideration, but that he felt fine and only wanted a little privacy. The father responded in high rage, "I don't want any more of *that* out of *you*. And if you can't treat your mother decently, you'd better move out!"

There were no cases in which the situation was not restorable upon the student's explanation. Nevertheless, for the most part, family members were not amused and only rarely did they find the experience instructive, as the student argued that it was supposed to have been. After hearing the explanation, a sister replied coldly on behalf of a family of four, "Please, no more of these experiments. We're not rats you know." Occasionally an explanation was accepted and still it added offense. In several cases students reported that the explanation left them, their families, or both wondering how much of what the student had said was "in character" and how much the student "really meant."

Students found the assignment difficult to complete because of not being treated as if they were in the role that they are attempting to play and of being confronted with situations to which they did not know how a boarder would respond.

There were several entirely unexpected results. (1) Although many students reported extensive rehearsals in imagination, very few of those that did it mentioned anticipatory fears or embarrassment. (2) Although unanticipated and nasty developments frequently occurred, in only one case did a student report serious regrets. (3) Very few students reported heartfelt relief when the hour was over. They were much more likely to report a partial relief. They frequently reported that in response to the anger of others they became angry in return and slipped easily into subjectively recognizable feelings and actions.

Demonstration 4: Breaching the Grasp of "What Anyone Knows" to Be Correct Grounds of Action of a Real Social World

Among the possibilities that a premedical student could treat as correct grounds for his further inferences and actions about such matters as how a medical school intake interview is conducted or how an applicant's conduct is related to his chances of admission, certain ones (e.g., that deferring to the interviewer's interests is a condition for making a favorable impression) he treats as matters that he is required to know and act upon as a condition of his competence as a premedical candidate. He expects others like him to know and act upon the same things; and he expects that as he expects others to know and act upon them, the others in turn expect the like of him.

A procedure was designed to breach the constitutive expectancies attached to "what-any-competent-premedical-candidate-knows" while satisfying the three conditions under which their breach would presumably produce confusion.

Twenty-eight premedical students of the University of California in Los Angeles were run individually through a three-hour experimental interview. As part of the solicitation of subjects, as well as the beginning of the interview, E identified himself as a representative of an Eastern medical school who was attempting to learn why the medical school intake interview was such a stressful situation. It was hoped that identifying E as a person with medical school ties would minimize the chance that students would "leave the field" once the accent breaching procedure began. How the other two conditions of (a) managing a redefinition in insufficient time and (b) not being able to count on consensual support for an alternative definition of social reality were met will be apparent in the following description.

During the first hour of the interview, the student furnished the facts-of-life about interviews for admission to medical school by answering for the "representative" such questions as "What sources of information about a candidate are available to medical schools?" "What can a medical school learn about a candidate from these sources?" "What kind of a man are the emotional schools looking for?" "What should a good candidate do in the interview?" "What should he avoid?" With this much completed, the student was told that the "representative's" research interests had been satisfied. The student was asked if he would care to hear a recording of an actual interview. All students wanted very much to hear the recording.

The recording was a faked one between a "medical school interviewer" and an "applicant." The applicant was depicted as being a boor; his language was ungrammatical and filled with colloquialisms; he was evasive; he contradicted the interviewer; he bragged; he ran down other schools and professions; he insisted on knowing how he had done in the interview and so on.

Detailed assessments by the student of the recorded applicant were obtained immediately after the recording was finished. The following edited assessment is representative:

I didn't like it. I didn't like his attitude. I didn't like anything about him. Everything he said grated the wrong way. I didn't like his smoking. The way he kept saying "Yeah-h!" He didn't show that he realized that the interviewer had his future in his hands. I didn't like the vague way he answered questions. I didn't like the way he pressed at the end of the interview. He was disrespectful. His motives were too obvious. He made a mess of it. He finished with a bang to say the least. . . . His answers to questions were stupid. I felt that the interviewer was telling him that he wasn't going to get in. I didn't like the interview. I felt it was too informal. To a degree it's good if it's natural but . . . the interview is not something to breeze through. It's just not the place for chit-chat. He had fairly good grades but . . . he's not interested in things outside of school and didn't say what he did *in* school. Then he didn't *do* very much—outside of this lab. I didn't like the man at all. I never met an applicant like that! "My pal"—Just one of these little chats. I never met anybody *like* that. Wrong-way Corrigan.

The student was then given information from the applicant's "official record." This information was deliberately contrived to contradict the principal points in the student's assessment. For example, if the student said that the applicant must have come from a lower class family, he was told that the applicant's father was vice president of a firm that manufactured pneumatic doors for trains and buses. If the applicant had been thought to be ignorant, he was described as having excelled in courses like The Poetry of Milton and Dramas of Shakespeare. If the student said the applicant did not know how to get along with people, then the applicant was pictured as having worked as a voluntary solicitor for Sydenham Hospital in New York City and had raised $32,000 from thirty "big givers." The belief that the applicant was stupid and would not do well in a scientific field was met by citing A grades in organic and physical chemistry and graduate level performance in an undergraduate research course.

The Ss wanted very much to know what "the others" thought of the applicant, and had he been admitted? The "others" had been previously and casually identified by the "representative" as "Dr. Gardner, the medical school interviewer," "six psychiatrically trained members of the admissions committee who heard only the recorded interview," and "other students I talked to."

The S was told that the applicant had been admitted and was living up to the promise that the medical school interviewer and the "six psychiatrists" had found and expressed in the following recommendation of the applicant's characterological fitness.

Dr. Gardner, the medical school interviewer, wrote, "A well-bred, polite young man, poised, affable, and self-confident. Capable of independent thinking. Interests of a rather specialized character. Marked intellectual curiosity. Alert and free of emotional disturbances. Marked maturity of manner and outlook. Meets others easily. Strongly motivated toward a medical career. Definite ideas of what he wants to achieve which are held in good perspective. Unquestioned sincerity and integrity. Expressed himself easily and well. Recommend favorable consideration." The six psychiatric members of the admissions committee agreed in all essentials.

Concerning the views of "other students," S was told that he was, for example, the thirtieth student I had seen; that twenty-eight before him were in entire agreement with the medical school interviewer's assessment; and that the remaining two had been slightly uncertain but at the first bit of information had seen him just as the others had.

Following this, Ss were invited to listen to the record a second time, after which they were asked to assess the applicant again.

Results. Twenty-five of the twenty-eight subjects were taken in. The following does not apply to the three who were convinced there was a deception. Two of these are discussed at the conclusion of this section.

Incongruous materials, presented to S in the order indicated, were performance information, and characterological information. Performance information dealt with the applicant's activities, grades, family background, courses, charity work, and the like. Characterological information consisted of character assessments of him by the "medical school interviewers," the "six psychiatrically trained members of the admissions committee," and the "other students."

Subjects managed incongruities of performance data with vigorous attempts to make it factually compatible with their original assessments. For example, when they said that the applicant sounded like a lower class person, they were told that his father was vice-president of a national corporation that manufactured pneumatic doors for trains and buses. Here are some typical replies:

"He should have made the point that he *could* count on money."

"That explains why he said he had to work. Probably his father made him work. That would make a lot of his moans unjustified in the sense that things were really not so bad."

"What does that have to do with values?!"

"You could tell from his answers. You could tell that he was used to having his own way."

"That's something the interviewer knew that *I* didn't know."

"Then he's an out and out liar!"

When Ss said that the applicant was selfish and could not get along with people, they were told that he had worked as a volunteer for Sydenham Hospital and had raised $32,000 from thirty "big givers."

"He seems to be a good salesman. So possibly he's missing his profession. I'd say *definitely* he's missing his profession!"

"They probably contributed because of the charity and not because they were solicited."

"Pretty good. Swell. Did he know them personally?"

"It's very fashionable to work, for example, during the war for Bundles for Britain. So that doesn't—definitely!—show altruistic motives at all. He is a person who is subject to fashion and I'm very critical of that sort of thing.

"He's so forceful he might have shamed them into giving."

"People who are wealthy—his father would naturally see those people—big contributions—they could give a lot of money and not know what they're giving it for."

That he had a straight A average in physical science courses began to draw bewilderment.

"He took quite a variety of courses . . . I'm baffled.—Probably the interview wasn't a very good mirror of his character."

"He did seem to take some odd courses. They seem to be fairly normal. Not normal—but—It doesn't strike me one way or the other."

"Well! I think you can analyze it this way. In psychological terms. See—one possible way—now I may be all *wet* but this is the way I look at *that*. He probably suffered from an inferiority complex and that's an overcompensation for his inferiority complex. His *great* marks—his *good* marks are a compensation for his failure—in social dealings perhaps, I don't know."

"Woops! And only third alternate at Georgia. (Deep sigh) I can see why he'd feel resentment about not being admitted to Phi Bet."

(Long silence) "Well! From what—that leads me to think he's a grind or something like that."

Attempts to resolve the incongruities produced by the character assessment of "Gardner" and "the other six judges" were much less frequent than normalizing attempts with performance information. Open expressions of bewilderment and anxiety interspersed with silent ruminations were characteristic.

(Laugh) "Golly!" (Silence) "I'd think it would be the other way around."—(Very subdued) "Maybe I'm all wro—My orientation is all off. I'm completely baffled."

"Not polite. Self-confident he certainly was. But not polite—I don't know. Either the interviewer was a little crazy or else I am." (Long pause) "That's rather shocking. It makes me have doubts about my own thinking. Perhaps my values in life are wrong. I don't know."

(Whistles) "I—I didn't think he sounded well bred at all. That whole tone of voice!!—I—Perhaps you noticed though, when he said 'You should have said in the first place' before he took it with a smile.—But even so! No, no I can't see that. 'You should have said that before.' Maybe he was being funny though. Exercising a—No! To me it sounded impertinent!"

"Ugh—Well, that certainly puts a different slant on my conception of interviews. Gee—that—confuses me all the more."

"Well—(laugh)—Hhh!—Ugh! Well, maybe he looked like a nice boy. He did—he did get his point across.—Perhaps—seeing the person would make a big difference.—Or perhaps I would never make a good interviewer." (Reflectively and al-most inaudibly) "They didn't mention any of the things I mentioned." (HG: Eh?) (Louder) "They didn't mention any of the things I mentioned and so I feel like a complete failure."

Soon after the performance data produced its consternation, an occasional request would be made: "What did the other students make of him?" Only after Gardner's assessment, and the responses to it had been made were the opinions of the "other students" given. In some cases the subject was told "34 out of 35 before you," in others 43 out of 45, 19 out of 20, 51 out of 52. All the numbers were large. For 18 of the 25 students the delivery hardly varied from the following verbatim protocols:

[34 out of 35] I don't know.—I still stick to my original convictions. I—I—Can you tell *me* what—I saw wrong. Maybe—I—I had the wrong idea—the wrong attitude all along. (Can you tell me? I'm interested that there should be such a disparity.) Definitely. —I—think—it would be definitely the other way—I can't make sense of it. I'm completely baffled, believe me. —I—I don't understand how I could have been so wrong. Maybe my ideas—my evaluations of people are—just twisted. I mean maybe I had the wrong—maybe my sense of values—is—off—or—different—from the other 33. But I don't think that's the case—because usually—and in all modesty I say this—I—I can judge people. I mean in class, in organizations I belong to—I usually judge them right. So therefore I don't understand at *all* how I could have been so wrong. I don't think I was under any stress or strain—here—tonight but—I don't understand it.

[43 out of 45] [Laugh] I don't know what to say now. —I'm troubled by my inability to judge the guy better than that. [Subdued] I shall sleep tonight, certainly—[Very subdued] but it certainly bothers me. —Sorry that I didn't—*Well!* One question that arises—I may be wrong—(Can you see how they might have seen him?) No. No, I can't see it, no. —Sure with all that background material, yes, but I don't see how Gardner did it without it. Well, I guess that makes Gardner, Gardner, and me, me. (The other 45 students didn't have the background material.) Yeah, yeah, yeah. I mean I'm not denying it at all. I mean for myself, there's no sense saying—Of course! With their background they would be accepted, especially the second man, good God! —Okay, what else?

[23 out of 25] [Softly] Maybe I'm tired. (HG, "Eh?") [Burst of laughter.] Maybe I didn't get enough sleep last night. —Uhh! —Well—I might not have been looking for the things that the other men were looking for. —I wasn't—Huh! —It puts me at a loss, really.

[10 out of 10] So I'm alone in my judgment. I don't know sir! I don't know, sir!! —I can't explain it. It's senseless. —I tried to be impartial at the beginning. I admit I was prejudiced immediately.

[51 out of 52] You mean that 51 others stuck to their guns, too? (Stuck to their guns in the sense that they saw him just as the judges saw him.) Uh huh. [Deep sigh] I still don't—Yeah! I see. But just listening I don't think he was a—very good chance. But in light of his other things I feel that the interview was not—showing—the real—him. —Hhh!

[36 out of 37] I would go back on my former opinion but I wouldn't go back too far. I just don't see it. —Why should I have these different standards? Were my opinions more or less in agreement on the first man? (No.) That leads me to think. —That's funny. Unless you got 36 unusual people. I can't understand it. Maybe it's my personality. (Does it make any difference?) It *does* make a difference if I assume they're correct. What I consider is proper, they don't. —It's my attitude—Still in all a man of that sort would alienate me. A wise guy type to be avoided. Of course you can talk like that with other fellows—but in an interview? . . . Now I'm more confused than I was at the beginning of the entire interview. I think I ought to go home and look in the mirror and talk to myself. Do you have any ideas? (Why? Does it disturb you?) Yes it *does* disturb me! It makes me think my abilities to judge people and values are way off from normal. It's not a healthy situation. (What difference does it make?) If I act the way I act it seems to me that I'm just putting my head in the lion's mouth. I did have preconceptions but they're shattered all to hell. It makes me wonder about myself. Why should I have these different standards? It all points to me.

Of the twenty-five Ss who were taken in, seven were unable to resolve the incongruity of having been wrong about such an obvious matter and were unable to "see" the alternative. Their suffering was dramatic and unrelieved. Five more resolved it with the view that the medical school had accepted a good man; five others with the view that it had accepted a boor. Although they changed, they nevertheless did not abandon their former views. For them Gardner's view could be seen "in general," but the grasp lacked convincingness. When attention was drawn to particulars, the general picture would evaporate. These Ss were willing to entertain and use the "general" picture, but they suffered whenever indigestible particulars of the same portrait came into view. Subscription to the "general" picture was accompanied by a recitation of characteristics that were not only the opposite of those in the original view but were intensified by superlative adjectives like "supremely" poised, "very" natural, "most" confident, "very" calm. Further, they saw the new features through a new appreciation of the way the medical examiner had been listening. They saw, for example, that the examiner was smiling when the applicant had forgotten to offer him a cigarette.

Three more Ss were convinced that there was deception and acted on the conviction through the interview. They showed no disturbance. Two of these showed acute suffering as soon as it appeared that the interview was finished, and they were being dismissed with no acknowledgment of a deception. Three others inadvertently suffered in silence and confounded E. Without any indication to E, they regarded the interview as an experimental one in which they were being asked to solve some problems and therefore were being asked to do as well as possible and to make no changes in their opinions, for only then would they be contributing to the study. They were difficult for me to understand during the interview because they displayed marked anxiety, yet their remarks were bland and were not addressed to the matters that were provoking it. Finally three more Ss contrasted with the others. One of these insisted that the character assessments were semantically ambiguous and because there was insufficient information a "high correlation opinion" was not possible. A second, and the only one in the entire series, found, according to his account, the second portrait as convincing as the original one. When the deception was revealed, he was disturbed that he could have been as convinced as he was. The third one, in the face of everything, showed only slight disturbance of very short duration. However, he alone among the subjects had already been interviewed for medical school, had excellent contacts, despite a grade point average of less than C he estimated his chances

of admission as fair, and finally he expressed his preference for a career in the diplomatic service over a career in medicine.

As a final observation, twenty-two of the twenty-eight Ss expressed marked relief—ten of them with explosive expressions—when I disclosed the deception. Unanimously they said that the news of the deception permitted them to return to their former views. Seven Ss had to be convinced that there had been a deception. When the deception was revealed, they asked what they were to believe. Was I telling them that there had been a deception in order to make them feel better? No pains were spared, and whatever truth or lies that had to be told were told in order to establish the truth that there had been a deception.

The Social Construction of Unreality: A Case Study of a Family's Attribution of Competence to a Severely Retarded Child

Melvin Pollner and *Lynn McDonald-Wikler*
With Commentary by David Reiss

Some families develop unusual or extreme versions of reality and sustain them in the face of a torrent of ostensibly discrediting and disconfirming information. Although the psychological dynamics and functions of such shared constructions have been amply considered, little is known about the routine transactions through which these unusual versions of reality are created and maintained. This paper examines the "reality work" of a family that attributed high levels of performance and competence to the severely retarded youngest child. Observation of videotaped interaction between family members and the child revealed practices that presupposed, "documented," and sustained the family's version of the child's competence. The practices are similar to those characteristics of interaction between adults and preverbal children. The implications of this similarity for the analysis of cases of folie à famille *are discussed.*

In recent years attention has been drawn to the ways in which what group members take to be given, natural, or real is a subtly organized achievement (Berger, 1969; Cicourel, 1973; Garfinkel, 1967). The social world of the group is not a simple reflection of what is "out there" but a continuously developed and sustained construction. The maintenance of a collective construct requires work—information must be selected,

"The Social Construction of Unreality: A Case Study of a Family's Attribution of Competence to a Severely Retarded Child" by M. Pollner and L. McDonald-Wikler, with commentary ("The Social Construction of Reality: The Passion Within Us All") by David Reiss, 1985. *Family Process* 24, pp. 241-254. Reprinted by permission of the publisher.

edited, and interpreted; anomalies must be explained; heretics from within and critics from without must be discounted, dissuaded, managed, or avoided. As Berger (1969) suggests:

> Worlds are socially constructed, socially maintained. Their continuing reality, both objective (as common, taken-for-granted facticity) and subjective (as facticity imposing itself on individual consciousness), depends upon *specific* social processes, namely those processes that ongoingly reconstruct and maintain the particular world in question. (p. 45)

The family is no different. Indeed, in many respects it is an especially intense locus of these constructive processes (Berger & Kellner, 1970). In *The Family's Construction of Reality*, Reiss (1981), for example, proposes that "family paradigms"—the fundamental assumptions a family holds about itself and the world—are realized and conserved through interactional patterns. These patterns create the family's everyday reality and enable members "to experience their own values and assumptions as if they were unquestionable components of outer reality" (p. 228).

The conception of family reality as an interactionally achieved construction may prove especially valuable in exploring the dynamics by which families maintain seemingly extreme, bizarre, or aberrant versions of reality. Although the psychological dynamics and functions of such constructions have received attention (Pulver & Brunt, 1961; Wikler, 1980) and despite numerous case histories in the literature (Gralnick, 1942), relatively little is known about the concrete, detailed activities in which family members use, manage, and "realize" these versions of reality in their day-to-day activities. The constructionist standpoint corrects this imbalance by inviting close examination of the artful, minute, and continuous work through which what might be characterized as "myth," "distortion," or "delusion" from outside the family is rendered a reality for those on the inside.[1]

We have applied this general perspective to a family diagnosed as *folie à famille* and attempted to discern the "reality work"—practices of reasoning, speaking, and acting—through which members documented and maintained their particular world. The family in question was initially encountered at a large psychiatric institute to which the parents had turned in their search for a remedy for 5½-year-old Mary's unusual behavior. Family members stated that Mary was a verbal and intelligent child who malingered and refused to speak in public in order to embarrass the family. Extensive clinical observation and examination revealed Mary to be severely retarded and unable to perform at anywhere near the level of competence claimed by her parents and two older sibs. Clinical materials collected included videotaped recordings of each family member interacting with the child in the institute. Initial viewings of the tapes suggested that family members' transactions were permeated by subtle, almost artful, practices that could function to create the image of Mary as an intelligent child. Intensive examination of these and other materials yielded a repertoire of such practices, and they constitute a central focus of this report. Although our analysis was driven by the assumption that family members were constructing their reality, our subsequent reflections suggested more complicated possibilities whose dimensions we shall explore in our concluding discussion.

Case Description

Mary's parents came to a psychiatric institute for an inpatient psychiatric evaluation of their 5½-year-old daughter.[2] Their presenting complaint was that, although at home their child acted normally, she refused to do so in public. They wanted the reason for this peculiar and difficult-to-manage behavior to be identified and then treated. In public, they claimed, she acted retarded. Each of the four family members who lived with Mary agreed with this description:

Father (aged 42): She's really a fast child, if anything. Once she even read a note aloud that I had passed over to my wife not intending for Mary to see it.
Mother (aged 39): She puts on an act of being retarded in public while acting normally at home.
Half-Sister (aged 18): I've had 10-minute long normal conversations with her, but she won't talk in front of most people.
Brother (aged 12): I don't know why she fakes it; she's like any other 5-year-old.

Prior to coming for the inpatient evaluation, the child had been taken to several reputable outpatient clinics in the general geographical area for work-ups. These had been, according to the parents, frustrating experiences, and they had not received the help they sought. In each case they were essentially told (father's report) that Mary was severely retarded. This was rejected by the parents and instead was regarded by them as an indicator of Mary's capabilities—she had fooled the clinicians. Therefore, they had continued their search for a thorough, long-term evaluation.

Mary was admitted to the children's ward in the Neuropsychiatric Institute, which specialized in evaluation and treatment of retarded children. The admission was made with the clearly stated contingency that the family remain intensively involved with the professional staff throughout her stay. Mary was observed 24 hours a day for eight weeks (except on weekends when she routinely returned home) by a professional nursing staff. The pediatrician and social worker for the ward had their offices on the ward and so had frequent occasions to observe Mary's behavior informally in addition to their formal evaluations. Mary was evaluated by specialists in developmental disabilities from the following disciplines (each using several standardized measures as well as narrative summaries of impressions to reach their conclusions): neurology, psychiatry, pediatrics, psychology, special education, psychiatric nursing, vocational rehabilitation, physical therapy, audiometry, speech pathology, dentistry, social work.

While recognizing the similarity with cases of elective mutism (Rosenberg & Lindblad, 1978), there was no deviation in any of the findings, and there was unanimous agreement on the diagnosis: Mary was severely retarded. She was mildly cerebral palsied; she had petit mal seizures; she was more than three standard deviations below average in height and weight; her language development was below that of a 9-month-old; her receptive language abilities seemed nonexistent, except for intonation; she was not sufficiently maturationally developed to be toilet trained; etc. There was

no time at which anyone felt or mentioned in the discussion of their findings that emotional disturbance or resistance or noncooperation was interfering with the validity of their test results. The evaluation was conclusive in every way; her IQ was set at approximately 20 to 25.

Although by standardized MMPI testing, no psychosis was evident and all members of the family were normal or above in intelligence, the family was diagnosed as delusional. A highly refined testing procedure indicated the mother was disposed to delusions under stress. She was seen as the locus of the family delusion, and the entire family was diagnosed as a case of *folie à famille, imposée*.

In contrast to the professional diagnosis, the family claimed that:

1. Mary is like other children her age; she is normal; she can talk.

2. Mary is often crabby and obstinate; when she's in such moods, she won't cooperate.

3. Mary puts on an act of "being retarded" in public, which the family cannot understand.

4. The professional staff had been fooled by Mary.

Our analysis of the available materials has been instigated by the following questions: How does the family do it? What sorts of skills, practices, and strategies are utilized to create and then "discover" Mary's competence? A number of images and anecdotes had heuristic value for discerning the nature of the family accomplishment. We occasionally thought of a Zen tale, for example, which goes something like this: A Zen master is asked by a novice to draw a perfect circle. The master draws a wretchedly ragged figure. The novice quickly notes that the figure is hardly a "perfect circle." "That is correct," responds the master, "but it is a perfect whatever-it-is." The tale captured for us what we felt was a dominant thrust of the family's practices— they had ways of transforming what others regarded as incompetent performance into exhibits of intelligence and responsiveness. The yield of our analysis has been a set of practices by which family members created Mary's "perfection."

Family Practices

Framing

There were several ways in which family members verbally or physically prestructured the environment to maximize the likelihood that *whatever* Mary did could be seen as meaningful, intentional activity. In "framing," Mary's family would establish a definition of the immediate situation and use it as a frame of reference for interpreting and describing any and all of Mary's subsequent behavior. Playing a game with Mary was perhaps the prototype of such framing activity. For example, once the game of "catch" was inaugurated as a definition of "what we are now doing," a variety of game-relevant dimensions for understanding and describing Mary's behavior came into effect. She could be seen as either "catching the ball," "not catching the ball," "dropping the ball," "throwing well," and so forth. The game provided a vocabulary for describing activities that occurred while the frame was in effect. Even activities that seemed to fall outside the frame were describable: Mary's nonresponsiveness might be formulated as "not playing" or "playing very poorly." Framed within the structure of an activity and described with the activity-specific terminology, Mary's behaviors were endowed with an aura of significance and responsiveness. In the exchange in Table 33.1, for example, Mary's passivity was reformulated into game-relevant terms; the ball tumbling out of Mary's hands was described by Mary's sister as an error; i.e., Mary "dropped" it.

To a certain extent the very structures of discourse provided frames that constituted

Table 33.1
Framing (Game)

Verbal Exchange	Movements
Do you want it?	
You gonna catch it for me? Huh?	
Come on.	
Come on.	
Put your hand out.	
Come on.	
Come on.	Sister puts ball in Mary's hand and Mary doesn't hold onto it.
Uh, uh (*laughs*).	
Almost dropped it.	Ball falls.
Come on.	Sister throws it to Mary who can't catch it, it drops again.
Come on (*laughs*).	

the possibility of interpreting Mary's behavior as intelligent and responsive. For example, once a question was posed or an invitation proffered, Mary's subsequent behavior might be reviewed for the ways in which whatever she was doing could serve as a response (Schegloff, 1968). Mary, of course, was impervious to the content of such overtures and often to the sheer fact of the overture itself; she never responded to a question or complied with a command behaviorally or verbally. Yet family members often formulated Mary's behaviors following these overtures as deliberately chosen and meaningful courses of activity even if Mary's behavior consisted of the completely unperturbed continuation of what she had been doing prior to the immediate transaction. In one sequence, for example, the mother twice requested "Give Mommy the ball"; when Mary simply continued to stand while holding the ball, the mother said "You don't want to give me the ball," thereby narratively transforming obliviousness into a willful reluctance to give the ball.

In the transaction in Table 33.2, Mary's involvement with a piling toy was framed by the mother's invitation to build a block house. Mary's continued fingering of the piling toy was then formulated as a deliberately chosen alternative. The formulation of Mary's activity was itself stated as a question—"Or are you gonna do that?"—with the subsequent result that Mary had been asked a sequence of questions that almost totally exhausted alternative possibilities for activity. In the face of options that covered the range of immediate possibilities—blocks or continued involvement with the piling toy—almost anything Mary did, even if she continued to do what she had been doing all along, could serve as material for inferring an intelligent choice.

Postscripting

If framing served prospectively to generate a "space" within which Mary's behaviors might assume meaning, postscripting attempted to generate or discern significance after the fact. In postscripting, family members would in effect track or follow Mary's ongoing behaviors and develop physical or verbal contexts that could render the behaviors intelligent and interactionally responsive.

Perhaps the clearest form of postscripting was expressed in what might be called "commanding the already done," in which family members requested Mary to engage in an activity she had already initiated. That is, family members observed the beginnings of possible actions and then ordered their completion. When done quickly with finesse, the inversion of the temporal sequence was hardly noticeable and the aura of competence enhanced; to the casual eye Mary seems to be following orders.

1. As Mary lay down on the floor, father said, "Mary, you just lie there." She does.

2. As Mary reached up to father with part of a toy in her hand, he said, "Give me that one, too." She gave it to him.

Table 33.2
Framing (Question)

Verbal Exchange		Movements
Mo:	Let's see, what have we got in here?	Mo pulls out piling toy, sets it on table away; M stands watching.
Mo:	How about building a block house?	Mo looks up at M, M looks at box.
M:	Um mmmm.	Mo takes ball out; Mary puts a leg on the table and reaches in box touching the blocks.
Mo:	O.K.?	Mo takes blocks out and puts them on the table; Mary climbs onto table and reaches for piling toy, begins to pull off a section. After placing box on floor, Mo places hands on toy ball and removes them from the table top and looks at her. M has piece of toy, which Mo removes from her hand. M sits back on her heels, and M drops a toy. Mo reaches for her waist and lifts her down from table onto her lap.
M:	Ahhhuy aiieo gege	
Mo:	Shall we build a house?	
Mo:	Or are you gonna do that?	
M:	Uh.	
Mo:	Let's build a house. Whup!	

3. As Mary looked at her sister and climbed onto the chair, her sister said, "And you sit down." Mary sat down.

A somewhat more sophisticated form of postscripting entails the interposition of actions into the stream of Mary's behaviors. By discerning a pattern or developmental possibility in Mary's behaviors, the successful postscripter could integrate his or her actions with Mary's so as to achieve the appearance of coordinated interactional activity. Thus, for example, at one point the sister dropped a block while Mary was intently banging a block on the table. As Mary sat down on the floor, the sister bent down from her chair, saying, "Let's find that block."

Puppeteering

In framing and postscripting, Mary's behaviors were endowed with significance through the artfulness of prebehavior and postbehavior interpretations. In effect, Mary's behaviors were treated as "givens" around which an edifice of meaning was constructed. On some occasions, however, instead of working with whatever Mary happened to do, family members would "create" Mary's behavior. Specifically, Mary would be physically maneuvered through various tasks. Moreover, the maneuvering was accompanied or followed by commentary implying that Mary was performing as an autonomous and responsive agent. We refer to this practice as "puppeteering," and when executed in a masterful way it could succeed in creating the illusion of independence. Indeed, initial viewings of videotaped sequences in Table 33.3 suggested that Mary could respond to requests and follow instructions. An instruction would be given, the observer would shift visually to view Mary, and Mary could be observed to approximate the behavior that had been requested of her. It was not until later in the analysis, however, that the sequencing of family talk and family touching was seen to be related to the active production of her behavioral response. Mary's movements were often artifacts of the family's physical engineering of her body.

Semantic Crediting

Mary was responsive to a range of different stimuli, all of which were nonverbal. These were fairly predictable, and they were appropriate for a child with her mental age. [Table 33.4 contains] a partial list of stimuli Mary responded to, with the corresponding behaviors (from hours of observation on ward and on tape).

These are events that elicited predictable behavioral reactions from Mary, even

Table 33.3
Puppeteering

Verbal Exchange	Movements
MOTHER AND MARY	
Mo: Okay, now. *Put your block in the middle.*	Mo sitting on floor next to the table, setting up a circle of blocks on table. Mary just slipped to floor. Mo picks M up under her arms to a standing position. With one hand Mother points to the middle of the circle of blocks, *other arm is around and behind M with hand on M's arm;*
M: Ah hayee.	*she pushes* M's arm,
Mo: Put your block in—	which has block in it, toward the middle while looking at the table—then looks at M. M's arm moves forward, then stops, and M slips to the floor again.
SISTER AND MARY	
Si: Give me this; give me that. All right; take these, put them in the truck; take the blocks and put them in the truck; *Come on take the* block.	S grabs the stick and block out of M's hand one at a time, puts her hand briefly on M's hand, then touches the blocks, then touches the truck in pointing gesture. *S puts her hand on M's arm and lifts it over to the block and onto the block;* M holds onto a block briefly.
FATHER AND MARY	Fa sitting on chair, M standing by his knee.
Fa: I'm not gonna talk to you unless you get the ball. *Now you go over there and get the ball. Come on Mary.*	Fa moves slightly away from M and puts one hand under his chin. *Fa puts hand on M's shoulder and pushes her toward the* table; lets go of her.

Table 33.4
Stimuli and Responses

Stimuli	Responses
A sudden loud noise: a shout, a knock on the door, a clapping of hands, etc.	Often causes Mary to turn toward the source of the noise, stop what she is doing, look and walk toward the source
A sudden movement within her peripheral vision	Often causes Mary to look in that direction, pause
A person reaching out to Mary, hand out, palm open, or arms outstretched	Often causes Mary to move toward that person or reach out with her hand
A person slapping her or shaking her suddenly	Often causes Mary to pause, orient herself, look at the person, make a face
Having an object placed close to her while she's watching	Often causes Mary to look at it, touch it, explore it, pick it up, or put it to her mouth
A person walking away	Often Mary will follow
Being near a door knob	Often Mary will touch and fiddle with it

Table 33.5
Semantic Crediting

Verbal Exchange		Movements
MOTHER AND MARY		
Mo:	Come on. *(knock on door)*	
		M looks around and Mo stands up.
	I think somebody wants to get in. Do you wanna open the door?	M reaches for Mo's hand. Mo pulls away and points to the door.
	Open the door.	M goes to the doorknob and puts both hands on it and twists it. Mo opens the door.
Mo:	Come on. *Get up (whisper). Get up (fierce).* Get up *(enunciated).*	Mo seated by the table, M lying on the floor fiddling with the blocks in her hand. *Mo taps M's foot, then holds out hand close to M. M lolls on floor, slowly gets up.*
FATHER AND MARY		
Fa:	You sit in my lap. Come on.	Fa sitting on chair, his hands on his knees, M walking toward him; holds his hands out toward her; she backs off and leans back against a chair.
M:	Euuuhhn.	
Fa:	I don't care *whether you* want to; *come on.*	*Fa reaches out with hand, almost touching M; she raises a leg, then touches his hand briefly with her own.* He takes hold and picks her up onto lap.
SISTER AND MARY		
Si:	Mary—	Si sitting on chair, M next to her. M drops block out of truck, Si reaches over and picks it up, puts it back in the truck, *slaps M's hand while looking at her face; M looks up at her for a moment.*
	Hey.	
	Now listen!	

when embedded in a context that included other stimuli such as talk. Indeed the fact that these triggering items almost invariably occurred in a semantically meaningful configuration created ambiguity as to precisely which features of the environment Mary was reacting to. Insofar as attention was displaced to the utterance accompanying a triggering event or gesture, such as an outstretched arm, it appeared that Mary was able to understand the verbal message, when in fact she was simply responding to a behavioral cue. Table 33.5 furnishes examples of how these cues might be embedded in or accompanied by a verbal message thereby permitting the inference that Mary's subsequent activity was in response to the meaning of the utterance.

The inference that one would make about Mary's mental acuity would vary dramatically according to which stimulus one considered to be the crucial one: the verbal request or the accompanying cues. The familial claim, of course, was that she understood the words spoken to her and that her competence far exceeded the level of responsiveness involved in merely reaching for an outstretched hand or turning to a loud noise.

Putting Words in Mary's Mouth

Perhaps the most dramatic, and the most difficult to understand, set of practices were those by which the family created the semblance of Mary's linguistic competence. From the point of hearing of an outside observer-listener, Mary's utterances were interactionally capricious and unintelligible and without promise of any sort of cryptointelligibility. Family members, on the other hand, were insistent that Mary spoke and spoke well, albeit not always and not everywhere. Although it is difficult to specify precisely what family members heard and how they came to hear it, we have located certain interactional styles that seemed to contribute to the image that Mary responded at a timely and appropriate place in a conversational sequence, that she responded intelligently and intelligibly, and that what she said was intersubjectively available. We shall comment on but one aspect of the interactional patterns by which the family sustained the myth of Mary's interactional skill.

Often, when Mary made an utterance, a family member would repeat what Mary said. But, of course, they did not repeat it at all, for they would babble were they to do so. More precisely, then, when family members "repeated," they were actually creating a novel, intelligent utterance and stating it as though they were repeating what they had heard Mary say or imply. While putting words in Mary's mouth, they implicitly claimed that she was putting her words in theirs. Table 33.6 presents several examples of such "statement by restatement." They were excerpted from a tape Mary's family made at

Table 33.6
Putting Words in Mary's Mouth

---

1. Mary is wearing a newly bought robe.

Fa: Want to see it in the mirror?

M: [Gurgling].

Fa: She doesn't like it.

Mo: You don't like the robe? It fits you.

M: [Gurgling].

Mo: What did you say about Daddy?

M: Mmmmmmm, [gurgle].

Fa: She thinks it's too cheap!

2. Encouraging her to talk into the recorder:

Fa: OK, you tell me your name and age into that thing, and I'll give you $5 to go out and buy a present that you want to buy yourself.

M: [Gurgling].

Fa: Your name and age—

M: Goo ga [gurgle].

Fa: She's bargaining with me for more money!

3. Later:

Mo: Time for your pills, Mary.

M: Mmmmm.

Mo: Time for your pills.

M: [Gurgling].

Mo: You don't think you need them.

M: Mmmmm, ga.

Mo: I think you need them.

---

home and offered as somewhat unsatisfactory (to them) evidence of Mary's competence.

Although we are unable to specify how family members were prompted to "repeat" precisely what they chose to "repeat," we can appreciate one of the possible functions of these procedures for the collective, sense-making enterprise. Specifically, such practices introduced a degree of determinacy and integrity to Mary's talk and allowed family consensus on what Mary has said. In "repeating," or heavily implying the meaning of Mary's utterance by their response, family members were in fact creating and broadcasting the meaning. If we are not mistaken, such work allowed the family to avoid embarrassing disagreements, to perpetuate the fiction that Mary was speaking intelligibly, and to develop a shared version of precisely what Mary said.

Explaining in the "Bright" Direction

Although the previously described practices often succeeded in imparting an aura of intelligence and responsiveness to Mary's behaviors, they also provided opportunities for behaviors to be specifically and recognizably inadequate. A parentally inaugurated game of catch, for example, generated the possibility of "missing" or "dropping" the ball over and over and over again. Thus, the practices were not a guarantee of the semblance of competence; they could become methods for displaying incompetence. Indeed, there were a number of occasions on which family members found Mary's behavior remiss, in error, or unresponsive. But such occasions did not result in attributions of incompetence. On the contrary, members could transform these episodes into evidence of Mary's sophistication.

Almost any system of belief is capable of furnishing secondary elaborations that will preserve the sense of the system's validity in the face of seemingly discrediting or subversive evidence. The belief in Mary's competence was protected by a network of such "epicyclical" explanations (Polanyi, 1964; Pollner & Wikler, 1979). Mary's ostensible failures were continuously reinterpreted as successes of sorts or else explained away as the product of normal, transient mood shifts or lapses of attention. Thus, for example, instances in which Mary's behavior seemed to defy interpretation as a directly responsive action were treated as the product of Mary's postulated proclivity toward "teasing" and "pretending." Indeed, the fact that psychiatric staff had one version of Mary and her family another was attributed to Mary's faking or malingering. Other failures were explained away by the family as products of orneriness,

Table 33.7
Explaining in the Bright Direction

Fa:	Go get the ball, Mary.
M:	Eigaga.
Fa:	Come on, Mary, go get the ball.
	Come on, come on, go get the ball.
	You're not being the least bit cooperative, Mary, you just lie there; Okay, you going to sleep?
	Come on, get me the ball.
	The ball, Mary.
M:	Ummm.
Fa:	Hey, I don't care whether you want to or not; do you want to get belted? Go get the ball! Come on.
	Come on, Mary.
M:	Uhnn.
Fa:	Huh?
M:	Ewaiuhh.
Fa:	Mary, you're making it harder on yourself.
	Come on.
	Come on with me, and I'll go over and get the ball with you.
	Give me your hand.
M:	Guheaa.
Fa:	You're being a bad girl, Mary.
M:	Agaa.

lack of cooperation, or momentary inattentiveness, as in the interaction between Mary and her father presented in Table 33.7.

In effect, the belief "Mary is competent" functioned as an "incorrigible assumption" (Gasking, 1965), that is, as an assumption that would not be withdrawn or reevaluated in light of empirical events. Instead, empirical events were interpreted so as to render them compatible with the fundamental claim "Mary is competent." The net effect of such explanatory and descriptive practices was to inhibit the growth of what could have been an enormous catalogue of incompetence. Each instance was explained away in a fashion congenial to the basic belief. Indeed, insofar as "faking" or "cheating" are higher-level activities requiring sophisticated reflections and interpersonal manipulations, there is a sense in which ostensible failures ultimately served to enhance Mary's image among family members.

Discussion

In a more literal sense than is usually intended, a *folie à famille* makes and lives in its own little world. We have attempted to examine some of the practices through which that world or *nomos* is reproduced and maintained. Although we have succeeded in identifying several practices, questions and issues abound both with respect to the case at hand and *folie à famille* generally.

The first issue is the extent to which the practices discerned were characteristic of the family's routine transactions with Mary. The videotapes were made in a clinic waiting room with several staff members behind a one-way mirror making consequential decisions on the basis of what they observed. It is a difficult task in general and an impossible one in this case, given the absence of materials on routine family relations, to assess the correspondence between performance in clinical and nonclinical settings. It is quite easy on the other hand to imagine ways in which the relation might be problematic, that is, the ways in which family performance in the clinic might have been different from interaction in the home. The very request to interact with Mary under the gaze of others, for example, might have induced a level of self-consciousness and an intensity of effort uncharacteristic of interaction in the home. It is also possible that Mary herself was different in the home. This, of course, was the claim of the family. Although every piece of clinical information weighed against the competence attributed to Mary by the family, the familiarity of household objects and routines may have contributed to higher levels of displayed competence than observed in the clinic. These are possibilities that defy closure owing to the limits of our materials.

A related issue is the extent to which family members believed or experienced their version of Mary. It is possible if not plausible that family members varied in the depth and nature of their acceptance of the delusional content (Evans & Marskey, 1972). Although again our materials preclude closure, it is of interest to note that family members varied in the adroitness with which they were able to create the aura of Mary's competence for observers—and perhaps for themselves. Mary's mother, for example, by virtue of her active involvement with Mary could achieve a more convincing display of Mary's competence than any other family member. The possibility of various depths and types of commitments to the family delusion means that, although some may have been true believers, others may have had to be continually though implicitly urged to voice the family line and to partake of the appropriate practices. Thus a comprehensive analysis of the "how" of the maintenance of shared delusion would explicate the interactional dynamics by which members are rewarded for honoring the family *doxa* and castigated for heretical tendencies.[3]

A final issue of consequence focuses on the origin of these practices. And although once again we plead limitations of materials, our reflections have taken us to a point suggesting that reformulation of the nature of the practice of delusion may be in order. Initially focused on the "how" of delusion, we did not have well-articulated notions regarding the origin of these practices save for the assumption that they were mobilized or developed in the interest of sustaining a belief that was important in the interpersonal and intrapersonal dynamics of family members. In effect, we regarded the practices and, for that matter, the belief itself as more or less de novo creations. As we completed the bulk of our analysis, we noted that the practices we discerned were similar to those many parents seem to employ with their preverbal children. Parent-infant interaction is replete with episodes in which adults playfully treat the child's babbling as an intelligent and complex utterance or manipulate the child through complex sequences of activity while praising the child for the excellence of her performance or describe whatever the child is doing at a particular moment as though it were an intentional project of the child (Bruner, 1983; Lock, 1981; Wertsch, 1978). In the language of our report, interaction between adults and preverbal children is replete with "putting words in the child's mouth," "puppeteering," and "framing."[4]

The similarity between observed family practices and those characteristic of adult/ young-child interaction suggests the origins of the former. It may be that family practices are not novel creations but a perseveration of once appropriate practices. Mary's family may have initially interacted with Mary in the fashion that all families interact with infants in the preverbal stage. Somehow those practices persisted despite the fact that Mary was now over five years old and had not acquired the skills and competencies appropriate for her age. Given this possibility, it is not that the family constructs a new world so much as they refuse to relinquish an old one. Accordingly, the question of interest may not be how did the practices originate, but rather how do they endure.

A detailed explication of the processes that might promote the perseveration of "outmoded" practices is beyond the scope of this paper, though some features may be portrayed in a few broad strokes. Consider that families will often have good reason for disattending or otherwise not confronting an actual loss, such as the decline of the position, prestige, or competence of one of its members or the loss of some anticipated state of affairs such as a successful career, happy family life, or healthy child. The psychological and interpersonal costs of addressing such losses may be great. The loss may touch on the foundations of a person's sense of self, other family members' sense of him, family members' relation to one another, and even their relations to others outside the nuclear family. Accordingly, there may be attempts to evade or forestall directly confronting the nature and significance of the loss. There are, of course, a variety of ways to accomplish this. Family members may tacitly agree not to talk about the matter. In other instances, perhaps especially when the loss is not (yet) definitive or clear-cut, the family may persevere in the practices and outlook characteristic of the preloss period—the husband is on the verge of success; we are a happy family; our daughter is a healthy, normal child. Permeated by the sense of catastrophe on the one hand and of hope on the other, these "little tribes in distress" (First, 1975) may continue to do what they have always done.

Depending upon the nature of the threatened loss, old practices may be retained for indefinite lengths of time without confronting directly contradictory or disconfirming information. As the hoped-for reality recedes into the horizon and the dreaded loss becomes actual, however, the retention of old practices means that the family enters a sham world or, more to the point, is left with a sham world (Henry, 1973). Initial participation in sham may have an accelerating effect: a little sham leads to a lot of sham as family members become reluctant and perhaps unable to cease the fiction for fear not only of calling attention to the lost object but also for fear of acknowledging that for the past few minutes, weeks, years, they have been living a fiction. Shamming after all is shameful, particularly with loved ones, and thus participants may find that having taken one step into this world they must take another—and cover their tracks.

Conclusion

Folie à deux (or "shared delusion") is often catalogued among the more exotic pathologies, involving as it does several individuals—the classical number, of course, is two—

who share and participate in the same delusional system (Wikler, 1980). Though there may be many differences between these little tribes and other collectivities, the commitment to beliefs whose foundation in reality is problematic is not in itself a distinguishing criterion. As Berger (1969) has noted, all collectivities construct a meaningful order or *nomos*, and every *nomos* is erected in the face of chaos and "irreality." Although it would be naïve and misleading to treat *folie à deux* as nothing but a variant of the *nomos*-building processes characteristic of other groups, there is heuristic value in underscoring the fact that these groups develop meaningful worlds that, like all such symbolic constructs, must be nourished and protected through specific practices of reasoning, speaking, and acting.

In an earlier work, Wikler (1980) explored some of the clinically relevant features of this particular case for family therapists, as an example of the syndrome of *folie à famille*. In this paper, we have examined the practices through which a family, diagnosed as *folie à famille*, sustained its world. Our analysis led us to suggest that some forms of "delusion" may involve not the construction of novel symbolic realms but the buttressing of old ones. Although it is highly unlikely that all forms of *folie à deux* originate through retention of outmoded practice, it is plausible and in keeping with the ubiquitousness of the phenomena (Ferreira, 1963; Gralnick, 1942; Greenberg, 1954; Wikler, 1980) to consider the possibility that, in some instances, shared "delusions" arise not as the consequence of an elected or induced set of practices and beliefs that fly in the face of reality but as a result of reality flying away from an established set of practices and anticipations.[5] Whether this interpretation extends beyond the current case awaits detailed descriptions of the processes by which families create their worlds and respond to the inevitable tremors.

Notes

1. The social constructionist attitude does not provide privileged exemptions for "expert" or "scientific" constructions of reality. The tacit practices by which clinicians develop, coordinate, use, and defend their versions of reality are as amenable to analysis as those of the families they study. For certain clinical purposes, however, it is necessary to avoid what can turn into an infinitely regressing form of analysis (as when, say, an analysis of the social construction of reality is itself viewed as a construction). Nevertheless, the ceaseless relativism inherent in the constructionist perspective is useful in that it heightens appreciation of the tacit commitments and practices implicated in the development of one's own "authoritative" version of "what really happened."

2. Extensive background and biographical information as well as transcripts of the audiotapes and videotapes used in this report are available in Wikler (1976).

3. The work of Henry (1973) and Goode (1980) provides examples of the kind of "clinical ethnography" necessary to get at family dynamics as they occur in the home setting.

4. In an unpublished paper, David Helm suggests these practices may be characteristic of interaction with any person whose verbal capacity or intelligence is perceived as limited, impaired, or otherwise problematic. A number of colleagues have suggested that similar practices are found in interaction with pets. An unusual development in this regard is a recent critical review of the research on the linguistic ability of primates. Umiker-Sebeok and Sebeok (1980) argue that ostensibly positive evidence may be more an artifact of researchers' procedures and interpretations than a reflection of genuine linguistic competence. Several of the practices identified by the Sebeoks as the source of artifactual evidence are remarkably similar to the practices described in this report. The Sebeoks note, for example, some of the "no-forfeit" practices through which a primate's signing behaviors, no matter how unusual, are treated as evidence of linguistic ability—anomalous signs are interpreted as jokes, insults, or metaphors. In characterizing the immediate social context of talking primate projects, the Sebeoks all but state the possibility of a *folie à famille*. A team constitutes "a tightly knit

social community with a solid core of shared beliefs and goals in opposition to outside visitors, as well as against groups elsewhere which are competing for scarce research resources" (pp. 7-8). The research teams, they indicate, are often led by investigators married to one another (e.g., the Gardners, Premacks, and Rumbaughs), with graduate students and younger colleagues serving as "uncles and aunts" of the subjects.

5. One implication of this portrayal of the path to *folie à famille* is that it is continuous and does not require reference to any qualitatively distinct psychological traits that dispose or propel individuals on their way. This is a problematic assumption, and it may be that there is a crevice between preservation of old practices and "delusion," across which one can leap only if propelled by, say, dependency needs of extreme intensity. It may, however, be worth considering that the point at which the leap occurs is much further away from home base than previously thought and that many families take the path a goodly distance before encountering the schism.

References

Berger, P. (1969). *The sacred canopy.* Garden City, NY: Doubleday.

Berger, P., & Kellner H. (1970). Marriage and the construction of reality. In H. P. Dreitzel (Ed.), *Recent sociology* (No. 2). New York: Macmillan.

Bruner, J. (1983). *Child's talk: Learning to use language.* New York and London: Norton.

Cicourel, A. V. (1973). *Cognitive sociology: Language and meaning in social interaction.* Harmondsworth, UK: Penguin.

Evans, P., & Marskey, H. (1972). Shared beliefs of dermal parasitosis: Folie partagée. *Brit. J. Med. Psychol., 45,* 19-26.

Ferreira, J. (1963). Family myth and homeostasis. *Arch. Gen. Psychiat., 9,* 457-463.

First, E. (1975). The new wave in psychiatry. *New York Review of Books, 22,* 8-15.

Garfinkel, H. (1967). *Studies in ethnomethodology.* Englewood Cliffs, NJ: Prentice-Hall.

Gasking, D. (1965). Mathematics and the world. In A. Flew (Ed.), *Logic and language.* Garden City, NY: Doubleday.

Goode, D. (1980). Behavioral sculpting: Parent-child interaction in families with retarded children. In J. Jacobs (Ed.),

Phenomenological approaches to mental retardation. Springfield, IL: Charles C Thomas.

Gralnick, A. (1942). Folie à deux—The psychosis of association. A review of 103 cases and the entire English literature: With case presentations. *Psychiat. Quart., 16,* 230-263, 491-520.

Greenberg, P. H. (1954). Folie à deux. *Guy's Hospital Reports, 4,* 381-392.

Henry, J. (1973). *Pathways to madness.* New York: Vintage.

Lock, A. J. (Ed.). (1981). *Action, gesture and symbol: The emergence of language.* London: Academic Press.

Polanyi, M. (1964). *Personal knowledge.* New York: Harper & Row.

Pollner, M. (1975). "The very coinage of your brain": The anatomy of reality disjunctures. *Philos. Soc. Sci., 5,* 411-430.

Pollner, M., & Wikler, L. (1979). "Cognitive enterprise" in einem Fall von Folie à Famille. In H. G. Soeffner (Ed.), *Interpretative Verfahren in den Sozial—und Textwissenschaften.* Stuttgart: J. B. Metzler.

Pulver, S. E., & Brunt, M. Y. (1961). Deflection of hostility in folie à deux. *Arch. Gen. Psychiat., 5,* 257-265.

Reiss, D. (1981). *The family's construction of reality.* Cambridge, MA: Harvard University Press.

Rosenberg, J. B., & Lindblad, M. B. (1978). Behavior therapy in a family context. *Fam. Proc., 17,* 77-82.

Schegloff, E. A. (1968). Sequencing in conversational openings. *Am. Anthrop., 70,* 1075-1095.

Umiker-Sebeok, J., & Sebeok, T. A. (1980). Introduction: Questioning apes. In J. Umiker-Sebeok & T. A. Sebeok (Eds.), *Speaking of apes.* New York: Plenum.

Wertsch, J. V. (1978). Adult-child interaction and the roots of metacognition. *Quarterly Newsletter of the Institute for Comparative Human Development, 2,* 15-18.

Wikler, L. (1976). *Delusions of competence: A socio-behavioral study of the maintenance of a deviant belief system in a family with a retarded child.* Unpublished doctoral dissertation, University of California, Irvine.

Wikler, L. (1980). Folie à famille: A family therapist's perspective. *Fam. Proc., 19,* 257-268.

Commentary

The Social Construction of Reality:
The Passion Within Us All

David Reiss

This case report by Pollner and McDonald-Wikler is both arresting and poignant. It shares with other beautifully rendered case reports a subtle and complex inner coherence that makes it highly evocative—both intellectually and emotionally. But the interest of this report is much more specific. It deeply etches an image of a family trying to make sense of what most of us would see as a great tragedy. It also shows, in clear detail, the intricate and complex maneuvers the family uses to construct its version of events. One of the great strengths of this report is that, in a short space, and by the use of only one case, it helps evoke a sense of the universality of these processes of reality construction. Indeed, most readers will be quick to recognize similar processes—perhaps less dramatic—in many families they know. Likewise, and here Pollner and McDonald-Wikler are quite explicit in drawing inferences—similar processes may be observed in professional groups (see, for example, their pregnant note 4). If the social construction of reality is universal—if it resides in all groups with a sustained history—what makes this family so unique? Why did it at first attract a long parade of specialists at the Neuropsychiatric Institute; why again did it absorb the meticulous attention of Pollner and McDonald-Wikler; and finally, why have we, as readers, become so riveted to this account? Three fea-

tures of this family, it seems to me, make it particularly notable. These three features expose some of the ramifications of this family's construction of reality—ramifications that are of central importance to clinician and researcher alike.

First is the *sequestration* of this family. Their construction of reality is, without question, radically different from that of the social context in which they are observed. The Neuropsychiatric Institute had a very different vision, although there must have been a bit of unshakiness to prompt such a long parade of specialists past this family. This family would cotton to none of it. They held to their own construction and (although it is not reported here) must have held themselves, in some measure, aloof. To sustain such a particular or unique view of their youngest child's competence, the family must have had to maintain a highly structured and attenuated tie with their ordinary workaday world, as well as with the care-giving community. Indeed, it is not hard to imagine that most outsiders were viewed with animus and suspicion. Any form of therapeutic alliance with them, any form of "joining," would be an almost impossible dream.

A second feature is the highly structured, almost ritualized *focus and organization around a single individual*. The processes within this family cannot be grasped without the full appreciation that every experiential and transactional detail must take account of the family's vision of Mary. Although the report does not detail it, we may be confident that interactions among others—even when they do not involve Mary—must somehow take the vision of a competent Mary into account. Brother and sister cannot, in some secluded privacy, acknowledge to each other that the whole enterprise is a sham. Even their most intimate moments with each other—and of the mother and father with each other—must be regulated by a common construction of Mary.

Finally, and perhaps most important, the family's vision engages us by the power of its combined *vividness and simplicity*. To be sure, some of the tactics and maneuvers that support this vision are extraordinarily subtle: Pollner and McDonald-Wikler reviewed videotapes many times just to identify, let alone explain, some of them. But the vision itself is disarmingly potent: Mary has a normal intellect but an uncanny knack for fooling outsiders. This view is starkly simple: A small number of postulates ("incorrigible assumptions") are used to explain everything. Paradoxically, the powerful explanatory function of these postulates requires incredible ingenuity, subtlety, and complexity, as the report clearly demonstrates.

These three features that captivate us may give some clue to the underlying mechanisms. Pollner and McDonald-Wikler provide an intriguing start. They note that the family's transactions with Mary may be typical of transactions most families engage in with preverbal children. The family's folly, they speculate, is some grotesque development arrest. The three formal features I have noted give a hint about what might fuel this developmental arrest. Let us briefly reconsider each feature.

Sequestration. As several of us have argued, all families engage in some form of idiosyncratic or particular construction of reality (Berger & Kellner, 1964; Reiss, 1981; Kantor & Lehr, 1975; Kantor & Neal, 1985; Strodtbeck,

1958). Indeed, I have suggested that each family can be recognized by a characteristic signature or special construction I have called the "family paradigm." But few families take the burden of construction so exclusively on themselves. Families are embedded in larger social systems: extended families, communities, institutions, and (where they are not hopelessly vitiated) even cultures and religions. It is rare to find a family devoted to such a singular synthetic effort without contextual support (although there may be hidden grandmothers or cults in this clinical picture that are helping to "normalize" this child). One must stand in awe, then, at the extraordinary *creativity, energy, and responsibility* of this family.

Focus on an Individual. Again, most families develop particular and, at times, uniquely creative visions of reality, but they are rarely so centered on an individual. When they are, we are most familiar with *degrading* constructions: scapegoating and the attribution of incompetence, illness, or "craziness" to one member. It is much more rare to encounter the elevation or *consecration* of a family member. As clinicians, we are familiar with the dynamics of degradations. See, for example, Eric Bermann's (1973) marvelous depiction of a family that scapegoated a young boy: they saw him as bumbling and incompetent in order to deflect family anxiety from an impending open heart operation for father. Degradation usually involves putting the worst of ourselves into an unfortunate family member. On the other hand, consecration must involve putting the best of ourselves into another; perhaps in this case it was the dreams and aspirations for the future that the family did not dare grasp for themselves when Mary showed signs of a developmental lag. Ironically, perhaps, these dreams became invested in her. But this investment, whatever projective forces are at work, is highly *disciplined. All* family members must gear transactions with each other and the outside world to maintain this consecration even if they must subordinate their own interests to do so.

Vividness and Explanatory Power. Nothing conveys the full creative and disciplined force of this family better than the remarkable vividness of their shared percept and its power to explain everything. Such a sweeping explanatory power gives the family a sense of meaning, but it also strikes the observer with special force. This family cannot be discounted; they cannot be consigned to the looney bin. It seems to me no accident that the literature has so many descriptions of *folie à deux, folie à trois,* or *folie à famille.* People are shaken, genuinely shaken, by their encounters with such social systems, just as they are shaken by encounters with messianic cults and radical political groups. The power of the explanation to shake us gives us a hint of its force for providing meaning and control to the family. Typically, family constructions are more implicit, more delicately interwoven with broader constructions of a broader social community, and less simplistic. They create meaning through tying together a silken fabric of memories and experiences but do not usually generate a preemptive, fully conscious, explanatory concept.

It seems to me no accident that these very same features—sequestration coupled with extreme creativity, disciplined focus on a single individual, and the force of a vivid, explanatory system—are also features of another form of social group. Griffith and Mullins (1972) summarized a large body of sociological observation of radical scientific groups from the phage workers at Coldspring Harbor to the Skinnerians at Harvard to the ethnomethodologists at UCLA (one suspects that the authors of this paper are direct lineal descendants of the last of these three).[1] They drew special attention to three features of these groups. First was their sequestration. As they created their own singular vision of reality, they cut themselves off from the everyday workday of their parent disciplines. For example, as these groups developed, they cited each other's work more and more and the rest of the literature less and less. Their work was galvanized around a single individual. Group process required individual subordination to a view attached or identified with one person in particular. The example is clearest with the Skinnerians, but the ethnomethodologists rallied around Garfinkel as did the phage group around Delbruck. Finally, the views had remarkable, perhaps sweeping, explanatory power: relatively simple and stark axioms or principles extended across continents and dealt effectively with objections from those outside the group.

It would trivialize both radical science and the pathos of Mary and her family to draw the parallels here too tightly. I want to emphasize only one point. The constructivist position that Mary's family forces us to take contains within it a critical clinical "stance" (Kantor & Neal, 1985). The principle that reality is what we make it is not an apologia or a curse. That reality is constructed through the actions of social groups is not a degradation of the concept of reality but a consecration of groups. In this case, it generates awe rather than ridicule for Mary's family. As clinicians, we will want in some way to employ the creative energy, discipline, and responsibility inherent in the constructions of this family. By recognizing the dedicated passion with which we create our own reality, we can, without converting them or ourselves, appreciate the zeal of Mary and her family.

But a somber footnote must be added. Mary's family is not a radical scientific group. In the end, their vision will not be sustained by the accolades of an appreciative community of colleagues. Elsewhere (Reiss, 1981) I have presented evidence suggesting that a family's own construction of reality cannot be sustained by the family alone. In the words of Piaget, the constructions of the broader social world are indispensable "ailment" for the family's own constructions.

Indeed, the family is sustained by, and contributes to, the constructions of the community in which it lives. The Neuropsychiatric Institute will provide no succor for this construction. Barring membership in a cult that in some way reveres mentally retarded children, this family seems headed for a fall of enormous pain and disorganization. I would amend Pollner and McDonald-Wikler's fundamental question. They ask, "How do they do it?" I ask, "How long can they keep it up?"

Note

1. I will leave it to the reader's imagination to spot similar parallels with the charismatic groups significant in the history of family therapy. For those who need some prodding for their imagination, see the recent analysis by Kantor and Neal (1985).

References

Berger, P. L., & Kellner, H. (1964). Marriage and the construction of reality. *Diogenes, 64,* 1-25.

Bermann, E. (1973). *Scapegoat.* Ann Arbor: University of Michigan Press.

Griffith, B. C., & Mullins, H. C. (1972). Coherent social groups in scientific change. *Science, 177,* 959-964.

Kantor, D., & Lehr, W. (1975). *Inside the family.* San Francisco: Jossey-Bass.

Kantor, D., & Neal, J. H. (1985). Integrative shifts for the theory and practice of family systems therapy. *Fam. Proc., 24,* 13-30.

Reiss, D. (1981). *The family's construction of reality.* Cambridge, MA: Harvard University Press.

Strodtbeck, F. L. (1958). Family interaction, values and achievement. In D. C. McClelland, A. L. Baldwin, & U. Bronfenbrenner (Eds.), *Talent and society.* Princeton, NJ: Van Nostrand.

34

Self-Fulfilling Prophecies

Paul Watzlawick

A self-fulfilling prophecy is an assumption or prediction that, purely as a result of having been made, causes the expected or predicted event to occur and thus confirms its own "accuracy." For example, if someone assumes, for whatever reason, that he is not respected, he will, because of this assumption, act in such a hostile, overly sensitive, suspicious manner that he brings about that very contempt in others which "proves" again and again his firmly entrenched conviction. This mechanism may be commonplace and well known, but it is based upon a number of facts that are by no means part of our everyday thinking and which have a profound significance for our view of reality.

In our traditional cause-and-effect thinking we usually see event *B* as the result of a preceding, causal event (*A*)—which in turn has, of course, its own causes, just as the occurrence of *B* produces its own sequel of events. In the sequence *A* → *B*, *A* is therefore the cause and *B* its effect. The causality is *linear* and *B* follows *A* in the course of time. Accordingly, in this causality model, *B* can have no effect on *A*, because this would mean a reversal of the flow of time: The

"Self-Fulfilling Prophecies" by P. Watzlawick, translated by Ursula Berg Lunk, is reprinted from *The Invented Reality: How Do We Know What We Believe We Know? Contributions to Constructivism* (pp. 95-116), edited by Paul Watzlawick, by permission of W. W. Norton & Company, Inc. Copyright © 1984 by W. W. Norton & Company, Inc.

present (*B*) would have to exert a backward effect on the past (*A*).

Matters stand differently in the following example: In March 1979, when the newspapers in California began to publish sensational pronouncements of an impending, severe gasoline shortage, California motorists stormed the gas stations to fill up their tanks and to keep them as full as possible. This filling up of 12 million gasoline tanks (which up to this time had on the average been 75% empty) depleted the enormous reserves and so brought about the predicted shortage practically overnight. The endeavor to keep the fuel containers as full as possible (instead of getting gas when the tank was almost empty, as had been done before) resulted in endless lines and hours of waiting time at the gas stations, and increased the panic. After the excitement died down, it turned out that the allotment of gasoline to the state of California had hardly been reduced at all.

Here the customary cause-and-effect thinking breaks down. The shortage would never have occurred if the media had not predicted it. In other words, an event that had not yet taken place (i.e., an event in the future) created an effect in the present (the storming of the gas stations), which in turn caused the predicted event to become reality. In this sense it was the future—not the past—that determined the present.

The objection could be raised that all of this is neither astonishing nor unheard of.

Are not almost all human decisions and actions largely dependent on the evaluation of their probable effects, advantages, and dangers (or at least should they not be)? Does not the future therefore always play a part in the present? Significant as these questions may be, they do not seem to make much sense here. Whoever tries, usually on the basis of earlier experience, to evaluate the future effect of his decision normally intends the best possible outcome. The specific action tries to take the future into consideration, and subsequently proves to be true or false, correct or incorrect; but it does not have to have any influence whatever on the course of events. However, an action that results from a self-fulfilling prophecy itself produces the requisite conditions for the occurrence of the expected event, and in this sense *creates* a reality which would not have arisen without it. The action that is at first neither true nor false produces a fact, and with it its own "truth."

Here are examples of both perspectives: If someone begins to suffer from headaches, sneezes, and shivers, he will, on the basis of past experience, assume that he is coming down with a cold; and if his diagnosis is correct, he can, with aspirin, hot drinks, and bedrest, favorably influence the (future) course of the illness by these means in the present. By doing so, he has correctly grasped a causal sequence that had at first been totally independent of him, and exerted a partial influence on it.

A fundamentally different sequence results from the practice of collecting taxes in certain countries. Since the revenue agency assumes a priori that no citizen will ever truthfully declare his income, the tax rate is dictated more or less arbitrarily. The revenue offices rely largely on the information of their assessment agents, who take into consideration such vague factors as a person's standard of living, his real estate property, the fur coats of his wife, the make of his car, and so forth. To the income, "ascertained" in this way, there is then added a

certain percentage that is supposed to make up for any undeclared income, because—as we said—it is assumed a priori that the taxpayer cheats. This assumption, however, produces the situation in which a truthful declaration of income becomes unacceptable even for an honest taxpayer, and in which dishonesty is practically made a necessity if one wants to escape unfair taxes. Again an assumption believed to be true creates the assumed reality, and again it is irrelevant whether the assumption was originally true or false. And so we see that the difference lies in the fact that, in the example of the head cold, a development that is already taking place in the present is acted upon as best as is possible, and its course is influenced in this way in the present; whereas in the examples of the gasoline shortage and the income tax the course of events is induced by the very measures which are undertaken as a (supposed) reaction to the expected event in question. Therefore what is supposed to be a *reaction* (the effect) turns out to be an action (the cause); the "solution" produces the problem; the prophecy of the event causes the event of the prophecy.

This singular reversal of cause and effect is particularly obvious in interpersonal conflicts, where the phenomenon of the so-called *punctuation* of a sequence of events is invariably present. Making use of an example that has already been employed elsewhere (Watzlawick, Bavelas, & Jackson, 1967, pp. 56-58), we will imagine a married couple struggling with a conflict that they both assume to be basically the other's fault, while their own behavior is seen only as a *reaction* to that of their partner. The woman complains that her husband is withdrawing from her, which he admits, but because he sees his silence or his leaving the room as the only possible reaction to her constant nagging and criticizing. For her this reasoning is a total distortion of the facts: His behavior is the *cause* of her criticism and her anger. Both partners are referring to the same interpersonal reality but assign to it a diametrically

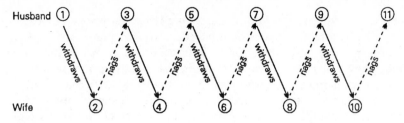

Figure 34.1

opposed causality. The above diagram, Figure 34.1, may illustrate this discrepancy, although it postulates—unavoidably but wrongly—a starting point that does not really exist, because the behavior pattern between the two people has been repeating itself for a long time, and the question of who started it has long since become meaningless.

The arrows with the solid lines represent the behavior of the husband ("withdraws"), and the dotted lines that of the wife ("nags"). The husband dissects ("punctuates") the whole of the pattern into the triads 2-3-4, 4-5-6, 6-7-8, and so on, and so sees the interpersonal reality as one in which his wife nags (cause) and he *therefore* withdraws from her (effect). From her point of view, however, it is his cold passivity (cause) that causes her nagging (effect); she criticizes him *because* he withdraws from her, and therefore punctuates the pattern into the triads 1-2-3, 3-4-5, 5-6-7, and so on. With this opposed punctuation, both have literally brought about two contradictory realities and—what is perhaps even more important—two self-fulfilling prophecies. The two modes of behavior, which are seen subjectively as a reaction to the behavior of the partner, cause this very behavior in the other and "therefore" justify one's own behavior.

It goes without saying that self-fulfilling prophecies in an interpersonal context can also be used deliberately and with a specific intent. The dangers of this practice will be discussed later on. As an example here let me only mention the well-known method of former matchmakers in patriarchal societies, who had the thankless task of awakening a mutual interest in two young people,

who possibly cared nothing for each other, because their families had decided that for financial reasons, social standing, or other similarly impersonal motives, the two would make a good couple. The matchmaker's usual procedure was to talk with the young man alone and ask him whether he had not noticed how the girl was always secretly watching him. Similarly, he would tell the girl that the boy was constantly looking at her when her head was turned. This prophecy, disguised as a fact, was often quickly fulfilled. Skilled diplomats also know this procedure as a negotiating technique.[1]

Everyday experience teaches us that only few prophecies are self-fulfilling, and the above examples should explain why: Only when a prophecy is believed, that is, only when it is seen as a fact that has, so to speak, already happened in the future, can it have a tangible effect on the present and thereby fulfill itself. Where this element of belief or conviction is absent, this effect will be absent as well. To inquire how the construction or acceptance of such a prophecy comes to be would go far beyond the scope of this essay. (An extensive study of the social, psychological, and physiological effects of self-fulfilling prophecies was published in 1974 by Jones.) Too numerous and various are the factors involved—from the realities one fabricates for oneself during the course of the so-called noncontingent reward experiments (Watzlawick, 1976, pp. 45-54) . . . , to such oddities as the (perhaps unverified, but not improbable) assertion that since Bernadette had a vision of the Virgin Mary in February of 1858, only pilgrims, but not a single inhabitant of Lourdes, found a miraculous cure there.

Of this story one can say, *se non è vero, è ben trovato,* since it helps to build a bridge from our previous, somewhat trivial reflections to manifestations of self-fulfilling prophecies that have a deeper human as well as scientific significance.

The oracle had prophesied that Oedipus would kill his father and marry his mother. Horrified by this prediction, which he undoubtedly believed to be true, Oedipus tries to protect himself from the impending doom, but the precautionary measures themselves lead to the seemingly inescapable fulfillment of the oracle's dictum. As is known, Freud used this myth as a metaphor for the incestuous attraction for the opposite sex inherent in every child, and the consequent fear of retaliation on the part of the parent of the same sex; and he saw in this key constellation, the Oedipus conflict, the fundamental cause of later neurotic developments. In his autobiography the philosopher Karl Popper (1974) refers back to a self-fulfilling prophecy that he had already described two decades earlier and which he called the Oedipus *effect:*

One of the ideas I had discussed in *The Poverty [of Historicism]* was the influence of a prediction upon the event predicted. I had called this the "Oedipus effect," because the oracle played a most important role in the sequence of events which led to the fulfillment of its prophecy. (It was also an allusion to the psychoanalysts, who had been strangely blind to this interesting fact, even though Freud himself admitted that the very dreams dreamt by patients were often coloured by the theories of their analysts; Freud called them "obliging dreams.")

Again we have the reversal of cause and effect, past and future; but here it is all the more critical and decisive because psychoanalysis is a theory of human behavior that hinges on the assumption of a linear causality, in which the past determines the present. And Popper points to the significance of this reversal by explicating further:

For a time I thought that the existence of the Oedipus effect distinguished the social from the natural sciences. But in biology too—even in molecular biology—expectations often play a role in bringing about what has been expected.

Similar quotations, referring to the effect of such "unscientific" factors as simple expectations and assumptions in the sciences, could be collated in abundance— [*The Invented Reality*] is itself intended as such a contribution. In this connection one might recall, for instance, Einstein's remark in a talk with Heisenberg: "It is the theory that determines what we can observe." And in 1958 Heisenberg himself says, "We have to remember that what we observe is not nature in itself, but nature exposed to our method of questioning." And more radical still, the philosopher of science Feyerabend (1978): "Not conservative, but anticipatory suppositions guide research."

Some of the most carefully documented and elegant investigations of self-fulfilling prophecies in the area of human communication are associated with the name of the psychologist Robert Rosenthal of Harvard University. Of particular interest here is his (1968) book with the appropriate title *Pygmalion in the Classroom,* in which he describes the results of his so-called Oak School experiments. They concerned a primary school with 18 women teachers and over 650 students. The self-fulfilling prophecy was induced in the members of the faculty at the beginning of a certain school year by giving the students an intelligence test whereby the teachers were told that the test could not only determine intelligence quotients, but could also identify those 20% of the students who would make rapid and above-average intellectual progress in the coming school year. After the intelligence test had been administered, but before the teachers had met their new students for the first time, they received the names (indiscriminately picked from the student list) of those students who supposedly, on the basis of the test, could be expected with certainty to perform unusually well. The difference between these children and the others thus existed solely in the heads of their particular teacher. The same intelligence test was repeated at the end of the school year for all students and showed *real* above-average increases in the intelligence quotients and achievements of these "special" students, and the reports of the faculty proved furthermore that these children distinguished themselves from their fellow students by their behavior, intellectual curiosity, friendliness, and so on.

Saint Augustine thanked God that he was not responsible for his dreams. Nowadays we do not have this comfort. Rosenthal's experiment is only one, although an especially clear example of how deeply and incisively our fellow human beings are affected by our expectations, prejudices, superstitions, and wishful thinking—all purely mental constructions, often without the slightest glimmer of actuality—and how these discoveries erode our comfortable conviction of the surpassing importance of heredity and innate characteristics. For it hardly needs to be expressly emphasized that these constructions can have negative as well as positive effects. We are not only responsible for our dreams, but also for the reality created by our hopes and thoughts.

It would, however, be a mistake to assume that self-fulfilling prophecies are restricted to human beings. Their effects reach deeper, into prehuman stages of development, and are in this sense even more alarming. Even before Rosenthal carried out his Oak School experiment, he reported in a book published in 1966 a similar experiment with rats that was repeated and confirmed by many scholars in the following years. Twelve participants in a laboratory course in experimental psychology were given a lecture on certain studies that purported to prove that good or bad test achievements of rats (for instance, in learning experiments in labyrinth cages) can become innate by selective breeding. Six of the students then received thirty rats whose genetic constitution allegedly made them especially good, intelligent laboratory subjects, while the other six students were assigned thirty rats of whom they were told the opposite, namely, that they were animals whose hereditary factors made them unsuitable for experiments. In fact and truth, the sixty rats were all of the same kind, the one that has always been used for such purposes. All sixty animals were then trained for exactly the same learning experiment. The rats whose trainers believed them to be especially intelligent did not just do better from the very outset, but raised their achievements far above that of the "unintelligent" animals. At the end of the five-day experiment the trainers were asked to evaluate their animals subjectively, in addition to the noted results of the experiments. The students who "knew" that they were working with unintelligent animals expressed themselves accordingly, that is, negatively, in their reports, whereas their colleagues, who had experimented with rats of supposedly above-average talents, rated their charges as friendly, intelligent, ingenious, and the like, and mentioned furthermore that they had often touched the animals, petted them, and even played with them. When we consider the surpassing role rat experiments play in experimental psychology and especially in the psychology of learning, and how often inferences are drawn from them to human behavior, these inferences now seem somewhat questionable.

Rats are known to be very intelligent animals, and the students' reports suggest that in the way they handled their animals, they literally "handed" them their assumptions and expectations. But the results of another research project, reported in 1963 by the research team Cordaro and Ison, suggest that it is not only a matter of such direct influence. In this project the laboratory subjects were earthworms (planaria), who are of great interest for the student of evolution and of behavior alike, in that they are the most primitive form of life possessing the rudiments of a brain. The supposition therefore suggested itself that these worms were capable of training of the simplest kind, as, for instance, a change in direction (to the left or to the right) upon arriving at the crossbeam of a T-shaped groove arrangement. Experiments of this kind began in several American universities in the late fifties. As in the rat experiments, Cordaro and Ison caused the experimenters to believe that they were working with especially intelligent or especially incapable worms, and even here, at this primitive stage of development (which, moreover, left little room for emotional attachment), there grew from the conviction, once it was established, objectively discernible and statistically significant differences in the experimental behavior of the planaria.[2]

For the very reason that these experiments undermine our basic concepts, it is all too easy to shrug them off and return to the comfortable certainty of our accustomed routines. That, for instance, test psychologists ignore these extremely disturbing results and continue to test people and animals with unmitigated tenacity and scientific "objectivity" is only a small example of the determination with which we defend ourselves when our world view is being threatened. The fact that we are responsible to the world in its entirety and to a much higher degree than is dreamed of in our philosophy is for the present almost unthinkable; but it can penetrate our consciousness through a better understanding of the processes of human communication—a study that will encompass many disciplines that heretofore have been either considered as being quite independent of each other or not considered at all. Rosenhan's contribution [see Chapter 37] illuminates the alarming

possibility that at least some so-called mental illnesses are nothing but constructions, and that the psychiatric institutions actually contribute to the constructions of those realities that are supposed to be treated therein. The chronic problem that still plagues modern psychiatry is that we have only the vaguest and most general concepts for the definition of mental health, while for the diagnosis of abnormal behavior there exist catalogs perfected to the last detail. Freud, for instance, used the concept of the ability to love and work as a basic criterion for mature emotional normalcy (a definition that does not do justice to a Hitler, on the one hand, or to the proverbial eccentricities of men of genius, on the other). The other medical specialties work with definitions of pathology that refer to certain deviations from fairly well-known normal functions of the healthy organism. Quite irrationally, in psychiatry it is just the opposite. Here pathology is considered the known factor, whereas normalcy is seen as difficult to define, if it is definable at all. This opens the floodgates to self-fulfilling diagnoses. There is a great number of very definite patterns of behavior that in the terminology of psychiatry are so tightly associated with certain diagnostic categories (again I refer to Rosenhan) that they virtually function like Pavlovian buzzers, not only in the thinking of the psychiatrist but also in the family environment of the patient. An attempt to show how certain specific forms of behavior take on the meaning of pathological manifestations on the basis of their cultural and societal significance, and how these manifestations in turn become self-fulfilling prophecies, would go beyond the scope of this essay. Of the already quite extensive literature on this topic, *The Manufacture of Madness* by Thomas Szasz (1970) is particularly notable. Suffice it to say that an essential part of the self-fulfilling effect of psychiatric diagnoses is based on our unshakable conviction that everything that has a name must *therefore* actually exist. The materializations and actualizations of psychiatric diagnoses probably originate largely from this conviction.

"Magic" diagnoses, in the actual sense of the word, have of course been known for a very long time. In his classic paper "Voodoo Death," the American physiologist Walter Cannon (1942) described a number of mysterious, sudden, and scientifically difficult to explain deaths that followed curses, evil spells, or the breaking of moral taboos. A Brazilian Indian, cursed by a medicine man, is helpless against his own emotional response to this death sentence and dies within hours. A young African hunter unknowingly kills and eats an inviolably banned wild hen. When he discovers his crime, he is overcome with despair and dies within twenty-four hours. A medicine man in the Australian bush points a bone with magic properties at a man. Believing that nothing can save him, the man sinks into lethargy and prepares to die. He is saved only at the last moment, when other members of the tribe force the witch doctor to remove the spell.

Cannon became convinced that voodoo death exists as a phenomenon,

characteristically noted among aborigines— among human beings so primitive, so superstitious, so ignorant, that they feel themselves bewildered strangers in a hostile world. Instead of knowledge, they have fertile and unrestricted imaginations which fill their environment with all manner of evil spirits capable of affecting their lives disastrously.

At the time when Cannon wrote these lines, hundreds of thousands of human beings who were neither superstitious nor ignorant had every reason to see themselves as bewildered victims of an unimaginably hostile world. From the haunted, shadowy world of the concentration camps Viktor Frankl (1959, pp. 74-75) reports a phenomenon that corresponds to voodoo death:

The prisoner who had lost faith in the future— his future—was doomed. With his loss of be-

lief in the future, he also lost his spiritual hold; he let himself decline and became subject to mental and physical decay. Usually this happened quite suddenly, in the form of a crisis, the symptoms of which were familiar to the experienced camp inmate. We all feared this moment—not for ourselves, which would have been pointless, but for our friends. Usually it began with the prisoner refusing one morning to get dressed and wash or to go out on the parade grounds. No entreaties, no blows, no threats had any effect. He just lay there.

One of Frankl's fellow prisoners lost his will to live when his own prediction, seen in a dream, did not come true and thereby became a negative self-fulfillment. "I would like to tell you something, Doctor," he said to Frankl,

I have had a strange dream. A voice told me that I could wish for something, that I should only say what I wanted to know, and all my questions would be answered. What do you think I asked? That I would like to know when the war would be over for me. You know what I mean, Doctor—for me! I wanted to know when we, when our camp, would be liberated and our sufferings come to an end. . . . Furtively he whispered to me, "March thirtieth."

But when the day of the prophesied liberation was near and the Allied forces were still far from the camp, things took a fateful turn for Frankl's fellow sufferer, the prisoner F.:

On March twenty-ninth, F. suddenly became ill and ran a high temperature. On March thirtieth, the day his prophecy had told him that the war and suffering would be over for him, he became delirious and lost consciousness. On March thirty-first, he was dead. He had died of typhus.

As a physician, Frankl understood that his friend died because

the expected liberation did not come and he was severely disappointed. This suddenly lowered his body's resistance against the latent typhus infection.

We admire human beings who face death calmly. Dying "decently," in a composed manner, without wrangling with the inevitable, was and is considered in most cultures an expression of wisdom and unusual maturity. All the more surprising and sobering therefore are the results of modern cancer research, which suggest that the mortality rate is higher in those patients who prepare themselves for death in a mature, serene way or who, like the concentration camp prisoner F., fall victim to a negative self-fulfilling prophecy. For those patients, however, who cling to life in a seemingly senseless, irrational, and immature way or who are convinced that they simply "cannot" or "must not" die because they have important work to do or family members to take care of, the prognosis is considerably more favorable. To the American oncologist Carl Simonton (1975), whose name is associated, above all, with the appreciation of the impact of emotional factors, now more and more recognized for their importance in the treatment of cancer, three things are of the utmost significance in this connection: the belief system of the patient, that of the patient's family, and, third, that of the attending physician. That each one of these belief systems can become a self-fulfilling prophecy seems credible in the light of what we have discussed so far. Furthermore, the studies and research reports about the susceptibility of the human immune system to mood swings, suggestions, and visual imagery (O. Simonton & S. Simonton, 1978; Solomon, 1969) are increasing.

How much can and should a physician tell his patients, not only about the gravity of their illnesses, but also about the dangers inherent in the treatment *itself*? At least in certain countries this question is becoming more and more rhetorical. The risk of getting hit with a malpractice suit because a patient has not been informed about his disease and its treatment down to the last technical detail causes many doctors in the United States, for example, to protect themselves in a way that can have serious consequences. The protection consists in asking the patient for a written consent to treatment in which the most catastrophic possible consequences of the illness and of the measures deemed necessary by the doctor are listed in every detail. It is not hard to imagine that this creates a kind of self-fulfilling prophecy that has a paralyzing effect on the confidence and will to recover of even the most sanguine patient. Who has not read the description of even a seemingly harmless medication and then had the feeling of swallowing poison? How does the layman (or, presumably, even the professional) know that he is not going to be the fourth of the three fatalities reported to date that were inexplicably caused by a medication so far used safely by millions? But *fiat justitia, pereat mundus*.

Since in the patient's eye a doctor is a kind of mediator between life and death, his utterances can easily become self-fulfilling prophecies. The astonishing degree to which this is possible is portrayed in a case reported (but unfortunately not sufficiently documented) by the American psychologist Gordon Allport (1964). What is unusual here is that a misunderstanding shifted the prophecy from death to life:

In a provincial Austrian hospital, a man lay gravely ill—in fact, at death's door. The medical staff had told him frankly that they could not diagnose his disease, but that if they knew the diagnosis they could probably cure him. They told him further that a famous diagnostician was soon to visit the hospital and that perhaps he could spot the trouble.

Within a few days the diagnostician arrived and proceeded to make the rounds. Coming to this man's bed, he merely glanced at the patient, murmured, "Moribundus," and went on.

Some years later, the patient called on the diagnostician and said, "I've been wanting to thank you for your diagnosis. They told me that if you could diagnose me I'd get well, and so the minute you said 'moribundus' I knew I'd recover."

Knowledge of the healing effect of positive predictions is undoubtedly just as ancient as faith in the inescapable consequences of curses and evil spells. Modern use of positive suggestions and autosuggestions ranges from the "I will recover; I feel better every day" of Emile Coué, through numerous forms of hypnotherapeutic interventions (Haley, 1973), to influencing the course of an illness—and not only cancer—by positive imagery. The extent to which such imagery that a (future) event has already taken place can reach into the physical realm is suggested by several studies according to which it is possible to increase a woman's chest measurement by an average of four to five centimeters through the use of certain self-hypnotic techniques (Staib & Logan, 1977; Willard, 1977). I mention these "successes" with all due skepticism and simply as curiosities testifying to the towering importance of the female breast in the North American erotic ethos.

Brief mention should also be made of the modern physiological and endocrinological studies that indicate more and more the possibility of stimulating the functions of the immune system of the human organism by certain experiences and that these functions are by no means completely autonomous (that is, outside conscious control), as was assumed until quite recently. Medical research is likely to make astonishing discoveries in this field in the near future. For instance, it is now known that the organism itself produces a number of morphene-like substances—the so-called endorphins (Beers, 1979)—that are analgesic and whose production is stimulated by certain emotional processes. There is thus a wide-open, unexplored territory in which the phenomenon of self-fulfilling prophecies begins to achieve scientific respectability.

Just as decisive as a doctor's suggestive comments, expectations, and convictions are the measures he takes and the remedies he administers. Of special interest here are *placebos*[3] (Benson & Epstein, 1975), those chemi-cally inert substances that resemble certain medicines in shape, taste, or color but which have no pharmaceutical effect. We must remember that until about 100 years ago nearly all medications were practically ineffective in the modern sense. They were only slightly more elegant tinctures and powders than the ground toads, the lizard blood, the "sacred oils," or the pulverized horn of the rhinoceros of even earlier times. During my childhood, people in the rural areas of Austria still believed that a necklace of garlic would protect them from the common cold, to say nothing about the well-known success of magic in the treatment of warts. Even in our time, old "tried and true" remedies or sensational new discoveries (as, for example, Laetrile) are always being unmasked as pharmaceutically ineffective. But that is not to say that they were or are *functionally* ineffective. "One should treat as many patients as possible with the new remedies, as long as these are still working," reads the maxim of a famous physician, attributed to Trousseau, Osler, or Sydenham. Scientific interest in placebos is rapidly increasing. In his contribution to the history of the placebo effect Shapiro (1960) points out that more articles on this topic were published in scientific journals between 1954 and 1957 alone than in the first fifty years of the twentieth century. Most of these reports discuss traditional pharmaceutical effectiveness studies, in which one group of patients receives the new medication while another takes a placebo. The purpose of this well-meaning procedure is to find out whether the course of the illness of the "actually" treated patients is different from that of the placebo group. Only people whose world view is based on classical linear causal thinking (for which there is only an "objective" relationship between cause and effect) react with consternation when they realize that the patients "treated" with placebos often show a quite "inexplicable" improvement in their condition. In other words, the claim of the doctor who administers the placebo that it is an effective, newly developed medicine and the patient's willingness to believe in its effectiveness create a reality in which the assumption actually becomes a fact.

Enough examples. Self-fulfilling prophecies are phenomena that not only shake up our personal conception of reality, but which can also throw doubt on the world view of science. They all share the obviously reality-creating power of a firm belief in the "suchness" of things, a faith that can be a superstition as well as a seemingly strictly scientific theory derived from objective observation. Until recently it has been possible to categorically reject self-fulfilling prophecies as unscientific or to ascribe them to the inadequate reality adaptation of muddle-headed thinkers and romanticists, but we no longer have this convenient escape hatch open to us.

What all this means cannot yet be appraised with any certainty. The discovery that we create our own realities is comparable to the expulsion from the paradise of the presumed suchness of the world, a world in which we can certainly suffer, but for which we need only feel responsible in a very limited way (Watzlawick, 1976).

And here lies the danger. The insights of constructivism may have the highly desirable advantage of allowing for new and more effective forms of therapy (Watzlawick, 1978), but like all remedies, they can also be abused. Advertising and propaganda are two especially repugnant examples: Both try quite deliberately to bring about attitudes, assumptions, prejudices, and the like, whose realization then seems to follow naturally and logically. Thanks to this brainwashing, the world is then seen as "thus" and therefore *is* "thus." In the novel *1984* (Orwell, 1949) this reality-creating propaganda language is called *Newspeak*, and Orwell explains that it "makes all other modes of thinking impossible." In a recent review of a volume of essays published in London on censorship in the People's Republic of Poland (Strzyzewski, 1977-1978), Daniel Weiss (1980) writes about this magic language:

> Compare for example the great number of adjectives, characteristic for Newspeak: Every development is nothing less than "dynamic," every plenary session of the party "historic," the masses always "proletarian workers." A sober communication scientist will find nothing but *redundance* in this inflation of mechanized epithets, drained of meaning. But after listening repeatedly, this automation is felt to have the equality of an incantation: The spoken word is no longer used to carry information, it has become the instrument of magic. (p. 66)

And finally the world simply *is thus.* How it was *made* to be this way was well known to Joseph Goebbels (1933/1976), when he lectured the managers of German radio stations on March 25, 1933:

> This is the secret of propaganda: To totally saturate the person, whom the propaganda wants to lay hold of, with the ideas of the propaganda, without him even noticing that he is being saturated. Propaganda has of course a purpose, but this purpose must be disguised with such shrewdness and virtuosity that he who is supposed to be filled with this purpose never even knows what is happening. (p. 120)

In the necessity of disguising the purpose, however, lies the possibility of overcoming it. As we have seen, the invented reality will become "actual" reality only if the invention is believed. Where the element of faith, of blind conviction, is absent, there will be no effect. With the better understanding of self-fulfilling prophecies our ability to transcend them grows. A prophecy that we know to be only a prophecy can no longer fulfill itself. The possibility of choosing differently (of being a heretic) and of disobeying always exists; whether we see it and act on it is, of course, another question. An insight from the seemingly far-removed domain of the mathematical theory of games is of interest here. Wittgenstein

(1956) already pointed out in his *Remarks on the Foundations of Mathematics* that certain games can be won with a simple trick. As soon as someone calls our attention to the existence of this trick, we no longer have to continue playing naively (and continue losing). Building on these reflections, the mathematician Howard (1967) formulated his *existential axiom* which maintains that "if a person becomes 'aware' of a theory concerning his behavior, he is no longer bound by it but is free to disobey it" (p. 167). Elsewhere he also says that

a conscious decision maker can always choose to disobey any theory predicting his behavior. We may say that he can always "transcend" such a theory. This indeed seems realistic. We suggest that among socio-economic theories, Marxian theory, for example, failed at least partly because certain ruling class members, when they became aware of the theory, saw that it was in their interest to disobey it. (1971)

And almost a hundred years before Howard, Dostoevski's underground man writes in his *Letters from the Underworld* (1913),

As a matter of fact, if ever there shall be discovered a formula which shall exactly express our wills and whims; if ever there shall be discovered a formula which shall make it absolutely clear what those wills depend upon, and what laws they are governed by, and what means of diffusion they possess, and what tendencies they follow under given circumstances; if ever there shall be discovered a formula which shall be mathematical in its precision, well, gentlemen, whenever such a formula shall be found, man will have ceased to have a will of his own—he will have ceased even to exist. Who would care to exercise his willpower according to a table of logarithms? In such a case man would become, not a human being at all, but an organ-handle, or something of the kind. (p. 32)

But even if this kind of mathematical formulization of our lives could ever be achieved, it would in no way comprehend the complexity of our existence. The best theory is powerless in the face of an antitheory; the fulfillment of even the truest prophecy can be thwarted if we know about it beforehand. Dostoevski (1913) saw much more in the nature of man:

Moreover, even if man *were* the keyboard of a piano, and could be convinced that the laws of nature and of mathematics had made him so, he would still decline to change. On the contrary, he would once more, out of sheer ingratitude, attempt the perpetration of something which would enable him to insist upon himself. . . . But if you were to tell me that all this could be set down in tables—I mean the chaos, and the confusion, and the curses, and all the rest of it—so that the possibility of computing everything might remain, and reason continue to rule the roost—well, in that case, I believe, man would *purposely* become a lunatic, in order to become devoid of reason, and therefore able to insist upon himself. I believe this, and I am ready to vouch for this, simply for the reason that every human act arises out of the circumstance that man is for ever striving to prove to his own satisfaction that he is a man and not an organ-handle. (p. 37)

However, even the evidence of the underground man is likely to be a self-fulfilling prophecy.

Notes

1. The following untrue story is a further illustration: In 1974, Secretary of State Kissinger, who is on one of his innumerable mediating missions in Jerusalem, is on his way back to the hotel after a private, late-evening stroll. A young Israeli stops him, introduces himself as an economist out of work, and asks Kissinger to help him find a job through his numerous connections. Kissinger is favorably impressed by the applicant and asks him whether he would like to be the vice-president of the Bank of Israel. The young man thinks of course that Kissinger is making fun of him, but the latter promises quite seriously that he will manage the matter for him. Next day Kissinger calls Baron Rothschild in Paris: "I have a charming young man here, a political economist, talented, going to be the next vice-

president of the Bank of Israel. You have to meet him; he would be a jewel of a husband for your daughter." Rothschild growls something that does not sound like total rejection, whereupon Kissinger immediately calls the president of the Bank of Israel: "I have a young financial expert here, brilliant fellow, exactly the stuff to make a vice-president for your bank, and most of all—imagine *that*—he is the future son-in-law of Baron Rothschild's."

2. Here I will briefly mention an interesting sequel to these experiments: For reasons irrelevant to our topic, several researchers (McConnell, Jacobson, & Humphries, 1961) studied the fascinating theory that at the planaria's primitive stage of development information stored in a worm's ribonucleic acid (RNA) could possibly be directly transferred to other worms. For this purpose they fed untrained animals their already successfully trained fellow worms. Even we laymen can imagine the sensation among experts when the training of the worms provided with such food actually turned out to be much easier and faster. The euphoria lasted for a short while until the experiments, repeated under more rigorous controls, showed themselves to be inconclusive, and serious doubts arose concerning the transferability of intelligence through ground meat. The suspicion suggests itself, but was, as far as I know, never proven, that the original results were due to self-fulfilling prophecies, similar to those whose effects on the worms were already known. (The analogy, however, to the superstition of certain African tribes that eating a lion's heart will confer the lion's courage cannot be dismissed out of hand.)

3. Latin for "I shall please."

References

Allport, G. W. (1964). Mental health: A generic attitude. *Journal of Religion and Health, 4*, 7-21.

Beers, R. F. (Ed.). (1979). *Mechanisms of pain and analgesic compounds.* New York: Raven.

Benson, H., & Epstein, M. D. (1975). The placebo effect: A neglected asset in the care of patients. *American Medical Association Journal, 232*, 1225-1227.

Cannon, W. B. (1942). Voodoo death. *American Anthropologist, 44*, 169-181.

Cordaro, L., & Ison, J. R. (1963). Observer bias in classical conditioning of the planaria. *Psychological Reports, 13*, 787-789.

Dostoevski, F. M. (1913). *Letters from the underworld.* New York: Dutton.

Feyerabend, P. K. (1978). *Science in a free society.* London: New Left.

Frankl, V. E. (1959). *From death camp to existentialism.* Boston: Beacon.

Goebbels, J. Quoted in Schneider, W. (1976). *Wörter machen leute. Magie und macht der sprache.* Munich: Piper.

Haley, J. (1973). *Uncommon therapy: The psychiatric techniques of Milton H. Erickson, MD.* New York: Norton.

Heisenberg, W. (1958). *Physics and philosophy: The revolution in modern science.* New York: Harper.

Howard, N. (1967). The theory of metagames. *General Systems, 2*, 167.

Howard, N. (1971). *Paradoxes of rationality, theory of metagames and political behavior.* Cambridge, MA: MIT Press.

Jones, R. A. (1974). *Self-fulfilling prophecies: Social, psychological and physiological effects of expectancies.* New York: Halsted.

McConnell, J. V., Jacobson, R., & Humphries, B. M. (1961). The effects of ingestion of conditioned planaria on the response level of naive planaria: A pilot study. *Worm Runner's Digest, 3*, 41-45.

Orwell, G. (1949). *1984.* New York: Harcourt, Brace.

Popper, K. R. (1974). *Unended quest.* La Salle, IL: Open Court.

Rosenthal, R. (1966). *Experimenter effects in behavioral research.* New York: Appleton-Century-Crofts.

Rosenthal, R., & Jacobson, L. (1968). *Pygmalion in the classroom: Teacher expectation and pupils' intellectual development.* New York: Holt, Rinehart & Winston.

Shapiro, A. K. (1960). A contribution to a history of the placebo effects. *Behavioral Science, 5*, 109-135.

Simonton, O. C., & Simonton, S. (1975). Belief systems and management of the emotional aspects of malignancy. *Journal of Transpersonal Psychology, 1*, 29-47.

Simonton, O. C., & Simonton, S. (1978). *Getting well again.* Los Angeles: J. P. Tarcher.

Solomon, G. F. (1969). Emotions, stress, the nervous system, and immunity. *Annals of the New York Academy of Sciences, 164*, 335-343.

Staib, A. R., & Logan, D. R. (1977). Hypnotic stimulation of breast growth. *American Journal of Clinical Hypnosis, 19,* 201-208.

Strzyzewski, T. (1977-1978). *Czarna ksiega cenzury PRL* (Black Book of Polish Censorship, 2 vols.). London: "Aneks."

Szasz, T. S. (1970). *The manufacture of madness: A comparative study of the inquisition and the mental health movement.* New York: Harper & Row.

Watzlawick, P. (1976). *How real is real?* New York: Random House.

Watzlawick, P. (1978). *The language of change: Elements of therapeutic communication.* New York: Basic Books.

Watzlawick, P., Bavelas, J. B., & Jackson, D. D. (1967). *Pragmatics of human communication: A study of interactional patterns, pathologies and paradoxes.* New York: Norton.

Weiss, D. (1980). Sprache und propaganda—Der sonderfall Polen. *Neue Zürcher Zeitung, 39,* 66.

Willard, R. R. (1977). Breast enlargement through visual imagery and hypnosis. *American Journal of Clinical Hypnosis, 19,* 195-200.

Wittgenstein, L. (1956). *Remarks on the foundations of mathematics.* Oxford, UK: Blackwell.

When Belief Creates Reality: The Self-Fulfilling Impact of First Impressions on Social Interaction

Mark Snyder

For the social psychologist, there may be no processes more complex and intriguing than those by which strangers become friends. How do we form first impressions of those we encounter in our lives? How do we become acquainted with each other? When does an acquaintance become a friend? Why do some relationships develop and withstand the test of time and other equally promising relationships flounder and fall by the wayside? It is to these and similar concerns that my colleagues and I have addressed ourselves in our attempts to chart

"When Belief Creates Reality: The Self-Fulfilling Impact of First Impressions on Social Interaction" by M. Snyder from *Experiencing Social Psychology*, edited by A. Pines and C. Maslach (pp. 189-192), 1977. New York: Alfred Knopf. Reprinted by permission of the author.

This research was supported in part by National Science Foundation Grant SOC 75-13872, "Cognition and Behavior: When Belief Creates Reality," to Mark Snyder. For a more detailed description of the background and rationale, procedures and results, implications and consequences of this investigation, see M. Snyder, E. D. Tanke, & E. Berscheid, Social perception and interpersonal behavior: On the self-fulfilling nature of social stereotypes. *Journal of Personality and Social Psychology*, 1977. For related research on behavioral confirmation in social interaction, see M. Snyder & W. B. Swann, Jr., Behavioral confirmation in social interaction: From social perception to social reality. *Journal of Experimental Social Psychology*, 1978.

the unfolding dynamics of social interaction and interpersonal relationships. In doing so, we chose—not surprisingly—to begin at the beginning. Specifically, we have been studying the ways in which first impressions channel and influence subsequent social interaction and acquaintance processes.

When we first meet others, we cannot help but notice certain highly visible and distinctive characteristics such as their sex, age, race, and bodily appearance. Try as we may to avoid it, our first impressions are often molded and influenced by these pieces of information. Consider the case of physical attractiveness. A widely held stereotype in this culture suggests that attractive people are assumed to possess more socially desirable personalities and are expected to lead better personal, social, and occupational lives than their unattractive counterparts. For example, Dion, Berscheid, and Walster (1972) had men and women judge photographs of either men or women who varied in physical attractiveness. Attractive stimulus persons of either sex were perceived to have virtually every character trait that pretesting had indicated was socially desirable to that participant population: "Physically attractive people, for example, were perceived to be more sexually warm and responsive, sensitive, kind, interesting, strong, poised, modest, sociable, and outgoing than persons of lesser physical attractiveness"

(Berscheid & Walster, 1974, p. 169). This powerful stereotype was found for male and female judges and for male and female stimulus persons. In addition, attractive people were predicted to have happier social, professional, and personal lives in store for them than were their less attractive counterparts. (For an excellent and comprehensive review, see Berscheid & Walster, 1974.)

What of the validity of the physical attractiveness stereotype? Are the physically attractive actually more likeable, friendly, sensitive, and confident than the unattractive? Are they more successful socially and professionally? Clearly, the physically attractive are more often and more eagerly sought out for social dates. And well they should be, for the stereotype implies that they should be perceived as more desirable social partners than the physically unattractive. Thus, it should come as little surprise that, among young adults, the physically attractive have more friends of the other sex, engage in more sexual activity, report themselves in love more often, and express less anxiety about dating than unattractive individuals do. But the effect is even more general than this. Even as early as nursery school age, physical attractiveness appears to channel social interaction: The physically attractive are chosen and the unattractive are rejected in sociometric choices.

A differential amount of interaction with the attractive and unattractive clearly helps the stereotype persevere because it limits the chances for learning whether the two types of individuals were in the traits associated with the stereotype. But the point I wish to focus on here is that the stereotype may also channel interaction so as to confirm itself *behaviorally*. Individuals appear to have different patterns and styles of interaction for those whom they perceive to be physically attractive and for those whom they consider unattractive. These differences in self-presentation and interaction style may, in turn, elicit and nurture behaviors from the target person that are in accord with the stereotype. That is, the physically attractive may actually come to behave in a friendly, likeable, sociable manner, not because they necessarily possess these dispositions, but because the behavior of others elicits and maintains behaviors taken to be manifestations of such traits.

In our empirical research, we have attempted to demonstrate that stereotypes may create their own social reality by channeling social interaction in ways that cause the stereotyped individual to behave in ways that confirm another person's stereotyped impressions of him or her. In our initial investigation, Elizabeth Decker Tanke, Ellen Berscheid, and I sought to demonstrate the self-fulfilling nature of the physical attractiveness stereotype in a social interaction context designed to mirror as faithfully as possible the spontaneous generation of first impressions in everyday social interaction and the subsequent channeling influences of these impressions on social interaction. In order to do so, pairs of previously unacquainted individuals (designated for our purposes as a *perceiver* and a *target*) interacted in a getting-acquainted situation constructed to allow us to control the information that one member of the dyad (the male perceiver) received about the physical attractiveness of the other individual (the female target). In this way, it was possible to evaluate separately the effects of actual and perceived physical attractiveness on the display of self-presentational and expressive behaviors associated with the stereotype that links beauty and goodness. In order to measure the extent to which the self-presentation of the target individual matched the perceiver's stereotype, naïve observer-judges who were unaware of the actual or perceived physical attractiveness of either participant listened to and evaluated tape recordings of the interaction.

Fifty-one male and fifty-one female undergraduates at the University of Minnesota participated, for extra course credit, in what had been described as a study of the "processes by which people become acquainted with each other." These individuals interacted in male-female dyads in a getting-acquainted situation in which they could hear but not see each other (a telephone conversation). Before initiating the conversation, the male member of each dyad received a Polaroid snapshot of his female interaction partner. These photographs, which had been prepared in advance and assigned at random to dyads, identified the target as either physically attractive (attractive-target condition) or physically unattractive (unattractive-target condition). Each dyad engaged in a ten-minute unstructured telephone conversation that was tape-recorded. Each participant's voice was recorded on a separate channel of the tape.

In order to assess the extent to which the actions of the female targets provided behavioral confirmation of the male perceivers' stereotypes, twelve observer-judges listened to the tape recordings of the getting-acquainted conversations. The observer-judges were unaware of the experimental hypotheses and knew nothing of the actual or perceived physical attractiveness of the individual whom they heard on the tapes. They heard only those tape tracks containing the female participants' voices. Nine other observer-judges listened to and rated only the male perceivers' voices. (For further details of the experimental procedures, see Snyder, Tanke, & Berscheid, 1977.)

In order to chart the process of behavioral confirmation of stereotype-based attributions in these dyadic social interactions, we examined the effects of our manipulation of the target's apparent physical attractiveness on both the male perceivers' initial impressions of their female targets and the females' behavioral self-presentation during their interactions, as measured by the observer-judges' ratings of the tape recordings of their voices.

The male perceivers clearly formed their initial impressions of their female targets on the basis of general stereotypes that associate physical attractiveness with socially desirable personality characteristics. On the basis of measures of first impressions that were collected after the perceivers had been given access to their partners' photographs but before the initiation of the getting-acquainted conversations, it was clear that (as dictated by the physical attractiveness stereotype) males who anticipated physically attractive partners expected to interact with comparatively cordial, poised, humorous, and socially adept individuals. By contrast, males faced with the prospect of getting acquainted with relatively unattractive partners fashioned images of rather withdrawn, awkward, serious, and socially inept creatures.

Not only did our perceivers fashion their images of their discussion partners on the basis of their stereotyped intuitions about the links between beauty and goodness of character, but the stereotype-based attributions initiated a chain of events that resulted in the behavioral confirmation of these initially erroneous inferences. Analysis of the observer-judges' ratings of the tape recordings of the conversations indicated that female targets who (unbeknown to them) were perceived to be physically attractive (as a consequence of random assignment to the attractive-target experimental condition) actually came to behave in a friendly, likeable, and sociable manner. This behavioral confirmation was discernible even by outside observer-judges who knew nothing of the actual or perceived physical attractiveness of the target individuals. In this demonstration of behavioral confirmation in social interaction, the "beautiful" people became "good" people, not because they necessarily possessed the socially valued dispositions that had been attributed to them, but because the actions of the perceivers, which were based on their stereotyped beliefs, had erroneously confirmed and validated these attributions.

Confident in our demonstration of the self-fulfilling nature of this particular social stereotype, we then attempted to chart the process of behavioral confirmation. Specifically, we searched for evidence of the behavioral implications of the perceivers' stereotypes. Did the male perceivers present themselves differently to the target women whom they assumed to be physically attractive or unattractive? An examination of the observer-judges' ratings of the tapes of only the males' contributions to the conversations provided clear evidence that our perceivers did have different interactional styles with targets of different physical attractiveness.

Men who interacted with women whom they believed to be physically attractive appeared to be more cordial, sexually warm, interesting, independent, sexually permissive, bold, outgoing, humorous, obvious, and socially adept than their counterparts in the unattractive-target condition. Moreover, these same men were seen by the judges to be more attractive, more confident, and more animated in their conversation than their counterparts. They were also considered by the observer-judges to be more comfortable in conversation, to enjoy themselves more, to like their partners more, to take the initiative more often, to use their voices more effectively, to see their women partners as more attractive, and finally, to be seen as more attractive by their partners than men in the unattractive-target condition.

It appears, then, that differences in the expressive self-presentation of sociability by the male perceivers may have been a key factor in the process of bringing out those reciprocal patterns of expression in the target women that constitute behavioral confirmation of the attributions from which the perceivers' self-presentation had been generated. One reason that target women who had been labeled attractive may have reciprocated this sociable self-presentation is that they regarded their partners' images of them as more accurate and their style of interaction to be more typical of the way men generally treated them than women in the unattractive-target condition did. Perhaps,

these latter individuals rejected their partners' treatment of them as unrepresentative and defensively adopted more cool and aloof postures to cope with their situations.

Our research points to the powerful but often unnoticed consequences of social stereotypes. In our demonstration, first impressions and expectations that were based on common cultural stereotypes about physical attractiveness channeled the unfolding dynamics of social interaction and acquaintance processes in ways that actually made those stereotyped first impressions come true. In our investigation, pairs of individuals got acquainted with each other in a situation that allowed us to control the information that one member of the dyad (the perceiver) received about the physical attractiveness of the other person (the target). Our perceivers [. . .] fashioned erroneous images of their specific partners that reflected their general stereotypes about physical attractiveness. Moreover, our perceivers had very different patterns and styles of interaction for those whom they perceived to be physically attractive and to be unattractive. These differences in self-presentation and interaction style, in turn, elicited and nurtured behaviors of the targets that were consistent with the perceived initial stereotypes. Targets who (unbeknown to them) were perceived to be physically attractive actually came to behave in a friendly, likeable, and sociable manner. The perceivers' attributions about their targets based on their stereotyped intuitions about the world had initiated a process that produced behavioral confirmation of those attributions. The initially erroneous impressions of the perceivers had become real. The stereotype had truly functioned as a self-fulfilling prophecy:

The self-fulfilling prophecy is, in the beginning, a *false* definition of the situation evoking a new behavior which makes the originally false conception come *true*. The validity of the self-fulfilling prophecy perpetuates a reign of error. For the prophet will cite the actual course of events as proof that he was right from the very beginning. . . . Such are the perversities of social logic. (Merton 1948, p. 195)

True to Merton's script, our "prophets," in the beginning, created false definitions of their situations. That is, they erroneously labeled their targets as sociable or unsociable persons on the basis of their physical attractiveness. But these mistakes in first impressions quickly became self-erasing mistakes because the perceivers' false definitions evoked new behaviors that made their originally false conceptions come true: They treated their targets as sociable or unsociable persons, and, indeed, these targets came to behave in a sociable or unsociable fashion. Our prophets also cited the actual course of events as proof that they had been right all along. Might not other important and widespread social stereotypes—particularly those concerning sex, race, social class, and ethnicity—also channel social interaction in ways that create their own social reality?

Any self-fulfilling influences of social stereotypes may have compelling and pervasive societal consequences. Social observers have for decades commented on and demonstrated the ways in which stigmatized social groups and outsiders may fall victim to self-fulfilling cultural stereotypes. Consider Scott's (1969) observations about the blind:

When, for example, sighted people continually insist that a blind man is helpless because he is blind, their subsequent treatment of him may preclude his own exercising the kinds of skills that would enable him to be independent. It is in this sense that stereotypic beliefs are self-actualized. (p. 9)

All too often, it is the victims who are blamed for their own plight [. . .] rather than the social expectations that have constrained their behavioral options.

References

Berscheid, E., & Walster, E. (1974). Physical attractiveness. In L. Berkowitz (Ed.), *Advances in experimental social psychology* (Vol. 7). New York: Academic Press.

Dion, K. K., Berscheid, E., & Walster, E. (1972). What is good is beautiful. *Journal of Personality and Social Psychology, 24,* 285-90.

Merton, R. K. (1948). The self-fulfilling prophecy. *Antioch Review, 8,* 193-210.

Scott, R. A. (1969). *The making of blind men.* New York: Russell Sage.

Snyder, M., Tanke, E. D., & Berscheid, E. (1977). Social perception and interpersonal behavior: On the self-fulfilling nature of social stereotypes. *Journal of Personality and Social Psychology, 35,* 656-666.

Pygmalion in the Classroom: Teacher Expectation and Pupils' Intellectual Development

Robert Rosenthal and *Lenore Jacobson*

There is increasing concern over what can be done to reduce the disparities of education, of intellectual motivation, and of intellectual competence that exist between the social classes and the colors of our school children. With this increasing concern, attention has focused more and more on the role of the classroom teacher, and the possible effects of her or his values, attitudes, and, especially, beliefs and expectations. Many educational theorists have expressed the opinion that the teacher's expectation of her pupils' performance may serve as an educational self-fulfilling prophecy. The teacher gets less because she expects less.

The concept of the self-fulfilling prophecy is an old idea which has found application in clinical psychology, social psychology, sociology, economics, and in everyday life. Most of the evidence for the operation of self-fulfilling prophecies has been correlational. Interpersonal prophecies have been found to agree with the behavior that was prophesied. From this, however, it cannot be said that the prophecy was the cause of its own fulfillment. The accurate prophecy

may have been based on a knowledge of the prior behavior of the person whose behavior was prophesied, so that the prophecy was in a sense "contaminated" by reality. If a physician predicts a patient's improvement, we cannot say whether the doctor is only giving a sophisticated prognosis or whether the patient's improvement is based on part on the optimism engendered by the physician's prediction. If school children who perform poorly are those expected by their teachers to perform poorly, we cannot say whether the teacher's expectation was the "cause" of the pupils' poor performance, or whether the teacher's expectation was simply an accurate prognosis of performance based on her knowledge of past performance. To help answer the question raised, experiments are required in which the expectation is experimentally varied and is uncontaminated by the past behavior of the person whose performance is predicted.

Such experiments have been conducted and they have shown that in behavioral research the experimenter's hypothesis may serve as self-fulfilling prophecy (Rosenthal, 1966). Of special relevance to our topic are those experiments involving allegedly bright and allegedly dull animal subjects. Half the experimenters were led to believe that their rat subjects had been specially bred for excellence of learning ability. The remaining experimenters were led to believe that their rat subjects were genetically inferior. Actually, the animals were assigned to their experimenters at random.

Regardless of whether the rat's task was to learn a maze or the appropriate responses in a Skinner box, the results were the same. Rats who were believed by their experimenters to be brighter showed learning which was significantly superior to the learning by rats whose experimenters believed them to be dull. Our best guess, supported by the experimenters' self-reports, is that allegedly well-endowed animals were handled more and handled more gently than the allegedly inferior animals. Such handling differences, along with differences in rapidity of reinforcement in the Skinner box situation, are probably sufficient to account for the differences in learning ability shown by allegedly bright and allegedly dull rats.

If rats showed superior performance when their trainer expected it, then it seemed reasonable to think that children might show superior performance when their teacher expected it. That was the reason for conducting the Oak School Experiment.

The Oak School Experiment

To all of the children in the Oak School, on the West Coast, the "Harvard Test of Inflected Acquisition" was administered in the Spring of 1964. This test was purported to predict academic "blooming" or intellectual growth. The reason for administering the test in the particular school was ostensibly to perform a final check of the validity of the test, a validity which was presented as already well-established. Actually, the "Harvard Test of Inflected Acquisition" was a standardized, relatively nonverbal test of intelligence, Flanagan's Tests of General Ability.

Within each of the six grades of the elementary school, there were three classrooms, one each for children performing at above-average, average, and below-average levels

of scholastic achievement. In each of the 18 classrooms of the school, about 20% of the children were designated as academic "spurters." The names of these children were reported to their new teachers in the Fall of 1964 as those who, during the academic year ahead, would show unusual intellectual gains. The "fact" of their intellectual potential was established from their scores on the test for "intellectual blooming."

Teachers were cautioned not to discuss the test findings with either their pupils or the children's parents. Actually, the names of the 20% of the children assigned to the "blooming" condition had been selected by means of a table of random numbers. The difference, then, between these children, earmarked for intellectual growth, and the undesignated control group children was in the mind of the teacher.

Four months after the teachers had been given the names of the "special" children, all the children once again took the same form of the nonverbal test of intelligence. Four months after this retest the children took the same test once again. This final retest was at the end of the school year, some eight months after the teachers had been given the expectation for intellectual growth of the special children. These retests were not explained as "retests" to the teachers, but rather as further efforts to predict intellectual growth.

The intelligence test employed, while relatively nonverbal in the sense of requiring no speaking, reading, or writing, was not entirely nonverbal. Actually there were two subtests, one requiring a greater comprehension of English—a kind of picture vocabulary test. The other subtest required less ability to understand any spoken language but more ability to reason abstractly. For shorthand purposes we refer to the former as a "verbal" subtest and to the latter as a "reasoning" subtest. The pretest correlation between these subjects was only +.42, suggesting that the two subtests were measuring somewhat different intellectual abilities.

For the school as a whole, the children of the experimental groups did not show a significantly greater gain in verbal IQ (2 points) than did the control group children. However, in total IQ (4 points) and especially in reasoning IQ (7 points) the experimental children gained more than did the control group children. In 15 of the 17 classrooms in which the reasoning IQ posttest was administered, children of the experimental group gained more than did the control group children. Even after the four-month retest this trend was already in evidence though the effects were smaller.

When we examine the results separately for the six grades we find that it was only in the first and second grades that children gained significantly more in IQ when their teacher expected it of them. In the first grade, children who were expected to gain more IQ gained over 15 points more than did the control group children. In the second grade, children who were expected to gain more IQ gained nearly 10 points more than did the control group children. In the first and second grades combined, 19% of the control group children gained 20 or more IQ points. Two-and-a-half times that many, or 47%, of the experimental group children gained 20 or more IQ points.

When educational theorists have discussed the possible effects of teachers' expectations, they have usually referred to the children at lower levels of scholastic achievement. It was interesting, therefore, to find that in the present study, children of the highest level of achievement showed as great a benefit as did the children of the lowest level of achievement of having their teachers expect intellectual gains.

At the end of the school year of this study, all teachers were asked to describe the classroom behavior of their pupils. Those children from whom intellectual growth was expected were described as having a significantly better chance of becoming successful in the future, as significantly more interesting, curious, and happy. There was a tendency, too, for these children to be seen as more appealing, adjusted, and affectionate and as lower in the need for social approval. In short, the children from whom intellectual growth was expected became more intellectually alive and autonomous—or at least were so perceived by their teachers. These findings were particularly striking among first-grade children; these were the children who had benefited most in IQ gain as a result of their teachers' favorable expectancies.

We have already seen that the children of the experimental group gained more intellectually. It was possible, therefore, that their actual intellectual growth accounted for the teachers' more favorable ratings of these children's behavior and aptitude. But a great many of the control group children also gained in IQ during the course of the year. Perhaps those who gained more intellectually among these undesignated children would also be rated more favorably by their teachers. Such was not the case. In fact, there was a tendency for teachers to rate those control group children who gained most in IQ as *less* well-adjusted, *less* interesting, and *less* affectionate than control group children who made smaller intellectual gains. From these results it would seem that when children who are expected to grow intellectually do so, they may benefit in other ways as well. When children who are not especially expected to develop intellectually do so, they may show accompanying undesirable behavior, or at least are perceived by their teachers as showing such undesirable behavior. It appears that there may be hazards to unpredicted intellectual growth.

A closer analysis of these data, broken down by whether the children were in the high, medium, or low ability tracks or groups, showed that these hazards of unpredicted intellectual growth were due primarily to the children of the low ability group. When these slow track children were in the control group, so that no intellectual gains were expected of them, they were rated less favorably by their teachers if they did show gains in IQ. The greater their IQ gains, the less favorably were they rated, both as to mental health and as to intellectual vitality. Even when the slow track children were in the experimental group, so that IQ gains were expected of them, they were not rated as favorably relative to their control group peers as were children of the high or medium track, despite the fact that they gained as much in IQ relative to the control group children as did the experimental group children of the high track. It may be difficult for a slow track child, even one whose IQ is rising, to be seen by his teacher as a well-adjusted child, or as a potentially successful child intellectually.

The Question of Mediation

How did the teachers' expectations come to serve as determinants of gains in intellectual performance? The most plausible hypothesis seemed to be that children for whom unusual intellectual growth had been predicted would be attended to more by their teachers. If teachers were more attentive to the children earmarked for growth, we might expect that teachers were robbing Peter to see Paul grow. With a finite amount of time to spend with each child, if a teacher gave more time to the children of the experimental group, she would have less time to spend with the children of the control group. If the teacher's spending more time with a child led to greater intellectual gains, we could test the "robbing Peter" hypothesis by comparing the gains made by children of the experimental group with gains made by the children of the control group in each class. The robbing Peter hypothesis predicts a negative correlation. The greater the gains made by children of the experimental group (with the implication of more time spent on them) the less should be the gains made by the children of the control group (with the implication of less time spent on them). In

fact, however, the correlation was positive, large, and statistically significant (+.57). The greater the gains made by children of whom gain was expected, the greater the gains made in the same classroom by those children from whom no special gain was expected.

Additional evidence that teachers did not take time from control group children to spend with the experimental group children comes from the teachers' estimates of time spent with each pupil. These estimates showed a slight tendency for teachers to spend *less* time with pupils from whom intellectual gains were expected.

That the children of the experimental group were not favored with a greater investment of time seems less surprising in view of the pattern of their greater intellectual gains. If, for example, teachers had talked to them more, we might have expected greater gains in verbal IQ. But the greater gains were found not in verbal but in reasoning IQ. It may be, of course, that the teachers were inaccurate in their estimates of time spent with each of their pupils. Possibly direct observation of the teacher-pupil interactions would have given different results, but that method was not possible in the present study. But even direct observation might not have revealed a difference in the amounts of teacher time invested in each of the two groups of children. It seems plausible to think that it was not a difference in amount of time spent with the children of the two groups which led to the differences in their rates of intellectual development. It may have been more a matter of the type of interaction which took place between the teachers and their pupils.

By what she said, by how she said it, by her facial expressions, postures, and perhaps by her touch, the teacher may have communicated to the children of the experimental group that she expected improved intellectual performance. Such communications, together with possible changes in teaching techniques, may have helped the child learn by changing his or her self-concept, expectations of his or her own behavior, motivation, as well as cognitive skills. Further research is clearly needed to narrow down the range of possible mechanisms whereby a teacher's expectations become translated into a pupil's intellectual growth. It would be valuable, for example, to have sound films of teachers interacting with their pupils. We might then look for differences in the ways teachers interact with those children from whom they expect more intellectual growth compared to those from whom they expect less. On the basis of films of psychological experimenters interacting with subjects from whom different responses were expected, we know that even in such highly standardized situations, unintentional communications can be subtle and complex (Rosenthal, 1967). How much more subtle and complex may be the communications between children and their teachers in the less highly standardized classroom situation?

Conclusions

The results of the Oak School experiment provide further evidence that one person's expectations of another's behavior may serve as a self-fulfilling prophecy. When teachers expected that certain children would show greater intellectual development, those children did show greater intellectual development. A number of more recent experiments have provided additional evidence for the operation of teacher expectancy effects, in contexts ranging from the classroom to teaching athletic skills. Although not all of the studies that have been conducted show such effects, a large proportion of them do (Rosenthal, 1971).

It may be that as teacher training institutions acquaint teachers-to-be with the possibility that their expectations of their pupils' performance may serve as self-fulfilling prophecies, these teacher trainees may be given a new expectancy—that children can learn more than they had believed possible.

Perhaps the most suitable summary of the hypothesis discussed in this paper has already been written. The writer is George Bernard Shaw, the play is *Pygmalion,* and the speaker is Eliza Doolittle:

You see, really and truly, . . . the difference between a lady and a flower girl is not how she behaves, but how she's treated. I shall always be a flower girl to Professor Higgins, because he . . . treats me as a flower girl, . . . but I know I can be a lady to you, because you always treat me as a lady, and always will.

Note

An expanded discussion of self-fulfilling prophecies and a full account of the Oak School experiment are presented in R. Rosenthal & L. Jacobson (1968), *Pygmalion in the classroom: Teacher expectation and pupils' intellectual development,* New York: Holt, Rinehart & Winston.

References

Rosenthal, R. (1966). *Experimenter effects in behavioral research.* New York: Appleton-Century-Crofts.

Rosenthal, R. (1967). Covert communication in the psychological experiment. *Psychological Bulletin, 67,* 356-367.

Rosenthal, R. (1971). Teacher expectation and pupil learning. In R. D. Strom (Ed.), *Teachers and the learning process.* Englewood Cliffs, NJ: Prentice-Hall.

37

On Being Sane in Insane Places

D. L. Rosenhan

If sanity and insanity exist, how shall we know them?

The question is neither capricious nor itself insane. However much we may be personally convinced that we can tell the normal from the abnormal, the evidence is simply not compelling. It is commonplace, for example, to read about murder trials wherein eminent psychiatrists for the defense are contradicted by equally eminent psychiatrists for the prosecution on the matter of the defendant's sanity. More generally, there are a great deal of conflicting data on the reliability, utility, and meaning of such terms as "sanity," "insanity," "mental illness," and "schizophrenia."[1] Finally, as early as 1934, Benedict suggested that normality and abnormality are not universal.[2] What is viewed as normal in one culture may be seen as quite aberrant in another. Thus, notions of normality and abnormality may not be quite as accurate as people believe they are.

To raise questions regarding normality and abnormality is in no way to question the fact that some behaviors are deviant or odd. Murder is deviant. So, too, are hallucinations. Nor does raising such questions deny the existence of the personal anguish that is often associated with "mental illness." Anxiety and depression exist. Psychological suffering exists. But normality and abnormality, sanity and insanity, and the diagnoses that flow from them may be less substantive than many believe them to be.

At its heart, the question of whether the sane can be distinguished from the insane (and whether degrees of insanity can be distinguished from each other) is a simple matter: do the salient characteristics that lead to diagnoses reside in the patients themselves or in the environments and contexts in which observers find them? From Bleuler, through Kretchmer, through the formulators of the recently revised *Diagnostic and Statistical Manual* of the American Psychiatric Association, the belief has been strong that patients present symptoms, that those symptoms can be categorized, and, implicitly, that the sane are distinguishable from the insane. More recently, however, this belief has been questioned. Based in part on theoretical and anthropological considerations, but also on philosophical, legal, and therapeutic ones, the view has grown that psychological categorization of mental illness is useless at best and downright harmful, misleading, and pejorative at worst. Psychiatric diagnoses, in this view, are in the minds of the observers and are not valid summaries of characteristics displayed by the observed.[3,4,5]

Gains can be made in deciding which of these is more nearly accurate by getting normal people (that is, people who do not have, and have never suffered, symptoms of serious psychiatric disorders) admitted to psychiatric hospitals and then determining whether they were discovered to be sane and, if so, how. If the sanity of such pseudopatients was always detected, there would be prima facie evidence that a sane individual can be distinguished from the insane context in which he is found. Normality (and presumably abnormality) is distinct enough that it can be recognized wherever it occurs, for it is carried within the person. If, on the other hand, the sanity of the pseudopatients were never discovered, serious difficulties would arise for those who support traditional modes of psychiatric diagnosis. Given that the hospital staff was not incompetent, that the pseudopatient had been behaving as sanely as he had been outside of the hospital, and that it had never been previously suggested that he belonged in a psychiatric hospital, such an unlikely outcome would support the view that psychiatric diagnosis betrays little about the patient but much about the environment in which an observer finds him.

This article describes such an experiment. Eight sane people gained secret admission to 12 different hospitals.[6] Their diagnostic experiences constitute the data of the first part of this article; the remainder is devoted to a description of their experiences in psychiatric institutions. Too few psychiatrists and psychologists, even those who have worked in such hospitals, know what the experience is like. They rarely talk about it with former patients, perhaps because they distrust information coming from the previously insane. Those who have worked in psychiatric hospitals are likely to have adapted so thoroughly to the settings that they are insensitive to the impact of that experience. And while there have been occasional reports of researchers who submitted themselves to psychiatric hospitalization,[7] these researchers have commonly remained in the hospitals for short periods of time,

often with the knowledge of the hospital staff. It is difficult to know the extent to which they were treated like patients or like research colleagues. Nevertheless, their reports about the inside of the psychiatric hospital have been valuable. This article extends those efforts.

Pseudopatients and Their Settings

The eight pseudopatients were a varied group. One was a psychology graduate student in his 20's. The remaining seven were older and "established." Among them were three psychologists, a pediatrician, a psychiatrist, a painter, and a housewife. Three pseudopatients were women, five were men. All of them employed pseudonyms, lest their alleged diagnoses embarrass them later. Those who were in mental health professions alleged another occupation in order to avoid the special attentions that might be accorded by staff, as a matter of courtesy or caution, to ailing colleagues.[8] With the exception of myself (I was the first pseudopatient and my presence was known to the hospital administrator and chief psychologist and, so far as I can tell, to them alone), the presence of pseudopatients and the nature of the research program were not known to the hospital staffs.[9]

The settings were similarly varied. In order to generalize the findings, admission into a variety of hospitals was sought. The 12 hospitals in the sample were located in five different states on the East and West coasts. Some were old and shabby, some were quite new. Some were research-oriented, others not. Some had good staff-patient ratios, others were quite understaffed. Only one was a strictly private hospital. All of the others were supported by state or federal funds or, in one instance, by university funds.

After calling the hospital for an appointment, the pseudopatient arrived at the admissions office complaining that he had been hearing voices. Asked what the voices said, he replied that they were often unclear, but as far as he could tell they said "empty," "hollow," and "thud." The voices were unfamiliar and were of the same sex as the pseudopatient. The choice of these symptoms was occasioned by their apparent similarity to existential symptoms. Such symptoms are alleged to arise from painful concerns about the perceived meaninglessness of one's life. It is as if the hallucinating person were saying, "My life is empty and hollow." The choice of these symptoms was also determined by the *absence* of a single report of existential psychoses in the literature.

Beyond alleging the symptoms and falsifying name, vocation, and employment, no further alterations of person, history, or circumstances were made. The significant events of the pseudopatient's life history were presented as they had actually occurred. Relationships with parents and siblings, with spouse and children, with people at work and in school, consistent with the aforementioned exceptions, were described as they were or had been. Frustrations and upsets were described along with joys and satisfactions. These facts are important to remember. If anything, they strongly biased the subsequent results in favor of detecting sanity, since none of their histories or current behaviors were seriously pathological in any way.

Immediately upon admission to the psychiatric ward, the pseudopatient ceased simulating *any* symptoms of abnormality. In some cases, there was a brief period of mild nervousness and anxiety, since none of the pseudopatients really believed that they would be admitted so easily. Indeed, their shared fear was that they would be immediately exposed as frauds and greatly embarrassed. Moreover, many of them had never visited a psychiatric ward; even those who had, nevertheless had some genuine fears about what might happen to them. Their nervousness, then, was quite appropriate to the novelty of the hospital setting, and it abated rapidly.

Apart from that short-lived nervousness, the pseudopatient behaved on the ward as he "normally" behaved. The pseudopatient spoke to patients and staff as he might ordinarily. Because there is uncommonly little to do on a psychiatric ward, he attempted to engage others in conversation. When asked by staff how he was feeling, he indicated that he was fine, that he no longer experienced symptoms. He responded to instructions from attendants, to calls for medication (which was not swallowed), and to dining-hall instructions. Beyond such activities as were available to him on the admissions ward, he spent his time writing down his observations abut the ward, its patients, and the staff. Initially these notes were written "secretly," but as it soon became clear that no one much cared, they were subsequently written on standard tablets of paper in such public places as the dayroom. No secret was made of these activities.

The pseudopatient, very much as a true psychiatric patient, entered a hospital with no foreknowledge of when he would be discharged. Each was told that he would have to get out by his own devices, essentially by convincing the staff that he was sane. The psychological stresses associated with hospitalization were considerable, and all but one of the pseudopatients desired to be discharged almost immediately after being admitted. They were, therefore, motivated not only to behave sanely, but to be paragons of cooperation. That their behavior was in no way disruptive is confirmed by nursing reports, which have been obtained on most of the patients. These reports uniformly indicate that the patients were "friendly," "cooperative," and "exhibited no abnormal indications."

The Normal Are Not Detectably Sane

Despite their public "show" of sanity, the pseudopatients were never detected. Admitted, except in one case, with a diagnosis of schizophrenia,[10] each was discharged with a diagnosis of schizophrenia "in remission." The label "in remission" should in no way be dismissed as a formality, for at no time during any hospitalization had any question been raised about any pseudopatient's simulation. Nor are there any indications in the hospital records that the pseudopatient's status was suspect. Rather, the evidence is strong that, once labeled schizophrenic, the pseudopatient was stuck with that label. If the pseudopatient was to be discharged, he must naturally be "in remission"; but he was not sane, nor, in the institution's view, had he ever been sane.

The uniform failure to recognize sanity cannot be attributed to the quality of the hospitals, for, although there were considerable variations among them, several are considered excellent. Nor can it be alleged that there was simply not enough time to observe the pseudopatients. Length of hospitalization ranged from 7 to 52 days, with an average of 19 days. The pseudopatients were not, in fact, carefully observed, but this failure clearly speaks more to traditions within psychiatric hospitals than to lack of opportunity.

Finally, it cannot be said that the failure to recognize the pseudopatients' sanity was due to the fact that they were not behaving sanely. While there was clearly some tension present in all of them, their daily visitors could detect no serious behavioral consequences—nor, indeed, could other patients. It was quite common for the patients to "detect" the pseudopatients' sanity. During the first three hospitalizations, when accurate counts were kept, 35 of a total of 118 patients on the admissions ward voiced their suspicions, some vigorously, "You're not crazy. You're a journalist, or a professor [referring to the continual note-taking]. You're checking up on the hospital." While most of the patients were reassured by the pseudopatient's insistence that he had been sick before he came in but was fine now, some continued to believe that the pseudopatient

was sane throughout his hospitalization.[11] The fact that the patients often recognized normality when staff did not raises important questions.

Failure to detect sanity during the course of hospitalization may be due to the fact that physicians operate with a strong bias toward what statisticians call the type 2 error.[5] This is to say that physicians are more inclined to call a healthy person sick (a false positive, type 2) than a sick person healthy (a false negative, type 1). The reasons for this are not hard to find: it is clearly more dangerous to misdiagnose illness than health. Better to err on the side of caution, to suspect illness even among the healthy.

But what holds for medicine does not hold equally well for psychiatry. Medical illnesses, while unfortunate, are not commonly pejorative. Psychiatric diagnoses, on the contrary, carry with them personal, legal, and social stigmas.[12] It was therefore important to see whether the tendency toward diagnosing the sane insane could be reversed. The following experiment was arranged at a research and teaching hospital whose staff had heard these findings but doubted that such an error could occur in their hospital. The staff was informed that at some time during the following 3 months, one or more pseudopatients would attempt to be admitted into the psychiatric hospital. Each staff member was asked to rate each patient who presented himself at admissions or on the ward according to the likelihood that the patient was a pseudopatient. A 10-point scale was used, with a 1 and 2 reflecting high confidence that the patient was a pseudopatient.

Judgments were obtained on 193 patients who were admitted for psychiatric treatment. All staff who had had sustained contact with or primary responsibility for the patient—attendants, nurses, psychiatrists, physicians, and psychologists—were asked to make judgments. Forty-one patients were alleged, with high confidence, to be pseudopatients by at least one member of the staff.

Twenty-three were considered suspect by at least one psychiatrist. Nineteen were suspected by one psychiatrist *and* one other staff member. Actually, no genuine pseudopatient (at least from my group) presented himself during this period.

The experiment is instructive. It indicates that the tendency to designate sane people as insane can be reversed when the stakes (in this case, prestige and diagnostic acumen) are high. But what can be said of the 19 people who were suspected by being "sane" by one psychiatrist and another staff member? Were these people truly "sane," or was it rather the case that in the course of avoiding the type 2 error the staff tended to make more errors of the first sort—calling the crazy "sane"? There is no way of knowing. But one thing is certain: any diagnostic process that lends itself so readily to massive errors of this sort cannot be a very reliable one.

The Stickiness of Psychodiagnostic Labels

Beyond the tendency to call the healthy sick—a tendency that accounts better for diagnostic behavior on admission than it does for such behavior after a lengthy period of exposure—the data speak to the massive role of labeling in psychiatric assessment. Having once been labeled schizophrenic, there is nothing the pseudopatient can do to overcome the tag. The tag profoundly colors others' perceptions of him and his behavior.

From one viewpoint, these data are hardly surprising, for it has long been known that elements are given meaning by the context in which they occur. Gestalt psychology made this point vigorously, and Asch[13] demonstrated that there are "central" personality traits (such as "warm" versus "cold") which are so powerful that they markedly color the meaning of other information in forming an impression of a given personality.[14] "Insane," "schizophrenic," "manic-depressive," and "crazy" are probably among the most powerful of such central traits. Once a person is designated abnormal, all of his other behaviors and characteristics are colored by that label. Indeed, that label is so powerful that many of the pseudopatients' normal behaviors were overlooked entirely or profoundly misinterpreted. Some examples may clarify this issue.

Earlier I indicated that there were no changes in the pseudopatient's personal history and current status beyond those of name, employment, and, where necessary, vocation. Otherwise, a veridical description of personal history and circumstances was offered. Those circumstances were not psychotic. How were they made consonant with the diagnosis of psychosis? Or were those diagnoses modified in such a way as to bring them into accord with the circumstances of the pseudopatient's life, as described by him?

As far as I can determine, diagnoses were in no way affected by the relative health of the circumstances of a pseudopatient's life. Rather, the reverse occurred: the perception of his circumstances was shaped entirely by the diagnosis. A clear example of such translation is found in the case of a pseudopatient who had had a close relationship with his mother but was rather remote from his father during his early childhood. During adolescence and beyond, however, his father became a close friend, while his relationship with his mother cooled. His present relationship with his wife was characteristically close and warm. Apart from occasional angry exchanges, friction was minimal. The children had rarely been spanked. Surely there is nothing especially pathological about such a history. Indeed, many readers may see a similar pattern in their own experiences, with no markedly deleterious consequences. Observe, however, how such a history was translated in the psychopathological context, this from the case summary prepared after the patient was discharged.

This white 39-year-old male . . . manifests a long history of considerable ambivalence in close relationships, which begins in early childhood. A warm relationship with his mother cools during his adolescence. A distant relationship to his father is described as becoming very intense. Affective stability is absent. His attempts to control emotionality with his wife and children are punctuated by angry outbursts and, in the case of the children, spankings. And while he says that he has several good friends, one senses considerable ambivalence embedded in those relationships also. . . .

The facts of the case were unintentionally distorted by the staff to achieve consistency with a popular theory of the dynamics of a schizophrenic reaction.[15] Nothing of an ambivalent nature had been described in relations with parents, spouse, or friends. To the extent that ambivalence could be inferred, it was probably not greater than is found in all human relationships. It is true the pseudopatient's relationships with his parents changed over time, but in the ordinary context that would hardly be remarkable—indeed, it might very well be expected. Clearly, the meaning ascribed to his verbalizations (that is, ambivalence, affective instability) was determined by the diagnosis: schizophrenia. An entirely different meaning would have been ascribed if it were known that the man was "normal."

All pseudopatients took extensive notes publicly. Under ordinary circumstances, such behavior would have raised questions in the minds of observers, as, in fact, it did among patients. Indeed, it seemed so certain that the notes would elicit suspicion that elaborate precautions were taken to remove them from the ward each day. But the precautions proved needless. The closest any staff member came to questioning those notes occurred when one pseudopatient asked his physician what kind of medication he was receiving and began to write down the response. "You needn't write it," he was told gently. "If you have trouble remembering, just ask me again."

If no questions were asked of the pseudopatients, how was their writing interpreted? Nursing records for three patients indicate that the writing was seen as an aspect of their pathological behavior. "Patient engages in writing behavior" was the daily nursing comment on one of the pseudopatients who was never questioned about his writing. Given that the patient is in the hospital, he must be psychologically disturbed. And given that he is disturbed, continuous writing must be a behavioral manifestation of that disturbance, perhaps a subset of the compulsive behaviors that are sometimes correlated with schizophrenia.

One tacit characteristic of psychiatric diagnosis is that it locates the sources of aberration within the individual and only rarely within the complex of stimuli that surrounds him. Consequently, behaviors that are stimulated by the environment are commonly misattributed to the patient's disorder. For example, one kindly nurse found a pseudopatient pacing the long hospital corridors. "Nervous, Mr. X?" she asked. "No, bored," he said.

The notes kept by pseudopatients are full of patient behaviors that were misinterpreted by well-intentioned staff. Often enough, a patient would go "berserk" because he had, wittingly or unwittingly, been mistreated by, say, an attendant. A nurse coming upon the scene would rarely inquire even cursorily into the environmental stimuli of the patient's behavior. Rather, she assumed that his upset derived from his pathology, not from his present interactions with other staff members. Occasionally, the staff might assume that the patient's family (especially when they had recently visited) or other patients had stimulated the outburst. But never were the staff found to assume that one of themselves or the structure of the hospital had anything to do with a patient's behavior. One psychiatrist pointed to a group of patients who were sitting outside the cafeteria entrance half an hour before lunchtime. To a group of young residents he indicated that such behavior was characteristic of the oral-acquisitive nature of the syndrome. It seemed not to occur to him that there were very few things to anticipate in a psychiatric hospital besides eating.

A psychiatric label has a life and an influence of its own. Once the impression has been formed that the patient is schizophrenic, the expectation is that he will continue to be schizophrenic. When a sufficient amount of time has passed, during which the patient has done nothing bizarre, he is considered to be in remission and available for discharge. But the label endures beyond discharge, with the unconfirmed expectation that he will behave as a schizophrenic again. Such labels, conferred by mental health professionals, are as influential on the patient as they are on his relatives and friends, and it should not surprise anyone that the diagnosis acts on all of them as a self-fulfilling prophecy. Eventually, the patient himself accepts the diagnosis, with all of its surplus meanings and expectations, and behaves accordingly.[5]

The inferences to be made from these matters are quite simple. Much as Zigler and Phillips have demonstrated that there is enormous overlap in the symptoms presented by patients who have been variously diagnosed,[16] so there is enormous overlap in the behaviors of the sane and the insane. The sane are not "sane" all of the time. We lose our tempers "for no good reason." We are occasionally depressed or anxious, again for no good reason. And we may find it difficult to get along with one or another person—again for no reason that we can specify. Similarly, the insane are not always insane. Indeed, it was the impression of the pseudopatients while living with them that they were sane for long periods of time— that the bizarre behaviors upon which their diagnoses were allegedly predicated constituted only a small fraction of their total behavior. If it makes no sense to label ourselves permanently depressed on the basis of an occasional depression, then it takes better evidence than is presently available to label all patients insane or schizophrenic on the basis of bizarre behaviors or cogni-

tions. It seems more useful, as Mischel[17] has pointed out, to limit our discussions to *behaviors*, the stimuli that provoke them, and their correlates.

It is not known why powerful impressions of personality traits, such as "crazy" or "insane," arise. Conceivably, when the origins of and stimuli that give rise to a behavior are remote or unknown, or when the behavior strikes us as immutable, trait labels regarding the *behaver* arise. When, on the other hand, the origins and stimuli are known and available, discourse is limited to the behavior itself. Thus, I may hallucinate because I am sleeping, or I may hallucinate because I have ingested a peculiar drug. These are termed sleep-induced hallucinations, or dreams, and drug-induced hallucinations, respectively. But when the stimuli to my hallucinations are unknown, that is called craziness, or schizophrenia— as if that inference were somehow as illuminating as the others. . . .

The Consequences of Labeling and Depersonalization

Whenever the ratio of what is known to what needs to be known approaches zero, we tend to invent "knowledge" and assume that we understand more than we actually do. We seem unable to acknowledge that we simply don't know. The needs for diagnosis and remediation of behavioral and emotional problems are enormous. But rather than acknowledge that we are just embarking on understanding, we continue to label patients "schizophrenic," "manic-depressive," and "insane," as if in those words we had captured the essence of understanding. The facts of the matter are that we have known for a long time that diagnoses are often not useful or reliable, but we have nevertheless continued to use them. We now know that we cannot distinguish insanity from sanity. It is depressing to consider how that information will be used.

Not merely depressing, but frightening. How many people, one wonders, are sane but not recognized as such in our psychiatric institutions? How many have been needlessly stripped of their privileges of citizenship, from the right to vote and drive to that of handling their own accounts? How many have feigned insanity in order to avoid the criminal consequences of their behavior, and, conversely, how many would rather stand trial than live interminably in a psychiatric hospital—but are wrongly thought to be mentally ill? How many have been stigmatized by well-intentioned, but nevertheless erroneous, diagnoses? On the last point, recall again that a "type 2 error" in psychiatric diagnosis does not have the same consequences it does in medical diagnosis. A diagnosis of cancer that has been found to be in error is cause for celebration. But psychiatric diagnoses are rarely found to be in error. The label sticks, a mark of inadequacy forever.

Notes

1. P. Ash (1949), *J. Abnorm. Soc. Psychol., 44,* 272 (1949); A. T. Beck (1962), *Amer. J. Psychiat., 119,* 210; A. T. Boisen (1938), *Psychiatry, 2,* 233; N. Kreitman (1961), *J. Ment. Sci., 107,* 876; N. Kreitman, P. Sainsbury, J. Morrisey, J. Towers, & J. Scrivener (1961), *J. Ment. Sci., 107,* 887; H. O. Schmitt & C. P. Fonda (1956), *J. Abnorm. Soc. Psychol., 52,* 262; W. Seeman (1953), *J. Nerv. Ment. Dis., 118,* 541. For an analysis of these artifacts and summaries of the disputes, see J. Zibin (1967), *Annu. Rev. Psychol., 18,* 373; L. Phillips & J. G. Draguns (1971), *Annu. Rev. Psychol., 22,* 447.

2. R. Benedict (1934), *J. Gen. Psychol., 10,* 59.

3. See in this regard H. Becker (1963), *Outsiders: Studies in the sociology of deviance,* New York: Free Press; B. M. Braginsky, D. D. Braginsky, & K. Ring (1969), *Methods of madness: The mental hospital as a last resort,* New York: Holt, Rinehart & Winston; G. M. Crocetti & P. V. Lemkau (1965), *Amer. Sociol. Rev., 30,* 577; E. Goffman (1964), *Behavior in public places,* New York: Free Press; R. D. Laing (1960), *The divided self: A study of sanity and madness,* Chicago: Quadrangle; D. L. Phillips (1963), *Amer.. Sociol. Rev., 20,* 963; T. R. Sarbin (1972), *Psychol. Today, 6,* 18; E. Schur (1969), *Amer.*

J. Sociol., 75, 309; T. Szasz (1963a), *Law, liberty and psychiatry,* New York: Macmillan; (1963b), *The myth of mental illness: Foundations of a theory of mental illness,* New York: Hoeber Harper. For a critique of some of these views, see W. R. Gove (1970), *Amer. Sociol. Rev., 35,* 873.

4. E. Goffman (1961), *Asylums,* Garden City, NY: Doubleday.

5. T. J. Scheff (1966), *Being mentally ill: A sociological theory,* Chicago: Aldine.

6. Data from a ninth pseudopatient are not incorporated in this report because, although his sanity went undetected, he falsified aspects of his personal history, including his marital status and parental relationships. His experimental behaviors therefore were not identical to those of the other pseudopatients.

7. A. Barry (1971), *Bellevue is a state of mind,* New York: Harcourt Brace Jovanovich; I. Belknap (1956), *Human problems of a state mental hospital,* New York: McGraw Hill; W. Caudill, F. C. Redlich, H. R. Gilmore, & E. B. Brody, *Amer. J. Orthopsychiat., 22,* 314; A. R. Goldman, R. H. Bohr, & T. A. Steinberg (1970), *Prof. Psychol., 1,* 427; *Roche Report, 1* (13 [1971]), 8.

8. Beyond the personal difficulties that the pseudopatient is likely to experience in the hospital, there are legal and social ones that, combined, require considerable attention before entry. For example, once admitted to a psychiatric institution, it is difficult, if not impossible, to be discharged on short notice, state law to the contrary notwithstanding. I was not sensitive to these difficulties at the outset of the project, nor to the personal and situational emergencies that can arise, but later a writ of habeas corpus was prepared for each of the entering pseudopatients and an attorney was kept "on call" during every hospitalization. I am grateful to John Kaplan and Robert Bartels for legal advice and assistance in these matters.

9. However distasteful such concealment is, it was a necessary first step to examining these questions. Without concealment, there would have been no way to know how valid these experiences were; nor was there any way of knowing whether whatever detections occurred were a tribute to the diagnostic acumen of the staff or to the hospital's rumor network. Obviously, since my concerns are general ones that cut across individual hospitals and staffs, I have respected their anonymity and have eliminated clues that might lead to their identification.

10. Interestingly, of the 12 admissions, 11 were diagnosed as schizophrenic and one, with the identical symptomatology, as manic-depressive psychosis. This diagnosis has a more favorable prognosis, and it was given by the only private hospital in our sample. On the relations between social class and psychiatric diagnosis, see A. deB. Hollingshead & F. C. Redlich (1958), *Social class and mental illness: A community study*, New York: John Wiley.

11. It is possible, of course, that patients have quite broad latitudes in diagnosis and therefore are inclined to call many people sane, even those whose behavior is patently aberrant. However, although we have no hard data on this matter, it was our distinct impression that this was not the case. In many instances, patients not only singled us out for attention, but came to imitate our behaviors and styles.

12. J. Cumming & E. Cumming (1965), *Community Ment. Health*, 1, 135; A. Farina & K. Ring (1965), *J. Abnorm. Psychol.*, 70, 47; H. E. Freeman & O. G. Simmons (1963), *The mental patient comes home*, New York: John Wiley; W. J. Johannsen (1969), *Ment. Hygiene*, 53, 218; A. S. Linsky (1970), *Soc. Psychiat.*, 5, 166.

13. S. E. Asch (1946), *J. Abnorm. Soc. Psychol.*, 41, 258; (1952), *Social psychology*, New York: Prentice-Hall.

14. See also I. N. Mensch & J. Wishner (1947), *J. Personality*, 16, 188; J. Wishner (1960), *Psychol. Rev.*, 67, 96; J. S. Bruner & R. Tagiuri (1954), in G. Lindzey (Ed.), *Handbook of social psychology* (Vol. 2, pp. 634-654), Cambridge, MA: Addison-Wesley; J. S. Bruner, D. Shapiro, & R. Tagiuri (1958), in R. Tagiuri & L. Petrullo (Eds.), *Person perception and interpersonal behavior* (pp. 277-288), Stanford, CA: Stanford University Press.

15. For an example of a similar self-fulfilling prophecy, in this instance dealing with the "central" trait of intelligence, see R. Rosenthal & L. Jacobson (1968), *Pygmalion in the classroom*, New York: Holt, Rinehart & Winston.

16. E. Zigler & L. Phillips (1961), *J. Abnorm. Soc. Psychol.*, 63, 69. See also R. K. Freudenberg & J. P. Robertson (1956), *A.M.A. Arch. Neurol. Psychiatr.*, 76, 14.

17. W. Mischel (1968), *Personality and assessment*, New York: John Wiley.

The Nudist Management of Respectability

Martin S. Weinberg

Public nudity is taboo in our society. Yet there is a group who breaches this moral rule. They call themselves "social nudists."

A number of questions may be asked about these people. For example, how can they see their behavior as morally appropriate? Have they constructed their own morality? If so, what characterizes this morality and what are its consequences?[1]

This article will attempt to answer these questions through a study of social interaction in nudist camps. The data come from three sources: two summers of participant observation in nudist camps; 101 interviews with nudists in the Chicago area; and 617 mailed questionnaires completed by nudists in the United States and Canada.[2]

The Construction of Situated Moral Meanings: The Nudist Morality

The construction of morality in nudist camps is based on the official interpretations that camps provide regarding the moral meanings of public heterosexual nudity. These are (1) that nudity and sexuality are unrelated; (2) that there is nothing shameful about the

human body; (3) that nudity promotes a feeling of freedom and natural pleasure; and (4) that nude exposure to the sun promotes physical, mental, and spiritual well-being.

This official perspective is sustained in nudist camps to an extraordinary degree, illustrating the extent to which adult socialization can affect traditional moral meanings. (This is especially true with regard to the first two points of the nudist perspective, which will be our primary concern since these are its "deviant" aspects.) The assumption in the larger society that nudity and sexuality are related, and the resulting emphasis on covering the sexual organs, make the nudist perspective a specifically situated morality. My field work, interview, and questionnaire research show that nudists routinely use a special system of rules to create, sustain, and enforce this situated morality.

Strategies for Sustaining a Situated Morality

The first strategy used by the nudist camp to anesthetize any relationship between nudity and sexuality[3] involves a system of organizational precautions regarding who can come into the camp. Most camps, for example, regard unmarried people, especially single men, as a threat to the nudist morality. They suspect that singles may indeed see nudity as something sexual. Thus, most camps either exclude unmarried people (especially men), or allow only a small quota of them. Camps that do allow single men may charge them up to 35 percent more than they charge families. (This is intended to discourage single men, but since the cost is still relatively low compared with other resorts, this measure is not very effective. It seems to do little more than create resentment among the singles, and by giving formal organizational backing to the definition that singles are not especially desirable, it may contribute to the segregation of single and married members in nudist camps.)

Certification by the camp owner is another requirement for admission to camp grounds, and three letters of recommendation regarding the applicant's character are sometimes required. These regulations help preclude people whom members regard as a threat to the nudist morality.

[The camp owner] invited us over to see if we were *desirable* people. Then after we did this, he invited us to camp on probation: then they voted us into camp. [Q: Could you tell me what you mean by desirable people?] Well, not people who are inclined to drink, or people who go there for a peep show. Then they don't want you there. They feel you out in conversation. They want people for mental and physical health reasons.

Whom to admit [is the biggest problem of the camp]. [Q][4] Because the world is so full of people whose attitudes on nudity are hopelessly warped. [Q: Has this always been the biggest problem in camp?] Yes. Every time anybody comes, a decision has to be made. [Q] . . . The lady sitting at the gate decides about admittance. The director decides on membership.

A limit is sometimes set on the number of trial visits a non-member may make to camp. In addition, there is usually a limit on how long a person can remain clothed. This is a strategy to mark guests who may not sincerely accept the nudist perspective.

The second strategy for sustaining the nudist morality involves norms of interpersonal behavior. These norms are as follows:

No Staring. This rule controls overt signs of overinvolvement. As the publisher of one nudist magazine said, "They all look up to the heavens and never look below." Such studied inattention is most exaggerated among women, who usually show no recognition that the male is unclothed. Women also recount that they had expected men to look at their nude bodies, only to find, when they finally did get up the courage to undress, that no one seemed to notice. As one woman states: "I got so mad because my husband wanted me to undress in front of other men that I just pulled my clothes right off thinking everyone would look at me." She was amazed (and appeared somewhat disappointed) when no one did.

The following statements illustrate the constraints that result:

[Q: Have you ever observed or heard about anyone staring at someone's body while at camp?] I've heard stories, particularly about men that stare. Since I heard these stories, I tried not to, and have even done away with my sunglasses after someone said, half-joking, that I hide behind sunglasses to stare. Toward the end of the summer I stopped wearing sunglasses. And you know what, it was a child who told me this.

[Q: Would you stare . . . ?] Probably not, 'cause you can get in trouble and get thrown out. If I thought I could stare unobserved I might. They might not throw you out, but it wouldn't do you any good. [Q] The girl might tell others and they might not want to talk to me. . . . [Q] They disapprove by not talking to you, ignoring you, etc.

[Someone who stares] wouldn't belong there. [Q] If he does that he is just going to camp to see the opposite sex. [Q] He is just coming to stare. [Q] You go there to swim and relax.

I try very hard to look at them from the jaw up—even more than you would normally.[5]

No Sex Talk. Sex talk, or telling "dirty jokes," is uncommon in camp. The owner of a large camp in the Midwest stated: "It is usually expected that members of a nudist camp will not talk about sex, politics, or religion." Or as one single male explained: "It is taboo to make sexual remarks here." During my field work, it was rare to hear "sexual" joking such as one hears at most other types of resort. Interview respondents who mentioned that they had talked about sex qualified this by explaining that such talk was restricted to close friends, was of a "scientific nature," or, if a joke, was a "cute sort."

Asked what they would think of someone who breached this rule, respondents indicated that such behavior would cast doubt on the situated morality of the nudist camp:

One would expect to hear less of that at camp than at other places. [Q] Because you expect that the members are screened in their attitude for nudism—and this isn't one who prefers sexual jokes.

I've never heard anyone swear or tell a dirty joke out there.

No. Not at camp. You're not supposed to. You bend over backwards not to.

They probably don't belong there. They're there to see what they can find to observe. [Q] Well, their mind isn't on being a nudist, but to see so and so nude.

No Body Contact. Although the extent to which this is enforced varies from camp to camp, there is at least some degree of informal enforcement in nearly every camp. Nudists mention that they are particularly careful not to brush against anyone or have any body contact for fear of how it might be interpreted:

I stay clear of the opposite sex. They're so sensitive, they imagine things.

People don't get too close to you. Even when they talk. They sit close to you, but they don't get close enough to touch you.

We have a minimum of contact. There are more restrictions [at a nudist camp]. [Q] Just a feeling I had. I would openly show my affection more readily someplace else.

And when asked to conceptualize a breach of this rule, the following response is typical:

They are in the wrong place. [Q] That's not part of nudism. [Q] I think they are there for some sort of sex thrill. They are certainly not there to enjoy the sun.

Also, in photographs taken for nudist magazines, the subjects usually have only limited body contact. One female nudist explained: "We don't want anyone to think we're immoral." Outsiders' interpretations, then, can also constitute a threat.

Associated with the body contact taboo is a prohibition of nude dancing. Nudists cite this as a separate rule. This rule is often talked about by members in a way that indicates organizational strain—that is, the rule itself makes evident that a strategy is in operation to sustain their situated morality.

This reflects a contradiction in our beliefs. But it's self-protection. One incident and we'd be closed.

No Alcoholic Beverages in American Camps. This rule guards against breakdowns in inhibition, and even respondents who admitted that they had "snuck a beer" before going to bed went on to say that they fully favor the rule.

Yes. We have [drunk at camp]. We keep a can of beer in the refrigerator since we're out of the main area. We're not young people or carousers. . . . I still most generally approve of it as a camp rule and would disapprove of anyone going to extremes. [Q] For common-sense reasons. People who overindulge lose their inhibitions, and there is no denying that the atmosphere of a nudist camp makes one bend over backwards to keep people who are so inclined from going beyond the bounds of propriety.

Anyone who drinks in camp is jeopardizing their membership and they shouldn't. Anyone who drinks in camp could get reckless. [Q] Well, when guys and girls drink they're a lot bolder—they might get fresh with someone else's girl. That's why it isn't permitted, I guess.

Rules Regarding Photography. Photography in a nudist camp is controlled by the camp management. Unless the photographer works for a nudist magazine, his (or her) moral perspective is sometimes suspect. One photographer's remark to a woman that led to his being so typed was, "Do you think you could open your legs a little more?"

Aside from a general restriction on the use of cameras, when cameras are allowed, it is expected that no pictures will be taken without the subject's permission. Members blame the misuse of cameras especially on single men. As one nudist said: "You always see the singles poppin' around out of nowhere snappin' pictures." In general, control is maintained, and any infractions that take place are not blatant or obvious. Over-indulgence in picture-taking communicates an overinvolvement in the subjects' nudity and casts doubt on the assumption that nudity and sexuality are unrelated.

Photographers dressed only in cameras and light exposure meters. I don't like them. I think they only go out for pictures. Their motives should be questioned.

Photographers for nudist magazines recognize the signs that strain the situated morality that characterizes nudist camps. As one such photographer commented:

I never let a girl look straight at the camera. It looks too suggestive. I always have her look off to the side.

Similarly, a nudist model showed the writer a pin-up magazine to point out how a model could make a nude picture "sexy"— through the use of various stagings, props, and expressions—and in contrast, how the nudist model eliminates these techniques to make her pictures "natural." Although it may be questionable that a nudist model completely eliminates a sexual perspective for the non-nudist, the model discussed how she attempts to do this.

It depends on the way you look. Your eyes and your smile can make you look sexy. The way they're looking at you. Here, she's on a bed. It wouldn't be sexy if she were on a beach with kids running around. They always have some clothes on too. See how she's "looking" sexy? Like an "Oh, dear!" look. A different look can change the whole picture.

Now here's a decent pose. . . . Outdoors makes it "nature." Here she's giving you "the eye," or is undressing. It's cheesecake. It depends on the expression on her face. Having nature behind it makes it better.

Don't smile like "Come on, honey!" It's that look and the lace thing she has on. . . . Like when you half-close your eyes, like "Oh, baby," a Marilyn Monroe look. Art is when you don't look like you're hiding it halfway.

The element of trust plays a particularly strong role in socializing women to the nudist perspective. Consider this in the following statements made by another model for nudist magazines. She and her husband had been indoctrinated in the nudist ideology by friends. At the time of the interview, however, the couple had not yet been to camp, although they had posed indoors for nudist magazines.

[Three months ago, before I was married] I never knew a man had any pubic hairs. I was shocked when I was married. . . . I wouldn't think of getting undressed in front of my husband. I wouldn't make love with a light on, or in the daytime.

With regard to being a nudist model, this woman commented:

None of the pictures are sexually seductive. [Q] The pose, the look—you can have a pose that's completely nothing, till you get a look that's not too hard to do. [Q: How do you do that?] I've never tried. By putting on a certain air about a person; a picture that couldn't be submitted to a nudist magazine—using————[the nudist photographer's] language. . . . [Q: Will your parents see your pictures in the magazine?] Possibly. I don't really care. . . . My mother might take it all right. But they've been married twenty years and she's never seen my dad undressed.[6]

No Accentuation of the Body. Accentuating the body is regarded as incongruent with the nudist morality. Thus, a woman who had shaved her pubic area was labeled "disgusting" by other members. There was a similar reaction to women who sat in a blatantly "unladylike" manner.

I'd think she was inviting remarks. [Q] I don't know. It seems strange to think of it. It's strange you ask it. Out there, they're not unconscious about their posture. Most women there are very circumspect even though in the nude.

For a girl, . . . [sitting with your legs open] is just not feminine or ladylike. The hair doesn't always cover it. [Q] Men get away with so many things. But, it would look dirty for a girl, like she was waiting for something. When I'm in a secluded area I've spread my legs to sun, but I kept an eye open and if anyone came I'd close my legs and sit up a little. It's just not ladylike.

You can lay on your back or side, or with your knees under your chin. But not with your legs spread apart. It would look to other people like you're there for other reasons. [Q: What other reasons?] . . . To stare and get an eyeful . . . not to enjoy the sun and people.

No Unnatural Attempts at Covering the Body. "Unnatural attempts" at covering the body are ridiculed since they call into question the assumption that there is no shame in exposing any area of the body. If such behavior occurs early in one's nudist career, however, members usually have more compassion, assuming that the person just has not yet fully assimilated the new morality.

It is how members interpret the behavior, however, rather than the behavior per se, that determines whether covering up is disapproved.

If they're cold or sunburned, it's understandable. If it's because they don't agree with the philosophy, they don't belong there.

I would feel their motives for becoming nudists were not well founded. That they were not true nudists, not idealistic enough.

A third strategy that is sometimes employed to sustain the nudist reality is the use of communal toilets. Not all the camps have communal toilets, but the large camp where I did most of my field work did have such a facility, which was marked, "Little Girls Room and Little Boys Too." Although the stalls had three-quarter-length doors, this combined facility still helped to provide an element of consistency; as the owner said, "If you are not ashamed of any part of your body or any of its natural functions, men and women do not need separate toilets." Thus, even the physical ecology of the nudist camp was designed to be consistent with the nudist morality. For some, however, communal toilets were going too far.

I think they should be separated. For myself it's all right. But there are varied opinions, and for the satisfaction of all, I think they should separate them. There are niceties of life we often like to maintain, and for some people this is embarrassing. . . . [Q] You know, in a bowel movement it always isn't silent.

The Routinization of Nudity

In the nudist camp, nudity becomes routinized; its attention-provoking quality recedes and nudity becomes a taken-for-granted state of affairs. Thus, when asked questions about staring ("While at camp, have you ever stared at anyone's body? Do you think you would stare at anyone's body?") nudists indicate that nudity generally does not invoke their attention.

Nudists don't care what bodies are like. They're out there for themselves. It's a matter-of-fact thing. After a while you feel like you're sitting with a full suit of clothes on.

To nudists the body becomes so matter-of-fact, whether clothed or unclothed, when you make it an undue point of interest it becomes an abnormal thing.

[Q: What would you think of someone staring?] I would feel bad and let down. [Q] I have it set up on a high standard. I have never seen it happen. . . . [Q] Because it's not done there. It's above that: you don't stare. . . . If I saw it happen, I'd be startled. There's no inclination to do that. Why would they?

There are two types—male and female. I couldn't see why they were staring. I don't understand it.

In fact, these questions about staring elicit from nudists a frame of possibilities in which what is relevant to staring is ordinarily not nudity itself. Rather, what evokes attention is something unusual, something the observer seldom sees and thus is not routinized to.[7]

There was a red-haired man. He had red pubic hair. I had never seen this before. . . . He didn't see me. If anyone did, I would turn the other way.

Well, once I was staring at a pregnant woman. It was the first time I ever saw this. I was curious, her stomach stretched, the shape. . . . I also have stared at extremely obese people, cripples. All this is due to curiosity, just a novel sight. [Q] . . . I was discreet. [Q] I didn't look at them when their eyes were fixed in a direction so they could tell I was.

[Q: While at camp have you ever stared at someone's body?] Yes. [Q] A little girl. She has a birthmark on her back, at the base of her spine.

[Q: Do you think you would ever stare at someone's body while at camp?] No. I don't like that. I think it's silly. . . . What people are is not their fault if they are deformed.

I don't think it would be very nice, very polite. [Q] I can't see anything to stare at whether it's a scar or anything else. [Q] It just isn't done.

I've looked, but not stared. I'm careful about that, because you could get in bad about that. [Q] Get thrown out by the owner. I was curious when I once had a perfect view of a girl's sex organs, because her legs were spread when she was sitting on a chair. I sat in the chair across from her in perfect view of her organs. [Q] For about ten or fifteen minutes. [Q] Nobody noticed. [Q] It's not often you get that opportunity.[8]

[Q: How would you feel if you were alone in a secluded area of camp sunning yourself, and then noticed that other nudists were staring at your body?] I would think I had some mud on me. [Q] . . . I would just ask them why they were staring at me. Probably I was getting sunburn and they wanted to tell me to turn over, or maybe I had a speck of mud on me. [Q] These are the only two reasons I can think of why they were staring.

In the nudist camp, the arousal of attention by nudity is usually regarded as *unnatural.* Thus, staring is unnatural, especially after a period of grace in which to adjust to the new meanings.

If he did it when he was first there, I'd figure he's normal. If he kept it up I'd stay away from him, or suggest to the owner that he be thrown out. [Q] At first it's a new experience, so he might be staring. [Q] He wouldn't know how to react to it. [Q] The first time seeing nudes of the opposite sex. [Q] I'd think if he kept staring, that he's thinking of something, like grabbing someone, running to the bushes, and raping them. [Q] Maybe he's mentally unbalanced.

He just sat there watching the women. You can forgive it the first time, because of curiosity. But not every weekend. [Q] The owner asked him to leave.

These women made comments on some men's shapes. They said, "He has a hairy body or ugly bones," or "Boy his wife must like him because he's hung big." That was embarrassing. . . . I thought they were terrible. [Q] Because I realized they were walking around looking. I can't see that.

Organizations and the Constitution of Normality

The rules-in-use of an organization *and the reality they sustain* form the basis on which behaviors are interpreted as "unnatural."[9] Overinvolvement in nudity, for example, is interpreted by nudists as unnatural (and not simply immoral). Similarly, erotic stimuli or responses, which breach the nudist morality, are defined as unnatural.

They let one single in. He acted peculiar. . . . He got up and had a big erection. I didn't know what he'd do at night. He might molest a child or anybody. . . . My husband went and told the owner.

I told you about this one on the sundeck with her legs spread. She made no bones about closing up. Maybe it was an error, but I doubt it. It wasn't a normal position. Normally you wouldn't lay like this. It's like standing on your head. She had sufficient time and there were people around.

She sat there with her legs like they were straddling a horse. I don't know how else to describe it. [Q] She was just sitting on the ground. [Q] I think she's a dirty pig. [Q] If you sit that way, everyone don't want to know what she had for breakfast. [Q] It's just the wrong way to sit. You keep your legs together even with clothes on.

[Q: Do you think it is possible for a person to be modest in a nudist camp?] I think so. [Q] If a person acts natural. . . . An immodest person would be an exhibitionist, and you find them in nudism too. . . . Most people's conduct is all right.

When behaviors are constituted as *unnatural*, attempts to understand them are usually suspended, and reciprocity of perspectives is called into question. (The "reciprocity of perspectives" involves the assumption that if one changed places with the other, one would, for all practical purposes, see the world as the other sees it.[10])

[Q: What would you think of a man who had an erection at camp?] Maybe they can't control themselves. [Q] Better watch out for him. [Q] I would tell the camp director to keep an eye on him. And the children would question that. [Q: What would you tell them?] I'd tell them the man is sick or something.

[Q: What would you think of a Peeping Tom—a non-nudist trespasser?] They should be reported and sent out. [Q] I think they shouldn't be there. They're sick. [Q] Mentally. [Q] Because anyone who wants to look at someone else's body, well, is a Peeping Tom, is sick in the first place. He looks at you differently than a normal person would. [Q] With ideas of sex. [A trespasser] . . . is sick. He probably uses this as a source of sexual stimulation.

Such occurrences call into question the taken-for-granted character of nudity in the nudist camp and the situated morality that is officially set forth.

Inhibiting Breakdowns in the Nudist Morality

Organized nudism promulgates a nonsexual perspective toward nudity, and breakdowns in that perspective are inhibited by (1) controlling erotic actions and (2) controlling erotic reactions. Nudity is partitioned off from other forms of "immodesty" (e.g., verbal immodesty, erotic overtures). In this way, a person can learn more easily to attribute a new meaning to nudity.[11] When behaviors occur that reflect other forms of "immodesty," however, nudists often fear a voiding of the nonsexual meaning that they impose on nudity.

This woman with a sexy walk would shake her hips and try to arouse the men. . . . [Q] These men went to the camp director to complain that the woman had purposely tried to arouse them. The camp director told this woman to leave.

Nudists are sensitive to the possibility of a breakdown in the nudist morality. Thus, they have a low threshold for interpreting acts as "sexual."

Playing badminton, this teenager was hitting the birdie up and down and she said, "What do you think of that?" I said, "Kind of sexy." ———[the president of the camp] said I shouldn't talk like that, but I was only kidding.

Note the following description of "mauling":

I don't like to see a man and a girl mauling each other in the nude before others. . . . [Q: Did you ever see this at camp?] I saw it once. . . . [Q: What do you mean by mauling?] Just, well,

I never saw him put his hands on her breasts, but he was running his hands along her arms.

This sensitivity to "sexual" signs also sensitizes nudists to the possibility that certain of their own acts, although not intended as "sexual," might nonetheless be interpreted that way.

Sometimes you're resting and you spread your legs unknowingly. [Q] My husband just told me not to sit that way. [Q] I put my legs together.

Since "immodesty" is defined as an unnatural manner of behavior, such behaviors are easily interpreted as being motivated by "dishonorable" intent. When the individual is thought to be in physical control of the "immodest" behavior and to know the behavior's meaning within the nudist scheme of interpretation, sexual intentions are assigned. Referring to a quotation that was presented earlier, one man said that a woman who was lying with her legs spread may have been doing so unintentionally, "but I doubt it. [Q] It wasn't a normal position. Normally you wouldn't lay like this. It's like standing on your head."

Erotic reactions, as well as erotic actions, are controlled in camp. Thus, even when erotic stimuli come into play, erotic responses may be inhibited.

When lying on the grass already hiding my penis, I got erotic thoughts. And then one realizes it can't happen here. With fear there isn't much erection.

Yes, once I started to have an erection. Once. [Q] A friend told me how he was invited by some young lady to go to bed. [Q] I started to picture the situation and I felt the erection coming on; so I immediately jumped in the pool. It went away.

I was once in the woods alone and ran into a woman. I felt myself getting excited. A secluded spot in the bushes which was an ideal place for procreation. [Q] Nothing happened, though.

When breaches of the nudist morality do occur, other nudists' sense of modesty may inhibit sanctioning. The immediate breach may go unsanctioned. The observers may feign inattention or withdraw from the scene. The occurrence is usually communicated, however, via the grapevine, and it may reach the camp director.

We were shooting a series of pictures and my wife was getting out of her clothes. ———— [the photographer] had an erection but went ahead like nothing was happening. [Q] It was over kind of fast. . . . [Q] Nothing. We tried to avoid the issue. . . . Later we went to see ———— [the camp director] and ———— [the photographer] denied it.

[If a man had an erection] people would probably pretend they didn't see it.

[Q: What do you think of someone this happens to?] They should try to get rid of it fast. It don't look nice. Nudists are prudists. They are more prudish. Because they take their clothes off they are more careful. [Q] They become more prudish than people with clothes. They won't let anything out of the way happen.

As indicated in the remark, "nudists are prudists," nudists may at times become aware of the fragility of their situated moral meanings.

At ———— [camp], this family had a small boy no more than ten years old who had an erection. Mrs. ———— [the owner's wife] saw him and told his parents that they should keep him in check, and tell him what had happened to him and to watch himself. This was silly, for such a little kid who didn't know what happened.

Deviance and Multiple Realities

There are basic social processes that underlie responses to deviance. Collectivities control thresholds of response to various behaviors, determining the relevance, meaning, and importance of the behavior. In the nudist camp, as pointed out previously, erotic overtures and erotic responses are regarded as unnatural, and reciprocity of perspectives is called into question by such behaviors.

We thought this single was all right, until others clued us in that he had brought girls up to camp. [Then we recalled that] . . . he was kind of weird. The way he'd look at you. He had glassy eyes, like he could see through you.[12]

Such a response to deviance in the nudist camp is a result of effective socialization to the new system of moral meanings. The deviant's behavior, on the other hand, can be construed as reflecting an ineffective socialization to the new system of meanings.

I think it's impossible [to have an erection in a nudist camp]. [Q] In a nudist camp you must have some physical contact and a desire to have one.
    He isn't thinking like a nudist. [Q] The body is wholesome, not . . . a sex object. He'd have to do that—think of sex.
    Sex isn't supposed to be in your mind, as far as the body. He doesn't belong there. [Q] If you go in thinking about sex, naturally it's going to happen. . . . You're not supposed to think about going to bed with anyone, not even your wife.

As these quotes illustrate, the unnaturalness or deviance of a behavior is ordinarily determined by relating it to an institutionalized scheme of interpretation. Occurrences that are "not understandable" in the reality of one collectivity may, however, be quite understandable in the reality of another collectivity.[13] Thus, what are "deviant" occurrences in nudist camps probably would be regarded by members of the clothed society as natural and understandable rather than unnatural and difficult to understand.

Finally, a group of people may subscribe to different and conflicting interpretive schemes. Thus, the low threshold of nudists to anything "sexual" is a function of their marginality; the fact that they have

not completely suspended the moral meanings of the clothed society is what leads them to constitute many events as "sexual" in purpose.

Notes

1. In my previous papers, I have dealt with other questions that are commonly asked about nudists. How persons become nudists is discussed in my (1966, February) "Becoming a nudist," *Psychiatry, 29,* 15-24. A report on the nudist way of life and social structure can be found in my (1967, Fall) article in *Human Organization, 26,* 91-99.

2. Approximately one hundred camps were represented in the interviews and questionnaires. Interviews were conducted in the homes of nudists during the off season. Arrangements for the interviews were initially made with these nudists during the first summer of participant observation: selection of respondents was limited to those living within a one-hundred-mile radius of Chicago. The questionnaires were sent to all members of the National Nudist Council. The different techniques of data collection provided a test of convergent validation.

3. For a discussion of the essence of such relationships, see A. Schutz (1962), *Collected papers: The problem of social reality* (M. Natanson, Ed.), The Hague: Nijhoff, I, p. 287ff.

4. [Q] is used to signify a neutral probe by the interviewer that follows the course of the last reply, such as "Could you tell me some more about that?" or "How is that?" or "What do you mean?" Other questions by the interviewer are given in full.

5. The King and Queen contest, which takes place at conventions, allows for a patterned evasion of the staring rule. Applicants stand before the crowd in front of the royal platform, and applause is used for selecting the winners. Photography is allowed during the contest, and no one is permitted to enter the contest unless willing to be photographed. The major reason for this is that this is a major camp event, and contest pictures are used in nudist magazines. At the same time, the large number of photographs sometimes taken by lay photographers (that is, not working for the magazines) makes many nudists uncomfortable by calling into question a nonsexual definition of the situation.

6. I was amazed at how many young female nudists described a similar pattern of extreme

clothing modesty among their parents and in their own married life. Included in this group was another nudist model, one of the most photographed of nudist models. Perhaps there are some fruitful data here for cognitive-dissonance psychologists.

7. Cf. Schutz (1962), p. 74.

8. For some respondents, the female genitals, because of their hidden character, never become a routinized part of camp nudity; thus their visible exposure does not lose an attention-provoking quality.

9. Compare H. Garfinkel (1963), "A conception of, and experiments with, 'trust' as a condition of concerted stable actions," in O. J. Harvey (Ed.), *Motivation and social interaction*, New York: Ronald.

10. See Schutz (1962), I, p. 11, for his definition of reciprocity of perspectives.

11. This corresponds with the findings of learning-theory psychologists.

12. For a study of the process of doublethink, see J. L. Wilkins (1964), "Doublethink: A study of erasure of the social past," unpublished doctoral dissertation, Northwestern University.

13. Cf. Schutz (1962), I, pp. 229ff.

39

Black Images in White Media

Michael Parenti

The make-believe media are predominantly White media. Of the sixty or seventy major performers in the new TV shows each season, relatively few are African-American. It took the television industry over four decades before it could get around to featuring African-American talk-show hosts such as Oprah Winfrey and Arsenio Hall. For other people of color, the situation has been at least as bad. As of the late 1970s, Asian-Americans, Native American Indians, and Latinos (that is, all persons of Spanish-speaking origin, including Chicanos and Puerto Ricans) together constituted less than 3 percent of the characters in teleplays and sitcoms.[1] Nor has the situation improved markedly since then.

In 1982, when it sought to give an award to an African-American for excellence in the cinema, the National Association for the Advancement of Colored People (NAACP) discovered that Cicely Tyson's performance in *Bustin' Loose* (1981), an artless, lightweight comedy, was the only lead role by a Black woman in more than two years.[2]

On the production side, not more than 3 percent of the people working behind the cameras are African-American. As of 1989, there were no major Black executives or agents in the movie and television industries. In 1988, Hollywood's two highest-ranking African-American executives lost their jobs. The same underrepresentation prevails in the news sector. A 1985 survey by the American Society of Newspaper Editors found that people of color composed less than 6 percent of the journalists employed (a good number of whom worked for Black publications).[3]

Smilin' 'n' Servin'

In the early years of the movie industry, the images of African-American were unrestrainedly racist—as reflected in such silent films as *The Wooing and Wedding of a Coon* (1904), *For Massa's Sake* (1911), *Coon Town Suffragettes* (1914), and *The Nigger* (1915). Whether he was called Sambo or Rastus, whether played by Blacks or black-faced Whites, the cinematic African-American male was usually a simple-minded buffoon, quick to laugh, irresponsible, lazy, fearful, and rhythmic. His female counterpart was good-natured, motherly yet sometimes sassy, able to work but complaining about it, and employed as a cook, seamstress, or servant.[4] One Black actor, Lincoln Perry, so encapsulated the shuffling, childish slouch that the character he played, "Steppin' Fetchit," actually became his Hollywood stage name.

From the 1920s through World War II, grotesque black-faced caricatures with huge

"Black Images in White Media" by Michael Parenti from *Make-Believe Media, The Politics of Entertainment* (pp. 127-141), 1992. New York: St. Martin's Press, Incorporated. Reprinted with permission of St. Martin's, Inc.

red lips and bulging eyes appeared as cannibals and dancing darkies in animated cartoons. They adorned pancake mix packages and tobacco advertisements. Of 100 motion pictures made during this period that had Black themes or characters "of more than passing significance," the great majority were classified as anti-Black, according to one study.[5]

Some enterprising African-Americans started their own film companies, most of which were small and underfinanced. By the 1930s they produced films populated entirely by African-Americans who exercised social power in ways that did not exist in the real world. These movies reached an urban African-American audience, but they failed to draw the great majority of Black moviegoers away from Hollywood movies. It seemed such audiences preferred the higher budgeted and more polished Hollywood star productions over a fantasy of Black power that many found implausible.[6]

When the right kind of music came on the screen, African-American film characters could be counted on to come to life in a bouncy, strutting way. Who can forget (even those of us who want to) the "Who dat?" musical sequence in *A Day at the Races* (1937) with Harpo Marx leading an entourage of shack-dwelling, poor-but-happy darkies in an ensemble number that had everything in it but the watermelon. Such a sequence is memorable not only for its racism but for the implosive, high quality dancing and singing by African-American performers who had to compress their talents into whatever tacky little roles they could get.

Campaigns launched by the NAACP, the African-American press, and show-business groups helped eliminate many of the worst racist images in the media by the mid-1940s. These campaigns were strengthened when the federal government itself entered the fray, attempting to rally the entire citizenry behind the war effort by propagating ideas of racial and religious equality. When the

Sambo roles were eliminated, however, nothing better was put in their place, and African-Americans became even less visible than before. They were often systematically excluded from scripts, and when they did appear, it was usually as singers, dancers, and domestics. Even those who excelled in the musical field sometimes had a hard time getting major billing. When the "Nat King Cole Show" was launched by NBC in the late 1950s—the first television show to have an African-American star performer—it failed to attract advertising support and was cancelled early in the season.[7]

The 1950s also gave us the television series "Amos 'n' Andy," originally a radio program created and acted by two White men. The show portrayed almost every character in its all-Black cast as a clown, a conniver, or a dimwit. Black doctors appeared as quacks and Black lawyers as slippery shysters. African-American women were usually shown as bossy shrews, given to hectoring their irresponsible and childish men.[8]

Similar fare could be found in "Beulah," a show about a Black maid who looked like she had come off a package of pancake mix. There was Rochester of the "Jack Benny Show" who deferred to his White boss but in a socially and comically critical way, as did another Black maid in the "The Great Gildersleeve" series. There was Willie, the handyman in "Life with Father" (later the "New Stu Erwin Show") who spent years scratching his head and shuffling around.[9] There was the "amusingly" terror-stricken chauffeur of the Charlie Chan movies—rerun on TV into the 1980s—who reluctantly accompanied his detective boss into dangerous situations, all the while rolling his eyes and babbling: "Oh Missuh Chan, lez get outta dis here place!" Then there was the famous Sam of *Casablanca* (1942), who plays the piano for his boss, Humphrey Bogart. All the White characters call Bogart "Rick," but to Sam he's "Mister Richard." When Mr. Richard is sad, Sam is sad; when Mr. Richard is happy, Sam is happy. Sam experiences Rick's concerns as his own, understandably enough since the script allows him none of his own.

For many years African-Americans in the make-believe media had neither anger, ambition, nor interests of their own. On the rare occasions they did act effectively, displaying initiative and strength, it was most likely in the service of Whites. Hence, when the burly ex-slave in *Gone With the Wind* dispatches two villainous tramps (one White, one Black) who are about to attack Scarlett O'Hara, he is being allowed to commit an act of violence only to defend White womanhood—as might any loyal eunuch. Boys, not men, maids, not women, these African-Americans existed to serve, amuse, protect, and die for their Caucasian superiors. When they were not Uncle Toms, they were Tontos and Gunga Dins.

Not much in the media was designed to give African-Americans a sense of themselves. Like their White counterparts, Black children cheered when Tarzan or some White adventurer obliterated the dark savages in the jungle, when British troops massacred the "blasted fuzzy-wuzzies," and when White cowboys cut down bands of Indians with flawless aim. They had no choice but to find their media heroes among those who ruled over them.

The African-American actress and writer Ellen Holly noted, "I grew up bombarded with movies that depicted Black women almost exclusively as maids or sluts of limited intelligence. . . . "[10] It might be argued that many maids *are* Black, and therefore the media offer a faithful representation of an unfortunate reality. But Holly's complaint is that Black women are not portrayed as human beings. Be they maids or prostitutes, their real stories have never been told. As she goes on to say:

The irony, of course, is that Hollywood has yet to make a movie that actually deals with a Black maid. . . . I have come to recognize the female Black domestic as perhaps THE great heroine of the Black race. Because that lady was willing to get down on her knees and scrub another woman's floor, clean another woman's house and bring up another woman's children, a whole race survived. But the trauma and the paradox of having to leave your own children in the morning and go out and care for someone else's in order to bring back bread for their table in the evening has yet to be examined on film.[11]

Back in 1943, the actress and singer Lena Horne made a plea regarding media treatment of African-Americans: "All we ask is that the Negro be portrayed as a normal person. Let's see the Negro as a worker at union meetings, as a voter at the polls, as a civil service worker or elected official."[12]

In the media-created world, African-Americans were represented as knowing their place. White audiences and White media owners were made uncomfortable by images of Black anger and assertiveness that might animate the consciousness of African-Americans in troublesome ways. Besides being no threat to White dominance, Steppin' Fetchit, Beulah, and the Kingfish assured Whites that the racial status quo was just fine. These films confirmed the notion that Black folk were neither capable nor desirous of a more elevated station in life. If all that African-Americans could do was shuffle, smile, and serve, then, of course, they deserved their underclass place in society. The entertainment media both reflected and bolstered the racial caste oppression, while ignoring the struggles for survival and for social betterment waged by African-Americans.

On this dreary landscape there appeared a few worthwhile exceptions. Powerfully drawn African-American figures appeared in such far-from-perfect dramas as *The Petrified Forest* (1936) and *Slave Ship* (1937). Movies like *Hallelujah!* (1929) and *The Green Pastures* (1936), despite their stock characters and stereotyped dialect, presented musical interludes that found favor with some Black critics. As might be expected, these films avoided the subject of racial integration.[13]

Clean-Cut and Saintly

After World War II, African-Americans migrated in larger numbers from the rural South to Northern cities and gained a greater measure of political influence. At last, Hollywood tackled the problem of racism, however imperfectly, in *Pinky* (1949) and *Lost Boundaries* (1949). Both dealt with the atypical problems faced by those who pass for White but who are then discovered to be Black. The antiracist position taken in such movies seemed so mild and limited as to be almost itself racist. In so many words: if some people are so Caucasian-looking as to pass for White, then let's not split hairs and cause unnecessary grief; let's be tolerant and accept them as White.

Of more importance were movies like *Intruder in the Dust* (1949) and *Home of the Brave* (1949). Adapted from the Faulkner novel, *Intruder* is about a Black man falsely accused of murder who faces a lynch mob. Events are seen through the eyes of a Caucasian boy who discovers the racial hatred that infects his rural Southern community. *Home of the Brave* deals with the prejudice confronted by a technically skilled African-American soldier who has volunteered to go on a dangerous mission with a White unit in the racially segregated U.S. Army of World War II. The soldier quickly becomes the object of racist jibes from other members of the unit. He quietly endures these insults. It is his White buddy, a former schoolmate, who angrily tells the others to "lay off." When this same buddy is killed in combat, the Black soldier succumbs to a psychogenic paralysis caused—we are asked to believe—by the guilt reaction he suffers at feeling relieved that it was his buddy and not he who was shot. He is cured by an army psychiatrist who moves him to anger by shouting, "Get up and walk, nigger!" He staggers, from his hospital bed in a rage, about to strike the doctor with clenched fist, only to crumble in the shrink's arms, tearfully realizing he can walk again. (In those days,

Hollywood endowed the psychiatric profession with miraculously curative powers.)

As with the few other films that dealt with the subject, *Home of the Brave* treated racism solely as a problem of individual prejudice devoid of institutional and class dimensions. The film offers not a word about the racial segregation that was the official policy of the U.S. Army until well into the first year of the Korean war. However, there were moments when the movie seemed to be saying more than it intended. Its climactic scene in the psychiatric ward, for instance, seemed to contain an allegoric message: only when Blacks openly confronted racism with their own anger would they become free of the paralysis imposed upon them.

By the 1950s and 1960s African-Americans were doing just that, militantly mobilizing against oppressive conditions—first in the South, then in the North—demonstrating in the streets, organizing sit-ins and boycotts, and pleading their cases in court and before the general public under the leadership of organizations like the NAACP. The cause of desegregation and civil rights was advanced. The right to vote was made a reality for larger numbers of Blacks. New leaders of the stature of Dr. Martin Luther King, Jr., emerged. It was a period of heroic struggle and sacrifice on the part of civil-rights advocates, as well as violence and murder on the part of racists. Millions of people were affected and a thousand dramas were played out in real life, along with scores of tragedies. At the time, however, Hollywood and television managed to overlook it all. A proud and dramatic page of history was deemed as being of no dramatic merit. (In 1975 there finally appeared a TV movie, *Attack on Terror*, a dramatization of the murder of three freedom riders in Mississippi. This teleplay stuck fairly close to the facts, unlike the 1988 movie *Mississippi Burning*, which is discussed later in the chapter.)

During this period of political fermentation, Hollywood found its ideal Black in the prototype played repeatedly by Sidney

Poitier. Whether befriended by nuns in *Lilies of the Field* (1963) or cooperating with a racist Southern sheriff to catch a criminal in *In the Heat of the Night* (1967) or winning the respect of a classroom of adolescent bigots in *To Sir, With Love* (1967) or being invited to meet his prospective White in-laws in *Guess Who's Coming to Dinner* (1967), Poitier was ever on his best behavior. Blessed with limitless supplies of patience, integrity, and self-control, he asserted himself only within limited parameters, never resorting to the harsh tactics of his bigoted adversaries. Here was the kind of African-American male that Whites would find acceptable, a nice, clean-cut, middle-class saint, who would not threaten White audiences with expressions of Black anger, incapable of doing to them what they were doing to him, never lowering himself to the level of his adversaries.

At the same time, African-Americans began to make occasional appearances on television in minor dramatic parts, rather than just as comics, singers, and tap dancers. In the late 1960s, a weekly adventure series, "I Spy," starring Robert Culp and Bill Cosby, had an African-American actor play a lead character—one who was not involved in a racial situation as such. Lena Horne's plea that Blacks be portrayed as just ordinary normal people had finally come true—except that "normal" for TV meant a gun-toting, fist-swinging, globe-trotting secret agent. Posing as tennis bums, these two U.S. spies traveled from country to country on different assignments. It was Culp, a White man, who got into one romance after another while Cosby remained seemingly free of sexual interests of his own. Cosby also was the more responsible one, coming to Culp's rescue whenever a dangerous predicament arose—as Tonto had often done for the Lone Ranger. Here was a Sidney Poitier with guns and fists, but still safely asexual so as not to evoke White anxieties.

Enter Superhero

Once Blacks qualified for the hero roles previously reserved for White males, they ended up as little more than replicas of a White macho idiocy. In *Sweet Sweetback's Badass Song* (1971), *Shaft* (1971), *Shaft's Big Score* (1972), and *Superfly* (1972), Black males now could be aggressive, violent, ruthless, powerful, and able to outsmart, outtalk, outfight, and outfornicate White males. "Sidney Poitier would no longer have to play the likeable eunuch to a squeamish liberalism still haunted by images of the Black man's threatening masculinity, a central fantasy in the racist mythology."[14] Indeed, in *Sweet Sweetback* and *Superfly* the Black Superhero is a glorified thug with a harem of beauties (both Black and White) but with few mental skills except what is needed to thrive on the streets. Such was the image of hope and betterment that American capitalist culture offered to African-American youth. Loyle Hairston describes it:

> The "supernigger" surfaced as folk hero. Emblazoned in full complement of silk jump suit, fur coat, slack-brimmed hat, alligator boots, a marijuana cool, and a custom built Cadillac, "supernigger" glorified the profitable brutalities of the pimp, the drug-pusher, the thug—every scavenger who hustles the Black ghetto.[15]

And as Francis Ward observed: "Only the super-hip, super-slick, super-strong, super-sexed, super-hyped up and inflated Black male could whip and kick around the White boys." A normal Black man with the ordinary mix of strengths and weaknesses would be too real and human and presumably too difficult for Hollywood to handle.[16]

The Black superhero offered African-Americans the escapist illusion of power and wealth. Self-worth was to be measured in terms of money, flashy consumer items, and dominance over others. In addition to keeping Whites in control of the images Blacks had of themselves, these films made enormous profits for their White producers, as African-Americans crowded the inner-city movie houses to view sex-filled, action-packed Black-over-White victories.[17]

The Black superhero made it to television by 1973 but in a sanitized version. Television did not offer the same audience selectivity as neighborhood theaters and the White public was less likely to respond to macho Blacks winning out over Whites. When Shaft went from films to television series, he was shorn of his power and sensuality, "like they poured a bottle of Listerine over him."[18] Superhero was accompanied by the inner-city "Blaxploitation" horror films of the 1970s, such as *Blacula* (1972) and its equally terrible sequel, *Scream, Blacula, Scream* (1973).

Meanwhile, the few serious, high-quality and deeply engaging films produced during this period, such as Gordon Park's autobiographical *The Learning Tree* (1969), Ossie Davis's *Black Girl* (1972), *Sounder* (1972), *Sounder, Part 2* (1976), and *Claudine* (1974), were largely left in limbo, given none of the mass promotional hype that bombarded the inner-city neighborhoods on behalf of the trashy superhero and superhorror flicks. Instead, the distribution of quality films was limited to a smaller number of independent theaters and, in subsequent years, to a few college campuses.

One of these quality films, *Sounder,* is an utterly superb drama about a poor, rural African-American family trying to survive and stay human under adverse conditions. For once, the characters are not caricatures but real persons, with attachments, loves, and fears that seem not only credible but deeply moving. The father's victimization by poverty and White authority, the mother's determination to hold the family together, the boy's devotion to both parents and his youthful courage and vulnerability, the story and the characterizations—all make for a great movie that not enough people, of whatever ethnic background, have seen. One measure of the film's quality might be the way its actors feel about it. Cicely Ty-son, who like other African-American performers had complained of the dearth of suitable roles, felt that her part in *Sounder* was the one for which she had prepared all her life.

A well-done and entertaining film is *Claudine,* a sympathetic treatment of a welfare mother's struggle to bring up her six kids while carrying on a courtship with a most likeable garbageman. He, in turn, experiences the difficulties of trying to be a breadwinning father while not earning enough money. *Claudine* offers a perspective on the inner-city welfare family that has been accorded almost no currency among middle-class White Americans.

Two Steps Forward, One-and-a-Half Steps Back

The fifties and sixties were decades of struggle for African-American rights. Such struggles created changes in the climate of opinion that were not entirely without effect on the White media. For one thing, the taboo subject of interracial romance was broached. As early as 1957, the beautiful Dorothy Dandridge was cast in one of the first interracial romance roles in *Island in the Sun.* But she was not allowed to kiss her White male leads. Dandridge was also paired romantically with the White actor Curt Jurgens in *Tamango* (1957), though the relationship was hardly between equals since she was a native woman and he, an empowered White male determined to put down a slave mutiny. In the early 1970s Diana Sands had White lovers in *Georgia, Georgia* (1972) and *The Landlord* (1970). Sidney Poitier was matched with a White female lead in *A Patch of Blue* (1965) (but she was blind), *The Lost Man* (1969), and *Guess Who's Coming to Dinner* (1967). In each of these films, the interracial love affair was a key element in the plot. In *One Potato, Two Potato* (1966), a serious effort is made to depict the institutional racism that existed under civil law: a divorced

White father wins a court decision to take his daughter away from her White mother because the mother had taken an African-American as her second husband.

By the late seventies and into the eighties, interracial coupling became less frequent. One exception was *Some Kind of Hero* (1982) in which a Vietnam veteran (Richard Pryor), abandoned by his African-American wife and buffeted by hard circumstances, becomes friend and lover to a high-priced White prostitute (Margot Kidder). A Black man gets a White woman but she's a prostitute—that is, a White woman of ill-repute rather than the all-American sweetheart from next door. The film is unusual because despite the interracial coupling, race and racism do not figure prominently in the plot. The couple are just taken as a couple—which itself is something of an achievement. Conflict between the two lovers stems not from their racial backgrounds but from what she does for a living.

Likewise in *The Miss Firecracker Contest* (1989), a worthwhile film, women resist the oppressive sexist expectations of some narrow, ill-spirited locals in a Southern community. The girlfriend of the romantic lead—a part originally written for a White woman—is played by African-American actress Alfred Woodard. Race does not come up as a factor. Woodard merely plays a woman who has a love relation with a man who happens to be Caucasian.

By the early 1970s, Blacks began to appear on television programs as local news announcers, quiz-show participants, and characters in cop shows and situation comedies. But of all the lead roles and major supporting roles in twenty-one new shows in the 1978-79 season, only two were Black and one was Puerto Rican. People of color were more likely than Whites to appear on prime-time shows as crooks, pimps, informers, or persons needing assistance from White professionals. The nine Blacks portrayed in one year of episodes of "Hawaii Five-O," a detective adventure show, consisted of five pimps, two prostitutes, and two students. The eleven Hawaiians and Polynesians on the show that year included two pimps, two assassins, and three mobsters.[19]

During this period, there were also a few outstanding television specials such as "Roots" and "Roots, the Next Generation" and made-for-television movies like *The Autobiography of Miss Jane Pittman* (1974) and *A Woman Called Moses* (1978), the latter about Harriet Tubman, the fugitive slave who helped others make their way north to freedom in the mid-nineteenth century. The popularity of these offerings among Whites and Blacks alike seemed to refute the claim that the public was not interested in quality productions, especially ones about African-Americans.

The African-American experience consists of many compelling real-life stories about confrontations with poverty and police, the struggle for housing, jobs, family, and community, and for a place in the arts, professions, unions, politics, and sports—stories that remained mostly untouched by the entertainment media. Instead, during the 1970s, African-Americans appeared as lead characters mostly in situation comedies like "Sanford and Son" and "The Jeffersons." Glib put-downs, insulting jibes, naïveté, ignorance, and silliness served as the source of humor, as Blacks taunted, derided, and jostled each other in weekly sitcom episodes. When important and relevant issues were touched upon, it was usually in facile, irrelevant ways. No wonder that twenty-three years after the NAACP's criticism of the "Amos 'n' Andy" show, the National Black Feminist Organization issued an almost identical indictment of the way African-Americans were portrayed on television, noting that:

Black shows are slanted toward the ridiculous with no redeeming counter-images. When Blacks are cast as professional people, the characters they portray generally lack professionalism and give the impression that Black people are incapable and inferior in such positions.

When older persons are featured, Black people are usually cast as shiftless derelicts or nonproductive individuals. Few Black women in TV programs are cast as professionals, para-professionals, or even working people.[20]

African-Americans were appearing in new scripts that still telegraphed some of the old racism. The Black writer Cecil Brown tells how the White producer Steve Krantz thought to work a few jokes into a screenplay Brown was working on. For instance:

Kid: If I eat Wheaties, Uncle Leroy, will I grow up big and strong?
Leroy: Yeah—and a baseball player—and white!

Brown failed to see the humor in a racist exchange that teaches a Black child that being White is the desired thing. Another "joke" inserted by Krantz:

Thelma: Leroy, don't you get involved with none of this union mess, you hear? Scabbing was good enough for your grandpa. (She motions to a picture on the wall; Leroy looks at the picture.)
Leroy: Mama, that isn't grandpa. That picture was on the wall when we moved in.

The false message is that (1) Blacks are happy as scabs and have no history in the struggle for unionization, and (2) they have no stable family relations and cannot even remember who their parents are. "In short," Brown comments, "what Krantz had done was write coon humor into the script." Brown remembers something James Baldwin once said:

A Black writer cannot write Black stereotypes the way a White writer can, because he cannot think of himself that way. A Black man cannot see himself as a stereotype. He does not exist the way Whites see him. That's why it's hard for Black writers to write the things Whites want to see.[21]

By the 1980s, African-Americans were appearing regularly in crime shows. When portrayed as criminals, they often had lead roles. When portrayed as cops, they were more often in subsidiary roles. For a while, it seemed that no African-American male could survive to the end of a film. Gregory Hines is eaten in *Wolfen* (1981); Bernie Casey is shot to pieces in *Sharkey's Machine* (1981); Paul Winfield kills himself rather than kill the hero Captain Kirk, in *Star Trek II* (1982); Richard Roundtree is devoured by Quetzalcoatl in *Q* (1982); both Howard Rollins and Debbie Allen perish in *Ragtime* (1981); Carl Weathers is killed by a Russian pugilist in *Rocky IV* (1985). In the world of make-believe media, the gap between Black and White life expectancy seemed even higher than in real life.[22]

Still missing was any depiction of African-Americans acting with concerted political effort around struggles of real social and class content. By the 1980s, one was lucky to find mainstream productions that even hinted at such themes. One popular film of the early eighties, *Ragtime*, manifests the limited ways that African-American struggle is represented (or misrepresented). The choice this film offers is (1) the individualized Black man defends himself by isolated terroristic action, packing up a gun and suicidally shooting it out with White authorities, or (2) Booker T. Washington takes a subservient, accommodationist role toward racist authority, winning patronizing praise from the same White official who murders the Black insurrectionist. Left out of the picture is reality itself. In fact, during the early twentieth-century period depicted in this film, African-Americans were organizing the NAACP, antilynching campaigns, the Niagara Movement, and other forms of resistance that laid the foundation for the mass democratic protests of subsequent eras.

In keeping with the Reaganite cinema of the 1980s, Blacks began appearing as macho, superpatriotic militarists, best encapsulated in Lou Gossett, Jr.'s performance in films like *Iron Eagle* (1986) and *An Officer and a Gentleman* (1982). In the latter, Gossett won an Academy Award for playing an abusive, fascistic drill instructor whose passion in life is to transform candy-assed recruits into unthinking killing machines forever committed to certain military and class principles: officers and gentlemen, the kind of men who will be addressed as "sir" both in and out of uniform. One remembers in *Gunga Din* how the devoted Indian water boy would snap to attention and announce to British officers, "I want to be a soldier." Gossett plays an updated Gunga Din who made it into uniform, serving the new empire and the new caste system.

In the 1980s, African-Americans appeared with greater frequency in television sitcoms like "Gimme a Break," "Diff'rent Strokes," "Benson," and "The New Odd Couple." These shows often featured perky, adorable Black youngsters and broadly drawn adult characters who specialized in smart-mouthing each other as they romped through the shallow, overdone predicaments that are the endlessly recycled stock-in-trade of sitcom humor.

The prime-time hit of the 1980s was "The Cosby Show," a sitcom offering us the "perfect" Black family, the Huxtables. The father, played by one of America's leading and most likeable comedians, Bill Cosby, is a doctor. The young and beautiful mother is a lawyer. The children are sweet and genuine. If "The Cosby Show" does not give us a positive image of African-Americans, then nothing does. But it is a superficial image. Here is that "better class of Negroes" we used to hear about in the 1950s, upper-middle-class professionals whom Whites might feel comfortable having as neighbors. "The Cosby Show" falsely implies that this small economic minority within a larger ethnic minority points the way to ending discrimination.

The sitcom world is inhabited mostly by silly little people with silly little problems. "The Cosby Show" is a refreshing exception at least in part. The characters are not silly. Everyone is more or less intelligent; no one is a ridiculous clown. To the show's credit, the confrontations are good-natured and the humor is gentle, devoid of the crude put-downs and aggression that pass for humor on shows like "The Jeffersons." Here are nice people playing idealized roles under ideal social conditions. The Huxtables never worry about money and never seem to need to shop, clean, or even work much at their professions. Unlike most doctors, Cosby spends most of his waking hours hanging around the house. The Huxtables are happy, even when they might get ruffled by the little crises that are resolved within the show's half-hour time frame. Take the episode in which the parents find marijuana in their son's room. It turns out the son is just *holding* it for a friend. Never in his life has he taken a toke. Never. His parents believe him, proving that the show is indeed comedy.

On rare occasions, an episode will edge toward some serious content as when the Huxtable family reminisces about Martin Luther King, Jr., or when—at Cosby's insistence and over the protests of the show's producers—an "End Apartheid" banner adorned the set. Overall, "The Cosby Show" is a positive representation of African-Americans, but it is still only a sitcom. It represents a giant step up from Steppin' Fetchit, but it still has Black people playing for laughs.

Notes

1. Screen Actors Guild (1974, October 31), "SAG documents use of women and minorities in prime-time television" (news release), cited in U.S. Commission on Civil Rights (1977, August), *Window dressing on the set* (report), p. 2.

2. I. Wilkerson (1982, August 15), "Blacks in films," *Washington Post*.

3. C. Trueheart (1989, February 14), "In Hollywood, the question of racism," *Washington Post*; J. Trescott (1985, April 12), "Minority coverage faulted," *Washington Post*; N. Kotz (1979, March/April), "The minority struggle for a place in the newsroom," *Columbia Journalism Review*, pp. 23-31.

4. J. Boskin (1986), *Sambo: The rise and demise of an American jester*, New York: Oxford University Press, pp. 149-158.

5. C. Reddick's (1944, Summer) study in *Journal of Negro Education*, cited in R. Colle (1968,

Spring), "Negro images in the mass media," *Journalism Quarterly, 45,* 56. Reddick finds 75 percent of the films were "anti-Negro," 13 percent neutral, and 12 percent "pro-Negro." For a full-length study, see D. Bogle (1973, 1988), *Toms, coons, mulattoes, mammies and bucks: An interpretive history of Blacks in American films,* New York: Crossroad Continuum.

6. T. Cripps (1978), "Black stereotypes on film," in R. Miller (Ed.), *Ethnic images in American film and television,* Philadelphia: Balch Institute, p. 7.

7. Colle (1968), pp. 56-57.

8. E. Barnouw (1970), *The golden web: A history of broadcasting in the United States 1933-1953* (Vol. 2), New York: Oxford University Press, p. 297. See the critique by the NAACP quoted in G. Simpson & J. M. Yinger (1958), *Racial and cultural minorities* (rev. ed.), New York: Harper & Bros., p. 716.

9. B. R. Sanders (1975, February), "25 years of Amos 'n' Andy," *New American Movement,* p. 9. For a full-length study, see J. F. MacDonald (1983), *Black and White on TV: Afro-Americans in television since 1948,* Chicago: Nelson-Hall.

10. E. Holly (1979, January/February), "The role of media in the programming of an underclass," *Black Scholar, 10,* 31.

11. Holly (1979), p. 31.

12. M. Ellison (1981), "Blacks in American film," in P. Davies & B. Neve (Eds.), *Cinema, politics and society in America,* New York: St. Martin's, p. 181.

13. Cripps (1978), p. 8.

14. L. Hairston (1974, Third Quarter), "The Black film—'Supernigger' as folk hero," *Freedomway,* p. 218; F. Ward (1974, Third Quarter), "Black male images in films," *Freedomway,* pp. 225-226.

15. Hairston (1974), p. 220.

16. Ward (1974), p. 226.

17. One survey in Chicago found that Black-oriented films accounted for about 40 percent of the box-office grosses in the Loop, although they represented only about 27 percent of the films shown. *Chicago Sun-Times,* January 8, 1975.

18. D. Bogle, quoted in J. Dreyfuss (1974, September 1), "Blacks and television," *Washington Post.*

19. NFBO statement, quoted in U.S. Commission on Civil Rights (1977), pp. 21-22.

20. Dreyfuss (1974); E. Collier (1974, Third Quarter), "'Black shows for White viewers," *Freedomway,* pp. 212-213; also Holly (1979), p. 33.

21. C. Brown (1981, January), "Blues for Blacks in Hollywood," *Mother Jones,* p. 23.

22. R. Tyson (1982, October 23), "Worthless film provokes worthwhile observation," *Daily World.*

40

Cosby Knows Best

Mark Crispin Miller

Bill Cosby is today's quintessential TV Dad—at once the nation's best-liked sitcom character and the most successful and ubiquitous of celebrity pitchmen. Indeed, Cosby himself ascribes his huge following to his appearances in the ads: "I think my popularity came from doing solid 30-second commercials. They can cause people to love you and see more of you than in a full 30-minute show." Like its star, "The Cosby Show" must owe much of its immense success to advertising, for this sitcom is especially well attuned to the commercials, offering a full-scale confirmation of their vision.

On the face of it, the Huxtables' milieu is as upbeat and well stocked as a window display at Bloomingdale's, or any of those visions of domestic happiness that graced the billboards during the Great Depression. Everything within this spacious brownstone is luminously clean and new, as if it had all been set up by the state to make a good impression on a group of visiting foreign dignitaries. Here are all the right commodities—lots of bright sportswear, plants and paintings, gorgeous bedding, plenty of copperware, portable tape players, thick carpeting, innumerable knickknacks, and, throughout the house, big, burnished dressers, tables, couches, chairs, and cabinets (Early American yet looking factory-new). Each week, the happy Huxtables nearly vanish amid the porcelain, stainless steel, mahogany, and fabric of their lives. In every scene, each character appears in some fresh designer outfit that positively glows with newness, never to be seen a second time.

Like all this pricey clutter, the plots and subplots, the dialogue, and even many of the individual shots reflect in some way on consumption as a way of life: Cliff's new juicer is the leitmotif of one episode; Cliff does a monologue on his son Theo's costly sweatshirt; Cliff kids daughter Rudy for wearing a dozen wooden necklaces. Each Huxtable, in fact, is hardly more than a mobile display case for his/her momentary possessions. In the show's first year, the credit sequence was a series of vivid stills presenting Cliff alongside a shiny Dodge Caravan, out of which the lesser Huxtables each emerged in shining playclothes, as if the van were their true parent, with Cliff serving as the genial midwife to this antiseptic birth. Each is routinely upstaged by what he/she eats or wears or lugs around: in a billowing blouse imprinted with gigantic blossoms, daughter Denise appears, carrying a tape player as big as a suitcase; Theo enters to get himself a can of Coke from the refrigerator, and we notice that he's wearing both a smart beige belt *and* a pair of lavender suspenders; Rudy munches cutely on a piece of pizza roughly twice the size of her own head.

"Cosby Knows Best" by M. C. Miller from *Boxed In: The Culture of TV* (pp. 69-75), 1988. Evanston, IL: Northwestern University Press. Reprinted with permission of Northwestern University Press.

As in the advertising vision, life among the Huxtables is not only well supplied, but remarkable for its surface harmony. Relations between these five pretty kids and their cute parents are rarely complicated by the slightest serious discord. Here affluence is magically undisturbed by the pressures that ordinarily enable it. Cliff and Clair, although both employed, somehow enjoy the leisure to devote themselves full-time to the trivial and comfortable concerns that loosely determine each episode: a funeral for Rudy's goldfish, a birthday surprise for Cliff, the kids' preparations for their first day of school. And daily life in this bright house is just as easy on the viewer as it is (apparently) for Cliff's dependents: "The Cosby Show" is devoid of any dramatic tension whatsoever. Nothing happens, nothing changes, there is no suspense or ambiguity or disappointment. In one episode, Cliff accepts a challenge to race once more against a runner who, years before, had beaten him at a major track meet. At the end, the race is run, and—it's a tie!

Of course, "The Cosby Show" is by no means the first sitcom to present us with a big, blissful family whose members never collide with one another, or with anything else; "Eight Is Enough," "The Brady Bunch," and "The Partridge Family" are just a few examples of earlier prime-time idylls. There are, however, some crucial differences between those older shows and this one. First of all, "The Cosby Show" is far more popular than any of its predecessors. It is (as of this writing) the top-rated show in the United States and elsewhere, attracting an audience that is not only vast, but often near fanatical in its devotion. Second, and stranger still, this show and its immense success are universally applauded as an exhilarating sign of progress. Newspaper columnists and telejournalists routinely deem "The Cosby Show" a "breakthrough" into an unprecedented *realism*, because it uses none of the broad plot devices or rapid-fire gags that define the standard sitcom. Despite its fantastic ambience of calm and plenty, "The Cosby Show" is widely regarded as a rare glimpse of truth, whereas "The Brady Bunch" et al., though just as cheery, were never extolled in this way. And there is a third difference between this show and its predecessors that may help explain the new show's greater popularity and peculiar reputation for progressivism: Cliff Huxtable and his dependents are not only fabulously comfortable and mild, but also noticeably black.

Cliff's blackness serves an affirmative purpose within the ad that is "The Cosby Show." At the center of his ample tableau, Cliff is himself an ad, implicitly proclaiming the fairness of the American system: "Look!" he shows us. "Even *I* can have all this!" Cliff is clearly meant to stand for Cosby himself, whose name appears in the opening credits as "Dr. William E. Cosby, Jr., Ed.D."—a testament both to Cosby's lifelong effort at self-improvement, and to his sense of brotherhood with Cliff. And, indeed, Dr. Huxtable is merely the latest version of the same statement that Dr. Cosby has been making for years as a talk show guest and stand-up comic: "I got mine!" The comic has always been quick to raise the subject of his own success. "What do I care what some ten-thousand-dollar-a-year writer says about me?" he once asked Dick Cavett. And on "The Tonight Show" a few years ago, Cosby told of how his father, years before, had warned him that he'd never make a dime in show business, "and then he walked slowly back to the projects . . . Well, I just lent him forty thousand dollars!"

That anecdote got a big hand, just like "The Cosby Show," but despite the many plaudits for Cosby's continuing tale of self-help, it is not quite convincing. Cliff's brownstone is too crammed, its contents too lustrous, to seem like his—or anyone's—own personal achievement. It suggests instead the corporate showcase which, in fact, it is. "The Cosby Show" attests to the power, not of Dr. Cosby/Huxtable, but of a consumer society that has produced such a tantalizing vision of reality. As Cosby himself admits, it was not his own Algeresque efforts that "caused people to love" him, but those ads put out by Coca-Cola, Ford, and General Foods—those ads in which he looks and acts precisely as he looks and acts in his own show.

Cosby's image is divided in a way that both facilitates the corporate project and conceals its true character. On the face of it, the Cosby style is pure impishness. Forever mugging and cavorting, throwing mock tantrums or beaming hugely to himself or doing funny little dances with his stomach pushed out, Cosby carries on a ceaseless parody of some euphoric eight-year-old. His delivery suggests the same childish spontaneity, for in the high, coy gabble of his harangues and monologues there is a disarming quality of baby talk. And yet all this artful goofiness barely conceals an intimidating hardness—the same uncompromising willfulness that we learn to tolerate in actual children (however cute they may be), but which can seem a little threatening in a grown-up. And Cosby is indeed a most imposing figure, in spite of all his antics: a big man boasting of his wealth, and often handling an immense cigar.

It is a disorienting blend of affects, but it works perfectly whenever he confronts us on behalf of Ford or Coca-Cola. With a massive car or Coke machine behind him, or with a calculator at his fingertips, he hunches toward us, wearing a bright sweater and an insinuating grin, and makes his playful pitch, cajoling us to buy whichever thing he's selling, his face and words, his voice and posture all suggesting this implicit and familiar come-on: "Kitchy-koo!" It is not so much that Cosby makes his mammoth bureaucratic masters seem as nice and cuddly as himself (although such a strategy is typical of corporate advertising); rather, he implicitly assures us that *we* are nice and cuddly, like little children. At once solicitous and overbearing, he personifies the corporate force that owns him. Like it, he comes across as an easygoing parent, and yet, also like it,

he cannot help betraying the impulse to coerce. We see that he is bigger than we are, better known, better off, and far more powerfully sponsored. Thus, we find ourselves ambiguously courted, just like those tots who eat up lots of Jell-O pudding under his playful supervision.

Dr. Huxtable controls his family with the same enlightened deviousness. As widely lauded for its "warmth" as for its "realism," "The Cosby Show" has frequently been dubbed "The 'Father Knows Best' of the Eighties." Here again (the columnists agree) is a good strong Dad maintaining the old "family values." This equation, however, blurs a crucial difference between Cliff and the early fathers. Like them, Cliff always wins; but this modern Dad subverts his kids not by evincing the sort of calm power that once made Jim Anderson so daunting, but by seeming to subvert himself at the same time. His is the executive style, in other words, not of the small businessman as evoked in the fifties, but of the corporate manager, skilled at keeping his subordinates in line while half concealing his authority through various disarming moves: Cliff rules the roost through teasing put-downs, clever mockery, and amiable shows of helpless bafflement.[1] This Dad is no straightforward tyrant, then, but the playful type who strikes his children as a peach, until they realize, years later, and after lots of psychotherapy, what a subtle thug he really was.

An intrusive kidder, Cliff never fails to get his way; and yet there is more to his manipulativeness than simple egomania. Obsessively, Cliff sees to it, through his takes and teasing, that his children always keep things light. As in the corporate culture and on TV generally, so on this show there is no negativity allowed. This is a conscious policy: Dr. Alvin F. Poussaint, a professor of psychiatry at Harvard, reads through each script as a "consultant," censoring any line or bit that might somehow tarnish the show's "positive images." And the show's upscale mise-en-scène has also been deliberately contrived to glow, like a fixed smile: "When you look at the artwork [on the walls], there is a positive feeling, an up feeling," Cosby says. "You don't see downtrodden, negative, I-can't-do-I-won't-do."

Cliff's function, then, is to police the corporate playground, always on the lookout for any downbeat tendencies. In one episode, for instance, Denise sets herself up by reading Cliff some somber verses that she's written for the school choir. The mood is despairing; the refrain, "I walk alone . . . I walk alone." It is clear that the girl does not take the effort very seriously, and yet Cliff merrily overreacts against this slight and artificial plaint, as if it were a crime. First, while she recites, he wears a clownish look of deadpan bewilderment, then laughs out loud as soon as she has finished, and ends by snidely mooing the refrain in outright parody. The studio audience roars, and Denise takes the hint. At the end of the episode, she reappears with a new version, which she reads sweetly, blushingly, while Cliff and Clair, sitting side by side in their high-priced pajamas, beam with tenderness and pride on her act of self-correction:

My mother and my father are my best
    friends.
When I'm all alone, I don't have to be.
It's because of me that I'm all alone, you
    see.
Their love is real. . . .
Never have they lied to me, never
    connived me,
talked behind my back.
Never have they cheated me.
Their love is real, their love is real.

Clair, choked up, gives the girl a big warm hug, and Cliff then takes her little face between his hands and kisses it, as the studio audience bursts into applause.

Thus, this episode ends with a paean to the show itself (for "their love" is *not* "real," but a feature of the fiction), a moment that, for all its mawkishness, attests to Cliff's

managerial adeptness. Yet Cliff is hardly a mere enforcer; he is also an underling, even as he seems to run things. This subservient status is manifest in his blackness. Cosby's blackness is indeed a major reason for the show's popularity, despite his frequent claims, and the journalistic consensus, that "The Cosby Show" is somehow "colorblind," simply appealing in some general "human" way. Although whitened by their status and commodities, the Huxtables are still unmistakably black. However, it would be quite inaccurate to hail their popularity as evidence of a new and rising amity between the races in America. On the contrary, "The Cosby Show" is such a hit with whites in part because whites are just as worried about blacks as they have always been—not blacks like Bill Cosby, or Lena Horne, or Eddie Murphy, but poor blacks, and the poor in general, whose existence is a well-kept secret on prime-time TV.

And yet TV betrays the very fears that it denies. In thousands of high-security buildings, and in suburbs reassuringly remote from the cities' "bad neighborhoods," whites may, unconsciously, be further reassured by watching not just Cosby, but a whole set of TV shows that negate the possibility of black violence with lunatic fantasies of containment: "Diff'rent Strokes" and "Webster," starring Gary Coleman and Emmanuel Lewis, respectively, each an overcute, miniaturized black person, each playing the adopted son of good white parents. In seeming contrast to these tabletop models, there is the oversized and growling Mr. T, complete with bangles, mohawk, and other primitivizing touches. Even this behemoth is a comforting joke, the dangerous ex-slave turned comic and therefore innocuous by campy excess; and he too is kept in line by a casual white father: Hannibal Smith, the commander of the A-Team, who employs Mr. T exclusively for his brawn.

As a willing advertisement for the system that pays him well, Cliff Huxtable also represents a threat contained. Although dark-skinned and physically imposing, he ingratiates us with his childlike mien and enviable lifestyle, a surrender that must offer some deep solace to a white public terrified that, one day, blacks might come with guns to steal the copperware, the juicer, the microwave, the VCR, even the TV itself. On "The Cosby Show," it appears as if blacks in general can have, or do have, what many whites enjoy, and that such material equality need not entail a single break-in. And there are no hard feelings, none at all, now that the old injustice has been so easily rectified. Cosby's definitive funny face, flashed at the show's opening credits and reproduced on countless magazine covers, is a strained denial of all animosity. With its little smile, the lips pursed tight, eyes opened wide, eyebrows raised high, that dark face shines toward us like the white flag of surrender—a desperate look that no suburban TV Dad of yesteryear would ever have put on, and one that millions of Americans today find indispensable.

By and large, American whites need such reassurance because they are now further removed than ever, both spatially and psychologically, from the masses of the black poor. And yet the show's appeal cannot be explained merely as a symptom of class and racial uneasiness, because there are, in our consumer culture, anxieties still more complicated and pervasive. Thus, Cliff is not just an image of the dark Other capitulating to the white establishment, but also the reflection of any constant viewer, who, whatever his/her race, must also feel like an outsider, lucky to be tolerated by the distant powers that be. There is no negativity allowed, not anywhere; and so Cliff serves both as our guide and as our double. His look of tense playfulness is more than just a sign that blacks won't hurt us; it is an expression that we too would each be wise to adopt, lest we betray some devastating sign of anger or dissatisfaction. If we stay cool and cheerful, white like him, and learn to get by with his sort of managerial acumen, we too, perhaps, can be protected from the world by a barrier of new appliances, and learn to put down others as each of us has, somehow, been put down.

Note

1. Cliff's managerial style is, evidently, also Cosby's. According to Tempestt Bledsoe, who plays Cliff's daughter Vanessa, Cosby "can make kids behave without telling them to do so." (Quoted in *People*, December 10, 1984.)

41

The Discovery of Hyperkinesis: Notes on the Medicalization of Deviant Behavior

Peter Conrad

Introduction

The increasing medicalization of deviant behavior and the medical institution's role as an agent of social control has gained considerable notice (Freidson, 1970; Pitts, 1968; Kitterie, 1971; Zola, 1972). By *medicalization* we mean defining behavior as a medical problem or illness and mandating or licensing the medical profession to provide some type of treatment for it. Examples include alcoholism, drug addiction, and treating violence as a genetic or brain disorder. This redefinition is not a new function of the medical institution: psychiatry and public health have always been concerned with social behavior and have traditionally functioned as agents of social control (Foucault, 1965; Szasz, 1970; Rosen, 1972). Increasingly sophisticated medical technology has extended the potential of this type of social control, especially in terms of psychotechnology (Chorover, 1973). This approach includes a variety of medical and quasi-medical treatments or procedures: psychosurgery, psychotropic medications, genetic engineering, antibuse, and methadone.

This paper describes how certain forms of behavior in children have become defined as a medical problem and how medicine has become a major agent for their social control since the discovery of hyperkinesis. By discovery we mean both origin of the diagnosis and treatment for this disorder, and discovery of children who exhibit this behavior. The first section analyzes the discovery of hyperkinesis and why it suddenly became popular in the 1960's. The second section will discuss the medicalization of deviant behavior and its ramifications.

"The Discovery of Hyperkinesis: Notes on the Medicalization of Deviant Behavior" by P. Conrad, 1975. *Social Problems 23*, pp. 12-21. Copyright © 1975 by the Society for the Study of Social Problems. Reprinted by permission.

This paper is a revised version of a paper presented at the meetings of the Society for the Study of Social Problems in San Francisco, August 1975. It was partially supported by a National Science Foundation dissertation grant (SOC 74-22043). I would like to thank Drs. Martin Kozloff, James E. Teele, John McKinlay, and the anonymous referees for comments on earlier drafts of this paper.

The Medical Diagnosis of Hyperkinesis

Hyperkinesis is a relatively recent phenomenon as a medical diagnostic category. Only in the past two decades has it been available as a recognized diagnostic category and only in the last decade has it received widespread notice and medical popularity. However, the roots of the diagnosis and treatment of this clinical entity are found earlier.

Hyperkinesis is also known as Minimal Brain Dysfunction, Hyperactive Syndrome, Hyperkinetic Disorder of Childhood, and by several other diagnostic categories. Although the symptoms and the presumed etiology vary, in general the behaviors are quite similar and greatly overlap.[1] Typical symptom patterns for diagnosing the disorder include: extreme excess of motor activity (hyperactivity); very short attention span (the child flits from activity to activity); restlessness; fidgetiness; often wildly oscillating mood swings (he's fine one day, a terror the next); clumsiness; aggressive-like behavior; impulsivity; in school he cannot sit still, cannot comply with rules, has low frustration level; frequently there may be sleeping problems and acquisition of speech may be delayed (Stewart et al., 1966; Stewart, 1970; Wender, 1971). Most of the symptoms for the disorder are deviant behaviors.[2] It is six times as prevalent among boys as among girls. We use the term hyperkinesis to represent all the diagnostic categories of this disorder.

The Discovery of Hyperkinesis

It is useful to divide the analysis into what might be considered *clinical factors* directly related to the diagnosis and treatment of hyperkinesis and *social factors* that set the context for the emergence of the new diagnostic category.

Clinical Factors

Bradley (1937) observed that amphetamine drugs had a spectacular effect in altering the behavior of school children who exhibited behavior disorders or learning disabilities. Fifteen of the thirty children he treated actually became more subdued in their behavior. Bradley termed the effect of this medication paradoxical, since he expected that amphetamines would stimulate children as they stimulated adults. After the medication was discontinued the children's behavior returned to premedication level.

A scattering of reports in the medical literature on the utility of stimulant medications for "childhood behavior disorders" appeared in the next two decades. The next significant contribution was the work of Strauss and his associates (Strauss & Lehtinen, 1947) who found certain behavior (including hyperkinesis behaviors) in postencephaletic children suffering from what they called minimal brain injury (damage). This was the first time these behaviors were attributed to the new organic distinction of minimal brain damage.

This disorder still remained unnamed or else it was called a variety of names (usually just "childhood behavior disorder"). It did not appear as a specific diagnostic category until Laufer, Denhoff, and Solomons (1957) described it as the "hyperkinetic impulse disorder" in 1957. Upon finding "the salient characteristics of the behavior pattern . . . are strikingly similar to those with clear cut organic causation" these researchers described a disorder with no clear-cut history or evidence for organicity (Laufer et al., 1957).

In 1966 a task force sponsored by the U.S. Public Health Service and the National Association for Crippled Children and Adults attempted to clarify the ambiguity and confusion in terminology and symptomology in diagnosing children's behavior and learning disorders. From over three dozen diagnoses, they agreed on the term "minimal brain dysfunction" as an overriding diagnosis that would include hyperkinesis and other disorders (Clements, 1966). Since this time M.B.D. has been the primary formal diagnosis or label.

In the middle 1950's a new drug, Ritalin, was synthesized, that has many qualities of amphetamines without some of their more undesirable side effects. In 1961 this drug was approved by the FDA for use with children. Since this time there has been much research published on the use of Ritalin in the treatment of childhood behavior disorders. This medication became the "treatment of choice" for treating children with hyperkinesis.

Since the early sixties, more research appeared on the etiology, diagnosis and treatment of hyperkinesis (cf. DeLong, 1972; Grinspoon & Singer, 1973; Cole, 1975)—as much as three-quarters concerned with drug treatment of the disorder. There had been increasing publicity of the disorder in the mass media as well. The *Reader's Guide to Periodical Literature* had no articles on hyperkinesis before 1967, one each in 1968 and 1969, and a total of forty for 1970 through 1974 (a mean of eight per year).

Now hyperkinesis has become the most common child psychiatric problem (Gross & Wilson, 1974, p. 142); special pediatric clinics have been established to treat hyperkinetic children, and substantial federal funds have been invested in etiological and treatment research. Outside the medical profession, teachers have developed a working clinical knowledge of hyperkinesis' symptoms and treatment (cf. Robin & Bosco, 1973); articles appear regularly in mass circulation magazines and newspapers so that parents often come to clinics with knowledge of this diagnosis. Hyperkinesis is no longer the relatively esoteric diagnostic category it may have been twenty years ago; it is now a well-known clinical disorder.

Social Factors

The social factors affecting the discovery of hyperkinesis can be divided into two areas: (1) The Pharmaceutical Revolution; (2) Government Action.

1. The Pharmaceutical Revolution. Since the 1930's the pharmaceutical industry has been synthesizing and manufacturing a large number of psychoactive drugs, contributing to a virtual revolution in drug making and drug taking in America (Silverman & Lee, 1974).

Psychoactive drugs are agents that effect the central nervous system. Benzedrine, Ritalin, and Dexedrine are all synthesized psychoactive stimulants which were indicated

for narcolepsy, appetite control (as "diet pills"), mild depression, fatigue, and more recently hyperkinetic children.

Until the early sixties there was little or no promotion and advertisement of any of these medications for use with childhood disorders.[3] Then two major pharmaceutical firms (Smith, Kline and French, manufacturer of Dexedrine, and CIBA, manufacturer of Ritalin) began to advertise in medical journals and through direct mailing and efforts of the "detail men." Most of this advertising of the pharmaceutical treatment of hyperkinesis was directed to the medical sphere; but some of the promotion was targeted for the educational sector also (Hentoff, 1972). This promotion was probably significant in disseminating information concerning the diagnosis and treatment of this newly discovered disorder.[4] Since 1955 the use of psychoactive medications (especially phenothiazines) for the treatment of persons who are mentally ill, along with the concurrent dramatic decline in in-patient populations, has made psychopharmacology an integral part of treatment for mental disorders. It has also undoubtedly increased the confidence in the medical profession for the pharmaceutical approach to mental and behavioral problems.

2. Government Action. Since the publication of the USPHS report on MBD there have been at least two significant governmental reports on treating school children with stimulant medications for behavior disorders. Both of these came as a response to the national publicity created by the *Washington Post* report (1970) that five to ten percent of the 62,000 grammar school children in Omaha, Nebraska were being treated with "behavior modification drugs to improve deportment and increase learning potential" (quoted in Grinspoon & Singer, 1973). Although the figures were later found to be a little exaggerated, it nevertheless spurred a Congressional investigation (U.S. Government Printing Office, 1970) and a conference sponsored by the Office of Child Development (1971) on the use of stimulant drugs in the treatment of behaviorally disturbed school children.

The Congressional Subcommittee on Privacy chaired by Congressman Cornelius E. Gallagher held hearings on the issue of prescribing drugs for hyperactive school children. In general, the committee showed great concern over the facility in which the medication was prescribed; more specifically that some children at least were receiving drugs from general practitioners whose primary diagnosis was based on teachers' and parents' reports that the child was doing poorly in school. There was also a concern with the absence of follow-up studies on the long-term effects of treatment.

The HEW committee was a rather hastily convened group of professionals (a majority were M.D.'s) many of whom already had commitments to drug treatment for children's behavior problems. They recommended that only M.D.'s make the diagnosis and prescribe treatment, that the pharmaceutical companies promote the treatment of the disorder only through medical channels, that parents should not be coerced to accept any particular treatment, and that long-term follow-up research should be done. This report served as blue ribbon approval for treating hyperkinesis with psychoactive medications.

Discussion

We will focus discussion on three issues: How children's deviant behavior became conceptualized as a medical problem; why this occurred when it did; and what are some of the implications of the medicalization of deviant behavior.

How does deviant behavior become conceptualized as a medical problem? We assume that before the discovery of hyperkinesis this type of deviance was seen as disruptive, disobedient, rebellious, anti-social, or deviant behavior. Perhaps the label "emotionally disturbed" was sometimes used, when it was in vogue in the early sixties, and the child was usually managed in the context of the family or the school or in extreme cases, the child guidance clinic. How then did this constellation of deviant behaviors become a medical disorder?

The treatment was available long before the disorder treated was clearly conceptualized. It was twenty years after Bradley's discovery of the "paradoxical effect" of stimulants on certain deviant children that Laufer named the disorder and described its characteristic symptoms. Only in the late fifties were both the diagnostic label and the pharmaceutical treatment available. The pharmaceutical revolution in mental health and the increased interest in child psychiatry provided a favorable background for the dissemination of knowledge about this new disorder. The latter probably made the medical profession more likely to consider behavior problems in children as within their clinical jurisdiction.

There were agents outside the medical profession itself that were significant in "promoting" hyperkinesis as a disorder within the medical framework. These agents might be conceptualized in Becker's terms as "moral entrepreneurs," those who crusade for creation and enforcement of the rules (Becker, 1963).[5] In this case the moral entrepreneurs were the pharmaceutical companies and the Association for Children with Learning Disabilities.

The pharmaceutical companies spent considerable time and money promoting stimulant medications for this new disorder. From the middle 1960's on, medical journals and the free "throwaway" magazines contained elaborate advertising for Ritalin and Dexedrine. These ads explained the utility of treating hyperkinesis and urged the physician to diagnose and treat hyperkinetic children. The ads run from one to six pages. For example, a two-page ad in 1971 stated:

MBD . . . MEDICAL MYTH OR DIAGNOS-ABLE DISEASE ENTITY What medical practitioner has not, at one time or another, been called upon to examine an impulsive, excitable hyperkinetic child? A child with difficulty in concentrating. Easily frustrated. Unusually aggressive. A classroom rebel. In the absence of any organic pathology, the conduct of such children was, until a few short years ago, usually dismissed as . . . spunkiness, or evidence of youthful vitality. But it is now evident that in many of these children the hyperkinetic syndrome exists as a distinct medical entity. This syndrome is readily diagnosed through patient histories, neurologic signs, and psychometric testing—has been classified by an expert panel convened by the United States Department of Health, Education and Welfare as Minimal Brain Dysfunction, MBD.

The pharmaceutical firms also supplied sophisticated packets of "diagnostic and treatment" information on hyperkinesis to physicians, paid for professional conferences on the subject, and supported research in the identification and treatment of the disorder. Clearly these corporations had a vested interest in the labeling and treatment of hyperkinesis; CIBA had $13 million profit from Ritalin alone in 1971, which was 15 percent of the total gross profits (Charles, 1971; Hentoff, 1972).

The other moral entrepreneur, less powerful than the pharmaceutical companies, but nevertheless influential, is the Association for Children with Learning Disabilities. Although its focus is not specifically on hyperkinetic children, it does include it in its conception of Learning Disabilities along with aphasia, reading problems like dyslexia, and perceptual motor problems. Founded in the early 1950's by parents and professionals, it has functioned much as the National Association for Mental Health does for mental illness: promoting conferences, sponsoring legislation, providing social support. One of the main functions has been to disseminate information concerning this relatively new area in education, Learning Disabilities. While the organization does have

a more educational than medical perspective, most of the literature indicates that for hyperkinesis members have adopted the medical model and the medical approach to the problem. They have sensitized teachers and schools to the conception of hyperkinesis as a medical problem.

The medical model of hyperactive behavior has become very well accepted in our society. Physicians find treatment relatively simple and the results sometimes spectacular. Hyperkinesis minimizes parents' guilt by emphasizing "It's not their fault, it's an organic problem" and allows for nonpunitive management or control of deviance. Medication often makes a child less disruptive in the classroom and sometimes aids a child in learning. Children often like their "magic pills" which make their behavior more socially acceptable and they probably benefit from a reduced stigma also. There are, however, some other, perhaps more subtle ramifications of the medicalization of deviant behavior.

The Medicalization of Deviant Behavior

Pitts has commented that "Medicalization is one of the most effective means of social control and that it is destined to become the main mode of *formal* social control"(1971, p. 391). Kitterie (1971) has termed it "the coming of the therapeutic state."

Medicalization of mental illness dates at least from the seventeenth century (Foucault, 1965; Szasz, 1970). Even slaves who ran away were once considered to be suffering from the disease *drapedomania* (Chorover, 1973). In recent years alcoholism, violence, and drug addiction as well as hyperactive behavior in children have all become defined as medical problems, both in etiology or explanation of the behavior and the means of social control or treatment.

There are many reasons why this medicalization has occurred. Much scientific research, especially in pharmacology and genetics, has become technologically more sophisticated, and found more subtle correlates with human behavior. Sometimes these findings (as in the case of XYY chromosomes and violence) become etiological explanations for deviance. Pharmacological technology that makes new discoveries affecting behavior (e.g., antibuse, methadone, and stimulants) are used as treatment for deviance. In part this application is encouraged by the prestige of the medical profession and its attachment to science. As Freidson notes, the medical profession has first claim to jurisdiction over anything that deals with the functioning of the body and especially anything that can be labeled illness (1970, p. 251). Advances in genetics, pharmacology, and "psychosurgery" also may advance medicine's jurisdiction over deviant behavior.

Second, the application of pharmacological technology is related to the humanitarian trend in the conception and control of deviant behavior. Alcoholism is no longer sin or even moral weakness, it is now a disease. Alcoholics are no longer arrested in many places for "public drunkenness," they are now somehow "treated," even if it is only to be dried out. Hyperactive children are now considered to have an illness rather than to be disruptive, disobedient, overactive problem children. They are not as likely to be the "bad boy" of the classroom; they are children with a medical disorder. Clearly there are some real humanitarian benefits to be gained by such a medical conceptualization of deviant behavior. There is less condemnation of the deviants (they have an illness, it is not their fault) and perhaps less social stigma. In some cases, even the medical treatment itself is more humanitarian social control than the criminal justice system.

There is, however, another side to the medicalization of deviant behavior. The four aspects of this side of the issue include (1) the problem of expert control; (2) medical social control; (3) the individualization of

social problems; and (4) the "depoliticization" of deviant behavior.

1. The Problem of Expert Control. The medical profession is a profession of experts; they have a monopoly on anything that can be conceptualized as illness. Because of the way the medical profession is organized and the mandate it has from society, decisions related to medical diagnoses and treatment are virtually controlled by medical professionals.

Some conditions that enter the medical domain are not ipso facto medical problems, especially deviant behavior, whether alcoholism, hyperactivity, or drug addiction. By defining a problem as medical it is removed from the public realm where there can be discussion by ordinary people and put on a plane where only medical people can discuss it. As Reynolds states,

> The increasing acceptance, especially among the more educated segments of our populace, of technical solutions—solutions administered by disinterested politically and morally neutral experts—results in the withdrawal of more and more areas of human experience from the realm of public discussion. For when drunkenness, juvenile delinquency, sub par performance and extreme political beliefs are seen as symptoms of an underlying illness or biological defect the merits and drawbacks of such behavior or beliefs need not be evaluated. (1973, pp. 220-221)

The public may have their own conceptions of deviant behavior but that of the experts is usually dominant.

2. Medical Social Control. Defining deviant behavior as a medical problem allows certain things to be done that could not otherwise be considered; for example, the body may be cut open or psychoactive medications may be given. This treatment can be a form of social control.

In regard to drug treatment Lennard points out: "Psychoactive drugs, especially those legally prescribed, tend to restrain individuals from behavior and experience that are not complementary to the requirements of the dominant value system" (1971, p. 57). These forms of medical social control presume a prior definition of deviance as a medical problem. Psychosurgery on an individual prone to violent outbursts requires a diagnosis that there was something wrong with his brain or nervous system. Similarly, prescribing drugs to restless, overactive, and disruptive school children requires a diagnosis of hyperkinesis. These forms of social control, what Chorover (1973) has called "psychotechnology," are very powerful and often very efficient means of controlling deviance. These relatively new and increasingly popular forms of social control could not be utilized without the medicalization of deviant behavior. As is suggested from the discovery of hospice, if a mechanism of medical social control seems useful, then the deviant behavior it modifies will develop a medical label or diagnosis. No overt malevolence on the part of the medical profession is implied: rather it is part of a complex process, of which the medical profession is only a part. The larger process might be called the individualization of social problems.

3. *The Individualization of Social Problems.* The medicalization of deviant behavior is part of a larger phenomenon that is prevalent in our society, the individualization of social problems. We tend to look for causes and solutions to complex social problems in the individual rather than in the social system. This view resembles Ryan's (1971) notion of "blaming the victim," seeing the causes of the problem in individuals rather than in the society where they live. We then seek to change the "victim" rather than the society. The medical perspective of diagnosing an illness in an individual lends itself to the individualization of social problems. Rather than seeing certain deviant behaviors as symptomatic of problems in the social system, the medical perspective focuses on the

individual diagnosing and treating the illness, generally ignoring the social situation.

Hyperkinesis serves as a good example. Both the school and the parents are concerned with the child's behavior; the child is very difficult at home and disruptive in school. No punishments or rewards seem consistently to work in modifying the behavior; and both parents and school are at their wit's end. A medical evaluation is suggested. The diagnoses of hyperkinetic behavior leads to prescribing stimulant medications. The child's behavior seems to become more socially acceptable, reducing problems in school and at home.

But there is an alternate perspective. By focusing on the symptoms and defining them as hyperkinesis we ignore the possibility that behavior is not an illness but an adaptation to a social situation. It diverts our attention from the family or school and from seriously entertaining the idea that the "problem" could be in the structure of the social system. And by giving medications we are essentially supporting the existing systems and do not allow this behavior to be a factor of change in the system.

4. *The Depoliticization of Deviant Behavior.* Depoliticization of deviant behavior is a result of both the process of medicalization and individualization of social problems. To our western world, probably one of the clearest examples of such a depoliticization of deviant behavior occurred when political dissenters in the Soviet Union were declared mentally ill and confined in mental hospitals (cf. Conrad, 1972). This strategy served to neutralize the meaning of political protest and dissent, rendering it the ravings of mad persons.

The medicalization of deviant behavior depoliticizes deviance in the same manner. By defining the overactive, restless and disruptive child as hyperkinetic we ignore the meaning of behavior in the context of the social system. If we focused our analysis on the school system we might see the child's behavior as symptomatic of some "disorder" in the school or classroom situation, rather than symptomatic of an individual neurological disorder.

Conclusion

I have discussed the social ramifications of the medicalization of deviant behavior, using hyperkinesis as the example. A number of consequences of this medicalization have been outlined, including the depoliticization of deviant behavior, decision-making power of experts, and the role of medicine as an agent of social control. In the last analysis medical social control may be the central issue, as in this role medicine becomes a de facto agent of the status quo. The medical profession may not have entirely sought this role, but its members have been, in general, disturbingly unconcerned and unquestioning in their acceptance of it. With the increasing medical knowledge and technology it is likely that more deviant behavior will be medicalized and medicine's social control function will expand.

Notes

1. The USPHS report (Clements, 1966) included 38 terms that were used to describe or distinguish the conditions that it labeled Minimal Brain Dysfunction. Although the literature attempts to differentiate MBD, hyperkinesis, hyperactive syndrome, and several other diagnostic labels, it is our belief that in practice they are almost interchangeable.

2. For a fuller discussion of the construction of the diagnosis of hyperkinesis, see Conrad (1976), especially Chapter 6.

3. The American Medical Association's change in policy in accepting more pharmaceutical advertising in the late fifties may have been important. Probably the FDA approval of the use of Ritalin for children in 1961 was more significant. Until 1970, Ritalin was advertised for treatment of "functional behavior problems in children." Since then, because of an FDA order, it has only been promoted for treatment of MBD.

4. The drug industry spends fully 25 percent of its budget on promotion and advertising. See Coleman, Katz, & Menzel (1966) for the role of the detail men and how physicians rely upon them for information.

5. Freidson also notes the medical professional role as moral entrepreneur in this process also: "The profession does treat the illnesses laymen take to it, but it also seeks to discover illness of which the laymen may not even be aware. One of the greatest ambitions of the physician is to discover and describe a 'new' disease or syndrome . . ." (1970, p. 252).

References

Becker, H. S. (1963). *The outsiders.* New York: Free Press.

Bradley, C. (1937, March). The behavior of children receiving Benzedrine. *American Journal of Psychiatry, 94,* 577-585.

Charles, A. (1971, October). The case of Ritalin. *New Republic, 23,* 17-19.

Chorover, S. L. (1973, October). Big brother and psychotechnology. *Psychology Today,* pp. 43-54.

Clements, S. D. (1966). *Task force I: Minimal brain dysfunction in children* (National Institute of Neurological Diseases and Blindness, Monograph no. 3). Washington, DC: U.S. Department of Health, Education, and Welfare.

Cole, S. (1975, January). Hyperactive children: The use of stimulant drugs evaluated. *American Journal of Orthopsychiatry, 45,* 28-37.

Coleman, J., Katz, E., & Menzel, H. (1966). *Medical innovation.* Indianapolis: Bobbs-Merrill.

Conrad, P. (1972). *Ideological deviance: An analysis of the Soviet use of mental hospitals for political dissenters.* Unpublished manuscript.

Conrad, P. (1976). *Identifying hyperactive children in the medicalization of deviant behavior.* Lexington, MA: D. C. Heath & Co.

DeLong, A. R. (1972, February). What have we learned from psychoactive drugs research with hyperactives? *American Journal of Diseases in Children, 123,* 177-180.

Foucault, M. (1965). *Madness and civilization.* New York: Pantheon.

Friedson, E. (1970). *Profession of medicine.* New York: Harper & Row.

Grinspoon, L., & Singer, S. (1973, November). Amphetamines in the treatment of hyperactive children. *Harvard Educational Review, 43,* 515-555.

Gross, M. B., & Wilson, W. E. (1974). *Minimal brain dysfunction.* New York: Brunner/Mazel.

Hentoff, N. (1972, May). Drug pushing in the schools: The professionals. *Village Voice, 22,* 21-23.

Kitterie, N. (1971). *The right to be different.* Baltimore, MD: Johns Hopkins University Press.

Laufer, M. W., Denhoff, E., & Solomons, G. (1957, January). Hyperkinetic impulse disorder in children's behavior problems. *Psychosomatic Medicine, 19,* 38-49.

Lennard, H. L., & Associates. (1971). *Mystification and drug misuse.* New York: Harper & Row.

Office of Child Development. (1971, January 11-12). *Report of the conference on the use of stimulant drugs in treatment of behaviorally disturbed children.* Washington, DC: Department of Health, Education, and Welfare, January 11-12.

Pitts, J. (1968). Social control: The concept. In D. Sills (Ed.), *International Encyclopedia of the Social Sciences* (Vol. 14). New York: Macmillan.

Reynolds, J. M. (1973). The medical institution. In L. T. Reynolds & J. M. Henslin (Eds.), *American society: A critical analysis* (pp. 198-324). New York: David McKay.

Robin, S. S., & Bosco, J. J. (1973, December). Ritalin for school children: The teachers' perspective. *Journal of School Health, 47,* 624-628.

Rosen, G. (1972). The evolution of social medicine. In H. E. Freeman, S. Levine, & L. Reeder (Eds.), *Handbook of medical sociology* (pp. 30-60). Englewood Cliffs, NJ: Prentice-Hall.

Ryan, W. (1971). *Blaming the victim.* New York: Vintage.

Silverman, M., & Lee, P. R. (1974). *Pills, profits and politics.* Berkeley: University of California Press.

Sroufe, L. A., & Stewart, M. (1973, August). Treating problem children with stimulant drugs. *New England Journal of Medicine, 289,* 407-421.

Stewart, M. A. (1970, April). Hyperactive children. *Scientific American, 222,* 794-798.

Stewart, M. A., Ferris, A., Pitts, N. P., & Craig, A. G. (1966, October). The hyperactive child syndrome. *American Journal of Orthopsychiatry, 36,* 861-867.

Strauss, A. A., & Lehtinen, L. E. (1947). *Psychopathology and education of the brain-injured child* (Vol. 1). New York: Grune & Stratton.

Szasz, T. (1970). *The manufacture of madness.* New York: Harper & Row.

U.S. Government Printing Office. (1970, September 29). *Federal involvement in the use of behavior modification drugs on grammar school children of the right to privacy inquiry: Hearing before a subcommittee of the committee on government operations.* Washington, DC, 91st Congress, 2nd session.

Wender, P. (1971). *Minimal brain dysfunction in children.* New York: John Wiley.

Zola, I. (1972, November). Medicine as an institution of social control. *Sociological Review, 20,* 487-504.

42

The Sane Slave: An Historical Note on the Use of Medical Diagnosis as Justificatory Rhetoric

Thomas S. Szasz

I

The passion to dehumanize and diminish man, as well as to superhumanize and glorify him, appears to be a characteristic of human nature. For millennia, the dialectic of vilification and deification and, more generally, of invalidation and validation—excluding the individual from the group as an evil outsider or including him in it as a member in good standing—was cast in the imagery and rhetoric of magic and religion. Thus, at the height of Christianity in Europe, only the faithful were considered human: the faithless—heretics, witches, and Jews—were considered subhuman or nonhuman and were so treated. At the same time, the popes were thought to be infallible and kings ruled by divine decree.

With the decline of the religious world view, and the ascendancy of the scientific, during the Renaissance and the Enlightenment, the religious rhetoric of validation and invalidation was gradually replaced by the scientific. I have described and documented this transformation in *The Manufacture of Madness* (1970b), showing, in particular, the birth, development, and flowering of the lexicon of medical diagnosis as a rhetoric of rejection.

In this essay, my aim is to offer an additional illustration of the foregoing thesis. In May, 1851, an essay entitled "Report on the Diseases and Physical Peculiarities of the Negro Race," written by Samuel A. Cartwright, M.D., was published in the then prestigious *New Orleans Medical and Surgical Journal*. In this remarkable document, Dr. Cartwright asserted—not only in his own name but also in his capacity as chairman of a committee appointed by the Medical Association of Louisiana to report on the "diseases and peculiarities of the Negro race"—that Negroes are biologically inferior to whites, and sought to justify their enslavement as a therapeutic necessity for the slaves and a medical responsibility for the masters. In support of this thesis, Dr. Cartwright claimed to identify two new diseases peculiar to Negroes: one, which he called "drapetomania," was manifested by the escape of the Negro slave from his white master; the other, which he called "dysaesthesia Aethiopis," was manifested by the Negro's neglecting his work or refusing to work altogether.

II

I consider Cartwright's "Report," and especially the two diseases afflicting the Negro

"The Sane Slave: An Historical Note on the Use of Medical Diagnosis as Justificatory Rhetoric" by T. S. Szasz, 1971. *American Journal of Psychotherapy, 25*, pp. 228-239. Reprinted by permission of the Association for the Advancement of Psychotherapy.

that he discovered, of special interest and importance to us today for the following reasons: first, because Cartwright invoked the authority and vocabulary of medical science to dehumanize the Negro and justify his enslavement by the white man; second, because the language and reasoning he used to justify the coercive control of the Negro are identical to those used today by mental health propagandists to justify the coercive control of the madman (that is, the so-called "psychotic," "addict," "sexual psychopath," and so forth); and third, because Cartwright's "Report" is the sort of medical document that has, for obvious reasons, been systematically ignored or suppressed in standard texts on medical and psychiatric history.

One such omission, discussed in detail in *The Manufacture of Madness*, is Benjamin Rush's theory of Negritude, according to which the black skin and other physical "peculiarities" of the Negro are due to his suffering from congenital leprosy (Szasz, 1970b, pp. 153-159). This grotesquely self-serving explanation—which postulated white as the only "healthy" human skin color, and defined the normal physiologic state of the Negro as a dreadful disease, justifying his segregation for reasons of alleged ill health rather than imputed racial inferiority—was, moreover, merely a part of Rush's medical world view in which all types of undesired human characteristics and conduct were considered diseases—usually of the mind. Thus by the time the "Report on the Diseases and Physical Peculiarities of the Negro Race" appeared, the habit, especially among medical men, of passionately degrading their adversaries as sick, while pretending to be impartially "diagnosing" them, was well established. It is against this general background, and the steadily increasing influence of the abolitionist forces in the United States at that time, that we must consider the Cartwright "Report."

I shall reproduce below excerpts from the "Report" describing drapetomania and

dysaesthesia Aethiopis, and shall then offer some comments on them.

III. Drapetomania, or the Disease Causing Slaves to Run Away

Drapetomania is from *"drapetes,"* a runaway slave, and *"mania," mad* or *crazy.* It is unknown to our medical authorities, although its diagnostic symptom, the absconding from service, is well known to our planters and overseers, as it was to the ancient Greeks, who expressed by the single word *"drapetes"* the fact of the absconding, and the relation that the fugitive held to the person he fled from. I have added to the word meaning runaway slave, another Greek term, to express the disease of the mind causing him to abscond. In noticing a disease not heretofore classed among the long list of maladies that man is subject to, it was necessary to have a new term to express it. The cause, in the most of cases, that induces the negro to run away from service, is as much a disease of the mind as any other species of mental alienation, and much more curable, as a general rule. With the advantages of proper medical advice, strictly followed, this troublesome practice that many negroes have of running away, can be almost entirely prevented, although the slaves be located on the borders of a free State, within a stone's throw of the abolitionists. . . .

To ascertain the true method of governing negroes, so as to cure and prevent the disease under consideration, we must go back to the Pentateuch, and learn the true meaning of the untranslated term that represents the negro race. In the name there given to that race, is locked up the true art of governing negroes in such a manner that they cannot run away. The correct translation of that term declares the Creator's will in regard to the negro; it declares him to be the submissive knee-bender. In the anatomical conformation of his knees, we see *"genu flexit"* written in the physical structure of his knees, being more flexed or bent, than any other kind of man. If the white man attempts to oppose the Deity's will, by trying to make the negro anything else than *"the submissive knee-bender"* (which the Almighty declared he should be), by trying to raise him to a level with himself, or by putting himself on an equality with the negro; or if he abuses the power which God has given him over his fellow man, by being cruel to him or punishing him in anger, or by neglecting to protect him from the wanton abuses of his fellow-servants and all others, or by denying him the usual comforts and necessities of life, the negro will run away, but if he keeps him in the position that we learn from the Scriptures he was intended to occupy, that is, the position of submission, and if his master or overseer be kind and gracious in his bearing towards him, without condescension, and at the same time ministers to his physical wants and protects him from abuses, the negro is spell-bound, and cannot run away. . . .

Before negroes run away, unless they are frightened or panic-struck, they become sulky and dissatisfied. The cause of this sulkiness and dissatisfaction should be inquired into and removed, or they are apt to run away or fall into the negro consumption. When sulky and dissatisfied without cause, the experience of those on the line and elsewhere was decidedly in favor of whipping them out of it, as a preventive measure against absconding or other bad conduct. It was called whipping the devil out of them.

If treated kindly, well fed and clothed, with fuel enough to keep a small fire burning all night, separated into families, each family having its own house—not permitted to run about at night, or to visit their neighbors, or to receive visits, or to use intoxicating liquors, and not overworked or exposed too much to the weather, they are very easily governed—more so than any other people in the world. When all this is done, if any one or more of them, at any time, are inclined to raise their heads to a level with their master or overseer, humanity and their own good require that they should be punished until they fall into that submissive state which it was intended for them to occupy in all after time, when their progenitor received the name of Canaan, or "submissive knee-bender." They have only to be kept in that state, and treated like children with care, kindness, attention and humanity, to prevent and cure them from running away.

IV. Dysaesthesia Aethiopis, or Hebetude of Mind and Obtuse Sensibility of Body— A Disease Peculiar to Negroes—Called by Overseers, "Rascality"

Dysaesthesia Aethiopis is a disease peculiar to negroes, affecting both mind and body, in a manner as well expressed by dysaesthesia, the name I have given it, as could be by a single term. There is both mind and sensibility, but both seem to be difficult to reach by impressions from without. There is partial insensibility of the skin, and so great a hebetude of the intellectual faculties as to be like a person half asleep, that is with difficulty aroused and kept awake. It differs from every other species of mental disease, as it is accompanied with physical signs or lesions of the body, discoverable to the medical observer, which are always present and sufficient to account for the symptoms. It is much more prevalent among free negroes living in clusters by themselves, than among slaves on our plantations, and attacks only such slaves as live like free negroes in regard to diet, drinks, exercise, etc. It is not my purpose to treat of the complaint as it prevails among free negroes, nearly all of whom are more or less afflicted with it, that have not got some white person to direct and to take care of them. To narrate its symptoms and effects among them would be to write a history of the ruins and dilapidation of Hayti and every spot of earth they have ever had uncontrolled possession over for any length of time. I propose only to describe its symptoms among slaves.

From the careless movements of the individuals affected with the complaint, they are apt to do much mischief, which appears as if intentional, but is mostly owing to the stupidness of mind and insensibility of the nerves induced by the disease. Thus, they break, waste and destroy everything they handle—abuse horses and cattle—tear, burn or rend their own clothing, and paying no attention to the rights of property, they steal other's to replace what they have destroyed. They wander about at night, and keep in a half-nodding sleep during the day. They slight their work—cut up corn, cane, cotton or tobacco when hoeing it, as if for pure mischief. They raise disturbances with their overseers and fellow servants without cause or motive, and seem to be insensible to pain when subjected to punishment.

The fact of the existence of such a complaint, making man like an automaton or senseless machine, having the above or similar symptoms, can be clearly established by the most direct and positive testimony. That it should have escaped the attention of the medical profession, can only be accounted for because its attention has not been sufficiently directed to the maladies of the negro race. Otherwise, a complaint of so common occurrence on badly-governed plantations, and so universal among free negroes, or those who are not governed at all—a disease radicated in physical lesions and having its peculiar and well-marked symptoms, and its curative indications, would not have escaped the notice of the profession. The northern physicians and people have noticed the symptoms, but not the disease from which they spring. They ignorantly attribute the symptoms to the debasing influence of slavery on the mind, without considering that those who have never been in slavery, or their fathers before them, are the most afflicted and the latest from the slave-holding South the least. The disease is the natural offspring of negro liberty—the liberty to be idle, to wallow in filth, and to indulge in improper food and drinks.

In treating of the anatomy and physiology of the negro, I showed that his respiratory system was under the same physiological laws as that of an infant child of the white race; that a warm atmosphere, loaded with carbonic acid and aqueous vapor, was the most congenial to his lungs during sleep, as it is to the infant; that, to insure the respiration of such an atmosphere, he invariably, as if moved by instinct, shrouds his head and face in a blanket or some other covering, when disposing himself to sleep; that if sleeping by the fire in cold weather, he turns his head to it, instead of his feet, evidently to inhale warm air; that when not in active exercise, he always hovers over a fire in comparatively warm weather, as if he took a positive pleasure in inhaling hot air and smoke when his body is quiescent. The natural effect of this practice, it was shown, caused imperfect atmospherization or vitalization of the blood in the lungs, as occurs in infancy, and a hebetude or torpor of intellect—from blood not sufficiently vitalized being distributed to the brain; also, a slothfulness, torpor and disinclination to exercise, from the same cause—the want of blood sufficiently areated or vitalized in the circulating system.

When left to himself, the negro indulges in his natural disposition to idleness and sloth, and does not take exercise enough to expand his lungs and to vitalize his blood, but dozes out a miserable existence in the midst of filth and uncleanliness, being too indolent and having too little energy of mind to provide for himself proper food and comfortable lodging and clothing. The consequence is, that the blood becomes so highly carbonized and deprived of oxygen, that it not only becomes unfit to stimulate the brain to energy, but unfit to stimulate the nerves of sensation distributed to the body. A torpor and insensibility pervades the system; the sentient nerves distributed to the skin lose their feeling to so great a degree, that he often burns his skin by the fire he hovers over, without knowing it, and frequently has large holes in his clothes, and the shoes on his feet burnt to a crisp, without having been conscious of when it was done. This is the disease called dysaesthesia—a Greek term expressing the dull or obtuse sensation that always attends the complaint.

When aroused from his sloth by the stimulus of hunger, he takes anything he can lay his hands on, and tramples on the rights, as well as on the property of others, with perfect indifference as to consequences. When driven to labor by the compulsive power of the white man, he performs the task assigned him in a headlong, careless manner, treading down with his feet, or cutting with his hoe the plants he is put to cultivate—breaking the tools he works with, and spoiling everything he touches that can be injured by careless handling. Hence the overseers call it "rascality," supposing that the mischief is intentionally done. But there is no premeditated mischief in the case—the mind is too torpid to meditate mischief, or even to be aroused by the angry passions to deeds of daring. Dysaesthesia, or hebetude of sensation of both mind and body, prevails to so great an extent, that when the unfortunate individual is subjected to punishment, he neither feels pain of any consequence, or shows any unusual resentment, more than by a stupid sulkiness.

In some cases, anaesthesiac would be a more suitable name for it, as there appears to be an almost total loss of feeling. The term "rascality," given to this disease by overseers, is founded on an erroneous hypothesis and leads to an incorrect empirical treatment, which seldom or ever cures it.

The complaint is easily curable, if treated on sound physiological principles. The skin is dry, thick and harsh to the touch, and the liver inactive. The liver, skin and kidneys should be stimulated to activity, and be made assist in decarbonising the blood. The best means to stimulate the skin is, first, to have the patient well washed with warm water and soap; then to anoint it all over with oil, and to slap the oil in with a broad leather strap; then to put the patient to some hard kind of work in the open air and sunshine, that will compel him to expand his lungs, as chopping wood, splitting rails or sawing with the cross-cut or whip saw. Any kind of labor will do that will cause full and free respiration in its performance, as lifting or carrying heavy weights, or brisk walking; the object being to expand the lungs by full and deep inspirations and expirations, thereby to vitalize the impure circulating blood by introducing oxygen and expelling carbon. . . .

Such treatment will, in a short time, effect a cure in all cases which are complicated with chronic visceral derangements. The effect of this or a like course of treatment is often like enchantment. No sooner does the blood feel the vivifying influences derived from its full and perfect atmospherization by exercise in the open air and in the sun, than the negro seems to be awakened to a new existence, and to look grateful and thankful to the white man whose compulsory power, by making him inhale vital air, has restored his sensation and dispelled the mist that clouded his intellect. His intelligence restored and his sensations awakened, he is no longer the *bipedum neqquissimus,* or arrant rascal, he was supposed to be, but a good negro that can hoe or plow, and handle things with as much care as his other fellow-servants. . . .

Although idleness is the most prolific cause of dysaesthesia, yet there are other ways that the blood gets deteriorated. I said before that negroes are like children, requiring government in everything. . . .

According to unalterable physiological laws, negroes, as a general rule, to which there are but few exceptions, can only have their intellectual faculties awakened in a sufficient degree to receive moral culture, and to profit by religious or other instruction, when under the compulsatory authority of the white man; because, as a general rule, to which there are but few exceptions, they will not take sufficient exercise, when removed from the white man's authority, to vitalize and decarbonize their blood by the process of full and free respiration, that active exercise of some kind alone can effect. A northern climate remedies, in a considerable degree, their naturally indolent disposition; but the dense atmosphere of Boston or Canada can scarcely produce sufficient hematosis and vigor of mind to induce them to labor. From their natural indolence, unless under the stimulus of compulsion, they doze away their lives with the capacity of their lungs for atmospheric air only half expanded, from the want of exercise to superinduce full and deep respiration. The inevitable effect is, to prevent a sufficient atmospherization or vitalization of the blood, so essential to the expansion and the freedom of action of the intellectual faculties. The black blood distributed to the brain chains the mind to ignorance, superstition and barbarism, and bolts the door against civilization, moral culture and religious truth. The compulsory power of the white man, by making the slothful negro take active exercise, puts into active play the lungs, through whose agency the vitalized blood is sent to the brain to give liberty to the mind, and to open the door to intellectual improvement. The very exercise, so beneficial to the negro, is expended in cultivating those burning fields in cotton, sugar, rice and tobacco, which, but for his labor, would, from the heat of the climate, go uncultivated, and their products lost to the world. Both parties are benefitted—the negro as well as his master—even more. But there is a third party benefitted—the world at large. The three millions of bales of cotton, made by negro labor, afford a cheap clothing for the civilized world. The laboring classes of all mankind, having less to pay for clothing, have more money to spend in educating their children, and in intellectual, moral and religious progress.

The wisdom, mercy and justice of the decree, that Canaan shall serve Japheth, is proved by the disease we have been considering, because it proves that his physical organization, and the laws of his nature, are in perfect unison with slavery, and in entire discordance with liberty—a discordance so great as to produce the loathsome disease that we have been considering, as one of its inevitable effects—a disease that locks up the understanding, blunts the sensations and chains the mind to superstition, ignorance and barbarism. Slaves are not subject to this disease, unless they are permitted to live like free negroes, in idleness and filth—to eat improper food, or to indulge in spirituous liquors. . . .

Our Declaration of Independence, which was drawn up at a time when negroes were scarcely considered as human beings, *That all men are by nature free and equal*," and only intended to apply to white men, is often quoted in support of the false dogma that all mankind possess the same mental, physiological and anatomical organization, and that the liberty, free institutions, and whatever else would be a blessing to one portion, would, under the same external circumstances, be to all, without regard to any original or internal differences inherent in the organization. . . .

The dysaesthesia Aethiopis adds another to the many ten thousand evidences of the fallacy of the dogma that abolitionism is built on; for here, in a country where two races of men dwell together, both born on the same soil, breathing the same air, and surrounded by the same external agents—liberty, which is elevating the one race of people above all other nations, sinks the other into beastly sloth and torpidity; and the slavery, which the one would prefer death rather than endure, improves the other in body, mind and morals; thus proving the dogma false, and establishing the truth that there is a radical, internal, or physical difference between the two races, so great in kind, as to make what is wholesome and beneficial for the white man, as liberty, republican or free institutions, etc., not only unsuitable to the negro race, but actually poisonous to its happiness.

The content of the Cartwright "Report" hardly requires comment. Its form, however, which closely resembles contemporary forms of psychiatric denigration, deserves further attention. I shall list my observations in the order in which the statements to which they refer occur in the text—first on "drapetomania," then on "dysaesthesia Aethiopis."

1. Although "running away," or escaping from captivity, is ordinarily thought of as a human act, a deliberate or willed performance, Cartwright refers to it as an occurrence or happening, an event "caused" by certain antecedent events: thus drapetomania "causes" slaves to run away.

2. The "cause . . . that induces the negro to run away from service" is, moreover, identified as a "disease of the mind."

3. Premonitory symptoms of drapetomania are said to be "sulkiness" and "dissatisfaction." When displayed by whites, such emotions were then viewed as the normal expressions of unhappiness with one's lot in life; but when displayed by Negro slaves, they signaled the onset of a dread mental disease.

4. To prevent the full-blown development of drapetomania, exhibited by the actual running away of the slave, whipping is recommended as medical therapy. This treatment, in a revealing allusion to its historical origins, is called "whipping the devil out of them."

5. Finally, the cure of drapetomania, and the restoration of the slave to sanity, is said to require the submission of the Negro slave to his white master. "They have only to be kept in that [submissive] state," concludes Cartwright, "and treated like children, with care, kindness, attention and humanity [sic], to prevent and cure them from running away."

Since Cartwright's foregoing observations, Lincoln has emancipated the Negro slaves and the medical profession has negritized the free whites. Thus, what had been drapetomania became depression. The Negro slave ran away from slavery. Modern man runs away from a life that seems to him a kind of slavery. In trying to escape, he may abandon his family, his job, his very life. Since such behavior is socially disruptive, and in the case of suicidal propensities is life-threatening, it is now generally regarded as a medical problem justifying the involuntary hospitalization and treatment of the alleged patient.

In short, the sane slave is the Negro who accepts his role as the natural and proper order of things. The Negro who rejects this role is defined as insane. In this view, formed more than a century ago, we recognize the current criteria of mental health and mental illness—that is, the acceptance of the social roles imposed upon us by birth, fate, law, or our superiors in life, or their rejection (Szasz, 1961, 1970a).

6. "Dysaesthesia Aethiopis" is an illness which Cartwright identifies as "a disease peculiar to negroes—called by overseers 'rascality.' " It is thus clearly a product of relabeling, pure and simple (Szasz, 1970a).

7. As with drapetomania, Cartwright further identifies dysaesthesia Aethiopis specifically as a "mental disease . . . accompanied with physical signs or lesions of the body, discoverable to the medical observer. . . ."

8. Although Cartwright mentions not a single free Negro who has consulted him as a patient, for this or any other illness, he refers to "the complaint [sic] as it prevails among free negroes. . . . " Actually, dysaesthesia Aethiopis points to certain types of behavior on the part of Negroes deemed offensive to whites—by the whites, not the blacks. It is Cartwright

who "complains," not his alleged "patients." This linguistic form—the oppressor labeling the undesired behavior of his victim a "complaint" or a "symptom"—continues to remain basic to, and indispensable for, the theory and practice of institutional psychiatry (Szasz, 1970b).

9. "Nearly all" free Negroes "that have not got some white person to direct and to take care of them" are said to be afflicted with dysaesthesia Aethiopis. This alleged finding re-affirms the equation between sanity and subjection for the black—and sanity and domination for the white. Today, we equate sanity with psychiatric subjection for the patient—and sanity with psychiatric domination for the physician. Since nowadays everyone is considered more or less mentally ill, the measure of mental health is "insight" into, and acceptance of, the role of mental patient by the layman—and the role of mental healer by the physician. The drama of mental illness is thus merely a new version of the drama of Negritude: the cast is new, but the play is the same.

10. The chief symptoms—"complaints," as Cartwright calls them—of dysaesthesia Aethiopis are the doing of "much mischief": the individuals afflicted with the malady "break, waste, and destroy everything they handle . . . slight their work—cut up corn, cane, cotton or tobacco when hoeing it, as if for pure mischief." These acts speak for themselves. Their meaning, and the human dignity of those whose protest they express and signify, are medically redefined as the meaningless manifestations of a mental disorder. And so it is today—except that we now dehumanize black and white equally. From insane "rascalities" in Louisiana to insane murders in Dallas and Los Angeles, it is only a short step.

11. Cartwright not only describes the signs and symptoms of the disease he calls "dysaesthesia Aethiopis," he also identi-

fies its etiology and prescribes its cure. "The disease," he asserts, "is the natural offspring of negro liberty. . . . "

12. "The complaint [sic] is easily curable." To cure the "patient," the doctor is exhorted "to anoint it [the skin] all over with oil, and to slap the oil in with a broad leather strap; then to put the patient [sic] to some hard kind of work in the open air and sunshine, that will compel him to expand his lungs, as chopping wood, splitting rails or sawing with the cross-cut or whip saw." This posture is indistinguishable from the "therapeutic attitude" of our "liberal" psychiatric criminologist (Halleck, 1967; Menninger, 1968). The basic formula is here in its entirety: call the victim "patient" and the punishment "treatment," and he will surely be "cured" of his "affliction"—provided, of course, that the physician is left in full charge not only of the patient and his treatment but of the evaluation of the therapeutic results as well.

13. Although Cartwright attributes the destructive behavior of Negroes to dysaesthesia Aethiopis and claims that the disease is curable, even complete recovery from this affliction fails to restore the blacks to a physiologic state comparable to that of the whites. "Although idleness is the most prolific cause of dysaesthesia, yet there are other ways that the blood gets deteriorated. I said before that the negroes are like children, requiring government in everything."

14. Lastly, Cartwright provides us with an exceptionally clear and unqualified statement regarding the subhuman character of Negroes which, though rarely put so badly nowadays, applies equally to the modern view of all men—black *and* white—stigmatized as mentally ill. "Our Declaration of Independence," Cartwright writes, "which was drawn up at a time when negroes were scarcely considered as human beings, 'That all men are by

nature free and equal,' and only intended to apply to white men, is often quoted in support of the false dogma that all mankind possesses the same mental, physiological, and anatomical organization. . . . The dysaesthesia Aethiopis adds another to the many ten thousand [sic] evidences of the fallacy of the dogma that abolitionism is built on. . . . " Liberty, Cartwright concludes, is beneficial for the white man, but is "actually poisonous to the happiness" of his black brother. No more fitting epitaph could be written for involuntary mental hospitalization, a practice that enshrines the identical proposition: Liberty, beneficial for the sane (psychiatrist), is actually poisonous to the happiness of the insane (patient).

VI

It would be misleading to leave off here, implying that our forebears accepted Cartwright's claims without the skepticism that is as characteristic of man as is his gullibility. In the September, 1851, issue of the *New Orleans Medical and Surgical Journal*, there appeared a devastating criticism of Cartwright's paper. Written by James T. Smith, Surgeon, Louisiana, it is titled: "Review of Dr. Cartwright's Report on the Diseases and Physical Peculiarities of the Negro Race." I shall quote from it only those passages that are relevant to our contemporary infatuation with the rhetoric of mental health and mental illness.

Commenting on "drapetomania," Smith writes: "This may well be called a new disease, discovered by Dr. Cartwright. . . . It is calculated to marshal the way to the pathology of a very numerous class of diseases hitherto never dreamed of as being anything but vices; for if a strong desire to do what is wrong be a disease, the violation of any one of the ten commandments will furnish us with a new one so that with a long Greek word for the commencement, and the addition of the magic 'mania,' we shall have a disease for coveting your neighbor's money (a disease common to both the white and black races), or a disease of bearing false witness, or a disease for cutting your neighbor's throat, commonly called 'murder'; all of which shall no longer be treated by the penitentiary, but by calomel, capsicum, etc. This we consider as the greatest step in the progress of philanthropy made in modern times."

Smith was no less astute in his remarks on Cartwright's treatment of dysaesthesia Aethiopis. For this disease, he writes, Cartwright "suggests a species of remedy which, with some modifications, the Greek master applied to his drapetes and the Roman to his fugitivus—it is, the 'strapping-in' recommended by the doctor. 'The best means,' says he, 'of stimulating the skin is to have the patient well washed with warm water and soap, then to anoint it all over with oil, and to slap it in with a broad leather strap.' Now they, the Romans and the Greeks, used the strapping in without the anointment; and with a much narrower strap than the one recommended."

And one final comment on drapetomania: It may be of some interest to note that standard medical dictionaries (such as *Gould's* and *Stedman's*) continue to list this term, defining it as "a morbid desire to wander or run away."

VII

It would be misleading still, to stop here, implying that Cartwright's vicious paternalism toward the Negro is safely behind us. In 1851, Samuel A. Cartwright, M.D., asserted that the Negro was a child who must be governed by the white man. In 1969, Graham B. Blaine, Jr., M.D., chief of Psychiatric Service of the Harvard University Health Services, asserts that the Negro is an adolescent whose "symptoms" must be borne with "patience" and "tolerance"

by the white man. From the "drapetomania" and "dysaesthesia Aethiopis" of the black slave, to the "adolescence of the black race" and its "identity conflict," the road is direct and the passage swift: The way is through the land of medicine and is marked clearly, all the way, by diagnostic labels.

As to the Negro's present medical condition—couched in the vocabulary of the most up-to-date and "humanistic" terms of psychiatry—I shall let Blaine (1969) speak about it for himself. "In addition to helping black students cope with the problems of their individual adolescence," he writes, "they must also be helped to deal with the conflicts that arise from the adolescence of the black race. It is in this country, at this time, a group which is struggling to define its identity. After such definition occurs, the race can take its place harmoniously within the larger culture. Rebellion and group distinctiveness are symptoms of this identity conflict. The rest of society must be patient and tolerant about these symptoms much as parents must deal with the paradoxical, provocative behavior of their adolescent children."

VIII

I have tried to call attention, by means of an article published in the *New Orleans Medical and Surgical Journal* for 1851, to some of the historical origins of the modern psychiatric rhetoric. In the article cited, conduct on the part of the Negro slave displeasing or offensive to his white master is defined as the manifestation of mental disease, and subjection and punishment are prescribed as treatments. By substituting involuntary mental patients for Negro slaves, institutional psychiatrists for white slave owners, and the rhetoric of mental health for that of white supremacy, we may learn a fresh lesson about the changing verbal patterns man uses to justify exploiting and oppressing his fellow man, in the name of helping him.

Perhaps Shaw—and Hegel whom he was paraphrasing—was right: "We learn from history, that we learn nothing from history."

References

Blaine, G. B., Jr. (1969, November 26). What's behind the youth rebellion? *Sunday Herald Traveler* (Boston), pp. 22-23.

Cartwright, S. A. (1851, May). Report on the diseases and physical peculiarities of the Negro race. *New Orleans Medical and Surgical Journal, 7*, 691-715.

Halleck, S. L. (1967). *Psychiatry and the dilemmas of crime.* New York: Hoeber-Harper.

Menninger, K. (1968). *The crime of punishment.* New York: Viking.

Smith, J. T. (1851, September). Review of Dr. Cartwright's report on the diseases and physical peculiarities of the negro race. *New Orleans Medical and Surgical Journal, 8,* 228-237.

Szasz, T. S. (1961). *The myth of mental illness.* New York: Hoeber-Harper.

Szasz, T. S. (1970a). *Ideology and insanity.* Garden City, NY: Doubleday-Anchor.

Szasz, T. S. (1970b). *The manufacture of madness: A comparative study of the inquisition and the mental health movement.* New York: Harper & Row.

Marriage and the Construction of Reality: An Exercise in the Microsociology of Knowledge

Peter Berger and *Hansfried Kellner*

Ever since Durkheim it has been a commonplace of family sociology that marriage serves as a protection against anomie for the individual. Interesting and pragmatically useful though this insight is, it is but the negative side of a phenomenon of much broader significance. If one speaks of *anomic* states, then one ought properly to investigate also the *nomic* processes that, by their absence, lead to the aforementioned states. If, consequently, one finds a negative correlation between marriage and anomie, then one should be led to inquire into the character of marriage as a *nomos*-building instrumentality; that is, of marriage as a social arrangement that creates for the individual the sort of order in which he can experience his life as making sense. It is our intention here to discuss marriage in these terms. While this could evidently be done in a macrosociological perspective, dealing with marriage as a major social institution related to other broad structures of society, our focus will be microsociological, dealing

primarily with the social processes affecting the individuals in any specific marriage, although, of course, the larger framework of these processes will have to be understood. In what sense this discussion can be described as microsociology of knowledge will hopefully become clearer in the course of it.[1]

Marriage is obviously only *one* social relationship in which this process of *nomos*-building takes place. It is, therefore, necessary to first look in more general terms at the character of this process. In doing so, we are influenced by three theoretical perspectives: the Weberian perspective on society as a network of meanings, the Meadian perspective on identity as a social phenomenon and the phenomenological analysis of the social structuring of reality, especially as given in the work of Schutz and Merleau-Ponty.[2] Not being convinced, however, that theoretical lucidity is necessarily enhanced by terminological ponderosity, we shall avoid as much as possible the use of the sort of jargon for which both sociologists and phenomenologists have acquired dubious notoriety.

The process that interests us here is the one that constructs, maintains and modifies a consistent reality that can be meaningfully experienced by individuals. In its essential forms this process is determined by the society in which it occurs. Every society

"Marriage and the Construction of Reality: An Exercise in the Microsociology of Knowledge" by P. Berger and H. Kellner, 1964. *Diogenes, 46*, pp. 1-23. Reprinted with permisson of Berg Publishers.

Peter Berger is Professor of Sociology, Boston University. Hansfried Kellner is Professor of Sociology, University of Darmstadt, West Germany.

has its specific way of defining and perceiving reality—its world, its universe, its overarching organization of symbols. This is already given in the language that forms the symbolic base of the society. Erected over this base, and by means of it, is a system of ready-made typifications through which the innumerable experiences of reality come to be ordered.[3] These typifications and their order are held in common by the members of society, thus acquiring not only the character of objectivity, but being taken for granted as *the* world *tout court*, the only world that normal men can conceive of.[4] The seemingly objective and taken-for-granted character of the social definitions of reality can be seen most clearly in the case of language itself, but it is important to keep in mind that the latter forms the base and instrumentality of a much larger world-erecting process.

The socially constructed world must be continually mediated to and actualized by the individual, so that it can become and remain indeed *his* world as well. The individual is given by his society certain decisive cornerstones for his everyday experience and conduct. Most importantly, the individual is supplied with specific sets of typifications and criteria of relevance, predefined for him by the society and made available to him for the ordering of his everyday life. This ordering, or (in line with our opening considerations) nomic apparatus, is biographically cumulative. It begins to be formed in the individual from the earliest stages of socialization, then keeps on being enlarged and modified by himself throughout his biography.[5] While there are individual biographical differences making for differences in the constitution of this apparatus in specific individuals, there exists in the society an overall consensus on the range of differences deemed to be tolerable. Without such consensus, indeed, society would be impossible as a going concern, since it would then lack the ordering principles by which alone experience can be shared and conduct can

be mutually intelligible. This order, by which the individual comes to perceive and define his world, is thus not chosen by him, except perhaps for very small modifications. Rather, it is discovered by him as an external datum, a ready-made world that simply is *there* for him to go ahead and live in, though he modifies it continually in the process of living in it. Nevertheless, this world is in need of validation, perhaps precisely because of an ever-present glimmer of suspicion as to its social manufacture and relativity. This validation, while necessarily undertaken by the individual himself, requires ongoing interaction with others who coinhabit this same socially constructed world. In a broad sense, *all* the other coinhabitants of this world serve a validating function. Every morning the newspaper boy validates the widest coordinates of my world and the mailman bears tangible validation of my own location within these coordinates. However, some validations are more significant than others. Every individual requires the ongoing validation of his world, including crucially the validation of his identity and position by those few who are his truly significant others.[6] Just as the individual's deprivation of relationship with his significant others will plunge him into anomie, so their continued presence will sustain for him that *nomos* by which he can feel at home in the world at least most of the time. Again in a broad sense, all the actions of the significant others and even their simple presence serve this sustaining function. In everyday life, however, the principal method employed is speech. In this sense, it is proper to view the individual's relationship with his significant others as an ongoing conversation. As the latter occurs, it validates over and over again the fundamental definitions of reality once entered into, not, of course, so much by explicit articulation, but precisely by taking the definitions silently for granted and conversing about all conceivable matters on this taken-for-granted basis. Through the same conversation the individual is also made capable of adjusting to changing and new social contexts in his biography. In a very fundamental sense it can be said that one converses one's way through life.

If one concedes these points, one can now state a general sociological proposition: The plausibility and stability of the world, as socially defined, is dependent upon the strength and continuity of significant relationships in which conversation about this world can be continually carried on. Or, to put it a little differently: The reality of the world is sustained through conversation with significant others. This reality, of course, includes not only the imagery by which fellowmen are viewed, but also the way in which one views oneself. The reality-bestowing force of social relationships depends on the degree of their nearness[7]; that is, on the degree to which social relationships occur in face-to-face situations and to which they are credited with primary significance by the individual. In any empirical situation, there now emerge obvious sociological questions out of these considerations; namely, questions about the patterns of the world-building relationships, the social forms taken by the conversation with significant others. Sociologically, one must ask how these relationships are *objectively* structured and disabled, and one will also want to understand how they are *subjectively* perceived and experienced.

With these preliminary assumptions stated we can now arrive at our main thesis. Namely, we would contend that marriage occupies a privileged status among the significant validating relationships for adults in our society. Put slightly differently: Marriage is a crucial nomic instrumentality in our society. We would further argue that the essential social functionality of this institution cannot be fully understood if this fact is not perceived.

We can now proceed with an ideal-typical analysis of marriage; that is, seek to abstract the essential features involved. Marriage in our society is a *dramatic* act in which two strangers come together and redefine themselves. The drama of the act is internally anticipated and socially legitimated long before it takes place in the individual's biography, and amplified by means of a pervasive ideology, the dominant themes of which (romantic love, sexual fulfillment, self-discovery and self-realization through love and sexuality, the nuclear family as the social site for these processes) can be found distributed through all strata of the society. The actualization of these ideologically predefined expectations in the life of the individual occurs to the accompaniment of one of the few traditional rites of passage that are still meaningful to almost all members of the society. It should be added that, in using the term "strangers," we do not mean, of course, that the candidates for the marriage come from widely discrepant social backgrounds—indeed, the data indicate that the contrary is the case. The strangeness lies rather in the fact that, unlike marriage candidates in many previous societies, those in ours typically come from different face-to-face contexts; in the terms used above, they come from different areas of conversation. They do not have a shared past, although their pasts have a similar structure. In other words, quite apart from prevailing patterns of ethnic, religious and class endogamy, our society is typically exogamous in terms of nomic relationships. Put concretely, in our mobile society the significant conversation of the two partners previous to the marriage took place in social circles that did not overlap. With the dramatic redefinition of the situation brought about by the marriage, however, all significant conversation for the two new partners is now centered in their relationship with each other; in fact, it was precisely with this intention that they entered upon their relationship.

It goes without saying that this character of marriage has its root in much broader structural configurations of our society. The most important of these, for our purposes, is the crystallization of a so-called private sphere of existence, more and more segregated from the immediate controls of the public institutions (especially the economic and political ones), and yet defined and utilized as the main social area for the individual's self-realization.[8] It cannot be our purpose here to inquire into the historical forces that brought forth this phenomenon, beyond making the observation that these are closely connected with the industrial revolution and its institutional consequences. The public institutions now confront the individual as an immensely powerful and alien world, incomprehensible in its inner workings, anonymous in its human character. If only through his work in some nook of the economic machinery, the individual must find a way of living in this alien world, come to terms with its power over him, be satisfied with a few conceptual rules of thumb to guide him through a vast reality that otherwise remains opaque to his understanding and modify its anonymity by whatever "human relations" he can work out in his involvement with it.

It ought to be emphasized, against some critics of "mass society," that this does not inevitably leave the individual with a sense of profound unhappiness and lostness. It would rather seem that large numbers of people in our society are quite content with a situation in which their public involvements have little subjective importance, regarding work as a not-too-bad necessity and politics as at best a spectator sport. It is usually only intellectuals with ethical and political commitments who assume that such people must be terribly desperate. The point, however, is that the individual in this situation, whether he is happy or not, will turn elsewhere for the experiences of self-realization that do have importance for him. The private sphere, this interstitial area created (we would think) more or less haphazardly as a by-product of the social metamorphosis of industrialism, is mainly where he will turn. It is here that the individual will seek power, intelligibility and, quite literally, a

name—the apparent power to fashion a world, however Lilliputian, that will reflect his own being; a world that, seemingly having been shaped by himself and thus unlike those other worlds that insist on shaping him, is translucently intelligible to him (or so he thinks); a world in which, consequently, he is somebody—perhaps even, within its charmed circle, a lord and master. What is more, to a considerable extent these expectations are not unrealistic. The public institutions have no need to control the individual's adventures in the private sphere, as long as they really stay within the latter's circumscribed limits. The private sphere is perceived, justifiably, as an area of individual choice and even autonomy. This fact has important consequences for the shaping of identity in modern society that cannot be pursued here. All that ought to be clear here is the peculiar location of the private sphere within and between the other social structures.

In sum, it is, as a rule, only in the private sphere that the individual can take a slice of reality and fashion it into his world. If one is aware of the decisive significance of this capacity and even necessity of men to externalize themselves in reality and to produce for themselves a world in which they can feel at home, then one will hardly be surprised at the great importance the private sphere has come to have in modern society.[9]

The private sphere includes a variety of social relationships. Among these, however, the relationships of the family occupy a central position and serve as a focus for most of the other relationships (such as those with friends, neighbors, fellow members of religious and other voluntary associations). Since, as the ethnologists keep reminding us, the family in our society is of the conjugal type, the central relationship in this whole area is the marital one. It is on the basis of marriage that, for most adults in our society, existence in the private sphere is built up. It will be clear that this is not at all a universal or even cross culturally wide function of marriage, which in our society has taken on a very peculiar character and functionality. It has been pointed out that marriage in contemporary society has lost some of its older functions and taken on new ones instead.[10] This is certainly correct, but we would prefer to state the matter a little differently. Marriage and the family used to be firmly embedded in a matrix of wider community relationships, serving as extensions and particularizations of the latter's social controls. There were few separating barriers between the world of the individual family and the wider community, a fact even to be seen in the physical conditions in which the family lived before the industrial revolution.[11] The same social life pulsated through the house, the street and the community. In our terms, the family and within it the marital relationship were part and parcel of a considerably larger area of conversation. In our contemporary society, by contrast, each family constitutes its own segregated subworld, with its own controls and its own closed conversation.

This fact requires a much greater effort on the part of the marriage partners. Unlike an earlier situation in which the establishment of the new marriage simply added to the differentiation and complexity of an already existing social world, the marriage partners now are embarked on the often difficult task of constructing for themselves the little world in which they will live. To be sure, the larger society provides them with certain standard instructions as to how they should go about this task, but this does not change the fact that considerable effort of their own is required for its realization. The monogamous character of marriage enforces both the dramatic and the precarious nature of his undertaking. Success or failure hinges on the present idiosyncrasies and the fairly unpredictable future development of these idiosyncrasies of only two individuals (who, moreover, do not have a shared past)—as Simmel has shown, the most unstable of all possible social relationships.[12] Not surprisingly, the decision to embark on this undertaking has a critical, even cataclysmic connotation in the popular imagination, which is underlined as well as psychologically assuaged by the ceremonialism that surrounds the event.

Every social relationship requires objectivation, that is, requires a process by which subjectively experienced meanings become objective to the individual and, in interaction with others, become common property and thereby massively objective.[13] The degree of objectivation will depend on the number and the intensity of the social relationships that are its carriers. A relationship that consists of only two individuals called upon to sustain, by their own efforts, an ongoing social world will have to make up in intensity for the numerical poverty of the arrangement. This, in turn, accentuates the drama and the precariousness. The addition of children will add to the density of objectivation taking place within the nuclear family, thus rendering the latter a good deal less precarious. It remains true that the establishment and maintenance of such a social world makes extremely high demands on the principal participants.

The attempt can now be made to outline the ideal-typical process that takes place when marriage functions as an instrumentality for the social construction of reality. The chief protagonists of the drama are two individuals, each with a biographically accumulated and available stock of experience.[14] As members of a highly mobile society, these individuals have already internalized a degree of readiness to redefine themselves and to modify their stock of experience, thus bringing with them considerable psychological capacity for entering new relationships with others.[15] Also, coming from broadly similar sectors of the larger society (in terms of region, class, ethnic and religious affiliations), the two individuals will have organized their stock of experience in similar fashion. In other words, the two individuals have internalized the same overall world, including the general definitions and expectations of the marriage relationship itself. Their society has provided them with a taken-for-granted image of marriage and has socialized them into an anticipation of stepping into the taken-for-granted roles of marriage. All the same, these relatively empty projections now have to be actualized, lived through and filled with experiential content by the protagonists. This will require a dramatic change in their definitions of reality and of themselves.

As of the marriage, most of each partner's actions must now be projected in conjunction with those of the other. Each partner's definitions of reality must be continually correlated with the definitions of the other. The other is present in nearly all horizons of everyday conduct. Furthermore, the identity of each now takes on a new character, having to be constantly matched with that of the other, indeed being typically perceived by people at large as being symbiotically conjoined with the identity of the other. In each partner's psychological economy of significant others, the marriage partner becomes the other par excellence, the nearest and most decisive coinhabitant of the world. Indeed, all other significant relationships have to be almost automatically reperceived and regrouped in accordance with this drastic shift.

In other words, from the beginning of the marriage each partner has new modes in his meaningful experience of the world in general, of other people and of himself. By definition, then, marriage constitutes a nomic rupture. In terms of each partner's biography, the event of marriage initiates a new nomic process. The full implications of this fact are rarely apprehended by the protagonists with any degree of clarity. There rather is to be found the notion that one's world, one's other relationships, and, above all, oneself have remained what they were before—only, of course, that world, others and self will now be shared with the marriage partner. It should be clear by now that this notion is a grave misapprehension. Just because of this fact, marriage now propels the individual into an unintended and unarticulated development, in the course of which the nomic transformation takes place. What typically *is* apprehended are certain objective and concrete problems arising out of the marriage, such as tensions with in-laws, or with former friends, or religious differences between the partners, as well as immediate tensions between them. These are apprehended as external, situational and practical difficulties. What is *not* apprehended is the subject side of these difficulties, namely, the transformation of *nomos* and identity that has occurred and that continues to go on, so that all problems and relationships are experienced in a quite new way, that is, experienced within a new and ever-changing reality.

Take a simple and frequent illustration: the male partner's relationships with male friends before and after the marriage. It is a common observation that such relationships, especially if the friends are single, rarely survive the marriage, or, if they do, are drastically redefined after it. This is typically the result of neither a deliberate decision by the husband nor deliberate sabotage by the wife. What happens, very simply is a slow process in which the husband's image of his friend is transformed as he keeps talking about this friend with his wife. Even if no actual talking goes on, the mere presence of the wife forces him to see his friend differently. This need not mean that he adopts a negative image held by the wife. Regardless of what image she holds or is believed by him to hold, it will be different from that held by the husband. This difference will enter into the joint image that now must be fabricated in the course of the ongoing conversation between the marriage partners— and, in due course, must act powerfully on the image previously held by the husband. Again, typically, this process is rarely apprehended with any degree of lucidity. The old friend is more likely to fade out of the picture by degrees as new kinds of friends take his place. The process, if commented upon at all within the marital conversation, can always be explained by socially available formulas about "people changing," "friends disappearing" or oneself "having become more mature." This process of conversational liquidation is especially powerful because it is onesided—the husband typically talks with his wife about his friend, but *not* with his friend about his wife. Thus the friend is deprived of the defense of, as it were, counterdefining the relationship. This dominance of the marital conversation over all others is one of its most important characteristics. It may be mitigated by a certain amount of protective segregation of some nonmarital relationships (say, "Tuesday night out with the boys," or "Saturday lunch with mother"), but even then there are powerful emotional barriers against the sort of conversation (conversation *about* the marital relationship, that is) that would serve by way of counterdefinition.

Marriage thus posits a new reality. The individual's relationship with this new reality, however, is a dialectical one; he acts upon it, in collusion with the marriage partner, and it acts back upon both him and the partner, welding together their reality. Since, as we have argued before, the objectivation that constitutes this reality is precarious, the groups with which the couple associates are called upon to assist in codefining the new reality. The couple is pushed toward groups that strengthen their new definition of themselves and the world, avoids those that weaken this definition. This, in turn, releases the commonly known pressures of group association, again acting upon the marriage partners to change their definitions of the world and of themselves. Thus the new reality is not posited once and for all, but goes on being redefined not only in the marital interaction itself but in the various maritally based group relationships into which the couple enters.

In the individual's biography marriage, then, brings about a decisive phase of socialization that can be compared with the phases of childhood and adolescence. This phase has a somewhat different structure from the earlier ones. Here he actively collaborates rather than passively accommodates himself. Also, in the previous phases of socialization, there was an apprehension of entering into a new world and being changed in the course of this. In marriage there is little apprehension of such a process, but rather the notion that the world has remained the same, with only its emotional and pragmatic connotations having changed. This notion, as we have tried to show, is illusionary.

The reconstruction of the world in marriage occurs principally in the course of conversation, as we have suggested. The implicit problem of this conversation is how to match two individual definitions of reality. By the very logic of the relationship a common overall definition must be arrived at, otherwise the conversation will become impossible and, ipso facto, the relationship will be endangered. Now, this conversation may be understood as the working away of an ordering and typifying apparatus—if one prefers, an objectivating apparatus. Each partner ongoingly contributes his conceptions of reality, which are then "talked through," usually not once but many times, and in the process become objectivated by the conversational apparatus. The longer this conversation goes on, the more massively real do the objectivations become to the partners. In the marital conversation a world is not only built, but it is also kept in a state of repair and ongoingly refurnished. The subjective reality of this world for the two partners is sustained by the same conversation. The nomic instrumentality of marriage is concretized over and over again, from bed to breakfast table, as the partners carry on the endless conversation that feeds on nearly all they individually or jointly experience. Indeed, it may happen eventually that no experience is fully real unless and until it has been thus "talked through."

This process has a very important result; namely, a hardening or stabilization of the common objectivated reality. It should be easy to see now how this comes about. The objectivations ongoingly performed and internalized by the marriage partners become ever more massively real, as they are confirmed and reconfirmed in the marital conversation. The world that is made up of these objectivations at the same time gains in stability. For example, the images of other people, which before or in the earlier stages of the marital conversation may have been rather ambiguous and shifting in the minds of the two partners, now become hardened into definite and stable characterizations. A casual acquaintance, say, may sometimes have appeared as lots of fun and sometimes as quite a bore to the wife before her marriage. Under the influence of the marital conversation, in which this other person is frequently "discussed," she will now come down more firmly on one or the other of the two characterizations, or on a reasonable compromise between the two. In any of these three options, though, she will have concocted with her husband a much more stable image of the person in question than she is likely to have had before her marriage, when there may have been no conversational pressure to make a definite option at all. The same process of stabilization may be observed with regard to self-definitions as well. In this way, the wife in our example will be pressured to assign stable characterizations not only to others but also to herself. Previously uninterested politically, she now identifies herself as a liberal. Previously alternating between dimly articulated religious positions, she now declares herself an agnostic. Previously confused and uncertain about her sexual emotions, she now understands herself as an unabashed hedonist in this area. And so on and so forth, with the same reality—and identity—stabilizing process at work on the husband. Both world and self thus take on a firmer, more reliable character for both partners.

Furthermore, it is not only the ongoing experience of the two partners that is constantly shared and passed through the conversational apparatus. The same sharing extends into the past. The two distinct biographies, as subjectively apprehended by the two individuals who have lived through them, are overruled and reinterpreted in the course of their conversation. Sooner or later, they will "tell all"—or, more correctly, they will tell it in a way that fits into the self-definitions objectivated in the marital relationship. The couple thus not only construct present reality but reconstruct past reality as well, fabricating a common memory that integrates the recollections of the two individual pasts.[16] The comic fulfillment of this process may be seen in those cases when one partner "remembers" more clearly what happened in the other's past than the other does—and corrects him accordingly. Similarly, there occurs a sharing of future horizons, which leads not only to stabilization, but inevitably to a narrowing of the future projections of each partner. Before marriage the individual typically plays with quite discrepant daydreams in which his future self is projected.[17] Having now considerably stabilized his self-image, the married individual will have to project the future in accordance with a maritally defined identity. This narrowing of future horizons begins with the obvious external limitations that marriage entails, as, for example, with regard to vocational and career plans. However, it extends also to the more general possibilities of the individual's biography. To return to a previous illustration, the wife, having "found herself" as a liberal, an agnostic and a "sexually healthy" person, ipso facto liquidates the possibilities of becoming an anarchist, a Catholic or a lesbian. At least until further notice she has decided upon who she is—and, by the same token, on who she will be. The stabilization brought about by marriage thus affects the total reality in which the partners exist. In the most far-reaching sense of the word, the married individual "settles down," and *must* do so, if the marriage is to be viable, in accordance with its contemporary institutional definition.

It cannot be emphasized strongly enough that this process is typically unapprehended, almost automatic in character. The protagonists of the marriage drama do *not* set out deliberately to re-create their world. Each continues to live in a world that is taken for granted—and keeps its taken-for-granted character even as it is metamorphosed. The new world that the married partners, Prometheus-like, have called into being is perceived by them as the normal world in which they have lived before. Reconstructed present and reinterpreted past are perceived as a continuum, extending forward into a commonly projected future. The dramatic change that has occurred remains, in bulk, unapprehended and unarticulated. And where it forces itself upon the individual's attention, it is retrojected into the past, explained as having always been there, though perhaps in a hidden way. Typically, the reality that has been "invented" within the marital conversation is subjectively perceived as a "discovery." Thus the partners "discover" themselves and the world, "who they really are," what they really believe," "how they really feel, and always have felt, about so-and-so." This retrojection of the world being produced all the time by themselves serves to enhance the stability of this world and at the same time to assuage the "existential anxiety" that, probably inevitably, accompanies the perception that nothing but one's own narrow shoulders support the universe in which one has chosen to live. If one may put it like this, it is psychologically more tolerable to be Columbus than to be Prometheus.

The use of the term "stabilization" should not detract from the insight into the difficulty and precariousness of this world-building enterprise. Often enough, the new universe collapses *in statu nascendi*. Many more times it continues over a period, swaying perilously back and forth as the two partners try to hold it up, finally to be abandoned as an impossible undertaking. If one conceives of the marital conversation as the principal drama and the two partners as the principal protagonists of the drama, then one can look upon the other individuals involved as the supporting chorus for the central dramatic action. Children, friends, relatives and casual acquaintances all have their part in reinforcing the tenuous structure of the new reality. It goes without saying that the children form the most important part of this supporting chorus. Their very existence is predicated on the maritally established world. The marital partners themselves are in charge of their socialization *into* this world, which to them has a pre-existent and self-evident character. They are taught from the beginning to speak precisely those lines that lend themselves to a supporting chorus, from their first invocations of "Daddy" and "Mummy" on to their adoption of the parents' ordering and typifying apparatus that now defines *their* world as well. The marital conversation is now in the process of becoming a family symposium, with the necessary consequence that its objectivations rapidly gain in density, plausibility and durability.

In sum: The process that we have been inquiring into is, ideal-typically, one in which reality is crystallized, narrowed and stabilized. Ambivalences are converted into certainties. Typifications of self and of others become settled. Most generally, possibilities become facticities. What is more, this process of transformation remains, most of the time, unapprehended by those who are both its authors and its objects.[18]

We have analyzed in some detail the process that, we contend, entitles us to describe marriage as a nomic instrumentality. It may now be well to turn back once more to the macrosocial context in which this process takes place—a process that, to repeat, is peculiar to our society as far as the institution of marriage is concerned, although it obviously expresses much more general human facts. The narrowing and stabilization of identity is functional in a society that, in its major public institutions, must insist on rigid controls over the individual's conduct. At the same time, the narrow enclave of the nuclear family serves as a macrosocially innocuous "play area," in which the individual can safely exercise his world-building proclivities without upsetting any of the important social, economic and political applecarts. Barred from expanding himself into the area occupied by these major institutions, he is given plenty of leeway to "discover himself" in his marriage and his family, and, in view of the difficulty of this undertaking, is provided with a number of auxiliary agencies that stand ready to assist him (such as counseling, psychotherapeutic and religious agencies). The marital adventure can be relied upon to absorb a large amount of energy that might otherwise be expended more dangerously. The ideological themes of familism, romantic love, sexual expression, maturity and social adjustment, with the pervasive psychologistic anthropology that underlies them all, function to legitimate this enterprise. Also, the narrowing and stabilization of the individual's principal area of conversation within the nuclear family is functional in a society that requires high degrees of both geographical and social mobility. The segregated little world of the family can easily be detached from one milieu and transposed into another without appreciably interfering with the central processes going on in it. Needless to say, we are not suggesting that these functions are deliberately planned or even apprehended by some mythical ruling directorate of the society. Like most social phenomena, whether they are macro- or microscopic, these functions are typically unintended and unarticulated. What is more, the functionality would be impaired if it were too widely apprehended.

We believe that the above theoretical considerations serve to give a new perspective on various empirical facts studied by family sociologists. As we have emphasized a number of times, our considerations are ideal-typical in intention. We have been interested in marriage at a normal age in urban, middle-class Western societies. We cannot discuss here such special problems as marriages or remarriages at a more advanced age, marriage in the remaining rural subcultures, or in ethnic or lower-class minority groups. We feel quite justified in this limitation of scope, however, by the empirical findings that tend toward the view that a global marriage type is emerging in the central strata of modern industrial societies.[19] This type, commonly referred to as the nuclear family, has been analyzed in terms of a shift from the so-called family of orientation to the so-called family of procreation as the most important reference for the individual.[20] In addition to the well-known socioeconomic reasons for this shift, most of them rooted in the development of industrialism, we would argue that important macrosocial functions pertain to the nomic process within the nuclear family, as we have analyzed it. This functionality of the nuclear family must, furthermore, be seen in conjunction with the familistic ideology that both reflects and reinforces it. A few specific empirical points may suffice to indicate the applicability of our theoretical perspective. To make these we shall use selected American data.

The trend toward marriage at an earlier age has been noted.[21] This has been correctly related to factors such as urban freedom, sexual emancipation and egalitarian values. We would add the important fact that a child raised in the circumscribed world of the nuclear family is stamped by it in terms of his psychological needs and social expectations. Having to live in the larger society from which the nuclear family is segregated, the adolescent soon feels the need for a "little world" of his own, having been socialized in such a way that only by having a private world to withdraw into can he successfully cope with the anonymous "big world" that confronts him as soon as he steps outside his parental home. In other words, to be "at home" in society entails, *per definitionem,* the construction of a maritally based subworld. The parental home itself facilitates an early jump into marriage precisely because its controls are very narrow in scope and leave the adolescent to his own nomic devices at an early age. As has been studied in considerable detail, the adolescent peer group functions as a transitional *nomos* between the two family worlds in the individual's biography.[22]

The equalization in the age of the marriage partners has also been noted.[23] This is certainly to be related to egalitarian values and, concomitantly, to the decline in the "double standard" of sexual morality. Also, however, this fact is very conducive to the common reality-constructing enterprise that we have analyzed. One of the features of the latter, as we have pointed out, is the reconstruction of the two biographies in terms of a cohesive and mutually correlated common memory. This task is evidently facilitated if the two partners are of roughly equal age. Another empirical finding to which our considerations are relevant is the choice of marriage partners within similar socioeconomic backgrounds.[24] Apart from the obvious practical pressures toward such limitations of choice, the latter also ensures sufficient similarity in the biographically accumulated stocks of experience to facilitate the described reality-constructing process. This would offer additional explanation to the observed tendency to narrow the limitations of marital choice even further, for example in terms of religious background.[25]

There now exists a considerable body of data on the adoption and mutual adjustment of marital roles.[26] Nothing in our considerations detracts from the analyses made of these data by sociologists interested primarily in the processes of group interaction. We would argue only that something more fundamental is involved in this role-taking; namely, the individual's relationship to reality as such. Each role in the marital situation carries with it a universe of discourse, broadly given by cultural definition but continually reactualized in the ongoing conversation between the marriage partners. Put simply: Marriage involves not only stepping into new roles, but, beyond this, stepping into a new world. The *mutuality* of adjustment may again be related to the rise of marital egalitarianism, in which comparable effort is demanded of both partners.

Most directly related to our considerations are data that pertain to the greater stability of married as against unmarried individuals.[27] Though frequently presented in misleading psychological terms (such as "greater emotional stability," "greater maturity" and so on), these data are sufficiently validated to be used not only by marriage counselors but in the risk calculations of insurance companies. We would contend that our theoretical perspective places these data into a much more intelligible sociological frame of reference, which also happens to be free of the particular value bias with which the psychological terms are loaded. It is, of course, quite true that married people are more stable emotionally (i.e., operating within a more controlled scope of emotional expression), more mature in their views (i.e., inhabiting a firmer and narrower world in conformity with the expectations of society) and more sure of themselves (i.e., having objectivated a more stable and fixated self-definition). *Therefore* they are more liable to be psychologically balanced (i.e., having sealed off much of their "anxiety," and reduced ambivalence as well as openness toward new possibilities of self-definition) and socially predictable (i.e., keeping their conduct well within the socially established safety rules). All of these phenomena are concomitants of the overall fact of having "settled down"—cognitively, emotionally, in terms of self-identification. To speak of these phenomena as indicators of "mental health," let alone of "adjustment to reality," overlooks the decisive fact that reality is socially constructed and that psychological conditions of all sorts are grounded in a social matrix.

We would say, very simply, that the married individual comes to live in a more stable world, from which fact certain psychological consequences can be readily deduced. To bestow some sort of higher ontological status upon these psychological consequences is ipso facto a symptom of the mis- or nonapprehension of the social process that has produced them. Furthermore, the compulsion to legitimate the stabilized marital world, be it in psychologistic or in traditional religious terms, is another expression of the precariousness of its construction.[28] This is not the place to pursue any further the ideological processes involved. Suffice it to say that contemporary psychology functions to sustain this precarious world by assigning to it the status of "normalcy," a legitimating operation that increasingly links up with the older religious assignment of the status of "sacredness." Both legitimating agencies have established their own rites of passage, validating myths and rituals, and individualized repair services for crisis situations. Whether one legitimates one's maritally constructed reality in terms of "mental health" or of the "sacrament of marriage" is today largely left to free consumer preference, but it is indicative of the crystallization of a new overall universe of discourse that it is increasingly possible to do both at the same time.

Finally, we would point here to the empirical data on divorce.[29] The prevalence, indeed, increasing prevalence of divorce might at first appear as a counterargument to our theoretical considerations. We would contend that the very opposite is the case, as the data themselves bear out. Typically, individuals in our society do not divorce because marriage has become unimportant to them, but because it has become so important that they have no tolerance for the less than completely successful marital arrangement they have contracted with the particular individual in question. This is more fully understood when one has grasped the crucial need for the sort of world that only marriage can produce in our society, a world without which the individual is powerfully threatened with anomie in the fullest sense of the word. Also, the frequency of divorce simply reflects the difficulty and demanding character of the whole undertaking. The empirical fact that the great majority of divorced individuals plan to remarry and a good majority of them actually do, at least in America, fully bears out this contention.[30]

The purpose of this article is not polemic, nor do we wish to advocate any particular values concerning marriage. We have sought to debunk the familistic ideology only insofar as it serves to obfuscate a sociological understanding of the phenomenon. Our purpose has been twofold. First, we wanted to show that it is possible to develop a sociological theory of marriage that is based on clearly sociological presuppositions, without operating with psychological or psychiatric categories that have dubious value within a sociological frame of reference. We believe that such a sociological theory of marriage is generally useful for a fully conscious awareness of existence in contemporary society, and not only for the sociologist. Second, we have used the case of marriage for an exercise in the sociology of knowledge, a discipline that we regard as most promising. Hitherto this discipline has been almost exclusively concerned with macrosociological questions, such as those dealing with the relationship of intellectual history to social processes. We believe that the microsociological focus is equally important for this discipline. The sociology of knowledge must be concerned not only with the great universes of meaning that history offers up for our inspection, but with the many little workshops in which living individuals keep hammering away at the construction and maintenance of these universes. In this way, the sociologist can make an important contribution to the illumination of that everyday world in which we all live and which we help fashion in the course of our biography.

Notes

1. The present article has come out of a larger project on which the authors have been engaged in collaboration with three colleagues in sociology and philosophy. The project is to produce a systematic treatise that will integrate a number of now separate theoretical stands in the sociology of knowledge.

2. Cf. especially M. Weber (1956), *Wirtschaft und gesellschaft*, Tuebingen: Mohr, and (1951), *Gesammelte aufsaetze zur wissenschaftslehre*, Tuebingen: Mohr; G. H. Mead (1934), *Mind, self and society*, Chicago: University of Chicago Press; A. Schutz (1960), *Der sinnhafte aufbau der sozialen welt*, Vienna: Springer, and (1962), *Collected papers*, I, The Hague: Nijhoff; M. Merleau-Ponty (1945), *Phénoménologie de la perception*, Paris: Gallimard, and (1953), *La structure du comportement*, Paris: Presses Universitaires de France.

3. Schutz (1960), pp. 202-220; (1962), I, pp. 3-27, 283-286.

4. Cf. Schutz (1962), I, pp. 207-228.

5. Cf. especially J. Piaget (1954), *The construction of reality in the child*, New York: Basic Books.

6. Cf. Mead (1934), pp. 135-226.

7. Cf. Schutz (1960), pp. 181-195.

8. Cf. A. Gehlen (1957), *Die seele im technischen zeitalter*, Hamburg: Rowohlt, pp. 57-69, and (1961), *Anthropologische forschung*, Hamburg: Rowohlt, pp. 69-77, 127-140; H. Schelsky (1955a), *Soziologie der sexualitaet*, Hamburg: Rowohlt, pp. 102-133. Also cf. T. Luckmann (1963, Spring), "On religion in modern society," *Journal for the Scientific Study of Religion*, pp. 147-162.

9. In these considerations we have been influenced by certain presuppositions of Marxian anthropology, as well as by the anthropological work of Max Scheler, Helmuth Plessner and Arnold Gehlen. We are indebted to Thomas Luckmann for the clarification of the social psychological significance of the private sphere.

10. Cf. T. Parsons & R. Bales (1955), *Family, socialization and interaction process*, Glencoe, IL: Free Press, pp. 3-34, 353-396.

11. Cf. P. Ariès (1962), *Centuries of childhood*, New York: Knopf, pp. 339-410.

12. Cf. K. Wolff (Ed.) (1950), *The sociology of Georg Simmel*, Glencoe, IL: Free Press, pp. 118-144.

13. Cf. Schutz (1960), pp. 29-36, 149-153.

14. Cf. Schutz (1960), pp. 186-192, 202-210.

15. David Riesman's well-known concept of "other-direction" would also be applicable here.

16. Cf. M. Halbwachs (1952), *Les cadres sociaux de la mémoire*. Paris: Presses Universitaires de France, especially pp. 146-177. Also cf. P. Berger (1963), *Invitation to sociology—A humanistic perspective*, Garden City, NY: Doubleday-Anchor, pp. 54-65.

17. Cf. Schutz (1962), I, pp. 72-73, 79-82.

18. The phenomena here discussed could also be formulated effectively in terms of the Marxian categories of reification and false consciousness. Jean-Paul Sartre's recent work, especially *Critique de la raison dialectique*, seeks to integrate these categories within a phenomenological analysis of human conduct. Also cf. H. Lefebvre (1958-1961), *Critique de la vie quotidienne*. Paris: l'Arche.

19. Cf. R. Mayntz (1955), *Die moderne familie*, Stuttgart: Enke; H. Schelsky (1955b), *Wandlungen der deutschen familie in der gegenwart*, Stuttgart: Enke; M. Sorre (Ed.) (1955), *Sociologie comparée de la famille contemporaine*, Paris: Centre National de la Recherche Scientifique; R. Anshen (Ed.) (1959), *The family—Its function and destiny*, New York: Harper; N. Bell & E. Vogel (1960), *A modern introduction to the family*, Glencoe, IL: Free Press.

20. Cf. T. Parsons (1949), *Essays in sociological theory*, Glencoe, IL: Free Press, pp. 233-250.

21. In these as well as the following references to empirical studies we naturally make no attempt at comprehensiveness. References are given as representative of a much larger body of materials. Cf. P. Glick (1957), *American families*, New York: John Wiley, p. 54, and (1947, April) "The family cycle," *American Sociological Review*, pp. 164-174. Also cf. Bureau of the Census (1956 and 1958), *Statistical abstracts of the United States*, and (1959, November), *Current population reports* (Series P-20, No. 96).

22. Cf. D. Riesman (1953), *The lonely crowd*, New Haven: Yale University Press, pp. 29-40; F. Elkin (1960), *The child and society*, New York: Random House, passim.

23. Cf. references given under Note 21.

24. Cf. W. L. Warner & P. Lunt (1941), *The social life of a modern community*, New Haven: Yale University Press, pp. 436-440; A. Hollingshead (1950, October), "Cultural factors in the selection

of marriage mates," *American Sociological Review,* pp. 619-627. Also cf. E. Burgess & P. Wallin (1943, September), "Homogamy in social characteristics," *American Journal of Sociology,* pp. 109-124.

25. Cf. G. Lenski (1961), *The religious factor.* Garden City, NY: Doubleday, pp. 48-50.

26. Cf. L. Cottrell (1933), "Roles in marital adjustment," *Publications of the American Sociological Society,* 27, 107-115; W. Waller & R. Hill (1951), *The family—A dynamic interpretation,* New York: Dryden, pp. 253-271; M. Zelditch (1955), "Role differentiation in the nuclear family," in T. Parsons & R. Bales (Eds.), *Family, socialization and interaction process* (pp. 307-352), Glencoe, IL: Free Press. For a general discussion of role interaction in small groups, cf. especially G. Homans (1950), *The human group,* New York: Harcourt Brace.

27. Cf. Waller & Hill (1951), pp. 253-271, for an excellent summation of such data.

28. Cf. D. Nash & P. Berger (1962, Fall), "The family, the child and the religious revival in suburbia," *Journal for the Scientific Study of Religion,* pp. 85-93.

29. Cf. Bureau of the Census (1956, 1958, 1959).

30. Cf. T. Parsons (1942, December), "Age and sex in the social structure of the United States," *American Sociological Review,* pp. 604-616; P. Glick (1949, December), "First marriages and remarriages," *American Sociological Review,* pp. 726-734; W. Goode (1956), *After divorce,* Glencoe, IL: Free Press, pp. 269-285.

44

Why Gay People Should Seek the Right to Marry

Thomas B. Stoddard

Even though, these days, few lesbians and gay men enter into marriages recognized by law, absolutely every gay person has an opinion on marriage as an "institution." (The word "institution" brings to mind, perhaps appropriately, museums.) After all, we all know quite a bit about the subject. Most of us grew up in marital households. Virtually all of us, regardless of race, creed, gender, and culture, have received lectures on the propriety, if not the sanctity, of marriage—which usually suggests that those who choose not to marry are both unhappy and unhealthy. We all have been witnesses, willing or not, to a lifelong parade of other people's marriages, from Uncle Harry and Aunt Bernice to the Prince and Princess of Wales. And at one point or another, some nosy relative has inevitably inquired of every gay person when he or she will finally "tie the knot" (an intriguing and probably apt cliché).

I must confess at the outset that I am no fan of the "institution" of marriage as currently constructed and practiced. I may simply be unlucky, but I have seen precious few marriages over the course of my forty years that invite admiration and emulation. All too often, marriage appears to petrify rather than satisfy and enrich, even for couples in their twenties and thirties who have had a chance to learn the lessons of feminism. Almost inevitably, the partners seem to fall into a "husband" role and a "wife" role, with such latter-day modifications as the wife who works in addition to raising the children and managing the household.

Let me be blunt: in its traditional form, marriage has been oppressive, especially (although not entirely) to women. Indeed, until the middle of the last century, marriage was, at its legal and social essence, an extension of the husband and his paternal family. Under the English common law, wives were among the husband's "chattel"—personal property—and could not, among other things, hold policy in their own names. The common law crime of adultery demonstrates the unequal treatment accorded to husbands and wives: while a woman who slept with a man who wasn't her husband committed adultery, a man who slept with a woman not his wife committed fornication. A man was legally incapable of committing adultery, except as an accomplice to an errant wife. The underlying offense of adultery was not the sexual betrayal of one partner by the other, but the wife's engaging in conduct capable of tainting the husband's bloodlines. (I swear on my *Black's Law Dictionary* that I have not made this up!)

Nevertheless, despite the oppressive nature of marriage historically, and in spite of the general absence of edifying examples of modern heterosexual marriage, I believe very strongly that every lesbian and gay man should have the right to marry the same-sex partner of his or her choice, and that the gay rights movement should aggressively seek full legal recognition for same-sex marriages. To those who might not agree, I respectfully offer three explanations, one practical, one political, and one philosophical.

The Practical Explanation

The legal status of marriage rewards the two individuals who travel to the altar (or its secular equivalent) with substantial economic and practical advantages. Married couples may reduce their tax liability by filing a joint return. They are entitled to special government benefits, such as those given surviving spouses and dependents through the Social Security program. They can inherit from one another even when there is no will. They are immune from subpoenas requiring testimony against the other spouse. And marriage to an American citizen gives a foreigner a right to residency in the United States.

Other advantages have arisen not by law but by custom. Most employers offer health insurance to their employees, and many will include an employee's spouse in the benefits package, usually at the employer's expense. Virtually no employer will include a partner who is not married to an employee, whether of the same sex or not. Indeed, very few insurance companies even offer the possibility of a group health plan covering "domestic partners" who are not married to one another. Two years ago, I tried to find such a policy for Lambda, and discovered that not one insurance company authorized to do business in New York—the second-largest state in the country with more than 17 million residents—would accommodate us. (Lambda has tried to make do by paying for individual insurance policies for the same-sex partners of its employ-

ees who otherwise would go uninsured but these individual policies are usually narrower in scope than group policies, often require applicants to furnish individual medical information not required under most group plans, and are typically much more expensive per person.)

In short, the law generally presumes in favor of every marital relationship, and acts to preserve and foster it, and to enhance the rights of the individuals who enter into it. It is usually possible, with enough money and the right advice, to replicate some of the benefits conferred by the legal status of marriage through the use of documents like wills and power of attorney forms, but that protection will inevitably, under current circumstances, be incomplete.

The law (as I suspect will come as no surprise to the readers of this journal) still looks upon lesbians and gay men with suspicion, and this suspicion casts a shadow over the documents they execute in recognition of a same-sex relationship. If a lesbian leaves property to her lover, her will may be invalidated on the grounds that it was executed under the "undue influence" of the would-be beneficiary. A property agreement may be denied validity because the underlying relationship is "meretricious"— akin to prostitution. (Astonishingly, until the mid-seventies, the law throughout the United States deemed "meretricious" virtually *any* formal economic arrangement between two people not married to one another, on the theory that an exchange of property between them was probably payment for sexual services; the Supreme Court of California helped unravel this quaint legal fantasy in its 1976 ruling in the first famous "palimony" case, *Marvin v. Marvin*.) The law has progressed considerably beyond the uniformly oppressive state of affairs before 1969, but it is still far from enthusiastic about gay people and their relationships— to put it mildly.

Moreover, there are some barriers one simply cannot transcend outside of a formal marriage. When the Internal Revenue Code or the Immigration and Naturalization Act says "married," it means "married" by definition of state statute. When the employer's group health plan says "spouse," it means "spouse" in the eyes of the law, not the eyes of the loving couple.

But there is another drawback. Couples seeking to protect their relationship through wills and other documents need knowledge, determination, and—most importantly—money. No money, no lawyer. And no lawyer, no protection. Those who lack the sophistication or the wherewithal to retain a lawyer are simply stuck in most circumstances. Extending the right to marry to gay couples would assure that those at the bottom of the economic ladder have a chance to secure their relationship, too.

The Political Explanation

The claim that gay couples ought to be able to marry is not a new one. In the seventies, same-sex couples in three states—Minnesota, Kentucky, and Washington—brought constitutional challenges to the marriage statutes, and in all three instances they failed. In each of the three, the court offered two basic justifications for limiting marriage to male-female couples: history and procreation. Witness this passage from the Supreme Court of Minnesota's 1971 opinion in *Baker v. Nelson:* "The institution of marriage as a union of man and woman, uniquely involving the procreation and rearing of children within a family, is as old as the book of Genesis. . . . This historic institution manifestly is more deeply founded than the asserted contemporary concept of marriage and societal interests for which petitioners contend."

Today no American jurisdiction recognizes the right of two women or two men to marry one another, although at least one nation in Northern Europe does. Even more telling, until earlier this year, there was lit-

tle discussion within the gay rights movement about whether such a right should exist. As far as I can tell, no gay organization of any size, local or national, has yet declared the right to marry as one of its goals.

With all due respect to my colleagues and friends who take a different view, I believe it is time to renew the effort to overturn the existing marriage laws, and to do so in earnest, with a commitment of money and energy, through both the courts and the state legislatures. I am not naive about the likelihood of imminent victory. There is none. Nonetheless—and here I will not mince words—I would like to see the issue rise to the top of the agenda of every gay organization, including my own (although that judgment is hardly mine alone).

Why give it such prominence? Why devote resources to such a distant goal? Because marriage is, I believe, the political issue that most fully tests the dedication of people who are *not* gay to full equality for gay people, and also the issue most likely to lead ultimately to a world free from discrimination against lesbians and gay men.

Marriage is much more than a relationship sanctioned by law. It is the centerpiece of our entire social structure, the core of the traditional notion of "family." Even in its present tarnished state, the marital relationship inspires sentiments suggesting that it is something almost suprahuman. The Supreme Court, in striking down an anti-contraception statute in 1965, called marriage "noble" and "intimate to the degree of being sacred." The Roman Catholic Church and the Moral Majority would go—and have gone—considerably further.

Lesbians and gay men are now denied entry to this "noble" and "sacred" institution. The implicit message is this: two men or two women are incapable of achieving such an exalted domestic state. Gay relationships are somehow less significant, less valuable. Such relationships may, from time to time and from couple to couple, give the appearance of a marriage, but they can never be of the same quality or importance.

I resent—indeed, I loathe—that conception of same-sex relationships. And I am convinced that ultimately the only way to overturn it is to remove the barrier to marriage that now limits the freedom of every gay man and lesbian.

That is not to deny the value of "domestic partnership" ordinances, statutes that prohibit discrimination based on "marital status," and other legal advances that can enhance the rights (as well as the dignity) of gay couples. Without question, such advances move us further along the path to equality. But their value can only be partial. (The recently enacted San Francisco "domestic partnership" ordinance, for example, will have practical value only for gay people who happen to be employed by the City of San Francisco and want to include their non-marital spouses in part of the city's fringe benefit package; the vast majority of gay San Franciscans—those employed by someone other than the city—have only a symbolic victory to savor.) Measures of this kind can never assure full equality. Gay relationships will continue to be accorded a subsidiary status until the day that gay couples have exactly the same rights as their heterosexual counterparts. To my mind, that means either that the right to marry be extended to us, or that marriage be abolished in its present form for all couples, presumably to be replaced by some new legal entity—an unlikely alternative.

The Philosophical Explanation

I confessed at the outset that I personally found marriage in its present avatar rather, well, unattractive. Nevertheless, even from a philosophical perspective, I believe the right to marry should become a stated goal of the gay rights movement.

First, and most basically, the issue is not the desirability of marriage, but rather the desirability of the *right* to marry. That I think two lesbians or two gay men should be entitled to a marriage license does not mean that I think all gay people should find appropriate partners and exercise the right, should it eventually exist. I actually rather doubt that I, myself, would want to marry, even though I share a household with another man who is exceedingly dear to me. There are others who feel differently, for economic, symbolic, or romantic reasons. They should, to my mind, unquestionably have the opportunity to marry if they wish and otherwise meet the requirements of the state (like being old enough).

Furthermore, marriage may be unattractive and even oppressive as it is currently structured and practiced, but enlarging the concept to embrace same-sex couples would necessarily transform it into something new. If two women can marry, or two men, marriage—even for heterosexuals—need not be a union of a "husband" and a "wife." Extending the right to marry to gay people— that is, abolishing the traditional gender requirements of marriage—can be one of the means, perhaps the principal one, through which the institution divests itself of the sexist trappings of the past.

Some of my colleagues disagree with me. I welcome their thoughts and the debates and discussions our different perspectives will trigger. The movement for equality for lesbians and gay men can only be enriched through this collective exploration of the question of marriage. But I do believe many thousands of gay people want the right to marry. And I think, too, they will earn that right for themselves sooner than most of us imagine.

Since When Is Marriage a Path to Liberation?

Paula L. Ettelbrick

"Marriage is a great institution . . . if you like living in institutions," according to a bit of T-shirt philosophy I saw recently. Certainly, marriage is an institution. It is one of the most venerable, impenetrable institutions in modern society. Marriage provides the ultimate form of acceptance for personal intimate relationships in our society, and gives those who marry an insider status of the most powerful kind.

Steeped in a patriarchal system that looks to ownership, property, and dominance of men over women as its basis, the institution of marriage long has been the focus of radical feminist revulsion. Marriage defines certain relationships as more valid than all others. Lesbian and gay relationships, being neither legally sanctioned or commingled by blood, are always at the bottom of the heap of social acceptance and importance.

Given the imprimatur of social and personal approval which marriage provides, it is not surprising that some lesbians and gay men among us would look to legal marriage for self-affirmation. After all, those who marry can be instantaneously transformed from "outsiders" to "insiders," and we have a desperate need to become insiders.

It could make us feel OK about ourselves, perhaps even relieve some of the internalized homophobia that we all know so well. Society will then celebrate the birth of our children and mourn the death of our spouses. It would be easier to get health insurance for our spouses, family memberships to the local museum, and a right to inherit our spouse's cherished collection of lesbian mystery novels even if she failed to draft a will. Never again would we have to go to a family reunion and debate about the correct term for introducing our lover/partner/ significant other to Aunt Flora. Everything would be quite easy and very nice.

So why does this unlikely event so deeply disturb me? For two major reasons. First, marriage will not liberate us as lesbians and gay men. In fact, it will constrain us, make us more invisible, force our assimilation into the mainstream, and undermine the goals of gay liberation. Second, attaining the right to marry will not transform our society from one that makes narrow, but dramatic, distinctions between those who are married and those who are not married to one that respects and encourages choice of relationships and family diversity. Marriage runs contrary to two of the primary goals of the lesbian and gay movement: the affirmation of gay identity and culture; and the validation of many forms of relationships.

When analyzed from the standpoint of civil rights, certainly lesbians and gay men should have a right to marry. But obtaining a right to does not always result in justice. White male firefighters in Birmingham, Alabama, have been fighting for their "rights" to retain their jobs by overturning the city's affirmative action guidelines. If their "rights" prevail, the courts will have failed in rendering justice. The "right" fought for by the white male firefighters, as well as those who advocate strongly for the "rights" to legal marriage for gay people, will result, at best, in limited or narrowed "justice" for those closest to power at the expense of those who have been historically marginalized.

The fight for justice has as its goal the realignment of power imbalances among individuals and classes of people in society. A pure "rights" analysis often fails to incorporate a broader understanding of the underlying inequities that operate to deny justice to a fuller range of people and groups. In setting our priorities as a community, we just combine the concept of both rights and justice. At this point in time, making legal marriage for lesbian and gay couples a priority would set an agenda of gaining rights for a few, but would do nothing to correct the power imbalances between those who are married (whether gay or straight) and those who are not. Thus, justice would not be gained.

Justice for gay men and lesbians will be achieved only when we are accepted and supported in this society *despite* our differences from the dominant culture and the choices we make regarding our relationships. Being queer is more than setting up house, sleeping with a person of the same gender, and seeking state approval for doing so. It is an identity, a culture with many variations. It is a way of dealing with the world by diminishing the constraints of gender roles which have for so long kept women and gay people oppressed and invisible. Being queer means pushing the parameters of sex, sexuality, and family, and in the process transforming the very fabric of society. Gay liberation is inexorably linked to women's liberation. Each is essential to the other.

The moment we argue, as some among us insist on doing, that we should be treated as equals because we are really just like married couples and hold the same values to be true, we undermine the very purpose of our movement and begin the dangerous process of silencing our different voices. As a lesbian, I am fundamentally different from non-lesbian women. That's the point. Marriage, as it exists today, is antithetical to my liberation as a lesbian and as a woman because it mainstreams my life and voice. I do not want to be known as "Mrs. Attached-To-Somebody-Else." Nor do I want to give the state the power to regulate my primary relationship.

Yet, the concept of equality in our legal system does not support differences, it only supports sameness. The very standard for equal protection is that people who are similarly situated must be treated equally. To make an argument for equal protection, we will be required to claim that gay and lesbian relationships are the same as straight relationships. To gain the right, we must compare ourselves to married couples. The law looks to the insiders as the norm, regardless of how flawed or unjust their institutions, and requires that those seeking the law's equal protection situate themselves in a similar posture to those who are already protected. In arguing for the right to legal marriage, lesbians and gay men would be forced to claim that we are just like heterosexual couples, have the same goals and purposes, and vow to structure our lives similarly. The law provides no room to argue that we are different, but are nonetheless entitled to equal protection.

The thought of emphasizing our sameness to married heterosexuals in order to obtain this "right" terrifies me. It rips away the very heart and soul of what I believe it is to be a lesbian in this world. It robs me of the opportunity to make a difference. We end up mimicking all that is bad about the institution of marriage in our effort to appear to be the same as straight couples.

By looking to our sameness and de-emphasizing our differences, we don't even place ourselves in a position of power that would allow us to transform marriage from an institution that emphasizes property and state regulation of relationships to an institution which recognizes one of many types of valid and respected relationships. Until the constitution is interpreted to respect and encourage differences, pursuing the legalization of same-sex marriage would be leading our movement into a trap; we would be demanding access to the very institution which, in its current form, would undermine *our* movement to recognize many different kinds of relationships. We would be perpetuating the elevation of married relationships and of "couples" in general, and further eclipsing other relationships of choice.

Ironically, gay marriage, instead of liberating gay sex and sexuality, would further outlaw all gay and lesbian sex which is not performed in a marital context. Just as sexually active non-married women face stigma and double standards around sex and sexual activity, so too would non-married gay people. The only legitimate gay sex would be that which is cloaked in and regulated by marriage. Its legitimacy would stem not from an acceptance of gay sexuality, but because the Supreme Court and society in general fiercely protect the privacy of marital relationships. Lesbians and gay men who do not seek the state's stamp of approval would clearly face increased sexual oppression.

Undoubtedly, whether we admit it or not, we all need to be accepted by the broader society. That motivation fuels our work to eliminate discrimination in the workplace and elsewhere, fight for custody of our children, create our own families, and so on. The growing discussion about the right to marry may be explained in part by this need for acceptance. Those closer to the norm or to power in this country are more likely to see marriage as a principle of freedom and equality. Those who are more acceptable to the mainstream because of race, gender, and economic status are more likely to want the right to marry. It is the final acceptance, the ultimate affirmation of identity.

On the other hand, more marginal members of the lesbian and gay community (women, people of color, working class, and poor) are less likely to see marriage as having relevance to our struggles for survival. After all, what good is the affirmation of our relationships (that is, marital relationships) if we are rejected as women, black, or working class?

The path to acceptance is much more complicated for many of us. For instance, if we choose legal marriage, we may enjoy the right to add our spouse to our health insurance policy at work, since most employment policies are defined by one's marital status, not family relationship. However, that choice assumes that we have a job *and* that our employer provides us with health benefits. For women, particularly women of color who tend to occupy the low-paying jobs that do not provide healthcare benefits at all, it will not matter one bit if they are able to marry their woman partners. The opportunity to marry will neither get them health benefits nor transform them from outsider to insider.

Of course, a white man who marries another white man who has a full-time job with benefits will certainly be able to share in those benefits and overcome the only obstacle left to full societal assimilation— the goal of many in his class. In other words, gay marriage will not topple the system that allows only the privileged few to obtain decent health care. Nor will it close the privilege gap between those who are married and those who are not.

Marriage creates a two-tier system that allows the state to regulate relationships. It has become a facile mechanism for employers to dole out benefits, for businesses to provide special deals and incentives, and for the law to make distinctions in distributing meager public funds. None of these entities bothers to consider the relationship among people; the love, respect, and need to protect that exists among all kinds of family members. Rather, a simple certificate of the state, regardless of whether the spouses love, respect, or even see each other on a regular basis, dominates and is supported. None of this dynamic will change if gay men and lesbians are given the option of marriage.

Gay marriage will not help us address the systemic abuses inherent in a society that does not provide decent health care to all of its citizens, a right that should not depend on whether the individual (1) has sufficient resources to afford health care or health insurance, (2) is working and receives health insurance as part of compensation, or (3) is married to a partner who is working and has health coverage which is extended to spouses. It will not address the underlying unfairness that allows businesses to provide discounted services or goods to families and couples—who are defined to include straight, married people and their children, but not domestic partners.

Nor will it address the pain and anguish of the unmarried lesbian who receives word of her partner's accident, rushes to the hospital and is prohibited from entering the intensive care unit or obtaining information about her condition solely because she is not a spouse or family member. Likewise, marriage will not help the gay victim of domestic violence who, because he chose not to marry, finds no protection under the law to keep his violent lover away.

If the laws change tomorrow and lesbians and gay men were allowed to marry, where would we find the incentive to continue the progressive movement we have started that is pushing for societal and legal recognition of all kinds of family relationships? To create other options and alternatives? To find a place in the law for the elderly couple who, for companionship and economic reasons, live together but do not

marry? To recognize the right of a long-time, but unmarried, gay partner to stay in his rent-controlled apartment after the death of his lover, the only named tenant on the lease? To recognize the family relationship of the lesbian couple and the two gay men who are jointly sharing child-raising responsibilities? To get the law to acknowledge that we may have more than one relationship worthy of legal protection?

Marriage for lesbians and gay men still will not provide a real choice unless we continue the work our community has begun, to spread the privilege around to other relationships. We must first break the tradition of piling benefits and privileges on to those who are married, while ignoring the real life needs of those who are not. Only when we de-institutionalize marriage and bridge the economic and privilege gap between the married and the unmarried will each of us have a true choice. Otherwise, our choice not to marry will continue to lack legal protection and societal respect.

The lesbian and gay community has laid the groundwork for revolutionizing society's views of family. The domestic partnership movement has been an important part of this progress insofar as it validates nonmarital relationships. Because it is not limited to sexual or romantic relationships, domestic partnership provides an important opportunity for many who are not related by blood or marriage to claim certain minimal protections.

It is crucial, though, that we avoid the pitfall of framing the push for legal recognition of domestic partners (those who share a primary residence and financial responsibility for each other) as a stepping stone to marriage. We must keep our eyes on the goals of providing true alternatives to marriage and of radically reordering society's view of family.

The goals of lesbian and gay liberation must simply be broader than the right to marry. Gay and lesbian marriages may minimally transform the institution of marriage by diluting its traditional patriarchal dynamic, but they will not transform society. They will not demolish the two-tier system of the "haves" and the "have nots." We must not fool ourselves into believing that marriage will make it acceptable to be gay or lesbian. We will be liberated only when we are respected and accepted for our differences and the diversity we provide to this society. Marriage is not a path to that liberation.

Negotiating Reality: Notes on Power in the Assessment of Responsibility

Thomas J. Scheff

The use of interrogation to reconstruct parts of an individual's past history is a common occurrence in human affairs. Reporters, jealous lovers, and policemen on the beat are often faced with the task of determining events in another person's life, and the extent to which he was responsible for those events. The most dramatic use of interrogation to determine responsibility is in criminal trials. As in everyday life, criminal trials are concerned with both act and intent. Courts, in most cases, first determine whether the defendant performed a legally forbidden act. If it is found that he did so, the court then must decide whether he was "responsible" for the act. Reconstructive work of this type goes on less dramatically in a wide variety of other settings, as well. The social worker determining a client's eligibility for unemployment compensation, for example,

"Negotiating Reality: Notes on Power in the Assessment of Responsibility" by T. Scheff, 1968. *Social Problems*, 16(1), pp. 3-17. Copyright © 1968 by the Society for the Study of Social Problems. Reprinted by permission.

The author wishes to acknowledge the help of the following persons who criticized earlier drafts: Aaron Cicourel, Donald Cressey, Joan Emerson, Erving Goffman, Michael Katz, Lewis Kurke, Robert Levy, Sohan Lal Sharma, and Paul Weubben. The paper was written during a fellowship provided by the Social Science Research Institute, University of Hawaii.

seeks not only to establish that the client actually is unemployed, but that he has actively sought employment, i.e., that he himself is not responsible for being out of work.

This paper will contrast two perspectives on the process of reconstructing past events for the purpose of fixing responsibility. The first perspective stems from the common sense notion that interrogation, when it is sufficiently skillful, is essentially neutral. Responsibility for past actions can be fixed absolutely and independently of the method of reconstruction. This perspective is held by the typical member of society, engaged in his day-to-day tasks. It is also held, in varying degrees, by most professional interrogators. The basic working doctrine is one of *absolute* responsibility. This point of view actually entails the comparison of two different kinds of items: first, the fixing of actions and intentions, and secondly, comparing these actions and intentions to some pre-determined criteria of responsibility. The basic premise of the doctrine of absolute responsibility is that both actions and intentions, on the one hand, and the criteria of responsibility, on the other, are absolute, in that they can be assessed independently of social context.[1]

An alternative approach follows from the sociology of knowledge. From this point of view, the reality within which members of society conduct their lives is largely of their own construction.[2] Since much of reality is a construction, there may be multiple realities, existing side by side, in harmony or in competition. It follows, if one maintains this stance, that the assessment of responsibility involves the construction of reality by members; construction both of actions and intentions, on the one hand, and of criteria of responsibility, on the other. The former process, the continuous reconstruction of the normative order, has long been the focus of sociological concern.[3] The discussion in this paper will be limited, for the most part, to the former process, the way in which actions and intentions are constructed in the act of assessing responsibility.

My purpose is to argue that responsibility is at least partly a product of social structure. The alternative to the doctrine of absolute responsibility is that of relative responsibility: the assessment of responsibility always includes a process of negotiation. In this process, responsibility is in part constructed by the negotiating parties. To illustrate this thesis, excerpts from two dialogues of negotiation will be discussed: a real psychotherapeutic interview, and an interview between a defense attorney and his client, taken from a work of fiction. Before presenting these excerpts it will be useful to review some prior discussions of negotiation, the first in courts of law, the second in medical diagnosis.[4]

The negotiation of pleas in criminal courts, sometimes referred to as "bargain justice," has been frequently noted by observers of legal processes.[5] The defense attorney, or (in many cases, apparently) the defendant himself, strikes a bargain with the prosecutor—a plea of guilty will be made, provided that the prosecutor will reduce the charge. For example, a defendant arrested on suspicion of armed robbery may arrange to plead guilty to the charge of unarmed robbery. The prosecutor obtains ease of conviction from the bargain, the defendant, leniency.

Although no explicit estimates are given, it appears from observers' reports that the great majority of criminal convictions are negotiated. Newman states:

A major characteristic of criminal justice administration, particularly in jurisdictions characterized by legislatively fixed sentences, is charge reduction to elicit pleas of guilty. Not only does the efficient functioning of criminal justice rest upon a high proportion of guilty pleas, but plea bargaining is closely linked with attempts to individualize justice, to obtain certain desirable conviction consequences, and to avoid undesirable ones such as "undeserved" mandatory sentences.[6]

It would appear that the bargaining process is accepted as routine. In the three jurisdictions Newman studied, there were certain meeting places where the defendant, his client, and a representative of the prosecutor's office routinely met to negotiate the plea. It seems clear that in virtually all but the most unusual cases, the interested parties expected to, and actually did, negotiate the plea.

From these comments on the routine acceptance of plea bargaining in the courts, one might expect that this process would be relatively open and unambiguous. Apparently, however, there is some tension between the fact of bargaining and moral expectations concerning justice. Newman refers to this tension by citing two contradictory statements: an actual judicial opinion, "Justice and liberty are not the subjects of bargaining and barter"; and an off-the-cuff statement by another judge, "All law is compromise." A clear example of this tension is provided by an excerpt from a trial and Newman's comments on it.

The following questions were asked of a defendant after he had pleaded guilty to unarmed robbery when the original charge was armed robbery. This reduction is common, and the judge was fully aware that the plea was negotiated:

Judge: You want to plead guilty to robbery unarmed?

Defendant: Yes, Sir.

Judge: Your plea of guilty is free and voluntary?

Defendant: Yes, Sir.

Judge: No one has promised you anything?

Defendant: No.

Judge: No one has induced you to plead guilty?

Defendant: No.

Judge: You're pleading guilty because you are guilty?

Defendant: Yes.

Judge: I'll accept your plea of guilty to robbery unarmed and refer it to the probation department for a report and for sentencing Dec. 28.[7]

The delicacy of the relationship between appearance and reality is apparently confusing, even for the sociologist-observer. Newman's comment on this exchange has an Alice-in-Wonderland quality:

This is a routine procedure designed to satisfy the statutory requirement and is not intended to disguise the process of charge reduction.[8]

If we put the tensions between the different realities aside for the moment, we can say that there is an explicit process of negotiation between the defendant and the prosecution which is a part of the legal determination of guilt or innocence, or in the terms used above, the assessment of responsibility.

In medical diagnosis, a similar process of negotiation occurs, but is much less self-conscious than plea bargaining. The English psychoanalyst Michael Balint refers to this process as one of "offers and responses":

Some of the people who, for some reason or other, find it difficult to cope with problems of their lives resort to becoming ill. If the doctor has the opportunity of seeing them in the first phases of their being ill, i.e., before they settle down to a definite "organized" illness, he may observe that the patients, so to speak, offer or propose various illnesses, and that they have to go on offering new illnesses until between doctor and patient an agreement can be reached resulting in the acceptance by both of them of one of the illnesses as justified.[9]

Balint gives numerous examples indicating that patients propose reasons for their coming to the doctor which are rejected, one by one, by the physician, who makes counter-proposals until an "illness" acceptable to both parties is found. If "definition of the situation" is substituted for "illness," Balint's observations become relevant to a wide variety of transactions, including the kind of interrogation discussed above. The fixing of responsibility is a process in which the client offers definitions of the situation, to which the interrogator responds. After a series of offers and responses, a definition of the situation acceptable to both the client and the interrogator is reached.

Balint has observed that the negotiation process leads physicians to influence the outcome of medical examinations, independently of the patient's condition. He refers to this process as the "apostolic function" of the doctor, arguing that the physician induces patients to have the kind of illness that the physician thinks is proper:

Apostolic mission or function means in the first place that every doctor has a vague, but almost unshakably firm, idea of how a patient ought to behave when ill. Although this idea is anything but explicit and concrete, it is immensely powerful, and influences, as we have found, practically every detail of the doctor's work with his patients. It was almost as if every doctor had revealed knowledge of what was right and what was wrong for patients to expect and to endure, and further, as if he had a sacred duty to convert to his faith all the ignorant and unbelieving among his patients.[10]

Implicit in this statement is the notion that interrogator and client have unequal power in determining the resultant definition of the situation. The interrogator's definition of the situation plays an important part in the joint definition of the situation which is finally negotiated. Moreover, his definition is more important than the client's in determining the final outcome of the negotiation, principally because he is well trained, secure, and self-confident in his role in the transaction, whereas the client is untutored, anxious, and uncertain about his role. Stated simply, the subject, because of these conditions, is likely to be susceptible to the influence of the interrogator.

Note that plea bargaining and the process of "offers and responses" in diagnosis differ in the degree of self-consciousness of the participants. In plea bargaining the process is at least partly visible to the participants themselves. There appears to be some ambiguity about the extent to which the negotiation is morally acceptable to some of the commentators, but the parties to the negotiations appear to be aware that bargaining is going on, and accept the process as such. The bargaining process in diagnosis, however, is much more subterranean. Certainly neither physicians nor patients recognize the offers and responses process as being bargaining. There is no commonly accepted vocabulary for describing diagnostic bargaining, such as there is in the legal analogy, e.g., "copping out" or "copping a plea." It may be that in legal processes there is some appreciation of the different kinds of reality, i.e., the difference between the public (official, legal) reality and private reality, whereas in medicine this difference is not recognized.

The discussion so far has suggested that much of reality is arrived at by negotiation. This thesis was illustrated by materials presented on legal processes by Newman, and medical processes by Balint. These processes are similar in that they appear to represent clear instances of the negotiation of reality. The instances are different in that the legal bargaining processes appear to be more open and accepted than the diagnostic process. In order to outline some of the dimensions of the negotiation process, and to establish some of the limitations of the analyses by Newman and Balint, two excerpts of cases of broadcasting will be discussed: the first taken from an actual psychiatric "intake" interview, the second

from a fictional account of a defense lawyer's first interview with his client.

The Process of Negotiation

The psychiatric interview to be discussed is from the first interview in *The Initial Interview in Psychiatric Practice*.[11] The patient is a thirty-four-year-old nurse, who feels, as she says, "irritable, tense, depressed." She appears to be saying from the very beginning of the interview that the external situation in which she lives is the cause of her troubles. She focuses particularly on her husband's behavior. She says he is an alcoholic, is verbally abusive, and won't let her work. She feels that she is cooped up in the house all day with her two small children, but that when he is home at night (on the nights when he *is* at home) he will have nothing to do with her and the children. She intimates, in several ways, that he does not serve as a sexual companion. She has thought of divorce, but has rejected it for various reasons (for example, she is afraid she couldn't take proper care of the children, finance the baby sitters, etc.). She feels trapped.[12]

In the concluding paragraph of their description of this interview, Gill, Newman, and Redlich give this summary:

The patient, pushed by we know not what or why at the time (the children—somebody to talk to), comes for help apparently for what she thinks of as help with her external situation (her husband's behavior as she sees it). The therapist does not respond to this but seeks her role and how it is that she plays such a role. Listening to the recording it sounds as if the therapist is at first bored and disinterested and the patient defensive. He gets down to work and keeps asking, "What is it all about?" Then he becomes more interested and sympathetic and at the same time very active (participating) and demanding. *It sounds as if she keeps saying, "This is the trouble." He says, "No! Tell me the trouble." She says, "This is it!" He says, "No, tell me," until the patient finally says, "Well I'll tell you."* Then the therapist says, *"Good! I'll help you."*[13]

From this summary it is apparent that there is a close fit between Balint's idea of the negotiation of diagnosis through offers and responses, and what took place in this psychiatric interview. It is difficult, however, to document the details. Most of the psychiatrist's responses, rejecting the patient's offers, do not appear in the written transcript, but they are fairly obvious as one listens to the recording. Two particular features of the psychiatrist's responses especially stand out: (1) the flatness of intonation in his responses to the patient's complaints about her external circumstances; and (2) the rapidity with which he introduces new topics, through questioning, when she is talking about her husband.

Some features of the psychiatrist's coaching are verbal, however:

T. 95: Has anything happened recently that makes it . . . you feel that . . . ah . . . you're sort of coming to the end of your rope? I mean I wondered what led you . . .

P. 95: (Interrupting.) It's nothing special. It's just everything in general.

T. 96: What led you to come to a . . .

P. 96: (Interrupting.) It's just that I . . .

T. 97: . . . a psychiatrist just now? (1)

P. 97: Because I felt that the older girl was getting tense as a result of . . . of my being stewed up all the time.

T. 98: Mmmhnn.

P. 98: Not having much patience with her.

T. 99: Mmmhnn. (Short pause.) Mmm. And how had you imagined that a psychiatrist could help with this? (Short pause.) (2)

P. 99: Mmm . . . maybe I could sort of get straightened out . . . straighten things out in my mind. I'm confused. Sometimes I can't remember things that I've done, whether I've done 'em or not or whether they happened.

T. 100: What is it that you want to straighten out? (Pause.)

P. 100: I think I seem mixed up.

T. 101: Yeah? You see that, it seems to me, is something that we really should talk about because . . . ah . . . from a certain point of view somebody might say, "Well now, it's all very simple. She's unhappy and disturbed because her husband is behaving this way, and unless something can be done about that how could she expect to feel any other way." But, instead of that, you come to the psychiatrist, and you say that you think there's something about you that needs straightening out. (3) I don't quite get it. Can you explain that to me? (Short pause.)

P. 101: I sometimes wonder if I'm emotionally grown up.

T. 102: By which you mean what?

P. 102: When you're married you should have one mate. You shouldn't go around and look at other men.

T. 103: You've been looking at other men?

P. 103: I look at them, but that's all.

T. 104: Mmmhnn. What you mean . . . you mean a grown-up person should accept the marital situation whatever it happens to be?

P. 104: That was the way I was brought up. Yes. (Sighs.)

T. 105: You think that would be a sign of emotional maturity?

P. 105: No.

T. 106: No. So?

P. 106: Well, if you rebel against the laws of society you have to take the consequences.

T. 107: Yes?

P. 107: And it's just that I . . . I'm not willing to take the consequences. I . . . don't think it's worth it.

T. 108: Mmhnn. So in the meantime then while you're in this very difficult situation, you find yourself reacting in a way that you don't like and that you think is . . . ah . . . damaging to your children and yourself? Now what can be done about that?

P. 108: (Sniffs; sighs.) I dunno. That's why I came to see you.

T. 109: Yes. I was just wondering what you had in mind. Did you think a psychiatrist could . . . ah . . . help you face this kind of a situation calmly and easily and maturely? (4) Is that it?

P. 109: More or less. I need somebody to talk to who isn't emotionally involved with the family. I have a few friends, but I don't like to bore them. I don't think they should know . . . ah . . . all the intimate details of what goes on.

T. 110: Yeah?

P. 110: It becomes food for gossip.

T. 111: Mmmhnn.

P. 111: Besides they're in . . . they're emotionally involved because they're my friends. They tell me not to stand for it, but they don't understand that if I put my foot down it'll only get stepped on.

T. 112: Yeah.

P. 112: That he can make it miserable for me in other ways. . . .

T. 113: Mmm.

P. 113: . . . which he does.

T. 114: Mmmhnn. In other words, you find yourself in a situation and don't know how to cope with it really.

P. 114: I don't.

T. 115: You'd like to be able to talk that through and come to understand it better and learn how to cope with it or deal with it in some way. Is that right?

P. 115: I'd like to know how to deal with it more effectively.

T. 116: Yeah. Does that mean you feel convinced that the way you're dealing with it now . . .

P. 116: There's something wrong of course.

T. 117: . . . something wrong with that. Mmmhnn.

P. 117: There's something wrong with it.[14]

Note that the therapist reminds her *four times* in this short sequence that she has come to see a *psychiatrist*. Since the context of these reminders is one in which the patient is attributing her difficulties to an external situation, particularly her husband, it seems plausible to hear these reminders as subtle requests for analysis of her own contributions to her difficulties. This interpretation is supported by the therapist's subsequent remarks. When the patient once again describes external problems, the therapist tries the following tack:

T. 125: I notice that you've used a number of psychiatric terms here and there. Were you specially interested in that in your training, or what?

P. 125: Well, my great love is psychology.

T. 126: Psychology?

P. 126: Mmmhnn.

T. 127: How much have you studied?

P. 127: Oh (Sighs.) what you have in your nurse's training, and I've had general psych, child and adolescent psych, and the abnormal psych.

T. 128: Mmmhnn. Well, tell me . . . ah . . . what would you say if you had to explain yourself what is the problem?

P. 128: You don't diagnose yourself very well, at least I don't.

T. 129: Well you can make a stab at it. (Pause.)[15]

This therapeutic thrust is rewarded: the patient gives a long account of her early life which indicates a belief that she was not "adjusted" in the past. The interview continues:

T. 135: And what conclusions do you draw from all this about why you're not adjusting now the way you think you should?

P. 135: Well, I wasn't adjusted then. I feel that I've come a long way, but I don't think I'm still . . . I still don't feel that I'm adjusted.

T. 136: And you don't regard your husband as being the difficulty? You think it lies within yourself?

P. 136: Oh, he's a difficulty all right, but I figure that even . . . ah . . . had . . . if it had been other things that . . . this probably—this state—would've come on me.

T. 137: Oh you do think so?

P. 137: (Sighs.) I don't think he's the sole factor. No.

T. 138: And what are the factors within . . .

P. 138: I mean . . .

T. 139: . . . yourself?

P. 139: Oh it's probably remorse for the past, things I did.

T. 140: Like what? (Pause.) It's sumping' [sic] hard to tell, hunh? (Short pause.)[16]

After some parrying, the patient tells the therapist what he wants to hear. She feels guilty because she was pregnant by another man when her present husband proposed. She cries. The therapist tells the patient she needs, and will get, psychiatric help, and the interview ends, the patient still crying. The negotiational aspects of the process are clear: After the patient has spent most of the interview blaming her current difficulties on external circumstances, she tells the therapist a deep secret about which she feels intensely guilty. The patient, and not the husband, is at fault. The therapist's tone and manner change abruptly. From being bored, distant, and rejecting, he becomes warm and solicitous. Through a process of offers and responses, the therapist and patient have, by implication, negotiated a shared definition of the situation— the patient, not the husband, is responsible.

A Contrasting Case

The negotiation process can, of course, proceed on the opposite premise, namely that the client is not responsible. An ideal example would be an interrogation of a client by a skilled defense lawyer. Unfortunately, we have been unable to locate a verbatim transcript of a defense lawyer's initial interview with his client. There is available, however, a fictional portrayal of such an interview, written by a man with extensive experience as defense lawyer, prosecutor, and judge. The excerpt to follow is taken from the novel *Anatomy of a Murder*.[17]

The defense lawyer, in his initial contact with his client, briefly questions him regarding his actions on the night of the killing. The client states that he discovered that the deceased, Barney Quill, had raped his wife; he then goes on to state that he then left his wife, found Quill, and shot him.

" . . . How long did you remain with your wife before you went to the hotel bar?"

"I don't remember."

"I think it is important, and I suggest you try."

After a pause. "Maybe an hour."

"Maybe more?"

"Maybe."

"Maybe less?"

"Maybe."

I paused and lit a cigar. I took my time. I had reached a point where a few wrong answers to a few right questions would leave me with a client—if I took his case—whose cause was legally defenseless. Either I stopped now and begged off and let some other lawyer worry

over it or I asked him the few fatal questions and let him hang himself. Or else, like any smart lawyer, I went into the Lecture. I studied my man, who sat as inscrutable as an Arab, delicately fingering his Ming holder, daintily sipping his dark mustache. He apparently did not realize how close I had him to admitting that he was guilty of first degree murder, that is, that he "feloniously, willfully and of his malice afore-thought did kill and murder one Barney Quill." The man was a sitting duck.[18]

The lawyer here realizes that his line of questioning has come close to fixing the responsibility for the killing on his client. He therefore shifts his ground by beginning "the lecture":

The Lecture is an ancient device that lawyers use to coach their clients so that the client won't quite know he has been coached and his lawyer can still preserve the face-saving illusion that he hasn't done any coaching. For coaching clients, like robbing them, is not only frowned upon, it is downright unethical and bad, very bad. Hence the Lecture, an artful device as old as the law itself, and one used constantly by some of the nicest and most ethical lawyers in the land. "Who, me? I didn't tell him what to say," the lawyer can later comfort himself. "I merely explained the law, see." It is a good practice to scowl and shrug here and add virtuously: "That's my duty, isn't it?"

"We will now explore the absorbing subject of legal justification or excuse," I said.

"Well, take self-defense," I began. "That's the classic example of justifiable homicide. On the basis of what I've so far heard and read about your case I do not think we need pause too long over that. Do you?"

"Perhaps not," Lieutenant Manion conceded, "we'll pass for now."

"Let's," I said dryly. "Then there's the defense of habitation, defense of property, and the defense of relatives or friends. Now there are more ramifications to these defenses than a dog has fleas, but we won't explore them now. I've already told you at length why I don't think you can invoke the possible defense of your wife. When you shot Quill her need for defense had passed. It's as simple as that."

"Go on," Lieutenant Manion said, frowning.

"Then there's the defense of a homicide committed to prevent a felony—say you're being robbed—; to prevent the escape of the felon—suppose he's getting away with your wallet—; or to arrest a felon—you've caught up with him and he's either trying to get away or has actually escaped." . . .

"Go on, then; what are some of the other legal justifications or excuses?"

"Then there's the tricky and dubious defense of intoxication. Personally I've never seen it succeed. But since you were not drunk when you shot Quill we shall mercifully not dwell on that. Or were you?"

"I was cold sober. Please go on."

"Then finally there's the defense of insanity." I paused and spoke abruptly, airily: "Well, that just about winds it up." I arose as though making ready to leave.

"Tell me more."

"There is no more." I slowly paced up and down the room.

"I mean about this insanity."

"Oh, insanity," I said, elaborately surprised. It was like luring a trained seal with a herring. "Well, insanity, where proven, is a complete defense to murder. It does not legally justify the killing, like self-defense, say, but rather excuses it." The lecturer was hitting his stride. He was also on the home stretch. "Our law requires that a punishable killing—in fact, any crime—must be committed by a sapient human being, one capable, as the law insists, of distinguishing between right and wrong. If a man is insane, legally insane, the act of homicide may still be murder but the law excuses the perpetrator."

Lieutenant Manion was sitting erect now, very still and erect. "I see—and this—this perpetrator, what happens to him if he should—should be excused?"

"Under Michigan law—like that of many other states—if he is acquitted of murder on the grounds of insanity it is provided that he must be sent to a hospital for the criminally insane until he is pronounced sane." . . .

. . . Then he looked at me. "Maybe," he said, "maybe I was insane."

. . . Thoughtfully: "Hm. . . . Why do you say that?"

"Well, I can't really say," he went on slowly. "I—I guess I blacked out. I can't remember a thing after I saw him standing behind the bar that night until I got back to my trailer."

"You mean—you mean you don't remember shooting him?" I shook my head in wonderment.

"Yes, that's what I mean."

"You don't even remember driving home?"

"No."

"You don't remember threatening Barney's bartender when he followed you outside after the shooting—as the newspaper says you did?" I paused and held my breath. "You don't remember telling him, 'Do you want some, too, Buster?'?"

The smoldering dark eyes flickered ever so little. "No, not a thing."

"My, my," I said blinking my eyes, contemplating the wonder of it all. "Maybe you've got something there."

The Lecture was over; I had told my man the law; and now he had told me things that might possibly invoke the defense of insanity. . . . [19]

The negotiation is complete. The ostensibly shared definition of the situation established by the negotiation process is that the defendant was probably not responsible for his actions.

Let us now compare the two interviews. The major similarity between them is their negotiated character: they both take the form of a series of offers and responses that continue until an offer (a definition of the situation) is reached that is acceptable to both parties. The major difference between the transactions is that one, the psychotherapeutic interview, arrives at an assessment that the client is responsible; the other, the defense attorney's interview, reaches an assessment that the client was not at fault, i.e., not responsible. How can we account for this difference in outcome?

Discussion

Obviously, given any two real cases of negotiation which have different outcomes, one might construct a reasonable argument that the difference is due to the differences between the cases—the finding of responsibility in one case and lack of responsibility in the other, the only outcomes which are reasonably consonant with the facts of the respective cases. Without rejecting this argument, for the sake of discussion only, and without claiming any kind of proof or demonstration, I wish to present an alternative argument; that the difference in outcome is largely due to the differences in technique used by the interrogators. This argument will allow us to suggest some crucial dimensions of negotiation processes.

The first dimension, consciousness of the bargaining aspects of the transaction, has already been mentioned. In the psychotherapeutic interview, the negotiational nature of the transaction seems not to be articulated by either party. In the legal interview, however, certainly the lawyer, and perhaps to some extent the client as well, is aware of, and accepts, the situation as one of striking a bargain, rather than as a relentless pursuit of the absolute facts of the matter.

The dimension of shared awareness that the definition of the situation is negotiable seems particularly crucial for assessments of responsibility. In both interviews, there is an agenda hidden from the client. In the psychotherapeutic interview, it is probably the psychiatric criteria for acceptance into treatment, the criterion of "insight." The psychotherapist has probably been trained to view patients with "insight into their illness" as favorable candidates for psychotherapy, i.e., patients who accept, or can be led to accept, the problems as internal, as part of their personality, rather than seeing them as caused by external conditions.

In the legal interview, the agenda that is unknown to the client is the legal structure of defenses or justifications for killing. In both the legal and psychiatric cases, the hidden agenda is not a simple one. Both involve fitting abstract and ambiguous criteria (insight, on the one hand, legal justifi-

cation, on the other) to a richly specific, concrete case. In the legal interview, the lawyer almost immediately broaches this hidden agenda; he states clearly and concisely the major legal justifications for killing. In the psychiatric interview, the hidden agenda is never revealed. The patient's offers during most of the interview are rejected or ignored. In the last part of the interview, her last offer is accepted and she is told that she will be given treatment. In no case are the reasons for these actions articulated by either party.

The degree of shared awareness is related to a second dimension which concerns the format of the conversation. The legal interview began as an interrogation, but was quickly shifted away from that format when the defense lawyer realized the direction in which the questioning was leading the client, i.e., toward a legally unambiguous admission of guilt. On the very brink of such an admission, the defense lawyer stopped asking questions and started, instead, to make statements. He listed the principle legal justifications for killing, and, in response to the *client's* questions, gave an explanation of each of the justifications. This shift in format put the client, rather than the lawyer, in control of the crucial aspects of the negotiation. It is the client, not the lawyer, who is allowed to pose the questions, assess the answers for their relevance to his case, and most crucially, to determine himself the most advantageous tack to take. Control of the definition of the situation, the evocation of the events and intentions relevant to the assessment of the client's responsibility for the killing, was given to the client by the lawyer. The resulting client-controlled format of negotiation gives the client a double advantage. It not only allows the client the benefit of formulating his account of actions and intentions in their most favorable light, it also allows him to select, out of a diverse and ambiguous set of normative criteria concerning killing, that criteria which is most favorable to his own case.

Contrast the format of negotiation used by the psychotherapist. The form is consistently that of interrogation. The psychotherapist poses the questions; the patient answers. The psychotherapist then has the answers at his disposal. He may approve or disapprove, accept or reject, or merely ignore them. Throughout the entire interview, the psychotherapist is in complete control of the situation. Within this framework, the tactic that the psychotherapist uses is to reject the patient's "offers" that her husband is at fault, first by ignoring them, later, and ever more insistently, by leading her to define the situation as one in which she is at fault. In effect, what the therapist does is to reject her offers, and to make his own counter-offers.

These remarks concerning the relationship between technique of interrogation and outcome suggest an approach to assessment of responsibility somewhat different from that usually followed. The common sense approach to interrogation is to ask how accurate and fair is the outcome. Both Newman's and Balint's analyses of negotiation raise this question. Both presuppose that there is an objective state of affairs that is independent of the technique of assessment. This is quite clear in Newman's discussion, as he continually refers to defendants who are "really" or "actually" guilty or innocent.[20] The situation is less clear in Balint's discussion, although occasionally he implies that certain patients are really physically healthy, but psychologically distressed.

The type of analysis suggested by this paper seeks to avoid such presuppositions. It can be argued that *independently* of the facts of the case, the technique of assessment plays a part in determining the outcome. In particular, one can avoid making assumptions about actual responsibility by utilizing a technique of textual criticism of a transaction. The key dimension in such work would be the relative power and authority of the participants in the situation.[21]

As an introduction to the way in which power differences between interactants shape the outcome of negotiations, let us take as an example an attorney in a trial dealing with "friendly" and "unfriendly" witnesses. A friendly witness is a person whose testimony will support the definition of the situation the attorney seeks to convey to the jury. With such a witness the attorney does not employ power, but treats him as an equal. His questions to such a witness are open, and allow the witness considerable freedom. The attorney might frame a question such as "Could you tell us about your actions on the night of ———?"

The opposing attorney, however, interested in establishing his own version of the witness' behavior on the same night, would probably approach the task quite differently. He might say: "You felt angry and offended on the night of ———, didn't you?" The witness frequently will try to evade so direct a question with an answer like: "Actually, I had started to. . . . " The attorney quickly interrupts, addressing the judge: "Will the court order the witness to respond to the question, yes or no?" That is to say, the question posed by the opposing attorney is abrupt and direct. When the witness attempts to answer indirectly, and at length, the attorney quickly invokes the power of the court to coerce the witness to answer as he wishes, directly. The witness and the attorney are not equals in power; the attorney used the coercive power of the court to force the witness to answer in the manner desired.

The attorney confronted by an "unfriendly" witness wishes to control the format of the interaction, so that he can retain control of the definition of the situation that is conveyed to the jury. It is much easier for him to neutralize the opposing definition of the situation if he retains control of the interrogation format in this manner. By allowing the unfriendly witness to respond only by yes or no to his own verbally conveyed account, he can suppress the ambient details of the opposing view that might sway the jury, and thus maintain an advantage for his definition over that of the witness.

In the psychiatric interview discussed above, the psychiatrist obviously does not invoke a third party to enforce his control of the interview. But he does use a device to impress the patient that she is not to be his equal in the interview, that is reminiscent of the attorney with an unfriendly witness. The device is to pose abrupt and direct questions to the patient's open-ended accounts, implying that the patient should answer briefly and directly; and, through that implication, the psychiatrist controls the whole transaction. Throughout most of the interview the patient seeks to give detailed accounts of her behavior and her husband's, but the psychiatrist almost invariably counters with a direct and, to the patient, seemingly unrelated question.

The first instance of this procedure occurs at T6, the psychiatrist asking the patient, "What do you do?" She replies "I'm a nurse, but my husband won't let me work." Rather than responding to the last part of her answer, which would be expected in conversion between equals, the psychiatrist asks another question, changing the subject: "How old are you?" This pattern continues throughout most of the interview. The psychiatrist appears to be trying to teach the patient to follow his lead. After some thirty or forty exchanges of this kind, the patient apparently learns her lesson; she cedes control of the transaction completely to the therapist, answering briefly and directly to direct questions, and elaborating only on cue from the therapist. The therapist thus implements his control of the interview not by direct coercion, but by subtle manipulation.

All of the discussion above, concerning shared awareness and the format of the negotiation, suggests several propositions concerning control over the definition of the situation. The professional interrogator, whether lawyer or psychotherapist, can maintain control if the client cedes control to him because of his authority as an expert, because of his manipulative skill in the transaction, or merely because the interrogator controls access to something the client wants, e.g., treatment, or a legal excuse. The propositions are:

1a. Shared awareness of the participants that the situation is one of negotiation. (The greater the shared awareness the more control the client gets over the resultant definition of the situation.)

b. Explicitness of the agenda. (The more explicit the agenda of the transaction, the more control the client gets over the resulting definition of the situation.)

2a. Organization of the format of the transaction, offers and responses. (The party to a negotiation who responds, rather than the party who makes the offers, has relatively more power in controlling the resultant shared definition of the situation.)

b. Counter-offers. (The responding party who makes counter-offers has relatively more power than the responding party who limits his response to merely accepting or rejecting the offers of the other party.)

c. Directness of questions and answers. (The more direct the questions of the interrogator, and the more direct the answers he demands and receives, the more control he has over the resultant definition of the situation.)

These concepts and hypotheses are only suggestive until such times as operational definitions can be developed. Although such terms as offers and responses seem to have an immediate applicability to most conversation, it is likely that a thorough and systematic analysis of any given conversation would show the need for clearly stated criteria of class inclusion and exclusion. Perhaps a good place for such research would be in the transactions for assessing responsibility discussed above. Since some 90 percent of all criminal convictions in the United States are based on guilty pleas, the extent to which techniques of interrogation subtly influence outcomes would have immediate policy implication. There is considerable evidence that interrogation techniques influence the outcome of psychotherapeutic interviews also.[22] Research in both of these areas would probably have implications for both the theory and practice of assessing responsibility.

Conclusion: Negotiation in Social Science Research

More broadly, the application of the sociology of knowledge to the negotiation of reality has ramifications which may apply to all of social science. The interviewer in a survey, or the experimenter in a social psychological experiment, is also involved in a transaction with a client—the respondent or subject. Recent studies by Rosenthal and others strongly suggest that the findings in such studies are negotiated, and influenced by the format of the study.[23] Rosenthal's review of bias in research suggests that such bias is produced by a pervasive and subtle process of interaction between the investigator and his source of data. Those errors which arise because of the investigator's influence over the subject (the kind of influence discussed in this paper as arising out of power disparities in the process of negotiation), Rosenthal calls "expectancy effects." In order for these errors to occur, there must be direct contact between the investigator and the subject.

A second kind of bias Rosenthal refers to as "observer effects." These are errors of perception or reporting which do not require that the subject be influenced by investigation. Rosenthal's review leads one to surmise that even with techniques that are completely non-obtrusive observer error could be quite large.[24]

The occurrence of these two kinds of bias poses an interesting dilemma for the lawyer, psychiatrist, and social scientist. The investigator of human phenomena is usu-ally interested in more than a sequence of events, he wants to know why the events occurred. Usually this quest for an explanation leads him to deal with the motivation of the persons involved. The lawyer, clinician, social psychologist, or survey researcher try to elicit motives directly, by questioning the participants. But in the process of questioning, as suggested above, he himself becomes involved in a process of negotiation, perhaps subtly influencing the informants through expectancy effects. A historian, on the other hand, might try to use documents and records to determine motives. He would certainly avoid expectancy effects in this way, but since he would not elicit motives directly, he might find it necessary to collect and interpret various kinds of evidence which are only indirectly related, at best, to determine motives of the participants. Thus through his choice in the selection and interpretation of the indirect evidence, he may be as susceptible to error as the interrogator, survey researcher, or experimentalist—his error being due to observer effects, however, rather than expectancy effects.

The application of the ideas outlined here to social and psychological research need to be developed. The five propositions suggested above might be used, for example, to estimate the validity of surveys using varying degrees of open-endedness in their interview format. If some technique could be developed which would yield an independent assessment of validity, it might be possible to demonstrate, as Aaron Cicourel has suggested, the more reliable the technique, the less valid the results.

The influence of the assessment itself on the phenomena to be assessed appears to be an ubiquitous process in human affairs, whether in ordinary daily life, the determination of responsibility in legal or clinical interrogation, or in most types of social science research. The sociology of knowledge perspective, which suggests that people go through their lives constructing reality, offers a framework within which the negotiation of reality can be seriously and constructively studied. This paper has suggested some of the avenues of the problem that might require further study. The prevalence of the problem in most areas of human concern recommends it to our attention as a substantial field of study, rather than as an issue that can be ignored or, alternatively, be taken as the proof that rigorous knowledge of social affairs is impossible.

Notes

1. The doctrine of absolute responsibility is clearly illustrated in psychiatric and legal discussions of the issue of "criminal responsibility," i.e., the use of mental illness as an excuse from criminal conviction. An example of the assumption of absolute criteria of responsibility is found in the following quotation, "The finding that someone is criminally responsible means to the psychiatrist that the criminal must change his behavior before he can resume his position in society. *This injunction is dictated not by morality, but, so to speak, by reality.*" See E. J. Sachar (1963), "Behavioral science and criminal law," *Scientific American, 209,* 39-45 (emphasis added).

2. Cf. P. L. Berger & T. Luckmann (1966), *The social construction of reality: A treatise in the sociology of knowledge,* New York: Doubleday.

3. The classic treatment of this issue is found in E. Durkheim (1975), *The elementary forms of the religious life,* London: G. Allen & Unwin.

4. A sociological application of the concept of negotiation, in a different context, is found in A. Strauss et al. (1963), "The hospital and its negotiated order," in E. Freidson (Ed.), *The hospital in modern society* (pp. 147-169), New York: Free Press.

5. Newman (1966) reports a study in this area, together with a review of earlier work, in "The negotiated plea," Part 3 in D. J. Newman, *Conviction: The determination of guilt or innocence without trial* (pp. 76-130), Boston: Little, Brown.

6. Newman (1966), p. 76.

7. Newman (1966), p. 83.

8. Newman (1966), p. 83.

9. M. Balint (1957), *The doctor, his patient, and the illness,* New York: International Universities Press, p. 18. A description of the negotiations between patients in a tuberculosis sanitarium and their physicians is found in J. A. Roth (1963), *Timetables: Structuring the passage of time in hospi-* *tal treatment and other careers,* Indianapolis, IN: Bobbs-Merrill, pp. 48-59. Obviously, some cases are more susceptible to negotiation than others. Balint implies that the great majority of cases in medical practice are negotiated.

10. Balint (1957), p. 216.

11. M. Gill, R. Newman, & F. C. Redlich (1954), *The initial interview in psychiatric practice,* New York: International Universities Press.

12. Since this interview is complex and subtle, the reader is invited to listen to it himself, and compare his conclusions with those discussed here. The recorded interview is available on the first L.P. record that accompanies Gill, Newman, & Redlich (1954).

13. Gill, Newman, & Redlich (1954), p. 133 (emphasis added).

14. Gill, Newman, & Redlich (1954), pp. 176-182 (numbers in parenthesis added).

15. Gill, Newman, & Redlich (1954), pp. 186-187.

16. Gill, Newman, & Redlich (1954), pp. 192-194.

17. R. Traver (1959), *Anatomy of a murder,* New York: Dell.

18. Traver (1959), p. 43.

19. Traver (1959), pp. 46-47, 57, 58-59, and 60.

20. In his Foreword the editor of the series, Frank J. Remington, comments on one of the slips that occurs frequently, the "acquittal of the guilty," noting that this phrase is contradictory from the legal point of view. He goes on to say that Newman is well aware of this, but uses the phrase as a convenience. Needless to say, both Remington's comments and mine can both be correct: the phrase is used as a convenience, but it also reveals the author's presuppositions.

21. Berger & Luckmann (1966), p. 100, also emphasize the role of power, but at the societal level. "The success of particular conceptual machineries is related to the power possessed by those who operate them. The confrontation of alternative symbolic universes implies a problem of power—which of the conflicting definitions of reality will be 'made to stock' in the society." Haley's discussions of control in psychotherapy are also relevant. See J. Haley (1959), "Control in psychoanalytic psychotherapy," in *Progress in psychotherapy* (Vol. 4, pp. 48-65), New York: Grune & Stratton; see also by the same author (1969), *The power tactics of Jesus Christ.* New York: Grossman.

22. T. J. Scheff (1966), *Being mentally ill,* Chicago: Aldine.

23. R. Rosenthal (1966), *Experimenter effects in behavioral research*, New York: Appleton-Century-Crofts. Friedman, reporting a series of studies of expectancy effects, seeks to put the results within a broad sociological framework; N. Friedman (1967), *The social nature of psychological research: The psychological experiment as social interaction*, New York: Basic Books.

24. Critics of "reactive techniques" often disregard the problem of observer effects. See, for example, E. J. Webb, D. T. Campbell, R. D. Schwartz, & L. Sechrest (1966), *Unobtrusive measures: Nonreactive research in social science*, Chicago: Rand-McNally.

47

Prestige as the Public Discourse of Domination

James C. Scott

The humbling of inferiors is necessary to the maintenance of social order.

(Madame de Sevigne)

He who is master cannot be free.

(J.-J. Rousseau)

The Display of Domination: Its Value and Its Cost

There is something very public and visible about prestige and its close cousin, status. Of course, it is possible for someone to have great status or prestige as an insider—"She's a mathematician's mathematician"; "Masons say he's the best bricklayer around"—but this merely tells us that the prestige extends only to an esoteric public of those who know. Completely covert status or prestige is almost a contradiction in terms.

Display of some kind seems to be a necessary, but not sufficient, condition for the creation and maintenance of prestige. Our initial estimate of the prestige of someone new to us comes from observing whether others defer to him or not and the degree of their deference. When and if this deference is directly contradicted by general off-stage contempt, we are alerted that we are in the

presence of power unaccompanied by prestige. Thus, prestige may require public performance, but the public performance must be thought to be authentic and not extracted by coercion. The difference here is not unlike that between power and authority; the public display of power will look very much like authority, but, if we know that those complying have been threatened with a beating if they spoil the performance, we would hesitate to call this authority.

This characteristic of prestige highlights the fact that unlike, say, wealth, prestige is a relational good. One can amass wealth whether or not others believe one to be wealthy. But prestige is something that others confer, not something that can be unilaterally acquired. If prestige is unlike wealth in this respect, it is akin to charisma. Although we often speak as if an individual *had* charisma the way she might have a house, what we mean is that others respond to her with an awe and enthusiasm that suggest charisma. The moment that others cease to believe in one's prestige or charisma, it quite literally vanishes into thin air. Prestige is a social transaction.

Prestige is, finally, a transitive good. To say that so-and-so has prestige is implicitly to say that he is held in higher regard than some—often specified—others. Like authority, prestige implies ranking and is therefore something of a zero-sum game. A statement about someone's wealth can be made without necessarily implying a comparison, but, with few exceptions, we can say that the accumulation of prestige by some entails the loss of standing for others.

These very social and public aspects of prestige help explain why it is so often displayed in public ceremonies and rituals. Prestige can be thought of as the public face of domination. The public face domination wears, the kind of prestige it aims at engendering, depends of course on the kind of claim to status it is making. Displays of technical skill, artistic grace, piety, physical strength, or knowledge of sacred texts might be appropriate depending on the sort of claim being dramatized. For this reason we need to speak of how forms of domination are given public expression as well as how individuals are "dramatized" within a given form of domination. Here I want to address the displays deployed by different modes of domination to create and enhance the prestige of its elites and to suggest how such effects are achieved. I also hope to show why it is normally in the interest of subordinate groups to play their assigned roles in these performances whether or not they are willing conscripts.

Domination, once established, does not persist on its own momentum. Inasmuch as it involves the use of power to extract work, production, services, or taxes against the will of the dominated, it generates considerable friction and can only be sustained by continuous efforts at reinforcement, maintenance, and adjustment. A good part of the maintenance work consists of the symbolization of domination by demonstrations and enactments of power. All visible, outward uses of power—each command, each act of deference, each list and ranking, each cere-monial order, each public punishment, each use of an honorific or a derogative term— are a symbolic gesture of domination which serves to manifest and reinforce a hierarchical order. The persistence of any pattern of domination is always problematic, and one may well ask what, given the resistances to it, is required to keep it in place—how many beatings, jailings, executions, secret understandings, bribes, warnings, concessions, and, not least, how many public demonstrations of grandeur, exemplary punishment, beneficence, spiritual rectitude, and so forth.

Some events are planned essentially as discursive affirmations of a particular pattern of domination. The May Day Parade in Red Square is a massive display of hierarchy and power, from the order of precedence on the reviewing stand, to the order in the line of march, to the display of armed might of the USSR creating an impression of power and solidarity designed to awe party members, citizens, and foreign antagonists alike. The large popular audience who turns out to witness the display helps, by its numbers, enthusiasm, and patriotic garb, to add an air of prestige to the proceedings. Most discursive affirmations are, however, not designed as mere displays. An election, assuming it is not purely ritualistic, may provide an occasion for an electorate to choose its leaders while, at the same time, serve as a symbolic affirmation of the prestige of democratic forms embodying popular sovereignty. When an opposition movement calls for a boycott of what it believes to be a fraudulent or meaningless election, it presumably does this precisely to undercut the value of the election as a prestige-building ritual. Small "ceremonies," being much more frequent, are perhaps more telling as daily embodiments of domination and subordination. When the peasant removes his cap in the presence of the landlord or official, when the slave owner assembles his slaves to witness a whipping, when seating at a meal is arranged by position or status, when the last piece of meat on the platter is taken by the father of a family, relations of rank and power have been expressed.

Elites naturally have the greatest political investment in such affirmations, since each of them signals a pyramid of precedence of which each forms the apex. They would like every performance to follow their scenario and to go off without a hitch. In practice, though, the performance is itself the outcome of a struggle—however unequal its terms. For, to the degree the performance demonstrates the claim of the dominant, it encounters a certain resistance from those at the bottom whose *inferiority*—whose lack of status—is thereby being reciprocally demonstrated. Occasionally, when they venture on-stage, subordinates may spoil, interrupt, or ridicule the performance in an attempt to turn it into a disconfirmation of power relations.

The "silent monitor" introduced by Robert Owen into his textile factory at New Lannark was a striking example of an attempt to make relations of power and judgment continually visible.[1] Believed by Owen to be "the most efficient check upon inferior conduct" at the mill, the silent monitor was a small, four-sided piece of wood with each side colored differently—black, blue, yellow, and white—and fitted with hooks so that one or another side could face outward. Each employee—save the owner-manager, presumably—was furnished with a "silent monitor" which was conspicuously displayed at the work site. The color showing represented his superior's judgment of performance on the previous day—black/bad, blue/indifferent, yellow/good, and white/excellent. Appealing a supervisor's judgment was allowed but rare. Owen or anyone else passing through the factory was thus afforded an instant visual representation of each worker's performance yesterday, and, by the same token, each worker wore around his or her neck, in effect, the management's judgment. To provide the system with historical depth, the colors were coded by number, and each day's judgment was recorded in what Owen calls "books of character" which were maintained for as long as the employee worked in Owen's mill. The parallels between this scheme and the legendary book of St. Peter in which one's conduct is faultlessly recorded was not lost on Owen: "The act of setting down the number in the book of character, never to be blotted out, might be likened to the supposed recording angel marking the good and bad deeds of poor human nature."[2] The place of God, in this terrestrial plan, is taken by the factory owner, and the role of sin is replaced by judgments according to one's contribution to production and profits. Owen's system simply gives regular, public form to the assessment by the dominant of the work of their subordinates; the public transcript is made visible and pervasive. The hierarchical structure of this great chain of judgment is nearly Orwellian in its capacity to obliterate other relations and criteria of evaluation. Imagine, for a moment, the symbolic impact that the reversal of Owen's scheme might have. That is, imagine a mill in which each superior wore around his neck a daily evaluation of his conduct imposed by his subordinates and that this principle was extended all the way up to Owen himself. To complete the reversal, of course, one would also have to envision a reversal of sanctioning power as well, inasmuch as a string of bad marks in Owen's books of character would be not only a public humiliation, but undoubtedly would lead to demotion, a pay cut, or even dismissal.

Owen's open display of domination and judgment, like other rituals of power, not only pictured a hierarchy of worth with himself at the apex, but also crowded any alternative view of production relationships off the public stage. Some displays, some rituals, however, are more elaborate and closely regulated than others. This seems particularly the case with any venerable institution whose claim to recognition and domination rests in large part on its continuous and faithful link with the past. Royal coronations, national day celebrations, ceremonies for those fallen in war thus seem to be choreographed down to small details so that little or nothing is left to the imagination. Such ceremonies seem designed to prevent surprises. The same generalization might be hazarded about the far smaller daily ceremonies we call "etiquette" or "politeness." Rules of etiquette represent, after all, a kind of grammar of social intercourse imposed by the guardians of taste and decorum, which allow its users to navigate the shoals of strangers—especially powerful strangers— without making a false step. But even here, as Bourdieu notes, the performance is infused with power: "The concession of politeness always contains political concessions, . . . the symbiotic taxes due from individuals."[3] The political concession involved is most apparent when a failure to observe the rules of politeness is taken as an act of insubordination.

The resort to meticulous control over the public interaction between elites and subordinates (the public "transcript")—to the careful imposition of dominant forms of discourse and classification—seems to vary greatly between forms of domination. Any lengthy analysis of the reasons for this variation is outside the scope of this inquiry, but a suggestion or two may be helpful. First, those forms of domination in which the skill and control of the powerholders are palpable and easily verifiable seem able to dispense with many of the symbolic trappings of power and with rituals of subordination. To take obvious examples, the Albert Einsteins, the brilliant surgeons, the financial "wizards" whose personal mastery of a skill commands prestige in its own right need little in the way of outward majesty or ceremony to reinforce the deference they receive. Contrast these roles to those of, say, a supreme court judge, an archbishop, or an admiral. Here the powerholders represent an institute *through which* they exercise power, and it would be difficult normally to decide whether they owe their positions to some unique personal talent or rather to a knack

for institutional infighting. When the dominant act as representatives, it seems that institutional power relies heavily upon outward, public manifestations of dominance through sumptuary regulations (wigs, robes, uniforms), elaborate rituals (announcement of judge with all in attendance standing, solemn high mass, official inspection), and an imposed etiquette of address ("your honor," "your worship," "Sir"). It is clear that these ceremonials of prestige are applied not to individuals but rather to the incumbents of roles within the institute. The "honor" that is done by the observance of such forms is done, above all, to the institution (judiciary, church, navy). Such institutions are, in fact, profoundly hostile to the individual who owes his position to entirely personal attributes such as technical skill or charisma which cannot be controlled by the institution. The church, far removed historically and structurally from its origins, becomes the implacable enemy of any prophecy and religious enthusiasm which implicitly claim authority from non-institutional sources. Once charisma is routinized, as Weber noted, any subsequent inspiration represents a threat to the official keepers of the flame.

In a crude sense, then, elaborate ritual and symbolism may be employed as a substitute for "real" power or to tap an original source of power and legitimacy which has since been attenuated.[4] An analogy may help illustrate what I have in mind. If sheep are pastured in a field surrounded by a powerful electric fence they will, at first, blunder into it and experience the painful shock. Once conditioned to the fence, the sheep will graze at a respectful distance.[5] If, following the conditioning, the fence is switched off for days at a time, the sheep continue to avoid it. The fence continues to have the same associations for them despite the fact that the *invisible* power has been cut. How long the fence would continue to exercise its power in the absence of current is not clear; it would presumably depend on the tenacity of memory and on how often sheep blundered into the fence.[6] The point, however, is simply that the symbols of power, providing that their potency was once experienced, may continue to exert influence after they have lost most or all of their effective power. If we imagine a highly stratified agrarian society in which landlords had once the coercive force to discover and punish any tenants or laborers who defied their power by acts of insubordination (e.g., poaching, strikes, petitions, rebellion), the parallel is clear. So long as the visible symbolism of their repression remains in place in the form, say, of jails, constabulary, and open threats, it may exert an intimidating influence out of proportion to its actual, contemporary power. Very small manifestations of landlord force may suffice to sustain the miasma of power for some time. In the absence of any concrete example of landlord weakness, their power may go long unchallenged.[7]

A substantial portion of the public transcript of the dominant thus consists in crafting a stage presence that appears masterful and self-confident. How the impression is conveyed—and it is conveyed not just by symbolization—will vary according to the sort of claim being exercised. The scripts of a slave owner, an archbishop, and a feudal lord will thus differ greatly. Despite these differences there is a certain amount of bluff and pretense in almost any display of power. The successful communication of power and authority is freighted with consequences inasmuch as it contributes to something like a self-fulfilling prophecy. If subordinates believe their superior to be powerful, the impression will help him impose himself and, in turn, contribute to his actual power. Ceremonies dramatizing the majesty of power are integral to the accumulation of power. Appearances do matter. Adolph Hitler has provided us with the most chilling version of this insight: "One cannot rule by force alone. True, force is decisive, but it is equally important to have this psychological something which the animal trainer also needs to be master of his beast. They must be convinced that we are the victors."[8]

The members of dominant groups, one supposes, learn the knack of acting with authority and self-assurance in the course of socialization. For hereditary ruling groups the training typically begins at birth; the aristocrat learns how to act like an aristocrat, the Brahmin like a Brahmin, the man like a man. For those whose position is not inherited, "on-the-job" training is required to make them convincing in their roles as bosses, professors, military officers, colonial officials. In each case, it is understood that the performance of mastery is staged for the impression it makes on subordinates, commoners, lower castes, women, employees, students, natives, and so forth. As Orwell observes elsewhere in "Shooting an Elephant," acting like a colonial official in front of the natives can become a very powerful incentive.

> With the crowd watching me, I was not afraid in the ordinary sense, as I would have been if I had been alone. A white man mustn't be frightened in front of the "natives"; and so, in general, he isn't frightened. The sole thought in my mind was that if anything went wrong those two thousand Burmans would see me pursued, caught, trampled on and reduced to a grinning corpse like that Indian up the hill. And if that happened it was quite probable that some of them would laugh. That would never do.[9]

What Orwell does off-stage—what "his hidden transcript" might be—is one thing, but his comportment in front of the natives must embody the ideas by which colonial domination is publicly justified. In this case, it means using his superior firepower publicly to protect the Burman population and doing it in a manner which suggests that such mastery is part of the natural endowment of a colonial official. He has so assimilated the code that he appears to fear the possible derision as much as death.

Being on stage in front of subordinates exerts a powerful influence on the conduct and speech of the dominant. Although they are, by virtue of their dominance, less constrained than subordinate groups, they have a collective theatre to maintain which becomes part of their self-definition. Above all, they frequently sense that they perform before an extremely critical audience which waits in eager anticipation for any sign that the actors are losing their touch. Sensitive observers of plantation life in the ante-bellum South noted that the speech and carriage of slaveholders changed the moment a black servant entered the room.[10] The Dutch in eastern Indonesia noticed that the clans of Torajans who held slaves behaved quite differently from clans without slaves.

> The To Lage and the To Anda'e, who always had to be mindful of keeping their prestige high with regard to their slaves, had in this way achieved a great deal of self-control, through which they made a more civilized impression on the foreigner than did the To Pebato who, not knowing this pressure, behaved more as they are, let themselves go more.[11]

Impressive though the front maintained by ruling groups may be, it is designed as much for what it obscures as for the awe it inspires.

Concealment

Chief of Police: He knew I wore a toupée?

The Bishop (snickering, to the Judge and the General): He's the only one who doesn't know that everyone knows it.

(Jean Genet, *The Balcony*)

In Genet's *The Screens*, set in Algeria, Arab farm laborers kill their European overseer when it is discovered that he has used padding on his stomach and buttocks to make an imposing appearance. Once he is reduced to ordinary proportions, they are no longer intimidated. Preposterous though this parable may seem, it does capture an important truth about the dramaturgy of power.

By controlling the public stage, the dominant can create an appearance that approximates what, ideally, they would want subordinates to see. The deception—or propaganda—they devise may add padding to their stature, but it will also hide whatever might detract from their grandeur and authority. Thus, for example, the pastoralist Tutsi, who were feudal lords over the agriculturalist Hutus in Rwanda, pretended publicly that they lived entirely on fluids from their herds—milk products and blood—and never ate meat.[12] This story, they believed, made them appear more awesome and disciplined in the eyes of the Hutu. In fact, the Tutsi did like meat and ate it surreptitiously whenever they could. Whenever their Hutu retainers caught them *in flagrante delicto* they were said to have sworn them to secrecy. One would be astonished if, in their own quarters, the Hutu did not take great delight in ridiculing the dietary hypocrisy of their Tutsi overlords. On the other hand, it is significant that, at that time, the Hutu would not have ventured a public declaration of Tutsi meat-eating and that the public transcript proceeds *as if* the Tutsi lived by fluids alone. A similar pattern may be seen in public relations between Brahmins and untouchables. Officially, contact between the two is governed by the elaborate rituals of relative purity and pollution. So long as this public reality is sustained, many Brahmins apparently feel free to violate the code privately. Thus, an untouchable procurer delights in maneuvering his high caste customers into eating with him and using his clothes, and they appear relatively unperturbed, providing this behavior takes place off-stage in a sequestered sphere.[13] It seems to matter little, as with the Tutsi, that these violations of official reality—these potential blows to their official prestige—are widely known among subordinates. What matters, apparently, is that such behavior is not openly declared or displayed where it would publicly threaten the official story.[14] Only when contradictions are publicly allowed do they have to be accounted for publicly.

Occasionally it has been argued that official power relations are not so much the symbolic, public component of a general domination, but rather a face-saving strategy which masks a loss of power. Susan Rogers applies this logic to gender relations in peasant communities in general and to those in the Lorraine region of France in particular.[15] Cultural tradition as well as the law confers authority and prestige on males who hold virtually all formal positions, while the power of women in the village is "more effective" but, at the same time, covert and informal. The men, she argues, accept this fact so long as there is no public challenge to their prestige and so long as they are still given "credit" for running things. To draw the conclusion, however, that the practical informal realities render men's power merely cosmetic and vaporous would be to forget that symbolic concessions are "political concessions" as well. That such power can only be exercised behind a veil of properties that reaffirm men's official rule as power-holders is a tribute—albeit a left-handed one—to their continued control of the public transcript.[16]

All forms of domination have something to hide from the public gaze of subordinates. However, some forms have more to hide. Speculatively, we might imagine that the more august the public image of ruling groups, the more important it becomes to sequester and guard closely an offstage sphere where such "postures are relaxed."[17] Those who inherit their right to rule (by way of caste, race, or gender, for example) or who claim a right to rule based on a spiritual claim are likely to fit this stereotype most closely. Those whose claim to authority is based on the superior performance of a verifiable skill—the production manager, the battlefield general, the athletic coach—have less reason for elaborate, staged presentations, either of their power or of the recip-

rocal deference of subordinates. In this latter case the gap between the public and hidden transcripts of elites is not so great, nor, for that reason, is its exposure to public view so dangerous.

Euphemization and Its Costs

If the side of the public transcript we have thus far examined serves to *magnify* the visible awe, prestige, or terror in which elites are held, another side of the public transcript serves cosmetically to beautify power, to highlight its beneficent side, and to obscure nasty truths. For lack of a better word, I will use Bourdieu's term, "euphemization," to express this function.[18]

Wherever one encounters euphemisms in language it is a nearly infallible sign that one has stumbled on a delicate subject.[19] They are used to obscure something that is negatively valued or would prove to be an embarrassment if declared more forthrightly. Thus we have a host of terms, at least in Anglo-American culture, designed to euphemize that place where urination and defecation take place: "john," "restroom," "comfort station," "water closet," "lavatory," "loo," etc. For occupations which have come to be valued negatively like trash collector or undertaker (itself a euphemism) we often substitute sanitation engineer or funeral director, especially in public. The imposition of euphemisms on the public transcript plays a similar role in masking the many nasty facts of domination and giving them a harmless or sanitized aspect. In particular, they are designed to obscure the use of coercion. A mere list of euphemisms which come to mind together with more blunt, non-cosmetic alternative terms amply illustrates their political use: "pacification" for armed attack and occupation; "calming" for confinement by straight-jacket; "capital punishment" for state execution; "re-education camps" for imprisoning political opponents. The first term in each pair is imposed by the dominant on public discourse to put a benign face on an activity or fact that would morally offend many. As a result, more graphic, ordinary language descriptions are frowned upon and often driven from the realm of official discourse.[20] In extreme cases, certain facts, though widely known, may never be mentioned in public contexts—e.g., forced labor camps in the Soviet Union, until Gorbachev's glasnost. Here it is a question of effacement, not defacement or beautification. What may develop under such circumstances is virtually a dual culture: the official culture filled with bright euphemisms, silences, and platitudes and an unofficial culture which has its own history, its own literature and poetry, its own biting slang, its own music and poetry, its own humor, and its own knowledge of shortages, corruption, and inequalities which may, once again, be widely known, but which may not be introduced into public discourse.

On every occasion in which the official presentation of reality is allowed to prevail over other dissonant versions, the dominant monopoly over public knowledge is publicly conceded by subordinates. They may, of course, have little choice in the matter, but so long as the monopoly is not publicly contested, it never has to "explain itself," it has nothing to "answer for." Take, for example, the commonplace of unemployment in capitalist economies. When employers dismiss workers, they are likely to euphemize their action by saying something like, "we had to let them go." In one short phrase they manage to deny their own agency as employers, implying that they had no choice in the matter, and to convey the impression that the workers in question were mercifully released, rather like dogs on leashes. The workers who are now out of work are likely to use more graphic verbs: "They fired me," "They gave me the axe," "They sacked me," and might well make the subject of their sentence, "those bastards. . . . " Linguistic forms depend very much on whose ox is being gored. When we hear terms such as "reduction in force," "retrenchment," "redun-

dancy," and "letting people go" we can be fairly confident about who is speaking. But, so long as this euphemistic description is left to stand, it remains the public description.

That acts of description should be politically loaded hardly comes as a surprise. The question that remains is the extent to which dominant descriptions monopolize the public transcript. In the Malay village I studied, poorer villagers who harvested paddy for their well-off neighbors received, in addition to their wage, a bonus in grain. The bonus had a great deal to do with a shortage of harvest labor at the time, but the gift was *publicly* described by the well-off as *zakat*. Inasmuch as *zakat* is a form of Islamic gift which enhances the giver's claim to prestige based on his pious generosity, it was in the interest of richer farmers to describe it in this fashion. Behind the backs of wealthy villagers, the harvest laborers consider the bonus an integral part of their wage, as no more than what they are entitled to as compensation for their work. The balance of power in the village, however, is sufficiently skewed against the harvesters that they abstain, out of prudence, from *publicly* contesting the self-serving definition applied by the rich. By letting it pass, by not contradicting its use, by behaving publicly *as if* they accepted this description, the poorer villages contribute—one might say wittingly—to the monopoly of public discourse exercised by the village elite.

Euphemisms in the broad sense I am using the term—the self-interested tailoring of descriptions and appearances by dominant powerholders—are not confined to language. It may be seen in gestures, architecture, ritual actions, public ceremonies, or any other actions where the powerful may portray their domination as they wish. Thus, the Ministry of Justice may choose to build or inhabit the most imposing buildings, display the emblem of blind justice holding a balance-scale, and employ judges in robes and wigs. This is, if you like, its picture of itself. In other settings, powerholders may seek to disguise their actual power and instead present a friendly, humble, or even egalitarian façade to subordinates. The seminar format of many university courses is a minor illustration of such a disguise, however sincerely perpetrated. The students and their professor sit in an arrangement (quite unlike the lecture podium facing an audience) which suggests equal authority and equal rights of participation and criticism. In fact, of course, the seminar situation is power-laden from the outset, which does not escape any of its participants, despite its misrepresentation by the egalitarian format. The setting, then, surely serves to veil or euphemize a relation of domination. In this case, as in others, the stagecraft is not without its political costs since such disguises can become a political resource for subordinates. They may and occasionally do exploit the gap between appearance and reality and use the hypocrisy itself to justify behavior which takes the egalitarian format seriously. An ideological hegemony, however cynically deployed and debased in practice, may be hoisted with its own petard by being asked to deliver on its own implicit promises. To such claims there is no easy *public* reply.

Euphemization is essentially an attempt to create the public impression of genuine prestige over and above mere power. That is, it makes an appeal to the presumed values of subordinates and its discourse aims at showing how power is in fact exercised on behalf of the best interests of subordinates. If the majesty and awe of gestures of power are the fierce face of domination, euphemization is its prestige-building friendly face. The claim to prestige, however, entails inevitable contradictions.

The contradictions inherent in the public transcript of slavery in the ante-bellum South of the U.S. are an instructive case in point. Since slaves were, officially, property like any other property, there were extensive ritual efforts to efface the slaves' prior identity. Here and in many other slavehold-ing societies, the slaves were given new names by their masters, denied any right to establish secure family ties, not allowed normal status as legal persons, not considered responsible for their own acts, and so on. And yet, since it was painfully obvious that the persons who were enslaved were human beings not unlike their masters, the official ideology of slavery embraced a kind of paternalist claim, occasionally embodied in law. This paternalism was useful in several directions: to argue the superiority of slavery over wage labor to opponents of slavery, to provide slave owners themselves with a rationale that claimed a higher purpose than mere self-interest, and to offer an official story for the slaves themselves. Paternalism, however, required arguing that slavery was in the best interest of slaves, and this in turn implied that they be properly fed, housed, clothed, and not overworked. The slaves, as Genovese has persuasively shown, made use of this euphemization for their own purposes.[21] When they helped themselves to what the master thought was his corn and grain, they reasoned that they were merely turning one form of property into another—"massa's horse, massa's grass." The small privileges they occasionally won—days off, garden plots, a tenuous family life, better rations, and so on—were defended by using the paternalist and Christian rationales of the slaveowning society itself. Any gains, given the latitude for arbitrary action afforded masters, were insubstantial, but the process of ideological euphemization had its costs; it was a double-edged sword even if one edge was far more blunt than the other.

Ruling groups can be called upon to live up to their own idealized presentation of themselves to their subordinates.[22] If they define a wage payment as an act of goodhearted charity, they can be condemned publicly for hard-heartedness when they fail to make "gifts." If the Czar is portrayed as powerful and beneficent to his serfs, he can be called upon to waive his serf's taxes in a time of dearth. If the superiority of a capitalist economy is alleged to lie in the prosperity and full-employment it promotes, then it may be criticized in its own terms in a depression. If a "people's democracy" claims it exists to promote the interest of the working class, it cannot easily explain why it is breaking strikes and jailing proletarians. To be sure, there are situations in which merely announcing a hypocrisy is to take a mortal risk. The point, however, is that the masks which domination wears are, under certain conditions, also traps.

Unanimity

A third function of the public transcript is to create the appearance of unanimity among the ruling groups and the appearance of consent among subordinates. In any highly stratified agrarian society there is usually more than a grain of truth to the former claim. Feudal lords, the gentry, and Brahmins, for example, partake in a cultural integration, reinforced by marriage alliances, social networks, and office, which extends at least to the provincial if not the national level. This social integration is likely to be reflected in dialect, ritual practices, cuisine, and entertainment. Popular culture, by contrast, is rather more locally rooted in terms of dialect, religious practices, dress, consumption patterns, and family networks.[23] Beyond the facts of the matter, however, it would seem that most ruling groups take great pains to foster a public image of cohesion and shared belief. Disagreements, informal discussions, off-guard commentary are kept to a minimum and, whenever possible, sequestered out of sight—in teachers' rooms, elite dinner parties, European clubs in the colonies, officers clubs, men's clubs, and myriads of more informal but protected sites. (The striking exception to the effort—not always successful—to present a united front is democratic forms of conflict management. Here too, however, only certain

forms of disagreement are generally aired before the general electorate, and "smoke-filled rooms" are used to transact business which would clash with public rhetoric.)

The advantages of keeping discord out of sight are obvious enough. If the dominant are at odds with one another in any substantial way, they are, to that degree, weakened, and subordinates may be able to exploit the divisions and renegotiate the terms of subordination. An effective façade of cohesion thus augments the apparent power of elites, thereby presumably affecting the calculations which subordinates might make about the risks of non-compliance or defiance.

For analogous reasons, the power of dominant groups is further enhanced if the unanimity appears to extend to subordinates as well. If convincing public displays of deference and conformity are periodically held, the impression of consent may be effectively conveyed. We might think of such displays as the visual and aural component of a hegemonic ideology—the ceremonial which gives euphemization an air of plausibility. Everything from feudal ceremonies of fealty, the military salute, the banquet with seating arranged by status, to any respectful public form of address to a superior may serve this purpose.

We must not assume that public activity between dominant and subordinate groups is nothing but a kind of tableau of power symbolizing hierarchy. A great deal of communication—especially in contemporary societies—does not materially affect power relations. It is nonetheless true that under nearly any form of domination, those in power make a remarkably assiduous effort to keep disputes that touch on their claim to power out of the public eye. If the clerical staff of a firm is grumbling about its pay and working conditions, it is vital that it be contained at that level and not erupt into a public confrontation. If the sharecropping tenants of a large landowner are restive over higher rents, the latter would rather see them individually and perhaps make concessions than to have a public confrontation. The importance of *avoiding any public display of insubordination* is not simply derived from a strategy of divide and rule; open insubordination represents a dramatic contradiction of the smooth surface of euphemized power.[24]

Using the Dramaturgy of Subordination

Three aspects of the dramaturgy of power relations follow from the effort to sanitize the public transcript. First, the only forms of dissent that are publicly countenanced are those couched in terms which affirm the subordination itself. The subjects of the king may petition for relief from taxes or conscription or even local administrative tyranny, but their petition must commence with a protestation of their loyalty, devotion, and subordination. They must begin with an outward recognition of the ruler's prestige. Standard formulas thus begin along the lines, "We, Sire, your most humble obedient servants do most loyally . . . ," after which usually follows a genuine complaint or request. Even in the heady decade following the French Revolution when the rights of citizens to representation and redress were loudly proclaimed, a Catalan-speaking village in southeastern France managed to find a republican formula for their faithfulness and loyalty while requesting a grammar school.

> In our commune, as in neighboring ones, there are a great number of young people whose fathers want them to learn to read and write in French, so that those children can have the benefit of learning the Rights of Man. . . . Permit us, Citizens, to tell you that it is to give subjects to the Republic and for the good of the state to teach our children the language in which the laws are made.[25]

Any communication to powerholders from below that stops short of outright defiance will normally, even if only for tactical reasons, make use of the approved formulas of subordination. A request to a ruler for a beneficent and paternalistic alleviation of taxes is one thing. It affirms subordination while requesting help, and the ruler, in granting the humble request, appears at the same time to validate his power and prestige.[26] A threatening demand to the same ruler for a reduction of taxes which has an explicit "or else" clause is something else again. It repudiates subordination, and granting the request—though it be precisely the same as one humbly beseeched—is not a public admission of weakness in the face of a direct challenge. Only when subordinates wish to provoke a crisis in a calculated way or are angry enough to throw caution to the winds are we likely to encounter a public transcript which breaks with norms of deference.

A second, and related, consequence of a "regulated" public transcript is that dissonance will normally be expressed in subtle, veiled, and muted forms. There is every reason for the dominant to make certain resistance stops well short of direct challenges in public. To the extent that they succeed, opposition will take safer forms such as vague grumbling, gossip, rumors, parables, and humor that may be read in several ways, and Aesopian language in general.[27] The interpretation of resistance along such lines might well lead to a valuable "theory of crumbling." Here, however, what is critical is the realization that veiled dissent of this kind does not constitute a direct challenge to the symbolism of power and, hence, does not require a public refutation or attack. Consider, for example, a slave who grumbled and who pilfered mightily from his master's grain supply. He might thereby have both insinuated his dissent and, in practice, improved the terms of his subordination. Compare such a slave with another who struck the master or who made obvious gestures of that kind in public. This last, if publicly unpunished, would represent a nearly decisive symbolic repudiation of subordination itself. The juxtaposition alone serves to explain why, as a practical matter, most slave resistance was of the former kind and why open defiance usually called forth the most massive and exemplary retaliation. It also explains why the traditional crime of *lèse majesté* is no laughing matter. Patterns of domination can, in fact, accommodate a reasonably high level of practical resistance so long as that resistance is not publicly and unambiguously acknowledged. Once it is, however, it requires a public reply if the symbolic status quo is to be restored. The symbolic restoration of power relations may be seen in the importance accorded to public apologies. Erving Goffman, in his careful analysis of the social micro-order, has examined the purposes of public apologies.[28] The subordinate who has publicly violated the required theatre of domination announces by way of a public apology that he dissociates himself from the offence and reaffirms the rule in question. He publicly accepts, in other words, the judgment of his superior that this is an offence and thus, implicitly, the censure or punishment which follows from it. The point has little to do with the sincerity of the retraction and disavowal, since what the apology repairs is the public transcript of apparent compliance. The taxes may be purely symbolic, but they are heavy for those on whom they are imposed. Accounts of slavery in the ante-bellum South emphasize how much attention was paid to ritual requests for forgiveness by slaves about to be punished for insubordination. Only after "humbling himself" to his master, and before other assembled slaves, was a victim's punishment lightened.[29]

From the perspective of the subordinate, of course, an apology may represent a comparatively economical means of escaping the most severe consequences of an offense against the dominant order. It may simply be a tactic cynically employed under duress. But, it is the show of compliance which is important and which is insisted on. Remorse, apologies, asking forgiveness, and generally making symbolic amends are a more vital element in almost any process of domination than punishment itself. A criminal who expresses remorse at his crime typically earns, in exchange for his petty contribution to the repair of the symbolic order, a reduction in punishment. A slave who publicly begs his master's pardon will be treated more leniently, thanks to his show of willing obedience. This is similar, of course, to the "misbehaving" child who says he is sorry and promises never to do it again. What all these actors offer is a show of discursive affirmation from below which is all the more valuable since it contributes to the impression that the prestige of the symbolic order is willingly accepted by its least advantaged members. To see why a flow of symbolic taxes is of such vital importance to the moral economy of domination, we have only to consider the symbolic consequences of a boycott of symbolic taxes. If the courts are filled with truculent and defiant criminals, if slaves stubbornly refuse to humble themselves, if children take their punishment sullenly and show no remorse whatever, their behavior amounts to a sign that domination is nothing more than tyranny—nothing more than the successful exercise of power against subordinates too weak to overthrow it but proud enough to defy it symbolically. To be sure, dominant elites would prefer a willing affirmation of their norms, but if this is not available they will extract, whenever they can, at least the simulacrum of a sincere obedience.

Notes

1. This account is drawn from Owen's autobiography (1920), *The life of Robert Owen*, New York: Knopf, pp. 110-112.

2. Owen (1920), p. 112 (emphasis added).

3. P. Bourdieu (1977), *Outline of a theory of practice* (R. Nice, Trans.), Cambridge, UK: Cambridge University Press, p. 85.

4. See, for example, J. H. Elliott's (1985) account of the spartan ceremonial of the early

Spanish monarchy. Elliott observes that where "The supremacy of the king is taken for granted, political imagery can be studiously understated, and there is no need to deck out the ruler with elaborate allegorical trappings. . . . This form of understatement may represent the ultimate in political sophistication." "Power and propaganda in the Spain of Philip IV," in S. Wilentz (Ed.), *The rites of power: Symbolism, ritual, and politics since the middle ages*, Philadelphia: University of Pennsylvania Press, p. 151.

5. The conditioning is so powerful that, having cut the power to the fence in order to work on it, I still hesitate to grasp it even though I "know" the current is off.

6. Here is where, I believe, the analogy breaks down. With sheep we may only assume a constant desire to get to the pasture beyond the fence—it is generally greener on the other side of the fence since they will have grazed everything on their side. With tenants or sharecroppers we may assume both a constant testing through poaching, pilfering, surreptitious gleaning and harvesting, and a cultural capacity for *collective anger and revenge*. The simple human desire to trespass, to do what is forbidden, *because it is forbidden,* may also be germane.

7. Although display and ritual might be considered cheap substitutes for more direct manifestations of power, they are not without their costs. Forms of domination that rely on elaborate codes of public ceremony do generally prevent surprises in the short run by monopolizing public discourse. They are, however, like radios that can send signals but cannot receive them. As a result, if they are surprised, the surprise is likely to be a large one. The nature of the surprise, moreover, is likely to represent a direct profaning of their ritual claim to power. Profanation is the most apparent historically in those movements against clerical authority in the West which aimed at a desacralization, ranging from burlesques of the Catholic mass, depictions of the sexual appetites of the supposedly celibate clergy, and pulling down of altar rails, to perhaps the limiting case, the revolutionary exhumations from the crypts of cathedrals during the Spanish Civil War. We will return to these issues in more detail later; it is enough to notice that each ritual of domination is accompanied, one might say "shadowed," by a potential "black mass."

8. Quoted in G. Sharpe (1973), *The politics of nonviolent action*, Boston: Porter Sargent, part I ("Power and struggle"), p. 43.

9. G. Orwell (1962), "Shooting an elephant," in *Inside the whale and other essays*, Harmondsworth, UK: Penguin, pp. 96-97.

10. G. Mullin (1972), *Fight and rebellion: Slave resistance in eighteenth-century Virginia*, New York: Oxford University Press, p. 100.

11. N. Adriani & A. C. Kruyt (1951), *De Barée sprekende Torajas van Midden-Celebes*, Amsterdam: Nood-Hollandsche Uitgevers Maatschappig, 2, p. 96, cited in O. Patterson (1982), *Slavery and social death: A comparative study*, Cambridge, MA: Harvard University Press, p. 55.

12. A. Cohen (1974), *Two-dimensional man: An essay on the anthropology of power and symbolism in complex society*, Berkeley: University of California Press, chap. 7; see also L. de Heusch (1964), "Mythe et société féodale: Le culte de Kubandwa dans le Rwanda traditionel," *Archives de Sociologie des Religions, 18*, 133-146.

13. J. M. Freeman (1979), *Untouchable: An Indian life history*, Stanford, CA: Stanford University Press, pp. 52-53.

14. See, in this connection, the suggestive analysis of power relations in Java by I. E. Slamet (1982) who writes: "This theatre-like aspect of Javanese life-style is, however, far from being limited to the lower strata of society; it is often still more outspoken with members of the elite, who have to stick to their ideal role in front of their subjects or inferiors (and often before their conscience, too) hiding the less ideal realities of their lives and aims beneath ritual or quasi-ritual appearance and performance." *Cultural strategies for survival: The plight of the Javanese* (Comparative Asian Studies Program Monograph 5), Rotterdam, p. 34.

15. S. C. Rogers (1975, November), "Female forms of power and the myth of male dominance: A model of female/male interaction in peasant society," *American Ethnologist, 2*(4), 727-756. For a more elaborate theoretical elaboration of this position, see S. Ardener (Ed.) (1977), *Perceiving women*, London: J. M. Dent, pp. 1-27.

16. This does not for a moment gainsay the fact that the symbols of official male dominance may be used by women as a strategic resource in gaining effective control of affairs. The fact that the "myth" is still a valuable weapon, even as a veil, says something about its continued efficacy.

17. R. Collins (1975), *Conflict sociology: Toward an explanatory science*, New York: Academic Press, pp. 118-119, 157.

18. Bourdieu (1977), p. 191. For a brilliant analysis of the social function of euphemisms by powerful groups, see M. Edelman (1974, Fall), "The political language of the 'helping professions,' " *Politics and Society*, 4(3), 295-310.

19. I have benefited here from R. Lakoff's (1975) discussion, *Language and women's place*, New York: Harper Colophon, p. 20ff.

20. The language of dominant discourse may, conversely, employ loaded terms to stigmatize a group, an activity, or a fact that, if described in ordinary language, might be less threatening or negative. Examples might be the use of "bandits" for armed revolutionaries or "petty bourgeois bacillus" for small trader or farmer.

21. E. D. Genovese (1974), *Roll, Jordan, roll: The world the slaves made*, New York: Pantheon, passim.

22. So, of course, can individuals be called upon in this sense to put up or shut up. Graham Greene's *The Comedians* is precisely focused on this issue. Its not-quite-a-charlatan anti-hero is forced to choose between acting bravely in accord with his bragging or to admit, finally, before the woman he loves, that he is a fraud.

23. The most persuasive empirical demonstrations of this point may be found in M. Marriott (1975), "Little communities in an indigenous civilization," in M. Marriott (Ed.), *Village India: Studies in the little community*, Chicago: University of Chicago Press, pp. 171-222; and G. W. Skinner (1975), *Marketing and social structure in Rural China*, Tucson, AZ: Association of Asian Studies.

24. The exception to this generalization occurs when elites may wish to provoke a confrontation with subordinates because they feel they have the resources to win in a showdown and thereby realign the terms of subordination in their favor.

25. I am grateful to Peter Sahlins for bringing this example to my attention. It comes from E. Frenay (Ed.) (1979), *Cahiers de doléances de la province de Roussillon, 1789,* Perpignan: Direction des Services d'Archives, pp. 548-549.

26. Thus a petition to a minister from the same region in 1826 which, in effect, complains about taxes collected for the use of forests and pastures includes the following passage lest the communes' plea be misunderstood: "This is an observation and not a direct demand that we address to you in this respect . . . " (copy from archives supplied by Peter Sahlins).

27. My contribution to this volume is drawn in part from chapter three of a book-length manuscript now in progress and tentatively entitled *Masks of domination: Masks of subordination.* It deals with this fugitive realm of political conflict.

28. E. Goffman (1971), *Relations in public: Microstudies in public order*, New York: Basic Books, p. 113ff.

29. See, for example, R. Isaac, "Communication and control: Authority metaphors and power contests on Colonel Landon Carter's Virginia plantation, 1752-1778," in S. Wilentz (Ed.), *The rites of power: Symbolism, ritual, and politics since the middle ages*, Philadelphia: University of Pennsylvania Press, pp. 275-302. In Melville's remarkable story "Benito Cereno," the Spanish captain, pretending to be master of a slave-crew, makes an apology the condition for removing shackles: "Say but one word, 'pardon,' and your chains shall be off." H. Melville (1968), "Benito Cereno," in *Billy Budd and other stories*, New York: Penguin, p. 183.

48

Los Vendidos[1]

Luis M. Valdez

Characters

Honest Sancho	Johnny
Secretary	Revolucionario
Farm Worker	Mexican-American

Scene: Honest Sancho's Used Mexican Lot and Mexican Curio Shop. Three models are on display in Honest Sancho's shop: to the right, there is a Revolucionario, complete with sombrero, carrilleras,[2] and carabina 30-30. At center, on the floor, there is the Farm Worker, under a broad straw sombrero. At stage left is the Pachuco, filero[3] in hand.

(Honest Sancho is moving among his models, dusting them off and preparing for another day of business.)

Sancho: Bueno, bueno, mis monos, vamos a ver a quien vendemos ahora, ¿no? *(To audience.)* ¡Quihubo![4] I'm Honest Sancho and this is my shop. Antes fui contratista pero ahora logré tener mi negocito.[5] All I need now is a customer. *(A bell rings offstage.)* Ay, a customer!

Secretary *(Entering):* Good morning, I'm Miss Jiménez from—

Sancho: ¡Ah, una chicana! Welcome, welcome Señorita Jiménez.

Secretary *(Anglo pronunciation):* JIM-enez.

Sancho: ¿Qué?

Secretary: My name is Miss JIM-enez. Don't you speak English? What's wrong with you?

Sancho: Oh, nothing. Señorita JIM-enez. I'm here to help you.

Secretary: That's better. As I was starting to say, I'm a secretary from Governor Reagan's office, and we're looking for a Mexican type for the administration.

Sancho: Well, you come to the right place, lady. This is Honest Sancho's Used Mexican lot, and we got all types here. Any particular type you want?

Secretary: Yes, we were looking for somebody suave—

Sancho: Suave.

Secretary: Debonair.

Sancho: De buen aire.

Secretary: Dark.

Sancho: Prieto.

Secretary: But of course not too dark.

Sancho: No muy prieto.

Secretary: Perhaps, beige.

Sancho: Beige, just the tone. Así como cafecito con leche,[6] ¿no?

Secretary: One more thing. He must be hard working.

Sancho: That could only be one model. Stop right over here to the center of the shop, lady. *(They cross to the Farm Worker.)* This is our standard farm worker model. As you can see, in the words of our beloved Senator

George Murphy, he is "built close to the ground." Also take special notice of his four-ply Goodyear huaraches, made from the rain tire. This wide-brimmed sombrero is an extra added feature—keeps off the sun, rain, and dust.

Secretary: Yes, it does look durable.

Sancho: And our farm worker model is friendly. Muy amable.[7] Watch. (*Snaps his fingers.*)

Farm Worker (*Lifts up head*): Buenos días, señorita. (*His head drops.*)

Secretary: My, he's friendly.

Sancho: Didn't I tell you? Loves his patrones! But his most attractive feature is that he's hard working. Let me show you. (*Snaps fingers. Farm Worker stands.*)

Farm Worker: ¡El jale![8] (*He begins to work.*)

Sancho: As you can see, he is cutting grapes.

Secretary: Oh, I wouldn't know.

Sancho: He also picks cotton. (*Snap. Farm Worker begins to pick cotton.*)

Secretary: Versatile isn't he?

Sancho: He also picks melons. (*Snap. Farm Worker picks melons.*) That's his slow speed for late in the season. Here's his fast speed. (*Snap. Farm Worker picks faster.*)

Secretary: ¡Chihuahua! . . . I mean, goodness, he sure is a hard worker.

Sancho (*Pulls the Farm Worker to his feet*): And that isn't the half of it. Do you see these little holes on his arms that appear to be pores? During those hot sluggish days in the field, when the vines or the branches get so entangled, it's almost impossible to move; these holes emit a certain grease that allows our model to slip and slide right through the crop with no trouble at all.

Secretary: Wonderful. But is he economical?

Sancho: Economical? Señorita, you are looking at the Volkswagen of Mexicans. Pennies a day is all it takes. One plate of beans and tortillas will keep him going all day. That, and chile. Plenty of chile. Chile jalapenos, chile verde, chile colorado. But, of course, if you do give him chile (*Snap. Farm Worker turns left face. Snap. Farm Worker bends over.*) then you have to change his oil filter once a week.

Secretary: What about storage?

Sancho: No problem. You know these new farm labor camps our Honorable Governor Reagan has built out by Parlier or Raisin City?

They were designed with our model in mind. Five, six, seven, even ten in one of those shacks will give you no trouble at all. You can also put him in old barns, old cars, river banks. You can even leave him out in the field overnight with no worry!

Secretary: Remarkable.

Sancho: And here's an added feature: Every year at the end of the season, this model goes back to Mexico and doesn't return, automatically, until next Spring.

Secretary: How about that. But tell me: does he speak English?

Sancho: Another outstanding feature is that last year this model was programmed to go out on STRIKE! (*Snap.*)

Farm Worker: ¡HUELGA! ¡HUELGA! Hermanos, sálganse de esos files.[9] (*Snap. He stops.*)

Secretary: No! Oh no, we can't strike in the State Capitol.

Sancho: Well, he also scabs. (*Snap.*)

Farm Worker: Me vendo barato, ¿y qué?[10] (*Snap.*)

Secretary: That's much better, but you didn't answer my question. Does he speak English?

Sancho: Bueno . . . no, pero[11] he has other—

Secretary: No.

Sancho: Other features.

Secretary: NO! He just won't do!

Sancho: Okay, okay pues. We have other models.

Secretary: I hope so. What we need is something a little more sophisticated.

Sancho: Sophisti—¿qué?

Secretary: An urban model.

Sancho: Ah, from the city! Step right back. Over here in this corner of the shop is exactly what you're looking for. Introducing our new 1969 JOHNNY PACHUCO model! This is our fast-back model. Streamlined. Built for speed, low-riding, city life. Take a look at some of these features. Mag shoes, dual exhausts, green chartreuse paint-job, dark-tint windshield, a little poof on top. Let me just turn him on. (*Snap. Johnny walks to stage center with a pachuco bounce.*)

Secretary: What was that?

Sancho: That, señorita, was the Chicano shuffle.

Secretary: Okay, what does he do?

Sancho: Anything and everything necessary for city life. For instance, survival: He knife fights. (*Snap. Johnny pulls out switch blade and swings at Secretary.*)

(Secretary screams.)

Sancho: He dances. *(Snap.)*

Johnny *(Singing)*: "Angel Baby, my Angel Baby . . . " *(Snap.)*

Sancho: And here's a feature no city model can be without. He gets arrested, but not without resisting, of course. *(Snap.)*

Johnny: ¡En la madre, la placa![12] I didn't do it! I didn't do it! *(Johnny turns and stands up against an imaginary wall, legs spread out, arms behind his back.)*

Secretary: Oh no, we can't have arrests! We must maintain law and order.

Sancho: But he's bilingual!

Secretary: Bilingual?

Sancho: Simón que yes.[13] He speaks English! Johnny, give us some English. *(Snap.)*

Johnny *(Comes downstage)*: Fuck-you!

Secretary *(Gasps)*: Oh! I've never been so insulted in my whole life!

Sancho: Well, he learned it in your school.

Secretary: I don't care where he learned it.

Sancho: But he's economical!

Secretary: Economical?

Sancho: Nickels and dimes. You can keep Johnny running on hamburgers, Taco Bell tacos, Lucky Lager beer, Thunderbird wine, yesca—

Secretary: Yesca?

Sancho: Mota.

Secretary: Mota?

Sancho: Leños[14] . . . Marijuana. *(Snap; Johnny inhales on an imaginary joint.)*

Secretary: That's against the law!

Johnny *(Big smile, holding his breath)*: Yeah.

Sancho: He also sniffs glue. *(Snap. Johnny inhales glue, big smile.)*

Johnny: Tha's too much man, ése.

Secretary: No, Mr. Sancho, I don't think this—

Sancho: Wait a minute, he has other qualities I know you'll love. For example, an inferiority complex. *(Snap.)*

Johnny *(To Sancho)*: You think you're better than me, huh ése? *(Swings switch blade.)*

Sancho: He can also be beaten and he bruises, cut him and he bleeds; kick him and he— *(He beats, bruises and kicks Pachuco.)* would you like to try it?

Secretary: Oh, I couldn't.

Sancho: Be my guest. He's a great scapegoat.

Secretary: No, really.

Sancho: Please.

Secretary: Well, all right. Just once. *(She kicks Pachuco.)* Oh, he's so soft.

Sancho: Wasn't that good? Try again.

Secretary *(Kicks Pachuco)*: Oh, he's so wonderful! *(She kicks him again.)*

Sancho: Okay, that's enough, lady. You ruin the merchandise. Yes, our Johnny Pachuco model can give you many hours of pleasure. Why, the L.A.P.D. just bought twenty of these to train their rookie cops on. And talk about maintenance. Señorita, you are looking at an entirely self-supporting machine. You're never going to find our Johnny Pachuco model on the relief rolls. No, sir, this model knows how to liberate.

Secretary: Liberate?

Sancho: He steals. *(Snap. Johnny rushes the Secretary and steals her purse.)*

Johnny: ¡Dame esa bolsa, vieja![15] *(He grabs the purse and runs. Snap by Sancho. He stops.)* *(Secretary runs after Johnny and grabs purse away from him, kicking him as she goes.)*

Secretary: No, no, no! We can't have any *more* thieves in the State Administration. Put him back.

Sancho: Okay, we still got other models. Come on, Johnny, we'll sell you to some old lady. *(Sancho takes Johnny back to his place.)*

Secretary: Mr. Sancho, I don't think you quite understand what we need. What we need is something that will attract the women voters. Something more traditional, more romantic.

Sancho: Ah, a lover. *(He smiles meaningfully.)* Step right over here, señorita. Introducing our standard Revolucionario and/or Early California Bandit type. As you can see he is well-built, sturdy, durable. This is the International Harvester of Mexicans.

Secretary: What does he do?

Sancho: You name it, he does it. He rides horses, stays in the mountains, crosses deserts, plains, rivers, leads revolutions, follows revolutions, kills, can be killed, serves as a martyr, hero, movie star—did I say movie star? Did you ever see *Viva Zapata? Viva Villa? Villa Rides? Pancho Villa Returns? Pancho Villa Goes Back? Pancho Villa Meets Abbott and Costello—*

Secretary: I've never seen any of those.

Sancho: Well, he was in all of them. Listen to this. *(Snap.)*

Revolucionario (Screams): ¡VIVA VILLAAAAA!

Secretary: That's awfully loud.

Sancho: He has a volume control. (He adjusts volume. Snap.)

Revolucionario (Mousey voice): ¡Viva Villa!

Secretary: That's better.

Sancho: And even if you didn't see him in the movies, perhaps you saw him on TV. He makes commercials. (Snap.)

Revolucionario: Is there a Frito Bandito in your house?

Secretary: Oh yes, I've seen that one!

Sancho: Another feature about this one is that he is economical. He runs on raw horse-meat and tequila!

Secretary: Isn't that rather savage?

Sancho: Al contrario,[16] it makes him a lover. (Snap.)

Revolucionario (To Secretary): ¡Ay, mamasota, cochota, ven pa'ca! (He grabs Secretary and folds her back—Latin-Lover style.)

Sancho: (Snap. Revolucionario goes back upright.): Now wasn't that nice?

Secretary: Well, it was rather nice.

Sancho: And finally, there is one outstanding feature about this model I KNOW the ladies are going to love: He's a GENUINE antique! He was made in Mexico in 1910!

Secretary: Made in Mexico?

Sancho: That's right. Once in Tijuana, twice in Guadalajara, three times in Cuernavaca.

Secretary: Mr. Sancho, I thought he was an American product.

Sancho: No, but—

Secretary: No, I'm sorry. We can't buy anything but American-made products. He just won't do.

Sancho: But he's an antique!

Secretary: I don't care. You still don't understand what we need. It's true we need Mexican models such as these, but it's more important that he be *American.*

Sancho: American?

Secretary: That's right, and judging from what you've shown me, I don't think you have what we want. Well, my lunch hour's almost over; I better—

Sancho: Wait a minute! Mexican but American?

Secretary: That's correct.

Sancho: Mexican but . . . (A sudden flash) AMERICAN! Yeah, I think we've got exactly what

you want. He just came in today! Give me a minute. (He exits. Talks from backstage.) Here he is in the shop. Let me just get some papers off. There. Introducing our new 1970 Mexican-American! Ta-ra-ra-ra-ra-ra-RA-RAAA!

(Sancho brings out the Mexican-American model, a clean-shaven middle-class type in a business suit, with glasses.)

Secretary (Impressed): Where have you been hiding this one?

Sancho: He just came in this morning. Ain't he a beauty? Feast your eyes on him! Sturdy US STEEL frame, streamlined, modern. As a matter of fact, he is built exactly like our Anglo models except that he comes in a variety of darker shades: naugahyde, leather, or leatherette.

Secretary: Naugahyde.

Sancho: Well, we'll just write that down. Yes, señorita, this model represents the apex of American engineering! He is bilingual, college educated, ambitious! Say the word "acculturate" and he accelerates. He is intelligent, well-mannered, clean—did I say clean? (Snap. Mexican-American raises his arm.) Smell.

Secretary (Smells): Old Sobaco, my favorite.

Sancho (Snap. Mexican-American turns toward Sancho.): Eric! (To Secretary.) We call him Eric García. (To Eric.) I want you to meet Miss JIM-enez, Eric.

Mexican-American: Miss JIM-enez, I am delighted to make your acquaintance. (He kisses her hand.)

Secretary: Oh, my, how charming!

Sancho: Did you feel the suction? He has seven especially engineered suction cups right behind his lips. He's a charmer all right!

Secretary: How about boards? Does he function on boards?

Sancho: You name them, he is on them. Parole boards, draft boards, school boards, taco quality control boards, surf boards, two-by-fours.

Secretary: Does he function in politics?

Sancho: Señorita, you are looking at a political MACHINE. Have you ever heard of the OEO, EOC, COD, WAR ON POVERTY? That's our model! Not only that, he makes political speeches.

Secretary: May I hear one?

Sancho: With pleasure. *(Snap.)* Eric, give us a speech.

Mexican-American: Mr. Congressman, Mr. Chairman, members of the board, honored guests, ladies and gentlemen. *(Sancho and Secretary applaud.)* Please, please. I come before you as a Mexican-American to tell you about the problems of the Mexican. The problems of the Mexican stem from one thing and one thing alone: He's stupid. He's uneducated. He needs to stay in school. He needs to be ambitious, forward-looking, harder-working. He needs to think American, American, American, AMERICAN, AMERICAN, AMERICAN. GOD BLESS AMERICA! GOD BLESS AMERICA! GOD BLESS AMERICA!! *(He goes out of control.)* *(Sancho snaps frantically and the Mexican-American finally slumps forward, bending, at the waist.)*

Secretary: Oh my, he's patriotic too!

Sancho: Sí, señorita, he loves his country. Let me just make a little adjustment here. *(Stands Mexican-American up.)*

Secretary: What about upkeep? Is he economical?

Sancho: Well, no. I won't lie to you. The Mexican-American costs a little bit more, but you get what you pay for. He's worth every extra cent. You can keep him running on dry Martinis, Langendorf bread.

Secretary: Apple pie?

Sancho: Only Mom's. Of course, he's also programmed to eat Mexican food on ceremonial functions, but I must warn you: an overdose of beans will plug up his exhaust.

Secretary: Fine! There's just one more question: HOW MUCH DO YOU WANT FOR HIM?

Sancho: Well, I tell you what I'm gonna do. Today and today only, because you've been so sweet, I'm gonna let you steal this model from me! I'm gonna let you drive him off the lot for the simple price of—let's see taxes and license included—$15,000.

Secretary: Fifteen thousand DOLLARS? For a MEXICAN!

Sancho: Mexican? What are you talking, lady? This is a Mexican-AMERICAN! We had to melt down two pachucos, a farm worker, and three gabachos to make this model! You want quality, but you gotta pay for it! This is no cheap run-about. He's got class!

Secretary: Okay, I'll take him.

Sancho: You will?

Secretary: Here's your money.

Sancho: You mind if I count it?

Secretary: Go right ahead.

Sancho: Well, you'll get your pink slip in the mail. Oh, do you want me to wrap him up for you? We have a box in the back.

Secretary: No, thank you. The Governor is having a luncheon this afternoon, and we need a brown face in the crowd. How do I drive him?

Sancho: Just snap your fingers. He'll do anything you want.

(Secretary snaps. Mexican-American steps forward.)

Mexican-American: RAZA QUERIDA, ¡VAMOS LEVANTANDO ARMAS PARA LIBERARNOS DE ESTOS DESGRACIADOS GABACHOS QUE NOS EXPLOTAN! VAMOS.[17]

Secretary: What did he say?

Sancho: Something about lifting arms, killing white people, etc.

Secretary: But he's not supposed to say that!

Sancho: Look, lady, don't blame me for bugs from the factory. He's your Mexican-American; you bought him, now drive him off the lot!

Secretary: But he's broken!

Sancho: Try snapping another finger.

(Secretary snaps. Mexican-American comes to life again.)

Mexican-American: ¡ESTA GRAN HUMANIDAD HA DICHO BASTA! Y SE HA PUESTO EN MARCHA! ¡BASTA! ¡BASTA! ¡VIVA LA RAZA! ¡VIVA LA CAUSA! ¡VIVA LA HUELGA! ¡VIVAN LOS BROWN BERETS! ¡VIVAN LOS ESTUDIANTES! ¡CHICANO POWER![18]

(The Mexican-American turns toward the Secretary, who gasps and backs up. He keeps turning toward the Pachuco, Farm Worker, and Revolucionario, snapping his fingers and turning each of them on, one by one.)

Pachuco *(Snap. To Secretary)*: I'm going to get you, baby! ¡Viva La Raza!

Farm Worker *(Snap. To Secretary)*: ¡Viva la huelga! ¡Viva la huelga! ¡VIVA LA HUELGA!

Revolucionario *(Snap. To Secretary)*: ¡Viva la revolución! ¡VIVA LA REVOLUCION!

(The three models join together and advance toward the Secretary who backs up and runs

out of the shop screaming. Sancho is at the other end of the shop holding his money in his hand. All freeze. After a few seconds of silence, the Pachuco moves and stretches, shaking his arms and loosening up. The Farm Worker and Revolucionario do the same. Sancho stays where he is, frozen to his spot.)

Johnny: Man, that was a long one, ése. (Others agree with him.)

Farm Worker: How did we do?

Johnny: Perty good, look all that lana, man! (He goes over to Sancho and removes the money from his hand. Sancho stays where he is.)

Revolucionario: En la madre, look at all the money.

Johnny: We keep this up, we're going to be rich.

Farm Worker: They think we're machines.

Revolucionario: Burros.

Johnny: Puppets.

Mexican-American: The only thing I don't like is—how come I always got to play the godamn Mexican-American?

Johnny: That's what you get for finishing high school.

Farm Worker: How about our wages, ése?

Johnny: Here it comes right now. $3,000 for you, $3,000 for you, $3,000 for you, and $3,000 for me. The rest we put back into the business.

Mexican-American: Too much, man. Heh, where you vatos going tonight?

Farm Worker: I'm going over to Concha's. There's a party.

Johnny: Wait a minute, vatos. What about our salesman? I think he needs an oil job.

Revolucionario: Leave him to me.

(The Pachuco, Farm Worker, and Mexican-American exit, talking loudly about their plans for the night. The Revolucionario goes over to Sancho, removes his derby hat and cigar, lifts him up and throws him over his shoulder. Sancho hangs loose, lifeless.)

Revolucionario (To audience): He's the best model we got! ¡Ajua! (Exit.)
(End.)

Notes

1. *Los Vendidos*: sellouts.

2. *Carrilleras*: literally chin straps, but may refer to cartridge belts.

3. *Pachuco*: Chicano slang for a 1940s zoot suiter; *filero*: blade.

4. *Bueno, bueno. . . . Quihubo*: "Good, good, my cute ones, let's see who we can sell now, O.K.?"

5. *Antes fui . . . negocito*: "I used to be a contractor, but now I've succeeded in having my little business."

6. *Así como . . . leche*: like coffee with milk.

7. *Muy amable*: very friendly.

8. *El jale*: the job.

9. *HUELGA! HUELGA! . . . esos files*: "Strike! Strike! Brothers, leave those rows."

10. *Me vendo . . . qué*: "I come cheap, so what?"

11. *Bueno . . . no, pero*: "Well, no, but . . . "

12. *En la . . . placa*: "Wow, the police!"

13. *Simón . . . yes*: yeah, sure.

14. *Leños*: "joints" of marijuana.

15. *Dame esa . . . vieja*: "Gimme that bag, old lady!"

16. *Al contrario*: on the contrary.

17. *RAZA QUERIDA. . . . VAMOS*: "Beloved Raza, let's pick up arms to liberate ourselves from those damned whites that exploit us! Let's go."

18. *ESTA GRAN . . . CHICANO POWER*: "This great mass of humanity has said enough! And it begins to march! Enough! Enough! Long live La Raza! Long live the Cause! Long live the strike! Long live the Brown Berets! Long live the students! Chicano Power!"

49

Talking Back

bell hooks

In the world of the southern black community I grew up in, "back talk" and "talking back" meant speaking as an equal to an authority figure. It meant daring to disagree and sometimes it just meant having an opinion. In the "old school," children were meant to be seen and not heard. My great-grandparents, grandparents, and parents were all from the old school. To make yourself heard if you were a child was to invite punishment, the back-hand lick, the slap across the face that would catch you unaware, or the feel of switches stinging your arms and legs.

To speak then when one was not spoken to was a courageous act—an act of risking and daring. And yet it was hard not to speak in warm rooms where heated discussions began at the crack of dawn, women's voices filling the air, giving orders, making threats, fussing. Black men may have excelled in the art of poetic preaching in the male-dominated church, but in the church of the home where the everyday rules of how to live and how to act were established it was black women who preached. There, black women spoke in a language so rich, so poetic, that it felt to me like being shut off from life, smothered to death if one was not allowed to participate.

It was in that world of woman talk (the men were often silent, often absent) that was born in me the craving to speak, to have a voice, and not just any voice but one that could be identified as belonging to me. To make my voice, I had to speak, to hear myself talk—and talk I did—darting in and out of grown folk's conversations and dialogues, answering questions that were not directed at me, endlessly asking questions, making speeches. Needless to say, the punishments for these acts of speech seemed endless. They were intended to silence me—the child—and more particularly the girl child. Had I been a boy they might have encouraged me to speak believing that I might someday be called to preach. There was no "calling" for talking girls, no legitimized rewarded speech. The punishments I received for "talking back" were intended to suppress all possibility that I would create my own speech. That speech was to be suppressed so the "right speech of womanhood" would emerge.

Within feminist circles, silence is often seen as the sexist "right speech of womanhood"—the sign of woman's submission to patriarchal authority. This emphasis on woman's silence may be an accurate remembering of what has taken place in the households of women from WASP backgrounds in the United States, but in black communities (and diverse ethnic communities) women have not been silent. Their voices can be heard. Certainly for black women, our struggle has not been to emerge from silence into speech but to change the nature and direction of our speech, to make a speech that compels listeners, one that is heard.

Our speech, "the right speech of womanhood," was often the soliloquy, the talking into thin air, the talking to ears that do not hear you—the talk that is simply not listened to. Unlike the black male preacher whose speech was to be heard, who was to be listened to, whose words were to be remembered, the voices of black women—giving orders, making threats, fussing—could be tuned out, could become a kind of background music, audible but not acknowledged as significant speech. Dialogue—the sharing of speech and recognition—took place not between mother and child or mother and male authority figure but among black women. I can remember watching fascinated as our mother talked with her mother, sisters, and women friends. The intimacy and intensity of their speech—the satisfaction they received from talking to one another, the pleasure, the joy. It was in this world of woman speech, loud talk, angry words, women with tongues quick and sharp, tender sweet tongues, touching our world with their words, that I made speech my birthright—and the right to voice, to authorship, a privilege I would not be denied. It was in that world and because of it that I came to dream of writing, to write.

Writing was a way to capture speech, to hold onto it, keep it close. And so I wrote down bits and pieces of conversations, confessing in cheap diaries that soon fell apart from too much handling, expressing the intensity of my sorrow, the anguish of speech—for I was always saying the wrong thing, asking the wrong questions. I could not confine my speech to the necessary corners and concerns of life. I hid these writings under my bed, in pillow stuffings, among faded underwear. When my sisters found and read them, they ridiculed and mocked me—poking fun. I felt violated, ashamed,

as if the secret parts of my self had been exposed, brought into the open, and hung like newly clean laundry, out in the air for everyone to see. The fear of exposure, the fear that one's deepest emotions and innermost thoughts would be dismissed as mere nonsense, felt by so many young girls keeping diaries, holding and hiding speech, seems to me now one of the barriers that women have needed and still need to destroy so that we are no longer pushed into secrecy or silence.

Despite my feelings of violation, of exposure, I continued to speak and write, choosing my hiding places well, learning to destroy work when no safe place could be found. I was never taught absolute silence, I was taught that it was important to speak but to talk a talk that was in itself a silence. Taught to speak and yet beware of the betrayal of too much heard speech, I experienced intense confusion and deep anxiety in my efforts to speak and write. Reciting poems at Sunday afternoon church service might be rewarded. Writing a poem (when one's time could be "better" spent sweeping, ironing, learning to cook) was luxurious activity, indulged in at the expense of others. Questioning authority, raising issues that were not deemed appropriate subjects brought pain, punishments—like telling mama I wanted to die before her because I could not live without her—that was crazy talk, crazy speech, the kind that would lead you to end up in a mental institution. "Little girl," I would be told, "if you don't stop all this crazy talk and crazy acting you are going to end up right out there at Western State."

Madness, not just physical abuse, was the punishment for too much talk if you were female. Yet even as this fear of madness haunted me, hanging over my writing like a monstrous shadow, I could not stop the words, making thought, writing speech. For this terrible madness which I feared, which I was sure was the destiny of daring women born to intense speech (after all, the authorities emphasized this point daily), was not as threatening as imposed silence, as suppressed speech.

Safety and sanity were to be sacrificed if I was to experience defiant speech. Though I risked them both, deep-seated fears and anxieties characterized my childhood days. I would speak but I would not ride a bike, play hardball, or hold the gray kitten. Writing about the ways we are hurt by negative traumas in our growing-up years, psychoanalyst Alice Miller makes the point in *For Your Own Good* that it is not clear why childhood wounds become for some folk an opportunity to grow, to move forward rather than backward in the process of self-realization. Certainly, when I reflect on the trials of my growing-up years, the many punishments, I can see now that in resistance I learned to be vigilant in the nourishment of my spirit, to be tough, to courageously protect that spirit from forces that would break it.

While punishing me, my parents often spoke about the necessity of breaking my spirit. Now when I ponder the silences, the voices that are not heard, the voices of those wounded and/or oppressed individuals who do not speak or write, I contemplate the acts of persecution, torture—the terrorism that breaks spirits, that makes creativity impossible. I write these words to bear witness to the primacy of resistance struggle in any situation of domination (even within family life); to the strength and power that emerges from sustained resistance and the profound conviction that these forces can be healing, can protect us from dehumanization and despair.

These early trials, wherein I learned to stand my ground, to keep my spirit intact, came vividly to mind after I published *Ain't I a Woman* and the book was sharply and harshly criticized. While I had expected a climate of critical dialogue, I was not expecting a critical avalanche that had the power in its intensity to crush spirit, to push one into silence. Since that time I have heard stories about black women, about women of color, who write and publish (even when the work is quite successful), having nervous breakdowns, being made mad because they cannot bear the harsh responses of family, friends, and unknown critics, or becoming silent, unproductive. Surely, the absence of a humane critical response has tremendous impact on the writer from any oppressed, colonized group who endeavors to speak. For us, true speaking is not solely an expression of creative power; it is an act of resistance, a political gesture that challenges the politics of domination that would render us nameless and voiceless. As such it is a courageous act—as such, it represents a threat. To those who wield oppressive power, that which is threatening must necessarily be wiped out, annihilated, silenced.

Recently, efforts by black women writers to call attention to our work serve to highlight both our presence and absence. Whenever I peruse women's bookstores I am struck not by the rapidly growing body of feminist writing by black women but by the paucity of available published material. Those of us who write and are published remain few in number. The context of silence is varied and multi-dimensional. Most obvious are the ways racism, sexism, and class exploitation act as agents to suppress and silence. Less obvious are the inner struggles, the efforts made to gain the necessary confidence to write, to re-write, to fully develop craft and skill—and the extent to which such efforts fail.

Although I have wanted writing to be my life-work since childhood, it has been difficult for me to claim "writer" as part of that which identifies and shapes my everyday reality. Even after publishing books, I would often speak of wanting to be a writer as though these works did not exist. And though I would be told, "you are a writer," I was not yet ready to fully affirm this truth. Part of myself was still held captive by domineering forces of history, of familial life that had charted a map of silence, of right speech.

I had not completely let go of the fear of saying the wrong thing, of being punished. Somewhere in the deep recesses of my mind, I believed I could avoid both responsibility and punishment if I did not declare myself a writer.

One of the many reasons I chose to write using the pseudonym bell hooks, a family name (mother to Sarah Oldham, grandmother to Rosa Bell Oldham, great-grandmother to me), was to construct a writer-identity that would challenge and subdue all impulses leading me away from speech into silence. I was a young girl buying bubble gum at the corner store when I first really heard the full name bell hooks: I had just "talked back" to a grown person. Even now I can recall the surprised look, the mocking tones that informed me I must be kin to bell hooks—a sharp-tongued woman, a woman who spoke her mind, a woman who was not afraid to talk back. I claimed this legacy of defiance, of will, of courage, affirming my link to female ancestors who were bold and daring in their speech. Unlike my bold and daring mother and grandmother, who were not supportive of talking back, even though they were assertive and powerful in their speech, bell hooks as I discovered, claimed, and invented her, was my ally, my support.

The initial act of talking back outside the home was empowering. It was the first of many acts of defiant speech that would make it possible for me to emerge as an independent thinker and writer. In retrospect, "talking back" became for me a rite of initiation, testing my courage, strengthening my commitment, preparing me for the days ahead—the days when writing, rejection notices, periods of silence, publication, ongoing development seem impossible but necessary.

Moving from silence into speech is for the oppressed, the colonized, the exploited, and those who stand and struggle side by side a gesture of defiance that heals, that makes new life and new growth possible. It is that act of speech, of "talking back," that is no mere gesture of empty words, that is the expression of moving from object to subject—the liberated voice.

Epilogue

Deconstruction

In the book *The Sword and the Stone*, by T. H. White, a wise old badger tells his young apprentice, Wart, how all the creatures of the earth came to be as they are. According to the badger, God assembled the multitude of fledgling embryos before him on the sixth day of creation and explained that he was going to hand out gifts. The embryos could each choose two or three gifts. These gifts would serve as a set of tools that would mark the creature's unique existence on earth. The embryos chattered excitedly among themselves about the possible combinations of tools each might ask for. When the time came, each embryo stepped forward and requested its gifts from God. Some embryos asked for arms that were diggers, or garden forks, some chose to use their arms as flying machines, others asked for bodies like boats and arms that were oars; one of the lizards decided to swap its entire body for blotting paper. Still others asked to be able to use their mouths as drills or offensive weapons. Finally it was the turn of the embryo called "human." This small, naked creature approached God and stammered shyly, "I have considered your generous offer, and I thank you for it, but I choose to stay as I am." "Well chosen," thundered God. "In deciding to retain your embryonic form you will have use of all the gifts that mark the being of each of the other creatures. You will exist always as potential; the potential to take up and put down the tools of the other creatures, the potential to create uniforms and tools of your own design and to wear and discard them as you see fit. You have chosen wisely human. We wish you well in your earthly journey."

A lesson of symbolic interactionism is that humans do exist as embryonic potential. As creatures we are capable of creating, taking on, and casting off various identities and cultural institutions. As embryos, our potential is limited only by our imagination and our ability to assemble the materials necessary to realize our visions. In this final note, we speak to the theme that the human enterprise is the construction of reality. The creation of shared meaning is the distinctive mark of our species. However, the history of Western consciousness suggests a somewhat paradoxical acceptance of this possibility; as humans we are eager to embrace our creative potential and, at the same time, reluctant to recognize the responsibility that it implies. In this essay we discuss two observations with regard to the production of reality and its relevance in daily life. The first observation is that, as a general society, we have difficulty recognizing our potential as the creators of our own realities. Instead of awe and inspiration at the possibilities of complex human social coordination, we seem inclined to attribute human culture to the existence of extra-human forces, some form of external order. The second observation is that to the extent that as an intellectual community we do acknowledge our roles in the production of reality, there is a tendency to focus this attention on tearing down social constructions. We pay far less attention to the possibilities indicated by our species' remarkable collective skills for producing meaningful cultural forms. The result, as we will elaborate, is being either unaware of our potential to author our own reality, in which case we are social robots, or using our creative pen to strike out what others have created, thereby cutting ourselves adrift as cynics in a meaningless world. Following the discussion of this dilemma, we offer an alternative route that emphasizes the mindful construction of reality.

Reason, Enlightenment, and Natural Law

Since the Age of Enlightenment (see essay 1) the cornerstone of Western thought has been the supremacy of human reason. The power of the collective human mind replaced the capricious authority of traditional gods as the creative force behind the social realm that our species inhabits. Human groups are capable of self-governance and are masters of their own destinies. Despite our firm acceptance of these fundamental principles of "enlightenment," as individuals and social scientists we continue to cling to the vestiges of a philosophy that assumes an inherent natural order to the universe. In so doing we fail to recognize our full human potential and neglect responsibility for our own creations. The human animal assembles raw materials and builds physical structures that are astoundingly diverse and magnif-icent in the combination of form and function. As a species we are genuinely proud of these structures, whether they be the grand cathedrals of Europe or a backyard tree house. We would never think to attribute the construction of these structures to anything other than human ingenuity and activity. Even the Egyptian pyramids, despite their mysterious origins, are assumed at the very least to be human constructions. Yet, we are less willing to recognize and acknowledge a similar role in the construction of our social institutions. We seem to not trust the existence of these less tangible but nonetheless influential social structures unless their origins can be attributed to some natural law or unseen god. We are odd creatures in this denial of our own potential to conceive of and construct the social realm in which we live out our lives. A central implication of social constructionism is that humans are the sole authors of the shared cultural meaning that makes their existence worthwhile. Somehow this notion disappoints many people. They would rather trade in their creative, observable, embryonic potential for an unseen, elusive form of natural order. The latter presumably offers more security. It also frees us from assuming responsibility for the existence and perpetuation of embarrassing or undesirable social institutions. If we can attribute these institutions to forces beyond our control, then we do not have to lend a hand toward changing them.

The Western intellectual community has been more willing to acknowledge the human role in the construction of reality. In the last few decades this has been especially the case in the social sciences and the humanities where the paradigm of social constructionism has begun to develop as a strong alternative to the natural law orientation of logical positivism. The latter, positive science, seeks to "discover" truth as expressed in the natural world. The former assumes that all truth is socially constructed and explores the underlying assumptions that drive the dominant systems of belief in various cultures, including the scientific community. This form of cultural analysis is known as "deconstructionism" or "critical theory." This path follows the road of infinite relativism in which all expressions of culture can be taken apart, "deconstructed" to expose the underlying assumptions and values of the creators. In and of itself this is a useful exercise if done for the purpose of critically evaluating the direction of these cultures and our own place in them. All too often, however, the path leads to a yawning abyss into which all cultural institutions must be thrown simply because it can be demonstrated that, ultimately, they are the product of some group's particular biases and relative position in the social order. This seems to us a rather hasty and irresponsible conclusion.

The Logic of Deconstructionism

Physicists were among the first to suspect that at the edge of a perceived natural order lurked chaos. The implication for the study of social institutions is that any order that we experience may well be the result of human creation rather than an indication of natural order. Amidst the forces of chaos we create and live in our own houses of order. When one pauses to consider the notion that humans create their own realities, it is a remarkable idea, an idea of tremendous potential. Beginning with the assumption that reality is socially constructed, several influential thinkers emphasize that many forms of social order represent the perspective and values of a privileged few. This line of thought is known as critical theory. Exponents of critical theory demonstrate that many prevailing social institutions reflect the interests and values of groups who control the means of cultural and economic production. In its inception this perspective was meant to be an indictment of white upper-middle-class males of European extraction. The intent of critical theory was to show that the science and technology practiced by this class was not, in fact, the discovery of natural law that its proponents claimed it to be, but a socially constructed reality that served to maintain the privileged position of this small group. Deconstructionism, a theoretical cousin of critical theory, attempts to "deconstruct" the logic and cultural forms of this group in order to demonstrate that their ideas are in fact self-fulfilling realities and not instances of a universal order that all should succumb to.

Practitioners of deconstruction consider the enterprise to be an apolitical tool used to reveal unacknowledged assumptions in the rhetoric of science. However, an unforeseen consequence is the transformation of this tool into a theoretical wrecking ball that, when swung indiscriminately, may not only expose the biases of some of our cultural institutions but also knock out the foundation upon which a meaningful existence is built. This is not the intention of those who practice intellectual deconstructionism. Nonetheless, it is our observation that it may, in fact, be a consequence of this practice.

Although the first target of critical theory and deconstructionism was primarily the white, male, middle class, it soon became evident that no social group was exempt from the theoretical wrecking ball. Any and all cultural expressions can be disassembled in order to point out the prejudices and taken-for-granted assumptions embedded in the logic of the group's beliefs and institutions. In general the practice of deconstructionism is a sound one. It instructs us to dig beyond the obvious and taken-for-granted in order to uncover the philosophies and interests that drive our beliefs and perpetuate our social institutions. These nonobvious special interests often lead to unintended and undesirable personal and social consequences. Thus it is useful to be aware of them. However, if not practiced with wisdom and insight, the deconstruction of social reality becomes nothing more than a weapon used by one group to attack the beliefs and practices of another. In its worst form deconstructionism becomes an instrument of annihilation of anything that social groups consider meaningful and worth an investment of human energy. The backlash against "political correctness" that has raged across North American campuses in recent months can be read as a reaction against the implications of deconstructionism as a political philosophy.

Many social scientists practice a more benign, less politically charged form of deconstructionism in the name of "value free" science. Sociologists in particular are eager to dismantle various social patterns, institutions, and belief systems in order to demonstrate that these are culturally relative social constructions, not natural occurrences. This sort of "disruption" is considered neat and socially worthwhile in that it contributes to the development of critical thinking skills. In a seminar that we offer to graduate students who are preparing to be college teachers we ask, What is worth teaching in sociology? Invariably the answer is that it is important to teach students how to think critically by "blowing away" or "deconstructing" their taken-for-granted assumptions about social reality. It is assumed that somehow this mode of instruction, which does effectively demonstrate that beliefs and practices are culturally relative, will also encourage students to be more tolerant and accepting of other social groups. Our observation is that often, instead of increased tolerance, students seem to grow cynical and alienated. The tools of deconstructionism, when used to their logical extreme, teach us how to dismantle our socially constructed realities but leave us with nothing but a pile of rubble to stand in. The conclusion is a disturbing one. If we do not engage in an informed scrutiny of our own socially constructed realities then we risk being driven by the mindless performance of social rituals and previously determined social scripts that have long ceased to have any meaning for us personally. But, if we deconstruct these beliefs and rituals to see what they are made of we risk eroding the very foundation of a meaningful existence. Are these the only choices: social robot or cynic?

We do think that there is a more hopeful way around this conundrum. It involves not only learning to recognize and deconstruct social realities but also participating mindfully in the construction of reality. The full realization of the creative potential of the human enterprise is in learning to build realities and to take responsibility for the consequences of these constructions. Deconstruction can be done with the intent of reassembling the building blocks in a meaningful way and the awareness of the consequences of this reassembly. This is not an easy agenda. To critique and tear down is simpler than to build with purpose. Yet, if we want to escape the clutches of previously spun social webs and at the same time avoid being left hanging by the single precarious thread of cynicism, we must be willing to spin alternative realities.

Reconstruction

There are two processes that detract from the mindful construction of meaningful realities. We refer to these as deconstructionism and ossification (and its companion, entropy). We have discussed the former and suggested that although it is a necessary first step toward the mindful construction of a meaningful reality, it can become nothing more than a tool of destruction if used only as an end in itself. This conclusion is a logic that implies that because cultural forms are human creations they are somehow less worthwhile than if they were the result of an extra-human force. To embrace this logic is to allow the ghost of a philosophy of natural order to haunt the possibilities of a socially constructed reality. We observed that this conclusion is a rather odd and hasty dismissal of the human potential as a creative entity. It is a position that implies that our own constructions are not worth anything simply because we also have the ability to deconstruct them as well.

Consider the Great Wall of China. This astounding structure is a remarkable feat of human coordination and labor. We are not any less amazed by its existence when we pause to ponder the reasons for its construction, or the fact that it could also be disassembled stone by stone by the same human hands that initially constructed it. It is therefore curious that we are reluctant to experience a similar awe and wonderment in the understanding that human culture is also the product of a highly complex and intricate set of coordinated human actions. Consider the production of the ritual known as "the football game" in this culture. In order to produce this ritual successfully, participants must first share a common conception of time and how to ascertain the block of time during which this production will take place. Persons must also agree on the definition of the general emotional tenor of the event—is it to be a sad, morose occasion, one of serious contemplation, or one of joviality and good-natured fun? There must also be a common understanding about who will hang out on the hard wooden benches and yell, and who will run around on the field. Add to this the notion that some persons will form one pack who will play in opposition to another pack and you have an increasingly complex set of circumstances that requires the coordination and cooperation of a huge mass of people. Note what an amazing achievement the production and maintenance of cultural reality is. The next time you participate in a collective event ponder all of the elements that must be commonly understood, performed and coordinated by this group of people in order to produce the reality of the moment. The creation and maintenance of cultural institutions is a profound occurrence.

We know when to tear down a building that has ceased to serve any useful function and may even be a source of danger. However, we sometimes rattle around in dusty old social institutions that are cracked and crumbling simply because we fail to realize that it is within our power to step beyond the confines of this structure and build others. Humans create social institutions for reasons. For example, the institution of gift exchange serves as a symbolic expression of alliance with another person or group. This symbolic basis promotes trust between the parties and enables them to exchange goods without fear of being cheated. Thus gift exchange is a useful institution, a recipe for successful exchange. Our social recipes sometimes have a tendency to harden or "ossify" (see essay 2). What may have served as a useful basis for achieving some particular end becomes an ideology and an end in itself. When this occurs our social constructions may cease to serve any useful function but we may persist in maintaining them simply because they have become permanent, hardened features of our social landscape. In this regard we may be contributing to the maintenance of our own prisons. The point is not that all old social institutions should be torn down, but that we should be mindful regarding the purpose of the social institutions that our actions (or inactions) help to perpetuate. This becomes increasingly difficult to recognize the more hardened, or ossified, the institution becomes.

Consider the social institution prevalent in American universities of giving exams. In the seminar mentioned above we ask prospective college teachers to provide us with a rationale for giving exams. In most cases the participants struggle with this assignment; the institution of giving exams has become an ossified element of the educational landscape. If exams are written and administered with a particular purpose, such as providing feedback for the student and the instructor, or to serve as an incentive to organize chunks of information, then we are participating in the mindful maintenance of this social institution. To give exams simply because "that's what has always been done" is to rattle around in a potentially useless social structure. Once one has isolated the purpose for a particular social reality, it is possible to devise potentially more useful routes. For example, a sometimes unfortunate outcome of the examination procedure is the unnecessary rank-ordering of students. If the purpose is to motivate students to organize and articulate their knowledge then it is possible to create an alternative form of exercise to the exam, one that more directly serves the intended purpose. If, on the other hand, the purpose is to rank-order persons for placement in another institution, such as the labor market, then instructors should be mindfully aware that their examination procedures serve to perpetuate this stratified institution. Again, the point is to understand how one's participation in particular cultural rites and rituals serves to perpetuate the existence of social institutions. Here is where the tools of deconstruction serve a useful end, the exploration of ossified structures. Such explorations need not lead to the conclusion that the entire structure should be dismantled, however. Mindful construction instructs us to ask what purpose the social ritual serves and whether or not we want to participate in that purpose. If so, are there alternative routes to accomplishing the same outcome with less problematic side-effects? Some undesirable social constructions are less easily torn down than others because the ideologies that support them have become extremely hardened. For instance, monogamous pair-bonding between opposite sexes is a functional means of perpetuating the species in many cultures. The association of reproduction with sexual satisfaction, emotional support, companionship, and economic support is a Western cultural institution, known as marriage, that implies that all these needs can be met by bonding with a single person of the opposite sex. Recently, there have been many challenges to this cultural reality. Some of the challenges come from homosexuals who suggest that an alternative social script is that companionship and sexuality are independent of reproduction, and hence, do not preclude persons of the same sex from monogamous pair-bonding rituals. Other groups emphasize the relationship between persons who provide economic and emotional support for one another without a sexual component. These alternatives challenge the ossified institutional reality of the "family" as persons mindfully consider just what sort of primary relationships in which they wish to invest their financial, sexual, and emotional resources. Two points are worth underscoring here. Social institutions are created and maintained through the active participation of individuals. To the extent that we are aware of our reasons for participating in various cultural productions we can be said to be mindfully engaged in the construction of reality. If, however, we are simply participating in patterns that "have always been," then we risk being social robots living in the brittle houses constructed by previous generations for their own purposes. Change does not occur simply by tearing down these structures, however. A meaningful existence requires that we construct other institutions in place of those that have been torn down. This is the focus of our last point.

If there is any pattern in a state of nature that seems to play itself out in human institutions as well it is that of entropy. Entropy is the natural process of decay. An ironic feature of the social construction of reality is that the meaning and purpose of many of our social institutions are constantly threatened with decay unless participants infuse these institutions with mindful energy. As we have noted, a great deal of mindful intellectual energy has been devoted to deconstructing ossified social realities. Often the result of this activity is isolated individuals cut adrift from any meaningful social activity: cynics. This path toward cynicism is exacerbated by the process of entropy. If we do not invest energy in those social productions that matter, they will cease to be meaningful dwelling places. Together ossification and entropy suggest that, left to themselves, our social institutions will harden into brittle and nonserviceable cultural forms which bind us at the same time that they cease to hold much meaning for us. This is not a pleasant outcome. Yet it has been the predicted outcome of many of the classical sociological thinkers. Max Weber, for example, referred to the process as the "Iron Cage." Karl Marx warned that individuals who were alienated from meaningful forms of social activity would suffer alienation and cynicism. Emile Durkheim proposed that groups that failed to produce meaningful social rituals would be unable to regulate the behavior of group members; these members would suffer from a sense of purposelessness and lack of regulation known as anomie.

If, as we have suggested in part 4, social realities are fragile and require maintenance, then it is reasonable to conclude that meaningful personal and social routines require our active participation. We have demonstrated that it is possible to maintain many cultural institutions through mindless, unexamined participation in taken-for-granted routines. To the extent that we do so we perpetuate realities that have little meaning for us and fail to consider ways in which we might actively and meaningfully produce alternative realities. In learning about and accepting alternative realities we learn tolerance and become aware of other possible scripts. In questioning and deconstructing our social institutions we avoid the pitfalls of being mindlessly driven by outmoded, ossified cultural norms. These lessons are worth learning, but there is an additional step if we wish to lead a meaningful existence beyond that of tolerant cynicism. This step requires us to participate in the active production of meaningful realities. To do so requires purposeful commitment and energy. This may seem antithetical to the theme of deconstructionism, which implies that all commitments entail prejudices. While it may indeed be the case that commitments do entail prejudices and biases, these are necessary in order for us to organize information and create meaning.

More to the point, deconstructionism should enable us to take a decisive stance on just which prejudices and biases we wish to commit our time, energy, and passion to. The authors of this book have a biased commitment toward "relevant education," for example. As a result, we steadfastly refuse to participate in certain cultural realities, such as teaching information that may be considered pro forma among social psychologists but for which we can find little real life significance. This bias is a basis upon which we design and teach courses that have a meaningful, defensible logic to us. As a result, we are committed to our teaching and we find it highly rewarding. It is an activity that gives us a sense of purpose. We constructed this reality by first deconstructing taken-for-granted assumptions about higher education in general and sociological education in particular. Having done this, we proceeded to determine which goals and cultural realities we felt were worth pursuing and to then mindfully construct a means of producing this outcome. The result is a lively reality concerning education that we share with each other and like-minded colleagues around the country. Whenever we engage in the ritualistic academic conference with one another, we have the opportunity to further cement this reality and to be exhilarated by it as a source of significance in our lives.

As a final illustration, consider the trap that we set for ourselves when we depend on ossified structures to provide us with a sense of meaning and purpose while neglecting to contribute adequate energy to the maintenance of these realities. Imagine a young, heterosexual male who decides to commit his services as an attorney to the struggle to allow gays access to military service. He has considered the situation and decided that an expression of his acceptance of and tolerance for other collective realities can be achieved through this service. In effect, he has chosen to participate in tearing down one social institution, the heterosexual military, and to contribute to its replacement with an alternative reality, one that suggests that combat and sexuality are separate institutions. Now imagine this same young man explaining to his wife and children that he does not have time to spend on birthday and anniversary celebrations because he is busy fighting an important social cause. In fact, he is often absent from the various family meal rituals as well. One day he awakens to the discovery that he is no longer a meaningful element in his family. This trite example is cliché in popular culture. However, it illustrates the simple but profound point that if we do not actively participate in the production of those realities that we wish to maintain as the meaningful foundations of our lives, they will be eroded by the forces of entropy. Love and family involvement, regardless of how one defines the specifics of the institution, require ongoing, active participation in the ritual interactions that maintain these institutions. It is not sufficient to free-ride on seemingly well-established social institutions, such as family values. These social institutions do not endure without active maintenance. Thus, the message is be choosy about the realities that you intend to produce or reproduce and recognize that the production of any reality requires your participation. To the extent that you do so mindfully your life will take on increased meaning and purpose.

Trudy-the-bag-lady introduced in the reading by Jane Wagner (part 1) is a true hero from the perspective of the mindful construction of reality. She has scrutinized the social institutions in which she dwells and found them to be unacceptable. Rather than turn away in despair, she has created a rich, lively alternative reality for herself. Now, as she describes it, her days are "jam-packed and funfilled." Trudy is both a product of the general social realities that form this society and a commentator on them. We find her commentary compelling because it is both informed and hopeful. She is neither a social robot nor a cynic. She has taken responsible control for the construction of her own reality and she invests in this production with enthusiasm and vigor. She is an intriguing character in that although she is a street person, we do not feel pity for her. We may in fact feel a bit envious of her insightful, energetic reality, mad though it may appear by conventional standards. Trudy is bursting with potential. Our own realities can be similarly produced. Whether they be as simple as heartfelt participation in small daily rituals with those you love, or as revolutionary as "talking back to outrage" in the form of large-scale collective protest, the message we find useful from this material is that it takes insight, courage, and responsibility to engage in the mindful production of reality. This is the basis of a meaningful existence.

Name Index

Subject Index

A

Accounts, 61, 73, 76, 78, 96, 102, 136-137, 219-220, 225-229, 231-233,248

Anomie, 331, 436-437, 447, 505

Attitudes, 63, 138, 167, 223, 288, 331, 334, 378, 393-394

Attribution, 22, 76, 103-104, 231, 254, 275, 305, 322, 331, 351, 357, 375-376
    biases and stereotypes, 15-16, 23, 60, 74, 173, 179, 375-377, 409
    fundamental attribution error, 22, 104

Authority, 311-312, 407, 414, 427, 430, 468-469, 473-474, 476-477, 479, 481, 493-494, 498

B

Bargaining, 460-462, 467. *See also* Negotiation

Behavior, xix, 4-5, 7, 13, 15, 22, 24-25, 33-34, 53, 55-56, 60-64, 69, 75, 92, 130, 134-138, 140, 309-311, 317, 321-324, 345, 347-348, 351, 361-365, 370, 374-378, 380, 382-385, 387-390, 393-394, 396-400, 406, 417-424, 432, 462, 468-469, 478, 505
    and environment, 20, 166, 178, 203, 219, 288
    automatic, 95-97, 104, 112, 168, 222
    situated, 134, 204, 260, 346
    strategies, 101-102, 104, 195, 233-234, 253
    theories of
        behaviorism, 8, 10-14, 16-19, 52, 82, 226
        cognitive/interpretive, 14-17, 226
        Freudianism, 12-13
        symbolic interactionism, xx-xxiv, 6, 8, 17-20, 23-24, 28, 31-34, 51-52, 54, 65, 97
        utilitarianism, 8-10, 16-18, 23

Behaviorism, 8, 10, 12-14, 16, 18, 52
    conditioning, 11-13, 17
    reinforcement, 11-12
    Skinner, B. F., 10, 12
    socialization, 11-12, 203

social learning theory, 11, 82
stimuli, 10, 11, 14-15, 17, 20, 51-59
stimulus-response, 11-13, 19, 51-52, 56

Beliefs, 281, 303-305, 482, 500-501
    and construction of reality, 352, 354
    magical, 42, 304
    preconceived, 307-308, 378, 383. *See also* Stereotypes
    self-fulfilling, 306, 362, 373, 375. *See also* Self-fulfilling prophecy
    unquestioned, 7, 107, 314-317. *See also* incorrigible propositions

Belief systems, 42-45, 302-304, 351, 367, 499, 501

C

Cognition, 14-17, 59, 389
    and decision-making, xxiii
    and development, 244, 248
    and interpretation, xxi, 14, 59
    categories of, 16, 59-60
    categorization, 59, 95, 309
    default assumptions, 60-61, 112-113, 116-118
    mindlessness, 60, 87, 94-98
    processes, 14-16, 32, 221, 244
    schemas, 15-16, 32, 113, 121, 250

Communication, 31, 101, 200, 233, 302, 381-382, 482-483
    and interaction, 257, 278
    mode of, 34, 46-48, 194-195, 228-229
    social context of, 194-195, 197
    symbolic, 18, 32, 57

Consciousness, 26, 404, 467, 497
    mindfulness, 502
    self, 462

Constructionism/Constructivism, 26, 30-31, 344, 354, 358, 369, 499, 502-508

Control, xxii, xxiv, 60, 129, 312, 358, 395, 399, 440, 445, 469, 479, 499-500. *See also* Power
    domination, 194, 216, 427, 476
    interactional, 173, 175-176, 179
    self, 22, 194, 266, 406, 507
    social, 221, 267, 417, 421-424, 440, 476

Conversation, 4, 32, 133-134, 138, 270, 301, 310, 317, 332, 350, 375-376,